W9-BEI-404

THE PURRFECT AAA MEMBER PERK

CAT CASH!

Travel between Portland, Maine and Yarmouth, Nova Scotia in just 5.5 hours on The CAT high-speed car ferry and earn CAT Cash - redeemable for onboard dining, drinks, and local souvenirs.*

Book your ADVENTURE ON THE CAT at ferries.ca using promo code **CAT18**.

THE CAT

Ferries.ca

*Some conditions apply. Earn $10 CAT Cash per person, to a maximum of $20 for one-way and $40 for round-trip reservations. Vouchers will be awarded at time of departure.

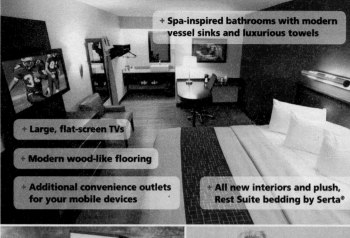

Pennsylvania

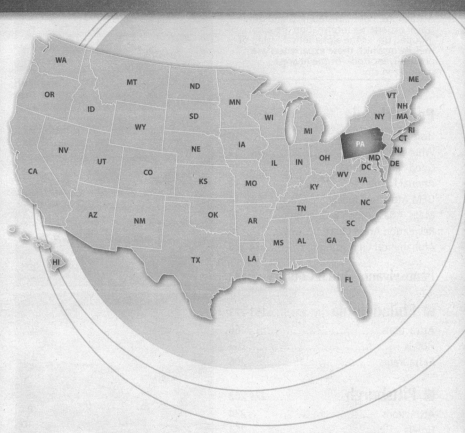

Published by AAA Publishing
1000 AAA Drive, Heathrow, FL 32746-5063
Copyright AAA 2018, All rights reserved

Advertising Rate and Circulation Information: (407) 444-8280

Printed in the USA by Quad/Graphics

This book is printed on paper certified by third-party standards for sustainably managed forestry and production.

 Printed on recyclable paper.
Please recycle whenever possible.

Stock #4674

CONTENTS

Get more travel information at
AAA.com/travelguides

Attractions, hotels, restaurants and other travel experience information are all grouped under the alphabetical listing of the city in which those experiences are physically located—or the nearest recognized city.

free to soak it all in

TripAssist travel insurance from Allianz Global Assistance can free you up to make the most of your vacation. Nothing will hold you back knowing that you and your travel plans are safe.

Talk to your AAA Travel Agent today for more information.

Using Your Guide

AAA TourBook guides are packed with travel insight, maps and listings of places to stay, play, eat and save. For more listings, more details and online booking, visit **AAA.com/travelguides**.

Helping You Make the Connection
Look for this symbol 🔗 throughout the guides for direct links to related content.

A to Z City Listings
Cities and places are listed alphabetically within each state or province. Attractions, hotels and restaurants are listed once — under the city in which they are physically located.

Cities that are considered part of a larger destination city or area have an expanded city header. The header identifies the larger region and cross-references pages that contain shared trip planning resources:

- Destination map – outline map of the cities that comprise a destination city or area
- Attraction spotting map – regional street map marked with attraction locations
- Hotel/restaurant spotting map and index – regional street map numbered with hotel and restaurant locations identified in an accompanying index

Cities that are not considered part of a larger destination city or area but have a significant number of listings may have these resources within the individual city section:

- Attraction spotting map
- Hotel/restaurant spotting map and index

Location Abbreviations
Directions are from the center of town unless otherwise specified, using these highway abbreviations:

Bus. Rte.=business route
CR=county road
FM=farm to market
FR=forest road
Hwy.=Canadian highway
I=interstate highway
LR=legislative route
R.R.=rural route
SR/PR=state or provincial route
US=federal highway

About Listed Establishments
AAA/CAA Inspected & Approved hotels and restaurants are listed on the basis of merit alone after careful evaluation and approval by full-time, professionally trained AAA inspectors. An establishment's decision to advertise in the TourBook guide has no bearing on its evaluation or rating; nor does inclusion of advertising imply AAA endorsement of products and services.

Information in this guide was believed accurate at the time of publication. However, since changes inevitably occur between annual editions, please contact your AAA travel professional, visit **AAA.com/travelguides** or download the free AAA Mobile app to confirm prices and schedules.

Attraction Listing Icons
SAVE AAA Discounts & Rewards® member discount

C Electric vehicle charging station on premises. Domestic station information provided by the U.S. Department of Energy. Canadian station information provided by Plug'n Drive Ontario.

GT Guided Tours available
A Camping facilities
¶1 Food on premises
X Recreational activities
P Pet friendly (Call for restrictions/fees.)
H Picnicking allowed

In select cities only:

T Mass transit station within 1 mile. Icon is followed by station name and AAA/CAA designated station number within listing.

GEM AAA/CAA travel experts may designate an attraction of exceptional interest and quality as a AAA GEM — a *Great Experience for Members*®. See GEM Attraction Index (listed on CONTENTS page) for a complete list of locations.

Consult the online travel guides at **AAA.com/travelguides** or visit AAA Mobile for additional things to do if you have time.

Hotel Listing Icons
May be preceded by CALL and/or SOME UNITS.

Member Information:

SAVE Member rates: discounted standard room rate or lowest public rate available at time of booking for dates of stay.

ECO Eco-certified by government or private organization.

EVC Electric vehicle charging station on premises. Domestic station information provided by the U.S. Department of Energy. Canadian station information provided by Plug'n Drive Ontario.

⊠ Smoke-free premises

In select cities only:

🚇 Mass transit station within 1 mile. Icon is followed by station name and AAA/CAA designated station number within listing.

Services:

✈ Airport transportation

🐾 Pet friendly (Call for restrictions/fees.)

🍴 Restaurant on premises

🍴+ Restaurant off premises

🍽 Room service for 2 or more meals

🍸 Full bar

👶 Child care

BIZ Business center

♿ Accessible features (Call property for available services and amenities.)

Activities:

🎰 Full-service casino

🏊 Pool

💪 Health club or exercise room on premises

In-Room Amenities:

HS High-speed Internet service

$HS High-speed Internet service (Call property for fees.)

🛜 Wireless Internet service

$🛜 Wireless Internet service (Call property for fees.)

🚫🛜 No wireless Internet service

🎬 Pay movies

🧊 Refrigerator

📟 Microwave

☕ Coffeemaker

🌀 No air conditioning

📺 No TV

☎ No telephones

Restaurant Listing Icons

SAVE AAA Discounts & Rewards® member discount

ECO Eco-certified by government or private organization.

EVC Electric vehicle charging station on premises. Domestic station information provided by the U.S. Department of Energy. Canadian station information provided by Plug'n Drive Ontario.

🌀 No air conditioning

♿ Accessible features (Call property for available services and amenities.)

⊘ Designated smoking section

B Breakfast

L Lunch

D Dinner

24 Open 24 hours

LATE Open after 11 p.m.

🐾 Pet friendly (Call for restrictions/fees.)

In select cities only:

🚇 Mass transit station within 1 mile. Icon is followed by station name and AAA/CAA designated station number within listing.

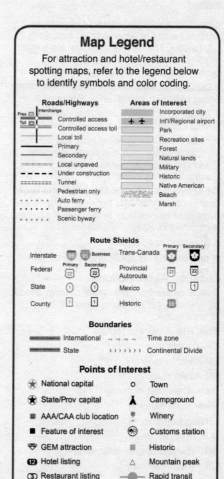

Map Legend

For attraction and hotel/restaurant spotting maps, refer to the legend below to identify symbols and color coding.

Roads/Highways

Interchange
Free — Toll
Controlled access
Controlled access toll
Local toll
Primary
Secondary
Local unpaved
Under construction
Tunnel
Pedestrian only
Auto ferry
Passenger ferry
Scenic byway

Areas of Interest

Incorporated city
✈ Int'l/Regional airport
Park
Recreation sites
Forest
Natural lands
Military
Historic
Native American
Beach
Marsh

Route Shields

Interstate — 95 — 95 Business — Trans-Canada (Primary/Secondary)
Federal — Primary 22 / Secondary 22 — Provincial Autoroute 22 / 22
State — 1 / 1 — Mexico 1 / 1
County — 1 / 1 — Historic 66

Boundaries

International — Time zone
State — Continental Divide

Points of Interest

★ National capital — o Town
★ State/Prov capital — ▲ Campground
■ AAA/CAA club location — ⚑ Winery
■ Feature of interest — ⊛ Customs station
▽ GEM attraction — ■ Historic
12 Hotel listing — △ Mountain peak
3 Restaurant listing — Rapid transit
🎓 College/University — Stations Metromover

Understanding the Diamond Ratings

Hotel and restaurant evaluations are unscheduled to ensure our professionally trained inspectors encounter the same experience members do.

- When an establishment is Diamond Rated, it means members can expect a good fit with their needs. The inspector assigns a rating that indicates the type of experience to expect.
- While establishments at high levels must offer increasingly complex personalized services, establishments at every level are subject to the same basic requirements for cleanliness, comfort and hospitality. Learn more at **AAA.com/diamonds**.

Hotels	Restaurants
Budget-oriented, offering basic comfort and hospitality.	Simple, economical food, often quick-serve, in a functional environment.
Affordable, with modestly enhanced facilities, décor and amenities.	Familiar food, often cooked to order, served in casual surroundings.
Distinguished, multifaceted with enhanced physical attributes, amenities and guest comforts.	Trendy cuisine, skillfully prepared and served, with expanded beverage options, in an enhanced setting.
Refined, stylish with upscale physical attributes, extensive amenities and high degree of hospitality, service and attention to detail.	Distinctive fine-dining. Creative preparations, skillfully served, often with wine steward, amid upscale ambience.

Ultimate luxury, sophistication and comfort with extraordinary physical attributes, meticulous personalized service, extensive amenities and impeccable standards of excellence.	Leading-edge cuisine of the finest ingredients, uniquely prepared by an acclaimed chef, served by expert service staff led by maître d' in extraordinary surroundings.

Guest Safety

Inspectors view a sampling of rooms during evaluations and, therefore, AAA/CAA cannot guarantee the presence of working locks and operational fire safety equipment in every guest unit.

Contacting AAA/CAA About the TourBook Guide

Tell us what you think about the content and format of the TourBook guide or about your experience at a listed hotel, restaurant or attraction. If your visit to an attraction, hotel or restaurant listed by AAA/CAA doesn't meet your expectations, please tell us about it **during your visit or within 30 days**. Be sure to save your receipts and other documentation for reference. Or, maybe you'd like to recommend a place you visited and would like AAA inspectors to consider.

Use the easy online form at **AAA.com/tourbookcomments** to send us the details.

Alternatively, you can email your comments to: memberrelations@national.aaa.com or submit them via postal mail to: AAA Member Comments, 1000 AAA Dr., Box 61, Heathrow, FL 32746.

Gettysburg National Military Park

Every state has its share of important "firsts," but if counting them were a game, Pennsylvania would be a tough player to beat.

Philadelphia was the first city in America to guarantee religious freedom. And if you've ever wondered about the first bank, stock exchange, hospital or zoo, each was established in Philly before anywhere else in the United States.

Some firsts heralded new hope: Pennsylvania was the first state to abolish slavery, and Dr. Jonas Salk developed a polio vaccine while at the University of Pittsburgh. Others have ushered in new ways of passing time. For instance, no one had ever eaten a banana split or played Bingo before each was first enjoyed in Pittsburgh.

You can see places associated with firsts. The Drake Well Museum in Titusville commemorates the spot where the world's first commercially successful oil well was drilled. Near Uniontown, Fort Necessity National

Pennsylvania

Battlefield preserves the site where the French and Indian War began, including the fort that Washington and his men built.

These Honored Dead

One of the most visited spots in Pennsylvania, Gettysburg National Military Park, commemorates the July 1863 battle in which 51,000 Union and Confederate soldiers were wounded, captured or killed. Soldiers' National Monument, one of thousands in the park, stands near the spot where Lincoln made his famous speech.

Three other parks in Pennsylvania memorialize significant earlier war battles. Washington Crossing Historic Park, near Trenton, N.J., preserves the site where Gen. George Washington and 2,500 soldiers crossed the Delaware River to attack German mercenaries during the American Revolution.

The following year, in 1777, Washington and the Continental Army settled down for a 6-month encampment at Valley Forge, where a brutal winter contributed to nearly 2,000 deaths of his ill-equipped men. The National Memorial Arch at Valley Forge National Historical Park pays tribute to these soldiers.

More than 2 decades before he led the United States to victory in the American Revolution, Washington commanded troops at Fort Necessity, the first battle of the French and Indian War. Fort Necessity National Battlefield encompasses this site along

National Memorial Arch at Valley Forge National Historical Park

with a reconstruction of the fort he built.

The Quaker State

The scene of such bloody conflict ironically began as an experiment in peaceful coexistence. In 1681, Quaker-convert William Penn established Pennsylvania as part of a "Holy Experiment" in applying Quaker principles to the practical business of governing a colony. Among those guiding beliefs was a commitment to religious tolerance.

If Penn were alive today in the state that bears his name, he would no doubt recognize his vision in the famed Pennsylvania Dutch Country. Here such religious groups as the Amish, Dunkers, Mennonites and others follow a simple, pastoral lifestyle that has changed little in the past 2 centuries.

More removed from the memories of epic battles won and lost on Pennsylvania soil is the natural tranquility of the Pocono Mountains. This highland wilderness of waterfalls, hiking trails and scenic overlooks has become a vacation playground for nature-hungry day-trippers from New York and Philadelphia and a favorite destination for honeymooners.

Even within the vast metropolis of Philadelphia you can forget conflict past and present at places like Fairmount Park, a lush oasis along the Schuylkill River's banks. Pittsburgh has its own enclaves of serenity—one such haven is a group of art, history and science museums collectively referred to as the Carnegie Museums of Pittsburgh.

Recreation

Practically any type of outdoor activity you can think of can be enjoyed in the Allegheny National Forest. Many recreation areas are near the 24-mile-long Allegheny Reservoir on the upper Allegheny River. Bradford and Warren are excellent starting points from which to explore this area. Among the forest's more than 200 miles of hiking trails is part of the constantly evolving North Country National Scenic Trail.

While the Allegheny Mountains are filled with challenging hiking terrain, other Pennsylvania paths offer easier walks, historic sites and bucolic scenery. The state's "rails to trails" program has converted unused railway lines into more than 1,800 miles of wide, fairly smooth byways. The Ridley Creek, Wissahickon Gorge and Wilderness Trails make wonderful day trips and are all located within a 30-minute drive of Philadelphia.

The most famous of Pennsylvania's trails is the Appalachian National Scenic Trail, which runs for 220 miles from the south central to the northeastern part of the state on its span from Georgia to Maine. It is especially popular with leaf-peepers; fall colors are at their peak here mid- to late October.

The commonwealth touts some of the best trout fishing in the eastern United States. Good fishing holes can be found along the Delaware River and around Lake Erie. Limestone streams flowing throughout the state present a challenge to fly-fishers.

Some of Pennsylvania's best white-water rafting is in Ohiopyle State Park, which contains more than 14 miles of the Youghiogheny River Gorge. Several outfitters are based in nearby Ohiopyle.

The high mountain meadows, thick wooded forests and flat farmlands of the 2,400-square-mile Pocono Mountain region offer eight ski resorts as well as opportunities for cross-country skiing, snowshoeing, snowmobiling, ice fishing and ice-skating.

The Poconos are also a choice spot for mountain biking. Lehigh Gorge Trail, suitable for beginners and intermediate riders, travels along the Lehigh River for 26 miles and stretches from the outlet of the Francis E. Walter Dam to Jim Thorpe. Casual cruisers opt for the maple-lined streets of US 6 through Milford, Hawley and Honesdale, which pass historic buildings, wildlife sanctuaries and numerous waterfalls.

Ski in the Poconos

Historic Timeline

1681 Quaker William Penn receives title to Pennsylvania in a land grant from England's King Charles II.

1731 Benjamin Franklin establishes the first public library in Philadelphia.

1776 The newly adopted Declaration of Independence is read to 8,000 people in Independence Square.

1787 The United States Constitution is signed in Philadelphia's Independence Hall.

1856 James Buchanan, the only Pennsylvanian who has served as president of the United States, is elected.

1863 Union forces defeat the Confederate Army in the Battle of Gettysburg.

1887 Punxsutawney Phil sees his shadow at the first official ceremony at Gobbler's Knob.

1889 The Johnstown flood kills more than 2,000 people.

1940 The first section of the Pennsylvania Turnpike, America's first high-speed, multilane highway, opens.

2001 United Airlines Flight 93 is hijacked by terrorists and crashes into a Somerset County field.

2007 An archeology dig is performed at the Philadelphia site of the original presidential residence, home to Washington and Adams.

What To Pack

Temperature Averages Maximum/Minimum	JANUARY	FEBRUARY	MARCH	APRIL	MAY	JUNE	JULY	AUGUST	SEPTEMBER	OCTOBER	NOVEMBER	DECEMBER
Allentown	39 / 21	41 / 24	50 / 31	61 / 39	72 / 49	80 / 58	85 / 63	83 / 62	76 / 54	65 / 42	54 / 35	43 / 27
Erie	33 / 20	36 / 21	45 / 28	56 / 38	67 / 49	76 / 59	80 / 64	79 / 63	72 / 56	61 / 46	49 / 36	39 / 27
Harrisburg	38 / 23	41 / 25	51 / 33	63 / 42	73 / 51	81 / 61	86 / 66	84 / 64	76 / 57	64 / 45	53 / 36	42 / 28
Philadelphia	39 / 25	42 / 28	51 / 35	62 / 44	72 / 55	81 / 64	86 / 70	84 / 69	77 / 61	66 / 49	55 / 40	44 / 31
Pittsburgh	37 / 20	39 / 21	50 / 29	62 / 38	71 / 48	80 / 56	85 / 62	83 / 60	76 / 53	64 / 41	53 / 33	42 / 25
Scranton	34 / 18	37 / 20	47 / 28	59 / 38	71 / 48	78 / 57	83 / 61	81 / 60	72 / 53	61 / 42	49 / 34	39 / 24

From the records of The Weather Channel Interactive, Inc.

Good Facts To Know

ABOUT THE STATE

POPULATION: 12,773,801.

AREA: 46,055 square miles; ranks 33rd.

CAPITAL: Harrisburg.

HIGHEST POINT: 3,213 ft., Mount Davis.

LOWEST POINT: Sea level, Delaware River.

TIME ZONE(S): Eastern. DST.

GAMBLING

MINIMUM AGE FOR GAMBLING: 21; 18 for pari-mutuel gambling.

REGULATIONS

TEEN DRIVING LAWS: Driving is not permitted 11 p.m.-5 a.m. During the first 6 months of driving, no more than one unrelated passenger under age 18, unless accompanied by a parent or guardian. After the first 6 months, no more than three unrelated passengers under 18, unless accompanied by a parent or guardian. Minimum age for unrestricted license is 17 years (with driver education). For more information about driver's license regulations phone (800) 932-4600, or (717) 412-5300 (outside Penn.).

SEAT BELT/CHILD RESTRAINT LAWS: Seat belts are required for driver and front-seat passengers ages 18 and over. Children ages 8-17 are required to be in a seat belt or child restraint. Children under age 8 must ride in a child safety seat or booster seat appropriate for their height and weight. Children under age 2 must be in a rear-facing restraint. AAA recommends the use of seat belts and appropriate child restraints for the driver and all passengers.

CELLPHONE RESTRICTIONS: Texting while driving is banned for all drivers.

HELMETS FOR MOTORCYCLISTS: Required for all drivers under age 21 and drivers over age 21 that have not completed a motorcycle safety course or have had a motorcycle license for less than 2 years. Required for passengers under age 21 and passengers of drivers required to wear helmets.

RADAR DETECTORS: Permitted. Prohibited for commercial vehicles.

MOVE OVER LAW: Driver is required to slow down and vacate the lane nearest stopped police, fire and rescue vehicles using audible or flashing signals. Law includes recovery vehicles, such as tow trucks, and utility vehicles within the first 72 hours after a declared emergency or until the expiration of a declared emergency, whichever is later.

FIREARMS LAWS: Vary by state or county. Contact Pennsylvania State Police Headquarters, 1800 Elmerton Ave., Harrisburg, PA 17110; phone (717) 783-5599.

SPECIAL REGULATIONS: Use of headlights is required in work zones in Pennsylvania.

HOLIDAYS

HOLIDAYS: Jan. 1 ▪ Martin Luther King Jr. Day, Jan. (3rd Mon.) ▪ Washington's Birthday/Presidents Day, Feb. (3rd Mon.) ▪ Memorial Day, May (last Mon.) ▪ July 4 ▪ Labor Day, Sept. (1st Mon.) ▪ Columbus Day, Oct. (2nd Mon.) ▪ Veterans Day, Nov. 11 ▪ Thanksgiving ▪ day after Thanksgiving ▪ Christmas.

MONEY

TAXES: Statewide sales tax is 6 percent; individual counties can levy additional increments. Pittsburgh levies a 5 percent amusements tax. The statewide lodging tax is 6 percent, with local options to allow additional increments.

VISITOR INFORMATION

INFORMATION CENTERS: I-276W in King of Prussia ▪ I-90W .5 mi. w. of N.Y. ▪ SR 15S 7 mi. s. of N.Y. ▪ I-79N 5 mi. n. of W. Va. ▪ I-80E w. of Farrell at the Ohio line ▪ I-80W at Delaware Water Gap ▪ I-70W at the Md. line near Warfordsburg ▪ I-70E near the W. Va. line ▪ I-83N at the Md. line s. of Shrewsbury ▪ I-81N s. of Greencastle near the Md. line ▪ I-84W just w. of Matamoras ▪ I-95N s. of Upland at the Del. line ▪ I-78W e. of Glendon at the N.J. line ▪ and I-81S s. of N.Y.'s Corbettsville. Daily 7-7. Closed some holidays.

FURTHER INFORMATION FOR VISITORS:
Pennsylvania Tourism Office, Department of Community and Economic Development
400 North St.
4th Floor, Commonwealth Keystone Building
Harrisburg, PA 17120-0225
(800) 847-4872

NATIONAL FOREST INFORMATION:
Allegheny National Forest
4 Farm Colony Dr.
Warren, PA 16365
(814) 723-5150
(877) 444-6777 (reservations)

FISHING AND HUNTING REGULATIONS:
Pennsylvania Fish and Boat Commission
1601 Elmerton Ave.
Harrisburg, PA 17110
(717) 705-7800 (Headquarters)
(877) 707-4085 (Fishing Licenses)

Pennsylvania Game Commission
2001 Elmerton Ave.
Harrisburg, PA 17110-9797
(717) 787-4250

Pennsylvania Annual Events

Please call ahead to confirm event details.

 Visit **AAA.com/travelguides/events** to find
AAA-listed events for every day of the year

JANUARY

- Orchid and Tropical Bonsai
  Show / Pittsburgh
  412-622-6914
- Mummers Parade
  Philadelphia
  215-336-3050
- Pennsylvania Farm Show
  Harrisburg
  717-787-5373

FEBRUARY

- Chocolate-Covered
  February / Hershey
  800-437-7439
- Jim Thorpe Winterfest
  Jim Thorpe
  888-546-8467
- Groundhog Day
  Punxsutawney
  814-618-5591

MARCH

- Philadelphia St. Patrick's
  Day Parade / Philadelphia
  215-983-7224
- PHS Philadelphia Flower
  Show / Philadelphia
  215-988-8800
- American Quilter's Society
  Quilt Show / Lancaster
  270-898-7903, ext. 146

APRIL

- International Spring Festival
  Lansdale
  215-362-2666
- Spring Blooms
  Kennett Square
  610-388-1000
- Kaleidoscope Art Festival
  Slippery Rock
  724-738-4721

MAY

- Spring Craft Fair / Leesport
  610-926-1307
- Memorial Day Parade and
  Ceremonies / Gettysburg
  717-334-6274
- Rhubarb Festival
  Intercourse
  717-768-8261

JUNE

- Pennsylvania State Laurel
  Festival / Wellsboro
  570-724-1926
- Delaware River Sojourn
  Bushkill
  609-883-9500
- Jubilee Day
  Mechanicsburg
  717-796-0811

JULY

- Kutztown Folk Festival
  Kutztown
  888-674-6136
- Pennsylvania Shakespeare
  Festival / Center Valley
  610-282-9455
- People's Choice Festival of
  Pennsylvania Arts
  Boalsburg
  814-692-1059

AUGUST

- Riverfest / Towanda
  570-265-2696
- Musikfest / Bethlehem
  610-332-1300
- Pennsylvania Renaissance
  Faire / Manheim
  717-665-7021, ext. 231

SEPTEMBER

- Whoopie Pie Festival
  Ronks
  717-687-8635
- Lancaster Liederkranz
  German Oktoberfest
  Manheim
  717-898-8451
- La Festa Italiana
  Scranton
  570-348-4921

OCTOBER

- Autumn Timber Festival
  East Stroudsburg
  570-421-7231
- Harvest Days / Lancaster
  717-569-0401
- Woolly Worm Festival
  Lewisburg
  570-594-4691

NOVEMBER

- Victorian Christmas
  Williamsport
  570-419-2989
- Christmas in Bethlehem
  Bethlehem
  610-332-1300
- Philadelphia Thanksgiving
  Day Parade / Philadelphia
  215-581-4502

DECEMBER

- Old Time Christmas
  Stroudsburg
  570-992-6161
- Country Christmas Village
  Lancaster
  717-569-0401
- Olde Time Christmas
  Jim Thorpe
  570-325-5810

American Quilter's Society
Quilt Show, Lancaster

Elfreth's Alley, Philadelphia

Ricketts Glen State Park,
Benton (Columbia County)

Fort Pitt Bridge, Pittsburgh

Spring Blooms, Kennett Square

Index: Great Experience for Members

AAA editor's picks of exceptional note

Old Economy Village

Brandywine River Museum of Art

State Capitol

Masonic Temple

See Orientation map on p. 26 for corresponding grid coordinates, if applicable.
*Indicates the GEM is temporarily closed.

ROADS/HIGHWAYS
INTERSTATE
CONTROLLED ACCESS
CONTROLLED ACCESS TOLL
TOLL ROAD
PRIMARY DIVIDED
PRIMARY UNDIVIDED
SECONDARY DIVIDED
SECONDARY UNDIVIDED
LOCAL DIVIDED
LOCAL UNDIVIDED
UNPAVED ROAD
UNDER CONSTRUCTION
TUNNEL
PEDESTRIAN ONLY
AUTO FERRY
PASSENGER FERRY
SCENIC BYWAY
10 DISTANCE BETWEEN MARKERS
EXIT NUMBER-FREE/TOLL
INTERCHANGE FULL/PARTIAL
WELCOME/INFORMATION CENTER
REST AREA/ SERVICE CENTER

BOUNDARIES
INTERNATIONAL
STATE
COUNTY
TIME ZONE
CONTINENTAL DIVIDE

ROAD SHIELDS
95 95 INTERSTATE/BUSINESS
22 22 22 U.S./STATE/COUNTY
127 127 FOREST/INDIAN
TRANS-CANADA
1 PROVINCIAL AUTOROUTE/ KING'S HIGHWAY
1 MEXICO
66 HISTORIC ROUTE 66
VT 41 REFERENCE PAGE INDICATOR

AREAS OF INTEREST
INDIAN
MILITARY
PARK
FOREST
GRASSLANDS
HISTORIC
INT'L/REGIONAL AIRPORT
INCORPORATED CITY

POINTS OF INTEREST
○ TOWN
⊛ NATIONAL CAPITAL
⊛ STATE/PROVINCIAL CAPITAL
■ AAA/CAA CLUB LOCATION
■ FEATURE OF INTEREST
▬ COLLEGE/UNIVERSITY
CUSTOMS STATION
HISTORIC
LIGHTHOUSE
MONUMENT/MEMORIAL
STATE/PROVINCIAL PARK
NATIONAL WILDLIFE REFUGE
SKI AREA
SPORTS COMPLEX
DAM

CITIES/TOWNS are color-coded by size, showing where to find AAA Approved and Diamond rated lodgings or restaurants listed in the AAA TourBook guides and on AAA.com:

- Red - major destinations and capitals; many listings
- Black - destinations; some listings
- Grey - no listings

ER054-16

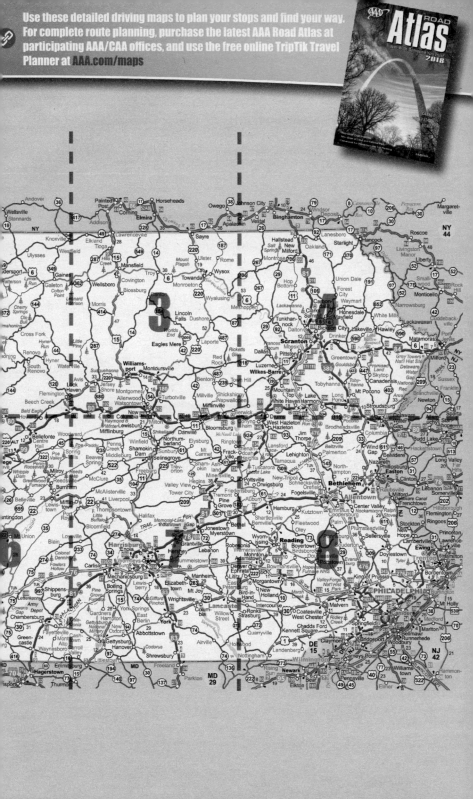

Use these detailed driving maps to plan your stops and find your way. For complete route planning, purchase the latest AAA Road Atlas at participating AAA/CAA offices, and use the free online TripTik Travel Planner at AAA.com/maps

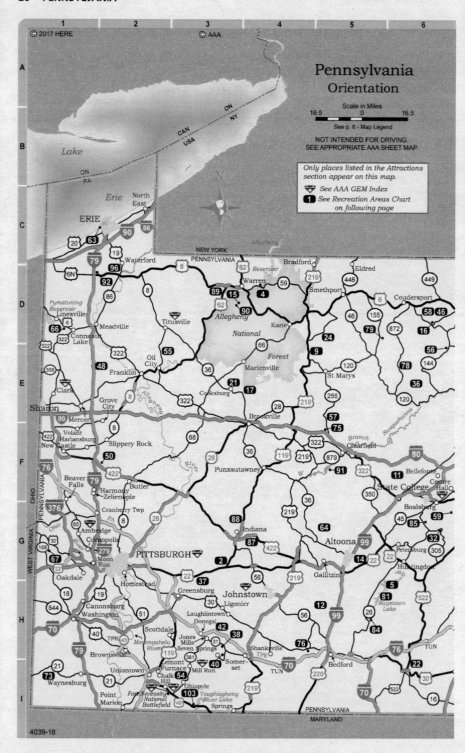

Pennsylvania
Orientation

Scale in Miles
16.5 0 16.5

See p. 6 - Map Legend

NOT INTENDED FOR DRIVING.
SEE APPROPRIATE AAA SHEET MAP.

Only places listed in the Attractions
section appear on this map.

⬩ See AAA GEM Index
1 See Recreation Areas Chart
on following page

4039-18

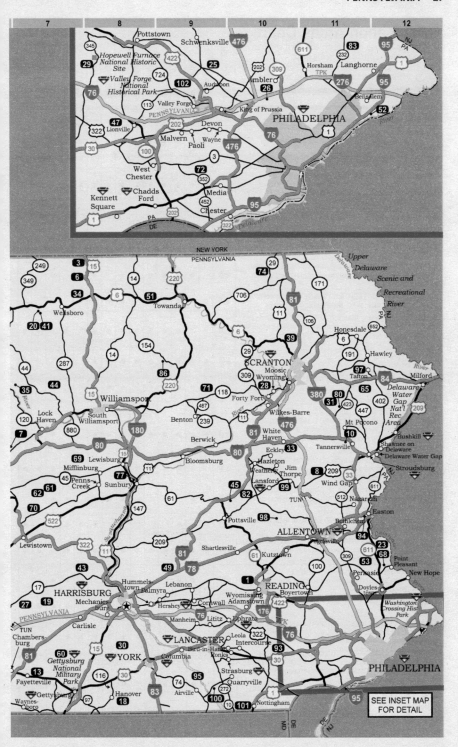

SEE INSET MAP FOR DETAIL

Recreation Areas Chart

The map location numerals in column 2 show an area's location on the preceding map.

🔗 Find thousands of places to camp at AAA.com/campgrounds

	MAP LOCATION	CAMPING	PICNICKING	HIKING TRAILS	BOATING	BOAT RAMP	BOAT RENTAL	FISHING	SWIMMING	PET FRIENDLY	BICYCLE TRAILS	WINTER SPORTS	VISITOR CENTER	LODGE/CABINS	FOOD SERVICE
NATIONAL FORESTS *(See place listings.)*															
Allegheny (D-3) 516,000 acres. Northwestern Pennsylvania. Cross-country skiing, geocaching, snowmobiling; all-terrain vehicle trails, horse trails.			●	●	●	●	●	●	●	●	●	●	●		●
NATIONAL RECREATION AREAS *(See place listings.)*															
Delaware Water Gap (E-12) 70,000 acres. Bird-watching, canoeing, cross-country skiing, horseback riding, hunting, kayaking, rafting, rock climbing, snowshoeing; tubing.			●	●	●	●		●	●	●	●	●	●		●
ARMY CORPS OF ENGINEERS															
Blue Marsh Lake (H-10) 6,276 acres 8 mi. n. of Reading on SR 183. Historic. Fishing, geocaching, horseback riding, hunting, iceboating, ice fishing, ice-skating, scuba diving, water skiing; volleyball courts. Food service is available Memorial Day-Labor Day.	❶		●	●	●	●		●	●	●	●	●	●		●
Conemaugh River Lake (G-3) 7,609 acres 8 mi. n. of New Alexandria off SR 981. Ball field, canoe launch, dam tours, interpretive trail, playground.	❷		●	●	●	●		●		●	●				
Cowanesque Lake (C-7) 3,200 acres 3 mi. w. of Lawrenceville off SR 15. Hunting, water skiing; amphitheater, playground.	❸	●	●	●	●	●		●	●	●	●		●		
Kinzua Dam & Allegheny Reservoir (D-4) 26,541 acres 6 mi. e. of Warren via US 6 and SR 59. Cross-country skiing, ice fishing, snowmobiling, water skiing; amphitheater, playground.	❹	●	●	●	●	●		●	●	●	●	●	●		
Raystown Lake (H-6) 29,300 acres s.w. of Huntingdon off SR 26. Water skiing; swimming beaches.	❺	●	●	●	●	●		●	●	●				●	●
Tioga-Hammond Lakes (D-7) 6,700 acres 12 mi. n. of Mansfield on US 15. Hunting, water skiing; archery trail, horseshoe pits, swimming beach.	❻	●	●	●	●	●		●	●	●	●		●		
STATE															
Bald Eagle (F-7) 5,900 acres off SR 150 to Main Park Rd. in Howard. Bird-watching, cross-country skiing, hunting, ice fishing, ice-skating, sledding, tobogganing; marina, swimming beach. Yurts available.	❼	●	●	●	●	●	●	●	●	●		●		●	
Beltzville (F-11) 3,002 acres 6 mi. e. of Lehighton off US 209. Bird-watching, cross-country skiing, hunting, iceboating, ice fishing, tobogganing, water skiing; swimming beach.	❽		●	●	●	●		●	●	●	●	●	●		●
Bendigo (E-5) 100 acres 3 mi. n.e. of Johnsonburg off US 219. Canoeing and kayaking, cross-country skiing, sledding, snowshoeing; canoe launch.	❾		●	●		●		●	●	●					
Big Pocono (F-11) 1,306 acres off I-80 exit 299 at Tannersville. Historic. Downhill skiing, horseback riding, hunting.	❿		●	●						●	●	●			●
Black Moshannon (F-6) 3,394 acres 9 mi. e. of Philipsburg on SR 504. Boating (electric motors only), cross-country skiing, hunting, iceboating, ice fishing, ice-skating, snowmobiling.	⓫	●	●	●	●	●	●	●	●	●	●	●	●	●	
Blue Knob (H-5) 6,128 acres .6 mi. n.w. of Pavia off SR 869. Cross-country skiing, downhill skiing, horseback riding, hunting, snowmobiling.	⓬	●	●	●				●	●	●	●	●	●	●	
Caledonia (I-7) 1,125 acres 4 mi. e. of Fayetteville on US 30. Historic. Cross-country skiing, golf (18 holes), hunting; theater.	⓭	●	●	●				●	●	●	●	●	●	●	
Canoe Creek (G-5) 958 acres 7 mi. e. of Hollidaysburg off US 22. Bird-watching, boating (electric motors only), cross-country skiing, disc golf (9 holes), horseback riding, hunting, iceboating, ice fishing, ice-skating, sledding.	⓮		●	●	●	●	●	●	●	●	●	●	●	●	
Chapman (D-3) 805 acres 5 mi. w. of Clarendon off US 6. Boating (electric motors only), cross-country skiing, hunting, ice fishing, ice-skating, sledding, snowmobiling; warming hut. Yurts available. **Note:** The park is undergoing a dam rehabilitation project, which may affect some day-use areas; phone (814) 723-0250 for updates.	⓯	●	●	●	●	●		●	●	●	●	●	●	●	●

Recreation Areas Chart

The map location numerals in column 2 show an area's location on the preceding map.

Find thousands of places to camp at AAA.com/campgrounds

	MAP LOCATION	CAMPING	PICNICKING	HIKING TRAILS	BOATING	BOAT RAMP	BOAT RENTAL	FISHING	SWIMMING	PET FRIENDLY	BICYCLE TRAILS	WINTER SPORTS	VISITOR CENTER	LODGE/CABINS	FOOD SERVICE
Cherry Springs (D-6) 48 acres 4 mi. e. of Coudersport on US 6, then 11 mi. s.e. on SR 44. Hunting, snowmobiling, stargazing.	**16**	•	•	•						•	•	•			
Clear Creek (E-4) 1,444 acres 4 mi. n. of Sigel off SR 949. Canoeing, cross-country skiing, hunting, sledding, snowshoeing; canoe launch, playground. Yurts available.	**17**	•	•	•	•	•	•	•	•	•		•		•	
Codorus (I-8) 3,452 acres 2 mi. e. of Hanover off SR 216. Cross-country skiing, disc golf (54 holes), horseback riding, hunting, iceboating, ice fishing, ice-skating, scuba diving, sledding, snowmobiling; horse trails, marina. Yurts available.	**18**	•	•	•	•	•	•	•	•	•		•	•	•	•
Colonel Denning (H-7) 273 acres 9 mi. n. of Newville off SR 233. Boating (non-powered boats only), canoeing, cross-country skiing, hunting, ice-skating, kayaking.	**19**	•	•	•	•			•	•	•		•	•	•	
Colton Point (D-7) 368 acres 5 mi. s. of Ansonia off US 6. Hunting, snowmobiling; interpretive center.	**20**	•	•	•				•		•		•			
Cook Forest (E-3) 7,182 acres 1 mi. n. of Cooksburg off SR 36. Canoeing, cross-country skiing, horseback riding, hunting, ice-skating, sledding, snowshoeing; canoe launch, craft center, horse rental, theater.	**21**	•	•	•	•		•	•		•		•	•	•	•
Cowans Gap (I-6) 1,085 acres n. of Fort Loudon off SR 75. Boating (electric motors only), cross-country skiing, hunting, ice fishing, ice-skating.	**22**	•	•	•	•		•	•	•	•		•	•	•	•
Delaware Canal (G-12) 60-mile area along SR 32; headquarters is in Upper Black Eddy. Bird-watching, canoeing, cross-country skiing, hunting, sledding.	**23**		•	•	•			•		•	•	•	•		
Elk (D-5) 3,192 acres 9 mi. e. of Wilcox. Boating (boats launched by hand only), hunting, iceboating, ice fishing.	**24**	•	•	•	•			•		•		•			
Evansburg (A-9) 3,349 acres 2 mi. e. of Collegeville on US 422. Cross-country skiing, golf (18 holes), horseback riding, hunting.	**25**	•	•	•				•		•	•	•	•		
Fort Washington (A-10) 493 acres at 500 Bethlehem Pike in Fort Washington. Bird-watching, cross-country skiing, disc golf (9 holes), sledding; observation deck, softball field.	**26**		•	•						•	•	•	•		
Fowlers Hollow (H-7) 104 acres 4 mi. s. of New Germantown off SR 274 on Upper Buck Ridge Rd. Cross-country skiing, horseback riding, hunting, mountain biking, snowmobiling.	**27**	•	•	•						•	•	•			
Frances Slocum (E-10) 1,035 acres 4 mi. e. of Dallas off SR 309. Boating (electric motors only), cross-country skiing, hunting, ice fishing, ice-skating, sledding.	**28**	•	•	•	•	•	•	•		•		•	•		
French Creek (A-8) 7,339 acres about 5 mi. n.e. of Elverson off SR 345 (Hopewell Rd.). Bird-watching, boating (electric motors only), cross-country skiing, disc golf, horseback riding, hunting, ice fishing, ice-skating, sledding; mountain bicycle trails. Yurts available.	**29**	•	•	•	•	•	•	•	•	•	•	•	•	•	•
Gifford Pinchot (H-8) 2,338 acres 2 mi. e. of Rossville off SR 74. Boating (electric motors only), cross-country skiing, disc golf (18 holes), horseback riding, hunting, iceboating, ice fishing, ice-skating; swimming beach. Yurts available.	**30**	•	•	•	•	•	•	•	•	•		•	•	•	•
Gouldsboro (E-11) 3,050 acres s. of Gouldsboro. Boating (electric motors only), cross-country skiing, hunting, ice fishing, ice-skating; mountain bicycle trails.	**31**	•	•	•	•	•	•	•	•	•	•	•		•	
Greenwood Furnace (G-6) 423 acres 5 mi. n.w. of Belleville on SR 305. Canoeing and kayaking only, cross-country skiing, hunting, ice fishing, ice-skating, snowmobiling.	**32**	•	•	•	•			•	•	•		•	•		
Hickory Run (F-10) 15,990 acres 5 mi. s.e. of White Haven on SR 534. Cross-country skiing, disc golf (19 holes), geocaching, hunting, ice fishing, ice-skating, snowmobiling; swimming beach.	**33**	•	•	•				•	•	•		•	•		
Hills Creek (D-7) 407 acres 7 mi. n.e. of Wellsboro off SR 6. Boating (electric motors only), cross-country skiing, hunting, ice fishing, ice-skating, sledding, tobogganing. Yurts available.	**34**	•	•	•	•	•	•	•	•	•		•	•	•	•
Hyner Run (E-7) 180 acres 7 mi. e. of Renovo off SR 120. Hang gliding, hunting, snowmobiling.	**35**	•	•	•				•	•	•		•	•	•	

Recreation Areas Chart

The map location numerals in column 2 show an area's location on the preceding map.

Find thousands of places to camp at AAA.com/campgrounds

	MAP LOCATION	CAMPING	PICNICKING	HIKING TRAILS	BOATING	BOAT RAMP	BOAT RENTAL	FISHING	SWIMMING	PET FRIENDLY	BICYCLE TRAILS	WINTER SPORTS	VISITOR CENTER	LODGE/CABINS	FOOD SERVICE
Kettle Creek (E-6) 1,793 acres 8 mi. n.w. of Westport off SR 120. Boating (electric motors only), cross-country skiing, horseback riding, hunting, ice fishing, sledding, snowmobiling; horse trail.	36	•	•	•	•	•		•		•	•	•	•		
Keystone (H-3) 1,190 acres 3 mi. s.e. of New Alexandria on SR 981. Bird-watching, boating (electric motors only), cross-country skiing, hunting, ice fishing, ice-skating, sledding.	37	•	•	•	•	•	•	•	•	•	•	•	•	•	•
Kooser (H-3) 250 acres 10 mi. w. of Somerset on SR 31. Cross-country skiing. **Note:** The park is undergoing a lake rehabilitation project, which may affect some day-use areas; phone (814) 445-7725 for updates.	38	•	•	•				•		•		•		•	•
Lackawanna (D-10) 1,411 acres 3 mi. n. of Waverly on SR 407. Boating (electric motors only), cross-country skiing, horseback riding, hunting, ice fishing, ice-skating, mountain biking, sledding, snowshoeing. Yurts available.	39	•	•	•	•	•	•	•	•	•	•	•	•	•	•
Laurel Hill (I-3) 3,935 acres 10 mi. w. of Somerset off SR 31 near Trent. Boating (electric motors only), cross-country skiing, hunting, ice fishing, mountain biking, sledding, snowmobiling, snowshoeing.	40	•	•	•	•	•	•	•	•	•	•	•	•	•	•
Leonard Harrison (D-7) 585 acres 10 mi. s.w. of Wellsboro off SR 660. Cross-country skiing, hunting.	41	•	•	•						•		•	•		
Linn Run (H-3) 612 acres 10 mi. s.e. of Ligonier off SR 711. Horseback riding, hunting, snowmobiling.	42		•	•				•		•		•		•	•
Little Buffalo (G-7) 830 acres 4 mi. s.w. of Newport off SR 34. Historic. Boating (electric motors only), cross-country skiing, hunting, ice fishing, ice-skating, sledding; playground.	43		•	•	•	•	•	•	•	•		•	•	•	
Little Pine (E-7) 2,158 acres 3 mi. n. of Waterville off SR 44. Boating (electric motors only), cross-country skiing, hunting, ice fishing, sledding, snowmobiling; shooting range, yurts.	44	•	•	•	•	•	•	•	•	•		•		•	
Locust Lake (F-10) 1,089 acres 3 mi. s. of Mahanoy City off I-81 exit 131A. Boating (electric motors only), hunting, ice fishing, ice-skating.	45	•			•			•	•	•		•			
Lyman Run (D-6) 595 acres 8 mi. s.w. of Galeton off US 6. Bird-watching, boating (electric motors only), geocaching, hunting, ice fishing, ice-skating, sledding, snowmobiling; all-terrain vehicle trails, swimming beach.	46	•	•	•	•	•		•	•	•		•	•	•	
Marsh Creek (B-8) 1,705 acres 5 mi. n.w. of Downingtown off SR 282. Bird-watching, cross-country skiing, horseback riding, hunting, iceboating, ice fishing, ice-skating, mountain biking, sailing, sledding; horse rental, lake tours.	47		•	•	•	•	•	•	•	•	•	•		•	•
Maurice K. Goddard (E-2) 2,856 acres 14 mi. w. of Franklin on US 62. Bird-watching, cross-country skiing, hunting, iceboating, ice fishing, ice-skating, sledding, snowmobiling.	48		•	•	•	•	•	•		•	•	•	•		
Memorial Lake (G-9) 230 acres 5 mi. n.e. of Grantville off US 22 and I-81. Boating (electric motors only), cross-country skiing, ice fishing, ice-skating, sailing.	49		•	•	•	•	•	•		•		•		•	
Moraine (F-2) 16,725 acres 8 mi. n.w. of Butler off US 422. Cross-country skiing, disc golf (18 holes), horseback riding, hunting, iceboating, ice fishing, ice-skating, sledding, snowmobiling, windsurfing; bicycle rental.	50		•	•	•	•	•	•	•	•	•	•	•		•
Mount Pisgah (D-8) 1,302 acres 10 mi. n.w. of Troy off US 6. Boating (electric motors only), cross-country skiing, hunting, ice fishing, ice-skating, snowmobiling.	51		•	•	•	•	•	•	•	•		•			•
Neshaminy (B-12) 330 acres near Croydon off SR 132.	52		•	•					•	•			•		•
Nockamixon (G-11) 5,283 acres 5 mi. e. of Quakertown off CRs 513 and 563. Cross-country skiing, disc golf (18 holes), horseback riding, hunting, ice fishing, ice-skating, sledding, windsurfing; horse rental.	53		•	•	•	•	•	•	•	•		•	•	•	•
Ohiopyle (I-3) 20,499 acres 14 mi. e. of Uniontown on SR 381. Boating (white-water rafting only), cross-country skiing, horseback riding, hunting, mountain biking, rock climbing, sledding, snowmobiling, tobogganing, whitewater rafting; natural water slides. Yurts available.	54	•	•	•	•	•		•		•	•	•	•	•	•

Recreation Areas Chart

The map location numerals in column 2 show an area's location on the preceding map.

Find thousands of places to camp at AAA.com/campgrounds

	MAP LOCATION	CAMPING	PICNICKING	HIKING TRAILS	BOATING	BOAT RAMP	BOAT RENTAL	FISHING	SWIMMING	PET FRIENDLY	BICYCLE TRAILS	WINTER SPORTS	VISITOR CENTER	LODGE/CABINS	FOOD SERVICE
Oil Creek (E-2) 7,007 acres 4 mi. n. of Oil City on SR 8 via signs. Historic. Canoeing, cross-country skiing, hunting, kayaking; waterfalls.	55	•	•	•	•			•		•	•	•	•		
Ole Bull (E-6) 132 acres 3 mi. s.w. of Oleona off SR 144. Cross-country skiing, hunting, mountain biking, snowmobiling.	56	•	•	•				•	•	•	•	•	•	•	
Parker Dam (E-5) 968 acres 4 mi. e. of Penfield off SR 153. Boating (electric motors only), cross-country skiing, geocaching, hunting, ice fishing, ice-skating, sledding, snowmobiling, snowshoeing.	57	•	•	•	•	•	•	•	•	•		•	•	•	•
Patterson (D-6) 10 acres off SR 44 between Cherry Springs and Sweden Valley. Hunting.	58	•	•	•							•	•			
Penn-Roosevelt (G-6) 41 acres 10 mi. w. of Milroy off US 322. Cross-country skiing, horseback riding, snowmobiling.	59	•	•	•						•		•			
Pine Grove Furnace (H-7) 696 acres at Pine Grove Furnace on SR 233. Boating (electric motors only), cross-country skiing, hunting, ice fishing, ice-skating, snowmobiling.	60	•	•	•	•	•	•	•	•	•		•	•	•	
Poe Paddy (F-7) 23 acres n.e. of Milroy off US 322. Canoeing, snowmobiling; canoe launch.	61	•	•	•		•		•		•		•			
Poe Valley (F-7) 620 acres 10 mi. n.e. of Milroy off US 322. Boating (electric motors only), cross-country skiing, hunting, ice fishing, snowmobiling.	62	•	•	•	•	•	•	•		•		•		•	•
Presque Isle (C-1) 3,200 acres 7 mi. n. of I-90 exit 18 on Peninsula Dr. (SR 832). Historic. Cross-country skiing, hunting, ice-boating, ice fishing, ice-skating, scuba diving, waterskiing; bike rentals, boat tours, marina, swimming beaches.	63		•	•	•	•	•	•	•	•	•	•	•		•
Prince Gallitzin (G-5) 7,335 acres 16 mi. n.w. of Altoona off SR 53. Cross-country skiing, disc golf (9 holes), horseback riding, hunting, iceboating, ice fishing, mountain biking, snowmobiling, tobogganing.	64	•	•	•	•	•	•	•	•	•		•	•	•	•
Promised Land (E-11) 2,971 acres 10 mi. n. of Canadensis on SR 390. Boating (electric motors only), cross-country skiing, geocaching, horseback riding, hunting, ice fishing, ice-skating, mountain biking, snowmobiling, snowshoeing.	65	•	•	•	•	•	•	•	•	•	•	•	•	•	•
Pymatuning (D-1) 21,122 acres 4 mi. n. of Jamestown off US 322. Cross-country skiing, disc golf (18 holes), hunting, iceboating, ice fishing, ice-skating, sledding, snowmobiling; water trail.	66	•	•		•	•	•	•	•	•		•	•	•	•
Raccoon Creek (G-1) 7,572 acres 2 mi. n. of Frankfort Springs on SR 18. Boating (electric motors only), cross-country skiing, horseback riding, hunting, ice fishing, ice-skating, sledding, snowmobiling.	67	•	•	•	•	•	•	•	•	•		•	•	•	•
Ralph Stover (G-12) 45 acres 9 mi. n.w. of New Hope on SR 32. Boating (white-water rafting only), rock climbing.	68		•	•	•			•		•					
Raymond B. Winter (F-7) 695 acres 20 mi. w. of Lewisburg on SR 192. Cross-country skiing, hunting, ice fishing, mountain biking, snowmobiling.	69	•	•	•				•	•	•	•	•	•		
Reeds Gap (G-7) 220 acres 13 mi. n.e. of Lewistown off US 322. Cross-country skiing, hunting.	70	•	•	•				•		•		•		•	
Ricketts Glen (E-9) 13,050 acres 4 mi. n. of Red Rock on SR 487. Boating (electric motors only), cross-country skiing, horseback riding, hunting, ice fishing, snowmobiling; beach, canoe and kayak rentals.	71	•	•	•	•	•	•	•	•	•		•	•	•	•
Ridley Creek (B-9) 2,606 acres 7 mi. e. of West Chester via SRs 3 or 352. Cross-country skiing, horseback riding, sledding; gardens.	72		•	•				•		•	•	•	•		
Ryerson Station (I-1) 1,164 acres 1 mi. s. of Wind Ridge off SR 21. Cross-country skiing, hunting, ice fishing, ice-skating, sledding, snowmobiling; swimming pool.	73	•	•	•				•	•	•		•	•	•	•
Salt Springs (D-10) 405 acres 1 mi. w. of Franklin Forks off SR 29. Primitive. Cross-country skiing, hunting, sledding.	74	•	•	•						•		•			
S.B. Elliott (F-5) 318 acres 9 mi. w. of Clearfield on SR 153. Cross-country skiing, hunting, snowmobiling.	75	•	•	•					•	•	•	•		•	

Recreation Areas Chart

The map location numerals in column 2 show an area's location on the preceding map.

🔗 Find thousands of places to camp at AAA.com/campgrounds

	MAP LOCATION	CAMPING	PICNICKING	HIKING TRAILS	BOATING	BOAT RAMP	BOAT RENTAL	FISHING	SWIMMING	PET FRIENDLY	BICYCLE TRAILS	WINTER SPORTS	VISITOR CENTER	LODGE/CABINS	FOOD SERVICE
Shawnee (H-4) 3,983 acres 9 mi. w. of Bedford off US 30. Boating (electric motors only), disc golf (9 holes), ice fishing, ice-skating, sledding, snowmobiling. Yurts available.	76	•	•	•	•	•	•	•	•	•	•	•	•	•	
Shikellamy (F-8) 132 acres 1 mi. n. of Shamokin Dam off SR 11; 3,000 acres off SR 147 between Sunbury and Northumberland. Bicycle rental, marina, scenic overlook.	77		•	•	•	•	•	•		•	•		•		
Sinnemahoning (E-6) 1,910 acres 10 mi. n. of Sinnemahoning on SR 872. Boating (electric motors only), cross-country skiing, hunting, ice fishing, ice-skating, snowmobiling.	78	•	•	•	•	•		•		•		•	•		
Sizerville (D-5) 386 acres at Sizerville off SR 155. Cross-country skiing, hunting, snowmobiling; swimming pool.	79	•	•	•					•	•		•			
Tobyhanna (E-11) 5,440 acres 2 mi. e. of Tobyhanna on SR 423. Boating (electric motors only), hunting, ice fishing, ice-skating, mountain biking, snowmobiling.	80	•	•	•	•	•	•	•	•	•	•	•			
Trough Creek (H-5) 554 acres 3 mi. n. of Entriken off SR 994. Cross-country skiing, hunting, snowmobiling.	81	•	•	•				•		•		•			
Tuscarora (F-10) 1,618 acres 5 mi. n.w. of Tamaqua off SR 309. Boating (electric motors only), hunting, ice fishing, ice-skating. Yurts available.	82	•	•	•	•	•		•	•	•		•			
Tyler (A-11) 1,711 acres 1.5 mi. w. of Newtown off SR 413. Boating (electric motors only), canoeing, cross-country skiing, disc golf (36 holes), horseback riding, ice fishing, ice-skating, sledding; theater.	83		•	•	•		•	•		•	•	•	•		
Warriors Path (H-5) 349 acres 1 mi. s. of Saxton on SR 26. Cross-country skiing, hunting.	84		•	•	•	•		•	•	•		•			
Whipple Dam (G-6) 256 acres 12 mi. s. of State College off SR 26. Boating (electric motors only), cross-country skiing, hunting, ice fishing, ice-skating, skiing, snowmobiling; volleyball court.	85		•	•	•	•	•	•	•	•		•			
Worlds End (E-9) 780 acres 7 mi. n.w. of Laporte on SR 154. Boating (white-water rafting only), cross-country skiing, hunting, snowmobiling.	86	•	•	•	•			•	•	•		•	•	•	•
Yellow Creek (G-4) 2,981 acres 12 mi. e. of Indiana on US 422. Cross-country skiing, hunting, iceboating, ice fishing, ice-skating, mountain biking, sledding, snowmobiling. Yurts available.	87	•	•	•	•	•		•	•	•	•	•	•		
OTHER															
Blue Spruce Park (G-3) 650 acres 6 mi. n. of Indiana on SR 110. Bird-watching, cross-country skiing, hunting, sledding; playgrounds, sports field, volleyball court.	88		•	•	•			•		•		•			
Buckaloons Access Area (D-3) 5 mi. w. of Warren at jct. US 6 and US 62. Horseback riding, hunting, scuba diving, tubing, water skiing, windsurfing; playground.	89	•	•	•	•	•		•		•	•				
Chapman Lake (D-4) 68 acres near Montdale. Boating (electric motors only), cross-country skiing, ice fishing, ice-skating, sledding, snowmobiling. **Note:** The lake is undergoing a dam rehabilitation project, which may affect some day-use areas; phone (814) 723-0250 for updates.	90	•	•	•	•	•		•	•	•		•		•	•
Curwensville Lake (F-5) 362 acres 3 mi. s. of Curwensville on SR 453. Ice fishing; dog park, marina.	91	•	•	•	•	•		•	•	•		•			•
Edinboro Lake (D-2) 245 acres on SR 99 in Edinboro. Water skiing; boat docks, fishing pier.	92	•	•		•	•	•	•		•				•	•
Hibernia Park (H-10) 900 acres 6 mi. n. of Coatesville on SR 82, then w. on Cedar Knoll Rd. Historic. Fishing pier, playground.	93	•	•	•				•		•		•	•		
Hugh Moore Park (G-11) 260 acres on SR 611 in Easton. Bicycle rental, mule-drawn boat tour, museum, playground. Boating is only permitted with rented canoes and paddleboats.	94		•	•	•		•				•		•		•
Lake Aldred (I-9) 5,000 acres 25 mi. s.e. of York on SR 425. Hunting, water skiing.	95	•	•	•	•	•		•		•					
Lake Leboeuf (D-2) 70 acres 2 blks. s. on Hazel St. in Waterford.	96	•	•		•	•	•								
Lake Wallenpaupack (E-11) 5,700 acres 10 mi. e. of Hamlin off SR 590. Bird-watching, ice fishing, water skiing; horse rental.	97	•	•	•	•	•	•	•	•	•	•	•	•	•	•

Recreation Areas Chart

The map location numerals in column 2 show an area's location on the preceding map.

Find thousands of places to camp at **AAA.com/campgrounds**

	MAP LOCATION	CAMPING	PICNICKING	HIKING TRAILS	BOATING	BOAT RAMP	BOAT RENTAL	FISHING	SWIMMING	PET FRIENDLY	BICYCLE TRAILS	WINTER SPORTS	VISITOR CENTER	LODGE/CABINS	FOOD SERVICE
Leaser Lake (G-10) 396 acres on SR 143 in Jacksonville. Boating (sailboats and boats with small electric motors only), cross-country skiing, horseback riding, ice fishing.	98		•	•	•	•		•				•			
Mauch Chunk Lake (F-10) 2,445 acres 4 mi. w. of Jim Thorpe. Boating (electric motors only), cross-country skiing, ice fishing; swimming beach.	99	•	•	•	•	•	•	•				•	•	•	•
Muddy Run (I-9) 700 acres 4 mi. w. of Buck on SR 372. Boating (electric motors only), canoeing, kayaking.	100	•	•	•	•	•		•		•	•				•
Nottingham (I-10) 651 acres .25 mi. s. of Nottingham at 150 Park Rd. Bird-watching, cross-country skiing; horseshoe pits, volleyball courts.	101	•	•	•					•		•	•			
Schuylkill Canal (A-9) 60 acres 3 mi. s. off US 422 on SR 29. Historic. Bird-watching, cross-country skiing, geocaching, horseback riding.	102	•	•	•							•	•	•		
Youghiogheny Reservoir (I-3) 3,915 acres 20 mi. s.e. of Uniontown on US 40. Hunting.	103	•	•		•	•	•	•	•	•	•	•			

ABBOTTSTOWN pop. 1,011

THE ALTLAND HOUSE INN AND SUITES   717/259-9535
💎💎 Historic Country Inn. **Address:** 1 Center Square 17301

WHERE TO EAT

THE ALTLAND HOUSE GRILL & PUB   717/259-9535
💎💎💎 American. Casual Dining. **Address:** 1 Center Square 17301

ABINGTON
• **Hotels & Restaurants map & index p. 192**
• **Part of Philadelphia area — see map p. 154**

KITCHEN BAR   215/576-9766   (97)
💎💎 American. Casual Dining. **Address:** 1482 Old York Rd 19001

LEE'S HOAGIE HOUSE   215/659-3322   (96)
💎 Sandwiches. Quick Serve. **Address:** 1656 Old York Rd 19001

ACME

BRADY'S RESTAURANT   724/423-4566
💎💎 American. Casual Dining. **Address:** 3242 State Rt 31 15610

ADAMSTOWN (H-10) pop. 1,789, elev. 980'
• **Hotels & Restaurants map & index p. 145**
• **Part of Pennsylvania Dutch Country area — see map p. 143**

Adamstown—called Antiques Capital, USA—and nearby Denver are considered gold mines by antiques lovers and collectors. Those shopping for furnishings or collectibles should not be disappointed.

Shopping: Between Adamstown and the nearby communities, there are nearly two dozen establishments selling antiques. Some of the shops are along SR 272 and can be accessed via the Pennsylvania Turnpike (I-76) exit 286. Some of the larger antique markets are Adamstown Antique Mall, Mad Hatter Antique Mall, Pine Hills Antique Mall, Renninger's Antique Market, Shupp's Grove, and Stoudt's Black Angus Antique Mall and Wonderful Good Market. Stoudtburg Village, off SR 272 on Stoudtburg Road, is a Bavarian-inspired village with more than 40 shops.

ADAMSTOWN INNS & COTTAGES   717/484-0800   **4**
💎💎💎 Historic Bed & Breakfast. **Address:** 144 W Main St 19501

Make the Connction

Find this symbol for places to look, book and save on AAA.com.

WHERE TO EAT

STOUDT'S BLACK ANGUS RESTAURANT
717/484-4386   (4)

💎💎
American Casual Dining $12-$39

AAA Inspector Notes: Victorian appointments decorate the casually upscale dining room, a favorite spot for special occasions. In addition to traditional German foods, such as Wiener schnitzel, the menu delivers steaks, crab cakes and delicious, homemade beer bread. The restaurant is also associated with the Stoudt Brewery and has a brewpub dispensing its products. **Features:** full bar, happy hour. **Reservations:** suggested. **Address:** 2800 N Reading Rd (SR 272) 19501 **Location:** I-76 (Pennsylvania Tpke) exit 286, 2.8 mi n on SR 272. (D)

ZIA MARIA'S ITALIAN RESTAURANT   717/336-1333   (5)
💎💎 Italian. Casual Dining. **Address:** 2350 N Reading Rd 17517

AIRVILLE (I-9) elev. 679'

On the grounds of the Indian Steps Museum, 205 Indian Steps Rd., is a giant holly tree that is more than 375 years old. Each year a small branch of the tree is broken off and presented to the Pennsylvania Power and Light Co. as payment of rent for the land occupied by the museum.

AKRON pop. 3,876
• **Hotels & Restaurants map & index p. 145**
• **Part of Pennsylvania Dutch Country area — see map p. 143**

BOXWOOD INN   717/859-3466   **15**
💎💎💎 Historic Bed & Breakfast. **Address:** 1320 Diamond St 17501

ALLEGHENY NATIONAL FOREST (D-4)
elev. 1,867'

Elevations in the forest range from 1,071 ft. at Baker Island near Tionesta to 2,245 ft. at Tracy Ridge Recreation Area. Refer to AAA maps for additional elevation information.

Allegheny National Forest extends 40 miles south from the New York-Pennsylvania border through the counties of Warren, Forest, Elk and McKean. The only national forest in Pennsylvania, its approximately 517,000 acres include 500 miles of fishing streams, 272 miles of hiking and cross-country ski trails, 300 miles of snowmobile trails and 108 miles of trail-bike and ATV routes. Several scenic drives traverse the area; contact the forest for recommended routes.

Six boat launches and a full-service marina provide access to the 12,000-acre Allegheny Reservoir *(see Warren p. 293 and Recreation Areas Chart)*, impounded by the Kinzua Dam *(see Warren p. 293 and Recreation Areas Chart)*. Water skiing is popular, and 10 of the forest's 21 campgrounds are on or near the shore. Six of these can be reached only by boat or on foot. Rimrock and Jake's Rocks overlooks offer picnicking and views of the dam and reservoir as well as spectacular displays of Pennsylvania's state flower, the mountain laurel, in June.

Several other picnic areas are available throughout the forest—some with unsupervised swimming facilities.

Another recreational activity is hunting for deer, bears, grouse and small game. Canoeing is popular on the Allegheny Wild and Scenic River, the Clarion River and, in the early spring, Tionesta Creek. Heart's Content, a 120-acre primeval tract of 300- to 400-year-old hemlock and beech trees, is 15 miles south of Warren.

The 8,663-acre Hickory Creek Wilderness provides opportunities for primitive camping, hiking, hunting, fishing and wildlife watching. Allegheny Islands Wilderness, comprised of seven islands totaling 368 acres in the Allegheny River, holds the distinction of being the smallest federally designated wilderness in the United States.

For more information contact the Forest Supervisor, Allegheny National Forest, 4 Farm Colony Dr., Warren, PA 16365. Phone (814) 728-6100. *See Recreation Areas Chart.*

ALLENTOWN (G-11) pop. 118,032, elev. 304'
- Hotels p. 40 • Restaurants p. 40
- Hotels & Restaurants map & index p. 37

Allentown is nestled in the Lehigh Valley along with Bethlehem *(see place listing p. 45)* and Easton *(see place listing p. 67)*. Allentown was originally incorporated as Northamptontown; German settlers played a key role in its development. The city later adopted the name of its founder, Colonial Pennsylvania Supreme Court Chief Justice William Allen.

After the Battle of Brandywine in 1777 George Washington had no hope of saving Philadelphia from the British. The Liberty Bell and the bells of Christ Church were secretly removed to Allentown to be hidden in Zion's Church. The church now houses the Liberty Bell Museum.

Allentown has 2,000 acres of park grounds; recreational opportunities can be found on the city's bike paths, hiking trails and golf courses. Fishing is permitted in rivers and streams. The Malcolm Gross Rose Garden and the Rose Garden, Parkway Boulevard and 27th Street, contain more than 100 varieties of roses, water plants and many other flowers. Peak bloom seasons are spring and fall. West Park features a fountain and war memorials surrounded by more than 200 types of trees; concerts are held in the summer at the band shell.

The city has three historic districts: Old Allentown; Old Fairgrounds; and West Park, which is centered around the city's first park and features Colonial Revival and Queen Anne architecture.

The 1,200-seat Miller Symphony Hall, 23 N. 6th St., is a renovated late 19th-century theater that is home to Allentown Symphony Orchestra. Musicals, theatrical events and symphony performances are given; phone (610) 432-6715 for the box office. The Civic Theatre of Allentown, 527 N. 19th St., offers live theater as well as independent and foreign films; phone (610) 432-8943.

Cedar Crest College and Muhlenberg College are institutions of higher education.

The Lehigh Valley IronPigs, Class AAA affiliate of the Philadelphia Phillies, play at Coca-Cola Park; phone (610) 841-7447.

Lehigh Valley SportsFest draws approximately 150,000 spectators and 10,000 amateur athletes, who compete in more than three dozen sporting events in parks across the city each July. In late August through early September the Great Allentown Fair, which supports the achievements of farmers, gardeners and homemakers, is held at the Allentown Fairgrounds. This annual event has been occurring since 1852 and features rides, games, shows and concerts; phone (610) 433-7541. Lights in the Parkway is a nearly 1.5-mile drive-through light display set to music along Lehigh Parkway, one of the city's parks, late November through late December; phone (610) 437-7530.

Lehigh County Historical Society operates the following nearby sites: Haines Mill Museum, 3600 Haines Mill Rd. in Cetronia; 1756 Troxell-Steckel Farmer Museum, 4229 Reliance St. in Egypt; and Lock Ridge Furnace Museum, 525 Franklin St. in Alburtis. For schedules phone (610) 435-1074.

Lehigh Valley Visitor Center: 840 Hamilton St., Suite 200, Allentown, PA 18101. **Phone:** (610) 882-9200.

Self-guiding tours: Brochures for the self-guiding Lehigh Valley Covered Bridges Tour, which leads past seven historic and picturesque bridges, are available at the convention and visitors bureau. Information about a local log cabin trail, the Lehigh Valley Wine Trail and bicycle trails also is available. Information about the Old Allentown historic district can be found at Lehigh Valley Visitor Center as well as at Old Allentown Preservation Association at 147 N. 10th St. and at City Hall.

Shopping: The Allentown Fairgrounds Farmers Market, 17th and Chew streets, features an Amish bakery, fresh produce, flowers, cheeses and specialty food items. It's open year-round Thursday through Saturday.

Lehigh Valley Mall, N. MacArthur Road and US 22, includes Boscov's, JCPenney and Macy's.

About 6.5 miles southeast of Allentown in Center Valley is The Promenade Shops at Saucon Valley, Center Valley Pkwy. and SR 309, which features more than 70 stores, including Banana Republic, Barnes & Noble, J. Jill and L.L. Bean.

AMERICA ON WHEELS MUSEUM, 5 North Front St. at jct. Hamilton St., presents creative exhibits portraying the many changes wheeled transportation has gone through over the years—from antique carriages to automobiles that run on alternative fuel sources. Cars, trucks, motorcycles and bicycles are displayed, and a gallery is dedicated to changing exhibits.

(See map & index p. 37.)

Some of the interactive exhibits included let visitors test their knowledge about mechanics' tools, have their photo taken while sitting in the driver's seat of a miniature race car, and learn about the options for powering cars in the future. The Kids' Car Service & Restoration Center offers children ages 12 and under a hands-on opportunity to learn about automobile maintenance.

Local history topics are tied into some of the exhibits. **Time:** Allow 1 hour, 30 minutes minimum. **Hours:** Tues.-Sat. 10-5, Sun. noon-5, Apr.-Dec.; Wed.-Sat. 10-4, Sun. noon-4, rest of year. Last ticket is sold 1 hour before closing. Closed major holidays. **Cost:** $10; $8 (ages 62+); $6 (ages 6-16); free (ages 0-12 Sun.). **Phone:** (610) 432-4200. GT

DA VINCI SCIENCE CENTER, 3145 Hamilton Blvd. Bypass, includes two floors of interactive science exhibits designed to entertain and inspire children under 13 and their families. A 72-foot dark tunnel, a saltwater marine tank, an animation station, a fossil wall and Newton riding chairs are featured. An area with activities designed for preschool children is available. Live and recorded programs also are offered throughout the year.

The lobby memorializes Leonardo da Vinci's design for a horse sculpture, which was completed more than 500 years later with the help of Allentown native Charles C. Dent and others. **Time:** Allow 3 hours minimum. **Hours:** Mon.-Sat. 10-5, Sun. noon-5. Closed Jan. 1, Easter, Thanksgiving and Christmas. **Cost:** $14.95; free (ages 0-2). **Phone:** (484) 664-1002.

DORNEY PARK AND WILDWATER KINGDOM is off I-78 exit 54, n.e. on Hamilton Blvd. (SR 222) and n. on Lincoln Ave. to jct.

Dorney Park Rd. With more than 134 years of operations, the site includes two parks spread across 200 acres and offers more than 100 attractions, thrill rides and shows. Dorney Park thrills guests with eight roller coasters, including Hydra: The Revenge, a floorless coaster; Talon: Grip of Fear, one of the Northeast's tallest inverted coasters; and Possessed, a U-shaped suspended impulse coaster. Planet Snoopy, inspired by the "Peanuts" comic strip, features 3.5 acres of rides and attractions that parents and children can enjoy together.

Wildwater Kingdom offers 28 waterslides, two tubing rivers, two giant wave pools, an aquatic fun house and three children's water-play areas. Family-friendly afternoon and scarier evening Halloween programs are offered weekends in fall months.

Time: Allow a full day. **Hours:** Both parks open daily, Memorial Day-Labor Day. Dorney Park also open Sat.-Sun., May 1-day before Memorial Day and day after Labor day-Oct. 28. Schedule may vary; phone to confirm. **Cost:** $58; $42 (under 48 inches tall and ages 62+); free (ages 0-2). Phone ahead to confirm rates. **Parking:** $20. **Phone:** (610) 395-3724. ⑪

LEHIGH VALLEY HERITAGE MUSEUM, 432 W. Walnut St., is the headquarters museum of the Lehigh County Historical Society. The museum collection includes thousands of artifacts and photographs, and the research library's collection contains nearly three million documents. The exhibit space comprises 13,000 square feet. Permanent exhibits focus on the history of Lehigh Valley and energy consumption.

Time: Allow 1 hour minimum. **Hours:** Museum Tues.-Sat. 10-4, Sun. noon-4. Library Tues.-Fri. 10-4. **Cost:** (includes admission to Historic Trout Hall, May-Sept.) $8; $3 (ages 2-11). **Phone:** (610) 435-1074. GT

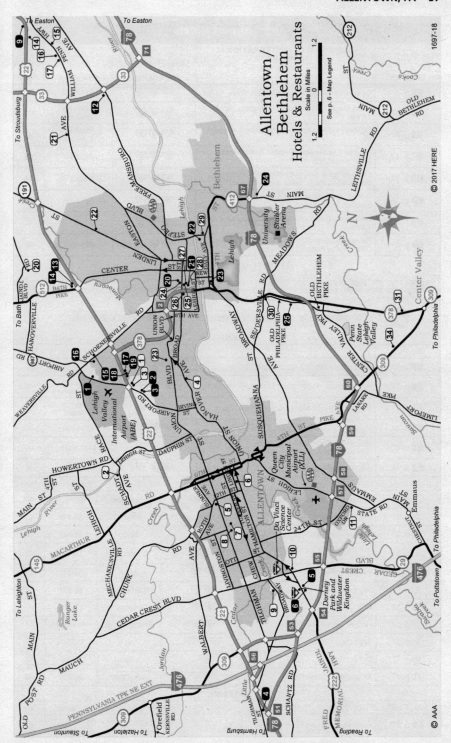

Allentown/
Bethlehem
Hotels & Restaurants

Scale in Miles

See p. 6 - Map Legend

© 2017 HERE

1697-18

© AAA

✈ Airport Hotels

Map Page	LEHIGH VALLEY INTERNATIONAL AIRPORT (Maximum driving distance from airport: 2.0 mi)	Diamond Rated	Rate Range	Page
1 p. 37	Days Hotel Allentown Airport/Lehigh Valley, 1.0 mi	♦♦♦	$80-$149	40
2 p. 37	Hilton Garden Inn Allentown Bethlehem Airport, 1.8 mi	♦♦♦	Rates not provided	40
3 p. 37	Staybridge Suites Allentown Bethlehem Airport, 1.8 mi	♦♦♦	Rates not provided	40
18 p. 37	Courtyard by Marriott Allentown Bethlehem/Lehigh Valley Airport, 2.0 mi	♦♦♦	$92-$347	45
19 p. 37	**Fairfield Inn & Suites by Marriott Allentown Bethlehem/Lehigh Valley Airport, 1.9 mi**	♦♦♦	$93-$243 [SAVE]	46
15 p. 37	Holiday Inn Express Hotel & Suites-Allentown area/Bethlehem Airport, 1.5 mi	♦♦♦	$99-$300	46
16 p. 37	Homewood Suites - Allentown/Bethlehem Airport, 1.3 mi	♦♦♦	$119-$349	46
17 p. 37	Residence Inn by Marriott Allentown Bethlehem/Lehigh Valley Airport, 2.0 mi	♦♦♦	$99-$347	46

Allentown/Bethlehem

This index helps you "spot" where approved hotels and restaurants are located on the corresponding detailed maps. Hotel daily rate range is for comparison only. Restaurant price range is a combination of lunch and/or dinner. Turn to the listing page for more information and consult display ads for special promotions.

 For more details, rates and reservations: AAA.com/travelguides/hotels

ALLENTOWN

Map Page	Hotels	Diamond Rated	Rate Range	Page
1 p. 37	Days Hotel Allentown Airport/Lehigh Valley	♦♦♦	$80-$149	40
2 p. 37	Hilton Garden Inn Allentown Bethlehem Airport	♦♦♦	Rates not provided	40
3 p. 37	Staybridge Suites Allentown Bethlehem Airport	♦♦♦	Rates not provided	40
4 p. 37	Holiday Inn Express & Suites Allentown West	♦♦♦	$85-$200	40
5 p. 37	Holiday Inn Express Hotel & Suites Allentown-Dorneyville	♦♦♦	$139-$269	40
6 p. 37	Allentown Comfort Suites	♦♦♦	$89-$244	40

Map Page	Restaurants	Diamond Rated	Cuisine	Price Range	Page
① p. 37	Ichiban Japanese Steak House	♦♦	Japanese	$10-$28	40
② p. 37	The Burger Shack	♦	Burgers	$6-$10	40
③ p. 37	Taste of Italy Ristorante	♦♦	Italian	$6-$27	40
④ p. 37	Stahley's Family Restaurant & Sports Bar	♦	American	$5-$20	40
⑤ p. 37	Bellissimo Ristorante	♦♦	Italian	$8-$25	40
⑥ p. 37	Bay Leaf Restaurant	♦♦	Asian Fusion	$8-$31	40
⑦ p. 37	Wert's Cafe	♦♦	American	$7-$22	40
⑧ p. 37	Henry's Salt Of The Sea	♦♦	Seafood Steak	$15-$40	40
⑨ p. 37	Grille 3501	♦♦♦	Asian	$10-$34	40
⑩ p. 37	Cali Burrito	♦	California	$4-$8	40
⑪ p. 37	A1 Japanese Steak House	♦♦	Japanese	$8-$28	40

EASTON

Map Page	Hotel	Diamond Rated	Rate Range	Page
9 p. 37	Holiday Inn Express Hotel & Suites	♦♦♦	Rates not provided	68

Map Page	Restaurants	Diamond Rated	Cuisine	Price Range	Page
⑭ p. 37	The James Eatery	♦♦	American	$6-$25	69
⑮ p. 37	Williams Family Restaurant	♦♦	American	$3-$16	69
⑯ p. 37	Nonna Lia Pizza Chef	♦♦	Italian	$6-$19	69
⑰ p. 37	Marblehead Grille and Chowder House	♦♦	Seafood	$13-$37	69

BETHLEHEM

Map Page	Hotels	Diamond Rated	Rate Range	Page
⑫ p. 37	**Courtyard by Marriott Bethlehem Lehigh Valley/I-78**	♦♦♦	$91-$385 SAVE	46
⑬ p. 37	**Best Western Lehigh Valley Hotel & Conference Center**	♦♦	$89-$159 SAVE	45
⑭ p. 37	Hampton Inn & Suites Bethlehem	♦♦♦	$119-$209	46
⑮ p. 37	Holiday Inn Express Hotel & Suites-Allentown area/Bethlehem Airport	♦♦♦	$99-$300	46
⑯ p. 37	Homewood Suites - Allentown/Bethlehem Airport	♦♦♦	$119-$349	46
⑰ p. 37	Residence Inn by Marriott Allentown Bethlehem/Lehigh Valley Airport	♦♦♦	$99-$347	46
⑱ p. 37	Courtyard by Marriott Allentown Bethlehem/Lehigh Valley Airport	♦♦♦	$92-$347	45
⑲ p. 37	**Fairfield Inn & Suites by Marriott Allentown Bethlehem/Lehigh Valley Airport**	♦♦♦	$93-$243 SAVE	46
⑳ p. 37	**Hyatt Place Bethlehem**	♦♦♦	$139-$249 SAVE	46
㉑ p. 37	Historic Hotel Bethlehem	♦♦♦	$179-$279	46
㉒ p. 37	**Sands Bethlehem**	♦♦♦♦	Rates not provided SAVE	46
㉓ p. 37	Comfort Suites University	♦♦♦	$115-$260	45
㉔ p. 37	Holiday Inn Express Hotel & Suites Bethlehem	♦♦♦	Rates not provided	46
㉕ p. 37	Wydnor Hall Inn	♦♦♦	Rates not provided	46

Map Page	Restaurants	Diamond Rated	Cuisine	Price Range	Page
⑳ p. 37	Hanoverville Roadhouse	♦♦	American	$7-$29	47
㉑ p. 37	Blue Grillhouse/Winebar	♦♦♦	Steak	$7-$47	46
㉒ p. 37	Stefano's Cafe	♦♦	Italian	$7-$26	47
㉓ p. 37	Red Hot Chinese Restaurant	♦♦	Szechuan	$7-$22	47
㉔ p. 37	Edge Restaurant and Lounge	♦♦♦	French	$15-$38	46
㉕ p. 37	Fegley's Bethlehem Brew Works	♦♦	American	$8-$22	47
㉖ p. 37	The Cafe	♦♦♦	Fusion	$5-$25	46
㉗ p. 37	Tapas on Main	♦♦	Spanish	$7-$24	47
㉘ p. 37	1741 on the Terrace	♦♦♦	American	$28-$38	46
㉙ p. 37	Burgers and More by Emeril	♦♦	Burgers	$5-$14	46
㉚ p. 37	Yianni's Taverna	♦♦	Greek	$14-$33	47
㉛ p. 37	Copperhead Grille	♦♦	American	$9-$23	46

CENTER VALLEY

Map Page	Restaurant	Diamond Rated	Cuisine	Price Range	Page
㉞ p. 37	Diana's Cafe & Catering	♦♦	American	$4-$11	55

(See map & index p. 37.)

ALLENTOWN COMFORT SUITES   (610)437-9100 **6**
▼▼▼ Hotel. **Address:** 3712 Hamilton Blvd 18103

COMFORT INN LEHIGH VALLEY WEST   (610)391-0344
▼▼ Hotel. **Address:** 7625 Imperial Way 18106

DAYS HOTEL ALLENTOWN AIRPORT/LEHIGH VALLEY
(610)266-1000 **1**
▼▼▼ Hotel. **Address:** 3400 Airport Rd 18109

HILTON GARDEN INN ALLENTOWN BETHLEHEM AIRPORT
610/443-1400 **2**
▼▼▼ Hotel. **Address:** 1787-B Air-   **AAA Benefit:**
port Rd 18109   Members save up to
                                       10%!

HOLIDAY INN EXPRESS & SUITES ALLENTOWN WEST
(610)530-5545 **4**
▼▼▼ Hotel. **Address:** 5630 Tilghman St 18104

HOLIDAY INN EXPRESS HOTEL & SUITES
ALLENTOWN-DORNEYVILLE   (610)437-9255 **5**
▼▼▼ Hotel. **Address:** 3620 Hamilton Blvd 18103

STAYBRIDGE SUITES ALLENTOWN BETHLEHEM AIRPORT
610/443-5000 **3**
▼▼▼ Extended Stay Hotel. **Address:** 1787-A Airport Rd 18109

WHERE TO EAT

A1 JAPANESE STEAK HOUSE   610/709-0998 **11**
▼▼ Japanese. Casual Dining. **Address:** 3300 Lehigh St,
Suite 320 18103

BAY LEAF RESTAURANT   610/433-4211 **6**
▼▼ Asian Fusion. Casual Dining. **Address:** 935 Hamilton St
18101

BELLISSIMO RISTORANTE   610/770-7717 **5**
▼▼ Italian. Casual Dining. **Address:** 1243 Tilghman St 18102

THE BURGER SHACK   610/443-2077 **2**
▼ Burgers. Quick Serve. **Address:** 2011 N 1st Ave 18052

CALI BURRITO   610/351-1791 **10**
▼ California. Quick Serve. **Address:** 3104 Hamilton Blvd 18103

GRILLE 3501   610/706-0100 **9**
▼▼▼ Asian. Fine Dining. **Address:** 3501 Broadway 18104

HENRY'S SALT OF THE SEA   610/434-2628 **8**
▼▼ Seafood Steak. Casual Dining. **Address:** 1926 W Allen St
18104

ICHIBAN JAPANESE STEAK HOUSE   610/266-7781 **1**
▼▼ Japanese. Casual Dining. **Address:** 1914 Catasauqua Rd
18109

STAHLEY'S FAMILY RESTAURANT & SPORTS BAR
610/433-2468 **4**
▼ American. Casual Dining. **Address:** 1826 Hanover Ave
18109

TASTE OF ITALY RISTORANTE   610/266-8011 **3**
▼▼ Italian. Casual Dining. **Address:** 1860 Catasauqua Rd
18109

WERT'S CAFE   610/439-0951 **7**
▼▼ American. Casual Dining. **Address:** 515 N 18th St 18104

ALTOONA (G-5) pop. 46,320, elev. 1,171'

Altoona was first settled in the mid-1700s. A series of stockades, including Fort Roberdeau, was
built to protect the region against Native American
raids. The region gained settlers and businesses
with the completion of the Pennsylvania Canal in
1834, and within several years, the demand for
lumber and coal gave rise to the railroad industry.
The Allegheny Portage Railroad was founded in Altoona in 1849 during construction of the first railroad
over the Alleghenies. For years the town's economy
depended on railroad building and repair shops, but
the area's economy has diversified and now includes manufacturing jobs.

PNG Field near Lakemont Park is home to Altoona's Class AA minor league baseball team, The
Curve, which is affiliated with the Pittsburgh Pirates;
phone (814) 943-5400 or (877) 992-8783 for ticket
information.

The 958-acre Canoe Creek State Park, 12 miles
east of Altoona, offers a wide assortment of summer
and winter activities: fishing, swimming, horseback
riding, boating, hiking, hunting, biking, cross-country
skiing, iceboating, ice fishing, ice-skating and tobog-
ganing. Environmental education and interpretive
programs for families also are offered; phone (814)
695-6807. *See Recreation Areas Chart.*

Explore Altoona: 1216 11th Ave., Suite 216, Altoona, PA 16601. **Phone:** (814) 943-4183 or (800)
842-5866.

Shopping: The major shopping center is Logan
Valley Mall, US 220 and Goods Lane. It features JC-
Penney, Macy's and Sears along with some 70
shops.

COMFORT SUITES ALTOONA   (814)942-2600
▼▼▼ Hotel. **Address:** 140 Stroehman Dr 16601

COURTYARD BY MARRIOTT ALTOONA   (814)312-1800
▼▼▼ Hotel. **Address:** 2 Convention   **AAA Benefit:**
Center Dr 16602   Members save 5%
                                       or more!

DAYS INN & SUITES   (814)944-4499
▼▼ Hotel. **Address:** 458 Sabbath Rest Rd 16601

HAMPTON INN-ALTOONA   (814)941-3500
▼▼▼ Hotel. **Address:** 180 Charlotte   **AAA Benefit:**
Dr 16601   Members save up to
                                       10%!

MICROTEL INN & SUITES BY WYNDHAM ALTOONA
(814)946-1400
▼▼ Hotel. **Address:** 1601 Valley View Blvd 16602

MOTEL 6 #1415   (814)946-7601
▼ Motel. **Address:** 1500 Sterling St 16602

QUALITY INN & SUITES   (814)944-9661
▼▼▼ Hotel. **Address:** 3306 Pleasant Valley Blvd 16602

SUPER 8 ALTOONA   (814)942-5350
▼▼ Motel. **Address:** 3535 Fairway Dr 16602

WHERE TO EAT

ALLEGRO   814/946-5216

◆◆◆
Italian
Casual Dining
$9-$35

AAA Inspector Notes: This quiet, family owned restaurant specializes in veal, steaks and pasta. The menu also includes seafood, Italian dishes and succulent filet mignon. Tiramisu and crème brûlée are the best bets among the homemade desserts. If your party includes four or more, you might consider ordering the traditional, family-style dinner. **Features:** full bar. **Reservations:** suggested, Fri & Sat. **Address:** 3926 Broad Ave 16601 **Location:** Jct Broad Ave and 40th St. D

FINELLI'S ITALIAN VILLA   814/943-8510
◆◆◆ Northern Italian. Casual Dining. **Address:** 1808 4th Ave 16602

AMBLER (A-10) pop. 6,417, elev. 217'
• Hotels & Restaurants map & index p. 192
• Part of Philadelphia area — see map p. 154

THE AMBLER ARBORETUM OF TEMPLE UNIVERSITY, 580 Meetinghouse Rd., features about a dozen garden areas and a greenhouse. The site was once part of the Pennsylvania School of Horticulture for Women, which was founded in 1910. It merged with Temple University in 1958. Among the gardens are several buildings from the former school; most are from the early 1900s, but the first dormitory/classroom building dates to the 1700s. Gravel walkways meander through the gardens. Highlights include the formal perennial garden and the woodland gardens. The latter was planted in the 1920s by the school's students and staff; its focus is trees—beech, dogwood, sycamore and tulip—many of which are tall enough to provide shade, but there are flowers and shrubs as well.

Maps for self-guided tours are available in garden kiosks and in the administration building. Guided tours available by reservation. **Time:** Allow 1 hour, 30 minutes minimum. **Hours:** Gardens open daily dawn-dusk. Administration building open Mon.-Fri. 8:30-5; building foyer open Sat.-Sun. 8:30-5. **Cost:** Donations. Guided tours $5. **Phone:** (267) 468-8000. GT

BRIDGET'S STEAKHOUSE   267/465-2000 82
◆◆◆ Steak. Fine Dining. **Address:** 8 W Butler Ave 19002

TRAX RESTAURANT AND CAFE   215/591-9777 83
◆◆◆ American. Fine Dining. **Address:** 27 W Butler Pike 19002

AMBRIDGE (G-1) pop. 7,050, elev. 700'
• Part of Pittsburgh area — see map p. 225

OLD ECONOMY VILLAGE, at 270 16th St. at jct. Church St., derives its title from the town of Oekonomie, built 1824-30 by the Harmony Society (*see Harmony p. 92*), a German communal group. Comprising 6.5 acres, the village contains 17 historic structures available for touring; the restored buildings showcase collections from the society. Historic formal gardens also are featured. A visitor center offers an orientation film, permanent and changing exhibits and a Works Progress Administration (WPA) mural depicting the Harmony Society. Staff is available to answer questions. Special events are offered throughout the year.

Time: Allow 2 hours minimum. **Hours:** Visitor center and self-guiding tours Wed.-Sat. 10-5, Sun. noon-5, Apr.-Dec. Closed major holidays and day after Thanksgiving. **Cost:** $10; $9 (ages 65+); $6 (ages 3-11); free (active military with ID). **Phone:** (724) 266-4500.

ARDMORE pop. 12,455
• Hotels & Restaurants map & index p. 192
• Part of Philadelphia area — see map p. 154

MIKADO THAI PEPPER   610/642-5951 125
◆◆ Asian. Casual Dining. **Address:** 64 E Lancaster Ave 19003

TIRED HANDS FERMENTARIA   484/413-2983 126
◆◆ American. Brewpub. **Address:** 35 Cricket Terrace 19003

AUDUBON (A-9) pop. 8,433, elev. 194'
• Part of Philadelphia area — see map p. 154

In the early 1900s some of the country's first feature-length motion pictures were produced a few miles east at a studio set up by Sigmund Lubin, a noted Philadelphia optician and movie producer. The lot, which accommodated 40 cowboys, 25 Native Americans and 100 horses, was used to film the "Battle of Shiloh," one of the first epic spectacles.

HOMEWOOD SUITES BY HILTON   (610)539-7300

◆◆◆
Extended Stay
Hotel
$119-$209

AAA Benefit: Members save up to 10%!

Address: 681 Shannondell Blvd 19403 **Location:** US 422 exit S Trooper Rd, 1.2 mi n. **Facility:** 123 efficiencies, some two bedrooms. 5 stories, interior corridors. **Terms:** 1-7 night minimum stay, cancellation fee imposed. **Pool:** heated outdoor. **Activities:** exercise room. **Guest Services:** valet and coin laundry, area transportation. **Featured Amenity:** breakfast buffet.

SAVE ◆ ☎ CALL ♿ ⬚ ✚ BIZ HS 🛜 ▤
▤ ▣ /SOME UNITS ▥

AVONDALE pop. 1,265
• Part of Philadelphia area — see map p. 154

THE FARM HOUSE RESTAURANT   610/268-2235
◆◆◆ Continental. Fine Dining. **Address:** 514 McCue Rd 19311

BALA-CYNWYD
• Hotels & Restaurants map & index p. 192
• Part of Philadelphia area — see map p. 154

AL DAR BISTRO   610/667-1245 129
◆◆ Mediterranean. Casual Dining. **Address:** 281 Montgomery Ave 19004

BARKEYVILLE pop. 207

QUALITY INN-BARKEYVILLE   (814)786-7901
♦♦ Motel. **Address:** 137 Gibb Rd 16038

WHERE TO EAT

KING'S FAMILY RESTAURANT   814/786-9494
♦♦ American. Casual Dining. **Address:** 5775 SR 8 16038

BARNESVILLE

COMFORT INN & SUITES   (570)773-5252
♦♦ Extended Stay Hotel. **Address:** 1252 Morea Rd 18214

BARTONSVILLE
- **Hotels & Restaurants map & index p. 266**
- **Part of Pocono Mountains Area — see map p. 264**

BAYMONT INN & SUITES   (570)476-1500 **39**

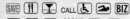

♦♦
Hotel
$90-$299

Address: 116 Turtlewalk Ln 18321 **Location:** I-80 exit 302B, 0.4 mi n. Located in a commercial area. **Facility:** 114 units. 2 stories, interior corridors. **Amenities:** safes. **Pool:** heated indoor. **Activities:** playground, game room, limited exercise equipment. **Guest Services:** coin laundry. **Featured Amenity: full hot breakfast.**

BEAR CREEK

BISCHWIND INN   570/332-8241
♦♦♦ Historic Bed & Breakfast. **Address:** 1 Coach Rd 18602

BEAVER pop. 4,531
- **Hotels & Restaurants map & index p. 246**
- **Part of Pittsburgh area — see map p. 225**

BERT'S WOODEN INDIAN   724/774-7992 **53**
♦♦ American. Casual Dining. **Address:** 308 Leopard Ln at Sharon Rd 15009

THE WOODEN ANGEL   724/774-7880 **54**
♦♦ American. Fine Dining. **Address:** 308 Leopard Ln at Sharon Rd 15009

BEAVER FALLS (F-1) pop. 8,987, elev. 787'
- **Part of Pittsburgh area — see map p. 225**

Beaver Falls, home to Geneva College, is along the banks of the Beaver River. When the Harmony Society purchased the site in 1859, an industrial boom began, which resulted in the area being referred to as a miniature Pittsburgh.

Beaver County Tourism: 121 Bradys Run Rd., Beaver Falls, PA 15010. **Phone:** (724) 770-2062 or (800) 342-8192.

BEAVER FALLS HISTORICAL SOCIETY MUSEUM is at 1301 Seventh Ave. (SR 18) in the basement of the Carnegie Free Library building. Historical items displayed include vintage fire department equipment, china, photo albums, clothing, 1800s Chinese cutlery and a Victorian-era room. **Time:** Allow 1 hour minimum. **Hours:** Mon.-Thurs.

10-2 and by appointment. Closed major holidays. Phone ahead to confirm schedule. **Cost:** Donations. **Phone:** (724) 494-2439 for the museum Mon.-Thurs., or (724) 846-4340 for the library. **GT**

MICROTEL INN & SUITES BY WYNDHAM BEAVER FALLS
(724)581-5273
♦♦ Hotel. **Address:** 2801 Darlington Rd 15010

PARK INN BY RADISSON BEAVER FALLS   724/846-3700
♦♦♦ Hotel. **Address:** 7195 Eastwood Rd 15010

WHERE TO EAT

GIUSEPPE'S TUSCANY GRILL   724/843-5656
♦♦ Italian. Casual Dining. **Address:** 7072 Big Beaver Blvd 15010

BEDFORD (H-5) pop. 2,841, elev. 1,060'

The Allegheny mountain area of Bedford was first settled in 1751 by Robert Ray, after whom Fort Raystown was named when it was built in 1758. Eventually the community was renamed in honor of the Duke of Bedford.

Several historic buildings have been preserved in Bedford, including the Espy House, which served as President Washington's headquarters in 1794 when he led Federal troops into western Pennsylvania to quell the Whiskey Rebellion. Also, the Anderson House, 137 E. Pitt St., was built 1814-15 and housed what is believed to be the first bank west of the Allegheny Mountains. The original bank vault still can be seen.

During the French and Indian War historic Forbes Road (US 30) was used by Gen. John Forbes on his way to capture Fort Duquesne, now known as Pittsburgh. The road winds through the farmlands and valleys of Bedford County and more than 14 covered bridges. Schellsburg Old Log Church, built in 1806, also is along Forbes Road.

In the early 1900s, Forbes Road became a vital link in nation's first transcontinental artery, the Lincoln Highway. Unusual tourist attractions and landmarks dotted the route, including an 18-foot-high coffee pot that lured travelers to a local luncheonette. Restored to its former glory, the architectural oddity can be seen on US 30, in the Bedford County Fairgrounds. This is one of many such sites commemorated by the Lincoln Highway Roadside Museum, a 200-mile, statewide heritage corridor that features historic buildings, road markers, exhibits and nostalgic murals. A brochure and driving tour map are available from the visitors bureau.

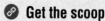

Free 2-hour guided tours of the downtown historic district are offered Fri. at 3:30, June-Oct.; phone (800) 765-3331.

Bedford County Visitors Bureau: 131 S. Juliana St., Bedford, PA 15522. **Phone:** (814) 623-1771 or (800) 765-3331.

Self-guiding tours: Brochures for walking, driving and bicycling tours are available at the visitors bureau.

FAIRFIELD INN & SUITES BY MARRIOTT BEDFORD
(814)623-3444

 Hotel. **Address:** 4436 Business Rt 220 15522

| **AAA Benefit:** Members save 5% or more! |

HAMPTON INN OF BEDFORD (814)624-0101

Hotel
$109-$189

AAA Benefit: Members save up to 10%!

Address: 4235 Business Rt 220 15522 **Location:** I-70/76 (Pennsylvania Tpke) exit 146, 0.5 mi s. **Facility:** 71 units. 4 stories, interior corridors. **Terms:** check-in 3:30 pm, 1-7 night minimum stay, cancellation fee imposed. **Pool:** heated indoor. **Activities:** hot tub, exercise room. **Guest Services:** valet laundry. **Featured Amenity:** breakfast buffet.

JUDY'S MOTEL-PA DUTCH HERITAGE (814)623-9118

 Motel. **Address:** 3521 Business Rt 220 15522

OMNI BEDFORD SPRINGS RESORT & SPA
(814)623-8100

Historic Resort Hotel
$129-$599

Address: 2138 Business Rt 220 15522 **Location:** I-70/76 (Pennsylvania Tpke) exit 146, 3.9 mi s. **Facility:** The resort, nestled in the Allegheny Mountains of southwest Pennsylvania, has a rich history and even a Revolutionary War flag mounted behind the front desk. Rooms are large with plush luxury bedding. 216 units, some two bedrooms. 4 stories, interior corridors. **Parking:** valet only. **Terms:** check-in 4 pm, 7 day cancellation notice-fee imposed, resort fee. **Amenities:** safes. **Dining:** 5 restaurants, also, The Crystal Room, The Frontier Tavern, see separate listings. **Pool:** heated outdoor, heated indoor. **Activities:** hot tub, fishing, regulation golf, tennis, recreation programs, bicycles, playground, lawn sports, trails, exercise room, spa. **Guest Services:** valet laundry, area transportation.

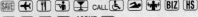

QUALITY INN BEDFORD (814)623-5188

 Hotel. **Address:** 4407 Business Rt 220 N 15522

THE CRYSTAL ROOM 814/623-8100
American. Fine Dining. **Address:** 2138 Business Rt 200 15522

ED'S STEAK HOUSE 814/623-8894
Steak. Casual Dining. **Address:** 4476 Business Rt 220 N 15522

THE FRONTIER TAVERN 814/623-8100
American. Casual Dining. **Address:** 2138 Business Rt 220 15522

THE GREEN HARVEST CO. CAFE 814/623-3465
Natural/Organic. Casual Dining. **Address:** 110 E Pitt St 15522

HOSS'S FAMILY STEAK & SEA 814/623-2793
Steak. Casual Dining. **Address:** 4308 Business Rt 220 15522

JEAN BONNET TAVERN 814/623-2250
American. Casual Dining. **Address:** 6048 Lincoln Hwy 15522

BELLEFONTE (F-6) pop. 6,187, elev. 747'

Bellefonte is built on several hills at the base of Bald Eagle Mountain. Many of the town's homes are fine examples of early Victorian architecture. Known as the Home of Governors, seven of the town's residents have become governors of Pennsylvania and other states. Several times per year, the Bellefonte Historical Railroad carries passengers through some of central Pennsylvania's most scenic landscapes; phone (814) 355-1053.

If you're interested in catch and release fly-fishing for trout, head to Fisherman's Paradise on Spring Creek Road, which parallels much of Spring Creek. A state fishing license is required; fishing is permitted daily dawn to dusk. For more information and location details phone (610) 369-0464 for Fisherman's Paradise, and (814) 359-5250 or (877) 707-4085 for the Pennsylvania Fish and Boat Commission.

Bellefonte Intervalley Area Chamber of Commerce: Train Station, 320 W. High St., Bellefonte, PA 16823. **Phone:** (814) 355-2917.

Self-guiding tours: A walking-tour brochure can be obtained from the chamber of commerce.

ECONO LODGE (814)355-5561
Motel. **Address:** 3482 Benner Pike 16823

REYNOLDS MANSION BED AND BREAKFAST (814)353-8407
Historic Bed & Breakfast. **Address:** 101 W Linn St 16823

BONFATTO'S 814/353-3330
Italian. Casual Dining. **Address:** 205 Park Pl, Suite 1 16823

BELLE VERNON pop. 1,093
• Part of Pittsburgh area — see map p. 225

COMFORT INN (724)929-3177
Hotel. **Address:** 4300 SR 51 S 15012

HAMPTON INN-BELLE VERNON   (724)929-8100
♦♦♦ Hotel. **Address:** 1525 Broad Ave Ext 15012

AAA Benefit: Members save up to 10%!

HOLIDAY INN EXPRESS & SUITES   (724)930-0100
♦♦♦ Hotel. **Address:** 181 Finley Rd 15012

BENSALEM (A-11) elev. 70'
• **Hotels & Restaurants map & index p. 192**
• **Part of Philadelphia area — see map p. 154**

Visit Bucks County: 3207 Street Rd., Bensalem, PA 19020. **Phone:** (215) 639-0300 or (800) 836-2825.

NATIONAL SHRINE OF SAINT KATHARINE DREXEL, 1663 Bristol Pike, houses the tomb of the founder of the Sisters of the Blessed Sacrament. Born into the wealthy Philadelphia Drexel family in 1858, Katharine Drexel devoted her life to the church and donated her $20 million inheritance to benefit African-Americans and Native Americans. **Hours:** Daily 10-5. Closed major holidays. **Cost:** Donations. **Phone:** (215) 244-9900.
🚊 Cornwells Heights, 254

BEST WESTERN PLUS PHILADELPHIA BENSALEM
(215)638-1500 **44**

♦♦♦♦ Hotel $89-$199

Best Western PLUS

AAA Benefit: Members save 5% to 15% and earn 10% bonus points!

Address: 3499 Street Rd 19020 **Location:** I-276 (Pennsylvania Tpke) exit 351, just s on US 1, then 0.3 mi e on SR 132. Located in a commercial area. **Facility:** 121 units. 2 stories, interior corridors. **Terms:** cancellation fee imposed. **Pool:** heated indoor. **Activities:** hot tub, exercise room. **Guest Services:** valet and coin laundry.

EXTENDED STAY AMERICA-PHILADELPHIA/BENSALEM
(215)633-6900 **47**
♦♦ Extended Stay Hotel. **Address:** 3216 Tillman Dr 19020

HAMPTON INN & SUITES PHILADELPHIA/BENSALEM
267/332-2200 **42**
♦♦♦ Hotel. **Address:** 3660 Street Rd 19020

AAA Benefit: Members save up to 10%!

HOLIDAY INN BENSALEM-PHILADELPHIA AREA
215/639-9100 **46**
♦♦♦ Hotel. **Address:** 3327 Street Rd 19020

HOLIDAY INN EXPRESS PHILADELPHIA NORTHEAST/BENSALEM   (215)245-5222 **48**
♦♦♦ Hotel. **Address:** 1329 Bristol Pike 19020

INN OF THE DOVE   215/638-3683 **43**
♦♦♦ Hotel. **Address:** 3901 Old Street Rd 19020

SLEEP INN & SUITES-BENSALEM   (215)244-2300 **45**
♦♦ Hotel. **Address:** 3427 Street Rd 19020

WHERE TO EAT

FISHER'S TUDOR HOUSE   215/244-9777 **90**
♦♦ American. Casual Dining. **Address:** 1858 Street Rd 19020

SPICE RACK   215/244-2566 **89**
♦♦ Indian. Casual Dining. **Address:** 2566 Knights Rd 19020

BENTLEYVILLE pop. 2,581
• **Part of Pittsburgh area — see map p. 225**

BEST WESTERN GARDEN INN   (724)239-4321

♦♦♦ Hotel $99-$129

Best Western

AAA Benefit: Members save 5% to 15% and earn 10% bonus points!

Address: 101 Gosai Dr 15314 **Location:** I-70 exit 32B, just s. **Facility:** 83 units. 3 stories, interior corridors. **Terms:** cancellation fee imposed. **Amenities:** safes. **Pool:** heated indoor. **Activities:** exercise room. **Guest Services:** valet and coin laundry. **Featured Amenity:** full hot breakfast.

HOLIDAY INN EXPRESS BENTLEYVILLE   (724)239-7700
♦♦♦ Hotel. **Address:** 25 Smita Ln 15314

WHERE TO EAT

KING'S FAMILY RESTAURANT   724/239-6202
♦♦ American. Casual Dining. **Address:** 206 Wilson Rd 15314

BENTON (COLUMBIA COUNTY) (E-9)
pop. 824, elev. 800'

RICKETTS GLEN STATE PARK is 11.3 mi. n. on SR 487. In the Glens Natural Area, 22 waterfalls are formed as Kitchen Creek winds through two deep gorges; Ganoga Falls is the tallest at 94 feet. There are 26 miles of hiking trails in the park. A full loop on the longest trail is 7 miles, and a 3-mile hike passes most of the falls. Other activities include snowmobiling, boating, fishing and swimming. *See Recreation Areas Chart.*

Hiking boots are recommended. Food is available Memorial Day-Labor Day. **Hours:** Daily dawn-dusk. Park office Mon.-Thurs. 8-4, Fri. 8 a.m.-9 p.m., Sat.-Sun. 8-6. **Cost:** Free. Fee for camping, cabins and boat rental. **Phone:** (570) 477-5675, or (888) 727-2757 for reservations.

BERWICK (F-9) pop. 10,477, elev. 505'

Berwick was founded as a religious refuge in 1786 by the Quaker Evan Owen, who named his community after Berwick-upon-Tweed, an English town on the Scottish border. Berwick is an industrial community that produces clothing, boxes, decorative ribbons, containers, snack foods, manufactured housing and metal parts.

BERWYN pop. 3,631
• Part of Philadelphia area — see map p. 154

RESIDENCE INN BY MARRIOTT PHILADELPHIA-VALLEY
FORGE   (610)640-9494
▼▼▼ Extended Stay Hotel. **Ad-**
dress: 600 W Swedesford Rd 19312   **AAA Benefit:**
                                        Members save 5%
                                        or more!

WHERE TO EAT

FRANKIE'S FELLINI CAFE   610/647-1737
▼▼ Italian. Casual Dining. **Address:** 678 Lancaster Ave
19312

LOTUS INN   610/725-8888
▼▼ Asian. Casual Dining. **Address:** 402 W Swedesford Rd
19312

NECTAR   610/725-9000
▼▼▼ Asian. Fine Dining. **Address:** 1091 Lancaster Ave
19312

QUINCY'S ORIGINAL LOBSTER ROLLS   484/328-3905
▼ Seafood. Quick Serve. **Address:** 414 W Swedesford Rd
19312

BETHEL (BERKS COUNTY)

COMFORT INN-BETHEL/MIDWAY   (717)933-8888
▼▼ Hotel. **Address:** 41 Diner Dr 19507

BETHEL PARK pop. 32,313
• Hotels & Restaurants map & index p. 246
• Part of Pittsburgh area — see map p. 225

CROWNE PLAZA HOTEL & SUITES PITTSBURGH
SOUTH   (412)833-5300 **113**

▼▼▼
Hotel
$119-$179

Address: 164 Ft Couch Rd 15241 **Lo-**
cation: 1 mi n on US 19. Opposite
South Hills Village Mall. 🚇 Bethel Village, 13. **Facility:** 179 units, some
kitchens. 2-8 stories, interior corridors.
Terms: cancellation fee imposed. **Pool:**
heated outdoor. **Activities:** exercise
room. **Guest Services:** valet and coin
laundry.

[SAVE] 🍴 🛏 🍸 CALL 🛗 🏊
🛠 [BIZ] 📶 ✉ 🚫 💻
/ SOME UNITS 🐾 🚪 🖥 🚃

BETHLEHEM (G-11) pop. 74,982, elev. 236'
• Restaurants p. 46
• Hotels & Restaurants map & index p. 37

Bethlehem is nestled in the Lehigh Valley along
with Allentown *(see place listing p. 35)* and Easton
(see place listing p. 67).

In 1741 a group of Moravian missionaries from
Europe arrived in what is now Bethlehem and established a community. They christened their settlement during the traditional vigils on Christmas Eve
with their patron, Count von Zinzendorf, who was
visiting from Europe. Many of the large stone buildings constructed by the Moravians are still in use;
the structures are considered among the finest examples of pre-Revolutionary German architecture in
the country. The visitor center offers guided tours of
the historic district.

Burnside Plantation, an 18th-century farm at 1461
Schoenersville Rd., was the first privately owned
Moravian residence in Bethlehem. Guided tours of
the grounds are offered throughout the year by appointment only; phone (610) 691-6055. Colonial Industrial Quarter, along Monocacy Creek at 459 Old
York Rd., is a restored 1700s industrial site that features a grist miller's house, a springhouse, a blacksmith's shop, the ruins of a pottery shop, a dye
house, a butchery and other historic structures. Visitors can watch blacksmiths at work in spring and
summer months. The 1810 Goundie House, at 501
Main St., is a Federalist-style brick home built by the
town's brewer. A kitchen, dining room and parlor
have been furnished in period, and changing exhibitions depict the story of 1800s Bethlehem. Phone
(610) 691-6055 for tour information for the Colonial
Industrial Quarter and the Goundie House.

Bethlehem is the home of three institutions of
higher education: Lehigh University, Moravian College and Northampton Community College. Moravian, established in 1742, is one of America's oldest
colleges, and Lehigh is a major research university.

🎭 Musikfest is a celebration of music, theater,
and arts and crafts held in the historic downtown
early- to mid-August. Celebrate the holiday season
at 🎭 Christkindlmarkt, which takes place on Main
and Spring streets late November to late December.

Historic Bethlehem Museums & Sites: 505 Main
St., Bethlehem, PA 18018. **Phone:** (610) 691-6055
or (800) 360-8687.

Self-guiding tours: Brochures of the Old Bethlehem historic district and tickets for guided walks of
the area are available at the visitor center.

BEST WESTERN LEHIGH VALLEY HOTEL &
CONFERENCE CENTER   (610)866-5800 **13**

▼▼
Hotel
$89-$159

 Best
Western.   **AAA Benefit:**
              Members save 5%
              to 15% and earn
              10% bonus points!

Address: 300 Gateway Dr 18017 **Loca-**
tion: US 22 exit Center St and SR 512.
Located in a commercial area. **Facility:**
192 units. 2 stories (no elevator),
interior/exterior corridors. **Terms:**
check-in 4 pm, cancellation fee imposed.
Dining: nightclub. **Pool:** outdoor. **Activ-**
ities: exercise room. **Guest Services:**
valet laundry.

[SAVE] 🐾 🍴 🛠 🍸 🏊 🛠

[BIZ] [HS] 📶 🚫 🚪 🖥 💻 / SOME UNITS 🐾

COMFORT SUITES UNIVERSITY   (610)882-9700 **23**
▼▼▼ Hotel. **Address:** 120 W 3rd St 18015

COURTYARD BY MARRIOTT ALLENTOWN BETHLEHEM/
LEHIGH VALLEY AIRPORT   (610)317-6200 **18**
▼▼▼ Hotel. **Address:** 2160 Motel   **AAA Benefit:**
Dr 18018   Members save 5%
                                      or more!

(See map & index p. 37.)

COURTYARD BY MARRIOTT BETHLEHEM LEHIGH VALLEY/I-78
(610)625-9500   **12**

Hotel
$91-$385

COURTYARD® Marriott

AAA Benefit: Members save 5% or more!

Address: 2220 Emrick Blvd 18020 **Location:** SR 33 exit Freemansburg Ave, just w. **Facility:** 138 units. 4 stories, interior corridors. **Terms:** cancellation fee imposed. **Pool:** heated indoor. **Activities:** hot tub, exercise room. **Guest Services:** valet and coin laundry, area transportation.

SAVE ✈ ▼ CALL ♿ 🛒 ⛨ BIZ HS 🛜 ✖ 🖥 ▯

/ SOME UNITS 📺

FAIRFIELD INN & SUITES BY MARRIOTT ALLENTOWN BETHLEHEM/LEHIGH VALLEY AIRPORT
(610)867-8681   **19**

Hotel
$93-$243

FAIRFIELD INN & SUITES Marriott

AAA Benefit: Members save 5% or more!

Address: 2140 Motel Dr 18018 **Location:** US 22 exit Airport Rd S, 0.8 mi se on Catasauqua Rd. Located in a commercial area. **Facility:** 103 units. 3 stories, interior corridors. **Terms:** cancellation fee imposed. **Pool:** outdoor. **Activities:** hot tub, exercise room. **Guest Services:** valet and coin laundry, area transportation. **Featured Amenity:** breakfast buffet.

SAVE ✈ ▮▮ CALL ♿ 🛒 ⛨ BIZ HS 🛜 ✖ 🖥 ▯ / SOME UNITS 📺

HAMPTON INN & SUITES BETHLEHEM   (610)868-2442   **14**
♦♦♦ Hotel. **Address:** 200 Gateway Dr 18017

AAA Benefit: Members save up to 10%!

HISTORIC HOTEL BETHLEHEM   (610)625-5000   **21**
♦ Historic Hotel. **Address:** 437 Main St 18018

HOLIDAY INN EXPRESS HOTEL & SUITES-ALLENTOWN AREA/BETHLEHEM AIRPORT   (610)882-2255   **15**
♦♦♦ Hotel. **Address:** 3375 High Point Blvd 18017

HOLIDAY INN EXPRESS HOTEL & SUITES BETHLEHEM
610/838-6110   **24**
♦♦♦ Hotel. **Address:** 2201 Cherry Ln 18015

HOMEWOOD SUITES - ALLENTOWN/BETHLEHEM AIRPORT
(610)264-7500   **16**
♦♦♦ Extended Stay Hotel. **Address:** 2031 Avenue C 18017

AAA Benefit: Members save up to 10%!

🔗 **For complete hotel, dining and attraction listings:**

AAA.com/travelguides

HYATT PLACE BETHLEHEM
(610)625-0500   **20**

Hotel
$139-$249

HYATT PLACE®

AAA Benefit: Members save 10%!

Address: 45 W North St 18018 **Location:** SR 378 exit 2 (Eighth Ave), just s, 0.7 mi w on Broad St, just n on Main St, then just w. **Facility:** 124 units. 6 stories, interior corridors. **Terms:** cancellation fee imposed. **Pool:** heated indoor. **Activities:** exercise room. **Guest Services:** valet laundry, area transportation. **Featured Amenity:** breakfast buffet.

SAVE ✈ ▼ CALL ♿ 🛒 ⛨ BIZ HS 🛜 ✖ 🎥 🖥 ▯ / SOME UNITS 📺

RESIDENCE INN BY MARRIOTT ALLENTOWN BETHLEHEM/ LEHIGH VALLEY AIRPORT   (610)317-2662   **17**
♦♦♦ Extended Stay Hotel. **Address:** 2180 Motel Dr 18018

AAA Benefit: Members save 5% or more!

SANDS BETHLEHEM
484/777-7690   **22**

Contemporary Resort Hotel
Rates not provided

Address: 77 Sands Blvd 18015 **Location:** I-78 exit 67, just off SR 412. **Facility:** After testing Lady Luck or enjoying one of the headlining events at this hotel, retreat back to your modern guest room with its pillow-top mattresses and upscale, glass-enclosed shower. 282 units. 10 stories, interior corridors. **Parking:** on-site and valet. **Amenities:** video games, safes. **Dining:** 8 restaurants, also, Burgers and More by Emeril, see separate listing. **Pool:** heated indoor. **Activities:** exercise room, spa. **Guest Services:** valet laundry.

SAVE ECO 🌀 ▮▮ ⛨ ▼ CALL ♿ 🛒 ⛨ BIZ 🛜 🎥

🖥 ▯

WYDNOR HALL INN   610/867-6851   **25**
♦♦♦ Bed & Breakfast. **Address:** 3612 Old Philadelphia Pike 18015

WHERE TO EAT

1741 ON THE TERRACE   610/625-5000   **28**
♦♦♦ American. Fine Dining. **Address:** 437 Main St 18018

BLUE GRILLHOUSE/WINEBAR   610/691-8400   **21**
♦♦♦ Steak. Fine Dining. **Address:** 4431 Easton Ave 18020

BURGERS AND MORE BY EMERIL   484/777-7777   **29**
♦♦ Burgers. Casual Dining. **Address:** 77 Sands Blvd 18015

THE CAFE   610/866-1686   **26**
♦♦♦ Fusion. Fine Dining. **Address:** 221 W Broad St 18018

COPPERHEAD GRILLE   610/282-4600   **31**
♦♦ American. Casual Dining. **Address:** 5737 Rt 378 N 18015

EDGE RESTAURANT AND LOUNGE   610/814-0100   **24**
♦♦ French. Fine Dining. **Address:** 74 W Broad St 18018

(See map & index p. 37.)

FEGLEY'S BETHLEHEM BREW WORKS   610/882-1300   25
♥♥ American. Brewpub. **Address:** 559 Main St 18018

HANOVERVILLE ROADHOUSE   610/837-1122   20
♥♥ American. Casual Dining. **Address:** 5001 Hanoverville Rd 18017

RED HOT CHINESE RESTAURANT   610/419-4159   23
♥♥ Szechuan. Casual Dining. **Address:** 2126 W Union Blvd 18018

STEFANO'S CAFE   610/866-8886   22
♥♥ Italian. Casual Dining. **Address:** 2970 Linden St 18017

TAPAS ON MAIN   610/868-8903   27
♥♥ Spanish. Casual Dining. **Address:** 500 Main St 18018

YIANNI'S TAVERNA   610/867-8821   30
♥♥ Greek. Casual Dining. **Address:** 3670 Old Philadelphia Pike 18015

BIRD-IN-HAND (H-9) pop. 402, elev. 360'

- Hotels p. 48 • Restaurants p. 48
- Hotels & Restaurants map & index p. 148
- Part of Pennsylvania Dutch Country area — see map p. 143

Bird-in-Hand took its name from a tavern sign that pictured a bird resting in a hand. Taverns of the period chose pictures over words because it was immediately recognizable to travelers, many of whom could not read. Four hotels have since stood on the site of the original Bird-in-Hand, which was built to serve travelers on the Philadelphia Turnpike.

Shopping: The Bird-in-Hand Farmers Market, 2710 Old Philadelphia Pike, is a great place to sample the area's specialty foods and crafts. The market is open Wed.-Sat. 8:30-5:30, July-Oct. Hours vary rest of year; phone (717) 393-9674.

The Old Village Store and Bird-in-Hand Village Antique Market, on SR 340, features an operating hardware store and an antique market with about 20 dealers. It is said to be one of the oldest hardware stores in the country. Phone (717) 278-1991.

ABE'S BUGGY RIDES, 2596 Old Philadelphia Pike, offers five different tours through Amish country in a horse-drawn Amish family carriage. The 1-hour ride and the 6.5-mile tour stop either at an Amish home or a Mennonite craft and bake shop. A 10-mile tour also is available by advance reservation. **Hours:** Mon.-Sat. 9-5, late Mar.-day after Thanksgiving (weather permitting). Hours vary; phone ahead. **Cost:** $10-$60; $5-$15 (ages 3-12). **Phone:** (717) 392-1794. GT 元

PLAIN & FANCY FARM, 1.5 mi. e. on SR 340 to 3121 Old Philadelphia Pike, is an interpretive cultural center on 10 acres where visitors can enjoy buggy rides and tours, explore crafts and gift shops and dine on fresh, farm-to-table Amish cuisine. **Hours:** Open daily 9-8, Apr.-Dec.; Sat.-Sun. 9-6,

mid-Mar. through Mar. 31. Phone ahead to confirm schedule. **Cost:** Varies per activity. **Phone:** (717) 768-4400. 11

Amish Country Homestead, 3121 Old Philadelphia Pike at Plain & Fancy Farm, is furnished to reflect the Amish way of life. Guided tours lasting 45 minutes take visitors through nine rooms on two stories and an adjoining one-room Amish school. Background information is provided on such topics as plain clothes, education and living without electricity.

Hours: Daily 10:45-4:45, late Mar.-Nov. 30; Sat. (also week before Christmas and week after Christmas) 10:45-4:15, in Dec. Last tour begins at closing. Closed Thanksgiving and Christmas. Phone ahead to confirm schedule. **Cost:** $12.95; $8.95 (ages 4-12). Combination ticket with The Amish Experience Theater $19.95; $14.95 (ages 4-12). **Phone:** (717) 768-8400, ext. 210. GT

Amish Country Tours at Plain & Fancy Farm is 1.5 mi. e. on SR 340 at 3121 Old Philadelphia Pike in Bird-in-Hand. The narrated 1.5-hour Farmlands shuttle bus tour includes views of scenic Amish farmlands in eastern Lancaster County and Amish-related stops. During the 3-hour Amish Visit In Person tour, visitors can observe and talk with the Amish at three different properties. Tours are limited to 14 passengers.

The VIP tour is limited to 14 passengers and is not recommended for young children. **Hours:** Farmland tour departs daily at 10, noon, 2 and 4, Apr.-Oct. VIP tour departs Mon.-Sat. at 5 (also at 10:30 and 2:30, July 1-Labor Day), mid-Apr. through Oct. 31. Phone ahead to confirm schedule. **Cost:** Farmland tour $29.95; $16.95 (ages 0-12). VIP tour $59.95; $39.95 (ages 6-16); ages 0-5 are not permitted. Reservations are recommended. **Phone:** (717) 768-8400, ext. 210. GT

The Amish Experience Theater, 3121 Old Philadelphia Pike at Plain & Fancy Farm, features a 30-minute multimedia presentation about a teenager who must choose between remaining in the modern, outside world or joining the Amish church and adopting the Amish lifestyle. Events from Amish history are re-created using special effects. Also featured are magic lantern shows, a form of entertainment featuring projected images that predate silent films.

Hours: Presentations are given daily 10-5, late Mar.-Nov. 30; Sat. (also week before Christmas and week after Christmas) 10-5, in Dec. Magic lantern shows are held in summer and on select days late Nov.-late Dec.; phone for schedule. Closed Thanksgiving and Christmas. Phone ahead to confirm schedule. **Cost:** $12.95; $8.95 (ages 4-12). Combination ticket with Amish Country Homestead $19.95; $14.95 (ages 4-12). **Phone:** (717) 768-8400, ext. 210.

(See map & index p. 148.)

AMISH COUNTRY MOTEL (717)768-8396 **41**
♦♦ Motel. **Address:** 3013 Old Philadelphia Pike (Rt 340) 17505

AMISH VIEW INN & SUITES (717)768-1162 **40**

♦♦♦♦
Hotel
$104-$214

Address: 3125 Old Philadelphia Pike (Rt 340) 17505 **Location:** On SR 340, 2 mi e. Located in a semi-rural area. **Facility:** 86 units, some two bedrooms and efficiencies. 3 stories, interior corridors. **Terms:** cancellation fee imposed. **Pool:** heated indoor. **Activities:** hot tub, game room, exercise room. **Guest Services:** coin laundry. **Featured Amenity:** full hot breakfast. *(See ad p. 117.)*

SAVE ❤ CALL ♿ 🚗 🛄
BIZ 🛜 ✕ 🖥 🖨 🖵
/SOME UNITS HS

BIRD-IN-HAND FAMILY INN (717)768-8271 **43**
♦♦ Hotel. **Address:** 2740 Old Philadelphia Pike (Rt 340) 17505

BIRD-IN-HAND VILLAGE INN & SUITES (717)768-1535 **42**
♦♦♦ Historic Country Inn. **Address:** 2695 Old Philadelphia Pike (Rt 340) 17505

LEAMAN'S LANCASTER COUNTRY LODGING
(717)656-7483 **39**
♦♦♦ Bed & Breakfast. **Address:** 155 Glenbrook Rd 17505

WHERE TO EAT

SMOKEHOUSE BBQ AND BREWS 717/431-8400 **31**

♦♦
Regional American Casual Dining
$7-$19

AAA Inspector Notes: A large gift shop of homemade wares and scrumptious desserts greets you before you enter the heart of this lively restaurant. The menu is filled with delicious pork, beef, chicken and turkey dishes cooked "low and slow" in a smoker lovingly known as "Lucille." A wide selection of locally produced beers and wines deliciously complements your meal. **Features:** full bar. **Address:** 3121 Old Philadelphia Pike (Rt 340) 17505 **Location:** On SR 340, 2 mi e; at Plain & Fancy Farm. L D CALL ♿

BLAIRSVILLE pop. 3,412, elev. 1,017'

HAMPTON INN & SUITES BLAIRSVILLE (724)459-5920
♦♦♦ Hotel. **Address:** 1762 Old William Penn Hwy 15717

AAA Benefit:
Members save up to 10%!

WHERE TO EAT

PIE CUCINA RISTORANTE 724/459-7145
♦♦ Italian. Casual Dining. **Address:** 181 E Brown St 15717

🔗 **Use the free online**

TripTik Travel Planner at

AAA.com/maps

BLAKESLEE elev. 1,677'
• **Part of Pocono Mountains Area — see map p. 264**

BEST WESTERN INN AT BLAKESLEE-POCONO
(570)646-6000

♦♦♦
Hotel
$72-$310

 Best Western.
AAA Benefit:
Members save 5% to 15% and earn 10% bonus points!

Address: 107 Parkside Ave 18610 **Location:** I-80 exit 284, just n. **Facility:** 85 units. 3 stories, interior corridors. **Terms:** cancellation fee imposed. **Pool:** heated indoor. **Activities:** sauna. **Guest Services:** coin laundry.

SAVE CALL ♿ 🚗 BIZ 🛜 ✕
🖵 /SOME UNITS 🐾 🖥

BLAWNOX pop. 1,432
• **Hotels & Restaurants map & index p. 246**
• **Part of Pittsburgh area — see map p. 225**

COMFORT INN & SUITES (412)963-0600 **63**
♦♦♦ Hotel. **Address:** 180 Gamma Dr 15238

BLOOMSBURG (F-9) pop. 14,855, elev. 530'

Its location on the Susquehanna River helped Bloomsburg emerge as an important player in the region's flourishing 19th-century iron industry. Today's downtown historic district features some 650 buildings that represent a variety of architectural styles from earlier eras.

Columbia-Montour Visitors Bureau: 121 Papermill Rd., Bloomsburg, PA 17815. **Phone:** (570) 784-8279 or (800) 847-4810.

BUDGET HOST PATRIOT INN 570/387-1776
♦♦ Motel. **Address:** 6305 Columbia Blvd 17815

COMFORT SUITES BLOOMSBURG (570)387-9100

♦♦♦
Hotel
$100-$229

Address: 120 Plaza Dr 17815 **Location:** I-80 exit 232 (SR 42), just e; in Buckhorn Plaza. **Facility:** 82 units, some efficiencies. 3 stories, interior corridors. **Pool:** heated indoor. **Activities:** game room, exercise room. **Guest Services:** valet and coin laundry. **Featured Amenity:** breakfast buffet.

SAVE ❤ ⓨ CALL ♿ 🚗 🛄
BIZ 🛜 ✕ 🖥 🖨 🖵
/SOME UNITS HS

ECONO LODGE (570)387-0490
♦♦ Hotel. **Address:** 189 Columbia Mall Dr 17815

FAIRFIELD INN & SUITES - BLOOMSBURG (570)416-2777
♦♦♦ Hotel. **Address:** 1065 Alliance Park Dr 17815

AAA Benefit:
Members save 5% or more!

HAMPTON INN BLOOMSBURG (570)380-1020

Hotel
$139-$229

AAA Benefit: Members save up to 10%!

Address: 255 Paper Mill Rd 17815 **Location:** I-80 exit 236 eastbound; exit 236A westbound, just sw. **Facility:** 70 units. 3 stories, interior corridors. **Terms:** 1-7 night minimum stay, cancellation fee imposed. **Pool:** heated indoor. **Activities:** hot tub, exercise room. **Guest Services:** valet and coin laundry. **Featured Amenity:** breakfast buffet.

THE INN AT TURKEY HILL (570)387-1500
Country Inn. **Address:** 991 Central Rd 17815

WHERE TO EAT

THE FARMHOUSE AT TURKEY HILL 570/387-1500
Regional American. Fine Dining. **Address:** 991 Central Rd 17815

LA FONTANA RISTORANTE & PIZZERIA 570/245-0057
Italian. Casual Dining. **Address:** 105 W Main St 17815

MARLEY'S BREWERY & GRILLE 570/784-9600
Comfort Food Pizza. Casual Dining. **Address:** 1323 Columbia Blvd 17815

TURKEY HILL BREWING COMPANY PUB & GRILLE
570/387-8422
American. Casual Dining. **Address:** 991 Central Rd 17815

BLUE BELL pop. 6,067
• **Hotels & Restaurants map & index p. 192**
• **Part of Philadelphia area — see map p. 154**

BLUE BELL INN 215/646-2010 (100)
Steak Seafood. Fine Dining. **Address:** 601 Skippack Pike 19422

BLUE MOUNTAIN

KENMAR MOTEL 717/423-5915
Vintage Motel. **Address:** 17788 Cumberland Hwy 17240

BOALSBURG (G-6) pop. 3,722, elev. 1,096'

An early stagecoach stop founded in 1808, Boalsburg has retained much of its original architecture and street layout.

Boalsburg lays claim as the site of the original Memorial Day, after a group of women honored those who died during the Civil War during a ceremony in 1864. Warrenton, Va., Charleston, S.C. and Savannah, Ga. also claim that they were the first to begin the holiday to honor soldiers who died in battle.

Shopping: The Village of Boalsburg offers taverns and quaint shops filled with antiques, art, flowers, crafts, gifts and collectibles. Many of the shops are in historic houses.

COLUMBUS CHAPEL AND BOAL MANSION MUSEUM is at 163 Boal Estate Dr. The Columbus Chapel was imported from Spain—where it was part of the Columbus Castle in Asturias—in 1909 by Col. Theodore Davis Boal, the husband of a descendant of Christopher Columbus. It features an admiral's desk said to have belonged to Columbus, 15th- and 16th-century artwork by European masters and two pieces of the cross on which Jesus Christ died. The mansion displays an array of Boal family items, including furnishings, papers, portraits, tools and weapons.

Time: Allow 1 hour, 30 minutes minimum. **Hours:** Tues.-Sun. 1:30-5, May-Oct.; other times by appointment. Phone ahead to confirm schedule. **Cost:** $10; $6 (ages 6-17); free (active military with ID). **Phone:** (814) 466-9266. (GT)

DUFFY'S TAVERN 814/466-6241
American. Casual Dining. **Address:** 113 E Main St 16827

BOILING SPRINGS pop. 3,225

BOILING SPRINGS TAVERN 717/258-3614
American. Casual Dining. **Address:** 1 E 1st St 17007

BOYERTOWN (H-11) pop. 4,055, elev. 386'

Known to the Pennsylvania Dutch who settled here as Boyer's Eck or Boyer's Corner, this community prospered because of its foundries and the craftsmen who manufactured caskets and vehicles. Today its orchards attract visitors.

Shopping: Several antique shops can be found in various areas throughout the town.

TWIN TURRETS INN 610/367-4513
Historic Bed & Breakfast. **Address:** 11 E Philadelphia Ave 19512

BRADDOCK HILLS pop. 1,880
• **Hotels & Restaurants map & index p. 246**
• **Part of Pittsburgh area — see map p. 225**

VELTRE'S PIZZA 412/271-3244 (76)
Pizza. Quick Serve. **Address:** 1268 Brinton Rd 15221

BRADFORD (C-4) pop. 8,770, elev. 1,437'
• **Hotels p. 50 • Restaurants p. 50**

Bradford was settled on the Tunungwant Creek in 1823 in the region known as the Tuna Valley but wasn't charted as a city until 1879. In 1871 oil was discovered and the price of land soared from 6.25 cents to $1,000 an acre. In less than 25 years the city boomed; residents sank wells everywhere. As the oil industry expanded in the area, the town became the world's first billion-dollar oil field. Bradford also has become a leader in manufacturing: Timber products, wooden toys, electronic parts, case knives and Zippo lighters are produced.

Of particular interest in the Downtown Bradford National Historic District are the Hooker-Fulton Building, a prime example of Art Deco architecture, and the still-operating Cline Oil Well on Main Street. Students at the University of Pittsburgh at Bradford campus can choose from more than 40 majors; phone (814) 362-7500. Bromeley Family Theater, 300 Campus Dr., presents a series of touring productions; phone (814) 362-5113 for ticket information.

One mile north of Bolivar Drive on the Seaward Avenue extension is Crook Farm, a collection of restored 19th-century buildings that includes a farmhouse, barn, carpenter shop, one-room schoolhouse, train depot and nature trails. Guided tours are available by appointment; phone (814) 362-3906 for information.

The Marilla Trail System is an interconnecting system of five trails: Marilla Bridges, Marilla Springs, Indian Pipe, White Pine and Hidden Valley. These trails offer raised boardwalks, covered bridges, wildlife viewing, fishing, canoeing and scenic hiking along Marilla Reservoir. Bradford is a launching site for hiking excursions within the Allegheny National Forest (see place listing p. 34 and Recreation Areas Chart) and New York's Allegany State Park, where there are more than 600 miles of trails available year-round.

Allegheny National Forest Visitors Bureau: 80 E. Corydon St., Bradford, PA 16701. **Phone:** (814) 368-9370 or (800) 473-9370.

ZIPPO/CASE MUSEUM, 1932 Zippo Dr., displays hundreds of rare production Zippo models and prototypes; interactive displays; and ZAC (Zippo and Case), an audio/kinetic ball machine with sound and motion. Visitors can watch technicians repair lighters at the Zippo Repair Clinic. **Hours:** Mon.-Sat. 9-5, Sun. 11-4. Closed Jan. 1-2, Easter, Thanksgiving and Christmas. **Cost:** Free. **Phone:** (814) 368-1932.

BEST WESTERN PLUS BRADFORD INN (814)362-4501

Hotel
$90-$160

AAA Benefit: Members save 5% to 15% and earn 10% bonus points!

Address: 100 Davis St S 16701 **Location:** US 219 exit Forman St southbound, just w to Davis St, then 0.3 mi s; exit Elm St northbound, just w. **Facility:** 112 units. 3 stories, interior corridors. **Terms:** cancellation fee imposed. **Pool:** heated outdoor. **Activities:** exercise room.

/ SOME UNITS

COMFORT INN-BRADFORD (814)368-6772
 Hotel. **Address:** 76 Elm St 16701

HOLIDAY INN EXPRESS BRADFORD (814)362-7090

Hotel
$109-$129

Address: 30 Tarport Dr Ext 16701 **Location:** US 219 exit Forman St, just w. **Facility:** 75 units. 3 stories, interior corridors. **Pool:** heated indoor. **Activities:** exercise room. **Guest Services:** coin laundry. **Featured Amenity:** continental breakfast.

THE LODGE AT GLENDORN 814/362-6511

Historic Country Inn
Rates not provided

Address: 1000 Glendorn Dr 16701 **Location:** US 219 exit Forman St, just s on Mechanic St, then 4.3 mi w on W Corydon St. Located in a quiet secluded area. **Facility:** On a forested 1,300-acre estate, this lodge specializes in rustic luxury with fresh flowers in your room upon check-in and homemade cookies, beverages and wood for your fireplace refreshed daily. 16 units. some kitchens, cabins and cottages. 1-2 stories (no elevator), interior/exterior corridors. **Pool:** heated outdoor. **Activities:** fishing, tennis, cross country skiing, snowmobiling, sledding, ice skating, recreation programs, bicycles, game room, lawn sports, picnic facilities, trails, exercise room, spa. **Guest Services:** valet laundry, area transportation. **Featured Amenity:** full hot breakfast.

THE MOUNTAIN LAUREL INN (814)362-8006
Historic Bed & Breakfast. **Address:** 136 Jackson Ave 16701

WHERE TO EAT

BEEFEATERS 814/362-9717
Steak. Casual Dining. **Address:** 27 Congress St 16701

BREEZEWOOD

DAYS INN BREEZEWOOD (814)735-4352
Motel. **Address:** 16407 Lincoln Hwy 15533

HOLIDAY INN EXPRESS BREEZEWOOD (814)735-7666
Hotel. **Address:** 16503 Lincoln Hwy 15533

QUALITY INN-BREEZE MANOR (814)735-4311
Motel. **Address:** 16621 Lincoln Hwy 15533

BRIDGEVILLE pop. 5,148
• Hotels & Restaurants map & index p. 246
• Part of Pittsburgh area — see map p. 225

HAMPTON INN 412/319-7706 103
Hotel. **Address:** 150 Old Pond Rd 15017

AAA Benefit: Members save up to 10%!

HOLIDAY INN EXPRESS 412/914-2000 104
Hotel. **Address:** 3053 Washington Pike 15017

WHERE TO EAT

KING'S FAMILY RESTAURANT 412/221-1119
American. Casual Dining. **Address:** 3049 Washington Pike 15017

(See map & index p. 246.)

LABELLA BEAN COFFEE HOUSE & EATERY
412/257-2202 107

⬙ American. Casual Dining. **Address:** 609 Washington Ave 15017

BROOKVILLE (F-4) pop. 3,924, elev. 1,230'

Brookville was settled about 1800 when Moses Knapp built a mill at the confluence of the North Fork and the Sandy Lick. Growth was slow, but in 1830 the town was named the county seat and settlement began in earnest. Between 1865 and 1874 Brookville had a thriving lumber industry and supplied all the lumber markets in Pittsburgh and along the Ohio. The arrival of the railroad in 1874 augmented industrial and commercial development.

Many of the town's 19th-century buildings have been preserved. Two such buildings are the 1867 three-story Greek Revival and Victorian Jefferson County Courthouse, Main and Pickering streets, and the Marlin Opera House, a 900-seat Italianate hall, which was in use 1884-1902.

PA Great Outdoors Visitors Bureau: 2801 Maplevale Rd., Brookville, PA 15825. **Phone:** (814) 849-5197.

Self-guiding tours: Maps detailing a walking tour of the historic district are available at the visitors bureau.

THE COURTHOUSE GRILLE & PUB   814/849-2557
⬙⬙ American. Casual Dining. **Address:** 209 Main St 15825

BROWNSVILLE (H-2) pop. 2,331, elev. 380'

Brownsville is part of the Laurel Highlands (*see place listing p. 122*). Dunlap Creek Bridge, built in 1839, was the first cast-iron bridge built in America; it crosses Dunlap Creek, carrying US 40 through downtown Brownsville and connecting High and Market streets. A metal truss bridge known as the Intercounty Bridge was built in 1917; it separates Fayette County from Washington County.

BRYN MAWR pop. 3,779, elev. 412'
- Hotels & Restaurants map & index p. 192
- Part of Philadelphia area — see map p. 154

TANGO   610/526-9500 132
⬙⬙⬙ American. Casual Dining. **Address:** 39 Morris Ave 19010

BUCKS COUNTY
- Part of Philadelphia area — see map p. 154

One of the commonwealth's largest and most historic counties, Bucks County stretches into the countryside surrounding northern Philadelphia. This quiet, wooded region bordering the Delaware River is replete with rolling hills, old stone houses and covered bridges. William Penn named the county for its resemblance to Buckinghamshire in England. An interesting driving tour covering much of Bucks County follows the Delaware River along SR 32.

The narrow, winding streets of Doylestown, once an overnight stagecoach stop between Philadelphia and Easton, capture Bucks County's historic charm, as do Fallsington and Washington Crossing Historic Park.

The Delaware Canal, on which construction was begun in 1817, flows through New Hope, an artists' and writers' colony settled along the river. New Hope is known for its natural settings, book and antiques shops, art galleries and cafés on the banks of both the river and the canal. The town also is home to one of the nation's oldest and most famous summer theaters, the Bucks County Playhouse; phone (215) 862-2121.

Some places and towns in Bucks County are Bensalem, Bristol, Buckingham, Chalfont, Doylestown, Fairless Hills, Feasterville, Lahaska, Lambertville, Langhorne, Levittown, Morrisville, New Hope, Newtown, Quakertown, Trevose, Warrington, Washington Crossing Historic Park and Yardley.

Visit Bucks County: 3207 Street Rd., Bensalem, PA 19020. **Phone:** (215) 639-0300 or (800) 836-2825.

BURNHAM pop. 2,054

QUALITY INN & SUITES OF LEWISTOWN
(717)248-4961

⬙⬙ ◆◆
Motel
$74-$270

Address: 13015 Ferguson Valley Rd 17009 **Location:** US 322 exit Burnham, just w. **Facility:** 111 units. 2 stories (no elevator), exterior corridors. **Pool:** outdoor. **Guest Services:** valet and coin laundry. **Featured Amenity:** breakfast buffet.

SAVE ⛔ 🍴 🍽 ➤ BIZ 🛜 ▭
/SOME UNITS 🐾 📵 ▭

SUPER 8 BURNHAM-LEWISTOWN
(717)242-8888

⬙⬙
Hotel
$60-$129

Address: 12886 Ferguson Valley Rd 17009 **Location:** US 322 exit Burnham, just w; 3.1 mi n of jct US 22 and 522. **Facility:** 57 units. 2 stories, interior corridors. **Terms:** 2 night minimum stay - seasonal and/or weekends, cancellation fee imposed. **Amenities:** safes. **Featured Amenity:** continental breakfast.

SAVE ⛔ 🛜 ✕ ▭
/SOME UNITS 📵 ▭

BUSHKILL (F-12) elev. 371'
- Part of Pocono Mountains Area — see map p. 264

Bushkill is best known for its scenic waterfalls nestled deep within the wooded mountains.

◆◆ **BUSHKILL FALLS,** 2 mi. n.w. off US 209 on Bushkill Falls Rd., is not just one but eight waterfalls that can be seen via a series of rustic trails and wooden stairs and bridges over a 2-mile area. The falls' source is Bushkill Creek, which descends through the Pocono Mountains to the Delaware River, passing rocky walls, rushing through gorges and over boulders and tumbling over misty precipices along the way. Lush foliage, ferns, mosses, verdant forested areas and wildflowers line the pathways.

A choice of four color-coded trails of varying difficulties provides access to the falls for all levels of hikers. The simplest and shortest, the Green Trail, is a brief 10- to 15-minute trek to a scenic overlook of the Main Falls, which cascades in a 100-foot drop. Follow the yellow markers for views of the Main Falls, the Lower Gorge Falls, Laurel Glen and the Upper Canyon; plan on spending about 45 minutes. Approximately 75 minutes on the Blue Trail takes hikers to Pennell Falls, while about 2.5 hours (and 2 miles) of hiking on the Red Trail covers all eight cataracts, including Bridal Veil Falls. Benches along the trails provide spots to rest for a bit.

The entrance to the trails is through an indoor wildlife exhibit featuring native animals in dioramas. Families with children will appreciate the 18-hole miniature golf course; paddleboat rides; fishing; gem mining and an exhibit showcasing the Native American lifestyle and featuring a life-size replica of a Lenni Lenape longhouse.

Comfortable, non-slip walking shoes and bottles of water are recommended. Pets must remain on a leash and not be left unattended. **Time:** Allow 2 hours minimum. **Hours:** Open daily at 9, Apr.-Nov. (weather permitting). Phone for closing times, which vary by season. Last admission 1 hour before closing. Closed Thanksgiving. Phone ahead to confirm schedule. **Cost:** $14.50; $13.50 (ages 62+); $8.50 (ages 4-10). Fees for activities are additional. **Phone:** (570) 588-6682.

SAVE **POCONO INDIAN MUSEUM,** off I-80 exit 309 then 8 mi. n. on US 209, depicts the lifestyle of the Delaware Indians and displays examples of their bark houses, pottery, food and weapons. Many of the items displayed were unearthed in the Delaware Water Gap area. A 30-minute self-guiding audio tour is available. **Time:** Allow 30 minutes minimum. **Hours:** Daily 10-6, during DST; 10-5:30, rest of year. Last admission 45 minutes before closing. Closed Thanksgiving and Christmas. Phone ahead to confirm schedule. **Cost:** $6; $3 (ages 6-16). **Phone:** (570) 588-9338.

BUTLER (F-2) pop. 13,757, elev. 1,040'
• Part of Pittsburgh area — see map p. 225

Butler County was named for Revolutionary War hero Gen. Richard Butler, who served with Gen. George Washington.

The county has more than 1,200 farms. Moraine State Park *(see Recreation Areas Chart),* 8 miles

northwest on US 422, offers year-round recreation, including boating, swimming, hiking, biking and cross-country skiing.

Butler County Chamber of Commerce: 101 E. Diamond St., Lower Level Suite 116, P.O. Box 1082, Butler, PA 16003-1082. **Phone:** (724) 283-2222.

THE MARIDON MUSEUM is downtown at 322 N. McKean St. An extensive collection of Chinese and Japanese art includes jade and ivory sculptures, landscape paintings, tapestries, silk prints and ink-on-paper scrolls. An impressive display of Meissen porcelain, with some items dating to the early 18th century, also is featured. The entire collection, which totals more than 800 art objects, was acquired and donated by Mary Phillips, a lifelong Butler resident.

Time: Allow 1 hour minimum. **Hours:** Wed.-Sat. 11-4; other times by appointment. Closed major holidays. **Cost:** $4; $3 (ages 60+ and students with ID); free (ages 0-7 with an adult). Reservations are recommended 1 week in advance for guided tours. **Phone:** (724) 282-0123. GT

FAIRFIELD INN & SUITES BY MARRIOTT BUTLER
(724)283-0009
▼▼▼ Hotel. **Address:** 200 Fairfield Ln 16001

AAA Benefit:
Members save 5% or more!

HAMPTON INN BUTLER 724/431-2400
▼▼▼ Hotel. **Address:** 610 Butler Crossing 16001

AAA Benefit:
Members save up to 10%!

LOCUST BROOK LODGE 724/283-8453
▼▼ Bed & Breakfast. **Address:** 179 Eagle Mill Rd 16001

WHERE TO EAT

THE BRICK HOUSE RESTAURANT 724/284-1159
▼▼ American. Casual Dining. **Address:** 118 N Main St 16001

FREEDOM FARMS SANDWICH SHOP 724/481-1444
▼ Sandwiches. Quick Serve. **Address:** 796 Pittsburgh Rd 16002

KING'S FAMILY RESTAURANT 724/282-1216
▼▼ American. Casual Dining. **Address:** 191 New Castle Rd 16001

RACHEL'S ROADHOUSE 724/841-0333
▼▼ American. Casual Dining. **Address:** 100 Fairfield Ln 16001

CAMP HILL pop. 7,888
• Hotels & Restaurants map & index p. 95

RADISSON HOTEL HARRISBURG 717/763-7117 31
▼▼▼ Hotel. **Address:** 1150 Camp Hill Bypass 17011

🔗 **For complete hotel, dining and attraction listings: AAA.com/travelguides**

(See map & index p. 95.)

WHERE TO EAT

CORK & FORK OSTERIA   717/317-9366 ㉗
♦♦ Italian. Casual Dining. **Address:** 4434 Carlisle Pike 17011

MASALA BISTRO   717/975-9091 ㉘
♦♦ Indian. Casual Dining. **Address:** 3401 Hartzdale Dr, Suite 120 17011

CANADENSIS
• **Hotels & Restaurants map & index p. 266**
• **Part of Pocono Mountains Area — see map p. 264**

BROOKVIEW MANOR INN   (570)595-2451 ⑬
♦♦♦ Bed & Breakfast. **Address:** 4534 Rt 447 18325

CANONSBURG (H-1) pop. 8,992, elev. 1,096'
• **Part of Pittsburgh area — see map p. 225**

Washington County Tourism Promotion Agency: 375 Southpointe Blvd., Suite 240, Canonsburg, PA, 15317. **Phone:** (724) 225-3010 or (866) 927-4969.

HILTON GARDEN INN PITTSBURGH/SOUTHPOINTE (724)743-5000

♦♦♦
Hotel
$119-$199

🏨 Hilton Garden Inn **AAA Benefit:** Members save up to 10%!

Address: 1000 Corporate Dr 15317 **Location:** I-79 exit 48, 0.3 mi w, then w on Southpointe Blvd. **Facility:** 175 units. 4 stories, interior corridors. **Terms:** 1-7 night minimum stay, cancellation fee imposed. **Pool:** heated indoor. **Activities:** exercise room. **Guest Services:** valet and coin laundry.

HOLIDAY INN EXPRESS - SOUTHPOINTE   724/743-4300
♦♦♦ Hotel. **Address:** 4000 Horizon Vue Dr 15317

HOMEWOOD SUITES PITTSBURGH-SOUTHPOINTE   (724)745-4663
♦♦♦ Extended Stay Hotel. **Address:** 3000 Horizon Vue Dr 15317

AAA Benefit: Members save up to 10%!

WHERE TO EAT

KING'S FAMILY RESTAURANT   724/745-2552
♦♦ American. Casual Dining. **Address:** 580 McClelland Rd 15317

CARBONDALE pop. 8,891

CARBONDALE GRAND HOTEL   570/536-6020
♦♦♦ Hotel. **Address:** 25 S Main St 18407

WHERE TO EAT

BEN-MAR RESTAURANT   570/282-5970
♦♦ Italian. Casual Dining. **Address:** 89 N Main St 18407

CARLISLE (H-7) pop. 18,682, elev. 469'
• **Hotels p. 54** • **Restaurants p. 54**

Founded in 1751, Carlisle was the home of James Smith, James Wilson and George Ross, three signers of the Declaration of Independence. The First Presbyterian Church, facing the town's main square, was built 1757-72. In this church the citizens of Carlisle chose Smith, Wilson and Ross to represent them at the Continental Congress. Mary Hays McCauley, the famous Molly Pitcher of the Battle of Monmouth, also lived in Carlisle. A life-size memorial in a cemetery on E. South Street marks her grave.

On Walnut Bottom Road, once a busy thoroughfare, is Two Mile House. This 1820 residence was built in the Federal style and served as a tavern 1826-1857. The house, which was named for its distance from the town square, features twelve rooms, ten of which have a fireplace. Tours may be arranged with the Cumberland County Historical Society; phone (717) 249-7610.

During the Confederate invasion in 1863 Gen. Richard S. Ewell's infantry corps, some of whom camped on the grounds of Dickinson College, occupied Carlisle for nearly 3 days. After their departure Union troops arrived but soon encountered additional Confederate cavalry under the command of Gen. Jeb Stuart, who ordered their surrender. The Union troops refused and the Confederates shelled the town until an urgent message from Gen. Robert E. Lee arrived directing all Confederate troops to converge on Gettysburg.

Originally founded as a British frontier outpost in 1757 to curb Native American attacks during the French and Indian war, Carlisle Barracks still serves as one of the oldest posts in the Army. The Carlisle Indian School, one of the first non-reservation schools for Native Americans, was established in 1879 at Carlisle Barracks, which is now the site of the U.S. Army War College. During its 39 years of existence the school attained an enrollment of more than 10,000 students representing all tribes in the United States. Jim Thorpe, winner of the pentathlon and the decathlon in the 1912 Olympic Games, attended the school. Monuments at the courthouse square, High and Hanover streets, honor Thorpe and Cumberland County's Civil War dead.

Activities at the 2,531-acre Kings Gap Environmental Education Center, 500 Kings Gap Rd., include hiking (18 miles of trails), hunting and birdwatching. Woodpeckers, great horned owls, white-tailed deer, snakes, turtles and wild turkeys are some of the park's inhabitants. Recreational and environmental education programs are offered throughout the year; the grounds are open daily dawn to dusk; offices are open weekdays 8-4; phone (717) 486-5031.

In nearby Boiling Springs, Allenberry Resort Inn and Playhouse is a 57-acre country estate that offers professional Broadway shows; phone (717) 258-3211.

Cumberland Valley Visitors Center: 33 W. High St., Carlisle, PA 17013. **Phone:** (888) 513-5130.

BEST WESTERN CARLISLE   (717)243-6200

Hotel
$70-$119

AAA Benefit: Members save 5% to 15% and earn 10% bonus points!

Address: 1155 Harrisburg Pike 17013 **Location:** I-76 (Pennsylvania Tpke) exit 226, just s. **Facility:** 72 units. 1 story, interior corridors. **Terms:** cancellation fee imposed. **Pool:** outdoor. **Activities:** exercise room. **Guest Services:** coin laundry.

SAVE 📶 CALL ♿ 🏊 🛗 BIZ
HS 📶 ✖ 🍴 📷 💻
/ SOME UNITS 🐾

COMFORT INN PA TURNPIKE-I-81   (717)706-3400
🔷🔷🔷 Hotel. **Address:** 77 Shady Ln 17013

COMFORT SUITES DOWNTOWN CARLISLE   (717)960-1000
🔷🔷🔷 Hotel. **Address:** 10 S Hanover St 17013

COUNTRY INN & SUITES BY CARLSON - CARLISLE, PA
                                        (717)241-4900

Hotel
$99-$239

Address: 1529 Commerce Ave 17015 **Location:** I-81 exit 44 (Plainfield Rd), s on SR 465 (Allen Rd), then left. **Facility:** 70 units. 3 stories, interior corridors. **Terms:** cancellation fee imposed. **Pool:** heated indoor. **Activities:** hot tub, exercise room. **Guest Services:** valet and coin laundry, area transportation. **Featured Amenity:** full hot breakfast.

SAVE 📶 CALL ♿ 🏊 🛗 BIZ
HS 📶 ✖ 🍴 📷 💻
/ SOME UNITS 🐾

DAYS INN CARLISLE-SOUTH   (717)258-4147
🔷🔷 Hotel. **Address:** 101 Alexander Spring Rd 17015

FAIRFIELD INN & SUITES BY MARRIOTT CARLISLE
                                        (717)243-2080
🔷🔷🔷 Hotel. **Address:** 1528 E Commerce Ave 17015

AAA Benefit: Members save 5% or more!

HAMPTON INN BY HILTON CARLISLE   (717)240-0200

Hotel
$114-$159

AAA Benefit: Members save up to 10%!

Address: 1164 Harrisburg Pike 17013 **Location:** I-76 (Pennsylvania Tpke) exit 226, just n; I-81 exit 52 (US 11) southbound; exit 52B northbound, 0.8 mi s. **Facility:** 97 units. 3 stories, interior corridors. **Terms:** 1-7 night minimum stay, cancellation fee imposed. **Pool:** heated indoor. **Activities:** hot tub, exercise room. **Guest Services:** valet and coin laundry. **Featured Amenity:** breakfast buffet.

SAVE CALL ♿ 🏊 🛗 BIZ HS 📶 ✖ 🍴 📷
💻 / SOME UNITS 🐾

HOLIDAY INN EXPRESS AND SUITES   717/240-0080
🔷🔷🔷 Hotel. **Address:** 1152 Harrisburg Pike 17013

PHEASANT FIELD BED & BREAKFAST   (717)258-0717

Historic Bed & Breakfast
$135-$255

Address: 150 Hickorytown Rd 17015 **Location:** I-76 (Pennsylvania Tpke) exit 226, 0.4 mi n on US 11, 2.3 mi right on S Middlesex Rd, 0.4 mi left on Ridge Dr, then right. Located in a quiet rural area. **Facility:** A former stop on the Underground Railroad, this serene, Federal-style, brick farmhouse is located near the Appalachian Trail. Guest rooms have modern amenities and are tastefully decorated. 8 units. 2 stories (no elevator), interior/exterior corridors. **Terms:** check-in 4 pm, 7 day cancellation notice-fee imposed. **Guest Services:** valet laundry. **Featured Amenity:** full hot breakfast.

SAVE 📶 ✖ 🚭 / SOME UNITS 🐾 🍴 📷 💻

RESIDENCE INN BY MARRIOTT HARRISBURG CARLISLE
                                        (717)610-9050

Extended Stay Hotel
$101-$261

Residence Inn Marriott

AAA Benefit: Members save 5% or more!

Address: 1 Hampton Ct 17013 **Location:** I-76 (Pennsylvania Tpke) exit 226, just n; I-81 exit 52 (US 11) southbound; exit 52B northbound, 0.8 mi s. **Facility:** 78 units, some two bedrooms, efficiencies and kitchens. 3 stories, interior corridors. **Terms:** cancellation fee imposed. **Pool:** heated indoor. **Activities:** hot tub, exercise room. **Guest Services:** valet and coin laundry. **Featured Amenity:** breakfast buffet.

SAVE 📶 CALL ♿ 🏊 🛗 BIZ HS 📶 ✖ 🍴
📷 💻 / SOME UNITS 🐾

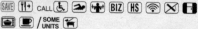
WHERE TO EAT

CAFE BRUGES   717/960-0223
🔷🔷 Belgian. Gastropub. **Address:** 16 N Pitt St 17013

HOSS'S FAMILY STEAK & SEA   717/258-4468
🔷 Steak. Casual Dining. **Address:** 1151 Harrisburg Pike 17013

MARKET CROSS PUB AND BREWERY   717/258-1234
🔷🔷 American. Casual Dining. **Address:** 113 N Hanover St 17013

MIDDLESEX DINER   717/241-2021
🔷🔷 American. Casual Dining. **Address:** 1803 Harrisburg Pike 17013

NORTH HANOVER GRILLE   717/241-5517
🔷🔷 American. Casual Dining. **Address:** 37 N Hanover St 17013

TRATTORIA PIATTO   717/249-9580
🔷🔷🔷 Italian. Fine Dining. **Address:** 22 W Pomfret St 17013

CARNEGIE pop. 7,972
• **Part of Pittsburgh area — see map p. 225**

KING'S FAMILY RESTAURANT   412/276-4544
🔷 American. Casual Dining. **Address:** 2100 Washington Pike 15106

CECIL
• **Part of Pittsburgh area — see map p. 225**

GOLDEN PIG   412/220-7170
🔷 Korean. Casual Dining. **Address:** 3201 Millers Run Rd 15321

CENTER VALLEY
• Hotels & Restaurants map & index p. 37

DIANA'S CAFE & CATERING   610/797-2525 (34)
♥♥ American. Casual Dining. **Address:** 4907 Rt 309 18034

CENTRE HALL (F-6) pop. 1,265, elev. 1,187'

PENN'S CAVE & WILDLIFE PARK, 5 mi. e. on SR 192 at 222 Penn's Cave Rd., is America's only all-water cavern and farm/nature/wildlife park. A 45-minute guided motorboat tour through the cavern features limestone formations. The site is still a working farm.

Also offered is a guided 90-minute tour of some of the 1,600 acres of the property's fields, farmland, grazing pastures and mountain trails. Highlights include bison, bobcats, white-tailed deer, elk, black bears, Texas longhorn cattle, timber wolves, bighorn sheep, a butterfly garden and a mountain lion den. A visitor center, a 4,800-square-foot Miner's Maze and gemstone panning also are offered. A 2-hour off-road jeep tour is available by advance reservation; restrictions apply.

Note: Caverns are not wheelchair accessible; 48 steps lead to the dock where tour boats are boarded. The cave's temperature is a constant 52 F. **Hours:** Cave tours depart daily 9-7, June-Aug.; daily 9-5, Apr.-May and Sept.-Oct.; daily 10-5 in Mar. and Nov.; Sat.-Sun. 11-5 in Feb. and Dec. Departure time for last cave tour varies; phone ahead. Wildlife Park tours available daily, Apr.-Oct.; Sat.-Sun., in Nov.; phone ahead to confirm schedule. Closed Thanksgiving and Christmas.

Cost: Cave tour $18.50; $17.50 (ages 65+); $15.50 (military with ID); $10.50 (ages 2-12); $7.50 (children of military ages 2-12). Wildlife Park tour $21.50; $20.50 (ages 65+); $15.50 (military with ID); $13 (ages 2-12); $8 (children of military ages 2-12). Combined cave and wildlife tour $31.99; $30.99 (ages 65+); $30 (military with ID); $17.99 (ages 2-12); $15 (children of military ages 2-12). Miners Maze $5.99; $2.99 (ages 2-12). Gemstone panning $10.50 (large bag); $5.95 (small bag). **Phone:** (814) 364-1664. GT ⑪ 🏕

CHADDS FORD (C-8) elev. 129'
• Part of Philadelphia area — see map p. 154

Chadds Ford is in the Brandywine Valley where the Revolutionary War engagement, the Battle of Brandywine, occurred. Chadds Ford also is home to the Wyeth family of artists. A river walk connects the Brandywine River Museum of Art *(see attraction listing)* with the circa 1725 John Chads House. The 1714 Barns-Brinton Tavern & House is nearby. Tours of the homes are given Sat. 11-3, Memorial Day weekend through Labor Day weekend, and by appointment. Contact the Chadds Ford Historical Society Barn Visitors Center, 1736 N. Creek Rd., for more information; phone (610) 388-7376. The visitor center, which was built to resemble the types of historic barns found in the area, has a small museum

with a combination of permanent and temporary exhibits pertaining to local history. The site is open Wed.-Fri., 10-4, year-round (also Sat. 11-4, Memorial Day-Labor Day).

GEM SAVE BRANDYWINE RIVER MUSEUM OF ART, on US 1 at 1 Hoffman's Mill Rd., is a 19th-century gristmill converted into a museum housing a collection of American art and illustration. Works by three generations of the Wyeth family are featured, with individual galleries devoted to N.C., Andrew and Jamie Wyeth. The galleries in the restored mill have original beams and pine floors. The museum grounds are landscaped with native plants and wildflowers.

Via a museum shuttle bus, visitors may take a 1-hour guided tour of the nearby Andrew Wyeth Studio, where the artist worked 1940-2008; the N.C. Wyeth house and studio, restored to their 1945 appearance, or Kuerner Farm, the inspiration for nearly 1,000 works completed during Andrew Wyeth's 70-year friendship with the Kuerner family.

Time: Allow 1 hour, 30 minutes minimum. **Hours:** Museum open daily 9:30-5. House and studio tours or Kuerner Farm tours are given early Apr. to mid-Nov. Food is available daily 10-3. Closed Thanksgiving and Christmas. **Cost:** $18; $15 (ages 65+); $6 (ages 6-18 and students with ID). Off-site tours additional $5-$8. Ages 0-5 are not permitted on off-site tours. **Phone:** (610) 388-2700, or (610) 388-8326 for off-site tour information. GT ⑪

BRANDYWINE RIVER HOTEL   (610)388-1200
♥♥ Hotel. **Address:** 1609 Baltimore Pike, Bldg 300 19317

WHERE TO EAT

THE GABLES AT CHADDS FORD   610/388-7700
♥♥♥ American. Fine Dining. **Address:** 423 Baltimore Pike 19317

CHALFONT pop. 4,009
• Part of Philadelphia area — see map p. 154

LOS SARAPES AUTHENTIC MEXICAN RESTAURANT & VILLA TEQUILA BAR   215/822-8858

◆◆
Mexican Casual Dining
$6-$25

AAA Inspector Notes: Traditionally prepared family recipes, including an extensive selection of beef, chicken and seafood dishes, are made from authentic ingredients. A buffet is set up for Sunday lunches. At the bar you'll find an extensive selection of Mexican beer and a wide variety of tequila offerings as well. **Features:** full bar, Sunday brunch, happy hour. **Reservations:** suggested. **Address:** 17 Moyer Rd 18914 **Location:** Just s of US 202. 🏠 Chalfont, 312. Ⓛ Ⓓ 🏕

CHALK HILL (I-2) pop. 141, elev. 2,000'

Chalk Hill is part of the Laurel Highlands (see place listing p. 122).

▼ FRANK LLOYD WRIGHT'S HOUSE ON KENTUCK KNOB, 6 mi. n. of US 40 at 723 Kentuck Rd. (Chalk Hill-Ohiopyle Rd.), was designed for Bernardine and I.N. Hagan in 1953 by renowned American architect Frank Lloyd Wright. The couple had admired Fallingwater, a house Wright had designed for the Kaufmann family, and asked him to design a house for them as well.

The house is one of Wright's Usonian designs and is constructed of tidewater red cypress and 800 tons of native sandstone; it appears to be part of the mountainous western Pennsylvania terrain. The design is based on a hexagonal grid with an open floor plan and expanses of glass, blurring the distinction between the indoor and outdoor spaces. The grounds include woodland trails with contemporary sculptures. A former greenhouse now serves as a visitor center. A guided 40-minute tour takes visitors around the exterior and through the interior of the home. The 90-minute in-depth tour shows visitors into secondary spaces of the home and highlights some of the collections on display. The Woodland Walk self-guiding tour explores the grounds and sculptures, providing views of the exterior of the house.

Time: Allow 1 hour, 30 minutes minimum. **Hours:** Guided tours are given Thurs.-Tues. 9-5, Wed. noon-5, Mar.-Oct.; Thurs.-Tues. 9-3, Wed. noon-3, in Nov.; Sat.-Sun. and day after Christmas-Dec. 31 10-3, in Dec. In-depth tours are offered daily; phone for schedule. Last Woodland Walk tour begins 1 hour before closing. Closed Jan. 1, Thanksgiving, Christmas Eve and Christmas. Phone ahead to confirm schedule. **Cost:** $25; $18 (ages 6-18 and students with ID). In-depth tour $65. Woodland Walk tour $15. Ages 0-5 are not permitted on interior house tours. Reservations are strongly recommended for guided tours. **Phone:** (724) 329-1901 for tour information. GT ✦

CHAMBERSBURG (I-6) pop. 20,268, elev. 613'

Nestled in the historic Cumberland Valley, Chambersburg experienced three raids by Confederate troops during the Civil War. The last incursion culminated in 1864 with the burning of the city after its refusal to pay an indemnity. In Memorial Square in the historic district is the five-tiered Memorial Fountain and its statue of a Union soldier; the memorial was dedicated in 1878 to honor Civil War soldiers. Facing south, the statue symbolizes protection against future invasions. Also in Memorial Square are Central Presbyterian Church, with its Tiffany glass windows, and the Franklin County Courthouse, which was rebuilt after the fire of 1864.

In the summer of 1859 Chambersburg served as a base of operations for abolitionist John Brown. His headquarters were at a local boarding house. Now known as the John Brown House, the building is at 225 E. King St.; phone (717) 264-1667 for schedule information.

Founding Fathers Park, on the historic site of Chambers Fort, has walkways and benches.

Chambersburg Heritage Center/Greater Chamber of Commerce: 100 Lincoln Way E., Chambersburg, PA 17201. **Phone:** (717) 264-7101.

Self-guiding tours: Brochures of walking and driving tours highlighting local historical sites are available at the chamber of commerce. Driving tour brochures are $1; walking tour brochures are free.

CHAMBERSBURG HERITAGE CENTER, 100 Lincoln Way E. on the town square, is housed in the restored white marble Valley National Bank Building. Two 10-minute films and exhibits about Native American tribes, the Revolutionary War, transportation and the Civil War showcase the town's history. Guided tours of the downtown historic area are offered. **Time:** Allow 1 hour minimum. **Hours:** Mon.-Fri. 8-5 (also Sat. 10-3, May-Oct.). Closed major holidays. **Cost:** Donations. Guided walking tour $3; with heritage center tour $5. Reservations are required for guided tours. **Phone:** (717) 264-7101. GT

HAMPTON INN BY HILTON CHAMBERSBURG
(717)261-9185

Hotel
$105-$189

AAA Benefit: Members save up to 10%!

Address: 955 Lesher Rd 17202 **Location:** I-81 exit 14, just e on SR 316. **Facility:** 121 units. 3 stories, interior corridors. **Terms:** 1-7 night minimum stay, cancellation fee imposed. **Pool:** heated outdoor. **Activities:** exercise room. **Guest Services:** valet laundry. **Featured Amenity:** continental breakfast.

HOLIDAY INN EXPRESS HOTEL & SUITES   717/709-9009
Hotel. **Address:** 1097 Wayne Ave 17201

LA QUINTA INN & SUITES CHAMBERSBURG   (717)446-0770
Hotel. **Address:** 199 Walker Rd 17201

RED LION INN & SUITES   717/263-9191
Hotel. **Address:** 1123 Lincoln Way E 17201

SLEEP INN & SUITES   (717)263-0596
Hotel. **Address:** 1435 Doron Dr 17202

WHERE TO EAT

BISTRO 71 RESTAURANT & BAR   717/261-0007
American. Casual Dining. **Address:** 71 N Main St 17201

CAFE D'ITALIA   717/262-4364
Italian. Casual Dining. **Address:** 9 N Main St 17201

COPPER KETTLE RESTAURANT   717/264-3109
American. Fine Dining. **Address:** 1049 Lincoln Way E 17201

KENZO JAPANESE & ASIAN FUSION RESTAURANT
717/263-0076
Japanese. Casual Dining. **Address:** 1495 Lincoln Way E, Suite 108 17202

MARIO'S ITALIAN RESTAURANT   717/263-9397
Italian. Casual Dining. **Address:** 831 Wayne Ave 17201

MONTEZUMA   717/709-1003
Mexican. Casual Dining. **Address:** 820 Wayne Ave 17201

THE ORCHARDS   717/264-4711
American. Fine Dining. **Address:** 1580 Orchard Dr 17201

ROSALIE'S FAB GRILL & WOOD-FIRED OVEN   717/262-4981
Italian Pizza Sandwiches. Casual Dining. **Address:** 1901 Scotland Ave 17201

VOLCANO JAPANESE RESTAURANT   717/504-8989
Japanese Sushi. Casual Dining. **Address:** 955 Wayne Ave 17201

CHESTER (C-10) pop. 33,972, elev. 23'
• Hotels & Restaurants map & index p. 192
• Part of Philadelphia area — see map p. 154

Settled by Swedes and Finns in 1644, Chester is one of the oldest settlements in Pennsylvania. Until its power waned in 1683, it was the most important town in the colony and the seat of its courts. The first meeting of the Pennsylvania Assembly was held in Chester in 1682, the year William Penn arrived.

The Caleb Pusey House, 2 miles west at 15 Race St. on Landingford Plantation in Upland, is a restored cottage built in 1683 of handmade bricks.

BEST WESTERN PLUS PHILADELPHIA AIRPORT SOUTH AT WIDENER UNIVERSITY   (610)872-8100 139

Hotel
$109-$139

Best Western PLUS. **AAA Benefit:** Members save 5% to 15% and earn 10% bonus points!

Address: 1450 Providence Ave (SR 320) 19013 **Location:** I-95 exit 6, just e to SR 320, follow signs. Across from Widener University. Chester T.C., 172. **Facility:** 60 units. 4 stories, interior corridors. **Terms:** cancellation fee imposed. **Amenities:** safes. **Activities:** exercise room. **Guest Services:** area transportation.

CHESTER SPRINGS elev. 275'
• Part of Philadelphia area — see map p. 154

MONTESANO BROTHERS   610/458-8065
Italian Sandwiches. Quick Serve. **Address:** 55 Seaboldt Way 19425

CLARION pop. 5,276, elev. 1,500'

HAMPTON INN-CLARION   (814)226-4444

Hotel
$109-$169

AAA Benefit: Members save up to 10%!

Address: 4 Hospital Dr 16214 **Location:** I-80 exit 62, just n. **Facility:** 72 units. 3 stories, interior corridors. **Terms:** 1-7 night minimum stay, cancellation fee imposed. **Pool:** heated indoor. **Activities:** exercise room. **Featured Amenity:** full hot breakfast.

PARK INN BY RADISSON - CLARION   814/226-8850
Hotel. **Address:** 45 Holiday Inn Rd 16214

QUALITY INN   (814)226-5230
Hotel. **Address:** 129 Dolby St 16214

WHERE TO EAT

BOB'S SUB & SANDWICH SHOP   814/226-7951
Sandwiches. Quick Serve. **Address:** 501 Main St 16214

RRR ROADHOUSE   814/227-2000
Steak. Casual Dining. **Address:** 22631 State Hwy 68 16214

CLARK (E-1) pop. 640, elev. 774'

TARA, just e. on SR 258 at 2844 Lake Rd., recalls the antebellum era of "Gone With the Wind." Spacious lawns, seasonal blossoms and a long veranda with white wicker furniture enhance the Southern atmosphere of this 1854 Greek Revival mansion, now an inn. Each room, named after a character from the Margaret Mitchell epic, is decorated with period furnishings and original works of art. Opulent chandeliers, Oriental rugs and a large collection of art and antiques create an atmosphere of Southern elegance. Tours are conducted by guides in Civil War-era costumes. **Time:** Allow 1 hour minimum. **Hours:** Tours depart Sat.-Sun. on the hour 10-2. Phone ahead to confirm schedule. **Cost:** $5. Reservations are strongly recommended. **Phone:** (724) 962-3535 or (800) 782-2803.

CLARKS SUMMIT pop. 5,116

COMFORT INN   (570)586-9100

Hotel
$80-$899

Address: 811 Northern Blvd 18411 **Location:** I-81 exit 194, on US 6 and 11; I-476 (Pennsylvania Tpke) exit 131. **Facility:** 65 units. 4 stories, interior corridors. **Guest Services:** valet laundry. **Featured Amenity:** full hot breakfast.

HAMPTON INN-CLARKS SUMMIT   (570)586-1515

Hotel
$119-$229

AAA Benefit: Members save up to 10%!

Address: 890 Northern Blvd 18411 **Location:** I-81 exit 194; I-476 (Pennsylvania Tpke) exit 131, 0.5 mi nw on US 6 and 11. Located in a commercial area. **Facility:** 68 units. 4 stories, interior corridors. **Terms:** 1-7 night minimum stay, cancellation fee imposed. **Pool:** heated indoor. **Activities:** hot tub, exercise room. **Guest Services:** valet and coin laundry. **Featured Amenity:** full hot breakfast.

NICHOLS VILLAGE HOTEL & SPA   570/587-1135
Boutique Hotel. **Address:** 1101 Northern Blvd 18411

RAMADA CLARKS SUMMIT-SCRANTON   (570)586-2730
Hotel. **Address:** 820 Northern Blvd 18411

WHERE TO EAT

STATE STREET GRILL   570/585-5590
New American. Casual Dining. **Address:** 114 S State St 18411

TULLY'S   507/586-2800
American. Casual Dining. **Address:** 820 Northern Blvd 18411

CLEARFIELD (F-5) pop. 6,215, elev. 1,100'

Visit Clearfield County: 208 Plaza Dr., Clearfield, PA 16830. **Phone:** (814) 765-5734.

BEST WESTERN PLUS CLEARFIELD   (814)768-1049

Hotel
$72-$170

Best Western PLUS

AAA Benefit: Members save 5% to 15% and earn 10% bonus points!

Address: 14424 Clearfield Shawville Hwy (Rt 879) 16830 **Location:** I-80 exit 120, just s. **Facility:** 69 units. 3 stories, interior corridors. **Terms:** cancellation fee imposed. **Pool:** heated indoor. **Activities:** hot tub, exercise room. **Guest Services:** valet and coin laundry. **Featured Amenity:** full hot breakfast.

CLEARFIELD RODEWAY INN   (814)765-7587

Motel
$55-$59

Address: 6259 Clearfield Woodland Hwy (US 322 E) 16830 **Location:** I-80 exit 120, 1.5 mi sw on SR 879, then 1.3 mi e. **Facility:** 34 units. 2 stories (no elevator), exterior corridors. **Featured Amenity:** continental breakfast.

COMFORT INN CLEARFIELD   (814)768-6400
Hotel. **Address:** 1821 Industrial Park Rd 16830

HAMPTON INN   (814)765-8300
Hotel. **Address:** 1777 Industrial Park Rd 16830

AAA Benefit: Members save up to 10%!

HOLIDAY INN EXPRESS HOTEL & SUITES CLEARFIELD   (814)768-7500
Hotel. **Address:** 1625 Industrial Park Rd 16830

SUPER 8-CLEARFIELD   (814)768-7580
Motel. **Address:** 14597 Clearfield Shawville Hwy (Rt 879) 16830

WHERE TO EAT

DUTCH PANTRY FAMILY RESTAURANT   814/765-2137
American. Casual Dining. **Address:** 14680 Clearfield Shawville Hwy 16830

MOENA   814/765-1564
Italian. Casual Dining. **Address:** 215 E Market St 16803

COATESVILLE pop. 13,100
• Part of Philadelphia area — see map p. 154

COURTYARD BY MARRIOTT PHILADELPHIA COATESVILLE/EXTON   (610)380-8700
Hotel. **Address:** 600 Manor Rd 19320

AAA Benefit: Members save 5% or more!

Get member rates and reservations at AAA.com/hertz

COLLEGEVILLE pop. 5,089, elev. 155'
• Part of Philadelphia area — see map p. 154

COURTYARD BY MARRIOTT PHILADELPHIA VALLEY FORGE/ COLLEGEVILLE   (484)974-2600
▼▼▼ Hotel. **Address:** 600 Campus Dr 19426

AAA Benefit: Members save 5% or more!

COLUMBIA (H-9) pop. 10,400, elev. 252'
• Hotels & Restaurants map & index p. 145
• Part of Pennsylvania Dutch Country area — see map p. 143

Founded in the early 1700s, Columbia is in the Susquehanna River Valley, a location that encouraged the development of the town's livelihood as a transportation and commercial center.

Susquehanna Valley Chamber of Commerce and Visitor Center: 445 Linden St., P.O. Box 510, Columbia, PA 17512. **Phone:** (717) 684-5249.

THE NATIONAL WATCH AND CLOCK MU-SEUM is off US 30 and SR 441 at 514 Poplar St. at jct. Fifth St. The museum, in a stately columned building, has what is said to be the largest collection of timepieces in North America as well as interactive exhibits that introduce visitors to horology, the study of time and timekeeping. After viewing a 10-minute introductory film explaining how clocks work, visitors enter the galleries through the Time Tunnel and begin a chronological examination of timekeeping and timepieces.

The history of timepieces is traced from Stonehenge to early water clocks to mechanisms used in early monasteries to clockmaking in the United States. Clockmaking in this country did not develop until after 1775, when tall case (grandfather) clocks were first made. During this time period, cabinets were made by a cabinetmaker and the clock mechanism by a clockmaker. One of the museum's finest collections is the large group of 18th- and 19th-century tall case clocks.

Other interesting displays include collections of European clocks, including German cuckoo clocks; vintage pocket watches; and old and new wristwatches. Sound effects accompany many exhibits, and murals and graphics provide background information about the timepieces displayed.

In addition, visitors can see timekeeping items from around the world including movements, tools and machinery; a cabinetmaker's workshop; a watch factory; a replica train master's office; a turn-of-the-20th-century watch and clock shop; and examples of various technological developments, from the earliest mechanical timepieces to the futuristic atomic clock. Temporary exhibits also are featured. A reference library and a computer-catalogued index are available.

Time: Allow 1 hour minimum. **Hours:** Tues.-Sat. 10-5, Sun. noon-4, Apr.-Nov. (also Mon. 10-5, Memorial Day-Labor Day); Tues.-Sat. 10-4, rest of year.

Closed Jan. 1, Easter, July 4, Thanksgiving and Christmas. **Cost:** $9; $8.50 (military with ID); $8 (ages 65+); $5 (ages 5-16); $23 (family, two adults and children under 18 in same household). **Phone:** (717) 684-8261.

TURKEY HILL EXPERIENCE, 301 Linden St. at jct. Third St., offers nine interactive exhibit areas showcasing the history and the inner workings of the Turkey Hill Dairy in Lancaster County. Though not a factory tour, visitors will learn how the company's ice cream and iced tea are made. They can milk a mechanical cow, design their own virtual ice cream flavor, make a Turkey Hill commercial and enjoy free samples of ice cream and iced tea. In the Taste Lab, ice cream lovers can add flavors, mix-ins and syrups to turn vanilla ice cream into their own custom flavor.

Time: Allow 1 hour, 30 minutes minimum. **Hours:** Daily 9:30-5, mid-June to early Sept.; daily 10-4 (also Sat.-Sun. 4-5), early Apr. to mid-June; daily 10-4, early Sept.-late Oct. Schedule varies rest of year; phone ahead. Closed Thanksgiving and Christmas. Phone ahead to confirm schedule. **Cost:** Turkey Hill Experience $9.95; $9.50 (ages 4-12 and 62+); free (military with ID). Combination ticket with Taste Lab $15.40; $14.95 (ages 4-12 and 62+); $5.45 (ages 0-3 and military with ID). Reservations are strongly recommended for Taste Lab. **Phone:** (844) 847-4884.

COMFORT INN LANCASTER COUNTY   (717)285-9100 **31**
▼▼ Hotel. **Address:** 3903 Abel Dr 17512

CONCORDVILLE
• Restaurants p. 60
• Part of Philadelphia area — see map p. 154

BEST WESTERN PLUS CONCORDVILLE HOTEL
                                             (610)358-9400

▼▼▼
Hotel
$115-$190

Best Western PLUS. **AAA Benefit:** Members save 5% to 15% and earn 10% bonus points!

Address: 780 Baltimore Pike 19331 **Location:** Jct US 322 W and 1. Located in a commercial area. **Facility:** 114 units, some two bedrooms. 5 stories, interior corridors. **Terms:** check-in 4 pm, cancellation fee imposed. **Amenities:** safes. **Dining:** Concordville Inn, see separate listing. **Pool:** heated indoor. **Activities:** game room, exercise room. **Guest Services:** valet and coin laundry, area transportation.

HAMPTON INN & SUITES CHADDS FORD   (610)358-9540
▼▼▼ Hotel. **Address:** 40 State Farm Dr 19342

AAA Benefit: Members save up to 10%!

WYNDHAM GARDEN GLEN MILLS   (610)358-1700

Hotel
$99-$365

Address: 1110 Baltimore Pike 19331 **Location:** Jct US 1 and 202. Located in a commercial area. **Facility:** 136 units, some two bedrooms and efficiencies. 5 stories, interior corridors. **Terms:** check-in 4 pm. **Amenities:** safes. **Pool:** outdoor. **Activities:** game room, exercise room. **Guest Services:** complimentary and valet laundry, area transportation. **Featured Amenity:** full hot breakfast.

SAVE 🍴 🍸 CALL 🐕 🏊 🚐 🛗
BIZ 🛜 ❌ 🔌 🖨 ▭
/ SOME UNITS HS

WHERE TO EAT

CONCORDVILLE INN   610/459-2230
🔷🔷 American. Casual Dining. **Address:** 780 Baltimore Pike 19331

CONNEAUT LAKE (D-1) pop. 653, elev. 1,083'

Conneaut Lake is Pennsylvania's largest natural lake and offers fishing, swimming, boating, water skiing and sailing.

CONSHOHOCKEN   pop. 7,833

• Hotels & Restaurants map & index p. 192
• Part of Philadelphia area — see map p. 154

RESIDENCE INN BY MARRIOTT PHILADELPHIA/ CONSHOHOCKEN   (610)828-8800 76

Extended Stay Hotel
$98-$276

Residence Inn Marriott
AAA Benefit: Members save 5% or more!

Address: 191 Washington St 19428 **Location:** I-76 (Schuylkill Expwy) exit 332 (SR 23), 0.3 mi over Fayette Bridge to Elm St, then just se along river. Located in a commercial area. 🚇 Conshohocken, 235. **Facility:** 137 units, some two bedrooms, efficiencies and kitchens. 6 stories, interior corridors. **Terms:** cancellation fee imposed. **Pool:** heated indoor. **Activities:** hot tub, exercise room.

Guest Services: valet and coin laundry, area transportation.

SAVE 🍴 🍸 CALL 🐕 🏊 🛗 BIZ HS 🛜 ❌
🔌 🖨 ▭ / SOME UNITS 🐾 🚲

WHERE TO EAT

BLACKFISH   610/397-0888 115
🔷🔷🔷 Continental. Fine Dining. **Address:** 119 Fayette St 19428

COYOTE CROSSING   610/825-3000 114
🔷🔷🔷 Mexican. Casual Dining. **Address:** 800 Spring Mill Ave 19428

EL LIMON   610/567-0120 116
🔷 Mexican. Casual Dining. **Address:** 103 Fayette St 19428

SPRING MILL CAFE   610/828-2550 113
🔷🔷🔷 French. Casual Dining. **Address:** 164 Barren Hill Rd 19428

COOKSBURG (E-3) elev. 1,197'

Cook Forest State Park is 1 mile north off SR 36. The park comprises some 7,182 acres of scenic drives and hiking trails set against the backdrop of the winding Clarion River. Once known as the "Black Forest," the area is famous for its stands of old growth forest and its abundance of deer. Canoeing and tubing are popular, as are camping, horseback riding, waterslides and winter sports. Mountain streams and reservoirs in the vicinity offer good trout fishing. *See Recreation Areas Chart.*

GATEWAY LODGE   814/744-8017
🔷🔷 Country Inn. **Address:** 14870 Rt 36 16217

WHERE TO EAT

GATEWAY LODGE   814/744-8017
🔷🔷 American. Casual Dining. **Address:** 14870 Rt 36 16217

CORAOPOLIS (G-1) pop. 5,677, elev. 722'

• Hotels & Restaurants map & index p. 246
• Part of Pittsburgh area — see map p. 225

Almost anyone who has ever spent a night at Pittsburgh International Airport hotel can say that they've been to Coraopolis—most of the hotels are in this suburb near the Ohio River. Big business also has a seat at the table in this Allegheny County town 15 miles northwest of downtown; it's the headquarters of Dick's Sporting Goods. A few miles away, in the heart of the borough itself, historic homes dot brick streets and a tall wrought iron clock and wooden gazebo can be found on the main corridor for shopping and business: 5th Avenue.

COURTYARD BY MARRIOTT PITTSBURGH AIRPORT
                                     (412)264-5000 71
🔷🔷🔷 Hotel. **Address:** 450 Cherrington Pkwy 15108
AAA Benefit: Members save 5% or more!

DOUBLETREE BY HILTON PITTSBURGH AIRPORT
                                     (412)329-1400 66
🔷🔷🔷 Hotel. **Address:** 8402 University Blvd 15108
AAA Benefit: Members save 5% or more!

EMBASSY SUITES BY HILTON PITTSBURGH INTERNATIONAL
AIRPORT   (412)269-9070 72
🔷🔷🔷 Hotel. **Address:** 550 Cherrington Pkwy 15108
AAA Benefit: Members save 5% or more!

HAMPTON INN PITTSBURGH AIRPORT (412)264-0020 67
🔷🔷🔷 Hotel. **Address:** 8514 University Blvd 15108
AAA Benefit: Members save up to 10%!

(See map & index p. 246.)

HYATT REGENCY PITTSBURGH INTERNATIONAL AIRPORT

(724)899-1234   **73**

Hotel
$99-$359

HYATT REGENCY®

AAA Benefit: Members save 10%!

Address: 1111 Airport Blvd 15231 **Location:** I-376 exit 53 (Airport Blvd), just n. Adjacent to airport. **Facility:** 336 units. 11 stories, interior corridors. **Parking:** on-site (fee). **Terms:** cancellation fee imposed. **Amenities:** safes. **Dining:** bellfarm Kitchen/Bar, see separate listing. **Pool:** heated indoor. **Activities:** sauna, hot tub, steamroom, exercise room. **Guest Services:** valet laundry, area transportation.

LA QUINTA INN PITTSBURGH AIRPORT   (412)269-0400   **68**
Hotel. **Address:** 8507 University Blvd 15108

PITTSBURGH AIRPORT SUPER 8   (412)264-7888   **69**
Motel. **Address:** 8991 University Blvd 15108

SHERATON PITTSBURGH AIRPORT HOTEL
(412)262-2400   **70**
Hotel. **Address:** 1160 Thorn Run Rd 15108

AAA Benefit: Members save 5% or more!

 WHERE TO EAT

ARMSTRONG'S RESTAURANT   412/262-9355   **70**
American. Casual Dining. **Address:** 1136 Thorn Run Rd 15108

BELLFARM KITCHEN/BAR   724/899-6050   **73**
American. Casual Dining. **Address:** 1111 Airport Blvd 15231

HYEHOLDE RESTAURANT   412/264-3116   **71**
Continental. Fine Dining. **Address:** 1516 Coraopolis Heights Rd 15108

KIYOSHI   412/269-2677   **69**
Asian. Casual Dining. **Address:** 6506 University Blvd 15108

WINGS, SUDS & SPUDS   412/264-1866   **72**
American. Casual Dining. **Address:** 8806 University Blvd 15108

CORNWALL   (H-9) pop. 4,112, elev. 620'

The Cornwall Ore Banks, on the knobs of South Mountain, Grassy Hill, Middle Hill and Big Hill, contain one of the most valuable deposits of iron ore in the East. The mines operated 1735-1972.

CORNWALL IRON FURNACE is off US 322, following markers on SR 419 to 94 Rexmont Rd. The furnace, built by Peter Grubb in 1742, operated until 1883. Structures on the grounds include the original furnace stack; the blast machinery; blowing tubs; wagon and blacksmith shops; the open-pit mine; and the ironmaster's mansion. Exhibits in the Charcoal House, now a visitor center, depict mining operations, charcoal making and iron making.

Time: Allow 1 hour, 15 minutes minimum. **Hours:** Thurs.-Sat. 9-5 (also Wed. 9-5, Memorial Day-Labor Day), Sun. noon-5. Last tour begins 1 hour, 45 minutes before closing. Closed major holidays except Memorial Day, July 4 and Labor Day. **Cost:** $8; $7 (ages 65+); $4 (ages 3-11). **Phone:** (717) 272-9711.

COUDERSPORT   (D-6) pop. 2,546, elev. 1,650'

Coudersport is a manufacturing community on the banks of the Allegheny River. It was founded by John Keating, an Irish mercenary who managed the Ceres Land Co., which owned most of the county. Keating gave 50 acres to each of the first 50 settlers and named the community after Jean Samuel Couderc, a Dutch banker. A monument to David Zeisberger, a Moravian missionary who camped nearby in October 1767, is in the county courthouse square at Second and Main streets.

WESTGATE INN   814/274-0400
Hotel. **Address:** 307 Rt 6 W 16915

CRABTREE   pop. 277

CARBONE'S   724/834-3430
Italian. Casual Dining. **Address:** 2582 Rt 119 15624

CRAFTON   pop. 5,951
• Hotels & Restaurants map & index p. 246
• Part of Pittsburgh area — see map p. 225

SAPPORO JAPANESE STEAKHOUSE   412/920-2988   **86**
Japanese. Casual Dining. **Address:** 4260 Steubenville Pike 15205

CRANBERRY

HOLIDAY INN EXPRESS HOTEL & SUITES

(814)677-2640

Hotel
$125-$149

Address: 225 Singh Dr 16319 **Location:** Jct US 322, just n on SR 257. Next to Cranberry Mall. **Facility:** 65 units. 3 stories, interior corridors. **Parking:** winter plug-ins. **Terms:** cancellation fee imposed. **Pool:** heated indoor. **Activities:** exercise room. **Guest Services:** coin laundry. **Featured Amenity:** continental breakfast.

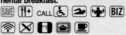

 WHERE TO EAT

EL TORO MEXICAN RESTAURANT   814/670-0532
Mexican. Casual Dining. **Address:** 7060 US 322 16319

CRANBERRY TOWNSHIP   (G-1)
• Hotels p. 62 • Restaurants p. 63
• Hotels & Restaurants map & index p. 246
• Part of Pittsburgh area — see map p. 225

North of Pittsburgh is the quickly growing community of Cranberry Township, at the crossroads of two

(See map & index p. 246.)

heavily traveled highways: I-76 and I-79. Though the name evokes images of the wild cranberries that once grew there along the banks of the Brush Creek, the only trace of those days are the descendants of the deer that ate them. The Pittsburgh Penguins opened a practice facility in 2015. Many local residents work at the sprawling Thorn Hill Industrial Park, and Cranberry Mall is a popular place of commerce.

BEST WESTERN PLUS PITTSBURGH/CRANBERRY TOWNSHIP   724/720-5600

[fyi] Hotel. Too new to rate, opening scheduled for March 2018. **Address:** 5001 Cranberry Springs Dr 16066 (See ad this page.)

| | AAA Benefit: Members save 5% to 15% and earn 10% bonus points! |

CANDLEWOOD SUITES   724/591-8666 **33**
◆◆◆ Extended Stay Hotel. **Address:** 20036 Rt 19 16066
CLARION INN   (724)772-1000 **34**
◆◆ Hotel. **Address:** 20003 Rt 19 16066
COMFORT INN CRANBERRY TOWNSHIP
                         (724)772-2700 **36**
◆◆◆ Hotel. **Address:** 924 Sheraton Dr 16066

COURTYARD BY MARRIOTT PITTSBURGH NORTH/ CRANBERRY WOODS   (724)776-1900 **29**

◆◆◆
Hotel
$80-$323

COURTYARD Marriott

AAA Benefit: Members save 5% or more!

Address: 150 Cranberry Woods Dr 16066 **Location:** I-79 exit 78 to Cranberry Woods Dr. **Facility:** 125 units. 5 stories, interior corridors. **Terms:** cancellation fee imposed. **Pool:** heated indoor. **Activities:** exercise room. **Guest Services:** complimentary and valet laundry.

[SAVE] [🍴] [♨] [▲] CALL [♿] [🏊] [✝]
[BIZ] [📶] [✖] [🔋] [💻]
/ SOME UNITS [📷]

DOUBLETREE CRANBERRY   (724)776-6900 **37**

◆◆◆
Hotel
$99-$179

DOUBLETREE BY HILTON

AAA Benefit: Members save 5% or more!

Address: 910 Sheraton Dr 16066 **Location:** I-76 (Pennsylvania Tpke) exit 28, 0.5 mi s on US 19; I-79 exit 76 (US 19) northbound; exit 78 southbound. **Facility:** 189 units. 5 stories, interior corridors. **Terms:** check-in 4 pm, 1-7 night minimum stay, cancellation fee imposed. **Amenities:** safes. **Pool:** heated outdoor, heated indoor. **Activities:** sauna, exercise room. **Guest Services:** valet and coin laundry.

[SAVE] [🍴] [♨] [▲] CALL [♿] [🏊] [✝] [BIZ] [HS] [📶]
[✖] [📷] [💻] / SOME UNITS [🦮] [🔋]

HAMPTON INN CRANBERRY   (724)776-1000 **28**
◆◆◆ Hotel. **Address:** 210 Executive Dr 16066

AAA Benefit: Members save up to 10%!

HILTON GARDEN INN PITTSBURGH/CRANBERRY
                         (724)779-9999 **25**
◆◆◆ Hotel. **Address:** 2000 Garden View Ln 16066

AAA Benefit: Members save up to 10%!

HOME2 SUITES BY HILTON PITTSBURGH CRANBERRY, PA
                         724/742-3800 **26**
◆◆◆ Extended Stay Hotel. **Address:** 1401 Cranberry Woods Dr 16066

AAA Benefit: Members save up to 10%!

⊘ **Where Diamonds make the difference:**
AAA.com/travelguides/hotels

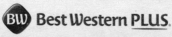

(See map & index p. 246.)

HYATT PLACE PITTSBURGH/CRANBERRY
(724)779-7900 **32**

▼▼▼▼
Hotel
$129-$649

HYATT PLACE
AAA Benefit: Members save 10%!

Address: 136 Emeryville Dr 16066 **Location:** I-76 (Pennsylvania Tpke) exit 28; I-79 exit 76 northbound, 0.7 mi n on US 19, then just w on Marguerite Dr. **Facility:** 127 units. 6 stories, interior corridors. **Terms:** cancellation fee imposed. **Amenities:** safes. **Pool:** heated indoor. **Activities:** exercise room. **Guest Services:** valet laundry. **Featured Amenity:** breakfast buffet.

[SAVE] [TI] [Y] CALL [&] [≈] [†] [BIZ] [🛜] [X] [🎥]
[🖥] [▣] / SOME UNITS [🐾] [HS]

PITTSBURGH MARRIOTT NORTH
(724)772-3700 **27**
▼▼▼▼ Hotel. **Address:** 100 Cranberry Woods Dr 16066

AAA Benefit: Members save 5% or more!

QUALITY INN
(724)772-0600 **31**
▼▼▼▼ Hotel. **Address:** 30 St. Francis Way 16066

RESIDENCE INN BY MARRIOTT PITTSBURGH CRANBERRY TOWNSHIP
(724)779-1000 **30**
▼▼▼▼ Extended Stay Hotel. **Address:** 1308 Freedom Rd 16066

AAA Benefit: Members save 5% or more!

SUPER 8-CRANBERRY
(724)776-9700 **35**
▼▼▼▼ Hotel. **Address:** 929 Sheraton Dr 16066

TOWNEPLACE SUITES BY MARRIOTT PITTSBURGH CRANBERRY TOWNSHIP
(724)779-7500 **24**
▼▼▼▼ Extended Stay Hotel. **Address:** 2020 Cool Springs Dr 16066

AAA Benefit: Members save 5% or more!

WHERE TO EAT

EAT'N PARK   724/776-4460
▼▼▼ American. Casual Dining. **Address:** 19085 Perry Hwy 16066

FIREBIRDS WOOD FIRED GRILL   724/831-5450 **47**
▼▼▼ Steak. Casual Dining. **Address:** 7300 Cranberry Springs Dr 16066

JUNIPER GRILL   724/591-8850 **48**
▼▼▼ American. Casual Dining. **Address:** 2030 Mackenzie Ste 800 Way 16066

MONTE CELLO'S CRANBERRY   724/772-3133 **46**
▼▼ Italian. Casual Dining. **Address:** 20325 Rt 19 Perry Hwy 16066

PIG IRON PUBLIC HOUSE   724/553-5592 **50**
▼▼▼ American. Gastropub. **Address:** 926 Sheraton Dr 16046

PRIMANTI BROS.   724/772-5757
▼▼ American. Casual Dining. **Address:** 200 Executive Dr 16066

TAMARIND   724/772-9191 **49**
▼▼ Indian. Casual Dining. **Address:** 10 St. Francis Way, Suite 6 16066

CRESCO
- Hotels & Restaurants map & index p. 266
- Part of Pocono Mountains Area — see map p. 264

CRESCENT LODGE   570/595-7486 **16**
▼▼▼▼ Country Inn. **Address:** 5854 Paradise Valley Rd 18326

WHERE TO EAT

CRESCENT LODGE   570/595-7486 **17**
▼▼▼▼ Continental. Casual Dining. **Address:** 5854 Paradise Valley Rd 18326

DANVILLE   pop. 4,699, elev. 456'

ABIGAIL HOUSE BED & BREAKFAST   570/284-4677
▼▼▼ Bed & Breakfast. **Address:** 12 Center St 17821

BEST WESTERN PLUS DANVILLE INN
(570)275-5750

▼▼▼
Hotel
$99-$159

Best Western PLUS
AAA Benefit: Members save 5% to 15% and earn 10% bonus points!

Address: 79 Old Valley School Rd 17821 **Location:** I-80 exit 224, just s. **Facility:** 58 units. 3 stories, interior corridors. **Terms:** cancellation fee imposed. **Pool:** heated indoor. **Activities:** exercise room. **Guest Services:** valet laundry. **Featured Amenity:** continental breakfast.

[SAVE] [TI+] CALL [&] [≈] [†] [BIZ]
[HS] [🛜] [X] [▣]
/ SOME UNITS [🐾] [🖥]

DANVILLE SUPER 8
(570)275-4640

▼▼▼
Motel
$65-$136

Address: 27 Sheraton Rd 17821 **Location:** I-80 exit 224, just sw on SR 54. **Facility:** 120 units. 3 stories (no elevator), exterior corridors. **Terms:** 3 day cancellation notice-fee imposed. **Activities:** game room, exercise room. **Guest Services:** coin laundry. **Featured Amenity:** continental breakfast.

[SAVE] [TI+] CALL [&] [†] [BIZ] [🛜]
[▣] / SOME UNITS [🐾] [HS] [🖥] [📷]

HAMPTON INN DANVILLE
(570)271-2500

▼▼▼
Hotel
$109-$220

Hampton by HILTON
AAA Benefit: Members save up to 10%!

Address: 97 Old Valley School Rd 17821 **Location:** I-80 exit 224, just s on SR 54. Located in a commercial area. **Facility:** 71 units. 3 stories, interior corridors. **Terms:** 1-7 night minimum stay, cancellation fee imposed. **Pool:** heated indoor. **Activities:** hot tub, exercise room. **Guest Services:** valet and coin laundry. **Featured Amenity:** breakfast buffet.

[SAVE] CALL [&] [≈] [†] [BIZ] [🛜] [X] [🖥] [📷] [▣]

WHERE TO EAT

OLD FORGE BREWING COMPANY   570/275-8151
▼▼ American. Casual Dining. **Address:** 298 Mill St 17821

DELAWARE WATER GAP (F-12) pop. 746, elev. 509'

- Hotels & Restaurants map & index p. 266
- Part of Pocono Mountains Area — see map p. 264

Tucked within the Delaware Water Gap National Recreation Area, the small town caters to those exploring the great outdoors. Businesses lining Main Street offer river trips, biking, kayaking and other recreational pursuits. One of the access points to the Appalachian Trail is near Main Street off Mountain Road; from the trailhead, hikers can venture to the top of Mount Minsi for a panorama of the Delaware Water Gap.

The Antoine Dutot Museum & Gallery, open 1-5 on weekends from Memorial Day weekend through Columbus Day, presents local history displays and art exhibits in a mid-19th-century brick schoolhouse; phone (570) 476-4240 for information. In early September, the Celebration of the Arts presents a weekend of jazz performances in a hillside amphitheater and at various venues throughout town; phone (570) 424-2210.

The Delaware River Scenic Drive, just outside town heading south on SR 611, affords views of the river cutting through an Appalachian Mountain ridge, known as a water gap. Drivers can pull off at Resort Point Overlook, Point of Gap Overlook and Arrow Island Overlook to enjoy the verdant scenery.

A Pennsylvania State Welcome Center providing local information is situated on Broad Street near its intersection with River Road.

DEER HEAD INN   570/424-2000 **35**
♥♥ Bed & Breakfast. **Address:** 5 Main St (SR 611) 18327

WATER GAP COUNTRY CLUB   (570)476-4653 **36**
♥♥ Historic Hotel. **Address:** 288 Mountain Rd 18327

WHERE TO EAT

APPLE PIE CAFE   570/476-9440 **45**
♥ Breakfast Sandwiches. Quick Serve. **Address:** 39 Broad St 18327

SYCAMORE GRILLE   570/426-1200 **46**
♥♥♥ American. Casual Dining. **Address:** 92 Main St 18327

DELAWARE WATER GAP NATIONAL RECREATION AREA (E-12) elev. 361'

- Part of Pocono Mountains Area — see map p. 264

Stretching for 40 miles along the Delaware River in New Jersey and Pennsylvania, Delaware Water Gap National Recreation Area encompasses nearly 70,000 acres. Popular with artists and wealthy vacationers during the late 1800s, the gap is a picturesque break in the Kittatinny Ridge of the Appalachian Mountains. The park is threaded by the Delaware River. Wooded Mount Tammany and Mount Minsi rise abruptly 1,200 feet above the river at the Water Gap.

More than 200 miles of scenic roads meander through the valleys and ridges of the park. Trails, wildlife, historic structures and waterfalls can be viewed along the way. A 27-mile portion of the Appalachian Trail winds its way along Kittatinny Ridge in New Jersey and Pennsylvania.

A variety of trails offer hiking, horseback riding and cross-country skiing opportunities. Camping is permitted in designated areas. Backcountry camping is permitted only along the Appalachian Trail, where regulations are in effect. Open fires are prohibited. On summer weekends lifeguards are on duty at Smithfield Beach, Milford Beach and Turtle Beach; the beaches charge a fee April through October. Canoeing, kayaking, boating and fishing (with state license) are permitted on the Delaware River. There are multiple access points; developed access points charge fees.

New Jersey's Millbrook Village, 12 miles north of Kittatinny Point Visitor Center along Old Mine Road, is a re-created rural community featuring residences and other buildings of the late 19th century. On weekends in summer interpreters in period dress demonstrate rural lifestyles; phone (908) 841-9531 on weekends Memorial Day weekend through Labor Day. During the Millbrook Days event in September, a hundred interpreters bring the village to life.

Raymondskill Falls, off US 209 at Milepost 18 on Raymondskill Road, is Pennsylvania's tallest waterfall. The upper falls are reached via a hike through a hemlock ravine, and the middle falls are reached via a hike with steep, uneven stairs. The upper falls hike is a quarter-mile round-trip, and the middle falls hike is a half-mile round-trip.

Dingmans Falls, Pennsylvania's second highest waterfall, is off Johnny Bee Road between Mileposts 12 and 13 on US 209 in Dingmans Ferry. A level, quarter-mile boardwalk leads to the bottom of the falls; for those who want to venture to the top, a steep, 240-step staircase awaits. The trail is open daily dawn-dusk (weather permitting); the road closes in winter due to snow and ice. Dingmans Falls Visitor Center offers information Wed.-Thurs. 9-5 and Fri.-Sun. 9-6, Memorial Day weekend through Labor Day. Phone (570) 828-6125 to confirm schedule.

Kittatinny Point Visitor Center, just off the I-80 toll bridge that crosses into New Jersey, has exhibits and free literature. The center is open Mon.-Tues. 9-5 and Fri.-Sun. 9-6, Memorial Day weekend through Labor Day. Phone (908) 496-4458 to confirm schedule.

Park headquarters is in Bushkill, Pa., 1 mile east of US 209 on River Road. It is open Mon.-Fri. 8:30-4:30; closed federal holidays. Phone (570) 426-2452.

Peters Valley School of Craft, at the junction of CR 615 and Old Mine Road near Layton, N.J., has several historic buildings that have been converted into studios for artisans, a gallery and a craft store; phone (973) 948-5202.

Pennsylvania's Pocono Environmental Education Center is off US 209 on Brisco Mountain Road, 7 miles north of Bushkill. The center offers guided treks, weekend ecology camps and naturalist-led activities; phone (570) 828-2319.

DELMONT pop. 2,686
• Part of Pittsburgh area — see map p. 225

HOLIDAY INN EXPRESS MURRYSVILLE/DELMONT
724/468-1050
♦♦♦ Hotel. **Address:** 6552 Rt 22 15626

SUPER 8 (724)468-4888
♦♦ Hotel. **Address:** 180 Sheffield Dr 15626

WHERE TO EAT

KING'S FAMILY RESTAURANT 724/468-6020
♦♦ American. Casual Dining. **Address:** 200 Sheffield Dr 15626

LAMPLIGHTER RESTAURANT 724/461-1031

♦♦
American
Casual Dining
$5-$30

AAA Inspector Notes: Breakfast is served all day at this family restaurant. The dining room offers fresh seafood; prime rib is served daily. Soup, bread and dessert are all homemade. The delicious Boston cream pie is moist and flavorful. On Sunday a dinner buffet is offered. American daredevil Evel Knievel ate here. **Features:** full bar, early bird specials, Sunday brunch, happy hour. **Reservations:** suggested. **Address:** 6566 William Penn Hwy 15626 **Location:** Just w of jct SR 66. [B] [L] [D] CALL [♿]

DENVER pop. 3,861
• Hotels & Restaurants map & index p. 145
• Part of Pennsylvania Dutch Country area — see map p. 143

COMFORT INN LANCASTER COUNTY NORTH
(717)336-7541 **34**
♦♦♦ Hotel. **Address:** 1 Denver Rd 17517

RED ROOF INN DENVER (717)336-4649 **35**
♦♦ Hotel. **Address:** 2017 N Reading Rd 17517

WHERE TO EAT

THE BLACK HORSE RESTAURANT & TAVERN
717/336-6555 **27**
♦♦ American. Casual Dining. **Address:** 2170 N Reading Rd 17517

DEVON (B-9) pop. 1,515, elev. 499'
• Part of Philadelphia area — see map p. 154

JENKINS ARBORETUM & GARDENS is off US 202 Devon/Valley Forge Rd. exit, .6 mi. s. on N. Valley Forge Rd. (which becomes Devon State Rd.), then .3 mi. w. to 631 Berwyn Baptist Rd. Azaleas, rhododendrons and wildflowers dominate the grounds of this 48-acre botanical garden, which include 1 mile of paved pathways lined with signs and labels informing visitors about the plants and ongoing ecological projects.

Animal residents include flying squirrels, foxes, green herons, kingfishers, owls, red-tailed hawks, turtles and more than 100 other bird species. A self-guiding map of the grounds is available in the John J. Willaman Education & Visitors Center. Educational activities are held and special exhibitions are on display throughout the year. Garden paths are not wheelchair accessible. Pets are not permitted. **Time:** Allow 1 hour, 30 minutes minimum. **Hours:** Gardens open daily 8

a.m.-sunset. Education center open daily 9-4. **Cost:** Free. **Phone:** (610) 647-8870. [🚐] Berwyn, 202

SHANGRILA 610/687-8838
♦♦♦ Asian. Fine Dining. **Address:** 120 W Swedesford Rd 19333

DICKSON CITY pop. 6,070

FAIRFIELD INN BY MARRIOTT-SCRANTON (570)346-3222
♦♦ Hotel. **Address:** 949 Viewmont Dr 18519

AAA Benefit:
Members save 5% or more!

HOLIDAY INN EXPRESS & SUITES 570/307-4437
♦♦♦ Hotel. **Address:** 1265 Commerce Blvd 18519

MICROTEL INN & SUITES BY WYNDHAM DICKSON CITY/SCRANTON (570)307-1200

♦♦♦
Hotel
$79-$114

Address: 232 Main St 18519 **Location:** I-81 exit 190, just n. **Facility:** 62 units. 3 stories, interior corridors. **Activities:** exercise room. **Guest Services:** valet and coin laundry. **Featured Amenity:** continental breakfast.

[SAVE] CALL [♿] [♿] [BIZ] [HS] [📶]
[✕] [📺] / SOME UNITS [🛏] [☕]

RESIDENCE INN BY MARRIOTT-SCRANTON (570)343-5121
♦♦ Extended Stay Hotel. **Address:** 947 Viewmont Dr 18519

AAA Benefit:
Members save 5% or more!

WHERE TO EAT

COLARUSSO'S COAL-FIRED PIZZA 570/489-2627
♦♦ Pizza. Casual Dining. **Address:** 1126 Commerce Blvd 18519

DONEGAL (H-3) pop. 120, elev. 1,811'
• Restaurants p. 66

Just off I-76, the small community of Donegal is part of the Laurel Highlands (see place listing p. 122) and is surrounded by the Laurel Mountains. It is convenient for hiking on the 70-mile Laurel Highlands Trail, which runs from Ohiopyle State Park to just northwest of Johnstown.

DAYS INN AT DONEGAL (724)593-7536
♦♦ Hotel. **Address:** 3620 Rt 31 15628

HOLIDAY INN EXPRESS & SUITES (724)593-1881

♦♦♦
Hotel
$109-$209

Address: 3695 SR 31 15628 **Location:** I-70/76 (Pennsylvania Tpke) exit 91, just e. **Facility:** 73 units. 3 stories, interior corridors. **Terms:** cancellation fee imposed. **Pool:** heated indoor. **Activities:** hot tub, exercise room. **Guest Services:** complimentary laundry. **Featured Amenity:** full hot breakfast.

[SAVE] [🍴] CALL [♿] [🚐] [♿] [BIZ]
[HS] [📶] [✕] [🛏] [☕] [📺]

WHERE TO EAT

OUT OF THE FIRE CAFE   724/259-8887
♦♦ American. Casual Dining. **Address:** 3784 SR 31 15628

DOWNINGTOWN pop. 7,891
- **Restaurants p. 66**
- **Part of Philadelphia area — see map p. 154**

THE OLIVE TREE GREEK MEDITERRANEAN GRILL
      610/873-7911
♦♦ Mediterranean. Casual Dining. **Address:** 379 W Uwchlan Ave 19335

DOYLESTOWN (H-12) pop. 8,380, elev. 351'
- **Part of Philadelphia area — see map p. 154**

Settled in 1735, Doylestown is in Bucks County *(see place listing p. 51)*, one of Pennsylvania's finest farming areas.

On the campus of Delaware Valley University at 700 E. Butler Ave. is the 60-acre Henry Schmieder Arboretum. The site, which is a nice place for picnics, is open daily dawn to dusk except for major holidays. Visitors should obtain a self-guiding tour map at the welcome center; phone (215) 489-2283. The best time to visit is late afternoons and weekends because there is less student activity.

Central Bucks Chamber of Commerce: Bailiwick Office Campus, Suite 23, 252 W. Swamp Rd., Doylestown, PA 18901. **Phone:** (215) 348-3913.

SAVE **JAMES A. MICHENER ART MUSEUM,** 138 S. Pine St., is in the renovated 1884 Bucks County prison. The permanent collection features Daniel Garber's 22-foot-mural, "A Wooded Watershed," as well as 19th- and 20th-century regional American art, including many fine pieces by Pennsylvania Impressionists. A permanent exhibit about author James A. Michener re-creates the Bucks County office where he wrote "Tales of the South Pacific." The Patricia D. Pfundt Sculpture Garden features items that pay homage to the area landscape. Nationally touring special exhibitions and regional artists also are showcased. Educational programs and music and dance performances are offered throughout the year.

Time: Allow 1 hour, 30 minutes minimum. **Hours:** Tues.-Fri. 10-4:30, Sat. 10-5, Sun. noon-5. Art reference library open by appointment. Sculpture garden closes 30 minutes before galleries. Food is available Tues.-Fri. 9-3, Sat. 10-3, Sun. noon-3. Closed major holidays. **Cost:** $18; $15 (ages 65+); $10 (college students with ID); $8 (ages 6-18). **Phone:** (215) 340-9800. 🍴 🚇 Doylestown, 315

SAVE **MERCER MUSEUM,** 84 S. Pine St. at jct. Ashland St., traces the pre-industrial history of the nation from colonization to the Civil War. Artifacts and implements from the 18th- and 19th centuries represent more than 60 crafts and trades. There also are folk art displays and changing exhibits. Changing exhibits are featured in the gallery.

Time: Allow 2 hours minimum. **Hours:** Museum Mon.-Sat. 10-5, Sun. noon-5. Library Tues.-Thurs. 1-5, Fri.-Sat. 10-5. Closed Jan. 1, Thanksgiving and Christmas. **Cost:** $15; $13 (ages 65+); $8 (ages 6-17). Combination ticket with Fonthill Castle $26; $15 (ages 6-17). **Phone:** (215) 345-0210. 🚇 Doylestown, 315

BOCCADITO   215/489-2525
♦♦ Small Plates. Casual Dining. **Address:** 12 S Main St 18901

HONEY   215/489-4200
♦♦♦ New American. Fine Dining. **Address:** 42 Shewell Ave 18901

DRUMS

HOLIDAY INN EXPRESS HOTEL & SUITES   570/788-8081
♦♦♦ Hotel. **Address:** 1 Corporate Dr 18222

DUBLIN pop. 2,158
- **Part of Philadelphia area — see map p. 154**

LUBERTO'S TRATTORIA   215/249-0688
♦ Italian. Casual Dining. **Address:** 169 N Main St 18917

DU BOIS pop. 7,794

BEST WESTERN INN & CONFERENCE CENTER
      (814)371-6200

Hotel
$60-$130

BW Best Western. **AAA Benefit:** Members save 5% to 15% and earn 10% bonus points!

Address: 82 N Park Pl 15801 **Location:** I-80 exit 97 eastbound, 2.5 mi e on DuBois Ave (US 219/SR 255), then just s; exit 101 westbound, 2.7 mi w on DuBois Ave (US 219/SR 255), then just s on US 219. Opposite DuBois Campus, Penn State. **Facility:** 55 units. 2-3 stories (no elevator), interior corridors. **Terms:** closed 12/24-12/26, cancellation fee imposed. **Activities:** playground, picnic facilities, exercise room. **Guest Services:** valet and coin laundry.

COMFORT SUITES DUBOIS   (814)375-6028
♦♦♦ Hotel. **Address:** 10 Lakeside Ave 15801

FAIRFIELD INN & SUITES BY MARRIOTT DU BOIS
      (814)371-2260

♦♦♦
Hotel
$73-$220

FAIRFIELD INN & SUITES Marriott **AAA Benefit:** Members save 5% or more!

Address: 2219 Bee Line Hwy 15801 **Location:** I-80 exit 101, 1 mi s on SR 255. **Facility:** 91 units. 3 stories, interior corridors. **Terms:** cancellation fee imposed. **Pool:** heated indoor. **Activities:** exercise room. **Guest Services:** coin laundry. **Featured Amenity:** continental breakfast.

HAMPTON INN - DU BOIS (814)375-1000
🛡️🛡️🛡️ Hotel. **Address:** 1582 Bee
Line Hwy 15801

AAA Benefit:
Members save up to
10%!

HOLIDAY INN EXPRESS & SUITES 814-371-8900
🛡️🛡️🛡️ Hotel. **Address:** 1690 Rich Hwy 15801

WHERE TO EAT

THE FORT WORTH RESTAURANT 814-371-7570
🛡️🛡️ Steak. Casual Dining. **Address:** 229 W Long Ave 15801

ITALIAN OVEN 814-371-6836
🛡️🛡️ Italian. Casual Dining. **Address:** 5548 Shaffer Rd 15801

LUIGIS RISTORANTE 814-375-9113
🛡️🛡️ Italian. Casual Dining. **Address:** 32 N Brady St 15801

THUNDERBIRD RESTAURANT & LOUNGE 814-371-0799
🛡️🛡️ American. Casual Dining. **Address:** 1 Thunderbird Rd 15851

DUNCANSVILLE pop. 1,233

COMFORT INN ALTOONA (814)693-1800
🛡️🛡️ Hotel. **Address:** 130 Patchway Rd 16635

WYE MOTOR LODGE 814-695-4407

💎
Motel
Rates not provided

Address: 200 Plank Rd 16635 **Location:** I-99 exit 31 (Plank Rd), 2.5 mi s. **Facility:** 36 units. 1 story, exterior corridors. **Guest Services:** coin laundry.

WHERE TO EAT

HOSS'S FAMILY STEAK & SEA 814-695-8543
🛡️ Steak. Casual Dining. **Address:** 110 Patchway Rd 16635

DUNMORE pop. 14,057

QUALITY INN SCRANTON (570)348-6101

🛡️🛡️🛡️
Hotel
$79-$179

Address: 1226 Oneill Hwy 18512 **Location:** I-81 exit 188 (Throop), just e at SR 347 N (Oneill Hwy). Located in a commercial area. **Facility:** 76 units. 4 stories, interior corridors. **Amenities:** safes. **Activities:** limited exercise equipment. **Guest Services:** coin laundry. **Featured Amenity:** continental breakfast.

SLEEP INN & SUITES (570)961-1116
🛡️🛡️ Hotel. **Address:** 102 Monahan Ave 18512

WHERE TO EAT

SIBIO'S RESTAURANT 570-961-9274
🛡️🛡️ Italian. Casual Dining. **Address:** 1240 Quincy Ave 18509

DUPONT pop. 2,711

HOLIDAY INN EXPRESS 570-654-3300
🛡️🛡️🛡️ Hotel. **Address:** 30 Concorde Dr 18641

EAST EARL pop. 1,144
• Hotels & Restaurants map & index p. 145

SHADY MAPLE SMORGASBORD 717/354-8222 [16]

💎💎
**American
Casual Dining
$10-$24**

AAA Inspector Notes: This excellent buffet, fresh and filling, offers such Pennsylvania Dutch cuisine as ham balls, stewed tomatoes, dried corn and noodle-based chicken pot pie. An ample dessert bar is filled with fresh-baked pies, cakes and cookies along with a wide variety of toppings. Specials change throughout the week and include prime rib on Wednesday. **Address:** 129 Toddy Dr 17519 **Location:** Jct SR 23, 0.9 mi e on US 322, just n.

Ⓑ Ⓛ Ⓓ CALL ♿

EAST GREENVILLE pop. 2,951
• Part of Philadelphia area — see map p. 154

JAVA GOOD DAY CAFE 267/923-5575
🛡️ Coffee/Tea. Casual Dining. **Address:** 231 Main St 18041

SCHULTHEIS CARRIAGE HOUSE 215/679-7700
🛡️ Continental. Casual Dining. **Address:** 745 Gravel Pike 18041

EAST NORRITON pop. 13,590
• Hotels & Restaurants map & index p. 192
• Part of Philadelphia area — see map p. 154

HYATT HOUSE PHILADELPHIA/PLYMOUTH MEETING
(610)313-9990 [59]

🛡️🛡️🛡️
**Extended Stay
Hotel
$94-$299**

H Y A T T house™
AAA Benefit: Members save 10%!

Address: 501 E Germantown Pike 19401 **Location:** I-476 exit 20, 2.5 mi w. Located in a commercial area. **Facility:** 131 efficiencies, some two bedrooms. 4 stories, interior corridors. **Terms:** cancellation fee imposed. **Pool:** heated outdoor. **Activities:** exercise room. **Guest Services:** valet and coin laundry, area transportation. **Featured Amenity:** breakfast buffet.

EASTON (G-11) pop. 26,800, elev. 211'
• Hotels p. 68 • Restaurants p. 69
• Hotels & Restaurants map & index p. 37

Easton is nestled in the Lehigh Valley along with Allentown *(see place listing p. 35)* and Bethlehem *(see place listing p. 45)*.

Easton served as a focal point of the Revolutionary War. The first public reading of the Declaration of Independence in the Colonies occurred on the steps of Northampton County Courthouse when it was in Centre Square. Easton also was the home of George Taylor, a signer of the Declaration of Independence. The Parson-Taylor House, a stone house built in 1757, still stands on S. 4th Street.

During the 19th century Easton became one of America's earliest industrial centers due to its strategic location at the confluence of the Delaware and

(See map & index p. 37.)

Lehigh rivers, the Morris Canal and five major railroads. It was during the height of the canal era that many of Easton's fine examples of American architecture were built.

Easton's industrial prosperity was reflected in the founding of Lafayette College in 1832. Daniel Chester French's bronze statue of the Marquis de Lafayette, the French aristocrat who fought with the American Colonists against the British, stands above the city on the Lafayette College campus.

Lehigh Valley Visitor Center—Easton at Sigal Museum: 342 Northampton St., Easton, PA 18042. **Phone:** (610) 253-1222.

Shopping: The downtown area surrounding the Crayola Experience features coffee houses, art galleries, antiques shops, restaurants, stores and historic architecture. Since 1752, the Easton Farmers Market has taken place downtown at Centre Square Sat. 9-1 May through December.

SAVE **CRAYOLA EXPERIENCE,** 30 Centre Sq., houses 28 interactive experiences on four floors. Guests can see how crayons are made in a live demonstration as well as learn the history and fun facts about crayons. The attraction offers a personalized crayon label station, a create-your-own coloring page activity, drip art stations where you can paint with melted wax, interactive digital art activities, a two-story crayon-themed playground and a live theater show. Themes for craft projects vary throughout the year, and changing exhibits also are presented.

Note: Backpacks are not permitted in the building. **Time:** Allow 3 hours minimum. **Hours:** Daily 10-6, Memorial Day-Labor Day; Mon.-Fri. 9:30-4, Sat.-Sun. 10-6, rest of year. Closed Easter, Thanksgiving and Christmas. Phone ahead to confirm schedule. **Cost:** $19.99; free (ages 0-2). Ages 0-15 must be with an adult. Additional fees for some craft activities. **Phone:** (610) 515-8000. [TI]

SAVE **NATIONAL CANAL MUSEUM,** in Hugh Moore Park at 2750 Hugh Moore Park Rd., contains interactive exhibits about the history and technology of Pennsylvania's 19th-century canals. Artifacts, photos and documents housed in the Emrick Center museum building reveal how the canals and the coal transported on them contributed to the Industrial Revolution.

The mule-drawn canal boat *Josiah White II* operates a 45-minute trip on a restored section of the Lehigh Canal. The canal's towpath allows foot and bicycle access to the park's working locks and 19th-century industrial ruins. During summer weekends an 1890s lock tender's house is staffed by a costumed interpreter.

The park offers picnic tables; a children's playground; and bicycle, paddleboat and canoe rentals. **Hours:** Park daily dawn-dusk. Museum Wed.-Sun.

11:30-4:30, first Sat. in June-Oct. 31. Boat tours depart on the hour noon-3. Phone ahead to confirm schedule and holiday closures. **Cost:** (includes boat tour) $12; $11 (senior citizens); $9 (ages 3-15). **Phone:** (610) 923-3548. [A]

SIGAL MUSEUM, 342 Northampton St., has permanent and changing exhibits about pre- and post-European settlement in the Easton/Bethlehem area. Exhibits illustrate the history of the area from 10,000 years ago to the present. Objects on display include documents, decorative arts, clothing, textiles, military memorabilia and farming implements. The Jane S. Moyer Genealogical Research Library is on-site as well. Docent-led tours and a self-guiding cell-phone audio tour are available.

Time: Allow 1 hour minimum. **Hours:** Museum Wed.-Sat. 10-4, Sun. noon-4. Library Wed.-Fri. 10-2:30. Closed Jan. 1, Easter, Memorial Day, July 4, Labor Day, Thanksgiving, day after Thanksgiving, Christmas and day after Christmas. Phone ahead to confirm schedule. **Cost:** $7; $6 (students with ID); $5 (ages 3-12, ages 55+ and active military with ID). Reservations are strongly recommended for the library. **Phone:** (610) 253-1222. [GT]

GRAND EASTONIAN SUITES HOTEL		(610)258-6350

WWW Hotel. **Address:** 140 Northampton St 18042

HAMPTON INN EASTON		(610)250-6500

WWW Hotel. **Address:** 3723 Easton-Nazareth Hwy 18045

AAA Benefit: Members save up to 10%!

HOLIDAY INN EXPRESS HOTEL & SUITES		610/923-9495 [9]

WWW Hotel. **Address:** 90 Kunkle Dr 18045

THE LAFAYETTE INN		(610)253-4500

WWW Historic Bed & Breakfast. **Address:** 525 W Monroe St 18042

QUALITY INN		(610)253-0546

WW Hotel. **Address:** 2415 Nazareth Rd 18042

TOWNEPLACE SUITES BY MARRIOTT-BETHLEHEM/ EASTON (610)829-2000

WWWW
Extended Stay Hotel
$87-$318

TOWNEPLACE — SUITES MARRIOTT

AAA Benefit: Members save 5% or more!

Address: 3800 Easton-Nazareth Hwy 18045 **Location:** SR 33 exit SR 248 (Easton-Nazareth Hwy), 0.6 mi w. **Facility:** 86 units, some two bedrooms, efficiencies and kitchens. 4 stories, interior corridors. **Terms:** check-in 4 pm, cancellation fee imposed. **Pool:** heated indoor. **Activities:** hot tub, exercise room. **Guest Services:** valet and coin laundry. **Featured Amenity:** continental breakfast.

(See map & index p. 37.)

WHERE TO EAT

THE JAMES EATERY   610/438-1339 [14]
👑👑 American. Casual Dining. **Address:** 190 S Greenwood Ave 18045

MARBLEHEAD GRILLE AND CHOWDER HOUSE
                                610/258-4301 [17]
👑👑 💎 Seafood. Casual Dining. **Address:** 4101 William Penn Hwy 18045

MORICI'S RESTAURANT   610/253-6257
👑👑 Italian. Casual Dining. **Address:** 218 Cattell St 18045

NONNA LIA PIZZA CHEF   610/258-5800 [16]
👑👑 Italian. Casual Dining. **Address:** 4011 William Penn Hwy 18045

PEARLY BAKER'S ALE HOUSE   610/253-9949
👑👑 American. Casual Dining. **Address:** 11 Centre Square 18042

RIVER GRILLE   610/923-5110
👑👑👑 American. Casual Dining. **Address:** 243 Northampton St 18042

WILLIAMS FAMILY RESTAURANT   610/253-8281 [15]
👑👑 American. Casual Dining. **Address:** 3630 William Penn Hwy 18045

EAST STROUDSBURG pop. 9,840, elev. 427'
• Hotels & Restaurants map & index p. 266
• Part of Pocono Mountains Area — see map p. 264

DAYS INN EAST STROUDSBURG   (570)424-1951 [42]

👑👑
Hotel
$60-$150

Address: 838 Seven Bridges Rd 18301 **Location:** I-80 exit 309, just n. **Facility:** 106 units. 2 stories (no elevator), exterior corridors. **Terms:** cancellation fee imposed. **Pool:** heated indoor. **Activities:** game room, exercise room. **Guest Services:** coin laundry.

🆂🅰🆅🅴 🍽 🛎 CALL 🅖 🛬 🏧
BIZ 📶 ✖ 📷 🖥 🖵 💻

QUALITY INN NEAR POCONO MOUNTAINS
                               (570)424-5451 [44]

👑👑👑
Hotel
$70-$139

Address: 320 Greentree Dr 18301 **Location:** I-80 exit 308, just se. **Facility:** 112 units. 2-3 stories (no elevator), interior/exterior corridors. **Terms:** cancellation fee imposed. **Dining:** The Roasted Tomato, see separate listing. **Activities:** limited exercise equipment. **Guest Services:** valet and coin laundry.

🆂🅰🆅🅴 🍽 🛎 CALL 🅖 BIZ 📶
🖥 💻 /SOME UNITS 🐾 🖵

SUPER 8 EAST STROUDSBURG   (570)424-7411 [43]
👑👑 Motel. **Address:** 340 Greentree Dr 18301

WHERE TO EAT

HOLY GUACAMOLE   570/420-1909 [25]
💎 Mexican. Quick Serve. **Address:** 107 Brown St 18301

PEPPE'S BISTRO   570/421-4460 [24]

👑👑👑👑
Northern Italian Casual Dining
$9-$33

AAA Inspector Notes: This updated modern, casual bistro is popular with locals, and it's easy to see why. The menu offers some familiar Italian favorites, pizzas and pastas as well as a few chef specialty entrées such as the veal chop stuffed with prosciutto and mozzarella or the sea bass with a crispy panko crust and lemon caper sauce. The staff is very friendly, and the atmosphere is relaxed and comfortable both in the dining room and the inviting lounge. **Features:** full bar, early bird specials, happy hour. **Reservations:** suggested, weekends. **Address:** 100 Eagle Valley Mall 18301 **Location:** Jct SR 447 N and Business Rt US 209; at Eagle Valley Mall. [D]

PETRIZZO'S RESTAURANT   570/588-6414 [29]
👑👑 Italian Pizza. Casual Dining. **Address:** 6171 Milford Rd 18302

THE ROASTED TOMATO   570/424-5451 [26]

👑👑 💎
American Casual Dining
$9-$22

AAA Inspector Notes: Nestled in the Pocono Mountains, this simple, but cozy restaurant is known for its weekend breakfast buffet and salad bar. On the dinner menu are such items as grilled marinated salmon, zesty crunchy cod, Mediterranean chicken, New York strip steak and baby back ribs. The lunch menu is a bit more casual with sandwiches and burgers offered. Service is laid back, but friendly and attentive. **Features:** full bar. **Address:** 320 Greentree Dr 18301 **Location:** I-80 exit 308, just se; in Budget Inn & Suites. [B] [L] [D]

EBENSBURG pop. 3,351

THE NOON-COLLINS INN   (814)472-4311

👑👑
Historic Bed & Breakfast
$100

Address: 114 E High St 15931 **Location:** Just e of jct High and Center sts; downtown. **Facility:** This 1834 restored historic Federal-style property resides in the heart of Ebensburg. Every room is thoughtfully arranged and decorated to reflect a cozy country style. 6 units. 2 stories (no elevator), interior corridors. **Terms:** 7 day cancellation notice-fee imposed. **Featured Amenity:** full hot breakfast. 🆂🅰🆅🅴 📶 ✖ ☎

QUALITY INN   (814)472-6100
👑👑👑 Hotel. **Address:** 111 Cook Rd 15931

ECKLEY (F-10) elev. 1,654'

ECKLEY MINERS' VILLAGE is off SR 940, following signs. This living-history museum is a 19th-century anthracite mining village with approximately 50 buildings. Exhibits, pictures and a 17-minute video presentation shown in the visitor center depict the lives of miners and their families. Some houses not open to the public are occupied by descendants of miners. Special events are offered and include Haunted Halloween Lantern Tours and Christmas at Eckley.

Time: Allow 2 hours minimum. **Hours:** Museum center Mon.-Sat. 9-5, Sun. noon-5. Guided walking tours are offered Mon.-Sat. at 11 and 2, Sun. at 2, Memorial Day weekend-Labor Day; Sat. at 11 and 2, Sun. at 2, day after Labor Day to mid-Oct. Closed holidays except Memorial Day, July 4 and Labor Day. Tours are given based on staff availability; phone ahead. **Cost:** (includes guided tour) $10; $9 (ages 65+); $8 (ages 3-12); $2 (active military with ID). Museum only $8; $7 (ages 65+); $6 (ages 3-12); free (active military with ID). **Phone:** (570) 636-2070. GT

EDINBORO pop. 6,438

COMFORT SUITES   (814)969-7000
Hotel. **Address:** 1007 Market Place Dr 16412

ELDRED (C-5) pop. 825, elev. 1,500'

ELDRED WWII MUSEUM is at 201 Main St. The war's history and its effect on the region is depicted with electronic exhibits, sound and light effects, dioramas, photographs, a dateline, documents and audiovisual history narrations. A sculpture exhibit recreates a local defense plant and honors the women who worked on its production line. A research library is included. **Time:** Allow 1 hour minimum. **Hours:** Tues.-Sat. 10-4, Sun. 1-4. **Cost:** $5; free (ages 0-18). **Phone:** (814) 225-2220 or (866) 686-9944.

ELIZABETHTOWN pop. 11,545, elev. 462'
• Hotels & Restaurants map & index p. 145
• Part of Pennsylvania Dutch Country area — see map p. 143

SURESTAY PLUS HOTEL ELIZABETHTOWN-HERSHEY   717/367-4000 24

Hotel
Rates not provided
Address: 147 Merts Dr 17022 **Location:** SR 283 exit Elizabethtown/Rheems. **Facility:** 82 units. 2 stories, interior corridors. **Activities:** exercise room. **Guest Services:** valet laundry. **Featured Amenity:** continental breakfast.
  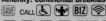 

Closest Lancaster County hotel to Hersheypark.

ELLWOOD CITY pop. 7,921
• Part of Pittsburgh area — see map p. 225

CHAPEL VALLEY ESTATE BED AND BREAKFAST   (724)201-0811
Bed & Breakfast. **Address:** 297 Chapel Dr 16117

WHERE TO EAT

SHAKESPEARE'S RESTAURANT & PUB AT OLDE STONEWALL GOLF COURSE   724/752-4653
American. Casual Dining. **Address:** 1495 Mercer Rd 16117

ENOLA pop. 6,111
• Hotels & Restaurants map & index p. 95

BEST WESTERN PLUS HARRISBURG WEST   (717)635-2523 28

Hotel
$75-$179
 Best Western PLUS. **AAA Benefit:** Members save 5% to 15% and earn 10% bonus points!

Address: 4900 Woodland Dr 17025 **Location:** I-81 exit 61, just w on Wertzville Rd, then just s on Good Hope rd. **Facility:** 66 units. 3 stories, interior corridors. **Terms:** off-site registration, cancellation fee imposed. **Amenities:** safes. **Pool:** outdoor. **Activities:** exercise room. **Guest Services:** valet and coin laundry. **Featured Amenity:** breakfast buffet.
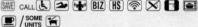

QUALITY INN ENOLA   (717)732-0785 27

Motel
$74-$560

Address: 501 N Enola Rd 17025 **Location:** I-81 exit 65, 1.7 mi s on US 11. **Facility:** 69 units. 2 stories (no elevator), interior corridors. **Amenities:** safes. **Activities:** exercise room. **Guest Services:** coin laundry. **Featured Amenity:** continental breakfast.

WHERE TO EAT

TAVERN ON THE HILL   717/732-2077 24
Steak Seafood. Fine Dining. **Address:** 109 Howard St 17025

VISAGGIO'S RISTORANTE   717/697-8082
Italian. Fine Dining. **Address:** 6990 Wertzville Rd 17025

AAA.com/campgrounds—
For overnights under the stars

EPHRATA (H-10) pop. 13,394, elev. 381'

- Hotels & Restaurants map & index p. 145
- Part of Pennsylvania Dutch Country area — see map p. 143

Ephrata Area Chamber of Commerce: 16 E. Main St., Suite 1, Ephrata, PA 17522. **Phone:** (717) 738-9010.

Shopping: The Green Dragon Farmers Market, 955 N. State St., offers a wide variety of goods at its indoor and outdoor stands Fri. 9-9, Mar.-Dec. (9-8, Jan.-Feb.).

EPHRATA CLOISTER, 632 W. Main St., was one of America's earliest communal societies. The cloister was established in 1732 by Conrad Beissel, a German immigrant who came to Pennsylvania to be able to worship freely under William Penn's policy of religious tolerance. The charismatic Beissel espoused a life of solitude and self-denial that included celibacy and Saturday as the main day of worship.

A small group of followers joined him, and at its height in the mid-18th century the community consisted of 80 celibate Brothers and Sisters and a group of approximately 200 known as the Householders, married family groups who supported Beissel with funds and assistance but were unwilling to live the austere life of the Brothers and Sisters.

The community of religious celibates practiced a Spartan, regimented lifestyle, emphasizing spiritual goals rather than material ones. They wore long white robes, ate only one meal a day, were allowed only 6 hours of sleep each night and built and occupied a distinctive group of European-style wooden buildings.

The cloister was an early center for publishing and printing, and the residents were known for their detailed hand-illuminated books and German-style calligraphy known as *Frakturschriften*. The self-reliant Brothers made their own ink and paper and had their own bindery. They also composed their own a cappella music and hymns. After Beissel's death in 1768, the community began to decline; the last celibate member died in 1813.

Nine of the original buildings on the 28-acre site have been restored and furnished to re-create the atmosphere of the 18th-century communal village. Following a 15-minute introductory film in the visitor center, 45-minute tours are conducted by knowledgeable costumed guides. The five-story, half-timbered meetinghouse and the four-story dormitory known as the Sisters' House can only be seen on the guided tour. Self-guided and cellphone tours also are available. Special events are offered throughout the year.

Time: Allow 1 hour, 30 minutes minimum. **Hours:** Mon.-Sat. 9-5, Sun. noon-5, Mar.-Dec.; Wed.-Sat. 9-5, Sun. noon-5, rest of year. Tours depart Mon.-Sat. at 10, noon, 2 and 3:30; Sun. at 12:30, 1:30, 2:30 and 3:30. Phone ahead to confirm tour times. Closed Jan. 1, Easter, Columbus Day, Veterans Day, Thanksgiving, day after Thanksgiving and Christmas. **Cost:** $10; $9 (ages 65+); $6 (ages 3-11). Phone ahead to confirm rates. **Phone:** (717) 733-6600. GT

HAMPTON INN & SUITES EPHRATA-MOUNTAIN SPRINGS
(717)733-0661   **7**

♥♥♥ Hotel. **Address:** 380 E Main St 17522

AAA Benefit: Members save up to 10%!

WHERE TO EAT

AROMAS DEL SUR   717/738-0101   **8**

♥♥ Colombian. Casual Dining. **Address:** 548 S State St 17522

ISAAC'S FAMOUS GRILLED SANDWICHES   717/733-7777

♥ Deli Sandwiches. Quick Serve. **Address:** 120 N Reading Rd 17522

ERIE (C-2) pop. 101,786, elev. 710'

- Hotels p. 73 • Restaurants p. 74

Pennsylvania's only port on the Great Lakes was founded in 1795 after the purchase of the Erie Triangle. The region's first inhabitants were the Eriez Indians, for whom the lake and city were named. In 1753 a French military expedition built Fort Presque Isle on the site of Erie and Fort LeBoeuf on the site of Waterford (see place listing p. 295). The French abandoned their forts in 1759; the next year the English took possession and rebuilt them.

Three years later the English were driven out by Native Americans led by Chief Pontiac, who destroyed both forts. The region remained free of Europeans until the spring of 1795, when 200 men from Gen. Anthony Wayne's army built a building on the bluff overlooking the bay. During the War of 1812 ships built at Erie under the command of Commodore Oliver Hazard Perry were instrumental in eliminating British naval control of the Great Lakes.

As the state's fourth largest city, modern Erie is a center of diversified industry and commerce that also offers a variety of entertainment and recreational opportunities. The Bayfront District, off the Bayfront Parkway via I-79 and I-90, is set against the backdrop of Presque Isle Bay. The cornerstone of the district is the Raymond M. Blasco M.D. Memorial Library, the Erie Maritime Museum and US Brig Niagara (see attraction listing) and the Bayfront Convention Center. Water-taxi service connects the Bayfront to Presque Isle State Park (see attraction listing) as well as Dobbins Landing and Liberty Park where outdoor concerts, festivals and performances are held seasonally; phone (201) 604-4799 for water taxi and (814) 455-7557 for Highmark Amphitheater at Liberty Park.

Erie's miles of inland waterways can be explored via private boats or sightseeing cruises. Boat rentals are available at many local marinas. Weekend sightseeing boat trips depart from the Perry Monument in Presque Isle State Park from mid-May through Sept. 30; phone (814) 836-0201 for reservations. Charter fishing services are generally available May through October.

A portion of the Seaway Trail, a scenic byway, includes SR 5, the Bayfront Parkway Loop and Peninsula Drive from West Sixth Street to Presque Isle State Park. It continues on into New York for some 450 miles paralleling Lake Erie, Niagara River and part of the St. Lawrence Seaway.

The city is home to the Class AA Erie SeaWolves, an affiliate of the Detroit Tigers. Baseball season runs April through September with games played at the 6,000-seat UPMC Park; phone (814) 456-1300. The Erie Otters, part of the Ontario Hockey League, play at the Erie Insurance Arena late September through mid-March; phone (814) 452-4857 or (814) 456-7070. The arena also is home to the Erie Bay-Hawks, November through May; the team is part of the NBA Development League and affiliated with the Atlanta Hawks; phone (814) 790-5600.

VisitErie-Erie Visitor Center: 301 Peninsula Dr., Erie, PA 16505. **Phone:** (814) 454-1000 or (800) 524-3743.

Shopping: The major shopping center in Erie is Millcreek Mall, US 19 and Interchange Road, featuring some 175 stores, including The Bon-Ton, Boscov's, JCPenney and Macy's. The mall complex also includes adjacent plazas. The Bayfront District offers gift shops.

BICENTENNIAL TOWER, 7 State St., was built at Dobbins Landing in 1995 to celebrate Erie's 200th birthday. The 187-foot tower overlooks the historic bay-front district and Presque Isle Bay. Visitors may take the elevator to the observation decks, which feature open-air and enclosed viewing areas; the highest one is at 138 feet.

Time: Allow 30 minutes minimum. **Hours:** Daily 9:30 a.m.-10 p.m., Memorial Day-Labor Day; daily 10-8, May 1 to day before Memorial Day; daily 10-6, mid-Apr. to late Apr. and day after Labor Day to Sept. 30; daily 10-5, Apr. 1 to mid-Apr.; Sat.-Sun. noon-4, rest of year. Phone ahead to confirm schedule. **Cost:** $4; $2 (ages 7-12); free (first Sun. of the month, excluding holidays). **Phone:** (814) 455-6055. ⧠

ERIE MARITIME MUSEUM AND US BRIG *NIAGARA* is at 150 E. Front St. just off Bayfront Pkwy. Regional maritime heritage with emphasis on the War of 1812 and the history of the USS *Michigan/Wolverine* is interpreted through interactive exhibits and multimedia presentations. In the Live Fire exhibit a section of a re-created wooden warship illustrates the rigors of fighting at sea. The *Niagara*, a re-creation of Oliver Hazard Perry's relief

flagship, sails frequently and operates as a sailing school vessel in summer months. Guided tours are available when it is in port.

Time: Allow 2 hours minimum. **Hours:** Mon.-Sat. 9-5, Sun. noon-5, Apr.-Sept.; Mon.-Sat. 9-5, in Oct.; Thurs.-Sat. 9-5, rest of year. Closed day after Thanksgiving and major holidays except Memorial Day, July 4 and Labor Day. Phone ahead to confirm availability of ship tour. **Cost:** (includes museum and ship when in port) $10; $8 (ages 66+); $5 (ages 3-11); free (active military with ID and immediate family). **Phone:** (814) 452-2744. GT ⧠

EXPERIENCE CHILDREN'S MUSEUM is at 420 French St. The museum's three floors offer hands-on art, science, reading and imaginative play exhibits for kids from toddlers to 10 years old. Exhibits include an interactive water table, a bedrock cave and a creativity center as well as Old Town, which features a doctor's office, a bank, a pizza kitchen and a kids' market. An outdoor children's discovery area features gardens and digging, building and painting activities.

Time: Allow 1 hour, 30 minutes minimum. **Hours:** Tues.-Sat. 10-5, Sun. 1-5. Closed major holidays. Phone ahead to confirm schedule. **Cost:** $7; $6 (ages 62+); free (ages 0-1). Phone ahead to confirm rates. **Phone:** (814) 453-3743.

PRESQUE ISLE STATE PARK is 7 mi. n. of I-90 exit 18 at 301 Peninsula Dr. (SR 832). This 3,200-acre peninsula on Lake Erie offers bicycling, boating, fishing, hiking, in-line skating and swimming. In winter, ice fishing, ice-skating and cross-country skiing are available (weather permitting). *See Recreation Areas Chart.* **Hours:** Park daily dawn-dusk. Boat tours are offered mid-May through Sept. 30. Phone ahead to confirm schedule. **Cost:** Free. **Phone:** (814) 833-7424. GT ⧠ ⧠ ⧠ ⧠

Tom Ridge Environmental Center is at 301 Peninsula Dr. at the entrance of Presque Isle State Park. The state-of-the-art facility was designed to be a green building with environmental-friendly features and includes 7,000 square feet of exhibit space. Two floors of exhibits and hands-on displays chronicle the natural history of the area. A 15-minute orientation film is shown in a 60-seat theater every 20 minutes. A 75-foot observation tower provides panoramic views of Lake Erie. The Big Green Screen, a 4-story, 45-foot-wide giant screen theater, presents science and entertainment films. Changing exhibits are offered throughout the year.

Time: Allow 2 hours minimum. **Hours:** Daily 10-6. Big Green Screen movies are shown on the hour 10-6. Food is available daily 11-4. Closed Jan. 1, Thanksgiving and Christmas. Phone ahead to confirm schedule. **Cost:** Center free. Big Green Screen movies $5-$7.50. **Phone:** (814) 833-7424. ⧠

SPLASH LAGOON INDOOR WATER PARK RESORT is off I-90 exit 24, then s. to 8091 Peach St. The indoor water park features waterslides, a wave pool, a lazy river, family whirlpools, a 1,000-gallon tipping bucket and a five-story interactive Tiki Tree House. The Tree Tops Ropes Course above the water park includes a tightrope, rickety bridges and balance beams. There also is an arcade and a laser tag facility.

Time: Allow 2 hours minimum. **Hours:** Hours vary; phone for schedule. **Cost:** May-Nov. $39.95; $29.95 (under 42 inches tall); $14.95 (spectator); free (ages 0-2). After 4 p.m. $29.95; $21.95 (under 42 inches tall); $12.95 (spectator); free (ages 0-2). Rest of year $45.95; $37.95 (under 42 inches tall); $19.95 (spectator). After 4 p.m. $37.95; $29.95 (under 42 inches tall); $17.95 (spectator); free (ages 0-2). Phone to confirm rates. Ropes course (one climb), Aqua Tumbler or Lazer Tag $7. **Phone:** (814) 217-1111 or (866) 377-5274. 🍴

BAYMONT INN & SUITES ERIE PA   (814)866-8808
▿▿▿ Hotel. **Address:** 8170 Perry Hwy 16509

COURTYARD BY MARRIOTT/ERIE AMASSADOR CONFERENCE CENTER   (814)860-8300
▿▿▿▿ Hotel. **Address:** 7792 Peach St 16509

AAA Benefit: Members save 5% or more!

COURTYARD BY MARRIOTT ERIE BAYFRONT
(814)636-1005

Hotel
$93-$449

COURTYARD Marriott

AAA Benefit: Members save 5% or more!

Address: 2 Sassafras Pier 16507 **Location:** Waterfront. I-90 exit 22B to Bayfront Connector; I-79 to Bayfront Pkwy. Next to convention center. **Facility:** 192 units. 5 stories, interior corridors. **Parking:** on-site (fee). **Terms:** cancellation fee imposed. **Dining:** 2 restaurants. **Pool:** heated outdoor, heated indoor. **Activities:** hot tub, exercise room. **Guest Services:** valet and coin laundry, boarding pass kiosk.

SAVE 🍴 🍸 CALL 🚹 🏊 🛗 BIZ 🛜 ✕ 🅿️
📱 / SOME UNITS 🐾 🖨️

GLASS HOUSE INN   (814)833-7751
▿▿ Motel. **Address:** 3202 W 26th St 16506

HAMPTON INN ERIE SOUTH   (814)866-6800
▿▿▿▿ Hotel. **Address:** 8050 Old Oliver Rd 16509

AAA Benefit: Members save up to 10%!

HILTON GARDEN INN   814/866-1390
▿▿▿ Hotel. **Address:** 2225 Downs Dr 16509

AAA Benefit: Members save up to 10%!

HOLIDAY INN EXPRESS HOTEL & SUITES   814/217-1100
▿▿▿ Hotel. **Address:** 8101 Peach St 16509

HOMEWOOD SUITES BY HILTON   (814)866-8292
▿▿▿ Extended Stay Hotel. **Address:** 2084 Interchange Rd 16565

AAA Benefit: Members save up to 10%!

LA QUINTA INN & SUITES   (814)864-1812
▿▿▿ Hotel. **Address:** 7820 Perry Hwy 16509

MICROTEL INN BY WYNDHAM ERIE   (814)864-1010
▿▿ 💎 Motel $59-$129

Address: 8100 Peach St 16509 **Location:** I-90 exit 24, just s. Across from indoor water park. **Facility:** 97 units. 3 stories, interior corridors. **Terms:** cancellation fee imposed. **Activities:** exercise room. **Guest Services:** valet and coin laundry. **Featured Amenity:** full hot breakfast.

SAVE 🍴 CALL 🚹 🛗 BIZ 🛜
/ SOME UNITS 🐾 🖨️

RED ROOF INN ERIE   (814)868-5246
▿▿ 💎 Motel $49-$170

Address: 7865 Perry Hwy 16509 **Location:** I-90 exit 27, just n on SR 97. **Facility:** 110 units. 2 stories (no elevator), interior/exterior corridors. **Amenities:** safes.

SAVE 🍴 CALL 🚹 🛜 ✕ 📱
/ SOME UNITS 🐾 🖨️ 🖨️

SHERATON ERIE BAYFRONT HOTEL   814/454-2005
▿▿▿ Hotel
Rates not provided

Ⓢ Sheraton

AAA Benefit: Members save 5% or more!

Address: 55 West Bay Dr 16507 **Location:** Waterfront. I-90 exit 22B to Bayfront Connector; I-79 to Bayfront Pkwy. Next to convention center. **Facility:** 200 units. 8 stories, interior corridors. **Parking:** on-site (fee). **Amenities:** safes. **Dining:** Bayfront Grille, see separate listing. **Pool:** heated indoor. **Activities:** hot tub, marina, fishing, exercise room. **Guest Services:** coin laundry.

SAVE 🍴 🍸 CALL 🚹 🏊 🛗 BIZ HS 🛜 ✕
🖨️ 📱 / SOME UNITS 🐾

SPRINGHILL SUITES BY MARRIOTT ERIE   (814)864-5000
▿▿▿ Hotel. **Address:** 2087 Interchange Rd 16509

AAA Benefit: Members save 5% or more!

TOWNEPLACE SUITES BY MARRIOTT ERIE   (814)866-7100
▿▿▿ Extended Stay Contemporary Hotel. **Address:** 2090 Interchange Rd 16565

AAA Benefit: Members save 5% or more!

WINGATE BY WYNDHAM   (814)860-3050
▿▿▿ Hotel. **Address:** 8060 Old Oliver Rd 16509

🍴 **What's for dinner?** AAA.com/travelguides/restaurants

WHERE TO EAT

1201 KITCHEN   814/464-8989
◆◆◆ Latin American Fusion Sushi. Fine Dining. **Address:** 1201 State St 16501

BAYFRONT GRILLE   814/454-2005
◆◆◆ American. Casual Dining. **Address:** 55 West Bay Dr 16507

CLOUD 9 WINE BAR   814/870-9007
◆◆◆ New American. Casual Dining. **Address:** 25 E 10th St, Suite 1 16501

LATINO'S RESTAURANT & BAR   814/452-1966
◆◆ Mexican. Casual Dining. **Address:** 1315 Parade St 16503

MAD MEX   814/520-5142
◆◆ Mexican. Casual Dining. **Address:** 5800 Peach St 16509

MI SCUZI   814/454-4533
◆◆ Italian. Casual Dining. **Address:** 2641 Myrtle St 16508

PICASSO'S THE ART OF FOOD   814/866-1183
◆ Sandwiches. Quick Serve. **Address:** 2060 Interchange Rd 16565

PINEAPPLE EDDIE SOUTHERN BISTRO   814/454-0700
◆◆ Southern American. Casual Dining. **Address:** 1402 W 10th St 16502

SYD'S PLACE   814/838-3089
◆◆ American. Casual Dining. **Address:** 2992 W Lake Rd 16505

ERWINNA
• Part of Philadelphia area — see map p. 154

GOLDEN PHEASANT INN   610/294-9595
◆◆◆◆ Historic Country Inn. **Address:** 763 River Rd 18920

WHERE TO EAT

GOLDEN PHEASANT INN   610/294-9595
◆◆◆ French. Fine Dining. **Address:** 763 River Rd 18920

ESSINGTON
• Hotels & Restaurants map & index p. 192
• Part of Philadelphia area — see map p. 154

THE CLARION HOTEL CONFERENCE CENTER
(610)521-9600 **132**

◆◆
Hotel
$139-$549

Address: 76 Industrial Hwy 19029 **Location:** I-95 exit 9A, 0.4 mi sw on SR 291. Located in a commercial area. **Facility:** 297 units. 7 stories, interior corridors. **Pool:** outdoor. **Activities:** exercise room. **Guest Services:** valet and coin laundry.

[SAVE] [↦] [¶¶] [↗] [Y] CALL[&]
[≋] [✈] [BIZ] [≋] [✕] [▼] [◻]
/SOME UNITS [▤] [◻]

HOLIDAY INN EXPRESS PHILADELPHIA AIRPORT
610/521-1200 **133**
◆◆◆ Hotel. **Address:** 101 Taylor Ave 19029

RED ROOF PLUS+ PHILADELPHIA AIRPORT
(610)521-5090 **130**

◆◆
Motel
$85-$109

Address: 49 Industrial Hwy 19029 **Location:** I-95 exit 9A, 0.3 mi sw on SR 291. Located in a commercial area. **Facility:** 135 units. 2-3 stories (no elevator), exterior corridors. **Amenities:** safes. **Guest Services:** coin laundry.

[SAVE] [¶¶+] CALL[&] [≋] [✕] [▼]
/SOME UNITS [🐾] [▤] [≋] [◻]

WYNDHAM GARDEN HOTEL PHILADELPHIA AIRPORT
(610)521-2400 **131**
◆◆◆ Hotel. **Address:** 45 Industrial Hwy 19029

EXTON   pop. 4,842
• Part of Philadelphia area — see map p. 154

DULING-KURTZ HOUSE & COUNTRY INN   (610)524-1830
◆◆ Historic Country Inn. **Address:** 146 S Whitford Rd 19341

HILTON GARDEN INN EXTON/WEST CHESTER   610/458-8822
◆◆◆ Hotel. **Address:** 720 Eagleview Blvd E 19341

AAA Benefit:
Members save up to 10%!

HOLIDAY INN EXPRESS EXTON/LIONVILLE   610/524-9000
◆◆◆ Hotel. **Address:** 120 N Pottstown Pike 19341

WHERE TO EAT

DULING-KURTZ HOUSE & COUNTRY INN   610/524-1830

◆◆◆
Continental
Fine Dining
$18-$42

AAA Inspector Notes: *Historic.* Friendly servers in formal attire go to great lengths to satisfy you at this 1830s country inn, which has seven intimate dining rooms appointed with lovely antiques. From the enclosed porch dining room you can see the small fountain and gazebo in the lovely gardens. As you browse the menu of veal, lamb and farm-raised game, take an extra minute to ponder hickory-smoked buffalo fillet with a pearl onion and pine nut sauce. **Features:** full bar, happy hour. **Reservations:** suggested. **Address:** 146 S Whitford Rd 19341 **Location:** Jct SR 100, 1 mi w on Business Rt US 30, 0.3 mi s. [≋] Whitford, 197.

[L] [D] [▥]

THE POUR HOUSE   610/280-7900
◆◆ American. Casual Dining. **Address:** 116 N Pottstown Pike 19341

RON'S ORIGINAL BAR & GRILLE   610/594-9900
◆◆ American. Gastropub. **Address:** 74 E Uwchlan Ave 19341

SHIP INN   610/363-7200
◆◆◆ Seafood Steak. Fine Dining. **Address:** 693 E Lincoln Hwy 19341

FAIRFIELD   pop. 507, elev. 531'

HISTORIC FAIRFIELD INN   717/642-5410
◆◆ Historic Bed & Breakfast. **Address:** 15 W Main St 17320

WHERE TO EAT

THE HISTORIC FAIRFIELD INN 1757   717/642-5410
◆◆ American. Casual Dining. **Address:** 15 W Main St 17320

FARMINGTON pop. 767

FALLING ROCK AT NEMACOLIN WOODLANDS RESORT
(724)329-6417

Boutique Resort Hotel
$249-$739

Address: 150 Falling Rock Blvd 15437 **Location:** On US 40. **Facility:** Frank Lloyd Wright-inspired architecture and natural décor set a graceful tone at this 2,000-acre hilltop resort where recreation is king and relaxation is queen; just a superb array of activities! 42 units. 3 stories, interior corridors. **Parking:** valet only. **Terms:** check-in 4 pm, 7 day cancellation notice. **Amenities:** safes. **Dining:** 2 restaurants, also, Aqueous, see separate listing. **Pool:** heated outdoor, heated indoor. **Activities:** hot tub, regulation golf, miniature golf, tennis, downhill & cross country skiing, recreation programs, kids club, bicycles, playground, game room, lawn sports, trails, health club, spa. **Guest Services:** valet laundry.

SAVE 🍴 🛎 ▽ 🏋 CALL ♿ 🏊 ▸◂ BIZ HS
🛜 ✕ 🐾

HISTORIC SUMMIT INN   724/438-8594
🔷🔷🔷 Historic Hotel. **Address:** 101 Skyline Dr 15437

NEMACOLIN WOODLANDS RESORT   (724)329-8555

Resort Hotel
$99-$569

Address: 1001 Lafayette Dr 15437 **Location:** On US 40. **Facility:** Nestled in the breathtaking Laurel Highlands, this multifaceted resort offers luxurious guest rooms, villas and townhouses. The traditional luxury décor blends with the modern art in the public areas. 283 units, some two bedrooms, kitchens, houses and condominiums. 4-5 stories, interior/exterior corridors. **Parking:** on-site and valet. **Terms:** check-in 4 pm, 7 day cancellation notice. **Amenities:** safes. **Dining:** 10 restaurants, also, Lautrec, see separate listing, entertainment. **Pool:** heated outdoor, heated indoor. **Activities:** sauna, hot tub, steamroom, fishing, regulation golf, miniature golf, tennis, downhill & cross country skiing, snowboarding, recreation programs, kids club, bicycles, playground, game room, lawn sports, picnic facilities, trails, health club, spa. **Guest Services:** valet laundry.

SAVE ⊞ 🍴 🛎 ▽ 🏋 CALL ♿ 🏊 ▸◂ BIZ
HS 🛜 🐾 /SOME UNITS 🦮 🍶 🖥 🖵

WHERE TO EAT

AQUEOUS   724/329-6417

American Fine Dining
$28-$72

AAA Inspector Notes: This chic dining room of stone and wood overlooks the 18th green of the resort's championship golf course and offers a wildly creative menu. The artful chef specializes in cutting-edge techniques that transforms luxury ingredients into distinctive displays—a traditional steak might be accented by a foie gras powder or a rich bisque served with a Parmesan powder. **Features:** full bar, patio dining. **Reservations:** suggested. **Address:** 150 Falling Rock Blvd 15437 **Location:** On US 40; in Falling Rock at Nemacolin Woodlands Resort. **Parking:** valet only.

B D CALL ♿

🔗 **Booth or table?**

AAA.com/travelguides/restaurants

LAUTREC   724/329-8555

🔷🔷🔷🔷🔷
French Fine Dining
$110-$270

AAA Inspector Notes: Fine dining is more than just good food prepared well. It's an experience for the senses, a culinary orchestra playing in perfect harmony, and you have front-row seats. This restaurant's elegant dining room, lush furnishings and attentive staff are key components to that luxury experience, but the ever-evolving menu of creative flavors and quality ingredients is the main event. I recommend taking the "leap of faith" and allowing the chef to prepare you a tasting menu that is sure to delight. **Features:** full bar, Sunday brunch. **Reservations:** suggested, weekends. **Address:** 1001 Lafayette Dr 15437 **Location:** On US 40; in Nemacolin Woodlands Resort. **Parking:** on-site and valet.

⊞ D CALL ♿

FAYETTEVILLE (I-7) pop. 3,128, elev. 792'

In Caledonia State Park *(see Recreation Areas Chart)*, Totem Pole Playhouse is a 450-seat theater that presents summer stock productions featuring nationally known actors, directors and designers. Performances are held May through August. Tickets are available at the box office starting in February; phone (717) 352-2164 or (888) 805-7056.

Also of interest in the park are artifacts and displays in the reconstructed Thaddeus Stevens' Blacksmith Shop and the Caledonia Iron Furnace. Recreational facilities include an Olympic-size swimming pool, an 18-hole golf course, nature trails and cross-country ski trails.

FERNDALE pop. 1,636
• Part of Philadelphia area — see map p. 154

FERNDALE INN   610/847-2662
🔷🔷🔷 American. Fine Dining. **Address:** 551 Church Hill Rd 18921

FOGELSVILLE (G-11) elev. 479'
• Restaurants p. 76

The regional transportation hub of Fogelsville is a suburb of Allentown, in Lehigh County. The village was named for a judge who opened a popular hotel there in 1798. Now I-78 and I-476 are the major crossroads that bring people to the region; often they are spending the night while visiting the wineries in nearby Breinigsville or the attractions in Allentown.

ALLENTOWN PARK HOTEL, AN ASCEND HOTEL COLLECTION MEMBER   (610)391-1500
🔷🔷🔷 Hotel. **Address:** 7471 Keebler Way 18106

THE CENTER AT HOLIDAY INN LEHIGH VALLEY
610/391-1000

🔷🔷🔷
Hotel
Rates not provided

Address: 7736 Adrienne Dr 18031 **Location:** I-78 exit 49A, 0.3 mi s on SR 100. **Facility:** 175 units. 3 stories, interior corridors. **Pool:** outdoor. **Activities:** exercise room. **Guest Services:** valet and coin laundry, area transportation.

SAVE ⬅ 🍴 🛎 ▽ CALL ♿
🏊 ▸◂ BIZ HS 🛜 ✕ 🍶
🖵 /SOME UNITS 🦮 🖥

GLASBERN   610/285-4723
▼▼▼ Historic Boutique Country Inn. **Address:** 2141 Packhouse Rd 18051

HAWTHORN SUITES BY WYNDHAM HOTELS   (610)366-9422
▼▼ Hotel. **Address:** 7720 Main St (I-78) 18051

HILTON GARDEN INN ALLENTOWN WEST   (610)398-6686
▼▼▼ Hotel. **Address:** 230 Sycamore Rd 18031

AAA Benefit:
Members save up to 10%!

SLEEP INN   (610)395-6603
▼▼ Hotel. **Address:** 327 Star Rd 18106

STAYBRIDGE SUITES-ALLENTOWN WEST   610/841-5100
▼▼▼ Extended Stay Hotel. **Address:** 327 Star Rd 18106

WHERE TO EAT

GLASBERN   610/285-4723
▼▼▼ American. Fine Dining. **Address:** 2141 Packhouse Rd 18051

MEDITERRANEAN CAFE & GRILL   610/391-0400
▼▼ Mediterranean. Casual Dining. **Address:** 7720 Main St 18051

STARLITE DINER   610/395-4031
▼▼ American. Casual Dining. **Address:** 233 N Rt 100 18051

FOREST HILLS pop. 6,518
• **Hotels & Restaurants map & index p. 246**
• **Part of Pittsburgh area — see map p. 225**

DREWS FAMILY RESTAURANT   412/271-1556   (79)
▼▼ American. Casual Dining. **Address:** 2060 Ardmore Blvd 15221

◆ FORT NECESSITY NATIONAL BATTLEFIELD (I-2) elev. 1,952'

Eleven miles east of Uniontown on US 40, Fort Necessity National Battlefield surrounds a reconstruction of the fort built by George Washington in 1754. The Battle of Fort Necessity, in which Washington led the Colonial Virginia Regiment alongside the British regulars from South Carolina against a strong force of French and Native Americans, occurred at the site on July 3, 1754. This was Washington's first major event in his military career and it marked the beginning of the French and Indian War.

Reconstructions of the fort, entrenchments and earthworks have been erected on their original sites. Picnic facilities are available. A visitor center features exhibits and a 20-minute video presentation. Mount Washington Tavern, on US 40 near the fort, is a restored 19th-century stagecoach inn. Visitor programs are available (weather permitting).

A mile west on US 40 is a monument marking the grave site of Gen. Edward Braddock. During the Battle of the Monongahela, Braddock was fatally wounded; his troops carried his body back as far as the site of the Old Orchard Camp, where he died. He was buried in the road that his men had built, and then the soldiers marched over the area to prevent the Native Americans from finding the body and

defiling it. George Washington, who had joined the campaign as a volunteer aide, officiated at Braddock's burial ceremony. In 1804 remains said to be those of Braddock were moved to the present grave site, marked by a monument.

Jumonville Glen, 7.5 miles from Fort Necessity, is reached via Jumonville Road (LR 26115), 2.5 miles north of US 40 at Mount Summit. It was the site of a 15-minute skirmish between French and British forces that led to the battle of Fort Necessity.

Park open daily dawn-dusk. Visitor center open daily 9-5; closed Jan. 1, Thanksgiving and Christmas. Jumonville Glen open daily dawn-dusk, May-Oct. Mount Washington Tavern open May 1-Oct. 31; phone ahead to verify hours. Admission is free. Phone (724) 329-5512.

FORT WASHINGTON pop. 5,446, elev. 174'
• **Hotels & Restaurants map & index p. 192**
• **Part of Philadelphia area — see map p. 154**

BEST WESTERN FORT WASHINGTON INN
(215)542-7930   **37**

▼▼▼
Hotel
$89-$105

BW Best Western.
AAA Benefit: Members save 5% to 15% and earn 10% bonus points!

Address: 285 Commerce Dr 19034 **Location:** I-276 (Pennsylvania Tpke) exit 339 (SR 309 S), just w on Pennsylvania Ave, just n to Commerce Dr, then 0.3 mi e. Located in a commercial area. 🅿 Fort Washington, 301. **Facility:** 105 units, some efficiencies. 4 stories, interior corridors. **Terms:** cancellation fee imposed. **Amenities:** safes. **Pool:** outdoor. **Activities:** exercise room. **Guest Services:** coin laundry.

[SAVE] 🍴 🍸 🏊 🛁 BIZ 📶 🔒 🛗 💻 / SOME UNITS 🐾 🚐

HILTON GARDEN INN PHILADELPHIA/FORT WASHINGTON   (215)646-4637   **39**

▼▼▼
Hotel
$99-$259

Hilton Garden Inn
AAA Benefit: Members save up to 10%!

Address: 530 W Pennsylvania Ave 19034 **Location:** I-276 (Pennsylvania Tpke) exit 339 (SR 309 S), just w. 🅿 Fort Washington, 301. **Facility:** 146 units. 6 stories, interior corridors. **Terms:** 1-7 night minimum stay, cancellation fee imposed. **Pool:** heated indoor. **Activities:** hot tub, exercise room. **Guest Services:** valet and coin laundry.

[SAVE] 🍸 CALL ♿ 🏊 🛁 BIZ
[HS] 📶 ✕ 🐾 🔒 🛗 💻 🚐

HOLIDAY INN EXPRESS & SUITES FT. WASHINGTON-PHILADELPHIA   (215)591-9000   **38**
▼▼▼ Hotel. **Address:** 432 W Pennsylvania Ave 19034

WHERE TO EAT

CANTINA FELIZ   215/646-1320   **86**
▼▼▼ Mexican. Casual Dining. **Address:** 424 S Bethlehem Pike 19034

FORTY FORT (E-10) pop. 4,214, elev. 554'

Built in 1790, the Nathan Denison House is 1 mile north via Wyoming Avenue at 35 Denison St. The house was built by Nathan Denison, a Revolutionary War colonel and later a Luzerne County judge. His 1717 ancestral homestead is in Mystic, Conn.

Col. Denison was among the first 40 settlers, for whom the Forty Fort settlement was named. Denison's property is considered to be the oldest frame dwelling in the Wyoming Valley. The restored house is mostly furnished with authentic 18th-century pieces. Events and programs of historical interest are presented throughout the year, concluding with an afternoon of Colonial hospitality in December. The house is open Sundays 1-4, Memorial Day weekend through September. Guided tours are available. Phone (570) 823-6244, ext. 3 for appointments or events information.

The 1807 Forty Fort Meeting House, 20 River St., was built by New England settlers from the Congregationalist, Presbyterian and Methodist congregations and was in use until the late 1840s. A cemetery dating to the late 18th century also is on the grounds; Col. Nathan Denison is among those interred here. The site is open Sundays and holidays 1-3 from Memorial Day weekend through late September; phone (570) 287-5214 to confirm schedule or to set up a tour by appointment.

FOXBURG pop. 183

THE FOXBURG INN HOTEL   724/659-3116

Hotel
$129-$199

Address: 20 Main St 16036 **Location:** I-80 exit 42; in town square. **Facility:** 24 units. 3 stories, exterior corridors. **Terms:** cancellation fee imposed. **Amenities:** safes. **Dining:** 2 restaurants. **Activities:** regulation golf, bicycles, trails.

FOX CHAPEL pop. 5,388
• Part of Pittsburgh area — see map p. 225

ATRIA'S RESTAURANT & TAVERN   412/963-1514
American. Casual Dining. **Address:** 1374 Freeport Rd 15238

FRACKVILLE pop. 3,805

COUNTRY INN & SUITES BY CARLSON - FRACKVILLE
                                      570/544-5201
Hotel. **Address:** 100 Keystone Blvd E 17901
HOLIDAY INN EXPRESS & SUITES FRACKVILLE
                                      570/874-1700
Hotel. **Address:** 958 Schuylkill Mall Rd 17931

FRANKLIN (VENANGO COUNTY) (E-2)
pop. 6,545, elev. 1,017'
• Restaurants p. 78

Franklin is believed to be the only city in Pennsylvania to have had four different forts within its boundaries. The town's history dates back to the French Fort Machault, built in 1753 near the confluence of French Creek and the Allegheny River. In 1760 the British built Fort Venango, which fell to the Native Americans during Pontiac's Conspiracy. American soldiers built Fort Franklin in 1787; it served as a defense against Native Americans. The fourth fort within the city, the Old Garrison, stationed federal troops 1796-99 and later served as the first jail of Venango County until 1819.

The county of Venango was established in 1800 with Franklin as the county seat. The town retained its rural atmosphere until the start of the oil boom in 1859. Drilling began in Franklin shortly after Edwin Drake's successful well came in near Titusville *(see place listing p. 289)*. Refineries were started, and Franklin's population more than tripled in the 1860s; three railroads came into the community, new businesses flourished, hotels were built and Franklin became a city in 1868.

Displays about local history can be seen at the Venango County Historical Society at 307 S. Park St. in the Egbert-Mullins-Koos House, a circa 1860 building; phone (814) 432-8260. Thirty Tiffany stained-glass windows adorn St. John's Episcopal Church on Buffalo Street; phone (814) 432-5161. The Barrow-Civic Theatre, a restored 1913 vaudeville house, features performing arts; phone (814) 437-3440 or (800) 537-7769.

Walking and bicycling can be enjoyed on the Allegheny River Trail and the Samuel Justis Trail.

Applefest, held Friday through Sunday the first full weekend in October, is an arts and crafts festival with live entertainment, a 5K race, an apple pie baking contest and an antique and classic car show. Apple orchards can be found in the surrounding area, but the main connection Franklin has with the fruit has to do with folk hero Johnny Appleseed's ties to the area. The festival draws nearly 100,000 to the Victorian downtown.

Franklin Area Chamber of Commerce: 1255 Liberty St., Franklin, PA 16323. **Phone:** (814) 432-5823.

Self-guiding tours: Booklets outlining a walking tour can be obtained at the chamber of commerce for $1.

Shopping: A farmers market is held on 12th Street on Wednesdays and Saturdays 8-1, May-Oct.

KNIGHTS INN   (814)432-2101
Hotel. **Address:** 847 Allegheny Blvd 16323

QUALITY INN & CONFERENCE CENTER   (814)437-3031

Hotel
$95-$300

Address: 1411 Liberty St 16323 **Location:** On US 62 and SR 8; center. **Facility:** 85 units. 5 stories, interior corridors. **Activities:** exercise room. **Guest Services:** valet and coin laundry. **Featured Amenity:** continental breakfast.

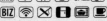

WHERE TO EAT

KING'S FAMILY RESTAURANT   814/437-6997
💎💎 American. Casual Dining. **Address:** 821 Allegheny Blvd 16323

FRIEDENS
• **Restaurants p. 78**

MOSTELLER'S COUNTRY CORRAL   814/445-7281
💎 American. Casual Dining. **Address:** 1207 Stoystown Rd 15541

GAINES
• **Restaurants p. 78**

LOG CABIN INN   814/435-8808
💎💎 Steak. Casual Dining. **Address:** 3501 Rt 6 16921

GALLITZIN (G-5) pop. 1,668, elev. 2,182'

ALLEGHENY PORTAGE RAILROAD NATIONAL HISTORIC SITE is off US 22 Gallitzin exit, following signs. Considered to be a 19th-century technological wonder, this site employed a series of inclined planes for transporting trains and canal boats over the Allegheny Mountains. Models, exhibits and artifacts depict its significance as a critical link in westward travel and trade.

An 1830s tavern, the Skew Arch Bridge, Incline Plane No. 6 and stone railroad ties can still be seen. Interpretive programs are offered in summer. **Time:** Allow 1 hour, 30 minutes minimum. **Hours:** Grounds daily dawn-dusk. Visitor center daily 9-5, mid-Apr. to mid-Nov.; Fri.-Sun. 9-5, rest of year; closed winter federal holidays. Phone ahead to confirm schedule. **Cost:** Free. **Phone:** (814) 886-6150. 🏛

GETTYSBURG (I-7) pop. 7,620, elev. 520'
• **Hotels p. 83** • **Restaurants p. 85**
• **Hotels & Restaurants map & index p. 81**

Marsh Creek Settlement was founded between two low ridges just north of the Mason-Dixon Line in the 1780s. Renamed Gettysburg in honor of Gen. James Gettys, the town grew quickly after being incorporated in 1806. Its square, at the crossroads of four major highways and several secondary roads, was a stopping point for travelers. This strategic location led to the town's involvement in one of the bloodiest battles of the Civil War *(see Gettysburg National Military Park p. 86)*.

Though the battlefield is the main draw for visitors, there are several reasons to venture downtown. On Lincoln Square, formed from Baltimore, Chambersburg, Carlisle and York streets, you'll find buildings from the Civil War era, including the David Wills House *(see attraction listing p. 86)*, where President Lincoln was a guest the evening before he delivered his Gettysburg Address on Nov. 19, 1863. Outside the building is a statue entitled " Return Visit" depicting Lincoln pointing toward the house and standing with a man dressed in late 20th-century attire who is reading a copy of the Gettysburg Address.

Not far from the Wills House is the restored Historic Gettysburg Lincoln Railroad Station at 35 Carlisle St. Original construction on the Italianate-style building was completed in 1859. During the battle of Gettysburg, it served as a hospital, and a few months later it was where Lincoln arrived in and departed from Gettysburg, but there is no proof that he ever actually went inside the station. There is proof, however, that he visited Gettysburg Presbyterian Church. The present building was built in 1963, but it contains the original pew, now marked with a plaque, in which Lincoln sat when he attended a patriotic service after the cemetery dedication. President and Mrs. Eisenhower were later members of the church and a plaque marks their pew as well.

Next to the railroad station is the Majestic Theater, built in 1925 in the Colonial Revival style and used for vaudeville shows and presentations of silent films. The interior boasts exquisite detail, from its custom-woven wool carpet to its pressed tin ceiling. Today films are shown and live performances are given. Two additional cinemas were added, and each was designed to have a 1950s look. For schedule information phone (717) 337-8200.

The small town is also home to the 200-acre campus of Gettysburg College, a liberal arts school with nearly 2,600 students. It is affiliated with the Lutheran faith and has its roots in abolitionist principles. Antislavery theologian Samuel Simon Schmucker founded the school—originally called Pennsylvania College—in 1832, and the institution eventually moved into Pennsylvania Hall, which was on land provided by abolitionist Thaddeus Stevens, who assisted in the Underground Railroad and began to establish American civil rights as a member of Congress. Pennsylvania Hall was used as a hospital during and after the battle. Another noteworthy building on campus is the admissions office, named Eisenhower House for the former president who served on the college's board of trustees and wrote his memoirs in the building.

In early July, Gettysburg Civil War Heritage Days features living-history encampments, reenactments, a book and paper show, a collectors' show, band concerts and a Civil War lecture series throughout Gettysburg and the Adams County area.

Destination Gettysburg: 1195 Baltimore Pike in the Gettysburg National Visitor Military Park Visitor Center, Gettysburg, PA 17325. A second location is the Visitor Information Center at 571 W. Middle St., Gettysburg, PA 17325. **Phone:** (717) 334-6274 or (800) 337-5015.

Self-guiding tours: Sightseeing excursions include a 14-block walking tour past 90 restored buildings. Driving tours include a 36-mile tour of the surrounding valley, and a 40-mile driving tour that explores East Cavalry Field, Victorian New Oxford and Early American East Berlin. Free brochures describing these tours are available from the Destination Gettysburg Information Center.

(See map & index p. 81.)

Shopping: Gettysburg shops lining Steinwehr Avenue and Baltimore, Chambersburg, Carlisle and York streets feature an assortment of antiques, books, collectibles, souvenirs and other specialty items. There also are more than a dozen art galleries.

Farmers markets are held downtown Saturdays 7 a.m.-1 p.m. and Thursdays 2-6 p.m. from late April through late October.

The Outlet Shoppes at Gettysburg, US 15 and SR 97, features a movie theater and dozens of stores, including Eddie Bauer, The Gap, Tommy Hilfiger and Van Heusen, in a village setting.

DAVID WILLS HOUSE—see Gettysburg National Military Park p. 86.

EISENHOWER NATIONAL HISTORIC SITE is accessible by a shuttle bus that departs from the Museum and Visitor Center at Gettysburg National Military Park on SR 97 at 1195 Baltimore Pike. The 231-acre Eisenhower farm was the only home ever owned by President Dwight D. Eisenhower and his wife Mamie. The house, grounds and buildings are preserved. Visitors can see the Eisenhower's formal living room, sun porch, original furniture and photographs as well as many of the president's paintings, gifts and other items. A 10-minute video presentation and exhibits about the president's life also are featured.

Among the dignitaries who visited the estate were Winston Churchill, Charles DeGaulle and Nikita Khrushchev. Self-guiding walking tours (with or without a cellphone audio tour) of the cattle barns, skeet shooting range and grounds are available. Summer programs include Ike and the Men of D-Day, a 30-minute interactive presentation featuring the weapons and equipment used for the invasion; Exploring Eisenhower, a ranger-led walking tour focusing on various topics relating to Eisenhower's life; and Hike With Ike, a ranger-led evening tour through downtown Gettysburg. Children ages 7-12 can participate in the Junior Secret Service Agent Program.

Hours: Twenty-minute tours of the grounds are conducted daily (weather permitting). A shuttle departs at regular intervals daily 9-4. Tickets are sold at the Museum and Visitor Center at Gettysburg National Military Park daily 8-6, Apr.-Oct.; 9-5, rest of year. Closed Jan. 1, Thanksgiving and Christmas. Phone ahead to confirm schedule. **Cost:** $9; $5 (ages 6-12). **Phone:** (717) 338-9114, or (717) 253-9256 for audio tour. GT

EXPLORE & MORE CHILDREN'S MUSEUM is .2 mi. s. on Baltimore Pike, then .1 mi. e. on High St. The museum offers a great variety of hands-on activities that focus on learning. The 1860s house features seven rooms, including an art room, an exploration room, a construction room and a re-creation of a period house. **Hours:** Mon.-Sat. 10-5,

Apr.-Sept.; Mon.-Tues. and Thurs.-Sat. 10-5, Sun. noon-5, rest of year. Closed major holidays. **Cost:** $7 (ages 2-14); $5 (adults). **Phone:** (717) 337-9151.

FARNSWORTH HOUSE INN & TOURS is at 401 Baltimore St. The 1810 house, which includes a brick portion that was added in 1833, has been restored to its 1863 appearance when it held Confederate sharpshooters during the 3-day siege in the Civil War. A south wall still holds more than 100 bullet holes. Weapons, bullets and artifacts from the house and battlefield are displayed in the attic area. The home was used by Union veterans during the 75th anniversary of the battle in 1938. Uniforms and props used by actors Sam Elliott and Tom Berenger from the 1993 film "Gettysburg" are also displayed.

Nightly ghost tours of Farnsworth House given by guides in period clothing include walks by other Gettysburg sites. A seated presentation in the cellar featuring ghost tales and stories about Victorian mourning is also offered nightly. Other offerings include In Their Shoes: A Day in the Life of a Soldier tour and Eat in Civil War Camp. Other tours also are available. The house can only be seen on a guided tour.

Time: Allow 1 hour minimum. **Hours:** House tours depart Fri.-Sat. at 4, Apr.-Nov. Ghost tour and seated presentation daily starting at 8 p.m., Apr.-Nov. Walking tour offered year-round (weather permitting); phone for schedule. A Day in the Life of a Soldier tour and Eat in Civil War Camp offered Apr.-Nov.; phone for schedule. Closed Jan. 1, Thanksgiving and Christmas. Phone ahead to confirm schedule. **Cost:** House tour $8. Ghost presentation $9-$50. **Phone:** (717) 334-8838. GT ⫯

GETTYSBURG BATTLEFIELD BUS TOURS, departing from 778 Baltimore St., offers 2-hour tours of the Gettysburg battlefield. Depending on the season and availability, tours take place aboard either a double-decker bus or an enclosed coach and are either led by a Gettysburg National Military Park guide or feature dramatized narration.

Hours: Daily 8-7, early June to mid-Aug.; 8-5, Mar. 1-early June and Sept.-Dec.; Sat.-Sun. 9-4, Jan.-Feb. Type of touring vehicle may vary; phone for details. Closed Jan. 1, Thanksgiving and Christmas. Phone ahead to confirm schedule. **Cost:** Audio tour $27; $16 (ages 6-12). Guided tour $35; $21 (ages 6-12). Phone ahead to confirm rates. **Phone:** (717) 334-6296 or (877) 680-8687. GT

GETTYSBURG BATTLE THEATRE, 571 Steinwehr Ave., offers an orientation program about the Battle of Gettysburg with a diorama, an electronic map and a film that features multimedia battle re-enactments. **Time:** Allow 1 hour minimum. **Hours:** Open daily at 9, July 4-Labor Day; phone for closing times and for schedule rest of year. **Cost:** $6.95; $6.25 (ages 60+ and military with ID); $3.50 (ages 6-12). **Phone:** (717) 334-6100. ⫯

(See map & index p. 81.)

GETTYSBURG SEMINARY RIDGE MUSEUM, 111 Seminary Ridge, is housed in a building that witnessed the Battle of Gettysburg and served as a field hospital during that battle. The Voices of Duty and Devotion exhibit details the first day of the Battle of Gettysburg along Seminary Ridge, showcases the nurses and doctors who treated the wounded, and tells stories about the fugitive slaves and African-Americans who served in the United States Colored Troops. The exhibit also focuses on the civic and spiritual debates related to faith and freedom that waged during the Civil War era to the present day. Murals, video screens, audio recordings and artifacts (including uniforms and weapons) are used throughout.

There is a 1-mile outdoor trail with interpretive signs on the campus, and cupola tours also are offered. **Time:** Allow 1 hour minimum for the museum; 1 hour, 30 minutes minimum for the museum and cupola. **Note:** Cupola tours require visitors to climb stairs. **Hours:** Daily 10-5, Mar.-Oct.; Fri.-Mon. 10-5, rest of year. Closed Jan. 1, Thanksgiving and Christmas. **Cost:** $9; $7 (ages 6-12 and 65+); $25 (family, up to four persons). Museum and cupola tour $29; $27 (ages 65+); $80 (family, up to four persons). Reservations are recommended for cupola tour. Ages 0-12 are not permitted in cupola. **Phone:** (717) 339-1300. [GT]

HISTORIC TOUR CO. tours depart from 55 Steinwehr Ave. Premier Gettysburg Battlefield Tours and Battlefield Tours for Kids—2 and 2.5 hours long—are conducted in vintage Yellowstone Park buses or 20-passenger coach buses. Other tours also are available.

Hours: Premier Gettysburg Battlefield Tour departs daily at 10, noon and 2. Battlefield Tour for Kids departs daily at 10:30 and 2:30. Phone ahead to confirm schedule. **Cost:** Premier Battlefield Tour $24.95; $12 (ages 6-18). Battlefield Tour for Kids $18 (per person); free (ages 0-3). Family discounts available. Reservations are recommended for battlefield tours. **Phone:** (717) 334-8000. [GT]

[SAVE] **JENNIE WADE HOUSE,** 548 Baltimore St., is the house in which the only civilian killed in the Battle of Gettysburg died. Guides in period attire lead visitors throughout the home, which is furnished as it might have been at the time of the historic battle.

Time: Allow 1 hour minimum. **Hours:** Daily 9-7, early June to mid-Aug.; Sun.-Thurs. 10-4, Fri. 10-6, Sat. 9-6 in Mar. and Nov.; Sun.-Thurs. 9-5, Fri.-Sat. 9-6 in Apr. and Sept.-Oct.; Fri. 10-4, Sat. 9-5, Sun. noon-5, in Dec. (hours vary Christmas week). Closed Thanksgiving and Christmas. Phone ahead to confirm schedule. **Cost:** $8.75; $6 (ages 6-12). Phone ahead to confirm rates. **Phone:** (717) 334-4100. [GT]

[SAVE] **LAND OF LITTLE HORSES FARM PARK,** 5 mi. w. off US 30 at 125 Glenwood Dr., features educational displays, events and performing animals. Petting and feeding areas are offered. **Hours:** Mon.-Sat. 10-5, Sun noon-5, June 1 to mid-Aug. Hours vary Apr.-May and mid-Aug. through Oct. 31. Phone ahead for show times. **Cost:** $15.95; $13.95 (ages 6-11); $11.95 (ages 2-5). **Phone:** (717) 334-7259. [II]

THE LINCOLN TRAIN MUSEUM, 425 Steinwehr Ave., features artifacts from early American history to the present day, railroad collections and interactive train layouts. Visitors take a simulated trip aboard the recreated Funeral Car United States as it follows the funeral route of President Abraham Lincoln through the post-Civil War countryside.

Time: Allow 1 hour minimum. **Hours:** Daily 9-9, June-July; daily 9-7 (also Fri.-Sat. 7-9 p.m.), Apr.-May and Aug.-Nov.; Thurs.-Mon. 10-5, rest of year. Last admission 1 hour before closing. Closed Jan. 1, Thanksgiving and Christmas. Phone ahead to confirm schedule. **Cost:** $7; $6 (military, police, fire and EMT personnel with ID); $5 (ages 65+); $4 (ages 6-12). **Phone:** (717) 334-5678.

SHRIVER HOUSE MUSEUM, 309 Baltimore St., is restored and furnished to its 1860s appearance. Guides in period costumes conduct tours and interpret the Shriver family's experience of living deep within Civil War battle lines. During the Battle of Gettysburg, Confederate sharpshooters took aim from positions in the attic; the house also served as a hospital for wounded soldiers. Visitors can explore the grounds before or after the guided tour. Candlelight tours are offered by reservation during the holiday season.

Time: Allow 45 minutes minimum. **Hours:** Sun.-Thurs. 10-5, Fri.-Sat. 10-6, Apr.-Oct.; Mon.-Thurs. noon-5, Sat. 10-6, Sun. 10-5, Nov. 1-Fri. before Thanksgiving; Sat. 10-5, Sun. 10-3, in Mar. Candlelight tours Thanksgiving to mid-Dec.; phone for tour times. Tour availability may be limited when groups with advance reservations are on-site; phone ahead to confirm schedule. **Cost:** $8.95; $6.95 (ages 7-12). **Phone:** (717) 337-2800. [GT]

STARS AND STRIPES TOURS meets passengers at select area hotels, attractions and campgrounds. The Washington, D.C. tour is a full-day narrated motor coach trip and includes visits to the World War II, Lincoln, Iwo Jima, Vietnam Veterans and Korean War Veterans memorials. Passengers are dropped off at the Smithsonian Institution for 3 hours of independent sightseeing. Other tours are available.

Hours: Tours depart Tues.-Thurs., June-Aug.; Wed.-Thurs. in May and Sept.-Oct. Departure times and length of trips may vary. Phone ahead to confirm schedule. **Cost:** $82; $76 (ages 4-12). **Phone:** (717) 528-1660 or (877) 723-1863. [GT]

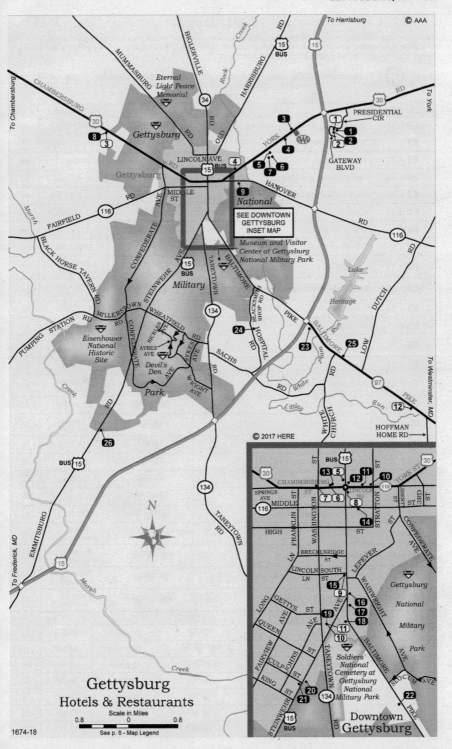

© AAA

Gettysburg
Hotels & Restaurants

Scale in Miles

0.8   0   0.8

See p. 6 - Map Legend

1674-18

Downtown
Gettysburg

© 2017 HERE

Gettysburg

This index helps you "spot" where approved hotels and restaurants are located on the corresponding detailed maps. Hotel daily rate range is for comparison only. Restaurant price range is a combination of lunch and/or dinner. Turn to the listing page for more information and consult display ads for special promotions.

 For more details, rates and reservations: AAA.com/travelguides/hotels

GETTYSBURG

Map Page	Hotels	Diamond Rated	Rate Range	Page
❶ p. 81	**Courtyard by Marriott Gettysburg**	♦♦♦	$68-$321 [SAVE]	83
❷ p. 81	**Wyndham Gettysburg**	♦♦♦	$119-$229 [SAVE]	85
❸ p. 81	Hampton Inn by Hilton	♦♦♦	$129-$249	85
❹ p. 81	**Hilton Garden Inn-Gettysburg**	♦♦♦	$119-$209 [SAVE]	85
❺ p. 81	**Days Inn Gettysburg**	♦♦	$42-$199 [SAVE]	83
❻ p. 81	**Super 8**	♦♦	$49-$209 [SAVE]	85
❼ p. 81	Quality Inn & Suites	♦♦	$75-$319	85
❽ p. 81	Inn at Herr Ridge	♦♦♦	$129-$259	85
❾ p. 81	Keystone Inn	♦♦♦	Rates not provided	85
❿ p. 81	The Swope Manor Bed & Breakfast	♦♦♦	Rates not provided	85
⓫ p. 81	The Brafferton Inn Bed & Breakfast	♦♦♦	$109-$249	83
⓬ p. 81	**Gettysburg Hotel**	♦♦♦	$109-$259 [SAVE]	83
⓭ p. 81	James Gettys Hotel	♦♦♦	Rates not provided	85
⓮ p. 81	The Gaslight Inn	♦♦♦	$145-$185	83
⓯ p. 81	Farnsworth House Inn	♦♦	Rates not provided	83
⓰ p. 81	The Brickhouse Inn	♦♦♦	$119-$219	83
⓱ p. 81	1863 Inn of Gettysburg	♦♦	Rates not provided	83
⓲ p. 81	Inn at Cemetery Hill	♦♦	$89-$250	85
⓳ p. 81	Gettystown Inn Bed & Breakfast	♦♦	$69-$195	85
⓴ p. 81	Quality Inn Gettysburg Battlefield	♦♦	$74-$239	85
㉑ p. 81	**Best Western Gettysburg**	♦♦♦	$84-$215 [SAVE]	83
㉒ p. 81	Comfort Suites Gettysburg	♦♦♦	$70-$340	83
㉓ p. 81	**Country Inn & Suites By Carlson** (See ad p. 84.)	♦♦	Rates not provided [SAVE]	83
㉔ p. 81	Baladerry Inn at Gettysburg	♦♦♦	Rates not provided	83
㉕ p. 81	The Lightner Farmhouse Bed & Breakfast	♦♦♦	Rates not provided	85
㉖ p. 81	Battlefield Bed & Breakfast Inn	♦♦♦	Rates not provided	83

Map Page	Restaurants	Diamond Rated	Cuisine	Price Range	Page
① p. 81	Appalachian Brewing Co.	♦♦	American	$9-$18	85
② p. 81	1863 Restaurant	♦♦♦	American	$9-$45	85
③ p. 81	Inn at Herr Ridge	♦♦♦	American	$23-$39	86
④ p. 81	La Bella Italia	♦♦	Italian	$8-$24	86
⑤ p. 81	The Pub and Restaurant	♦♦	American	$11-$37	86
⑥ p. 81	The Parrot Bistro	♦♦	American	$7-$31	86
⑦ p. 81	Food 101 Gettysburg	♦♦	American	$8-$17	85

Map Page	Restaurants (cont'd)	Diamond Rated	Cuisine	Price Range	Page
⑧ p. 81	Blue and Gray Bar and Grill	◈◈	American	$8-$23	85
⑨ p. 81	Farnsworth House	◈◈	American	$17-$41	85
⑩ p. 81	Alexander Dobbin Dining Rooms in the Dobbin House	◈◈◈	American	$25-$36	85
⑪ p. 81	Springhouse Tavern at the Dobbin House	◈◈	American	$9-$29	86
⑫ p. 81	Olivia's Restaurant	◈◈	Mediterranean	$10-$26	86

1863 INN OF GETTYSBURG   717/334-6211   **17**
◈◈ Hotel. **Address:** 516 Baltimore St 17325

BALADERRY INN AT GETTYSBURG   717/337-1342   **24**
◈◈◈ Historic Bed & Breakfast. **Address:** 40 Hospital Rd 17325

BATTLEFIELD BED & BREAKFAST INN   717/334-8804   **26**
◈◈◈ Historic Bed & Breakfast. **Address:** 2264 Emmitsburg Rd 17325

BEST WESTERN GETTYSBURG   (717)334-1188   **21**

◈◈◈
Hotel
$84-$215

BW **Best Western.** **AAA Benefit:** Members save 5% to 15% and earn 10% bonus points!

Address: 301 Steinwehr Ave 17325 **Location:** 1 mi s on US 15 business route, just s of jct SR 134. **Facility:** 81 units, some two bedrooms. 3 stories, interior/exterior corridors. **Terms:** 3 night minimum stay - seasonal, cancellation fee imposed. **Amenities:** safes. **Pool:** heated indoor. **Activities:** exercise room. **Guest Services:** coin laundry.

[SAVE] [📶] CALL [♿] [🚐] [👨‍👩‍👧] [BIZ]

[HS] [📶] [✕] [🔌] [🖥] [💻]

THE BRAFFERTON INN BED & BREAKFAST   (717)337-3423   **11**
◈◈◈ Historic Bed & Breakfast. **Address:** 44 York St 17325

THE BRICKHOUSE INN   (717)338-9337   **16**
◈◈◈ Historic Bed & Breakfast. **Address:** 452 Baltimore St 17325

COMFORT SUITES GETTYSBURG   (717)334-6715   **22**
◈◈◈ Hotel. **Address:** 945 Baltimore Pike 17325

COUNTRY INN & SUITES BY CARLSON
717/337-9518   **23**

◈◈
Hotel
Rates not provided

Address: 1857 Gettysburg Village Dr 17325 **Location:** US 15 exit SR 97, just e. Next to factory outlet stores. **Facility:** 83 units. 3 stories, interior corridors. **Pool:** heated indoor. **Activities:** hot tub, exercise room. **Guest Services:** coin laundry. **Featured Amenity:** breakfast buffet. *(See ad p. 84.)*

[SAVE] [📶] CALL [♿] [🚐] [👨‍👩‍👧]

[BIZ] [HS] [📶] [✕] [🔌] [🖥]

[💻] / [SOME UNITS] [🐾]

COURTYARD BY MARRIOTT GETTYSBURG
(717)334-5600   **1**

◈◈◈
Hotel
$68-$321

COURTYARD Marriott **AAA Benefit:** Members save 5% or more!

Address: 115 Presidential Cir 17325 **Location:** US 15 exit York St, just e on US 30. **Facility:** 152 units. 5 stories, interior corridors. **Terms:** cancellation fee imposed. **Pool:** heated indoor. **Activities:** hot tub, exercise room. **Guest Services:** complimentary laundry.

[SAVE] [📶] [Y] CALL [♿] [🚐] [👨‍👩‍👧]

[BIZ] [HS] [📶] [✕] [🔌] [💻]

/ [SOME UNITS] [🖥]

DAYS INN GETTYSBURG   (717)334-0030   **5**

◈◈
Hotel
$42-$199

Address: 865 York Rd 17325 **Location:** 1 mi e on US 30. **Facility:** 112 units. 5 stories, interior corridors. **Terms:** check-in 4 pm, cancellation fee imposed. **Pool:** outdoor. **Activities:** exercise room. **Guest Services:** coin laundry. **Featured Amenity:** continental breakfast.

[SAVE] [📶] [🚐] [👨‍👩‍👧] [BIZ] [📶] [✕]

[🔌] [🖥] [💻]

FARNSWORTH HOUSE INN   717/334-8838   **15**
◈◈ Historic Bed & Breakfast. **Address:** 401 Baltimore St 17325

THE GASLIGHT INN   717/337-9100   **14**
◈◈◈ Historic Bed & Breakfast. **Address:** 33 E Middle St 17325

GETTYSBURG HOTEL   (717)337-2000   **12**

◈◈◈
Historic Hotel
$109-$259

Address: One Lincoln Square 17325 **Location:** On US 30; center of downtown. **Facility:** Established in 1797, this restored hotel has a ballroom that was once a bank. Guest rooms are traditionally decorated with many modern comforts and amenities. 119 units, some two bedrooms. 6 stories, interior corridors. **Parking:** on-site (fee). **Terms:** check-in 4 pm, 3 day cancellation notice. **Pool:** outdoor. **Activities:** exercise room.

[SAVE] [📶] [Y] CALL [♿] [🚐]

[👨‍👩‍👧] [BIZ] [📶] [✕] [💻]

/ [SOME UNITS] [🔌] [🖥]

GETTYSBURG HOTEL *Established 1797*

Walking distance to the battlefield, attractions, shops & restaurants. Located in Historic Downtown.

(See map & index p. 81.)

(See map & index p. 81.)

GETTYSTOWN INN BED & BREAKFAST   (717)334-2100   **19**
♦♦♦ Historic Country Inn. **Address:** 89 Steinwehr Ave 17325

HAMPTON INN BY HILTON   (717)338-9121   **3**
♦♦♦ Hotel. **Address:** 1280 York Rd 17325
AAA Benefit: Members save up to 10%!

HILTON GARDEN INN-GETTYSBURG
(717)334-2040   **4**

♦♦♦
Hotel
$119-$209

Hilton Garden Inn
AAA Benefit: Members save up to 10%!

Address: 1061 York Rd 17325 **Location:** 0.9 mi e on US 30. Located in a commercial area. **Facility:** 88 units. 4 stories, interior corridors. **Terms:** 1-7 night minimum stay, cancellation fee imposed. **Pool:** heated indoor. **Activities:** hot tub, exercise room. **Guest Services:** valet and coin laundry.

HOLIDAY INN EXPRESS & SUITES GETTYSBURG
(717)420-2686
[fyi] Hotel. Too new to rate. **Address:** 1871 Gettysburg Village Dr 17325 **Location:** US 15 exit SR 97. **Amenities:** 99 units. *(See ad p. 84.)*

INN AT CEMETERY HILL   (717)334-9281   **18**
♦♦ Motel. **Address:** 613 Baltimore St 17325

INN AT HERR RIDGE   (717)334-4332   **8**
♦♦♦ Historic Country Inn. **Address:** 900 Chambersburg Rd 17325

JAMES GETTYS HOTEL   717/337-1334   **13**
♦♦♦ Historic Bed & Breakfast. **Address:** 27 Chambersburg St 17325

KEYSTONE INN   717/337-3888   **9**
♦♦♦ Historic Bed & Breakfast. **Address:** 231 Hanover St 17325

THE LIGHTNER FARMHOUSE BED & BREAKFAST
717/337-9508   **25**
♦♦♦ Historic Bed & Breakfast. **Address:** 2350 Baltimore Pike 17325

QUALITY INN & SUITES   (717)337-2400   **7**
♦♦ Hotel. **Address:** 871 York Rd 17325

QUALITY INN GETTYSBURG BATTLEFIELD
(717)334-1103   **20**
♦♦ Motel. **Address:** 380 Steinwehr Ave 17325

SUPER 8
(717)337-1400   **6**

♦♦
Motel
$49-$209

Address: 869 York Rd 17325 **Location:** 1 mi e on US 30. **Facility:** 50 units. 2 stories (no elevator), interior corridors. **Terms:** cancellation fee imposed. **Amenities:** safes. **Pool:** heated indoor. **Activities:** hot tub. **Guest Services:** complimentary laundry. **Featured Amenity:** continental breakfast.

THE SWOPE MANOR BED & BREAKFAST
717/398-2655   **10**
♦♦♦ Historic Bed & Breakfast. **Address:** 58-60 York St 17325

WYNDHAM GETTYSBURG
(717)339-0020   **2**

♦♦♦
Hotel
$119-$229

Address: 95 Presidential Cir 17325 **Location:** US 15 exit York St, just e on US 30. **Facility:** 248 units. 6 stories, interior corridors. **Terms:** cancellation fee imposed. **Amenities:** safes. **Dining:** 1863 Restaurant, see separate listing. **Pool:** heated indoor. **Activities:** hot tub, exercise room. **Guest Services:** complimentary laundry, rental car service.

WHERE TO EAT

1863 RESTAURANT   717/339-0020   **2**
♦♦♦ American. Fine Dining. **Address:** 95 Presidential Cir 17325

ALEXANDER DOBBIN DINING ROOMS IN THE DOBBIN HOUSE   717/334-2100   **10**
♦♦♦ American. Casual Dining. **Address:** 89 Steinwehr Ave 17325

APPALACHIAN BREWING CO.   717/398-2419   **1**
♦♦ American. Brewpub. **Address:** 70 Presidential Cir 17325

BLUE AND GRAY BAR AND GRILL   717/334-1999   **8**
♦♦ American. Casual Dining. **Address:** 2 Baltimore St 17325

FARNSWORTH HOUSE   717/334-8838   **9**
♦♦ American. Casual Dining. **Address:** 401 Baltimore St 17325

FOOD 101 GETTYSBURG   717/334-6080   **7**
♦♦ American. Casual Dining. **Address:** 101 Chambersburg St 17325

(See map & index p. 81.)

INN AT HERR RIDGE   717/334-4332 ③

**American
Fine Dining
$23-$39**

AAA Inspector Notes: *Historic.* Fireplaces lend to the appeal of this 1816 public house's four dining rooms, which are decorated with antiques and lanterns. Gourmet cuisine is prepared and served in a refined atmosphere. Small plates include baked baby Brie with seasonal changes and crab and corn chowder. Satisfying main entrées include pork, chicken, seafood and filet mignon with seasonal accompaniments. A 4-course prix fixe menu is available, as well as wine pairings. **Features:** full bar. **Reservations:** suggested, weekends. **Address:** 900 Chambersburg Rd 17325 **Location:** 1.7 mi w on US 30. 🅱 D

LA BELLA ITALIA   717/334-1978 ④

🍷🍷 Italian. Casual Dining. **Address:** 402 York St 17325

OLIVIA'S RESTAURANT   717/359-9357 ⑫

🍷🍷 Mediterranean. Casual Dining. **Address:** 3015 Baltimore Pike 17325

THE PARROT BISTRO   717/337-3739 ⑥

🍷🍷 American. Casual Dining. **Address:** 35 Chambersburg St 17325

THE PUB AND RESTAURANT   717/334-7100 ⑤

🍷🍷 American. Casual Dining. **Address:** 21 Lincoln Square 17325

SPRINGHOUSE TAVERN AT THE DOBBIN HOUSE
                                          717/334-2100 ⑪

🍷🍷 American. Casual Dining. **Address:** 89 Steinwehr Ave 17325

▼GEM GETTYSBURG NATIONAL MILITARY PARK (I-7) elev. 495'

• Attractions map p. 87

Gettysburg National Military Park virtually surrounds the town of Gettysburg; the main entrance is at the Museum and Visitor Center at 1195 Baltimore Pike. The park comprises the Gettysburg battlefield, where one of the most important and hotly contested battles of the Civil War was fought July 1-3, 1863. It also was the bloodiest battle of the war, resulting in 51,000 wounded, captured or killed.

The Federal Army of the Potomac, under Major Gen. George Meade, met the Confederate Army of Northern Virginia, under Gen. Robert E. Lee. Some 168,000 soldiers were at Gettysburg. The battlefield covers 25 square miles.

After his victory at Chancellorsville, Va., Lee invaded Pennsylvania, hoping to draw the Union Army away from Richmond. On the morning of July 1 two Confederate brigades attacked Gen. John Buford's cavalry division. Fierce fighting followed, and the Union forces were driven back to the heights south of town, known as Cemetery Hill, Cemetery Ridge and Culp's Hill. That night the armies moved into battle position. Confederate assaults on both Union flanks gained some ground late the next day in some of the heaviest fighting of the battle.

On the third day, after a heavy 2-hour artillery barrage, a Confederate force advanced on the center of the Union line in the face of deadly fire that shattered their ranks. They retreated on the evening of July 4, ending the last major offensive of Lee's army and presaging the war's outcome 22 months later.

On Nov. 19, 1863, President Lincoln dedicated Soldiers' National Cemetery on the battlefield, delivering his most famous speech, the Gettysburg Address.

There are now more than 1,300 monuments and memorials, three observation towers and 31 miles of marked avenues.

On Cemetery Ridge, Meade, commander of the Union forces, is depicted on his horse. His headquarters on Taneytown Road is preserved. In the spring, summer and fall there are interpretive walks to the National Cemetery as well as to other battlefield sites.

Many states have erected monuments in the park. The Virginia memorial is surmounted by a statue of Lee, and the North Carolina memorial was designed and carved by Gutzon Borglum, sculptor of Mount Rushmore.

The park roads are open daily 6 a.m.-10 p.m., Apr.-Oct.; 6 a.m.-7 p.m., rest of year. Phone (717) 334-1124, or (877) 874-2478 for advance ticket purchases.

DAVID WILLS HOUSE is at 8 Lincoln Sq. on the downtown square, within Gettysburg National Military Park. The site reveals what Gettysburg was like during the weeks after the Civil War battle through displays, two interactive exhibits and two films. Much of the recovery phase was centered around the three-story brick house of David Wills, a prominent lawyer. From here local women cared for wounded soldiers, and state leaders convened to discuss burial options for the Union casualties. Pennsylvania's governor, Andrew Curtin, placed Wills in charge of organizing a national cemetery.

On Nov. 2, 1863, Wills wrote to President Lincoln, inviting him to deliver "a few appropriate remarks" at the cemetery's dedication on Nov. 19. To many people's amazement, the president accepted and arrived the evening before the event. Mr. and Mrs. Wills welcomed him into their home, where they were hosting a dinner for nearly three dozen guests. That night from his bedroom (Mrs. Wills had prepared her own for the president), he completed the Gettysburg Address he would give the next day.

The museum collection features original furnishings, including the bed Lincoln slept in, and the saddle he used on his trip to the cemetery. A model with 260 buildings is a powerful visual representation of the 1863 town. Photography is permitted. **Time:** Allow 45 minutes minimum. **Hours:** Daily 10-5, May-Aug.; Wed.-Mon. 10-4, Mar.-Apr. and Sept.-Oct.; Sat.-Sun. 10-4, Nov.-Dec. and mid- to late Feb. Closed Thanksgiving and Christmas. Phone ahead to confirm schedule. **Cost:** $7; $6 (ages 65+); $4 (ages 6-12). **Phone:** (717) 334-2499 or (866) 486-5735.

▼GEM **DEVIL'S DEN**, off Warren Ave. and just w. of Little Round Top within Gettysburg National Military Park, is a group of huge boulders from which Capt. James Smith's Union troops were driven in Gen. James Longstreet's attack July 2, 1863. The

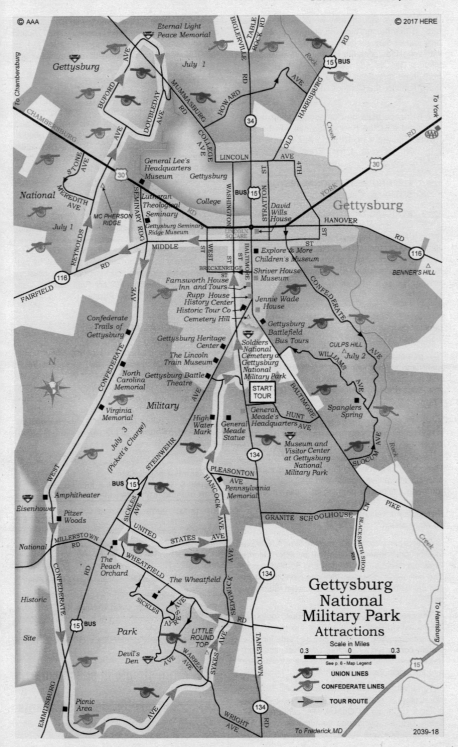

© AAA

© 2017 HERE

Eternal Light
Peace Memorial

To Chambersburg

Gettysburg

July 1

BIGLERVILLE RD

TABLE ROCK RD

BUFORD AVE

MUMMASBURG RD

HOWARD AVE

DOUBLEDAY AVE

COLLEGE AVE

Rock Creek

OLD HARRISBURG AVE

BUS 15

To York

RD

AAA

RD 30

CHAMBERSBURG

34

LINCOLN

AVE

4TH

STONE AVE

30

MEREDITH AVE

General Lee's
Headquarters
Museum

Gettysburg

WASHINGTON ST

BUS 15

STRATTON ST

1ST

YORK

David Wills
House

Gettysburg

National

July 1

MC PHERSON
RIDGE

SEMINARY RDG

Lutheran
Theological
Seminary

College

LINCOLN
SQUARE

HANOVER

ST

RD 116

Reynolds

Gettysburg Seminary
Ridge Museum

MIDDLE

WEST ST

BENNER'S HILL

116

FAIRFIELD

RD

BRECKENRIDGE ST

Explore & More
Children's Museum

Shriver House
Museum

CONFEDERATE AVE

Confederate
Trails of
Gettysburg

CONFEDERATE AVE

Farnsworth House
Inn and Tours

Rupp House
History Center

Historic Tour Co

Cemetery Hill

BALTIMORE ST

Jennie Wade
House

Gettysburg
Battlefield
Bus Tours

CULPS HILL

July 2

WILLIAMS AVE

N

Gettysburg Heritage
Center

The Lincoln
Train Museum

Gettysburg Battle
Theatre

North
Carolina
Memorial

Military

Soldiers
National
Cemetery a
Gettysburg
National
Military Park

START
TOUR

BALTIMORE

Spanglers
Spring

SLOCUM AVE

Virginia
Memorial

July 3
(Pickett's Charge)

High
Water
Mark

General
Meade
Statue

General
Meade's
Headquarters

HUNT AVE

Museum and
Visitor Center
at Gettysburg
National
Military Park

Rock Creek

MT PIKE

WEST

BUS 15

STEINWEHR AVE

SICKLES AVE

134

PLEASONTON
AVE

Pennsylvania
Memorial

HANCOCK AVE

GRANITE SCHOOLHOUSE

BLACKSMITH SHOP

Amphitheater

Eisenhower

Pitzer
Woods

MILLERSTOWN RD

UNITED STATES AVE

National

Historic

RD

The Peach
Orchard

WHEATFIELD

SICKLES AVE

AYRES AVE

The Wheatfield

SEDGWICK RD

134

To Harrisburg

15

15 BUS

Site

Park

Devil's
Den

LITTLE
ROUND
TOP

WARREN AVE

SYKES AVE

TANEYTOWN RD

Gettysburg
National
Military Park
Attractions

Scale in Miles

0.3   0.3

See p. 6 – Map Legend

EMMITSBURG

Picnic
Area

WRIGHT AVE

134

To Frederick, MD

UNION LINES

CONFEDERATE LINES

TOUR ROUTE

15

2039-18

Union soldiers thought they would be at an advantage at this height, but with little room at the top, only four of their six guns could be used and there was very little space left for ammunition supplies or infantry. The Confederate troops eventually attacked from three directions at the same time, and after much fighting, the Confederates took control of the site.

A barricade used by Confederate sharpshooters who fired on Little Round Top still can be seen. **Hours:** Daily 6 a.m.-10 p.m., Apr.-Oct.; 6 a.m.-7 p.m., rest of year. **Cost:** Free. **Phone:** (717) 334-1124.

 EISENHOWER NATIONAL HISTORIC SITE—see Gettysburg p. 79.

 ETERNAL LIGHT PEACE MEMORIAL, on Oak Ridge in the northwest section of Gettysburg National Military Park, commemorates the Battle of Gettysburg. The project was suggested by Union and Confederate veterans in 1913, and after funding difficulties and construction delays were resolved, it was dedicated by President Franklin D. Roosevelt on the 75th anniversary of the battle on July 3, 1938. Some Civil War veterans attended the ceremony, which drew an estimated 250,000 people. Perhaps another 100,000 would-be visitors were stuck in nearby traffic.

A perpetual flame burns at the top of the monument, and an inscription reads, "Peace Eternal in a Nation United." **Hours:** Park daily 6 a.m.-10 p.m., Apr.-Oct.; 6 a.m.-7 p.m., rest of year. **Cost:** Free. **Phone:** (717) 334-1124.

 MUSEUM AND VISITOR CENTER AT GETTYSBURG NATIONAL MILITARY PARK is at 1195 Baltimore Pike, adjacent to the battlefield. The Civil War, particularly the Battle of Gettysburg, is chronicled through archival materials, artifacts, interactive exhibits and a 42-foot high, 377-foot-long cyclorama painting of Pickett's Charge. "The Battle of Gettysburg," by French artist Paul Philippoteaux was painted 1883-84 with the help of 20 other artists.

Guests can watch the 22-minute film "A New Birth of Freedom," featuring narration by actors Morgan Freeman, Marcia Gay Harden and Sam Waterston. The museum's collection includes more than 1 million items, though not all are displayed. Temporary exhibits also are offered.

The center serves as the starting point for tours of the battlefield. Both self-guiding and guided tours are available. Arrangements can be made for a personally conducted 2-hour tour with a licensed battlefield guide. Ranger programs are offered April through December.

Time: Allow 2 hours minimum. **Hours:** Daily 8-6, Apr.-Oct.; 9-5, rest of year. Closed Jan. 1, Thanksgiving and Christmas. **Cost:** Visitor center free. Museum, film and cyclorama combination ticket $15; $14 (ages 65+ and military veterans with ID); $10 (ages 6-12); free (active military with ID). Museum-only tickets and combination passes with battlefield bus tour are available. **Phone:** (717) 334-1124, or (877) 874-2478 for advance ticket purchases and battlefield tour reservations. GT ❚⫶❚

 SOLDIERS' NATIONAL CEMETERY AT GETTYSBURG NATIONAL MILITARY PARK, at 97 Taneytown Rd., just n. of the museum and visitor center, consists of 17 acres and contains the graves of 3,555 Union Civil War dead, 1,600 of them unknown. The Soldiers' National Monument stands near the spot where President Lincoln delivered his immortal dedication address Nov. 19, 1863, to some 15,000 people. Veterans from the Civil War through the Vietnam War, along with their dependents, are buried here.

Since the official closing in 1972, no more burials except for the dependents of those veterans already interred are possible. Interpretive walks are given seasonally. Self-guiding walking tour brochures for the cemetery and other battlefield sites may be purchased at the Museum and Visitor Center bookstore at Gettysburg National Military Park. **Hours:** Daily dawn-dusk. **Cost:** Free. **Phone:** (717) 334-1124. GT

RECREATIONAL ACTIVITIES
Horseback Riding
• **Confederate Trails of Gettysburg** 2-hour horseback tours depart from McMillan Woods Youth Campground's parking area on W. Confederate Ave., within Gettysburg National Military Park. **Hours:** Tours are offered Fri.-Wed., Apr.-Nov. (weather permitting). Schedules vary; phone to confirm departure times. **Cost:** Reservations are required. **Phone:** (717) 476-7428 or (866) 907-0633. GT

GIBSONIA pop. 2,733
• Hotels & Restaurants map & index p. 246
• Part of Pittsburgh area — see map p. 225

QUALITY INN & SUITES PITTSBURGH-GIBSONIA
(724)444-8700 **40**
▼▼ Motel. **Address:** 5137 William Flynn Hwy 15044

WHERE TO EAT

EAT'N PARK   724/443-7280
▼▼ American. Casual Dining. **Address:** 5143 SR 8 15044

KING'S FAMILY RESTAURANT   724/443-4280
▼▼ American. Casual Dining. **Address:** 112 Northtowne Square 15044

 From simple to spectacular:

AAA.com/travelguides/restaurants

GLEN MILLS elev. 230'
• Part of Philadelphia area — see map p. 154

THE INN AT GRACE WINERY   610/459-4711

Historic Bed & Breakfast
Rates not provided

Address: 50 Sweetwater Rd 19342 **Location:** US 1, 2 mi w on Valley Rd, 0.6 mi s. **Facility:** Set on 50 acres, this beautifully decorated B&B features upscale cottage suites spread throughout the property as well as comfortable guest rooms in the historic 18th-century manor house. 15 units, some two bedrooms, kitchens and cottages. 1-2 stories (no elevator), interior/exterior corridors. **Pool:** outdoor. **Activities:** hot tub, exercise room. **Featured Amenity: continental breakfast.**

SAVE 🚲 🏥 BIZ 🛜 ✕
/SOME UNITS 🏰 🅱 📷 💻

WHERE TO EAT

BLUEFIN SUSHI AND ASIAN CUISINE   610/459-2055
💎💎 Japanese. Casual Dining. **Address:** 1102 Baltimore Pike 19342

GORDONVILLE pop. 508
• Hotels & Restaurants map & index p. 148
• Part of Pennsylvania Dutch Country area — see map p. 143

AFTER EIGHT B&B   (717)687-3664 **52**
💎💎💎 Historic Bed & Breakfast. **Address:** 2942 Lincoln Hwy E 17529

HARVEST DRIVE FAMILY INN   717/768-7186 **50**

Motel
Rates not provided

Address: 3368 Harvest Dr 17529 **Location:** 0.5 mi w on SR 340, 0.7 mi s on Clearview Rd, then just w. **Facility:** 50 units. 1-2 stories (no elevator), exterior corridors. **Activities:** playground, picnic facilities. **Guest Services:** coin laundry.

SAVE 🍴 🛜 ✕ 🅱 📷 💻
/SOME UNITS 🐾

MOTEL 6-LANCASTER #4174   717/687-3880 **51**
💎💎 Motel. **Address:** 2959 Lincoln Hwy E 17529

GRANTVILLE elev. 531'

DAYS INN GRANTVILLE-HERSHEY   (717)469-0631
💎💎 Motel. **Address:** 252 Bow Creek Rd 17028

HAMPTON INN-GRANTVILLE/HARRISBURG/HERSHEY   (717)469-7689
💎💎💎 Hotel. **Address:** 255 Bow Creek Rd 17028

AAA Benefit: Members save up to 10%!

HOLIDAY INN HARRISBURG-HERSHEY AREA, I-81   (717)469-0661

💎💎💎 **Hotel**
$99-$229

Address: 604 Station Rd 17028 **Location:** I-81 exit 80, just w. **Facility:** 200 units. 4 stories, interior corridors. **Terms:** check-in 4 pm, cancellation fee imposed. **Dining:** 2 restaurants, entertainment. **Pool:** outdoor, heated indoor. **Activities:** hot tub, exercise room. **Guest Services:** valet and coin laundry, area transportation. *(See ad p. 105.)*

SAVE 🚭 🍴 🏊 🍸
CALL 🔗 🚲 🏥 BIZ 🛜
✕ 💻 /SOME UNITS 🏰 🅱 📷

Holiday Inn

Located just minutes to Hersheypark and attractions!

GREENCASTLE pop. 3,996

COMFORT INN   (717)597-8164
💎💎 Hotel. **Address:** 50 Pine Dr 17225

GREENSBURG (H-3) pop. 14,892, elev. 1,114'
• Hotels p. 90 • Restaurants p. 90

Greensburg is part of the Laurel Highlands *(see place listing p. 122)*. Incorporated in 1799, Greensburg was named in honor of Revolutionary War Gen. Nathanael Greene. A monument and marker for Gen. Arthur St. Clair, who served as president of the Continental Congress and was the first governor of the Northwest Territory, is in St. Clair Park.

In the early 1900s, Greensburg joined dozens of other small towns linked across the nation by the newly created Lincoln Highway. Known today as US 30, its heritage sites across the state are commemorated by the Lincoln Highway Roadside Museum. This 200-mile corridor features historic buildings, architectural oddities, exhibits and nostalgic murals. A brochure and driving tour map are available from the Lincoln Highway Heritage Corridor office at 3435 US 30E in Latrobe; phone (724) 879-4241.

The Five Star Trail, which is along the Southwestern Pennsylvania Railroad corridor and accommodates walkers, bikers and cross-country skiers, begins at Lynch Field and continues 6 miles south to Hillis Street in Youngwood. Just before the southern terminus, the trail branches east at Depot Street and continues about 1.5 miles to connect with Westmoreland County Community College and then to Armburst. For brochures or more information contact Westmoreland County Parks and Recreation, 194 Donohoe Rd., Greensburg, PA 15601; phone (724) 830-3950.

Westmoreland County Chamber of Commerce: 241 Tollgate Hill Rd., Greensburg, PA 15601. **Phone:** (724) 834-2900.

Shopping: Westmoreland Mall, US 30 and Donohoe Rd., features The Bon-Ton, JCPenney, Macy's and Sears.

COURTYARD BY MARRIOTT PITTSBURGH GREENSBURG
(724)834-3555
WWW Hotel. **Address:** 700 Powerline Dr 15601

AAA Benefit:
Members save 5%
or more!

HAMPTON INN GREENSBURG (724)838-8800
WWW Hotel. **Address:** 1000 Towne Square Dr 15601

AAA Benefit:
Members save up to
10%!

HOLIDAY INN EXPRESS & SUITES 724/837-1400
WWW Hotel. **Address:** 137 Blair St 15601

RAMADA HOTEL AND CONFERENCE CENTER GREENSBURG
(724)836-6060
WWW Hotel. **Address:** 100 Ramada Inn Dr 15601

WHERE TO EAT

BLACK ROK ALE HOUSE 724/205-6408
W American. Brewpub. **Address:** 6026 Old Route 30 15601

KING'S FAMILY RESTAURANT 724/523-5371
WW American. Casual Dining. **Address:** 6297 Lincoln Hwy 15601

LITTLE E'S PIZZERIA 724/834-7336
WW Pizza. Casual Dining. **Address:** 807 Highland Ave 15601

PRIMANTI BROS. 724/689-1300
W American. Casual Dining. **Address:** 830 E Pittsburgh St 15601

ROBOKYO JAPANESE STEAKHOUSE AND SUSHI
724/834-7423
WWW Japanese. Casual Dining. **Address:** 910 E Pittsburgh St 15601

VALLOZZI'S RESTAURANT 724/836-7663
WWW Italian. Casual Dining. **Address:** 855 Georges Station Rd E 15601

VISTA PLATEAU RESTAURANT 724/836-6060
WW American. Casual Dining. **Address:** 100 Sheraton Dr 15601

GET THE APP

Download today. Connect every day.
AAA.com/mobile
CAA.ca/mobile

GREEN TREE pop. 4,432
- **Hotels & Restaurants map & index p. 246**
- **Part of Pittsburgh area — see map p. 225**

CROWNE PLAZA PITTSBURGH WEST-GREEN TREE
412/922-8100 **95**
WWW Hotel. **Address:** 401 Holiday Dr 15220

DOUBLETREE BY HILTON PITTSBURGH-GREEN TREE
(412)922-8400 **97**

WWW
Hotel
$99-$149

DOUBLETREE
BY HILTON

AAA Benefit:
Members save 5% or
more!

Address: 500 Mansfield Ave 15205 **Location:** I-376 exit 67, 1.1 mi nw to Mansfield Ave. **Facility:** 460 units. 7 stories, interior corridors. **Terms:** 1-7 night minimum stay, cancellation fee imposed. **Amenities:** safes. **Dining:** 2 restaurants. **Pool:** heated outdoor, heated indoor. **Activities:** hot tub, exercise room. **Guest Services:** valet laundry, area transportation. **Featured Amenity:** breakfast buffet.

HAMPTON INN PITTSBURGH GREEN TREE
(412)922-0100 **96**
WWW Hotel. **Address:** 555 Trumbull Dr 15205

AAA Benefit:
Members save up to
10%!

HOLIDAY INN EXPRESS HOTEL & SUITES PITTSBURGH WEST-GREENTREE 412/922-7070 **94**
WWW Hotel. **Address:** 875 Green Tree Rd 15220

WHERE TO EAT

TAMARIND SAVORING INDIA 412/278-4848 **96**
WW Indian. Casual Dining. **Address:** 2101 Greentree Rd 15220

GROVE CITY (E-2) pop. 8,322, elev. 1,245'

Eastern Mercer County's first gristmill, built in 1799 by Valentine Cunningham, drew settlers to the village then known as Pine Grove. Several historical markers downtown on Broad Street describe noteworthy buildings, events and people related to Grove City. Three murals depict scenes related to the town's history; one is at 118 S. Broad St., one is at 201 S. Broad St. and the other is at 232 S. Broad St. Today's Grove City is a prosperous community best known as the home of Grove City College.

Grove City Area Chamber of Commerce: 119 S. Broad St., Grove City, PA 16127. **Phone:** (724) 458-6410.

Shopping: Downtown offers more than a dozen small shops, but the big draw is Grove City Premium Outlets, I-79 and SR 208, where retailers include Banana Republic, Calvin Klein, Gap, J. Crew, Nike and Polo Ralph Lauren.

BEST WESTERN GROVE CITY INN   (724)748-5836

  Best Western.

Hotel
$89-$199

AAA Benefit: Members save 5% to 15% and earn 10% bonus points!

Address: 1924 Leesburg Grove City Rd 16127 **Location:** I-79 exit 113, just w. Across from outlet mall. **Facility:** 60 units. 2 stories (no elevator), interior corridors. **Terms:** 3 day cancellation notice-fee imposed. **Amenities:** safes. **Pool:** heated indoor. **Activities:** sauna, hot tub. **Guest Services:** coin laundry.

SAVE ⊞ CALL ⬆ 🔁 BIZ HS
📶 ⊠ 🖥 🖨 💻

HAMPTON INN & SUITES OF GROVE CITY   (724)748-5744
Hotel. **Address:** 4 Holiday Blvd 16127

AAA Benefit: Members save up to 10%!

HOLIDAY INN EXPRESS   724/748-5514
Hotel. **Address:** 21 Holiday Blvd 16127

TERRA NOVA HOUSE B&B   (724)450-0712
Historic Bed & Breakfast. **Address:** 322 W Poplar St 16127

WHERE TO EAT

EAT'N PARK   724/748-5911
American. Casual Dining. **Address:** 1911 Leesburg Grove City Rd 16127

KING'S FAMILY RESTAURANT   724/748-1015
American. Casual Dining. **Address:** 1920 Leesburg Grove City Rd 16127

GWYNEDD
• Part of Philadelphia area — see map p. 154

WILLIAM PENN INN   215/699-9272
Continental. Fine Dining. **Address:** 1017 Dekalb Pike 19436

HALLSTEAD pop. 1,303

COLONIAL BRICK INN & SUITES   570/879-2162

Motel
$98-$140

Address: 25161 SR 11 18822 **Location:** I-81 exit 230 (Great Bend-Hallstead), just w. Located in a light-commercial area. **Facility:** 53 units, some kitchens. 2 stories (no elevator), interior corridors. **Parking:** winter plug-ins.

SAVE ⊞ 📶 🖥 🖨 💻
/ SOME UNITS 🐾

Easy On, Easy Off Great Bend Exit, I-81, golf & ski packages, in plaza with many restaurants.

HAMBURG pop. 4,289

MICROTEL INN & SUITES BY WYNDHAM HAMBURG   (610)562-4234
Hotel. **Address:** 50 Industrial Dr 19526

WHERE TO EAT

HECKY'S SUB SHOP   610/562-4500
Sandwiches. Quick Serve. **Address:** 315 State St 19526

HAMLIN elev. 555'
• Part of Pocono Mountains Area — see map p. 264

COMFORT INN-POCONO LAKES REGION   (570)689-4148
Hotel. **Address:** 117 Twin Rocks Rd 18427

HANOVER (YORK COUNTY) (I-8)
pop. 15,289, elev. 599'
• Restaurants p. 92

In its early days, Hanover was called Digg's Choice or Rogue's Roost, names that originated from the many outlaws who migrated to the area due to the lack of law enforcement that ensued after the Pennsylvania-Maryland boundary dispute. In 1763 Col. Richard McAllister founded the town by drawing up a formal plan; hence it was called McAllister's Town. In order to gain favor with Germans who occupied the land, McAllister named it Hanover, meaning "on the high banks." The town was incorporated as a borough in 1815.

On June 30, 1863, the first Civil War battle north of the Mason-Dixon Line was fought in Hanover when Union generals Hugh Kilpatrick and George Custer defeated Confederate general J.E.B. Stuart and prevented him from reaching Gettysburg until the day after that major battle.

Hanover is the base for several industries that produce furniture, machine tools and such foods as potato chips and pretzels. The city's most famous product, however, is the horse. Just south on SR 194, Hanover Shoe Farms, is one of the largest Standardbred horse breeders in the world. The 4,000-acre farm, founded in 1926, is home to some 1,100 horses, many of which are record-breaking trotters and pacers. The grounds and buildings are open daily 8-4 for self-guiding tours; phone (717) 637-8931.

A variety of concerts and theater events are presented at the Eichelberger Performing Arts Center, 195 Stock St.; phone (717) 637-7086. Two miles east of town is Codorus State Park *(see Recreation Areas Chart)*, which offers a 1,275-acre lake with 26 miles of shoreline. Swimming, boating, fishing, camping and picnicking are popular activities. Also in the area are nature trails and snowmobiling and sledding facilities.

Hanover Area Chamber of Commerce: 146 Carlisle St., Hanover, PA 17331. **Phone:** (717) 637-6130.

HAMPTON INN BY HILTON (717)633-1117
♦♦♦ Hotel. **Address:** 309 Wilson Ave 17331

AAA Benefit: Members save up to 10%!

HANOVER SUPER 8 (717)630-8888
♦♦ Hotel. **Address:** 40 Wetzel Dr 17331

HOLIDAY INN EXPRESS 717/637-1228
♦♦♦ Hotel. **Address:** 305 Wilson Ave 17331

WHERE TO EAT

WAREHOUSE GOURMET BISTRO & BREW PUB
717/451-9898
♦♦ American. Casual Dining. **Address:** 7 Pennsylvania Ave 17331

HARLANSBURG (F-1) elev. 1,125'

HARLANSBURG STATION MUSEUM OF TRANSPORTATION, jct. US 19 and SR 108, showcases transportation history from railroading and seafaring days to the era of air travel. A replica of a train station was built to house four 80-foot-long train cars, which have been set up with an array of artifacts, including rail memorabilia, photographs and railroad lanterns as well as a model train display. A baggage wagon, postal buggy and a collection of train tracks and gauges are on the grounds.

The maritime history area includes vintage river tow boats and model boats, automotive history is presented through memorabilia like signs and collectible toy cars and trucks, and aviation exhibits cover commercial and military aircraft history as well as the air mail program. **Time:** Allow 45 minutes minimum. **Hours:** Tues.-Sat. 10-5, Sun. noon-5, June-Aug.; Sat. 10-5, Sun. noon-5, Mar.-May and Sept.-Dec. Closed major holidays. **Cost:** $5; $4 (ages 0-12). **Phone:** (724) 652-9002. GT

HARMARVILLE
• **Hotels & Restaurants map & index p. 246**
• **Part of Pittsburgh area — see map p. 225**

HAMPTON INN & SUITES PITTSBURGH/HARMARVILLE
412/423-1100 **56**
♦♦♦ Hotel. **Address:** 2805 Freeport Rd 15238

AAA Benefit: Members save up to 10%!

HOLIDAY INN EXPRESS 412/828-9300 **55**
♦♦♦ Hotel. **Address:** 10 Landings Dr 15238

TOWNEPLACE SUITES BY MARRIOTT (412)423-1900 **57**
♦♦♦ Extended Stay Contemporary Hotel. **Address:** 2785 Freeport Rd 15238

AAA Benefit: Members save 5% or more!

WHERE TO EAT

KING'S FAMILY RESTAURANT 412/826-9170
♦♦ American. Casual Dining. **Address:** 5 Alpha Dr E 15238

PRIMANTI BROS. 412/826-9680
♦ American. Casual Dining. **Address:** 6 Anchor Dr 15238

HARMONY (F-1) pop. 890, elev. 913'
• **Part of Pittsburgh area — see map p. 225**

George Rapp and his Harmony Society set up their first communal settlement on Connoquenessing Creek in 1804. During the following 10 years about 100 members died and were buried in a little graveyard. The graves, according to custom, were not marked. This cemetery and a number of substantial brick buildings remain from the original settlement.

In 1814 the society migrated to Indiana and founded New Harmony; 10 years later they returned to Pennsylvania and established the community of Old Economy, later renamed Ambridge (see place listing p. 41).

LOG CABIN INN 724/452-4155
♦♦ American. Casual Dining. **Address:** 430 Perry Hwy (US 19) 16037

HARRISBURG (H-8) pop. 49,528, elev. 358'
• **Hotels p. 98 • Restaurants p. 100**
• **Hotels & Restaurants map & index p. 95**

Around 1710 John Harris established a trading post in the area that is now Harrisburg; in 1733 he obtained a grant of 800 acres of land. His son, John Harris Jr., the founder of Harrisburg, and William Maclay, Pennsylvania's first U.S. senator, laid out the town in 1785, including four acres in what now is Capitol Park with hopes of it becoming the commonwealth's capital.

Incorporated as a borough in 1791, Harrisburg officially replaced Lancaster as the state capital in 1812. Today's Capitol Complex includes the ornate Capitol Building, The State Museum of Pennsylvania, plazas and fountains, and landscaped areas open to the public. An early residence, the 1766 John Harris/Simon Cameron Mansion, was built by the city's founder and later expanded in 1863 by Simon Cameron, a former U.S. senator and President Lincoln's first secretary of war. Mansion tours are available Tues.-Fri. year-round, and the second and fourth Sun. of the month in July and August. The house also includes a library with documents relating to local history and genealogical information; phone (717) 233-3462.

Paxton Presbyterian Church, at Paxtang Boulevard and Sharon Street, is one of the oldest Presbyterian churches still in use in the United States. The present structure dates from 1740. In the sanctuary are the baptismal font and pulpit light holder that have been in use for more than 200 years. The archives contain a pewter communion set that was used as early as 1734.

The adjacent cemetery, which dates from the early 1700s, contains the graves of John Harris Jr.; Rev. John Elder, the fighting parson of the Revolution; and William Maclay. A brochure describing a self-guiding tour of the graveyard is available.

City Island is in the middle of the Susquehanna River across from downtown. Owned by the city and operated by its Parks and Recreation Department,

(See map & index p. 95.)

this setting offers nature trails, a swimming beach and a playground. Also in the park are commercial amusement and recreational facilities. The Harrisburg Senators, a AA league baseball team affiliated with the Washington Nationals, play here at FNB Field; phone (717) 231-4444. Events also take place on the island.

The Capital Area Greenbelt, a 20-mile parkway used for bicycling, jogging, walking and nature studies, loops around the city and passes through many scenic parks. Reservoir Park, 22nd and Market streets, has art galleries, gardens, plazas, fountains, playgrounds, basketball courts and other facilities. Riverfront Park, along a 5-mile stretch of scenic waterfront, features sunken gardens, public art and various memorials. Other recreational facilities are in Italian Lake Park, 3rd and Division streets. Phone (717) 255-3020 for more information.

The Pennsylvania Farm Show Complex & Expo Center covers 14 acres at N. Cameron and Maclay streets; phone (717) 787-5373. Among the many events held here are the Pennsylvania Farm Show and Pennsylvania Auto Show in January, the Great American Outdoor Show in February, and the Pennsylvania National Horse Show in October.

Free City Island brochures and area maps are available from Visit Hershey & Harrisburg; phone (717) 231-7788.

Visit Hershey & Harrisburg: 3211 North Front St., Harrisburg, PA 17101. **Phone:** (717) 231-7788 or (877) 727-8573.

Shopping: Two major malls are Colonial Park, US 22 and Colonial Road, and Harrisburg at I-83 and Paxton Street. The former has more than 70 stores, including The Bon-Ton, Boscov's and Sears; the latter offers nearly 70 stores, including Macy's. Nearby Camp Hill has Capital City at the Highland Park exit off US 15, featuring JCPenney and Macy's.

The historic Broad Street Market is open Thurs.-Fri. 7-6 and Sat. 7-4. This farmers market, which sells fresh produce, meat, poultry, confections and food, has been operating since 1860 and is housed in two buildings dating from 1863 and 1874. The market is one-half mile north of the Capitol Complex, at 1233 N. 3rd St.; phone (717) 236-7923.

THE NATIONAL CIVIL WAR MUSEUM, at 1 Lincoln Cir. at Reservoir Park, is reportedly the only museum in the nation to cover the entire American Civil War from beginning to end. In bringing history to life, the museum includes collections of Union and Confederate artifacts, life-size dioramas and audiovisual presentations.

Seventeen galleries focus on the multitude of human experiences that made up the war. From slavery, to camp life, to the turmoil of 19th-century politics, the museum immerses visitors in the Civil War, with an equal emphasis given to both sides of the conflict.

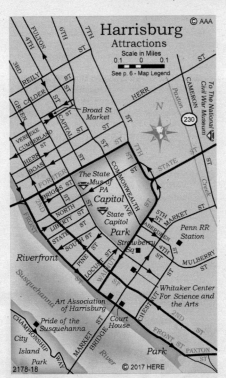

Harrisburg Attractions

Scale in Miles
0.1   0   0.1

See p. 6 - Map Legend

© 2017 HERE

Time: Allow 1 hour, 30 minutes minimum. **Hours:** Mon.-Sat. 9-5 (also Wed. 5-8), Sun. 10-5, Memorial Day weekend-Labor Day; Mon.-Sat. 10-5 (also Wed. 5-8), Sun. noon-5, rest of year. Closed Jan. 1, Easter, Thanksgiving and Christmas. **Cost:** $12; $11 (ages 60+); $10 (students ages 6+ and military with ID); $44 (family, two adults and three students). **Phone:** (717) 260-1861.

THE PENNSYLVANIA NATIONAL FIRE MUSEUM, 1820 N. 4th St., is in a restored 1899 firehouse. The collection, which includes items spanning the 18th-through 21st centuries, features an 1867 carriage, interactive displays, a stovepipe hat collection and firefighters' apparatus and uniforms. Various fire safety videos are shown. **Time:** Allow 30 minutes minimum. **Hours:** Tues.-Sat. 10-4, Sun. 1-4. Closed major holidays. **Cost:** $6; $5 (ages 60+ and students with ID); $20 (family, adults and children in same household). **Phone:** (717) 232-8915.

STATE CAPITOL is on Capitol Hill. A magnificent building in a 13-acre park, the Capitol covers 2 acres and contains more than 600 rooms. The 272-foot dome, bronze doors, statuary, mural paintings and stained-glass windows are notable features. The marble grand staircase is designed after the one in the Paris Grand Opera House. Flanking the central entrance are two groups of statuary by the Pennsylvania-born sculptor George Grey Barnard. The welcome center, in the East Wing of the Capitol, offers interactive exhibits.

(See map & index p. 95.)

Note: All visitors must pass through metal detectors; all bags and packages will be X-rayed and are subject to hand inspection. The security screening may require a whole body pat-down. **Hours:** Thirty-minute guided tours are offered Mon.-Fri. every half-hour 8:30-4, Sat.-Sun. and most holidays at 9, 11, 1 and 3. Welcome center open Mon.-Fri. 8:30-4:30. Food is available Mon.-Fri. 7:30-2. Closed Jan. 1, Easter, Thanksgiving and Christmas. Phone ahead to confirm schedule. **Cost:** Free. **Phone:** (717) 787-6810 or (800) 868-7672. GT ▯

THE STATE MUSEUM OF PENNSYLVANIA, 300 North St., presents Pennsylvania's heritage from the Earth's beginning to the present. Archeological artifacts, decorative arts, fine art galleries and industrial and technological innovations can be seen. A Civil War exhibit includes Peter F. Rothermel's 1870 "The Battle of Gettysburg: Pickett's Charge" painting. Curiosity Connection is a hands-on learning environment for children ages 5 and younger. Additional features are Nature Lab, Mammal Hall, a restored mastodon skeleton and a planetarium.

Time: Allow 2 hours minimum. **Hours:** Wed.-Sat. 9-5, Sun. noon-5. Curiosity Connection Wed.-Sat. 10-4, Sun. noon-4. Phone ahead for planetarium show schedule. Closed federal and state holidays. **Cost:** Museum $7; $6 (ages 65+); $5 (ages 1-11); free (retired military with ID and active military with ID and immediate family). Planetarium additional $3. **Phone:** (717) 787-4980.

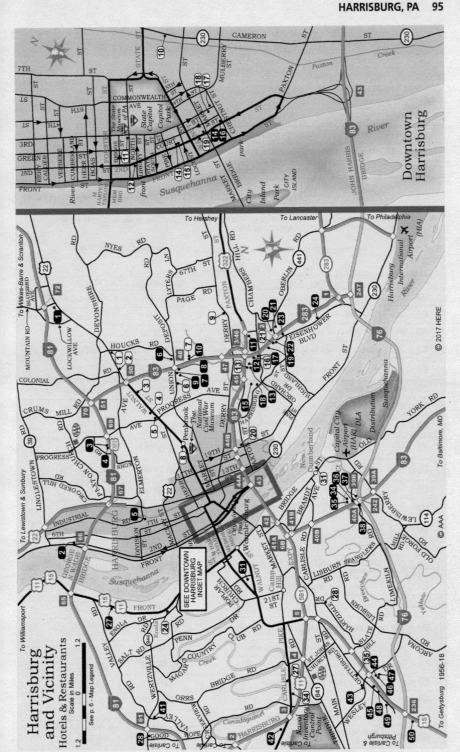

Downtown Harrisburg

Harrisburg
and Vicinity
Hotels & Restaurants
Scale in Miles
See p. 6 - Map Legend

© 2017 HERE

✈ Airport Hotels

Map Page	**HARRISBURG INTERNATIONAL AIRPORT** (Maximum driving distance from airport: 6.6 mi)	Diamond Rated	Rate Range	Page
24 p. 95	**Best Western Plus Harrisburg East Inn & Suites, 5.5 mi**	◈◈◈	$89-$209 [SAVE]	98
21 p. 95	Red Lion Hotel Harrisburg Hershey, 6.3 mi	◈◈	$89-$199	99
23 p. 95	**Red Roof Inn Harrisburg - Hershey, 6.4 mi**	◈◈	$50-$126 [SAVE]	99
20 p. 95	**Sheraton Harrisburg Hershey, 6.3 mi**	◈◈◈	$99-$399 [SAVE]	100
19 p. 95	Sleep Inn & Suites Harrisburg/Hershey, 6.6 mi	◈◈◈	$89-$208	100

Harrisburg and Vicinity

This index helps you "spot" where approved hotels and restaurants are located on the corresponding detailed maps. Hotel daily rate range is for comparison only. Restaurant price range is a combination of lunch and/or dinner. Turn to the listing page for more information and consult display ads for special promotions.

 For more details, rates and reservations: AAA.com/travelguides/hotels

HARRISBURG

Map Page	Hotels	Diamond Rated	Rate Range	Page
1 p. 95	Comfort Inn Harrisburg/Hershey	◈◈	$69-$194	99
2 p. 95	Days Inn Harrisburg North	◈◈	$80-$140	99
3 p. 95	Hampton Inn & Suites Harrisburg North	◈◈◈	$99-$229	99
4 p. 95	SpringHill Suites by Marriott Harrisburg/Hershey	◈◈◈	$84-$329	100
5 p. 95	Staybridge Suites Harrisburg	◈◈◈	Rates not provided	100
6 p. 95	Hampton Inn Harrisburg East (Hershey Area)	◈◈◈	$119-$245	99
7 p. 95	Holiday Inn Express Harrisburg East	◈◈◈	$99-$199	99
8 p. 95	**Country Inn & Suites By Carlson, Harrisburg at Union Deposit Rd**	◈◈◈	Rates not provided [SAVE]	99
9 p. 95	Fairfield Inn & Suites by Marriott-Harrisburg/Hershey	◈◈◈	$78-$263	99
10 p. 95	**Best Western Premier The Central Hotel & Conference Center**	◈◈◈	$99-$209 [SAVE]	98
11 p. 95	Residence Inn by Marriott Harrisburg-Hershey	◈◈◈	$93-$353	99
12 p. 95	Homewood Suites by Hilton-Harrisburg East (Hershey Area)	◈◈◈	$139-$449	99
13 p. 95	Hilton Garden Inn Harrisburg East	◈◈◈	$109-$219	99
14 p. 95	Hilton Harrisburg	◈◈◈	$199-$279	99
15 p. 95	**TownePlace Suites by Marriott Harrisburg Hershey**	◈◈◈	$98-$295 [SAVE]	100
16 p. 95	**Crowne Plaza Harrisburg-Hershey**	◈◈◈	$129-$249 [SAVE]	99
17 p. 95	Econo Lodge	◈	Rates not provided	99
18 p. 95	**Candlewood Suites Harrisburg-Hershey**	◈◈◈	Rates not provided [SAVE]	98
19 p. 95	Sleep Inn & Suites Harrisburg/Hershey	◈◈◈	$89-$208	100
20 p. 95	**Sheraton Harrisburg Hershey**	◈◈◈	$99-$399 [SAVE]	100
21 p. 95	Red Lion Hotel Harrisburg Hershey	◈◈	$89-$199	99
22 p. 95	Courtyard by Marriott-Harrisburg/Hershey	◈◈◈	$118-$312	99
23 p. 95	**Red Roof Inn Harrisburg - Hershey**	◈◈	$50-$126 [SAVE]	99
24 p. 95	**Best Western Plus Harrisburg East Inn & Suites**	◈◈◈	$89-$209 [SAVE]	98

Map Page	Restaurants	Diamond Rated	Cuisine	Price Range	Page
① p. 95	El Rodeo	◆◆	Mexican	$7-$17	100
② p. 95	The Wild Tomato Pizzeria	◆	American	$7-$20	100
③ p. 95	Gabriella Italian Restaurant	◆◆	Italian	$11-$25	100
④ p. 95	Progress Grill	◆◆	American	$14-$38	100
⑤ p. 95	M Sushi House and Restaurant	◆◆	Japanese	$9-$23	100
⑥ p. 95	Empire Asian Bistro	◆◆	Asian	$7-$30	100
⑦ p. 95	O'Reilly's Tap Room and Kitchen	◆◆	American	$9-$24	100
⑧ p. 95	Meiji	◆◆	Vietnamese	$7-$11	100
⑨ p. 95	Pho Kim's	◆◆	Vietnamese	$7-$12	100
⑩ p. 95	Appalachian Brewing Co	◆◆	American	$8-$16	100
⑪ p. 95	Mangia Qui	◆◆	Italian	$9-$32	100
⑫ p. 95	The Fire House Restaurant	◆◆	American	$8-$42	100
⑬ p. 95	Tomato Pie Café	◆◆	American	$4-$11	100
⑭ p. 95	Cafe Fresco	◆◆	American	$9-$30	100
⑮ p. 95	Stock's on 2nd	◆◆	American	$11-$34	100
⑯ p. 95	Lancaster Brewing Company	◆◆	American	$7-$26	100
⑰ p. 95	Bricco	◆◆◆	International	$11-$40	100
⑱ p. 95	El Sol Mexican Restaurant	◆◆	Mexican	$9-$25	100
⑲ p. 95	Bacco Pizzeria and Wine Bar	◆◆	Italian	$7-$22	100
⑳ p. 95	Bangkok 56 Thai Cuisine	◆◆	Thai	$10-$16	100
㉑ p. 95	Leeds Restaurant and Lounge	◆◆	American	$8-$40	100

ENOLA

Map Page	Hotels	Diamond Rated	Rate Range	Page
㉗ p. 95	**Quality Inn Enola**	◆◆	$74-$560 [SAVE]	70
㉘ p. 95	**Best Western Plus Harrisburg West**	◆◆	$75-$179 [SAVE]	70

Map Page	Restaurant	Diamond Rated	Cuisine	Price Range	Page
㉔ p. 95	Tavern on the Hill	◆◆◆	Steak Seafood	$17-$40	70

CAMP HILL

Map Page	Hotel	Diamond Rated	Rate Range	Page
㉛ p. 95	Radisson Hotel Harrisburg	◆◆◆	Rates not provided	52

Map Page	Restaurants	Diamond Rated	Cuisine	Price Range	Page
㉗ p. 95	Cork & Fork Osteria	◆◆	Italian	$10-$16	53
㉘ p. 95	Masala Bistro	◆◆	Indian	$9-$18	53

NEW CUMBERLAND

Map Page	Hotels	Diamond Rated	Rate Range	Page
㉞ p. 95	Holiday Inn Express New Cumberland	◆◆◆	Rates not provided	137
㉟ p. 95	Fairfield Inn & Suites by Marriott Harrisburg West	◆◆◆	$80-$276	137
㊱ p. 95	La Quinta Inn & Suites	◆◆◆	$69-$169	137
㊲ p. 95	Clarion Hotel & Conference Center Harrisburg West	◆◆	$85-$209	137
㊳ p. 95	**Best Western Plus New Cumberland Inn & Suites**	◆◆◆	$94-$189 [SAVE]	137

Map Page	Restaurant	Diamond Rated	Cuisine	Price Range	Page
31 p. 95	Yak n' Yeti	♦♦♦	Nepali	$5-$12	137

MECHANICSBURG

Map Page	Hotels	Diamond Rated	Rate Range	Page
41 p. 95	Holiday Inn Express & Suites Harrisburg West/Mechanicsburg	♦♦♦	Rates not provided	130
42 p. 95	Park Inn by Radisson Harrisburg West	♦♦	$69-$399	130
43 p. 95	Comfort Inn Mechanicsburg/Harrisburg South	♦♦	$84-$214	130
44 p. 95	Hampton Inn by Hilton-Harrisburg West	♦♦♦	$99-$199	130
45 p. 95	**Courtyard by Marriott Harrisburg West/Mechanicsburg**	♦♦♦	$71-$260 [SAVE]	130
46 p. 95	Homewood Suites by Hilton-Harrisburg West	♦♦♦	$104-$329	130
47 p. 95	TownePlace Suites by Marriott	♦♦♦	$89-$340	130
48 p. 95	Country Inn & Suites by Carlson Harrisburg West	♦♦♦	$99-$179	130
49 p. 95	Econo Lodge	♦♦	$60-$125	130
50 p. 95	Wingate by Wyndham Mechanicsburg/Harrisburg West	♦♦♦	$109-$209	130

Map Page	Restaurants	Diamond Rated	Cuisine	Price Range	Page
34 p. 95	Pho 7 Spice	♦♦	Vietnamese	$6-$12	130
35 p. 95	Cafe Magnolia	♦♦	American	$5-$27	130

BEST WESTERN HARRISBURG HERSHEY HOTEL
(717)652-0101

Hotel
$79-$209

Best Western. AAA Benefit: Members save 5% to 15% and earn 10% bonus points!

Address: 7500 Allentown Blvd 17112 **Location:** I-81 exit 77, 1 mi s on SR 39, then 1.2 mi w on US 22. **Facility:** 56 units. 3 stories, interior corridors. **Terms:** cancellation fee imposed. **Pool:** heated indoor. **Activities:** exercise room. **Guest Services:** coin laundry.

[SAVE] [✗] CALL [♿] [≈] [♦] [BIZ]
[HS] [≈] [✗] [♦] [▯] [▭]

BEST WESTERN PLUS HARRISBURG EAST INN & SUITES
(717)985-1600 24

Hotel
$89-$209

Best Western PLUS AAA Benefit: Members save 5% to 15% and earn 10% bonus points!

Address: 1344 Eisenhower Blvd 17111 **Location:** I-76 (Pennsylvania Tpke) exit 247, just n. **Facility:** 84 units. 4 stories, interior corridors. **Terms:** check-in 4 pm, cancellation fee imposed. **Activities:** hot tub, exercise room. **Guest Services:** coin laundry. **Featured Amenity:** breakfast buffet.

[SAVE] CALL [♿] [♦] [BIZ] [HS] [≈]
[✗] [♦] [▯] [▭] / SOME UNITS [🐾]

BEST WESTERN PREMIER THE CENTRAL HOTEL & CONFERENCE CENTER
(717)561-2800 10

Hotel
$99-$209

 PREMIER BEST WESTERN. AAA Benefit: Members save 5% to 15% and earn 10% bonus points!

Address: 800 E Park Dr 17111 **Location:** I-83 exit 48, just e on Union Deposit Rd, then 0.5 mi s. **Facility:** 174 units. 3 stories, interior corridors. **Terms:** cancellation fee imposed. **Amenities:** safes. **Dining:** O'Reilly's Tap Room and Kitchen, see separate listing. **Pool:** heated indoor. **Activities:** game room, exercise room. **Guest Services:** valet and coin laundry, area transportation.

[SAVE] [✈] [♦] [♦] [♦] CALL [♿] [≈] [♦] [BIZ] [≈]
[✗] [♦] [▯] [▭] / SOME UNITS [🐾]

CANDLEWOOD SUITES HARRISBURG-HERSHEY
717/561-9400 18

Extended Stay Hotel
Rates not provided

Address: 413 Portview Dr 17111 **Location:** I-83 exit 45, 0.7 mi on Paxton St, then 0.4 mi s. **Facility:** 71 efficiencies. 4 stories, interior corridors. **Pool:** heated indoor. **Activities:** hot tub, exercise room. **Guest Services:** complimentary and valet laundry.

[SAVE] CALL [♿] [≈] [♦] [BIZ] [HS]
[≈] [✗] [♦] [▯] [▭]
/ SOME UNITS [🐾]

HARRISBURG, PA 99

(See map & index p. 95.)

COMFORT INN HARRISBURG/HERSHEY (717)657-2200 **1**
Hotel. **Address:** 5680 Allentown Blvd 17112

COMFORT SUITES HUMMELSTOWN/HERSHEY
(717)566-3000

Hotel
$109-$339

Address: 320 Milroy Rd 17036 **Location:** I-283 exit 3C, 3.4 mi e on US 322. **Facility:** 80 units. 4 stories, interior corridors. **Terms:** check-in 4 pm. **Amenities:** safes. **Pool:** heated indoor. **Activities:** exercise room. **Guest Services:** coin laundry. **Featured Amenity: full hot breakfast.**

COUNTRY INN & SUITES BY CARLSON, HARRISBURG AT UNION DEPOSIT RD   717/558-9200 **8**

Hotel
Rates not provided

Address: 1025 Peiffers Ln 17109 **Location:** I-83 exit 48, just w. **Facility:** 78 units. 5 stories, interior corridors. **Pool:** heated indoor. **Activities:** hot tub, exercise room. **Guest Services:** valet and coin laundry. **Featured Amenity: full hot breakfast.**

COURTYARD BY MARRIOTT-HARRISBURG/HERSHEY
(717)558-8544 **22**
Hotel. **Address:** 725 Eisenhower Blvd 17111

> **AAA Benefit:** Members save 5% or more!

CROWNE PLAZA HARRISBURG-HERSHEY

Hotel
$129-$249

Address: 23 S 2nd St 17101 **Location:** Jct Chestnut St; downtown. **Facility:** 260 units. 10 stories, interior corridors. **Parking:** valet only. **Terms:** check-in 4 pm, cancellation fee imposed. **Pool:** heated indoor. **Activities:** exercise room. **Guest Services:** valet and coin laundry.

DAYS INN HARRISBURG NORTH (717)233-3100 **2**
Motel. **Address:** 3919 N Front St 17110

ECONO LODGE 717/561-1885 **17**
Motel. **Address:** 495 Eisenhower Blvd 17111

FAIRFIELD INN & SUITES BY MARRIOTT-HARRISBURG/HERSHEY (717)412-4326 **9**
Hotel. **Address:** 1018 Briarsdale Rd 17109

> **AAA Benefit:** Members save 5% or more!

HAMPTON INN & SUITES HARRISBURG NORTH
(717)540-0900 **3**
Hotel. **Address:** 30 Capital Dr 17110

> **AAA Benefit:** Members save up to 10%!

HAMPTON INN HARRISBURG EAST (HERSHEY AREA)
(717)545-9595 **6**
Hotel. **Address:** 4230 Union Deposit Rd 17111

> **AAA Benefit:** Members save up to 10%!

HILTON GARDEN INN HARRISBURG EAST
(717)635-7299 **13**
Hotel. **Address:** 3943 TecPort Dr 17111

> **AAA Benefit:** Members save up to 10%!

HILTON HARRISBURG (717)233-6000 **14**
Hotel. **Address:** One N 2nd St 17101

> **AAA Benefit:** Members save 5% or more!

HOLIDAY INN EXPRESS HARRISBURG EAST
(717)561-8100 **7**
Hotel. **Address:** 4021 Union Deposit Rd 17109

HOLIDAY INN EXPRESS HARRISBURG NE - HERSHEY
(717)540-8400

Hotel
$69-$229

Address: 7744 Linglestown Rd 17112 **Location:** I-81 exit 77, 0.5 mi w. **Facility:** 80 units. 3 stories, interior corridors. **Terms:** cancellation fee imposed. **Pool:** heated indoor. **Activities:** hot tub, exercise room. **Guest Services:** coin laundry. **Featured Amenity: continental breakfast.**

HOMEWOOD SUITES BY HILTON-HARRISBURG EAST
(HERSHEY AREA) (717)909-4663 **12**
Extended Stay Hotel. **Address:** 3990 TecPort Dr 17111

> **AAA Benefit:** Members save up to 10%!

LA QUINTA INN & SUITES HARRISBURG HERSHEY
(717)566-7666
Hotel. **Address:** 265 N Hershey Rd 17112

RED LION HOTEL HARRISBURG HERSHEY
(717)939-7841 **21**
Hotel. **Address:** 4751 Lindle Rd 17111

RED ROOF INN HARRISBURG - HERSHEY
(717)939-1331 **23**

Motel
$50-$126

Address: 950 Eisenhower Blvd 17111 **Location:** I-283 exit 2, just e. **Facility:** 110 units. 2 stories (no elevator), interior/exterior corridors. **Amenities:** safes.

RESIDENCE INN BY MARRIOTT HARRISBURG-HERSHEY
(717)561-1900 **11**
Extended Stay Hotel. **Address:** 4480 Lewis Rd 17111

> **AAA Benefit:** Members save 5% or more!

(See map & index p. 95.)

SHERATON HARRISBURG HERSHEY

(717)564-5511 **20**

Hotel
$99-$399

AAA Benefit:
Members save 5%
or more!

Address: 4650 Lindle Rd 17111 **Location:** I-283 exit 2, just e. **Facility:** 347 units. 10 stories, interior corridors. **Terms:** cancellation fee imposed. **Amenities:** safes. **Pool:** heated outdoor, heated indoor. **Activities:** hot tub, exercise room. **Guest Services:** valet and coin laundry, area transportation.

SLEEP INN & SUITES HARRISBURG/HERSHEY

(717)564-8888 **19**

Hotel. **Address:** 631-A Eisenhower Blvd 17111

SPRINGHILL SUITES BY MARRIOTT HARRISBURG/HERSHEY

(717)540-5100 **4**

Hotel. **Address:** 15 Capital Dr 17110

AAA Benefit:
Members save 5%
or more!

STAYBRIDGE SUITES HARRISBURG

717/233-3304 **5**

Extended Stay Hotel. **Address:** 920 Wildwood Park Dr 17110

TOWNEPLACE SUITES BY MARRIOTT HARRISBURG HERSHEY

(717)558-0200 **15**

Extended Stay Hotel
$98-$295

TOWNEPLACE
SUITES
MARRIOTT

AAA Benefit:
Members save 5%
or more!

Address: 450 Friendship Rd 17111 **Location:** I-83 exit 45, 0.7 mi on Paxton St, then 0.3 mi s. Near a shopping mall and restaurants. **Facility:** 107 units, some two bedrooms, efficiencies and kitchens. 4 stories, interior corridors. **Terms:** check-in 4 pm, cancellation fee imposed. **Pool:** heated indoor. **Activities:** hot tub, exercise room. **Guest Services:** valet and coin laundry. **Featured Amenity:** continental breakfast.

WHERE TO EAT

APPALACHIAN BREWING CO   717/221-1080 **10**
American. Casual Dining. **Address:** 50 N Cameron St 17101

BACCO PIZZERIA AND WINE BAR   717/234-7508 **19**
Italian. Gastropub. **Address:** 20 N 2nd St 17101

BANGKOK 56 THAI CUISINE   717/236-2931 **20**
Thai. Casual Dining. **Address:** 1917 Paxton St 17104

THE BLUE MOOSE BAR AND GRILLE   717/651-9493
American. Casual Dining. **Address:** 6791 Linglestown Rd 17112

BRICCO   717/724-0222 **17**
International. Casual Dining. **Address:** 31 S 3rd St 17101

CAFE FRESCO   717/236-2599 **14**
American. Casual Dining. **Address:** 215 N 2nd St 17101

EL RODEO   717/652-5340 **1**
Mexican. Casual Dining. **Address:** 4659 Jonestown Rd 17109

EL SOL MEXICAN RESTAURANT   717/901-5050 **18**
Mexican. Casual Dining. **Address:** 18 S 3rd St 17101

EMPIRE ASIAN BISTRO   717/558-9258 **6**
Asian. Casual Dining. **Address:** 3819 Union Deposit Rd 17109

THE FIRE HOUSE RESTAURANT   717/234-6064 **12**
American. Casual Dining. **Address:** 606 N 2nd St 17101

GABRIELLA ITALIAN RESTAURANT   717/540-0040 **3**
Italian. Casual Dining. **Address:** 3907 Jonestown Rd 17109

HERSHEY ROAD FAMILY RESTAURANT   717/545-2529
American. Casual Dining. **Address:** 257 N Hershey Rd 17112

LANCASTER BREWING COMPANY   717/564-4448 **16**
American. Casual Dining. **Address:** 469 Eisenhower Blvd 17111

LEEDS RESTAURANT AND LOUNGE   717/564-4654 **21**
American. Casual Dining. **Address:** 750 Eisenhower Blvd 17111

MANGIA QUI   717/233-7358 **11**
Italian. Casual Dining. **Address:** 272 North St 17101

MEIJI   717/213-9300 **8**
Vietnamese. Casual Dining. **Address:** 2306 Walnut St 17103

M SUSHI HOUSE AND RESTAURANT   717/545-8885 **5**
Japanese. Casual Dining. **Address:** 3402 Walnut St 17109

O'REILLY'S TAP ROOM AND KITCHEN   717/564-2700 **7**
American. Casual Dining. **Address:** 800 E Park Dr 17111

PHO KIM'S   717/836-7562 **9**
Vietnamese. Casual Dining. **Address:** 5490 Derry St 17111

PROGRESS GRILL   717/652-7348 **4**
American. Fine Dining. **Address:** 3526 Walnut St 17109

STOCK'S ON 2ND   717/233-6699 **15**
American. Casual Dining. **Address:** 211 N 2nd St 17101

TOMATO PIE CAFÉ   717/836-7051 **13**
American. Casual Dining. **Address:** 3950 Tecport Dr 17111

THE WILD TOMATO PIZZERIA   717/545-6435 **2**
American. Quick Serve. **Address:** 4315 Jonestown Rd 17109

HAWLEY (E-11) pop. 1,211, elev. 906'
• Part of Pocono Mountains Area — see map p. 264

Chamber of the Northern Poconos: 2512 US 6, Hawley, PA 18428. **Phone:** (570) 226-3191.

THE LODGE AT WOODLOCH

570/685-8500

★★★ ★★★
Resort Hotel
Rates not provided

Address: 109 River Birch Ln 18428 **Location:** Waterfront. Jct US 6, 6.3 mi e on SR 590 E. **Facility:** This four-seasons destination sits on 150 private, natural wooded acres and offers luxurious rooms and baths. Extensive public areas and grounds all overlook a gorgeous private lake. 57 units. 3 stories, interior corridors. **Parking:** valet only. **Terms:** check-in 4 pm. **Amenities:** safes. **Dining:** entertainment. **Pool:** heated indoor. **Activities:** sauna, hot tub, self-propelled boats, fishing, regulation golf, recreation programs, bicycles, trails, health club, spa. **Guest Services:** complimentary laundry, area transportation. **Featured Amenity: full hot breakfast.**

THE SETTLERS INN AT BINGHAM PARK   (570)226-2993
★★★ Historic Country Inn. **Address:** 4 Main Ave 18428

SILVER BIRCHES   570/226-4388
★★★ Historic Vintage Resort Hotel. **Address:** 205 Rt 507 18428

TANGLWOOD RESORTS   (570)226-6161

★★★
Resort
Condominium
$90-$165

Address: 9 Crest Dr 18428 **Location:** Waterfront. I-84 exit 26, 5.1 mi n on SR 390, then 1.3 mi n on SR 507 to jct US 6. **Facility:** This condo-style resort offers activities both in and around the immediate area, at Lake Wallenpaupack. Handsome contemporary suites are spacious and kitchens offer guests a chance to prepare meals. 75 condominiums. 1-2 stories (no elevator), exterior corridors. **Terms:** check-in 4 pm, 2 night minimum stay - seasonal and/or weekends, cancellation fee imposed, resort fee. **Pool:** outdoor. **Activities:** motor boats, boat dock, fishing, tennis, recreation programs, game room. **Guest Services:** coin laundry.

WHERE TO EAT

THE BOAT HOUSE RESTAURANT   570/226-5027
★★ American. Casual Dining. **Address:** 141 Rt 507 18428

THE DOCK ON WALLENPAUPACK   570/226-2124
★★ American. Casual Dining. **Address:** 205 Rt 507 18428

GRESHAM'S CHOP HOUSE   570/226-1500
★★★ Steak. Casual Dining. **Address:** 2495 Route 6 18428

THE SETTLERS INN AT BINGHAM PARK   570/226-2993

★★★
Regional
American
Fine Dining
$9-$38

AAA Inspector Notes: Local organic ingredients and products, including fresh herbs from the owner's garden, are used in such menu preparations as the grilled pork tenderloin with rhubarb ginger chutney or pasture-raised chicken roulade with fresh mozzarella, local tomatoes and basil aïoli. All the creations are served in the pale warm glow of the amber lamps in the Arts and Crafts-style dining room or on the covered porch overlooking the gardens. **Features:** full bar, patio dining, Sunday brunch. **Reservations:** suggested. **Address:** 4 Main Ave 18428 **Location:** On Main Ave (US 6), 0.3 mi w.

 B L D

HAZLETON (F-10) pop. 25,340, elev. 1,624'

The first seven miles of the Greater Hazleton Rails to Trails follows old rail bed—the 1842 Delaware Susquehanna and Schuylkill line—on SR 93 (E. Broad St.) and includes picnic areas, benches, flowers and plants.

The Greater Hazleton Historical Society & Museum, 55 N. Wyoming St., is open by appointment and contains exhibits relating to Native Americans, the mining and railroad industries, music, sports, the military and the life of native son, actor Jack Palance. Reservations must be made one week in advance; phone (570) 455-8576.

Greater Hazleton Chamber of Commerce: 8 W. Broad St. (mezzanine level), Hazleton, PA 18201. **Phone:** (570) 455-1509.

RAMADA INN HAZLETON   (570)455-2061
★★ Hotel. **Address:** 1221 N Church St 18202

RED ROOF INN & SUITES HAZLETON   (570)454-2494

★★
Hotel
$85-$98

Address: 1341 N Church St 18202 **Location:** I-80 exit 262, 6 mi s on SR 309. Located in a commercial area. **Facility:** 77 units, some kitchens. 1-3 stories (no elevator), interior/exterior corridors. **Pool:** heated outdoor. **Activities:** playground. **Guest Services:** valet and coin laundry. **Featured Amenity: continental breakfast.**

RESIDENCE INN BY MARRIOTT-HAZLETON   (570)455-9555
★★★ Extended Stay Hotel. **Address:** 1 Station Circle Dr 18202

AAA Benefit:
Members save 5%
or more!

WHERE TO EAT

OVALON BAR & GRILL   570/454-0853
★★ Italian. Casual Dining. **Address:** 254 N Wyoming St 18201

HERMITAGE pop. 16,220, elev. 1,076'

COMBINE BROTHERS BAR & GRILLE   724/983-1057
★★ Italian. Casual Dining. **Address:** 2376 S Hermitage Rd (SR 18) 16148

HERSHEY (H-9) pop. 14,257, elev. 423'
• Hotels p. 104 • Restaurants p. 106

The aroma of chocolate pervades Hershey, a name synonymous with the confection. In the rich Lebanon Valley, the town was founded in 1903 by Milton S. Hershey, who planned and built an attractive industrial community. The Hershey Foods Corp. factory is one of the largest chocolate and cocoa plants in the world.

The 550-acre campus of Penn State Milton S. Hershey Medical Center, on US 322 at 500 University Dr., includes Penn State College of Medicine, Penn State Hershey Children's Hospital, Penn State Hershey Cancer Institute and other health facilities; phone (717) 531-8521.

Giant Center, a 12,500-seat arena, is home to the Hershey Bears AHL hockey club. Hersheypark Stadium presents outdoor sports events and concerts; it

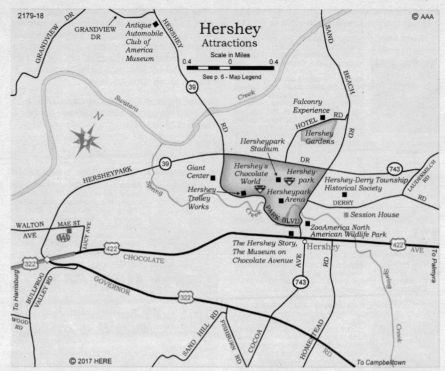

2179-18

GRANDVIEW DR

GRANDVIEW DR

Antique Automobile Club of America Museum

Hershey
Attractions
Scale in Miles
0.4   0   0.4
See p. 6 - Map Legend

© AAA

Swatara

Creek

39

Falconry Experience

RD

HOTEL

Hersheypark Stadium

Hershey Gardens

Hershey's Chocolate World

Hershey-park

DR

743

HERSHEYPARK

39

Giant Center

Spring

Hershey Trolley Works

Hersheypark Arena

Hershey-Derry Township Historical Society

DERRY

LAUDERMILCH RD

RD

Creek

PARK BLVD

Session House

WALTON AVE

MAE ST

LUCY AVE

422

CHOCOLATE

ZooAmerica North American Wildlife Park

322

To Harrisburg

BULLFROG VALLEY RD

GOVERNOR

322

The Hershey Story, The Museum on Chocolate Avenue

Hershey

AVE

RD

422   AVE

To Palmyra

Spring

743

WOOD RD

SAND HILL RD

FISHBURN RD

COCOA

HOMESTEAD   RD

Creek

© 2017 HERE

To Campbelltown

---

seats 30,000. Next to the stadium is Star Pavilion, an 8,000-seat amphitheater that features musical events in summer. Phone (717) 534-3911 for additional information for all venues.

One-hour tours of Hershey Theatre, built by Milton S. Hershey in 1933, are given Friday mornings at 11 a.m. (also Sunday at 1 p.m., Memorial Day weekend through Labor Day). The performing arts center features Broadway shows and other entertainers; phone (717) 534-3405.

Shopping: SAVE Tanger Outlet Center, 46 Outlet Sq., offers nearly 60 stores, including Ann Taylor Factory Store, Calvin Klein, Coach, J. Crew, Reebok and Tommy Hilfiger.

SAVE **ANTIQUE AUTOMOBILE CLUB OF AMERICA MUSEUM** is 1 mi. n. of Hersheypark Dr. on US 39W. Eight decades of antique cars, motorcycles and memorabilia are presented in themed exhibits. The Museum of Bus Transportation depicts the evolution of public transit and how it influenced the development of modern society; nearly a dozen buses are displayed. A large collection of Tucker Automobiles and related artifacts are also on display. Visitors can sit behind the wheel of a Tucker vehicle. Other highlights include an interactive assembly line exhibit and From Roads to Rails, a model train display.

Time: Allow 1 hour minimum. **Hours:** Daily 9-5. Last admission 1 hour before closing. Closed Jan. 1,

Thanksgiving, Christmas Eve and Christmas. **Cost:** $12; $11 (ages 61+); $9 (ages 4-12). **Phone:** (717) 566-7100.

HERSHEY-DERRY TOWNSHIP HISTORICAL SOCIETY is at 40 Northeast Dr. Hershey's history before and after the arrival of the chocolate factory and park is showcased through artifacts and a research library. Highlights include a re-creation of the home office of Maj. Dick Winters, an exhibit about the Hershey Bears hockey team franchise and a children's discovery area. During the Christmas holiday, an extensive collection of model trains is on display. Guided tours are available by appointment. **Time:** Allow 30 minutes minimum. **Hours:** Mon., Wed. and Fri. 9-4:30, first and third Sat. of the month 9-1 (also some extended hours Nov.-Dec.). **Cost:** $4; $2 (ages 4-12); $5 (family). **Phone:** (717) 520-0748. GT

GEM SAVE **HERSHEYPARK,** just off SR 743 and US 422, dates to 1907 when the park was founded by Milton S. Hershey as a recreational gathering place for employees of his chocolate company and residents of the town of Hershey. The park's appearance has changed over the past century but has retained its original charm.

There are now more than 70 rides and attractions, including 13 roller coasters. At Hershey Triple Tower, each of the three towers offers a different ride experience. Coasters include Laff Trakk, an indoor, spinning "glow coaster"; Fahrenheit, a vertical lift coaster with a 97-degree drop; Great Bear, a steel looping coaster; Storm Runner, a hydraulic launch coaster with inversions; Skyrush, the park's tallest, fastest and longest coaster; and Comet, a classic wooden coaster built in 1946. Daily entertainment includes live singing and dancing shows and a marine mammal presentation. The Boardwalk at Hersheypark, a water play area reminiscent of the beaches and boardwalks of the Northeast, features more than a dozen attractions, including The Shore, a 378,000-gallon wave pool, and Intercoastal Waterway, a lazy river. Admission to ZooAmerica North American Wildlife Park *(see attraction listing)* also is included.

In April the park opens up for a 2-weekend preview called Springtime in the Park, and on weekends in mid-October the park celebrates Halloween with Hersheypark in the Dark. From mid-November through December 31, more than 4 million lights transform the park into a festive holiday wonderland for Hersheypark Christmas Candylane.

Lockers are available, and day-use kennels are available during park hours. **Time:** Allow 4 hours minimum. **Hours:** Open daily at 10, Memorial Day-Labor Day; select Sat.-Sun. at 10, day after Labor Day-Sept. 30; select days at 10, early May-day before Memorial Day. Closing times vary; phone ahead. Phone for Springtime in the Park and Christmas Candylane schedules. **Cost:** (includes ZooAmerica North American Wildlife Park) $66.95; $43.95 (ages 3-8 and 55-69); $26.95 (ages 70+). Sunset admission (after 3 when park closes at 6, after 4 when park closes at 8, after 5 when park closes at 10 and 11) $31.95; $27.95 (ages 3-8 and 55-69); $18.45 (ages 70+). Other admission packages, including multiday options, are available. Phone ahead to confirm rates. **Phone:** (800) 437-7439. ⊓

Falconry Experience is at The Hotel Hershey, 100 Hotel Rd. During the 1.5-hour Falconry Experience, guests will see simulated hunt demonstrations and birds in flight. Falconry, now a field sport, is a 4,000-year-old technique where hunters used trained birds of prey to hunt game for food. Falconers provide background on falconry and willing participants can hold a bird of prey.

Hours: Wed.-Mon. 11-12:30, Memorial Day-Labor Day; Sat.-Sun. 11-12:30, Apr. 1-day before Memorial Day and day after Labor Day-Dec. 31 (also Fri. after Thanksgiving); by appointment rest of year. Winter and holiday schedule varies based on availability. **Cost:** $75; $25 (ages 0-15). Reservations are required. **Phone:** (717) 534-8860 for in-season reservations, or (717) 575-0948 for off-season reservations.

ZooAmerica North American Wildlife Park is at 201 Park Ave., opposite Hersheypark. This 11-acre zoo depicts native plants and animals from five North American regions: Big Sky Country, The Great Southwest, Eastern Woodlands, Southern Swamps, and Northlands. ZooAmerica cares for more than 200 animals representing 75 species. Visitors can pre-register to take the 2-hour After-Hours Tour, conducted by flashlight, to see animal buildings and the health center at night as well as to feed an otter, touch a reptile and hold a bird of prey. They also can pre-register to take the 2-hour Early Bird Tour to explore outdoor exhibits, feed select animals and watch an enrichment activity with mountain lions. A photography tour also is available.

Hours: Park open daily. Opening and closing times vary; phone ahead. After-Hours Tour departs Wed. and Sat. at 8, Apr.-Sept.; at 6, rest of year. Early Bird Tour departs Tues., Fri. and Sun. at 8, year-round. Closed Thanksgiving and Christmas. Phone ahead to confirm schedule. **Cost:** $11.50; $9.50 (ages 3-8 and 55+). Admission to zoo included with Hersheypark ticket on same day. After-Hours or Early Bird tour $49 (ages 3+); reservations with 72-hour notice are required. **Phone:** (717) 534-3900. GT ⊓ 🎟

🔺 **HERSHEY'S CHOCOLATE WORLD** is at 101 Chocolate World Way. This is the official visitor center of The Hershey Co. A tour explains the chocolate-making process from harvesting cocoa beans to packaging the finished product and includes a free sample. The "4D Chocolate Mystery" show features many special effects.

You can probably guess what goes on at the Chocolate Tasting Experience. This 30-minute session combines chocolate lore with the opportunity to taste a variety of chocolate types. Desserts, including Hershey's S'mores, can be created at Hershey's Dessert Creation Studio. For a more involved experience, visitors can head to the Create Your Own Candy Bar area to experience a real factory environment and create and make their own candy bar, including the packaging design.

Note: Three hours of free parking is available. **Time:** Allow 30 minutes minimum. **Hours:** Open daily at 9; phone ahead to verify closing times. Closed Christmas. **Cost:** Tour free. "4D Chocolate Mystery" $7.95; $6.95 (ages 3-12). Hershey's Create Your Own Candy Bar $19.95. Fees for candy and dessert creations vary. Phone ahead to confirm rates. **Phone:** (717) 534-4900. ⊓

Hershey Trolley Works tours depart from the main lobby inside Hershey's Chocolate World at 101 Chocolate World Way. The 1-hour Chocolate & History Tour takes visitors through the town while sharing information about Milton Hershey. It includes a stop at Founders Hall at the Milton Hershey School. The 45-minute Summer Trolley also takes visitors around town, but there is entertainment provided by two actors who reveal aspects of the time when Mr. Hershey lived; sing-alongs and mini chocolates are in abundance. Three seasonal tours also are offered—Trick or Treat Trolley, Holly Jolly Trolley and Sweet Lights Trolley.

Hours: Chocolate & History Tour runs daily, year-round. Summer Trolley runs daily, Memorial Day-Labor Day. Trick or Treat tour is offered select days, in Oct. Holly Jolly Trolley and Sweet Lights Trolley tours are offered select days, Nov.-Dec. (weather permitting). Phone for departure times. Closed Christmas. Phone ahead to confirm schedule. **Cost:** Chocolate & History Tour and seasonal tours $15.95; $12.95 (ages 3-12). Sweet Lights tour $10.95 (ages 3+). **Phone:** (717) 534-4900. GT

THE HERSHEY STORY, THE MUSEUM ON CHOCOLATE AVENUE is downtown at 63 W. Chocolate Ave. (US 422). This museum features exhibits about Milton S. Hershey's life, including his chocolate factory, the town he created and his philanthropic legacy. In the lobby, visitors can sample various flavors of single-origin warm drinking chocolate "flights" at Tastings. Chocolate Lab classes explore the qualities of chocolate and explain techniques of working with chocolate like tempering, dipping and molding.

Time: Allow 1 hour, 30 minutes minimum. **Hours:** Open daily 9-7, mid-June through Labor Day; 9-5, Feb. 1 to mid-June and day after Labor Day-Dec. 31; 10-5, rest of year. Closes early Christmas Eve. Closed Thanksgiving and Christmas. Phone ahead to confirm schedule. **Cost:** Museum $12.50; $11.50 (ages 62+); $9 (ages 3-12); free (active military with ID). Chocolate Lab $12.50; $11.50 (ages 62+); $9 (ages 4-12); $7.50 (active military with ID). Combination Museum and Chocolate Lab $20; $19 (ages 62+); $15 (ages 4-12); $7.50 (active military with ID). A fee is charged for Tastings. A combination ticket with Hershey Gardens is available. Ages 0-3 are not permitted in the lab. **Phone:** (717) 534-8939. ⑪

INDIAN ECHO CAVERNS—see Hummelstown p. 107.

COMFORT INN AT THE PARK   (717)566-2050

Hotel
$89-$399

Address: 1200 Mae St 17036 **Location:** Jct US 322, 422 and SR 39 (Hersheypark Dr); just off Hersheypark Dr. **Facility:** 125 units, some two bedrooms. 7 stories, interior corridors. **Terms:** check-in 4 pm. **Amenities:** safes. **Pool:** heated indoor. **Guest Services:** coin laundry. **Featured Amenity:** full hot breakfast.

Friendly staff. Quiet location. Near the attractions!

DAYS INN HERSHEY   (717)534-2162

Hotel
$110-$300

Address: 350 W Chocolate Ave 17033 **Location:** On US 422; center. **Facility:** 89 units. 4 stories, interior corridors. **Terms:** check-in 4 pm. **Amenities:** safes. **Pool:** heated indoor. **Activities:** hot tub, game room, exercise room. **Guest Services:** valet and coin laundry, area transportation. **Featured Amenity:** continental breakfast.

FAIRFIELD INN & SUITES BY MARRIOTT-HERSHEY
          (717)520-5240

◆◆◆ Hotel. **Address:** 651 Areba Ave 17033

AAA Benefit: Members save 5% or more!

HAMPTON INN & SUITES HERSHEY   (717)533-8400

Hotel
$109-$279

AAA Benefit: Members save up to 10%!

Address: 749 E Chocolate Ave 17033 **Location:** 0.9 mi e on US 422. **Facility:** 110 units, some efficiencies. 3 stories, interior corridors. **Terms:** check-in 4 pm, 1-7 night minimum stay, cancellation fee imposed. **Pool:** heated indoor. **Activities:** hot tub, exercise room. **Guest Services:** valet and coin laundry. **Featured Amenity:** full hot breakfast.

HAMPTON INN & SUITES HERSHEY NEAR THE PARK
          717/566-3369

◆◆◆ Hotel. **Address:** 195 Hershey Rd 17036

AAA Benefit: Members save up to 10%!

HERSHEY LODGE   (717)533-3311

Hotel
$129-$499

Address: 325 University Dr 17033 **Location:** Jct US 322, 2.5 mi w on US 422. **Facility:** 665 units, some two bedrooms. 2-5 stories, interior/exterior corridors. **Parking:** on-site and valet. **Terms:** check-in 4 pm, 3 day cancellation notice-fee imposed. **Amenities:** safes. **Dining:** 5 restaurants. **Pool:** outdoor, heated indoor. **Activities:** sauna, hot tub, miniature golf, tennis, recreation programs, game room, trails, exercise room. **Guest Services:** valet laundry, rental car service, area transportation.

HILTON GARDEN INN HERSHEY (717)566-9292

Hotel
$124-$439

 AAA Benefit: Members save up to 10%!

Address: 550 E Main St 17036 **Location:** Just nw of jct US 322, 422 and SR 39 (Hersheypark Dr). **Facility:** 112 units. 3 stories, interior corridors. **Terms:** 1-7 night minimum stay, cancellation fee imposed. **Pool:** heated indoor. **Activities:** hot tub, exercise room. **Guest Services:** valet and coin laundry.

HOLIDAY INN EXPRESS - HERSHEY/HUMMELSTOWN
717/583-0500

Hotel
Rates not provided

Address: 610 Walton Ave 17036 **Location:** Just nw of jct US 322, 422 and SR 39 (Hersheypark Dr); just off Hersheypark Dr. **Facility:** 78 units. 3 stories, interior corridors. **Pool:** heated indoor. **Activities:** hot tub, exercise room. **Guest Services:** valet and coin laundry. **Featured Amenity: full hot breakfast.**

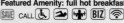

THE HOTEL HERSHEY (717)533-2171

Classic Historic Hotel
$229-$599

Address: 100 Hotel Rd 17033 **Location:** Jct US 322, 2.3 mi n on SR 39 (Hersheypark Dr). **Facility:** Set on a hill overlooking 300 acres of lush, manicured grounds, this hotel is styled after a 19th-century Mediterranean palace. The luxurious rooms are spacious, with elegantly designed furnishings. 276 units, some two bedrooms and cottages. 1-5 stories, interior corridors. **Parking:** onsite and valet. **Terms:** check-in 4 pm, 3 day cancellation notice-fee imposed. **Amenities:** safes. **Dining:** 3 restaurants, also, The Circular, Trevi 5, see separate listings. **Pool:** heated outdoor, heated indoor. **Activities:** sauna, hot tub, steamroom, cabanas, miniature golf, tennis, recreation programs, kids club, bicycles, playground, game room, trails, health club, spa. **Guest Services:** valet laundry, area transportation.

HOWARD JOHNSON INN (717)533-9157

Hotel
$67-$270

Address: 845 E Chocolate Ave 17033 **Location:** 1 mi e on US 422. **Facility:** 52 units. 1-2 stories (no elevator), interior/exterior corridors. **Terms:** check-in 4 pm, cancellation fee imposed. **Dining:** What If...of Hershey, see separate listing. **Pool:** heated outdoor. **Activities:** exercise room. **Guest Services:** coin laundry. **Featured Amenity: continental breakfast.**

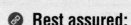

RODEWAY INN & SUITES (717)533-7054
Motel. **Address:** 43 W Areba Ave 17033

SPRINGHILL SUITES BY MARRIOTT HERSHEY
(717)583-2222
Hotel. **Address:** 115 Museum Dr 17033

AAA Benefit: Members save 5% or more!

🔗 **Rest assured:**

AAA.com/travelguides/hotels

▼ See AAA listing p. 89 ▼

WHITE ROSE MOTEL   717/533-9876
♥♥ Motel. **Address:** 1060 E Chocolate Ave 17033

WHERE TO EAT

THE CHOCOLATE AVENUE GRILL   717/835-0888
♥♥ American. Casual Dining. **Address:** 114 W Chocolate Ave
17033

THE CIRCULAR   717/534-8800

**Continental
Fine Dining
$23-$49**

AAA Inspector Notes: You'll be awed
by the dining room's breathtaking views
of the property's gardens and reflecting
pools. The kitchen expertly prepares sophisticated American and continental
specialties, focusing heavily on steaks
and chops. Start out with the classic lob-
ster bisque, but save room for the sinful chocolate desserts. The
expansive wine list is available for viewing on your iPad, including suggestions for the perfect food pairing. The restaurant
schedule may vary seasonally. **Features:** full bar, Sunday
brunch, happy hour. **Reservations:** suggested. **Address:** 100
Hotel Rd 17033 **Location:** Jct US 322, 2.3 mi n on SR 39 (Hersheypark Dr); in The Hotel Hershey. **Parking:** on-site and valet.

Ⓑ Ⓛ Ⓓ

DEVON SEAFOOD + STEAK   717/508-5460
♥♥♥ Seafood. Fine Dining. **Address:** 27 W Chocolate Ave
17033

THE HERSHEY PANTRY   717/533-7505
♥♥ American. Casual Dining. **Address:** 801 E Chocolate Ave
17033

HOULIHAN'S   717/534-3110
♥♥♥ American. Casual Dining. **Address:** 27 W Chocolate
Ave 17033

SODA JERK DINER & DAIRY BAR   717/566-7707
♥♥ American. Casual Dining. **Address:** 403 E Main St 17036

TREVI 5   717/534-8800
♥♥♥ Italian. Casual Dining. **Address:** 100 Hotel Rd 17033

WHAT IF...OF HERSHEY   717/533-5858
♥♥♥ International. Casual Dining. **Address:** 845 E
Chocolate Ave 17033

HOLLIDAYSBURG pop. 5,791

THE DREAM FAMILY RESTAURANT   814/696-3384
♥♥ American. Casual Dining. **Address:** 1500 Allegheny St
16648

HOMESTEAD (G-2) pop. 3,165, elev. 787'
• **Hotels & Restaurants map & index p. 246**
• **Part of Pittsburgh area — see map p. 225**

Homestead, which lies in the Rivers of Steel National Heritage Area in southwestern Pennsylvania,
was the setting for a labor strike that held national
interest in 1892. The Amalgamated Association of
Iron and Steel Workers held out against Carnegie
Steel Co. from June 29-Nov. 21 despite the arrival of
300 Pinkerton guards by barge on July 6; 12 men
lost their lives in the confrontation between the
guards and the laborers, families and supporters. In
the end the strikers lost. Visitors can still see rem-
nants of the steel era like the pump house and
smokestacks, but the main draw now is the Monongahela River waterfront's shopping and
entertainment.

The Rivers of Steel National Heritage Area operates the Carrie Blast Furnace Tour, a 2-hour guided
walking tour through the former U.S. Steel Homestead Works in Braddock. Visitors learn about the
iron-making process and the construction of the 92-
foot tall furnaces that at one time produced 1,000
tons of iron a day. Tours are offered May-Oct.;
phone (412) 464-4020 for more information.

Shopping: The Waterfront is a shopping and entertainment locale that has taken over the land once
occupied by the Homestead steel mill.

COURTYARD BY MARRIOTT PITTSBURGH-WATERFRONT
(412)462-7301 Ⓐ Ⓐ 91
♥♥♥ Hotel. **Address:** 401 W Waterfront Dr 15120

AAA Benefit:
Members save 5%
or more!

HAMPTON INN & SUITES PITTSBURGH WATERFRONT
(412)462-4226 90
♥♥♥ Hotel. **Address:** 301 W Waterfront Dr 15120

AAA Benefit:
Members save up to
10%!

WHERE TO EAT

MITCHELL'S FISH MARKET   412/476-8844 89
♥♥♥ Seafood. Casual Dining. **Address:** 185 W Waterfront
Dr 15120

P.F. CHANG'S CHINA BISTRO   412/464-0640 90
♥♥♥ Chinese. Fine Dining. **Address:** 148 W Bridge St
15120

HONESDALE (D-11) pop. 4,480, elev. 982'
• **Part of Pocono Mountains Area — see map
p. 264**

Established in 1828 as a terminal for canal
barges carrying coal to New York markets, Honesdale was the site of the first use of a commercial
steam locomotive in the United States. Imported
from England, the locomotive Stourbridge Lion
made its trial run on Aug. 8, 1829. Too heavy for the
rails, it was withdrawn from service. A full-size replica can be seen in the Wayne County Historical Society Museum.

Weekend excursions on the Stourbridge rail line
are offered by the Delaware Lackawaxen & Stourbridge Railroad Company from Memorial Day
weekend through the fall foliage season, with some
holiday-themed trips in December. Departure times
vary; phone (570) 470-2697 for information.

Chamber of the Northern Poconos: 32 Commercial St., Suite 200, Honesdale, PA 18431. **Phone:**
(570) 253-1960.

HOPEWELL FURNACE NATIONAL
HISTORIC SITE (A-8) elev. 472'

Hopewell Furnace National Historic Site is about
5 miles south of Birdsboro on SR 345 and also is accessible via the Morgantown exit off the Pennsylvania Turnpike, using SRs 23 and 345. The 848-
acre site is one of the finest examples of an early

American 18th- and 19th-century iron-making community.

Englishman William Bird was prominent in the early iron industry in Pennsylvania. His son Mark built Hopewell Furnace on French Creek in 1771. Around the furnace developed a small industrial settlement where many of the employees lived in tenant houses. A resident manager lived on the site in the ironmaster's mansion.

The furnace cast pig iron, hollowware, stoves and many other items; during the Revolutionary War it produced cannon and shot. The furnace operated until 1883, when more advanced technology made it unprofitable.

Many of the structures have been restored and refurnished. The waterwheel, blast machinery, bridge house, cooling shed, barn, store, ironmaster's mansion and tenant houses can be seen. The ruin of an 1853 anthracite furnace has been uncovered and stabilized.

A visitor center features an audiovisual program and an exhibit area with original iron castings produced at Hopewell Furnace and tools associated with the operation of 18th- and 19th-century cold-blast charcoal furnaces. Allow 2 hours minimum. Daily 9-5, mid-May to early Oct. (also Memorial Day, July 4, Labor Day and Columbus Day); Wed.-Sun., 9-5, rest of year. Closed Jan. 1, Martin Luther King Jr. Day, Presidents Day, Thanksgiving and Christmas. Admission free. Phone (610) 582-8773.

HORSHAM (A-11) pop. 14,842, elev. 249'
• Hotels & Restaurants map & index p. 192
• Part of Philadelphia area — see map p. 154

SAVE **GRAEME PARK**, .5 mi. w. off US 611 at 859 County Line Rd., was the home of Sir William Keith, the provincial governor of Pennsylvania 1717-26. Built during his years as governor, the well-preserved stone house is a fine example of 18th-century architecture. The home is furnished with period pieces and contains original paneling and flooring. Writer Elizabeth Graeme Fergusson also lived in the house 1739-93.

Time: Allow 1 hour minimum. **Hours:** Grounds daily dawn-dusk. House open Fri.-Sat. 10-4, Sun. noon-4. Last tour begins 1 hour before closing. Closed Jan. 1, Easter, day after Thanksgiving and Christmas. **Cost:** Grounds free. House tour $6; $5 (ages 65+); $3 (ages 3-11). **Phone:** (215) 343-0965. GT ⊼

DAYS INN-HORSHAM/PHILADELPHIA   (215)674-2500 **26**
♦♦ Hotel. **Address:** 245 Easton Rd 19044

EXTENDED STAY AMERICA-PHILADELPHIA/HORSHAM
(215)784-9045 **28**
♦♦ Extended Stay Hotel. **Address:** 114 Welsh Rd 19044

RESIDENCE INN BY MARRIOTT-WILLOW GROVE
(215)443-7330 **27**
♦♦♦♦ Extended Stay Hotel. **Address:** 3 Walnut Grove Dr 19044

AAA Benefit:
Members save 5%
or more!

WHERE TO EAT

IRON ABBEY GASTROPUB   215/956-9600
♦♦ American. Gastropub. **Address:** 680 N Easton Rd 19044

LEE'S HOAGIE HOUSE   215/674-8000
♦ Sandwiches. Quick Serve. **Address:** 870 Easton Rd 19044

HUMMELSTOWN (H-8) pop. 4,538, elev. 384'

SAVE **INDIAN ECHO CAVERNS**, off US 322, offers a 45-minute guided, narrated tour amid the natural beauty of stalagmites, stalactites, columns, flowstone and lakes. The caverns are electronically lighted, contain level pathways and maintain a constant temperature of 52 degrees Fahrenheit. Visitors may pan for gemstones at Gem Mill Junction or interact with goats in the petting zoo.

Guests who cannot walk through the caverns can enjoy a non-walking video tour. **Note:** Backpacks and large bags are prohibited inside the caverns. Two covered picnic pavilions are available. **Hours:** Daily 9-5, Memorial Day-Labor Day; 10-4, rest of year. Closed Jan. 1, Thanksgiving and Christmas. **Cost:** $18; $16 (ages 62+); $10 (ages 2-11). Phone ahead to confirm rates. Reservations are recommended for non-walking video tour. **Phone:** (717) 566-8131. GT ⊼

HOAGEEZ   717/566-1314
♦ Sandwiches. Quick Serve. **Address:** 422 Walton Ave 17036

HUNTINGDON (G-6) pop. 7,093, elev. 630'
• Hotels p. 108 • Restaurants p. 108

Near Huntingdon is Raystown Lake (see Recreation Areas Chart), the largest man-made lake wholly within Pennsylvania. Recreation available at the lake includes hunting, boating, camping, swimming and fishing, especially for smallmouth and largemouth bass, striped bass and lake trout. Wildlife inhabiting the area includes deer, turkeys, grouse and squirrels.

SAVE **LINCOLN CAVERNS**, 3 mi. w. on US 22 at 7703 William Penn Hwy., offers 1-hour interpretive tours through two crystal caverns that display a variety of formations. Children may pan for gemstones in a sluice. Nature trails also are available.

Cavern temperature is 52 degrees Fahrenheit. A light jacket is recommended. **Hours:** Guided tours are offered daily 9-6, July 1-Labor Day; daily 9-5, Memorial Day weekend-June 30; daily 9-4, Apr. 1-late May and early Sept.-Oct. 31 (also some extended weekends in Oct.); Thurs.-Mon. 9-4 in Mar. and Nov.; Sat.-Sun. 11-3, in Dec.; by appointment rest of year. Closed Thanksgiving and Christmas. **Cost:** Tour $15.98; $14.98 (ages 65+); $9.98 (ages 4-12). Tour and gem panning $14.98 (ages 4-12, mid-Mar. to mid-Nov. only). Phone ahead to verify rates. **Phone:** (814) 643-0268. GT ▲ ⏏

COMFORT INN   (814)643-1600
♥♥ Hotel. **Address:** 100 S 4th St 16652

FAIRFIELD INN & SUITES BY MARRIOTT HUNTINGDON
(814)643-3672

Hotel
$86-$263

FAIRFIELD INN & SUITES Marriott   **AAA Benefit:** Members save 5% or more!

Address: 9970 Shaner Blvd 16652 **Location:** US 22 exit SR 26 (Everett); jct US 22 and Raystown Rd. **Facility:** 80 units. 3 stories, interior corridors. **Terms:** cancellation fee imposed. **Pool:** indoor. **Activities:** exercise room. **Guest Services:** valet and coin laundry. **Featured Amenity:** breakfast buffet.

SAVE CALL 🛗 🚼 🐾 BIZ HS
🛜 ✕ 🖥 /SOME UNITS 🛗 🖨

THE INN AT SOLVANG   814/643-3035
♥♥♥ Bed & Breakfast. **Address:** 10611 Standing Stone Rd 16652

THE MILL STONE MANOR   814/643-0108
♥♥ Motel. **Address:** 11979 William Penn Hwy 16652

WHERE TO EAT

HOSS'S FAMILY STEAK & SEA   814/643-6939
♥ Steak. Casual Dining. **Address:** 9016 William Penn Hwy 16652

HUNTINGDON VALLEY
• **Hotels & Restaurants map & index p. 192**
• **Part of Philadelphia area — see map p. 154**

WHITE ELEPHANT RESTAURANT   215/663-1495 103
♥♥♥ Thai. Casual Dining. **Address:** 759 Huntingdon Pike 19006

INDIANA (INDIANA COUNTY) (G-3)
pop. 13,975, elev. 1,310'

Indiana was founded in 1805 when George Clymer of Philadelphia, a signer of the Declaration of Independence, donated 250 acres of land for county buildings. Later, before the Civil War, Indiana became an important station on the Underground Railroad. In more recent history, the town was the birthplace and childhood home of actor Jimmy Stewart. A bronze statue of the actor, unveiled for his 75th birthday, stands on the lawn of the Indiana County Courthouse on Philadelphia Street. Crosswalk audio clips at 7th and 9th streets and Philadelphia and 9th streets feature safety tips and personal tidbits from Jimmy Stewart (thanks to a voice impersonator).

Northern Indiana County is Amish country. Horse-drawn buggies are common sights, as are Christmas trees—more than one million trees per year are marketed by local growers in the area.

Historic buildings can be seen on the campus of Indiana University of Pennsylvania. John Sutton Hall, built in 1875, houses University Museum's changing art exhibits and displays; phone (724) 357-2397.

Year-round recreational opportunities include hunting, fishing and boating. For information about game areas phone the Pennsylvania Game Commission Southwest Regional office at (724) 238-9523. For fishing information and boating regulations phone the Pennsylvania Fish and Boat Commission regional office at (814) 443-9841. Yellow Creek State Park *(see Recreation Areas Chart)* is about 12 miles east of town. The Ghost Town, Hoodlebug and West Penn trails offer nearly 65 miles of rails-to-trails that give hikers and bikers the opportunity to pass through scenic areas, historic sites and other natural attractions. Maps are available at the Indiana County Tourist Bureau and at the Indiana County Parks & Trails office, 1128 Blue Spruce Rd. in Blue Spruce Park; phone (724) 463-7505 for the tourist bureau or (724) 463-8636 for the parks and trails office.

Indiana County Tourist Bureau: 2334 Oakland Ave., Indiana, PA 15701. **Phone:** (724) 463-7505.

The office is in Indiana Mall.

Shopping: Yarnick Farm Market, in business for more than 35 years, is open daily 9-6 at 155 Thomas Covered Bridge Rd. Indiana County Farmers Market, downtown at 8th and Church streets, is open Sat. 9-noon and at Wayne Avenue across from the Kovalchick Complex Wed. 3-5:30, June through October. The town also features antique and specialty shops.

THE JIMMY STEWART MUSEUM, 835 Philadelphia St. at jct. 9th St., on the third floor of the Indiana Free Library, is dedicated to the life and career of film icon Jimmy Stewart. Displays include original movie posters and photo stills; family photographs; and items reflecting his personal, public and military life. A film is shown in a 50-seat theater.

Time: Allow 2 hours minimum. **Hours:** Mon.-Sat. 10-4, Sun. noon-4. Matinees are offered Sat.-Sun.; phone for times. Closed federal holidays. Phone ahead to confirm schedule. **Cost:** $8; $7 (ages 50+, military with ID and college students with ID); $6 (ages 7-17). **Phone:** (724) 349-6112.

BEST WESTERN INDIANA INN   724/349-4600

Hotel
Rates not provided

BW Best Western.   **AAA Benefit:** Members save 5% to 15% and earn 10% bonus points!

Address: 111 Plaza Rd 15701 **Location:** US 422 exit SR 286, just n. **Facility:** 67 units. 3 stories, interior corridors. **Amenities:** safes. **Activities:** exercise room.

SAVE 🍴 CALL 🛗 🚼 BIZ HS
🛜 ✕ 🛗 🖨 🖥

DAYS INN INDIANA (724)465-7000

Hotel. **Address:** 1350 Indian Springs Rd 15701

HAMPTON INN INDIANA (724)349-7700

Hotel. **Address:** 1275 Indian Springs Rd 15701

AAA Benefit: Members save up to 10%!

PARK INN BY RADISSON (724)463-3561

Hotel. **Address:** 1395 Wayne Ave 15701

WHERE TO EAT

BENJAMIN'S 724/465-4446

Mediterranean. Casual Dining. **Address:** 458 Philadelphia St 15701

INDUSTRY pop. 1,835

• **Part of Pittsburgh area — see map p. 225**

WILLOWS INN 724/643-4500

fyi Motel. Under major renovation, scheduled to be completed July 2018. **Last Rated:** **Address:** 1830 Beaver Midland Rd 15052

WHERE TO EAT

WILLOWS INN FAMILY SMORGASBORD 724/643-4500

fyi American. Casual Dining. Under major renovation, scheduled to be completed July 2018. **Last rated:** **Address:** 1830 Beaver Midland Rd 15052

INTERCOURSE (H-10) pop. 1,274, elev. 436'

• **Restaurants p. 110**
• **Hotels & Restaurants map & index p. 148**
• **Part of Pennsylvania Dutch Country area — see map p. 143**

In the heart of Pennsylvania Dutch Country, Intercourse was founded in 1754. First called Cross Keys after a local tavern, the town was renamed in 1814. Its name is believed to have evolved from either the entrance to the old racecourse (the Entercourse) just outside of town or from the joining, or intercourse, of the Old Kings Highway and the Wilmington-Erie Road.

Shopping: Amish and Mennonite crafts, including such items as quilts, toys and tablecloths, can be found at the Old Country Store on Old Philadelphia Pike. Across the street Kitchen Kettle Village contains more than 40 stores offering Amish and other handmade items as well as antiques, food and furniture.

BEST WESTERN PLUS INTERCOURSE VILLAGE INN & SUITES (717)768-3636 35

Hotel
$119-$299

AAA Benefit: Members save 5% to 15% and earn 10% bonus points!

Address: 3610 E Newport Rd 17534 **Location:** SR 772, just se of SR 340. **Facility:** 89 units, some two bedrooms. 3 stories, interior corridors. **Terms:** check-in 4 pm, cancellation fee imposed. **Pool:** heated indoor. **Activities:** hot tub, exercise room, spa. **Guest Services:** complimentary laundry. **Featured Amenity:** continental breakfast. *(See ad this page.)*

SAVE CALL BIZ HS

THE INN & SPA AT INTERCOURSE VILLAGE 717/768-2626 36

Historic Bed & Breakfast. **Address:** 3542 Old Philadelphia Pike 17534

▼ See AAA listing this page ▼

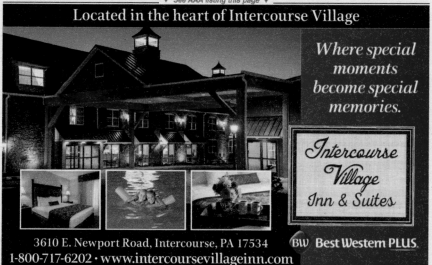

(See map & index p. 148.)

THE INN AT KITCHEN KETTLE VILLAGE   717/768-8261 **34**
◆◆◆ Country Inn. **Address:** 3529 Old Philadelphia Pike 17534

TRAVELERS REST MOTEL   (717)768-8731 **33**
◆◆ Motel. **Address:** 3701 Old Philadelphia Pike (Rt 340) 17534

WHERE TO EAT

THE KLING HOUSE RESTAURANT   717/768-2746 **28**
◆◆ Regional American. Casual Dining. **Address:** 3529 Old Philadelphia Pike 17534

IRWIN pop. 3,973
• Restaurants p. 110
• Part of Pittsburgh area — see map p. 225

PASQUALINO'S ITALIAN EATERY   724/864-9600
◆◆ Italian. Casual Dining. **Address:** 8711 Rt 30 15642

JEANNETTE pop. 9,654, elev. 1,033'
• Restaurants p. 110
• Part of Pittsburgh area — see map p. 225

MAURO'S RISTORANTE & LOUNGE   724/523-3391
◆◆ Italian. Casual Dining. **Address:** 202 Baughman Ave 15644

JENNERSTOWN pop. 695

GREEN GABLES RESTAURANT   814/629-9201
◆◆ American. Casual Dining. **Address:** 7712 Somerset Pike 15547

JERMYN pop. 2,169

WINDSOR INN   570/876-4600
◆ American. Casual Dining. **Address:** 669 Washington Ave 18433

JIM THORPE (F-10) pop. 4,781, elev. 531'
• Part of Pocono Mountains Area — see map p. 264

In the foothills of the Pocono Mountains, the town of Jim Thorpe was named after the famous Olympic athlete who won each pentathlon event but the javelin throw in the 1912 Olympic Games in Stockholm. He was later stripped of his honors because of previous professional sports activities.

In response to Thorpe's widow's search for a memorial for him, two Pennsylvania communities— Mauch Chunk and East Mauch Chunk—joined by incorporating as Jim Thorpe in the mid-1950s. The new community gave the man a final and fitting memorial, while also gaining economic stability for itself. Jim Thorpe was reinstated in the Olympic records in 1982, and the medals he won in the 1912 games were presented to his family. The Jim Thorpe Memorial is a half-mile east on SR 903.

St. Mark's & St. John's Episcopal Church, on Race Street, contains Italian marble altars, brass gas standards flanking the baptismal font and Tiffany stained-glass windows. Guided tours are available Memorial Day weekend through October; phone (570) 325-2241.

Mauch Chunk Lake Park *(see Recreation Areas Chart)* offers recreational opportunities, including picnicking, hiking, boating, fishing, swimming and cross-country skiing.

Concerts are often held at Penn's Peak at 325 Maury Rd.; phone (610) 826-9000 or (866) 605-7325.

THE INN AT JIM THORPE   (570)325-2599
◆◆◆ Historic Country Inn. **Address:** 24 Broadway 18229

WHERE TO EAT

BROADWAY GRILLE AND PUB   570/732-4343
◆◆ American. Casual Dining. **Address:** 24 Broadway 18229

STONE ROW PUB & EATERY   570/732-0465
◆◆ New International. Casual Dining. **Address:** 45-47 Race St 18229

JOHNSTOWN (H-4) pop. 20,978, elev. 1,178'

Four times disastrous floods have claimed Johnstown, which is in a deep, irregular valley formed by Stony Creek and the Little Conemaugh and Conemaugh rivers. The first two floods, in 1862 and 1889, were a result of the collapse of the South Fork Dam, about 12 miles east on the Conemaugh. Some of the older buildings still show high water marks of the 1889 disaster, one of the country's worst peacetime catastrophes. Debris held behind a stone bridge area caught fire and added to the losses, which included some 2,200 lives. The Path of the Flood Trail is a hiking/biking trail following the roughly 14-mile path of the 1889 flood. The trail begins in Ehrenfeld and then joins the National Park Service's Staple Bend Tunnel Site for a short distance. There is about a .75-mile gap until it picks up again just past the Franklin Ballfield area to Pershing Avenue/Clapboard Run Road; the route then continues into Johnstown and ends at the Johnstown Flood Museum. Kiosks and interpretive panels along the way detail the devastating event. For more information about the route contact the Cambria County Conservation & Recreation Authority, (814) 472-2110, or the visitors bureau, (814) 536-7993.

In 1936 a third flood caused a great deal of damage to the city and its environs. A fourth flood occurred in July 1977, when heavy rains caused rivers and streams to overflow throughout the Conemaugh Valley. Once again damage was severe.

Conemaugh Gap, a gorge cut by the Conemaugh River as it passes through Laurel Hill Ridge Mountain, extends 7 miles and is about 1,700 feet deep.

Pasquerilla Performing Arts Center at the University of Pittsburgh at Johnstown stages plays, dance performances and concerts as well as productions for children; phone (814) 269-7200 or (800) 846-2787. The Johnstown Symphony Orchestra also provides musical entertainment; its 1,000-seat theater is at the performing arts center; phone (814) 535-6738.

Greater Johnstown/Cambria Convention and Visitors Bureau: 111 Roosevelt Blvd., Suite A, Johnstown, PA 15906. **Phone:** (814) 536-7993 or (800) 237-8590.

Shopping: The Johnstown Galleria, SR 219, has nearly 80 specialty stores, including The Bon-Ton, Boscov's, JCPenney and Sears. In addition, numerous shops line Scalp Avenue.

 FRANK & SYLVIA PASQUERILLA HERITAGE DISCOVERY CENTER is at 201 6th Ave.; the parking lot entrance is at jct. Broad St. and 7th Ave. The center presents the experiences of Southern and Eastern European immigrants whose arrival at the turn of the 20th century shaped the region's culture, economy and industry. Daily experiences, difficulties and accomplishments are depicted through several fictional immigrants who give personal accounts of events in their lives. Some of the scenes depicted are an Italian funeral, a Ukrainian wedding, a bar mitzvah, an ethnic social club and a butcher shop.

Interactive exhibits about coal mines and steel mills also are featured. The Iron & Steel Gallery presents additional exhibits about the steel industry. It also shows the film "Mystery of Steel," which chronicles Johnstown's 19th-century history as a technological innovator in steelmaking. The Johnstown Children's Museum is housed here as well.

Time: Allow 1 hour, 30 minutes minimum. **Hours:** Tues.-Sat. 10-5, Sun. noon-5, Apr.-Oct.; Wed.-Sat. 10-5, Sun. noon-5, rest of year. Closed Jan. 1, Easter, Thanksgiving and Christmas. **Cost:** $9; $7 (ages 3-18 and 62+). Combination ticket with Johnstown Children's Museum and Johnstown Flood Museum (valid up to 5 days after ticket is purchased) $12; $10 (ages 3-18 and 62+). **Phone:** (814) 539-1889.

SAVE **Johnstown Children's Museum** is at 201 6th Ave. at jct. Broad St. and 7th Ave., on one floor of the Frank & Sylvia Pasquerilla Heritage Discovery Center. Many of the interactive exhibits introduce children to local history topics, including mining and steel mills. There is a water room where youngsters can learn about dams, rain, fish and municipal plumbing; a rooftop garden with native Pennsylvania plants; an area to learn about maps and city planning; role play and dress-up activities; and a coal mine-theme climbing structure.

Time: Allow 1 hour minimum. **Hours:** Tues.-Sat. 10-5, Sun. noon-5, Apr.-Oct.; Wed.-Sat. 10-5, Sun. noon-5, rest of year. Closed Jan. 1, Easter, Thanksgiving and Christmas. **Cost:** $9; $7 (ages 3-18 and 62+). Combination ticket with Frank & Sylvia Pasquerilla Heritage Discovery Center and Johnstown Flood Museum (valid up to 5 days after ticket is purchased) $12; $10 (ages 3-18 and 62+). **Phone:** (814) 539-1889.

JOHNSTOWN FLOOD MUSEUM is at 304 Washington St. at Walnut St. This 1891 building was one of the first Carnegie libraries, built with a donation from philanthropist Andrew Carnegie. The museum chronicles the cause and course of events prior to, during and after the devastating flood of May 31, 1889, and features the 26-minute 1989 Academy Award-winning documentary film "The Johnstown Flood." Oklahoma houses, prefabricated structures designed for Oklahoma Territory homesteaders, were used for emergency housing after the flood; an original is displayed.

A 24-foot, 3-D relief map with sound effects and animation illustrates the devastation wrought by the 40-foot-high wall of water. Some 2,200 people were killed as it swept through the Conemaugh Valley, destroying everything in its path. Another exhibit is dedicated to the relief provided by the American Red Cross, including the efforts of the group's founder, Clara Barton. Recovered artifacts also are displayed.

Time: Allow 1 hour, 30 minutes minimum. **Hours:** Tues.-Sat. 10-5, Sun. noon-5, Apr.-Oct.; Wed.-Sat. 10-5, Sun. noon-5, rest of year. Film is shown every hour. Closed Jan. 1, Easter, Thanksgiving and Christmas. **Cost:** $9; $7 (ages 3-18 and 62+). Combination ticket with Frank & Sylvia Pasquerilla Heritage Discovery Center and Johnstown Children's Museum (valid up to 5 days after ticket is purchased) $12; $10 (ages 3-18 and 62+). **Phone:** (814) 539-1889.

HAMPTON INN	(814)262-7700
▼▼▼ Hotel. **Address:** 129 Commerce Ct 15904	**AAA Benefit:** Members save up to 10%!
HOLIDAY INN DOWNTOWN	814/535-7777
▼▼▼ Hotel. **Address:** 250 Market St 15901	
QUALITY INN & SUITES	(814)266-3678
▼▼▼ Hotel. **Address:** 455 Theatre Dr 15904	
SLEEP INN	(814)262-9292
▼▼ Hotel. **Address:** 453 Theatre Dr 15904	
SUPER 8 JOHNSTOWN	(814)535-5600
▼▼ Hotel. **Address:** 627 Solomon Run Rd 15904	

WHERE TO EAT

HARRIGAN'S CAFE & WINE DECK	814/361-2620
▼▼ American. Casual Dining. **Address:** 250 Market St 15901	

JONES MILLS (H-3) elev. 1,560'

Jones Mills is part of the Laurel Highlands (see place listing p. 122).

LOG CABIN LODGE & SUITES	724/593-8200
▼▼ Motel. **Address:** 288 Rt 711 15646	

JONESTOWN pop. 1,905

COMFORT INN LEBANON VALLEY-FT. INDIANTOWN GAP
(717)865-8080

Motel
$54-$249

Address: 16 Marsanna Ln 17038 **Location:** I-81 exit 90, just w. **Facility:** 51 units. 3 stories, interior corridors. **Pool:** outdoor. **Activities:** exercise room. **Guest Services:** coin laundry, area transportation.

DAYS INN LEBANON/FORT INDIANTOWN GAP   (717)865-4064
Hotel. **Address:** 3 Everest Ln 17038

FAIRFIELD INN & SUITES BY MARRIOTT LEBANON VALLEY
(717)865-4234
Hotel. **Address:** 4 Fisher Ave 17038

AAA Benefit: Members save 5% or more!

KANE (D-4) pop. 3,730, elev. 2,020'

Located in northwestern Pennsylvania, Kane was founded in 1863 by Gen. Thomas L. Kane, who recruited the renowned Bucktail Regiment for Civil War combat. ArtWorks at the Depot, 1 S. Fraley St., is an art gallery and store housed in the historic railroad depot; it's open weekends late May through late December. The Allegheny National Forest *(see place listing p. 34 and Recreation Areas Chart)* surrounds the city and offers year-round recreation.

KENNETT SQUARE (C-8) pop. 6,072, elev. 260'
• Part of Philadelphia area — see map p. 154

The Brandywine Valley Tourist Information Center, just outside the gates of Longwood Gardens, is housed in a 19th-century Quaker meetinghouse and offers exhibits, video presentations and a wide range of visitor information. Across the street is a Quaker cemetery begun in the mid-1800s.

Chester County Conference and Visitors Bureau: 300 Greenwood Rd., Kennett Square, PA 19348. **Phone:** (484) 770-8550.

LONGWOOD GARDENS is 3 mi. n.e. at jct. US 1 and SR 52. Once the country estate of industrialist Pierre S. du Pont, Longwood is famous for its superb grounds that include elaborate fountains, two lakes, meadows, woodlands, 20 outdoor formal and informal gardens and a conservatory. The Peirce-du Pont House, occupied by du Pont until 1954, contains an exhibit tracing the 300-year historical and horticultural evolution of Longwood Gardens through photographs, artifacts, video and family home movies.

Fountains, a water lily display and more than 11,000 types of plants are the main summer outdoor attractions. Masses of flowering plants adorn the 4-acre heated conservatory, which is particularly colorful November through April. Special events are offered throughout the year, including fireworks and fountains shows.

Time: Allow 2 hours minimum. **Hours:** Grounds daily 9-6. Closing times may vary; phone ahead to confirm schedule. **Cost:** $23; $20 (ages 62+ and college students with ID); $12 (ages 5-18). Admission may be higher on peak days during the Christmas season. Advance ticket purchase is recommended. **Phone:** (610) 388-1000.

FAIRFIELD INN & SUITES BY MARRIOTT KENNETT SQUARE BRANDYWINE VALLEY
(610)444-8995
Hotel. **Address:** 719 E Baltimore Pike 19348

AAA Benefit: Members save 5% or more!

HILTON GARDEN INN KENNETT SQUARE   (610)444-9100
Hotel. **Address:** 815 E Baltimore Pike 19348

AAA Benefit: Members save up to 10%!

KENNETT HOUSE BED & BREAKFAST   (610)444-9592
Bed & Breakfast. **Address:** 503 W State St 19348

WHERE TO EAT

TWO STONES PUB   610/444-3940
American. Sports Bar. **Address:** 843 E Baltimore Pike 19348

KING OF PRUSSIA (B-9) pop. 19,936, elev. 200'
• Restaurants p. 114
• Part of Philadelphia area — see map p. 154

For Philadelphia locals, King of Prussia isn't just a southeastern suburb—it refers to a shopping mecca by the same name. The King of Prussia Mall is one of the largest in the country, and has high-end options like Tiffany's and Neiman Marcus as well as mass market retailers like Dick's Sporting Goods. The region is highly populated because it's a crossroads for four major roads. Its unusual name can be linked to King Frederick II of Prussia; his name was the inspiration for the King of Prussia Inn, built initially as a cottage by Quakers, and later used as a place of respite for Gen. George Washington.

Valley Forge Tourism & Convention Board: 1000 First Ave., Suite 101, King of Prussia, PA 19406. **Phone:** (610) 834-1550.

Get the scoop from AAA inspectors:
AAA.com/travelguides/restaurants

BEST WESTERN PLUS THE INN AT KING OF PRUSSIA
(610)265-4500

Hotel
$99-$189

 Best Western PLUS **AAA Benefit:** Members save 5% to 15% and earn 10% bonus points!

Address: 127 S Gulph Rd 19406 **Location:** I-76 (Pennsylvania Tpke) exit 326 (Valley Forge Rd), 1.3 mi e to jct US 202 N and S Gulph Rd; Schuylkill Expwy exit 328A (Mall Blvd), just e. Opposite King of Prussia Mall. **Facility:** 168 units. 2-3 stories, interior corridors. **Terms:** cancellation fee imposed. **Pool:** heated outdoor. **Activities:** hot tub, exercise room. **Guest Services:** valet and coin laundry.

CASINO HOTEL TOWER-VALLEY FORGE RESORT
610/265-1500

Hotel. **Address:** 1210 1st Ave 19406

CROWNE PLAZA PHILADELPHIA/KING OF PRUSSIA
(610)265-7500

Hotel
$109-$269

Address: 260 Mall Blvd 19406 **Location:** I-76 (Pennsylvania Tpke) exit 326 (Valley Forge Rd), 1 mi e; Schuylkill Expwy exit 328A (Mall Blvd), just n; just w off US 202 N. Next to a shopping mall. **Facility:** 225 units. 5 stories, interior corridors. **Terms:** cancellation fee imposed. **Activities:** exercise room. **Guest Services:** valet laundry, area transportation.

DOUBLETREE BY HILTON PHILADELPHIA VALLEY FORGE
(610)337-1200

Hotel
$109-$209

 DOUBLETREE BY HILTON **AAA Benefit:** Members save 5% or more!

Address: 301 W Dekalb Pike 19406 **Location:** I-76 (Pennsylvania Tpke) exit 326 (Valley Forge Rd), 1.4 mi ne on US 202 N. **Facility:** 327 units. 9 stories, interior corridors. **Terms:** 1-7 night minimum stay, cancellation fee imposed. **Amenities:** safes. **Pool:** heated outdoor. **Activities:** exercise room. **Guest Services:** valet laundry, area transportation.

For complete hotel, dining and attraction listings:

AAA.com/travelguides

FAIRFIELD INN BY MARRIOTT PHILADELPHIA/VALLEY FORGE
(610)337-0700

Hotel
$77-$252

 FAIRFIELD INN & SUITES Marriott **AAA Benefit:** Members save 5% or more!

Address: 258 Mall Blvd 19406 **Location:** I-76 (Pennsylvania Tpke) exit 326 (Valley Forge Rd); Schuylkill Expwy exit 328A (Mall Blvd), just off US 202 N. Next to King of Prussia Mall. **Facility:** 80 units. 5 stories, interior corridors. **Terms:** cancellation fee imposed. **Activities:** exercise room. **Guest Services:** valet laundry. **Featured Amenity:** continental breakfast.

HAMPTON INN PHILADELPHIA/KING OF PRUSSIA
(610)962-8111

Hotel. **Address:** 530 W Dekalb Pike 19406

AAA Benefit: Members save up to 10%!

HOLIDAY INN EXPRESS HOTEL & SUITES-KING OF PRUSSIA
(610)768-9500

Hotel. **Address:** 260 N Gulph Rd 19406

HYATT HOUSE PHILADELPHIA/KING OF PRUSSIA
(610)265-0300

Extended Stay Hotel
$109-$349

HYATT house™ **AAA Benefit:** Members save 10%!

Address: 240 Mall Blvd 19406 **Location:** I-76 (Pennsylvania Tpke) exit 326 (Valley Forge Rd), 1 mi n of jct US 202 on Gulph Rd. **Facility:** 147 units, some efficiencies. 4 stories, interior corridors. **Terms:** cancellation fee imposed. **Pool:** heated indoor. **Activities:** hot tub, exercise room. **Guest Services:** valet and coin laundry, area transportation. **Featured Amenity:** breakfast buffet.

HYATT PLACE PHILADELPHIA/KING OF PRUSSIA
(484)690-3000

Hotel
$99-$349

HYATT PLACE' **AAA Benefit:** Members save 10%!

Address: 440 American Ave 19406 **Location:** I-76 (Pennsylvania Tpke) exit 326 (Valley Forge Rd); Schuylkill Expwy exit 328A (Mall Blvd), 1.3 mi n on N Gulph Rd, 1 mi ne on 1st Ave, then just e. Located in a commercial area. **Facility:** 129 units. 6 stories, interior corridors. **Terms:** cancellation fee imposed. **Pool:** heated indoor. **Activities:** hot tub, exercise room. **Guest Services:** valet and coin laundry, area transportation. **Featured Amenity:** breakfast buffet.

INN OF KING OF PRUSSIA
610/962-0700

Hotel. Under major renovation, scheduled to be completed March 2018. **Last Rated:** **Address:** 550 W Dekalb Pike 19406

RADISSON VALLEY FORGE HOTEL   610/337-2000
 Hotel. **Address:** 1160 1st Ave 19406

SHERATON VALLEY FORGE   (484)238-1800

Hotel
$99-$399

Sheraton

AAA Benefit:
Members save 5%
or more!

Address: 480 N Gulph Rd 19406 **Location:** I-76 (Pennsylvania Tpke) exit 326 (Valley Forge Rd), 0.5 mi w. Located in a commercial area. **Facility:** 180 units. 6 stories, interior corridors. **Terms:** cancellation fee imposed. **Amenities:** safes. **Dining:** Ralph's of South Philly, see separate listing. **Pool:** heated indoor. **Activities:** hot tub, exercise room. **Guest Services:** valet laundry, area transportation.

SPRINGHILL SUITES BY MARRIOTT PHILADELPHIA/VALLEY FORGE/KING OF PRUSSIA   (610)783-1400
 Hotel. **Address:** 875 Mancill Mill Rd 19406

AAA Benefit:
Members save 5%
or more!

WHERE TO EAT

THE CAPITAL GRILLE   610/265-1415
 Steak. Fine Dining. **Address:** 236 Mall Blvd 19406

CREED'S SEAFOOD & STEAKS   610/265-2550
 Continental. Fine Dining. **Address:** 499 N Gulph Rd 19406

MAGGIANO'S LITTLE ITALY   610/992-3333
 Italian. Fine Dining. **Address:** 205 Mall Blvd 19406

MICHAEL'S DELICATESSEN & RESTAURANT   610/265-3265
 American. Casual Dining. **Address:** 130 Town Center Rd 19406

MISTRAL KOP   610/768-1630
 American. Casual Dining. **Address:** 160 N Gulph Rd 19406

PEPPERS ITALIAN RESTAURANT AND BAR   610/265-2416
 Italian. Casual Dining. **Address:** 239 Town Center Rd 19406

RALPH'S OF SOUTH PHILLY   484/238-1990
 Italian. Fine Dining. **Address:** 480 N Gulph Rd 19406

SULLIVAN'S STEAKHOUSE   610/878-9025
 Steak. Fine Dining. **Address:** 700 W Dekalb Pike 19406

KITTANNING pop. 4,044

HOLIDAY INN EXPRESS & SUITES   724/543-5200
 Hotel. **Address:** 13 Hilltop Plaza 16201

QUALITY INN ROYLE   (724)543-1159
 Motel. **Address:** 405 Butler Rd 16201

WHERE TO EAT

KING'S FAMILY RESTAURANT   724/545-3340
 American. Casual Dining. **Address:** 16 Hilltop Plaza 16201

KULPSVILLE pop. 8,194
• **Part of Philadelphia area — see map p. 154**

HOLIDAY INN LANSDALE   215/368-3800
 Hotel. **Address:** 1750 Sumneytown Pike 19443

KUTZTOWN (G-10) pop. 5,012, elev. 423'

Kutztown was settled in 1771 by Pennsylvania Germans and named for founder George Kutz. An 1892 schoolhouse at White Oak and Normal avenues portrays a classroom and library of the era. On display are Keith Haring sketches, antique toys and a 1799 newspaper announcing George Washington's death. It is open Sun. 1-3, late Nov.-late Jan.; phone (610) 683-7697. Also in town is Kutztown State University.

The Kutztown Folk Festival celebrates the town's heritage with traditional food, crafts and family entertainment. The celebration begins at the Kutztown Fairgrounds the Saturday before July 4 and continues through the following Sunday; phone (888) 674-6136.

Northeast Berks Chamber of Commerce: 110 W. Main St., P.O. Box 209, Kutztown, PA 19530. **Phone:** (610) 683-8860.

Shopping: Renninger's Antique & Farmers Market, 740 Noble St., is open Fri.-Sat. (antique market Sat. only).

PENNSYLVANIA GERMAN CULTURAL HERITAGE CENTER, .5 mi. s. off US 222 at 22 Luckenbill Rd., is a museum that highlights the history of early German immigrants. On its 30 acres is an 1830 one-room schoolhouse, an 1810 stone farmhouse, a 19th-century barn and washhouse and two reconstructed 18th-century log houses. Also on the premises is a genealogy and cultural library. **Time:** Allow 1 hour minimum. **Hours:** Mon.-Fri. 10-noon and 1-4. Closed major holidays. **Cost:** Library $5. Grounds only free. Tours by donation. Reservations are required. **Phone:** (610) 683-1589. GT

LACKAWAXEN elev. 687'
• **Part of Pocono Mountains Area — see map p. 264**

1870 ROEBLING INN ON THE DELAWARE   (570)685-7900
 Historic Bed & Breakfast. **Address:** 155 Scenic Dr 18435

WHERE TO EAT

SUMMIT RESTAURANT AT MASTHOPE MOUNTAIN
570/685-1173
 American. Casual Dining. **Address:** 192 Karl Hope Blvd 18435

LAHASKA elev. 315'
• **Part of Philadelphia area — see map p. 154**

GOLDEN PLOUGH INN   215/794-4004
 Country Inn. **Address:** Rt 202 & Street Rd 18931

BUTTONWOOD GRILL   215/794-4040
 American. Casual Dining. **Address:** Rt 202 & Street Rd
18931

COCK 'N BULL RESTAURANT   215/794-4000

American
Casual Dining
$7-$34

AAA Inspector Notes: The atmosphere bustles at this cozy restaurant, a family favorite for traditional food. The Thursday King Henry's feast buffet lays out a sumptuous selection. An eclectic collection of folk art contributes to the bright appeal of the dining room. **Features:** full bar, Sunday brunch. **Reservations:** suggested, for dinner. **Address:** SR 263 & Street Rd 18931 **Location:** In Peddler's Village. Ⓛ Ⓓ CALL 👤

EARL'S BUCKS COUNTY   215/794-4020

American
Casual Dining
$9-$44

AAA Inspector Notes: This sophisticated steak and seafood house is quite upscale. A granite-topped bar with a brushed-aluminum front contributes to the cosmopolitan, urban atmosphere, and a high-energy lounge hops with live entertainment on select days. The menu features the finest Black Angus steaks from Omaha, fresh seafood flown in daily, selections from a raw bar and an extensive wine collection. A two- or three-course lunch option is available 11 am-4 pm, Monday through Saturday. **Features:** full bar, happy hour. **Reservations:** suggested, for dinner. **Address:** 2400 Street Rd 18931 **Location:** In Peddler's Village.

Ⓛ Ⓓ CALL 👤

LAKE ARIEL elev. 1,434'
• Part of Pocono Mountains Area — see map
p. 264

TWIN ROCKS DINER   570/689-9112

American
Casual Dining
$7-$15

AAA Inspector Notes: Popular with locals and tourists alike, the informal restaurant—family-owned and -operated since 1976—is welcoming to families. The menu centers on home-cooked food, which is simply prepared and flavorful. Service is friendly and attentive. **Address:** 117 Twin Rocks Rd 18436 **Location:** I-84 exit 17, just n on SR 191. Ⓑ Ⓛ Ⓓ

LAKE HARMONY elev. 1,870'
• Part of Pocono Mountains Area — see map
p. 264

NICK'S LAKE HOUSE   570/722-2500
 American. Casual Dining. **Address:** 110 S Lake Dr 18624

LAKEVILLE
• Part of Pocono Mountains Area — see map
p. 264

COVE HAVEN RESORT   570/226-4506

Resort Hotel
Rates not provided

Address: 194 Lakeview Dr 18438 **Location:** Waterfront. Just off SR 590, 7 mi w of jct US 6; on Lake Wallenpaupack. **Facility:** This spacious couples-only resort has many accommodations with in-room pools, steam baths and fireplaces. Heart-shaped hot tubs also are offered in many of the king units. 256 units. 1-2 stories (no elevator), interior/exterior corridors. **Terms:** check-in 3:30 pm, age restrictions may apply. **Dining:** 2 restaurants, nightclub, entertainment. **Pool:** heated outdoor, heated indoor. **Activities:** sauna, hot tub, steamroom, self-propelled boats, fishing, miniature golf, tennis, sledding, ice skating, bicycles, game room, lawn sports, trails, health club, massage.

SAVE 🍴 🐾 ▽ 🐟 ♿ 📶 🎿 🛄 💻

LAMAR pop. 562

HAMPTON INN & SUITES OF LAMAR   (570)726-3939
▽▽▽ Hotel. **Address:** 24 Hospitality Ln 16848

AAA Benefit:
Members save up to 10%!

QUALITY INN MILL HALL   (570)726-4901
▽▽ Hotel. **Address:** 31 Hospitality Ln 17751

LANCASTER (H-9) pop. 59,322, elev. 377'
• Hotels p. 117 • Restaurants p. 119
• Hotels & Restaurants map & index p. 145, 148
• Part of Pennsylvania Dutch Country area — see
map p. 143

During the Revolutionary War Lancaster was the largest inland city in the Colonies. It was capital of the nation for 1 day on Sept. 27, 1777, when Congress stopped in Lancaster as it fled Philadelphia after the Battle of Brandywine *(see Chadds Ford p. 55)*. Lancaster was the state capital 1799-1812.

The city is in the heart of Lancaster County and is known for its Amish and Mennonite population, its picturesque and productive farms and its heaping platters of Pennsylvania Dutch food. The Discover Lancaster Visitors Center, off US 30, presents a brief orientation to the area through multimedia displays, brochures, maps and an art gallery.

Discover Lancaster Visitors Center: 501 Greenfield Rd., Lancaster, PA 17601. **Phone:** (717) 299-8901 or (800) 723-8824.

Shopping: Farmers markets at various locations around town offer such delicacies as souse, schmiercase, cup cheese, schnitz, old-fashioned Bavarian pretzels and shoofly pie. **Central Market**, Penn Sq., has been operating since the 1730's in what is said to be the oldest farmers market building in the country. Visitors can shop for fresh fruits, vegetables, flowers, meats and baked goods. The site is open Tues. and Fri. 6-4 and Sat. 6-2.

Lancaster has a large number of factory outlets, including the SAVE Tanger Outlet Center, featuring

(See maps & indexes p. 145, 148.)

more than 85 outlet stores and **Rockvale Square Factory Outlet Village**, at SR 30E and SR 896, another large center with nearly 80 factory stores. Several specialty shops are located on Lincoln Highway E.

HANDS-ON HOUSE, CHILDREN'S MUSEUM is at 721 Landis Valley Rd. The museum encourages learning through imaginative play. Interactive exhibits include a child-size grocery store, a post office, a machine shop and assembly line as well as an indoor farm exhibit with a tractor and cow. The Clubhouse offers changing activities. Face painting and a play garden also are offered.

Picnic facilities are limited; phone ahead for availability. **Time:** Allow 2 hours minimum. **Hours:** Mon.-Sat. 10-5, Sun. noon-5, Memorial Day-Labor Day; Tues.-Fri. 11-4, Sat. 10-5, Sun. noon-5, rest of year. Closed major holidays. **Cost:** $9.50. Children under 16 must be with an adult. **Phone:** (717) 569-5437. Ⓐ

LANDIS VALLEY VILLAGE & FARM MUSEUM is 2.5 mi. n. on Oregon Pike (SR 272), following signs to 2451 Kissel Hill Rd. This living-history complex interprets 1740-1940 Pennsylvania German rural life with a mixture of modern and historic buildings on more than 100 acres. An orientation film program and exhibits are offered at the visitor center.

Brothers Henry and George Landis, both devoted collectors of historic memorabilia, founded the museum in 1925 in the barn of their Landis Valley homestead in order to preserve the heritage and culture of the Pennsylvania German region and their family; their collection eventually grew to more than 100,000 items.

From arrowheads gathered in their childhood, the brothers' collections expanded to include decorative arts and examples of early implements and tools used by their farming ancestors that were rapidly being replaced by more modern, mass-produced items. The museum continued to expand and eventually historic buildings (and some new ones) were acquired and moved to the site.

At the 1870s Landis Brothers House visitors can see the brothers' Victorian home interpreted as it might have appeared around the turn of the 20th century. The house originally belonged to the brothers' parents. The Erisman House, which dates

to the 1800s, was moved from Lancaster to the village. In its current setting it is interpreted as the modest home of a seamstress.

Though built in 1941, the stone Tavern, with its huge kitchen and nearby barroom, was constructed to resemble one of the inns prevalent in this area in the early 19th century. An exhibit of Pennsylvania rifles, powder horns, handguns and gunsmithing tools can be seen at the Gun Shop, another of the "newer" buildings. The Country Store is stocked with items typical of a rural store of the early 1900s. Other buildings include a blacksmith shop, a schoolhouse and a barn.

Interpreters dressed in period clothing are stationed at many of the buildings and provide insights into everyday life. Traditional craft and trades demonstrations also are given. Special events are held throughout the year.

Time: Allow 2 hours minimum. **Hours:** Tues.-Sat. 9-5, Sun. noon-5, mid-Mar. through Dec. 31; Wed.-Sat. 9-5, Sun. noon-5, rest of year. Closed Jan. 1, Martin Luther King Jr. Day, Presidents Day, Columbus Day, Veterans Day, Thanksgiving, day after Thanksgiving and Christmas. Phone ahead to confirm schedule. **Cost:** $12; $10 (ages 65+); $8 (ages 3-11). Additional fees may be charged during special events. **Phone:** (717) 569-0401. Ⓐ

PRESIDENT JAMES BUCHANAN'S WHEATLAND is at 1120 Marietta Ave. (SR 23). Wheatland, home of the 15th U.S. president James Buchanan from 1848-68, highlights the life of America's only bachelor president and the only Pennsylvanian to hold the office. During Buchanan's presidential years the home served as his personal retreat and offered respite from public life. He conducted his 1856 campaign from here, and it also served as Democratic Party headquarters. From the front porch he accepted his party's nomination and the general election results.

Tours of the 1828 Federal-style mansion include public and private rooms furnished in period. Interpreters in period dress help illustrate Buchanan's life and times. The grounds include gardens, a carriage house, ice house and privy. Living history and Yuletide tours also are offered.

Time: Allow 1 hour minimum. **Hours:** House tours are offered Mon.-Sat. on the hour 10-3. Yuletide program offered Nov.-Dec. Closed week before Thanksgiving, Dec. 31-early Jan. and major holidays except Presidents Day. Phone ahead to confirm schedule. **Cost:** (includes LancasterHistory.org galleries at 230 N. President Ave.) $15; $13 (ages 65+); $8 (ages 11-17); $35 (family, two adults and two children). Reservations are recommended. **Phone:** (717) 392-4633. GT

(See maps & indexes p. 145, 148.)

AUSTRALIAN WALKABOUT INN B&B   (717)464-0707 **22**
◆◆◆ Historic Bed & Breakfast. **Address:** 837 Village Rd 17602

COMFORT INN LANCASTER - ROCKVALE OUTLETS
(717)293-9500 **20**
◆◆◆ Hotel. **Address:** 24 S Willowdale Dr 17602

COMFORT SUITES AMISH COUNTRY   (717)299-7000 **15**
◆◆◆ Hotel. **Address:** 2343 Lincoln Hwy E (US 30 E) 17602

CONTINENTAL INN   (717)299-0421 **16**

◆◆◆
Hotel
$75-$145

Address: 2285 Lincoln Hwy E 17602 **Location:** On US 30 (Lincoln Hwy), 5 mi e. Adjacent to an amusement park. **Facility:** 165 units. 2 stories (no elevator), interior/exterior corridors. **Pool:** outdoor, heated indoor. **Activities:** sauna, hot tub, tennis, playground, game room, lawn sports, picnic facilities. **Guest Services:** coin laundry. (See ad p. 118.)

SAVE 🍽 🍸 🏊 BIZ 🛜 ✕ 🔌 💻

CORK FACTORY HOTEL   (717)735-2075 **8**
◆◆◆ Historic Hotel. **Address:** 480 New Holland Ave, Suite 3000 17602

COUNTRY INN & SUITES BY CARLSON
(717)299-4460 **17**

◆◆◆
Hotel
$89-$299

Address: 2260 Lincoln Hwy E 17602 **Location:** On US 30 (Lincoln Hwy), 5 mi e. Located in a commercial area. **Facility:** 78 units, some two bedrooms. 4 stories, interior corridors. **Terms:** check-in 4 pm, cancellation fee imposed. **Amenities:** safes. **Pool:** heated indoor. **Activities:** hot tub, exercise room. **Guest Services:** coin laundry. **Featured Amenity:** continental breakfast.

SAVE 🍽 CALL ♿ 🏊 👨‍👩‍👧 BIZ 🛜 ✕ 🔌 💻 / SOME UNITS HS

COUNTRY INN OF LANCASTER   717/393-3413 **13**

◆◆◆
Hotel
Rates not provided

Address: 2133 Lincoln Hwy E 17602 On US 30 (Lincoln Hwy), 4.5 mi e. Located in a commercial area. **Facility:** 125 units. 2 stories, interior corridors. **Pool:** heated indoor. **Activities:** hot tub. **Guest Services:** complimentary and valet laundry. **Featured Amenity:** continental breakfast.

SAVE 🍽 🚶 🍸 CALL ♿ 🏊 BIZ 🛜 ✕ 🔌 💻 / SOME UNITS 🍳

COUNTRY LIVING INN   717/295-7295 **7**
◆◆ Country Inn. **Address:** 2406 Old Philadelphia Pike 17602

COURTYARD BY MARRIOTT-LANCASTER
(717)393-3600 **6**

◆◆◆
Hotel
$94-$287

COURTYARD Marriott.
AAA Benefit: Members save 5% or more!

Address: 1931 Hospitality Dr 17601 **Location:** US 30 (Lincoln Hwy) exit Greenfield Rd, just n, then just e on Hempstead Rd. **Facility:** 133 units. 5 stories, interior corridors. **Terms:** cancellation fee imposed. **Pool:** heated indoor. **Activities:** hot tub, exercise room. **Guest Services:** valet and coin laundry, boarding pass kiosk.

SAVE 🍴 🍸 CALL ♿ 🏊 👨‍👩‍👧 BIZ 🛜 ✕ 🔌 💻 💻 / SOME UNITS 🐾

▼ See AAA listing p. 48 ▼

The Adults-only, Grand King room type

▼ See AAA listing p. 117 ▼

DOUBLETREE RESORT BY HILTON HOTEL LANCASTER   (717)464-2711   **23**

WWW
Resort Hotel
$109-$180

AAA Benefit:
Members save 5% or more!

Address: 2400 Willow Street Pike 17602 **Location:** On US 222, 3.8 mi s. **Facility:** Guests can enjoy upscale guest suites while also partaking in the extensive recreational facilities, including a 35-acre, nine-hole golf course and a water park. 185 units, some two bedrooms. 5 stories, interior corridors. **Terms:** check-in 4 pm, 1-7 night minimum stay, cancellation fee imposed. **Pool:** heated indoor. **Activities:** hot tub, regulation golf, recreation programs, game room, exercise room. **Guest Services:** valet and coin laundry, area transportation.

[SAVE] [🔧] [❗] [👤] [🍽] CALL [♿] [🛏] [👪] [BIZ]
[📶] [✉] [🔒] [💻]

DOUBLETREE RESORT
BY HILTON
LANCASTER

Enjoy Hilton hospitality, in the heart of the Pennsylvania Dutch Country.

EDEN RESORT & SUITES, BW PREMIER COLLECTION
(717)569-6444   **4**

WWWW Boutique Resort Hotel. **Address:** 222 Eden Rd 17601

AAA Benefit: Members save 5% to 15% and earn 10% bonus points!

FAIRFIELD INN & SUITES BY MARRIOTT LANCASTER
(717)581-1800   **2**

WWWW Hotel. **Address:** 150 Granite Run Dr 17601

AAA Benefit: Members save 5% or more!

FAIRFIELD INN & SUITES BY MARRIOTT LANCASTER EAST AT THE OUTLETS   (717)295-9100   **18**

WWWW Hotel. **Address:** 2270 Lincoln Hwy E 17602

AAA Benefit: Members save 5% or more!

FULTON STEAMBOAT INN   717/299-9999   **19**

WWWW Hotel. **Address:** 2510 Lincoln Hwy E 17602

HAMPTON INN-LANCASTER   (717)299-1200   **5**

WWWW Hotel. **Address:** 545 Greenfield Rd 17601

AAA Benefit: Members save up to 10%!

HAWTHORN SUITES BY WYNDHAM
(717)290-7100   **12**

WWW
Hotel
$90-$170

Address: 2045 Lincoln Hwy 17602 **Location:** Jct US 30 (Lincoln Hwy). Located in a commercial area. **Facility:** 73 units. 3 stories, interior corridors. **Terms:** check-in 4 pm, cancellation fee imposed. **Activities:** exercise room. **Guest Services:** valet and coin laundry. **Featured Amenity:** continental breakfast.

[SAVE] [👤] CALL [♿] [👪] [BIZ] [📶]
[✉] [🔒] [🍽] [💻] /SOME UNITS [🐾]

(See maps & indexes p. 145, 148.)

HERITAGE HOTEL LANCASTER   (717)898-2431

Hotel
$135-$165

Address: 500 Centerville Rd 17601 **Location:** 5 mi w on US 30 (Lincoln Hwy) exit Centerville Rd, just nw. Located in a commercial area next to dinner theater. **Facility:** 165 units. 3 stories, interior corridors. **Terms:** 3 day cancellation notice-fee imposed. **Pool:** outdoor. **Activities:** exercise room.

HILTON GARDEN INN LANCASTER   (717)560-0880

Hotel. **Address:** 101 Granite Run Dr 17601

AAA Benefit: Members save up to 10%!

HOMEWOOD SUITES BY HILTON LANCASTER   (717)381-4400

Extended Stay Hotel. **Address:** 200 Granite Run Dr 17601

AAA Benefit: Members save up to 10%!

KING'S COTTAGE BED AND BREAKFAST   (717)397-1017

Historic Bed & Breakfast. **Address:** 1049 E King St 17602

LANCASTER ARTS HOTEL   (717)299-3000

Historic Boutique Hotel
$169-$369

Address: 300 Harrisburg Ave 17603 **Location:** US 30 (Lincoln Hwy) exit Harrisburg Pike, 1.5 mi s; just n of jct Mulberry St. **Facility:** This former tobacco warehouse features comfortable rooms that highlight the unique character of the building. Enjoy the large doses of local artwork creatively displayed throughout the property. 63 units. 5 stories, interior corridors. *Bath:* shower only. **Terms:** cancellation fee imposed. **Activities:** exercise room. **Guest Services:** valet laundry. **Featured Amenity:** continental breakfast.

THE LANCASTER BED AND BREAKFAST   717/293-1723

Historic Bed & Breakfast. **Address:** 1105 E King St 17602

LANCASTER MARRIOTT AT PENN SQUARE   (717)239-1600

Hotel
$125-$303

AAA Benefit: Members save 5% or more!

Address: 25 S Queen St 17603 **Location:** US 222 S to US 30 (Lincoln Hwy) exit Walnut St, left on Prince St, then left on King St. **Facility:** 301 units. 19 stories, interior corridors. **Parking:** on-site (fee) and valet. **Terms:** check-in 4 pm, cancellation fee imposed. **Amenities:** safes. **Pool:** heated indoor. **Activities:** exercise room. **Guest Services:** valet laundry.

WINGATE BY WYNDHAM LANCASTER   (717)299-6604

Hotel
$109-$205

Address: 2110 Lincoln Hwy E (Rt 30 E) 17602 **Location:** On US 30 (Lincoln Hwy), 4.3 mi e. **Facility:** 70 units. 3 stories, interior corridors. **Amenities:** safes. **Activities:** hot tub, exercise room. **Featured Amenity:** full hot breakfast.

WHERE TO EAT

ARTHUR'S TERRACE RESTAURANT   717/569-6444
American. Casual Dining. **Address:** 222 Eden Rd 17601

THE BELVEDERE INN   717/394-2422
Continental. Fine Dining. **Address:** 402 N Queen St 17603

THE BRASSERIE RESTAURANT & BAR   717/299-1694

American
Casual Dining
$10-$29

AAA Inspector Notes: *Historic.* This restaurant in a converted 1925 home contains five small dining rooms and a bar that once was the judge's bench from the old city courthouse. Menu items typically reflect casual American cuisine with some specialty house options, including the award-winning baked tomato bisque, gourmet burgers and crab cakes. The outdoor patio in the back is a wonderful place to soak in some sun while enjoying your meal in the summer months. **Features:** full bar. **Reservations:** suggested, weekends. **Address:** 1679 Lincoln Hwy E 17602 **Location:** 2 mi e on SR 462.

CHECKERS BISTRO   717/509-1069
French. Casual Dining. **Address:** 398 Harrisburg Ave #700 17603

DJ'S TASTE OF THE 50S   717/509-5050
American. Casual Dining. **Address:** 2410 Old Philadelphia Pike 17602

EL SERRANO RESTAURANTE   717/397-6191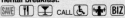
Mexican. Casual Dining. **Address:** 2151 Columbia Ave 17603

FOUR54 GRILL   717/390-2626
American. Quick Serve. **Address:** 454 New Holland Ave 17602

GIBRALTAR   717/397-2790
Seafood. Fine Dining. **Address:** 931 Harrisburg Pike 17603

HORSE INN RESTAURANT   717/392-5528
American. Casual Dining. **Address:** 540 E Fulton St 17602

(See maps & indexes p. 145, 148.)

ISAAC'S FAMOUS GRILLED SANDWICHES

Deli Sandwiches. Quick Serve.

LOCATIONS:
Address: 1559 Manheim Pike 17601 **Phone:** 717/560-7774
Address: 25 N Queen St, Suite 101 17603
Phone: 717/394-5544
Address: 245 Centerville Rd 17603 **Phone:** 717/393-1199
Address: 565 Greenfield Rd 17601 **Phone:** 717/393-6067

ISSEI NOODLE   717/449-6800 (15)

Asian Noodles. Casual Dining. **Address:** 44 N Queen St 17603

LANCASTER BREWING COMPANY   717/391-6258 (8)

Regional American. Casual Dining. **Address:** 302 N Plum St 17603

LANCASTER BREWING COMPANY TAPROOM & GRILL
717/826-9555 (12)

American. Brewpub. **Address:** 2323 Lincoln Hwy E 17602

MANOR BUFFET   717/290-8181 (13)

Asian. Buffet Style. **Address:** 2090 Lincoln Hwy E 17602

THE PRESSROOM   717/399-5400 (16)

American. Casual Dining. **Address:** 26-28 W King St 17603

RICE & NOODLES   717/481-7461 (2)

Vietnamese. Quick Serve. **Address:** 1238 Lititz Pike 17601

STOCKYARD INN   717/394-7975 (4)

Steak
Seafood
Fine Dining
$8-$45

AAA Inspector Notes: The former home of President James Buchanan, this converted restaurant carries out a Colonial theme with the help of large murals, candlelight, background music and freshly cut flowers. Expect traditional cuisine such as chicken croquettes and baked flounder. **Features:** full bar, patio dining. **Reservations:** suggested. **Address:** 1147 Lititz Pike 17601 **Location:** 0.5 mi s of US 30 (Lincoln Hwy) on US 222 S. L D

TOBIAS S FROGG   717/394-8366 (18)

American. Casual Dining. **Address:** 1766 Columbia Ave 17603

TONY WANG'S CHINESE RESTAURANT
717/399-1915 (14)

Chinese
Casual Dining
$6-$24

AAA Inspector Notes: This quaint storefront serves cuisine inspired by Cantonese specialties; an extensive takeout menu is offered. Among tasty examples are sliced chicken with broccoli in garlic sauce and General Tso's chicken, in which large chunks of marinated spring chicken are deep fried and sauteed with scorched red peppers in a tangy sauce. Bring your favorite wine or pop into the beer shop next door if you'd like to enjoy a glass with your meal. **Reservations:** suggested, weekends. **Address:** 2217 Lincoln Hwy E (Rt 30) 17602 **Location:** On US 30 (Lincoln Hwy), 4.7 mi e. L D

VENICE PIZZA & PASTA   717/396-1100 (1)

Italian. Quick Serve. **Address:** 3079 Columbia Ave 17603

LANGHORNE (A-12) pop. 1,622, elev. 103'
• Hotels & Restaurants map & index p. 192
• Part of Philadelphia area — see map p. 154

SESAME PLACE is at 100 Sesame Rd. This family theme park based on the show "Sesame Street" offers a variety of interactive attractions for all ages. The fun includes the Neighborhood Street Party parade, water play activities in The Count's Splash Castle, live stage shows, the Vapor Trail roller coaster, character meet-and-greets, and exciting rides in Elmo's World. Oscar's Wacky Taxi roller coaster debuts for the 2018 season.

Swimwear is required for water attractions. Stroller, wheelchair and locker rentals are available. Pets (with the exception of service animals) are not permitted. **Time:** Allow 5 hours minimum. **Hours:** Opens daily at 10, early June-Labor Day; Fri.-Sun. (also Memorial Day) at 10, in May; Sat.-Sun. at 10, day after Labor Day-Oct. 31; select days at 1, mid-Nov. through Dec. 31. Closing times vary. Phone ahead to confirm schedule. **Cost:** $70; free (ages 0-1). Prices may vary. Character dining is available for an additional fee. **Parking:** $18-$30. **Phone:** (215) 702-3566.

COURTYARD BY MARRIOTT PHILADELPHIA-LANGHORNE
(215)945-7980

Hotel. **Address:** 5 E Cabot Blvd 19047

AAA Benefit:
Members save 5%
or more!

HOLIDAY INN EXPRESS-LANGHORNE OXFORD VALLEY   215/757-4500

Hotel
Rates not provided

Address: 3101 Cabot Blvd W 19047 **Location:** I-95 exit 46A (Oxford Valley Rd), just e off US 1 N; 0.5 mi n of Sesame Place. Located in a commercial area. **Facility:** 88 units. 4 stories, interior corridors. **Pool:** outdoor. **Activities:** exercise room. **Guest Services:** area transportation. **Featured Amenity:** full hot breakfast.

RED ROOF INN PHILADELPHIA OXFORD VALLEY
(215)750-6200

Motel
$69-$140

Address: 3100 Cabot Blvd W 19047 **Location:** I-95 exit 46A (Oxford Valley Rd), just e off US 1 N; 0.5 mi n of Sesame Place. **Facility:** 91 units. 3 stories, exterior corridors. **Amenities:** safes.

(See map & index p. 192.)

RESIDENCE INN BY MARRIOTT PHILADELPHIA LANGHORNE
(215)946-6500

Residence Inn Marriott

Extended Stay Hotel
$82-$416

AAA Benefit: Members save 5% or more!

Address: 15 E Cabot Blvd 19047 **Location:** I-95 exit 46A (Oxford Valley Rd), just e off US 1 N; 0.5 mi n of Sesame Place. **Facility:** 100 units, some two bedrooms, efficiencies and kitchens. 4 stories, interior corridors. **Terms:** cancellation fee imposed. **Pool:** heated indoor. **Activities:** hot tub, picnic facilities, exercise room. **Guest Services:** valet and coin laundry, area transportation. **Featured Amenity:** breakfast buffet.

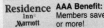

SHERATON BUCKS COUNTY HOTEL
(215)547-4100

Hotel
$119-$229

Sheraton

AAA Benefit: Members save 5% or more!

Address: 400 Oxford Valley Rd 19047 **Location:** I-95 exit 46A (Oxford Valley Rd), 0.8 mi e to exit off US 1 N. Opposite Sesame Place. **Facility:** 186 units. 15 stories, interior corridors. **Terms:** cancellation fee imposed. **Amenities:** safes. **Pool:** heated indoor. **Activities:** hot tub, exercise room. **Guest Services:** valet laundry, area transportation.

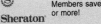

SPRINGHILL SUITES BY MARRIOTT   (215)891-5501
▼▼▼ Hotel. **Address:** 200 N Buckstown Dr 19047

AAA Benefit: Members save 5% or more!

WHERE TO EAT

J. B. DAWSON'S   215/702-8119 76
▼▼ American. Casual Dining. **Address:** 92 N Flowers Mill Rd 19047

LANSDALE pop. 16,269
• Part of Philadelphia area — see map p. 154

COURTYARD BY MARRIOTT PHILADELPHIA LANSDALE
(215)412-8686
▼▼▼ Hotel. **Address:** 1737 Sumneytown Pike 19446

AAA Benefit: Members save 5% or more!

HOMEWOOD SUITES BY HILTON-LANSDALE   (215)362-6400
▼▼▼ Extended Stay Hotel. **Address:** 1200 Pennbrook Pkwy 19446

AAA Benefit: Members save up to 10%!

WHERE TO EAT

UMAI JAPANESE RESTAURANT   215/855-5544
▼▼ Japanese. Casual Dining. **Address:** 220 Pennbrook Pkwy 19446

LANSFORD (F-10) pop. 3,941, elev. 1,134'
• Part of Pocono Mountains Area — see map p. 264

 NO. 9 MINE & MUSEUM is off SR 209, following signs to 9 Dock St. A battery-operated mine car transports visitors 1,600 feet horizontally into the mountainside where anthracite coal was mined 1855-1972. No. 9, owned by Lehigh Coal & Navigation Co., was said to be the world's oldest continuously operated coal mine.

You'll need to duck and bend over as you climb into the bright yellow metal mine car, which noisily clanks and rumbles its way into the dark, dank, chilly world of the coal miners and their search for black gold.

A guided walking tour leads down a maze of narrow, dimly lit passageways, as the dangers and hard work required to bring the coal to the surface are related. This is a no-frills tour. Deposits of rust can be seen above and on the sides of the walls, and water drips, forming puddles of water on the floor.

You'll see the muleway (the path taken by the mules that were lowered into the mine to haul the heavy carloads of coal out before electric/battery motors came into use); a "hospital" cut into the stone of the mine (more like a room with a cot, some chairs, bandages, crutches and blankets); and the 900-foot-deep elevator shaft used to transfer the miners and loaded coal cars to the surface.

Above ground, the museum is housed in a former wash shanty, where miners would hang their clothes from the ceiling. You'll also see a kitchen typical of a miner's home, photographs, tools and mining memorabilia.

Note: A jacket or sweater and comfortable closed-toe walking shoes are recommended; the mine temperature averages 52 to 54 degrees Fahrenheit. **Time:** Allow 2 hours minimum. **Hours:** Museum open Wed.-Sun. 11-4, June-Aug.; Fri.-Sun. 11-4, in May; Sat.-Sun. 11-4, Sept.-Oct. Mine tours depart on the hour 11-3 (weather permitting). Phone ahead to confirm schedule. **Cost:** (includes mine and museum) $10; $6.50 (ages 5-10); free (ages 0-4). Museum only, $3. **Phone:** (570) 645-7074. GT

LATROBE pop. 8,338

SPRINGHILL SUITES BY MARRIOTT LATROBE   (724)537-7800
▼▼▼ Hotel. **Address:** 115 Arnold Palmer Dr 15650

AAA Benefit: Members save 5% or more!

WHERE TO EAT

CHEF MARK'S PALATE   724/879-8146
▼▼ American. Casual Dining. **Address:** 1032 US 30 15650

DENUNZIO'S ITALIAN CHOPHOUSE AND SINATRA BAR
724/539-3980
▼▼ Italian. Casual Dining. **Address:** 148 Aviation Ln 15650

DISALVO'S STATION RESTAURANT   724/539-0500
💎💎 Italian. Casual Dining. **Address:** 325 McKinley Ave 15650

LAUGHLINTOWN (H-3) elev. 1,289'

Laughlintown is part of the Laurel Highlands *(see place listing this page).*

LAUREL HIGHLANDS

In Southwestern Pennsylvania, the Laurel Highlands cover a 3,000-square-mile region in the Allegheny Mountain foothills, which includes Fayette, Somerset and Westmoreland counties. Once the exclusive country retreat of Pittsburgh's wealthy industrialists, it is now a popular four-season resort area. Its mountain vistas, rolling countryside and recreational rivers yield a wide range of activities and experiences.

Inspired by the surrounding natural beauty, renowned architect Frank Lloyd Wright left his touch on the area with two landmark homes, Fallingwater *(see attraction listing p. 132)* and House on Kentuck Knob *(see attraction listing p. 56).* Nearby is Fort Necessity National Battlefield, built by George Washington in 1754 *(see place listing p. 76).*

Excellent white-water rafting is possible on the Youghiogheny River, which runs southeastward from McKeesport to the Maryland border *(see Ohiopyle p. 140).* Boating on Conemaugh Lake and Youghiogheny Reservoir also is popular. The Laurel and Chestnut ridges of the Allegheny Mountains provide for excellent stream fishing in season as well as downhill and cross-country skiing in winter. The region also offers more than 25 hiking, bicycling and horse trails and some 30 golf courses. Cyclists can travel 150 continuous miles on the Great Allegheny Passage *(see Insider Info p. 140),* which runs through the heart of the Laurel Highlands, connecting Cumberland, Md., to the Pittsburgh riverfront.

In warmer months photographers appreciate the profusion of wildflowers; mountain laurel blooms at higher elevations for about 3 weeks in June. The fall foliage is at its peak mid- to late October. Views are dramatic along the Laurel Highlands Scenic Byway—begin at Farmington, follow SR 381 north through Ohiopyle State Park onto SR 711, continue north at Normalville, then end the trip with a stop for ice cream in historic Ligonier. Forbes State Forest in the central highlands and Mount Davis, the state's highest point, also provide great vistas.

Another scenic route, the Pennsylvania Turnpike/I-76, traverses the region. Exits 67, 75, 91 and 110 off I-76, and exit 27 off I-70 provide direct access to Laurel Highlands.

Laurel Highlands Visitors Bureau: 120 E. Main St., Ligonier, PA 15658. **Phone:** (724) 238-5661 or (800) 333-5661.

LEBANON (LEBANON COUNTY) (H-9)
pop. 25,477, elev. 466'

A community of German agricultural and English industrial origins, Lebanon was founded in 1750 and named after the White Mountain of Biblical times.

Lebanon's historic churches include the 1792 Tabor United Church of Christ at 10th and Walnut streets and the 1760 Salem Lutheran Church at Eighth and Willow streets. Both churches are open for tours by appointment.

North of Lebanon off SR 72 at Tunnel Hill Road is Union Canal Tunnel, one of the oldest tunnels in the United States. When it was completed in 1827, the tunneling through 729 feet of rock was considered an engineering marvel. The feat completed the canal between Harrisburg and Reading.

Visit Lebanon Valley Visitors Center: 31 S. 8th St., Lebanon, PA 17042. **Phone:** (717) 277-0100.

LEBANON COUNTY HISTORICAL SOCIETY is at 924 Cumberland St. The organization's Stoy Museum, which can only be seen on a guided tour, contains such reconstructed rooms as a drugstore, one-room schoolhouse, Victorian parlor and general store as well as exhibits about early industries and regional crafts. The front part of the building, constructed in the 1780s as a residence, was used from 1813-1818 as the county courthouse, where James Buchanan, the 15th U.S. president, practiced law as a young attorney. The building also houses the Hauck Research Archives.

Time: Allow 1 hour, 30 minutes minimum. **Hours:** Building open Tues.-Fri. 10-5, Sat. 10-2. Ninety-minute museum tours are given Sat. at 11 and by appointment. Closed major holidays. **Cost:** Museum $6; $5 (ages 65+); $3 (ages 6-17). Library $6. **Phone:** (717) 272-1473. GT

BERRY PATCH BED AND BREAKFAST   (717)865-7219
💎💎💎 Bed & Breakfast. **Address:** 115 Moore Rd 17046

WHERE TO EAT

GIN MILL   717/273-2729
💎💎 American. Casual Dining. **Address:** 324 E Cumberland St 17042

LEECHBURG pop. 2,156

KING'S FAMILY RESTAURANT   724/842-0361
💎💎 American. Casual Dining. **Address:** 315 Hyde Park Rd 15656

LEHIGHTON pop. 5,500
• Part of Pocono Mountains Area — see map p. 264

COUNTRY INN & SUITES BY CARLSON   (610)379-5066
💎💎💎
Hotel
$99-$300

Address: 1619 Interchange Rd 18235 **Location:** I-476 (Pennsylvania Tpke NE Ext) exit 74 (US 209), just w. **Facility:** 63 units. 3 stories, interior corridors. **Terms:** cancellation fee imposed. **Pool:** heated indoor. **Activities:** hot tub, exercise room. **Guest Services:** coin laundry. **Featured Amenity:** continental breakfast.

HAMPTON INN LEHIGHTON (JIM THORPE AREA)
(610)377-3400

WWWW Hotel. **Address:** 877 Interchange Rd 18235

AAA Benefit: Members save up to 10%!

PJ WHELIHAN'S PUB & RESTAURANT 610/377-1819
WW American. Casual Dining. **Address:** 101 Harrity Rd 18235

LEMONT FURNACE (I-2) elev. 1,040'

COAL AND COKE HERITAGE CENTER on US 119 at 2201 University Dr., on the grounds of Penn State Fayette, The Eberly Campus, in the lower level of the library. This museum chronicles the local coal and coke industries, which fueled the Pittsburgh steel industry, through an extensive collection of items donated by families of former industry employees. The technical aspect of the industry is presented along with the human element of the workers—the problems and opportunities they encountered, the communities ("patches") they formed, and the ethnic and cultural backgrounds of the immigrants as well as the African Americans who arrived from the South. The collection includes artifacts, clothing and photographs.

Among the items in the research archives are documents, maps, newspapers and oral histories. **Time:** Allow 30 minutes minimum. **Hours:** Mon.-Fri. 10-3 when school is in session, mid-Jan. to mid-Dec. Research archives by appointment. Phone ahead to confirm schedule. **Cost:** Donations. **Phone:** (724) 430-4158.

LEOLA (H-10) elev. 430'
• Hotels & Restaurants map & index p. 145, 148
• Part of Pennsylvania Dutch Country area — see map p. 143

MASCOT ROLLER MILLS AND RESSLER FAMILY HOME is 3.4 mi. s.e. off SR 23 to jct. Stumptown and Newport rds. A mill has been on this site since the mid-1730s, and it was owned and operated by three generations of the Ressler family 1865-1977. The mill also acted as the town's post office 1890-1934.

Guided tours of the operational mill offer information about early rural life as well as the milling process; old equipment can be seen. The 1855 house features period antiques. **Time:** Allow 1 hour, 30 minutes minimum. **Hours:** Mon.-Sat. 10-4, May 1 to mid-Oct. Closed major holidays. **Cost:** Free. **Phone:** (717) 656-7616. GT

🐾 **Booth or table?**

AAA.com/travelguides/restaurants

THE INN AT LEOLA VILLAGE (717)656-7002 ⑳

WWWWW
Historic Boutique Hotel
$169-$369

Address: 38 Deborah Dr 17540 **Location:** On SR 23; center. Located in a commercial area. **Facility:** A romantic country-inn ambience characterizes this property. Each room is individually decorated with elegant wood furnishings and luxe bedding. A full-service spa and a restaurant are on site. 62 units, some two bedrooms and kitchens. 1-3 stories (no elevator), interior/exterior corridors. **Terms:** cancellation fee imposed, resort fee. **Amenities:** *Some;* safes. **Dining:** 2 restaurants, also, TE, see separate listing. **Pool:** outdoor. **Activities:** sauna, exercise room, spa. **Guest Services:** valet and coin laundry, area transportation.

GRACIE'S ON WEST MAIN 717/556-0004 ㉕
WW American. Casual Dining. **Address:** 264 W Main St 17540

TÈ 717/556-8715 ㉔

WWWWW
Italian Fine Dining
$129-$189

AAA Inspector Notes: In an intimate dining space formerly used for afternoon tea, guests can choose from either a five- or nine-course prix fixe menu of innovative Italian cuisine. Extras that further enhance the experience include a selection of cheeses from a roving cart, expert wine pairings and multiple chef accoutrements between courses. A highly refined staff pampers guests while artfully timing each course for a relaxing and memorable meal. **Features:** full bar. **Reservations:** required. Formal attire. **Address:** 38 Deborah Dr 17540 **Location:** On SR 23; center; in The Inn at Leola Village. 📧 D CALL ♿

LEVITTOWN pop. 52,983
• Hotels & Restaurants map & index p. 192
• Part of Philadelphia area — see map p. 154

RAMADA INN (215)946-1100 ㊶

WW
Hotel
$69-$119

Address: 6201 Bristol Pike 19057 **Location:** I-276 (Pennsylvania Tpke) exit 358, just n. Located in a commercial area. **Facility:** 120 units. 2 stories (no elevator), interior corridors. **Amenities:** safes. **Pool:** outdoor. **Activities:** playground, exercise room. **Guest Services:** coin laundry. **Featured Amenity:** breakfast buffet.

LEWISBURG (F-8) pop. 5,792, elev. 460'
• Hotels p. 124 • Restaurants p. 124

Lewisburg, on the West Branch of the Susquehanna River, is noted for its late Federal and Victorian architecture. It also is a college town: Bucknell University is a private liberal arts college.

Susquehanna River Valley Visitors Bureau: 81 Hafer Rd., Lewisburg, PA 17837. **Phone:** (570) 524-7234 or (800) 525-7320.

Shopping: An interesting shopping center is Shops at Country Cupboard, 3 miles north on SR 15. It offers gifts, home decor items, greenhouse and outdoor items, and specialty foods. Another unusual collection of shops is Ard's Farm, 6 miles west of SR 15 on SR 45, offering gourmet foods and local produce. Roller Mills Antique Center, 517 St. Mary St., features 400 antiques dealers in a restored 1883 flour mill. The Street of Shops, in a restored woolen mill at 100 N. Water St., is home to 375 unique boutique-style shops offering artwork, handcrafted items, collectibles, antiques and vintage furniture.

BEST WESTERN PLUS COUNTRY CUPBOARD INN
(570)524-5500

Hotel
$120-$260

 Best Western PLUS

AAA Benefit: Members save 5% to 15% and earn 10% bonus points!

Address: 7701 Westbranch Hwy (US 15) 17837 **Location:** I-80 exit 210A (US 15/New Columbia), 4.8 mi s on US 15. Located in a commercial area. **Facility:** 136 units. 3 stories, interior corridors. **Terms:** 3 day cancellation notice-fee imposed. **Dining:** Country Cupboard Restaurant, see separate listing. **Pool:** heated outdoor, heated indoor. **Activities:** sauna, hot tub, exercise room. **Guest Services:** valet and coin laundry. **Featured Amenity:** full hot breakfast.

COMFORT SUITES
(570)524-8000
 Hotel. **Address:** 4775 Westbranch Hwy 17837

COUNTRY INN & SUITES BY CARLSON
(570)524-6600

Hotel
$99-$170

Address: 134 Walter Dr 17837 **Location:** I-80 exit 210A (US 15/New Columbia), 4.8 mi s on US 15. **Facility:** 81 units. 3 stories, interior corridors. **Terms:** cancellation fee imposed. **Pool:** heated indoor. **Activities:** hot tub, exercise room. **Guest Services:** valet and coin laundry. **Featured Amenity:** breakfast buffet.

HAMPTON INN
(570)522-8500

Hotel
$129-$199

 Hampton by HILTON

AAA Benefit: Members save up to 10%!

Address: 140 International Dr 17837 **Location:** I-80 exit 210A (US 15/New Columbia), 5 mi s, then just w. **Facility:** 70 units. 4 stories, interior corridors. **Terms:** 1-7 night minimum stay, cancellation fee imposed. **Pool:** heated indoor. **Activities:** hot tub, exercise room. **Guest Services:** valet and coin laundry. **Featured Amenity:** continental breakfast.

 **WHERE TO EAT**

COUNTRY CUPBOARD RESTAURANT
570/523-3211
 American. Casual Dining. **Address:** 101 Hafer Rd 17837

ELIZABETH'S AN AMERICAN BISTRO
570/523-8088
 American. Casual Dining. **Address:** 412 Market St 17837

LEWISBURG HOTEL
570/523-7800
 American. Casual Dining. **Address:** 136 Market St 17837

REBA & PANCHO'S A MODERN AMERICAN RESTAURANT
570/522-7006
 New American. Casual Dining. **Address:** 2006 W Market St 17837

TEMPERANCE HOUSE
570/524-2558
 American. Casual Dining. **Address:** 50 N 2nd St 17837

LEWISTOWN (G-7) pop. 8,338, elev. 495'

Lewistown, named in honor of Quaker legislator William Lewis, was a thriving Native American community prior to its incorporation in 1795. European immigrants later settled in the region; their traces are still visible at many local historical sites. The borough lies within a scenic region: To the east is Lewistown Narrows, a 6-mile section of land through which the Juniata River flows; the river meets the Susquehanna River some 35 miles downstream. The river offers year-round fishing, recreation and natural beauty.

The Stone Arch Bridge, curiously constructed without a keystone, was once part of the early turnpike that connected Harrisburg and Pittsburgh. The arch is off US 22/322W Lewistown exit on Jacks Creek Road. North of Lewistown is the Seven Mountain District, known for good hunting and fishing. Kishacoquillas Valley, also called the Big Valley, is 8 miles north of Lewistown on SR 655W and is home to a large Amish population. Amish and Mennonites sell produce, plants, flowers, antiques and handcrafted items in this 25-mile-long valley. Farmers markets, flea markets and livestock auctions are held June-October.

The Pennsylvania State Fire Academy is in Lewistown. Firefighters from Pennsylvania and other states attend classes throughout the year.

The original county courthouse, built in 1843, is on Monument Square and is home to the chamber of commerce and visitors bureau and the Mifflin County Historical Society. Nearby is McCoy House, the 1874 birthplace and home of soldier-statesman Maj. Gen. Frank Ross McCoy. It now houses a museum. Tours are offered Tues. 10-2, May-Sept. and other times by appointment; phone (717) 242-1022.

Juniata River Valley Chamber of Commerce & Visitors Bureau: One W. Market St., Lewistown, PA 17044. **Phone:** (717) 248-6713.

LIGONIER (H-3) pop. 1,573, elev. 1,201'

Part of the Laurel Highlands (see place listing p. 122), Ligonier is sheltered by Laurel Mountain to the east and Chestnut Ridge to the west. It is a quiet, picturesque village with a turn-of-the-20th-century atmosphere. Steeped in history, the town was a key British defense post during the French and Indian War. In the early 1800s it served as a stagecoach stop along the new Philadelphia-Pittsburgh Turnpike, which a century later became part of the Lincoln Highway.

Quaint shops and eateries border the town square, where a Victorian bandstand on a grassy lawn is surrounded by benches and pretty flora. Metered parking is available for those eager to explore the downtown area on foot. Boutiques, taverns and antique dealers also are dotted along Main Street, branching off the town square. You'll encounter the occasional coffee shop or ice cream parlor tucked in between novelty shops and art galleries displaying hand-crafted works. The commercial area eventually gives way to tidy historic homes with well-manicured lawns and flower gardens.

Live stage productions, children's theater shows, concerts and movies are offered at the Diamond Theatre of Ligonier, 210 W. Main St.; phone (724) 238-2929. The musically inclined can witness some fancy guitar picking at the Laurel Highlands Bluegrass Festival, held in late June just northeast of town at the Ligonier Township Fire Department's fairgrounds. Exhibits relating to Eastern Orthodox Christianity as well as Middle Eastern and Eastern European culture are featured at the Antiochian Heritage Museum, 6 miles north of US 30 on SR 711; phone (724) 238-3677.

Ligonier is one of many places included along a statewide heritage corridor known as the Lincoln Highway Heritage Corridor. This 200-mile stretch of US 30 features some 250 landmarks, both historical and whimsical, commemorating the colorful history of the nation's first coast-to-coast highway. The Lincoln Highway Experience museum at 3435 SR 30 E. in nearby Latrobe offers a 13-minute orientation film about the highway and exhibits, including quirky roadside signs and antique gas pumps. A 60-page driving tour map is included with the $7 admission; phone (724) 879-4241. Free brochures and tour maps also are available at the Laurel Highlands Visitors Bureau; phone (724) 238-5661. Another pleasant drive, the Laurel Highlands Scenic Byway, extends from SR 711 in Ligonier to Donegal; travelers can view hilly, bucolic countryside dotted by farms along this stretch.

CHAMPION LAKES B&B AND GOLF CLUB   724/238-5440
♥♥ Bed & Breakfast. **Address:** 4743 Rt 711 15923

LINCOLN FALLS

MORGAN CENTURY FARM   570/924-4909
♥♥♥ Bed & Breakfast. **Address:** 7043 Rt 154 18616

LINESVILLE (D-1) pop. 1,040, elev. 1,034'

Pymatuning Reservoir arcs through Crawford County for 16 miles, its south end near Jamestown on US 322 and its northern apex near Linesville on US 6. Its western shore curves into Ohio. Pymatuning State Park *(see Recreation Areas Chart)* surrounds the Pennsylvania shoreline. At the spillway in the park visitors can buy bread to feed the fish; the

site is known as the place where the fish are reputedly so numerous that ducks walk on the fishes' backs. The lake is home to bass, bluegill, crappie, muskellunge, perch and walleye. Recreational activities include hunting and fishing.

The upper part of the reservoir is a state waterfowl sanctuary. A number of islands mark this part of the reservoir. Cabins, campgrounds and boat rentals are available at Pymatuning State Park; phone (724) 932-3142 for information.

Pymatuning Holeshot Raceway, 15729 Maple Rd., offers dirt bike, ATV and quad racing competitions April through October; phone (814) 683-5655.

LIONVILLE (B-8) elev. 541'
• Part of Philadelphia area — see map p. 154

Though it is considered a suburb of Philadelphia, Lionville is almost as close to Reading, and King of Prussia is its closest next big neighbor. Largely residential Lionville is also often linked to its southern neighbor of Exton, because the two towns share a zip code. Nearby, you can go boating, fishing or have a summer picnic in picturesque Marsh Creek State Park; try cross-country skiing or sledding in the winter.

CLARION HOTEL   (610)363-1100
fyi Hotel. Under major renovation, scheduled to be completed April 2018. **Last Rated:** ♥♥♥ **Address:** 815 N Pottstown Pike 19341

COMFORT SUITES EXTON   (610)594-4770
♥♥♥ Hotel. **Address:** 700 W Uwchlan Ave 19341

EXTENDED STAY AMERICA-PHILADELPHIA/EXTON
          (610)524-7185
♥♥ Extended Stay Hotel. **Address:** 877 N Pottstown Pike (Rt 100) 19353

FAIRFIELD INN BY MARRIOTT PHILADELPHIA WEST CHESTER/EXTON   (610)524-8811
♥♥♥ Hotel. **Address:** 5 N Potts-town Pike 19341

| AAA Benefit: |
| Members save 5% or more! |

HAMPTON INN EXTON/DOWNINGTOWN   (610)363-5555
♥♥♥ Hotel. **Address:** 4 N Potts-town Pike 19341

| AAA Benefit: |
| Members save up to 10%! |

RESIDENCE INN BY MARRIOTT PHILADELPHIA GREAT VALLEY/EXTON   (610)594-9705
♥♥ Extended Stay Hotel. **Address:** 10 N Pottstown Pike 19341

| AAA Benefit: |
| Members save 5% or more! |

WHERE TO EAT

ARTHUR'S STEAKHOUSE RESTAURANT   610/363-1100
♥♥ American. Casual Dining. **Address:** 815 N Pottstown Pike 19341

ISAAC'S FAMOUS GRILLED SANDWICHES   484/875-5825
♥ Deli Sandwiches. Quick Serve. **Address:** 630 W Uwchlan Ave 19341

TACO MAYA   610/363-3081
Mexican. Quick Serve. **Address:** 221 Eagleview Blvd 19341

LITITZ (H-9) pop. 9,369, elev. 360'
- Hotels & Restaurants map & index p. 145
- Part of Pennsylvania Dutch Country area — see map p. 143

Dedicated in 1756 as a Moravian community, Lititz was named for the place in Bohemia where the Moravian Church was founded in 1456. Until 1855 the entire community was owned by the church. Linden Hall, one of the oldest girls' residence schools in the United States, was founded by Moravians in 1746. Originally a day school, it began boarding students in 1794. The Lititz Moravian Archives Museum, at Church Square and Main Street, provides guided tours of the church buildings by appointment May through October; phone (717) 626-8515.

Lititz Springs Park, on SR 501 just north of jct. SR 772, is illuminated by thousands of candles on July 4. The celebration dates from the early days of the town's settlement.

Self-guiding tours: A brochure outlining a walking tour of historic buildings and houses on E. Main Street is available from the Lititz Historical Foundation at the Johannes Mueller House, 137 E. Main St.

ALDEN HOUSE BED & BREAKFAST   717/627-3363 11
Historic Bed & Breakfast. **Address:** 62 E Main St 17543

HOLIDAY INN EXPRESS & SUITES   717/625-2366 12

Hotel
Rates not provided

Address: 101 Crosswinds Dr 17543 **Location:** 1.4 mi s on SR 501 (Lititz Pike), just w on Trolley Run Rd. **Facility:** 90 units. 3 stories, interior corridors. **Pool:** heated indoor. **Activities:** exercise room. **Guest Services:** valet and coin laundry. **Featured Amenity:** continental breakfast.

SWISS WOODS BED & BREAKFAST   717/627-3358 10
Bed & Breakfast. **Address:** 500 Blantz Rd 17543

WHERE TO EAT

ISAAC'S FAMOUS GRILLED SANDWICHES   717/625-1181
Deli Sandwiches. Quick Serve. **Address:** 4 Trolley Run Rd 17543

KANPAI ASIAN KITCHEN   717/626-9366 11
Asian. Casual Dining. **Address:** 1032 Lititz Pike 17543

KNIGHT AND DAY DINER   717/490-6198 12
American. Casual Dining. **Address:** 3140 Lititz Pike 17543

MOJO ASIAN CUISINE & SUSHI BAR   717/509-3888 13
Asian. Casual Dining. **Address:** 245 Bloomfield Dr 17543

LOCK HAVEN (F-7) pop. 9,772, elev. 563'

Lock Haven was laid out at the site of Fort Reed, which had once protected frontier settlers from the Native Americans. The 1778 evacuation of the fort during a fierce Native American raid became known as the great runaway. During the 19th century Lock Haven was a major lumber center and an important port on the Pennsylvania Canal.

Clinton County Economic Partnership: 212 N. Jay St., Lock Haven, PA 17745. **Phone:** (570) 748-5782 or (888) 388-6991.

Self-guiding tours: Guided walking tours are offered by appointment at the Ross Library at 232 W. Main St. Tour schedules and themes vary; phone (570) 748-3321.

PIPER AVIATION MUSEUM, One Piper Way, chronicles the life of William T. Piper Sr., founder of Piper Aircraft, and his contribution to the airline industry's demand for light personal aircraft. His company once boasted three manufacturing facilities in Pennsylvania and two in Florida. The museum includes aircraft, artifacts, models, advertising, historic photographs and archives.

Guided tours are available with 1-week advance reservation. **Time:** Allow 1 hour minimum. **Hours:** Mon.-Fri. 9-4, Sat. 10-4, Sun. noon-4, Mar.-Dec.; by appointment rest of year. Closed major holidays. **Cost:** $6; $5 (ages 55+); $3 (ages 7-16). **Phone:** (570) 748-8283. GT

BEST WESTERN LOCK HAVEN   (570)748-3297

Hotel
$119-$199

Best Western. **AAA Benefit:** Members save 5% to 15% and earn 10% bonus points!

Address: 101 E Walnut St 17745 **Location:** US 220 exit 111 (SR 120 W), just w. **Facility:** 67 units. 4 stories, interior corridors. **Terms:** closed 12/24 & 12/25, cancellation fee imposed. **Activities:** exercise room. **Guest Services:** valet and coin laundry.

FAIRFIELD INN & SUITES BY MARRIOTT LOCK HAVEN
(570)748-1580

Hotel
$104-$396

FAIRFIELD INN & SUITES. Marriott. **AAA Benefit:** Members save 5% or more!

Address: 50 Spring St 17745 **Location:** US 220 exit 109 (Mill Hall), 2 mi n on SR 150 (Bellefonte Ave), just w. **Facility:** 65 units. 3 stories, interior corridors. **Terms:** cancellation fee imposed. **Pool:** heated indoor. **Activities:** hot tub, exercise room. **Guest Services:** valet and coin laundry. **Featured Amenity:** breakfast buffet.

WHERE TO EAT

DUTCH HAVEN RESTAURANT   570/748-7444
American. Casual Dining. **Address:** 201 E Bald Eagle St 17745

LUDWIGS CORNER
• Part of Philadelphia area — see map p. 154

LUDWIG'S GRILLE AND OYSTER BAR   610/458-5336

🔻🔻 Seafood. Casual Dining. **Address:** 2904 Conestoga Rd 19343

LUZERNE pop. 2,845

ANDY PERUGINO'S RESTAURANT   570/288-5337

🔻🔻 Italian. Casual Dining. **Address:** 258 Charles St 18709

MACUNGIE pop. 3,074, elev. 390'

BEAR CREEK MOUNTAIN RESORT & CONFERENCE CENTER
610/682-7100

🔻🔻🔻 Boutique Resort Hotel. **Address:** 101 Doe Mountain Ln 18062

WHERE TO EAT

THE GRILLE AT BEAR CREEK   610/641-7149

🔻🔻 American. Casual Dining. **Address:** 101 Doe Mountain Ln 18062

MALVERN (B-9) pop. 2,998, elev. 561'
• Part of Philadelphia area — see map p. 154

Just southwest of Valley Forge is the borough of Malvern—now a small town marked by a red brick train station taking commuters to Philadelphia via SEPTA. But in September 1777, it was the site of the Battle of Paoli, during the American Revolution. (The town of Paoli *(see page p. 141.)* itself is just to the east.) There were few actual casualties, but the brutal tactics by the British during the surprise attack on Washington's Army led to the most common nickname of the battle: The Paoli Massacre. Today the 40-acre Paoli Battlefield Historical Park is the site of celebrations throughout the year, including what is said to be the oldest Memorial Day parade in the country.

COURTYARD BY MARRIOTT - PHILADELPHIA GREAT VALLEY/MALVERN   (610)993-2600

🔻🔻🔻 Hotel. **Address:** 280 Old Morehall Rd 19355

| **AAA Benefit:** Members save 5% or more! |

THE DESMOND HOTEL AND CONFERENCE CENTER MALVERN   610/296-9800

🔻🔻🔻 Hotel. **Address:** 1 Liberty Blvd 19355

EXTENDED STAY AMERICA-PHILADELPHIA GREAT VALLEY
(610)240-0455

🔻🔻 Extended Stay Hotel. **Address:** 300 Morehall Rd (SR 29) 19355

HAMPTON INN GREAT VALLEY/MALVERN   (610)699-1300

🔻🔻🔻 Hotel. **Address:** 635 Lancaster Ave 19355

| **AAA Benefit:** Members save up to 10%! |

🔗 **Discover member savings around the world: AAA.com/discounts**

HOLIDAY INN EXPRESS MALVERN FRAZER
(610)651-0400

🔻🔻🔻🔻
Hotel
$99-$169

Address: 1 Morehall Rd 19355 **Location:** Jct US 30 at SR 29. 🖼 Malvern, 199. **Facility:** 88 units. 4 stories, interior corridors. **Terms:** cancellation fee imposed. **Activities:** exercise room. **Guest Services:** valet laundry. **Featured Amenity: full hot breakfast.**

SAVE 🛏️ CALL 🦽 🛜 BIZ 🛜
✕ 🍴 📷 📺 🚌

HOMEWOOD SUITES BY HILTON   (610)296-3500

🔻🔻🔻 Extended Stay Hotel. **Address:** 12 E Swedesford Rd 19355

| **AAA Benefit:** Members save up to 10%! |

SHERATON GREAT VALLEY HOTEL   610/524-5500

🔻🔻🔻
Hotel
Rates not provided

Sheraton

| **AAA Benefit:** Members save 5% or more! |

Address: 707 E Lancaster Ave 19355 **Location:** Jct US 202 and 30 E. Located in a commercial area. **Facility:** 193 units. 5 stories, interior corridors. **Amenities:** *Some:* safes. **Pool:** heated indoor. **Activities:** hot tub, exercise room. **Guest Services:** valet and coin laundry, area transportation.

SAVE 🛏️ 🍽️ CALL 🦽 🏊 👥
BIZ 🛜 ✕ 🍴 📷 📺

/SOME UNITS 🐾 HS

SONESTA ES SUITES MALVERN   610/296-4343

🔻🔻🔻
Extended Stay Hotel
Rates not provided

Address: 20 S Morehall Rd 19355 **Location:** Jct US 30 and SR 29, just nw. Located in a commercial area. 🖼 Malvern, 199. **Facility:** 120 units, some two bedrooms, efficiencies and kitchens. 2 stories (no elevator), interior/exterior corridors. **Terms:** check-in 4 pm. **Amenities:** safes. **Pool:** outdoor. **Activities:** exercise room. **Guest Services:** valet and coin laundry, area transportation. **Featured Amenity: breakfast buffet.**

SAVE 🛏️ CALL 🦽 🏊 🛜 BIZ
HS 🛜 ✕ 📷 📺

/SOME UNITS 🐾 🚌

WHERE TO EAT

ANTHONY'S PIZZA AND ITALIAN RESTAURANT 610/647-7400

🔻🔻 Italian. Casual Dining. **Address:** 127 W King St 19355

DIXIE PICNIC   484/320-8024

🔻 Southern American. Quick Serve. **Address:** 215 Lancaster Ave 19355

HISTORIC GENERAL WARREN INNE   610/296-3637

🔻🔻🔻 Continental. Fine Dining. **Address:** 9 Old Lancaster Rd 19355

THE HUNT ROOM   610/296-9800

🔻🔻🔻 Regional American. Fine Dining. **Address:** 1 Liberty Blvd 19355

MARGARET KUO'S MANDARIN   610/647-5488
♥♥ Chinese. Casual Dining. **Address:** 190 Lancaster Ave 19355

MANHEIM (H-9) pop. 4,858, elev. 400'
• Hotels & Restaurants map & index p. 145
• Part of Pennsylvania Dutch Country area — see map p. 143

Baron Henry William Stiegel, along with Charles and Alexander Stedman, founded Manheim in 1762. The trio bought the land from Mary Norris, granddaughter of James Logan. Logan was William Penn's secretary and was given the 720 acres from Penn's widow and sons in 1734. Stiegel also was the originator of Stiegel glass, which is blown and colored. Its three types include enameled, pattern-molded, and cut and engraved.

The 🏵 Pennsylvania Renaissance Faire is held on the grounds of the 35-acre 19th-century Mount Hope Estate and Winery, .5 mi. s. of the Pennsylvania Tpke. exit 266 on SR 72, weekends August through October (also Labor Day). The grand traditions of the 16th century, including arts, literature and music, are re-created with artisans, jousters, merchants, more than 90 daily stage performances and hundreds of people in Elizabethan costumes. Each weekend offers its own theme. Food—including contemporary and ethnic fare as well as fare that would have been served during the era—is available.

Manheim Area Chamber of Commerce: 15 E. High St., Manheim, PA 17545. **Phone:** (717) 665-6330.

HAMPTON INN & SUITES MOUNT JOY/LANCASTER WEST
    717/653-5515 **20**
♥♥♥ Hotel. **Address:** 2301 Strickler Rd 17545

| **AAA Benefit:** Members save up to 10%! |

HAMPTON INN-MANHEIM   (717)665-6600 **18**
♥♥♥ Hotel. **Address:** 2764 Lebanon Rd 17545

| **AAA Benefit:** Members save up to 10%! |

ENJOY THE FREEDOM
Extend your safe driving years.
SENIORDRIVING.AAA.COM
SENIORSDRIVING.CAA.CA

LANCASTER INN & SUITES   (717)665-5440 **19**
♥♥ Hotel. **Address:** 1475 Lancaster Rd 17545

WHERE TO EAT

THE CAT'S MEOW   717/664-3370 **19**
♥♥ American. Casual Dining. **Address:** 215 S Charlotte St 17545

FORKLIFT AND PALATE   717/537-6205 **20**
♥♥ American. Casual Dining. **Address:** 2913 Spooky Nook Rd 17545

MANSFIELD pop. 3,625

HAMPTON INN & SUITES   (570)662-7500
♥♥♥♥ Hotel. **Address:** 98 Dorsett Heights 16933

| **AAA Benefit:** Members save up to 10%! |

MICROTEL INN & SUITES BY WYNDHAM MANSFIELD
    (570)662-9300
♥♥ Hotel. **Address:** 90 Dorsett Heights 16933

QUALITY INN & SUITES   (570)662-3000
♥♥ Hotel. **Address:** 300 Gateway Dr 16933

WHERE TO EAT

LAMB'S CREEK   570/662-3222
♥♦ American. Casual Dining. **Address:** 200 Gateway Dr 16933

MARIENVILLE (E-4) pop. 3,137, elev. 1,732'

Marienville, cradled between the half-million-acre Allegheny National Forest *(see place listing p. 34 and Recreation Areas Chart)* and the 7,182-acre virgin timber Cook Forest State Park *(see Recreation Areas Chart)*, is attractive to outdoor enthusiasts year-round.

THE FOREST LODGE & CAMPGROUND   814/927-8790
♥ Motel. **Address:** 44078 Rt 66 16239

MARIETTA   pop. 2,588, elev. 259'
- **Hotels & Restaurants map & index p. 145**
- **Part of Pennsylvania Dutch Country area — see map p. 143**

RAILROAD HOUSE RESTAURANT BED & BREAKFAST
717/426-4141   **30**

♦♦ American. Casual Dining. **Address:** 280 W Front St 17547

MARSHALLS CREEK
- **Hotels & Restaurants map & index p. 266**
- **Part of Pocono Mountains Area — see map p. 264**

POCONO PALACE RESORT   570-588-6692   **7**

Resort Hotel
Rates not provided

Address: 5241 Milford Rd (Rt 209) 18335 **Location:** I-80 exit 309, 7.4 mi n on SR 209. Located in a rural area. **Facility:** Live it up in your 1970s disco-era guest room at this classic couples-only, all-inclusive resort. Eight varieties of room types are available, including lakeside chalets and multi-level suites. 188 units. 1-4 stories, interior/exterior corridors. **Terms:** check-in 3:30 pm, age restrictions may apply. **Dining:** 2 restaurants, nightclub, entertainment. **Pool:** heated outdoor, heated indoor. **Activities:** sauna, hot tub, steamroom, motor boats, fishing, regulation golf, miniature golf, tennis, cross country skiing, snowmobiling, recreation programs, bicycles, game room, trails, exercise room, massage.

WHERE TO EAT

ALASKA PETE'S   570/223-8575   **10**

♦♦♦ Seafood Steak. Casual Dining. **Address:** 151 Seven Bridge Rd 18335

BIG "A" GRILLEHOUSE   570/223-1700   **9**

♦♦ Italian Steak Seafood. Casual Dining. **Address:** One Fox Run Ln 18302

LANDMARK RESTAURANT   570/426-1370   **11**

♦ New Breakfast Comfort Food. Casual Dining. **Address:** 809 Seven Bridges Rd 18301

MATAMORAS   pop. 2,469
- **Part of Pocono Mountains Area — see map p. 264**

BEST WESTERN INN AT HUNT'S LANDING
(570)491-2400

Hotel
$109-$189

Best Western
AAA Benefit: Members save 5% to 15% and earn 10% bonus points!

Address: 120 Rt 6 & 209 18336 **Location:** I-84 exit 53, just s. **Facility:** 109 units. 4 stories, interior corridors. **Terms:** cancellation fee imposed. **Pool:** heated indoor. **Activities:** fishing, recreation programs in season, limited exercise equipment. **Guest Services:** coin laundry. **Featured Amenity:** full hot breakfast.

HAMPTON INN   (570)491-5280

♦♦♦ Hotel. **Address:** 122 Westfall Town Dr 18336

AAA Benefit: Members save up to 10%!

MAYFIELD   pop. 1,807

ALEXANDER'S FAMILY RESTAURANT   570/876-9993

♦♦ American. Casual Dining. **Address:** 604 Rt 6 18433

MCELHATTAN   pop. 598

RESTLESS OAKS   570/769-7385

♦♦ American. Casual Dining. **Address:** 119 Pine Mountain Rd 17748

MEADVILLE   (D-1) pop. 13,388, elev. 1,078'
- **Restaurants p. 130**

The invention of the hookless fastener by Whitcomb L. Judson in Chicago came to the attention of Meadville's Col. Lewis Walker in 1893. Impressed by the new idea, Walker persuaded Judson to build a machine to produce the fastener. After several years of failure, Walker moved the enterprise to Meadville, where Gideon Sundback invented the fastener as it is currently known. The fastener did not become a commercial success, however, until 1923, when the B.F. Goodrich Co. decided to put it on a new line of galoshes. The popular new galoshes were called Zippers, a name that has evolved to mean the fastener itself.

The first direct primary took place here in 1842, and use of this system eventually spread across the country.

Of architectural interest is the Unitarian Church in Diamond Park. Built in 1835, it is a fine example of Greek Revival architecture. The Meadville Market House on Market Street has been used as an open-air marketplace since its founding about 1870 and is said to be the state's oldest continuously operating such marketplace; it is the cultural hub of the community. The Meadville Council on the Arts occupies the second floor.

If you head 13 miles northeast on SR 77 then just south to 17620 John Brown Rd. in Guys Mills, you'll reach the site of the John Brown Tannery, which was operated by the abolitionist 1825-35. All that remains of the tannery are its 8-foot stone walls. Interpretive markers at the site guide visitors to different points of interest, including the graves of Brown's first wife and two of their sons.

Crawford County Convention and Visitors Bureau: 16709 Conneaut Lake Rd., Meadville, PA 16335. **Phone:** (814) 333-1258 or (800) 332-2338.

HAMPTON INN   (814)807-1446

♦♦♦ Hotel. **Address:** 11446 N Dawn Dr 16335

AAA Benefit: Members save up to 10%!

HOLIDAY INN EXPRESS   (814)724-6012
▼▼▼ Hotel. **Address:** 18240 Conneaut Lake Rd 16335

QUALITY INN MEADVILLE   (814)333-8883
▼▼ Motel. **Address:** 17259 Conneaut Lake Rd 16335

WHERE TO EAT

CHOVY'S ITALIAN CASUAL   814/724-1286
▼▼ Italian. Casual Dining. **Address:** 18228 Conneaut Lake Rd 16335

COMPADRES MEXICAN RESTAURANT   814/336-6633
▼▼ Mexican. Casual Dining. **Address:** 17345 Conneaut Lake Rd 16335

KING'S FAMILY RESTAURANT   814/333-8938
▼▼ American. Casual Dining. **Address:** 16494 Conneaut Lake Rd 16335

MECHANICSBURG (H-8) pop. 8,981, elev. 433'
• Hotels & Restaurants map & index p. 95

AMERICA'S MUSEUM & RESEARCH FACILITY FOR ROLLS-ROYCE AND BENTLEY MOTOR-CARS, 189 Hempt Rd., provides guided tours of its collection of Rolls-Royce and Bentley automobiles (about 12 are usually displayed) and related historical items. A noncirculating library features books, technical manuals, handbooks, sales literature, periodicals and other historic documents.

Time: Allow 1 hour minimum. **Hours:** Mon.-Fri. 10-3:30; last tour begins 30 minutes before closing. Schedule may vary; phone ahead to confirm. **Cost:** Donations. **Phone:** (717) 795-9400. [GT]

COMFORT INN MECHANICSBURG/HARRISBURG SOUTH
                                                (717)766-3700 **43**
▼▼ Hotel. **Address:** 1012 Wesley Dr 17055

COUNTRY INN & SUITES BY CARLSON HARRISBURG WEST
                                                (717)796-0300 **48**
▼▼ Hotel. **Address:** 4943 Gettysburg Rd 17055

COURTYARD BY MARRIOTT HARRISBURG WEST/ MECHANICSBURG   (717)766-9006 **45**

▼▼▼
Hotel
$71-$260

COURTYARD **Marriott**

AAA Benefit: Members save 5% or more!

Address: 4921 Gettysburg Rd 17055 **Location:** I-76 (Pennsylvania Tpke) exit 236, 1 mi n to Rossmoyne Rd/Wesley Dr, just w, then 0.5 mi s. **Facility:** 91 units. 3 stories, interior corridors. **Terms:** cancellation fee imposed. **Pool:** heated indoor. **Activities:** hot tub, exercise room. **Guest Services:** valet and coin laundry, boarding pass kiosk.
[SAVE] [Y] CALL [&] [≈] [✚] [BIZ]
[📶] [✕] [🛄] [🖥] [💻] [/SOME UNITS] [HS]

ECONO LODGE   (717)766-4728 **49**
▼▼ Motel. **Address:** 650 Gettysburg Rd 17055

⊘ **From simple to spectacular:**
AAA.com/travelguides/restaurants

HAMPTON INN BY HILTON-HARRISBURG WEST
                                                (717)691-1300 **44**
▼▼▼ Hotel. **Address:** 4950 Ritter Rd 17055

AAA Benefit: Members save up to 10%!

HOLIDAY INN EXPRESS & SUITES HARRISBURG WEST/ MECHANICSBURG   717/732-8800 **41**
▼▼▼ Hotel. **Address:** 2055 Technology Pkwy 17050

HOLIDAY INN EXPRESS HARRISBURG SW-MECHANICSBURG   (717)790-0924
▼▼ Hotel. **Address:** 6325 Carlisle Pike 17050

HOMEWOOD SUITES BY HILTON-HARRISBURG WEST
                                                (717)697-4900 **46**
▼▼▼ Extended Stay Hotel. **Address:** 5001 Ritter Rd 17055

AAA Benefit: Members save up to 10%!

PARK INN BY RADISSON HARRISBURG WEST
                                                (717)697-0321 **42**
▼▼ Hotel. **Address:** 5401 Carlisle Pike 17050

TOWNEPLACE SUITES BY MARRIOTT   (717)691-1400 **47**
▼▼ Extended Stay Hotel. **Address:** 4915 Ritter Rd 17055

AAA Benefit: Members save 5% or more!

WINGATE BY WYNDHAM MECHANICSBURG/HARRISBURG WEST   (717)766-2710 **50**
▼▼ Hotel. **Address:** 385 Cumberland Pkwy 17055

WHERE TO EAT

BLACK N' BLEU   717/458-8105
▼▼ American. Casual Dining. **Address:** 6108 Carlisle Pike 17050

CAFE MAGNOLIA   717/901-9700 **35**
▼▼ American. Casual Dining. **Address:** 4700 Gettysburg Rd 17055

HELLENIC KOUZINA   717/766-2990
▼▼ Greek. Casual Dining. **Address:** 500 E Main St 17055

ISAAC'S FAMOUS GRILLED SANDWICHES
▼ Deli Sandwiches. Quick Serve.
LOCATIONS:
Address: 4940 Ritter Rd 17055 **Phone:** 717/766-1111
Address: 6520 Carlisle Pike 17050 **Phone:** 717/795-1925

PHO 7 SPICE   717/412-7155 **34**
▼▼ Vietnamese. Casual Dining. **Address:** 4830 Carlisle Pike 17050

MEDIA (C-9) pop. 5,327, elev. 210'
• Part of Philadelphia area — see map p. 154

Media, named for its central location in Delaware County, was laid out in 1848 after being designated county seat. Midway between Philadelphia and Wilmington, Del., it has remained a thriving business and government center.

Just south on Rose Valley Road in an 1840 gristmill is the 1923 Hedgerow Theatre, one of the oldest repertory theaters in the country; phone (610) 565-4211. Another sign of the past still rumbles along State Street—an early 20th-century trolley that takes passengers to shops, restaurants and the Delaware County Courthouse. On Wednesday evenings from May to September, a portion of State

Street is closed to traffic for Dining Under the Stars, an event sponsored by local restaurants. Several music festivals occur throughout the year, including the Americana Roots Ramble in April, the State Street Blues Stroll in June and the Jazz by Night Celebration in November.

Destination Delco: 1501 N. Providence Rd., Media, PA 19063. **Phone:** (610) 565-3679.

MENDENHALL
• Part of Philadelphia area — see map p. 154

INN AT MENDENHALL, AN ASCEND HOTEL COLLECTION
(610)388-2100
▼▼▼ Hotel. **Address:** 323 Kennett Pike (Rt 52) 19357

WHERE TO EAT

MENDENHALL INN   610/388-1181
▼▼▼ Continental. Fine Dining. **Address:** 323 Kennett Pike (Rt 52) 19357

MERCER (E-1) pop. 2,002, elev. 1,006'

Founded near the banks of the Neshannock Creek in 1803, Mercer was named for Brig. Gen. Hugh Mercer, a Scottish physician who moved to America and fought in the Revolutionary War. The city is a light industrial center in a farming region.

Mercer Area Chamber of Commerce: 143 N. Diamond St., Mercer, PA 16137. **Phone:** (724) 662-4185.

CANDLEWOOD SUITES GROVE CITY   724/748-6900
▼▼▼ Extended Stay Contemporary Hotel. **Address:** 37 Holiday Blvd 16137

TOWNEPLACE SUITES BY MARRIOTT GROVE CITY
MERCER/OUTLETS   724/748-6322
▼▼▼ Extended Stay Hotel. **Ad-** **dress:** 231 Westside Square Dr 16137

> **AAA Benefit:** Members save 5% or more!

WHERE TO EAT

IRON BRIDGE INN   724/748-3626
▼▼ American. Casual Dining. **Address:** 1438 Perry Hwy 16137

MY BROTHER'S PLACE   724/748-3840
▼▼ American. Casual Dining. **Address:** 2058 Leesburg Grove City Rd 16137

RACHEL'S ROADHOUSE   724/748-3193
▼▼ American. Casual Dining. **Address:** 1553 Perry Hwy 16137

MIDDLETOWN (DAUPHIN COUNTY)

ALFRED'S VICTORIAN RESTAURANT   717/944-5373
▼▼▼ Continental. Fine Dining. **Address:** 38 N Union St 17057

MIFFLINBURG (F-8) pop. 3,540, elev. 583'

Established in 1792 and renamed in honor of Governor Thomas Mifflin in 1827, Mifflinburg was a buggy-making town. Between 1841 and 1924, 75 independent buggy makers called this borough home. Because of the quality of its product, the town produced more buggies per capita than any other Pennsylvania town, as many as 6,000 vehicles annually. In fact, in 1880 the town came to be known by the nickname "Buggy Town."

CARRIAGE CORNER RESTAURANT   570/966-3866
▼▼ American. Casual Dining. **Address:** 257 E Chestnut St 17844

MIFFLINTOWN pop. 936

ECONO LODGE   (717)436-5981

Motel
$69-$224

Address: 29 Stop Plaza Dr 17059 **Location:** Jct US 322/22 and SR 35. **Facility:** 47 units, some kitchens. 2 stories (no elevator), interior/exterior corridors.
SAVE ⑪ BIZ HS 🛜 ⬛ ⬜ / SOME UNITS ⬜

MIFFLINVILLE pop. 1,253

SUPER 8 - MIFFLINVILLE   (570)759-6778
▼▼ Motel. **Address:** 450 W 3rd St 18631

MILFORD (E-12) pop. 1,021, elev. 492'
• Hotels p. 132 • Restaurants p. 132
• Part of Pocono Mountains Area — see map p. 264

Situated along the early Milford-Owego Turnpike, the village became an important transportation stop during the nation's 19th-century westward expansion. Today numerous historic buildings, tree-lined streets and country inns make it a pleasant vacation stop. The Columns is a Victorian mansion housing the museum of the Pike County Historical Society. The artifact collection includes the flag that supposedly was used to cradle President Lincoln's head after he was shot at Ford's Theatre; several tests have confirmed its authenticity. Native Americans and Underground Railroad are other local history topics that are showcased. The museum is downtown at 608 Broad St. and is usually open Wednesdays and weekends 1-4; phone (570) 296-8126.

Pike County Chamber of Commerce: 209 E. Harford St., Milford, PA 18337. **Phone:** (570) 296-8700.

Self-guiding tours: Information about driving tours of the area is available from the chamber of commerce.

Shopping: Milford has a large variety of antique and specialty shops.

GREY TOWERS NATIONAL HISTORIC SITE is .5 mi. w. on US 6, then .3 mi s.w. on Old Owego Tpke. This 1886 estate was the summer home of conservationist Gifford Pinchot, a former Pennsylvania governor and first chief of the USDA Forest Service. Designed to resemble a French château, the stone mansion is built of native materials and furnished in 1920s style. Guided 1-hour tours of the first floor are given. Visitors may wander through the restored gardens and walking trails on their own. Special tours and events are offered.

Pets are not permitted in the mansion. **Time:** Allow 1 hour, 30 minutes minimum. **Hours:** Grounds daily dawn-dusk, year-round. Guided tours of the mansion and gardens are offered Thurs.-Mon. on the hour 11-4, Memorial Day weekend-Oct. 31. The Sat.-Sun. tour at 4 includes three floors. **Cost:** Guided tour $8; $7 (ages 62+); $5 (ages 12-17). **Phone:** (570) 296-9630. [GT] [🏛]

HOTEL FAUCHÈRE   (570)409-1212
♦♦♦ ♦♦♦ Historic Hotel. **Address:** 401 Broad St 18337

MYER COUNTRY MOTEL   570/296-7223
♦♦ Cottage. **Address:** 600 Rt 6 & 209 18337

SCOTTISH INNS   (570)491-4414

♦♦
Motel
$65-$125

Address: 274 Rt 6 & 209 18337 **Location:** I-84 exit 53, 1 mi s. Located in a semi-rural area. **Facility:** 18 units. 1 story, exterior corridors. **Terms:** 3 day cancellation notice-fee imposed.

[SAVE] [🍴] [📶] [✕] [🔌] [🗄] [💻]

WHERE TO EAT

APPLE VALLEY FAMILY RESTAURANT   570/296-6831
♦♦ American. Casual Dining. **Address:** 104 Rt 6 18337

BAR LOUIS   570/409-1212
♦♦♦ New American. Casual Dining. **Address:** 401 Broad St 18337

MILFORD DINER   570/296-8611
♦♦ American. Casual Dining. **Address:** 301 Broad St 18337

VILLAGE DINER   570/491-2819
♦♦ Comfort Food. Casual Dining. **Address:** 268 Rt 6 & 209 18337

WATER WHEEL CAFE   570/296-2383
♦♦ Comfort Food. Casual Dining. **Address:** 150 Water St 18337

MILL RUN (I-3) elev. 1,383'

Mill Run is part of the Laurel Highlands (*see place listing p. 122*).

◤GEM FALLINGWATER, on SR 381 at 1491 Mill Run Rd., was a weekend home designed by Frank Lloyd Wright in 1935 and was entrusted to Western Pennsylvania Conservancy in 1963. Constructed of reinforced concrete and native stone, the house is dramatically cantilevered over a waterfall. The famous house blends so well with the mountainous terrain that it seems to grow out of its site. It has been acclaimed by the American Institute of Architects. Self-guiding grounds tours, 1-hour guided house tours, 2-hour in-depth tours and other special tours are offered. A visitor center is on-site.

Hours: Thurs.-Tues. 10-4, early Mar.-late Nov.; Sat.-Sun. 11:30-3, in Dec. Grounds daily 10-3, year-round (weather permitting). Phone for in-depth and other special tour schedules. All tours are available weather permitting. Closed Jan. 1, Thanksgiving, Christmas Eve and Christmas. **Cost:** $33; $20 (ages 6-12). In-depth tour $83. Grounds-only pass $10. Advanced ticket purchase is required to guarantee tour availability; discounts are applied to advance ticket purchases. Ages 0-5 are not permitted on regular tour. Ages 0-8 are not permitted on in-depth and other special tours. **Phone:** (724) 329-8501. [GT] [🍴]

MILROY pop. 1,498

BEST WESTERN NITTANY INN MILROY   (717)667-9595

♦♦
Hotel
$69-$90

[BW] Best Western. **AAA Benefit:** Members save 5% to 15% and earn 10% bonus points!

Address: 5 Commerce Dr 17063 **Location:** US 322 exit Milroy, just e. **Facility:** 41 units. 2 stories, interior corridors. **Terms:** cancellation fee imposed. **Pool:** heated outdoor. **Activities:** exercise room. **Guest Services:** valet and coin laundry.

[SAVE] [🍴] [🍸] [🏊] [💪] [BIZ] [📶] [✕] [🔌] [🗄] [💻] / SOME UNITS [🐾]

MOHNTON pop. 3,043

EMILY'S   610/856-7887
♦♦ American. Casual Dining. **Address:** 3790 Morgantown Rd 19540

MONACA pop. 5,737
- **Hotels & Restaurants map & index p. 246**
- **Part of Pittsburgh area — see map p. 225**

COMFORT SUITES   (724)728-9480 [49]
♦♦♦ Hotel. **Address:** 1523 Old Brodhead Rd 15061

FAIRFIELD INN & SUITES BY MARRIOTT   (724)888-2696 [50]
♦♦♦ Hotel. **Address:** 1438 Brodhead Rd 15061   **AAA Benefit:** Members save 5% or more!

HAMPTON INN BEAVER VALLEY/PITTSBURGH
           (724)774-5580 [52]
♦♦♦ Hotel. **Address:** 202 Fairview Dr 15061   **AAA Benefit:** Members save up to 10%!

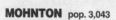

(See map & index p. 246.)

HOLIDAY INN EXPRESS HOTEL & SUITES-CENTER TOWNSHIP
(724)728-5121 **51**

Hotel
$104-$139

Address: 105 Stone Quarry Rd 15061 **Location:** I-376 exit 39 (SR 18 N/Frankfort Rd), just n. **Facility:** 66 units. 4 stories, interior corridors. **Pool:** heated indoor. **Activities:** hot tub, exercise room. **Guest Services:** valet and coin laundry. **Featured Amenity:** breakfast buffet.

WHERE TO EAT

BOWSER'S   724/774-5536 **57**
American. Casual Dining. **Address:** 1493 Old Brodhead Rd 15061

KING'S FAMILY RESTAURANT   724/774-7760
American. Casual Dining. **Address:** 1451 N Brodhead Rd 15061

RAINALDI'S RESTAURANT   724/774-1877 **58**
Italian. Casual Dining. **Address:** 201 Fairview Dr 15061

MONROEVILLE pop. 28,386, elev. 1,204'
- Hotels & Restaurants map & index p. 246
- Part of Pittsburgh area — see map p. 225

COMFORT SUITES MONROEVILLE   (412)373-0911 **19**
Contemporary Hotel. **Address:** 2731 Mosside Blvd 15146

COURTYARD BY MARRIOTT PITTSBURGH MONROEVILLE
(412)856-8680 **18**

Hotel
$90-$340

COURTYARD Marriott **AAA Benefit:** Members save 5% or more!

Address: 3962 William Penn Hwy 15146 **Location:** I-76 (Pennsylvania Tpke) exit 57, 1 mi w on US 22. **Facility:** 98 units. 4 stories, interior corridors. **Terms:** check-in 4 pm, cancellation fee imposed. **Pool:** heated indoor. **Activities:** hot tub, exercise room. **Guest Services:** valet and coin laundry. (See ad p. 259.)

DOUBLETREE BY HILTON HOTEL PITTSBURGH - MONROEVILLE CONVENTION CENTER
(412)373-7300 **21**

Hotel
$109-$189

DOUBLETREE BY HILTON **AAA Benefit:** Members save 5% or more!

Address: 101 Mall Blvd 15146 **Location:** I-76 (Pennsylvania Tpke) exit 57, 2 mi w on US 22. Adjacent to Monroeville Mall. **Facility:** 191 units. 15 stories, interior corridors. **Terms:** 1-7 night minimum stay, cancellation fee imposed. **Pool:** heated indoor. **Activities:** hot tub, exercise room. **Guest Services:** valet laundry.

EXTENDED STAY AMERICA PITTSBURGH-MONROEVILLE
(412)856-8400 **16**
Extended Stay Hotel. **Address:** 3851 Northern Pike 15146

HAMPTON INN MONROEVILLE/PITTSBURGH
(412)380-4000 **14**
Hotel. **Address:** 3000 Mosside Blvd 15146

AAA Benefit: Members save up to 10%!

HOLIDAY INN PITTSBURGH-MONROEVILLE
412/372-1022 **15**
Hotel. **Address:** 2750 Mosside Blvd 15146

RED ROOF PLUS+ PITTSBURGH EAST - MONROEVILLE
(412)856-4738 **20**

Motel
$52-$157

Address: 2729 Mosside Blvd 15146 **Location:** I-76 (Pennsylvania Tpke) exit 57; I-376 exit 84A, 0.8 mi s on SR 48. **Facility:** 116 units. 3 stories, exterior corridors. **Amenities:** safes. **Guest Services:** coin laundry.

SPRINGHILL SUITES BY MARRIOTT PITTSBURGH MONROEVILLE
(412)380-9100 **17**

Hotel
$79-$245

SPRINGHILL SUITES MARRIOTT **AAA Benefit:** Members save 5% or more!

Address: 122 Daugherty Dr 15146 **Location:** I-76 (Pennsylvania Tpke) exit 57; I-376 exit 84A, 0.5 mi s on SR 48. **Facility:** 86 units. 4 stories, interior corridors. **Terms:** check-in 4 pm, cancellation fee imposed. **Pool:** heated indoor. **Activities:** exercise room. **Guest Services:** valet and coin laundry. (See ad p. 259.)

WHERE TO EAT

BLAZE PIZZA   412/229-8522 **39**
Pizza. Casual Dining. **Address:** 3939 William Penn Hwy 15146

DAD'S PUB & GRUB   412/856-5666 **41**
American. Gastropub. **Address:** 4320 Northern Pike 15146

EIGHTY ACRES KITCHEN & BAR   412/519-7304 **38**
New American. Casual Dining. **Address:** 1910 New Texas Rd 15239

GATEWAY GRILL   412/372-2977 **42**
American. Casual Dining. **Address:** 4251 Northern Pike 15146

KING'S FAMILY RESTAURANT   412/373-3110
American. Casual Dining. **Address:** 4310 Northern Pike 15146

RUDY'S SUBMARINES   412/372-9738 **40**
Sandwiches. Quick Serve. **Address:** 3942 William Penn Hwy (US 22) 15146

TAIPEI -TOKYO   412/373-5464 **43**
Chinese. Casual Dining. **Address:** 304 Mall Blvd 15146

MONTGOMERYVILLE pop. 12,624
• Part of Philadelphia area — see map p. 154

COURTYARD BY MARRIOTT
PHILADELPHIA-MONTGOMERYVILLE   (215)699-7247

Hotel
$73-$263

 **AAA Benefit:** Members save 5% or more!

Address: 544 Dekalb Pike 19454 **Location:** Jct SR 309, just s. Across from Montgomery Mall. **Facility:** 102 units. 4 stories, interior corridors. **Terms:** cancellation fee imposed. **Activities:** hot tub, exercise room. **Guest Services:** valet and coin laundry, boarding pass kiosk.

QUALITY INN MONTGOMERYVILLE   (215)361-3600
Hotel. **Address:** 678 Bethlehem Pike 18936

RESIDENCE INN BY MARRIOTT PHILADELPHIA/
MONTGOMERYVILLE   (267)468-0111

Extended Stay Hotel
$64-$284

Residence Inn Marriott **AAA Benefit:** Members save 5% or more!

Address: 1110 Bethlehem Pike 19454 **Location:** I-276 (Pennsylvania Tpke) exit 339, 6.5 mi n on SR 309. **Facility:** 96 units, some two bedrooms, efficiencies and kitchens. 3 stories, interior corridors. **Terms:** cancellation fee imposed. **Pool:** heated indoor. **Activities:** exercise room. **Guest Services:** valet and coin laundry. **Featured Amenity:** full hot breakfast.

WHERE TO EAT

BACCO   215/699-3361
Southern Italian. Casual Dining. **Address:** 587 Dekalb Pike 19454

IRON HILL BREWERY & RESTAURANT   267/708-2000
American. Casual Dining. **Address:** 1460 Bethlehem Pike 19454

MONTOURSVILLE pop. 4,615

JOHNSON'S CAFÉ   570/368-8351
American. Casual Dining. **Address:** 334 Broad St 17754

MOON RUN (G-1) elev. 1,122'
• Hotels & Restaurants map & index p. 246
• Part of Pittsburgh area — see map p. 225

Moon Run is a bedroom community west of Pittsburgh, and it's growing quickly as its metropolitan footprint expands. Locals and visitors alike flock to the 500,000 square feet of shopping space at the Robinson Town Centre, anchored by HomeGoods, Marshall's and Swedish furniture (and meatball) expert IKEA. The residential neighborhood itself still retains its small-town charm with activities at the local library, fund-raisers for the volunteer fire department and community pet events.

CANDLEWOOD SUITES   (412)787-7770 **85**
Extended Stay Hotel. **Address:** 100 Chauvet Dr 15275

COMFORT SUITES   (412)494-5750 **80**
Hotel. **Address:** 750 Aten Rd 15108

FAIRFIELD INN & SUITES BY MARRIOTT PITTSBURGH AIRPORT/ROBINSON TOWNSHIP   (412)859-9070 **81**
Hotel. **Address:** 1004 Sutherland Dr 15205

AAA Benefit: Members save 5% or more!

HOLIDAY INN EXPRESS & SUITES - PITTSBURGH AIRPORT   412/788-8400 **87**
Hotel. **Address:** 5311 Campbells Run Rd 15205

HOMEWOOD SUITES BY HILTON   412/490-0440 **76**
Extended Stay Hotel. **Address:** 2000 GSK Dr 15108

AAA Benefit: Members save up to 10%!

HYATT PLACE PITTSBURGH AIRPORT
   (412)494-0202 **84**

Hotel
$79-$259

HYATT PLACE
AAA Benefit: Members save 10%!

Address: 6011 Campbells Run Rd 15205 **Location:** I-376 exit 60B (Crafton/SR 60 S), just w. **Facility:** 127 units. 6 stories, interior corridors. **Terms:** cancellation fee imposed. **Amenities:** safes. **Pool:** heated indoor. **Activities:** exercise room. **Guest Services:** valet laundry, area transportation. **Featured Amenity:** breakfast buffet.

MAINSTAY SUITES/SLEEP INN PITTSBURGH AIRPORT
   (412)490-7343 **83**
Extended Stay Hotel. **Address:** 1000 Park Lane Dr 15275

PITTSBURGH AIRPORT MARRIOTT   (412)788-8800 **79**

Hotel
$79-$314

MARRIOTT **AAA Benefit:** Members save 5% or more!

Address: 777 Aten Rd 15108 **Location:** I-376 exit 58 (Montour Run Rd), just n. **Facility:** 318 units. 15 stories, interior corridors. **Terms:** cancellation fee imposed. **Pool:** heated indoor. **Activities:** exercise room. **Guest Services:** valet and coin laundry, boarding pass kiosk, area transportation.

PITTSBURGH COMFORT INN   (412)922-7555 **77**
Hotel. **Address:** 4770 Steubenville Pike 15205

(See map & index p. 246.)

RESIDENCE INN BY MARRIOTT PITTSBURGH AIRPORT CORAOPOLIS   (412)787-3300   82

♦♦♦ Extended Stay Hotel. **Address:** 1500 Park Lane Dr 15275

AAA Benefit:
Members save 5%
or more!

SPRINGHILL SUITES BY MARRIOTT - PITTSBURGH AIRPORT   (412)494-9446   86

♦♦♦ Hotel. **Address:** 239 Summit Park Dr 15275

AAA Benefit:
Members save 5%
or more!

TOWNEPLACE SUITES PITTSBURGH AIRPORT/ROBINSON TOWNSHIP   (412)494-4000   78

♦♦♦ Extended Stay Hotel. **Address:** 1006 Sutherland Dr 15205

AAA Benefit:
Members save 5%
or more!

WHERE TO EAT

DITKA'S RESTAURANT   412/722-1555   83

♦♦♦ Steak. Fine Dining. **Address:** 1 Robinson Plaza 15205

MAD MEX   412/494-5656

♦♦ Mexican. Casual Dining. **Address:** 2 Robinson Plaza 15205

PLAZA AZTECA MEXICAN RESTAURANT   412/787-8888

♦♦ Mexican. Casual Dining. **Address:** 1000 Sutherland Dr 15205

PRIMANTI BROS.   412/921-6677

♦ American. Casual Dining. **Address:** 4501 Steubenville Pike 15205

YA FEI   412/788-9388   82

♦♦ Chinese. Casual Dining. **Address:** 1980 Park Manor Blvd 15205

MOOSIC (E-10) pop. 5,719, elev. 636'

Lackawanna County Convention and Visitors Bureau: 99 Glenmaura National Blvd., Moosic, PA 18507. **Phone:** (570) 496-1701 or (800) 229-3526.

MONTAGE MOUNTAIN WATERPARK, 1000 Montage Mountain Rd., offers a wave pool, lazy river, children's pool, waterslides and bumper boats. The facility also has batting cages and a miniature golf course. ZipRider (a zipline) is available on weekends. **Time:** Allow 4 hours minimum. **Hours:** Daily noon-6, Memorial Day-Labor Day weekend (weather permitting). ZipRider Fri.-Sun.; phone ahead. Phone ahead to confirm schedule. **Cost:** $24.99; $20.99 (under 48 inches tall); free (ages 0-2). An additional fee is charged for ZipRider. Phone ahead to confirm

rates. **Phone:** (570) 969-7669 or (855) 754-7946. ⑪ 🏝

RECREATIONAL ACTIVITIES
Skiing and Snowboarding

• [SAVE] **Montage Mountain Resort** is at 1000 Montage Mountain Rd. Snow tubing, air boarding and 26 cross-country trails also are offered. **Hours:** Mon.-Fri. 9-9 (also Fri. 9-10 p.m.), Sat. 8:30 a.m.-10 p.m., Sun. 8:30 a.m.-9 p.m., Dec.-Mar. (weather permitting). **Phone:** (570) 969-7669 or (855) 754-7946. ⑪

MARZONI'S BRICK OVEN AND BREWING   570/342-7027

♦♦ Comfort Food Pizza. Brewpub. **Address:** 26 Montage Mountain Rd 18507

MORGANTOWN pop. 826

HOLIDAY INN   610/286-3000

♦♦♦ Hotel. **Address:** 6170 Morgantown Rd 19543

WHERE TO EAT

THE WINDMILL RESTAURANT   610/286-5980

♦♦ American. Casual Dining. **Address:** 2838 Main St 19543

MORRISVILLE pop. 8,728, elev. 21'
• **Part of Philadelphia area — see map p. 154**

QUALITY INN & SUITES NJ STATE CAPITAL AREA
(215)428-2600

♦♦♦
Hotel
$74-$189

Address: 7 S Pennsylvania Ave 19067 **Location:** US 1 exit Pennsylvania Ave, just n. Located in a commercial area. **Facility:** 59 units. 2 stories, interior corridors. **Amenities:** safes. **Pool:** outdoor. **Activities:** limited exercise equipment. **Guest Services:** coin laundry. **Featured Amenity:** full hot breakfast.

WHERE TO EAT

CAFE ANTONIO   215/428-1733

♦♦♦ Italian Pizza. Casual Dining. **Address:** 107 E Trenton Ave 19067

MOUNT JOY pop. 7,410, elev. 360'
• **Hotels & Restaurants map & index p. 145**
• **Part of Pennsylvania Dutch Country area — see map p. 143**

THE CATACOMBS   717/653-2056   23

♦♦ American. Casual Dining. **Address:** 102 N Market St 17552

COUNTRY TABLE RESTAURANT   717/653-4745   24

♦♦ Regional American. Casual Dining. **Address:** 740 E Main St 17552

🔗 **Dreaming of s'mores and starry nights?**

AAA.com/campgrounds

MOUNT LEBANON pop. 33,137

- Hotels p. 136 • Restaurants p. 136
- Hotels & Restaurants map & index p. 246
- Part of Pittsburgh area — see map p. 225

SPRINGHILL SUITES BY MARRIOTT PITTSBURGH MT. LEBANON   (412)563-6300   100

Hotel
$93-$273

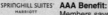 SPRINGHILL SUITES MARRIOTT **AAA Benefit:** Members save 5% or more!

Address: 611 Washington Rd 15228 **Location:** Jct SR 19. Mt Lebanon, 42. **Facility:** 108 units. 7 stories, interior corridors. **Terms:** cancellation fee imposed. **Pool:** heated indoor. **Activities:** exercise room. **Guest Services:** valet and coin laundry. *(See ad p. 260.)*

SAVE CALL 🛁 🐟 BIZ HS
🛜 ✕ 🍴 🖥 🖨 🚌

WHERE TO EAT

DEBLASIO'S   412/531-3040   99
Italian. Casual Dining. **Address:** 1717 Cochran Rd 15220

IL PIZZAIOLO   412/344-4123   100
Italian. Casual Dining. **Address:** 703 Washington Rd 15228

MOUNT PLEASANT pop. 4,454

- Hotels p. 136 • Restaurants p. 136
- Part of Pittsburgh area — see map p. 225

HOLIDAY INN EXPRESS   (724)547-2095
Hotel. **Address:** 250 Bessemer Rd 15666

WHERE TO EAT

VILLAGE RESTAURANT   724/547-3529
Italian. Casual Dining. **Address:** 236 W Main St 15666

MOUNT POCONO (F-11) pop. 3,170, elev. 1,658'

- Hotels & Restaurants map & index p. 266
- Part of Pocono Mountains Area — see map p. 264

From a hundred viewpoints at and near Mount Pocono, the colossal notch of the Delaware Water Gap is plainly visible, even though it is 25 miles away. Southwest of town is Pocono Raceway, where two annual NASCAR 400 automobile races and other motorsports races are held.

MOUNT AIRY CASINO RESORT   (570)243-4800   20

Contemporary Resort Hotel
$99-$699

Address: 312 Woodland Rd 18344 **Location:** I-380 exit 3, 1.8 mi e on SR 940, 2 mi s on SR 611, then just e. **Facility:** Setting the bar high for lodgings in the Poconos area, this casino resort offers upscale accommodations and colorful amenities, including an impressive indoor/outdoor pool complex and luxury spa. 188 units. 6 stories, interior corridors. **Parking:** on-site and valet. **Terms:** check-in 4 pm, cancellation fee imposed, resort fee. **Amenities:** safes. **Dining:** 5 restaurants, also, Guy Fieri's Mt. Pocono Kitchen, see separate listing, nightclub, entertainment. **Pool:** heated outdoor, heated indoor. **Activities:** sauna, hot tub, steamroom, cabanas, regulation golf, snowmobiling, recreation programs in season, lawn sports, trails, health club, spa. **Guest Services:** valet laundry, area transportation.

SAVE 🎰 🍴 🍸 CALL 🛁 🐟 BIZ HS
🛜 ✕ 🎥 🖨 / SOME UNITS 🍴 🖥

PARADISE STREAM RESORT   570/839-8881   19

Resort Hotel
Rates not provided

Address: Rt 940 & Carlton Rd 18344 **Location:** Waterfront. I-380 exit 3 (SR 940), 5 mi e, then just w of SR 390. Located in a semi-rural area. **Facility:** This couples-resort, with all-inclusive meal options, offers accommodations from lakeside villas to thoroughly over the top champagne-tower suites. 143 units. 1 story, exterior corridors. **Terms:** check-in 3:30 pm, age restrictions may apply. **Dining:** 2 restaurants, nightclub, entertainment. **Pool:** heated outdoor, heated indoor. **Activities:** hot tub, self-propelled boats, fishing, miniature golf, tennis, recreation programs, bicycles, game room, trails, exercise room, spa. **Guest Services:** coin laundry, area transportation.

SAVE 🍴 🎣 🍸 CALL 🛁 🐟 👥 🛜 🎥 🍴
🖨

WHERE TO EAT

BAILEYS RIB & STEAKHOUSE   570/839-9678   20
Steak. Casual Dining. **Address:** 604 Pocono Blvd 18344

GUY FIERI'S MT. POCONO KITCHEN   570/580-9990   21
New Comfort Food. Casual Dining. **Address:** 312 Woodland Rd 18344

MOUNTVILLE pop. 2,802

- Hotels & Restaurants map & index p. 145
- Part of Pennsylvania Dutch Country area — see map p. 143

MAINSTAY SUITES   (717)285-2500   28

Extended Stay Hotel
$69-$209

Address: 314 Primrose Ln 17554 **Location:** US 30 (Lincoln Hwy) exit Mountville, just n on Stoney Battery Rd, just w on Highland Dr, then just s. Located in a light-commercial area. **Facility:** 71 efficiencies, some two bedrooms. 3 stories, interior corridors. **Pool:** heated outdoor. **Activities:** exercise room. **Guest Services:** coin laundry. **Featured Amenity:** continental breakfast.

SAVE CALL 🛁 🐟 BIZ HS
🛜 🍴 🖥 🖨 / SOME UNITS 🐕

SLEEP INN & SUITES LANCASTER COUNTY   (717)285-0444   27

Hotel
$75-$190

Address: 310 Primrose Ln 17554 **Location:** US 30 (Lincoln Hwy) exit Mountville, just n on Stoney Battery Rd, just w on Highland Dr, then just s. Located in a light-commercial area. **Facility:** 80 units. 3 stories, interior corridors. *Bath:* shower only. **Pool:** heated indoor. **Activities:** hot tub, exercise room. **Featured Amenity:** full hot breakfast.

SAVE 🍴 CALL 🛁 🐟 BIZ
HS 🛜 ✕ 🖥 / SOME UNITS 🍴 🖥

MURRYSVILLE pop. 20,079

- Part of Pittsburgh area — see map p. 225

ATRIA'S RESTAURANT & TAVERN   724/733-4453
American. Casual Dining. **Address:** 4869 William Penn Hwy 15668

MYERSTOWN   pop. 3,062

MOTEL SKANDIA   717/866-6447
Motel. **Address:** 922 E Lincoln Ave 17067

WHERE TO EAT

COUNTRY FARE RESTAURANT BAKERY & DELI
                                                 717/866-9043
American. Casual Dining. **Address:** 498 E Lincoln Ave
17067

NAZARETH   (G-11) pop. 5,746, elev. 530'

The area was originally part of a 5,000-acre tract of land owned as a feudal estate by the William Penn family. In 1740 evangelist George Whitefield purchased the land. He employed Peter Boehler and a small band of Moravians, a group of Protestants from Germany, to oversee the construction of what is now called the Whitefield House, at 214 E. Center St. The house now contains the Moravian Historical Society's Museum and Research Library; phone (610) 759-5070. The following year the Moravians bought the property and Nazareth remained exclusively a Moravian settlement for more than a century. Nazareth Hall, built in 1755, was a boys' military academy 1759-1929.

Nazareth-Bath Regional Chamber of Commerce and Visitor Center: 201 N. Main St., P.O. Box 173, Nazareth, PA 18064. **Phone:** (610) 759-9188.

CLASSIC VICTORIAN ESTATE INN   610/759-8276
Historic Bed & Breakfast. **Address:** 35 N New St 18064

WHERE TO EAT

HANA SUSHI   610/759-2810
Japanese Sushi. Casual Dining. **Address:** 6 Belvidere St
18064

NEWBURG INN   610/759-8528
American. Casual Dining. **Address:** 4357 Newburg Rd
18064

NEW CASTLE   (F-1) pop. 23,273, elev. 806'

Visit Lawrence County: 229 S. Jefferson St., New Castle, PA 16101. **Phone:** (724) 654-8408 or (888) 284-7599.

HAMPTON INN & SUITES NEW CASTLE   (724)656-0000
Contemporary Hotel. **Ad-**
dress: 2608 W State St 16101   **AAA Benefit:**
                                        Members save up to
                                        10%!

SUPER 8   (724)658-8849
Hotel. **Address:** 1699 New Butler Rd (US Business 422)
16101

WHERE TO EAT

ELHAM RESTAURANT   724/652-6611
Mediterranean. Casual Dining. **Address:** 2001 E Washington
St 16101

KING'S FAMILY RESTAURANT   724/656-0699
American. Casual Dining. **Address:** 2541 W State St
16101

NEW COLUMBIA   pop. 1,013

HOLIDAY INN EXPRESS   (570)568-1100

Hotel
$99-$229

Address: 160 Commerce Park Dr 17856 **Location:** I-80 exit 210A (US 15/New Columbia), just s. Located in a quiet area. **Facility:** 101 units. 3 stories, interior corridors. **Pool:** heated indoor. **Activities:** hot tub, exercise room. **Guest Services:** valet and coin laundry. **Featured Amenity:** breakfast buffet.

SAVE ｜↑↓ CALL ⬚ ⬚ ⬚ BIZ
⬚ ✕ ⬚
/SOME UNITS ⬚ ⬚ ⬚

NEW CUMBERLAND   pop. 7,277
• Hotels & Restaurants map & index p. 95

BEST WESTERN PLUS NEW CUMBERLAND INN &
SUITES   (717)774-4440   38

Hotel
$94-$189

Best Western PLUS. **AAA Benefit:** Members save 5% to 15% and earn 10% bonus points!

Address: 702 Limekiln Rd 17070 **Location:** I-83 exit 40A, just w. **Facility:** 64 units. 3 stories, interior corridors. **Terms:** 2 night minimum stay - seasonal, cancellation fee imposed. **Pool:** heated indoor. **Activities:** hot tub, exercise room. **Guest Services:** valet and coin laundry.

SAVE ｜↑↓ CALL ⬚ ⬚ ⬚ BIZ
HS ⬚ ⬚ ⬚ /SOME UNITS ⬚

CLARION HOTEL & CONFERENCE CENTER HARRISBURG
WEST   (717)774-2721   37
Hotel. **Address:** 148 Sheraton Dr 17070

FAIRFIELD INN & SUITES BY MARRIOTT HARRISBURG
WEST   (717)774-0100   35
Hotel. **Address:** 185 Beacon
Hill Blvd 17070   **AAA Benefit:**
                                        Members save 5%
                                        or more!

HOLIDAY INN EXPRESS NEW CUMBERLAND
                                            717/774-6400   34
Hotel. **Address:** 190 Beacon Hill Blvd 17070

LA QUINTA INN & SUITES   (717)774-8888   36
Hotel. **Address:** 130 Limekiln Rd 17070

WHERE TO EAT

YAK N' YETI   717/774-0333   31
Nepali. Casual Dining. **Address:** 213 3rd St 17070

NEW HOLLAND   pop. 5,378
• Restaurants p. 138
• Hotels & Restaurants map & index p. 145, 148
• Part of Pennsylvania Dutch Country area — see
map p. 143

COMFORT INN AMISH COUNTRY   (717)355-9900   27
Hotel. **Address:** 626 W Main St 17557

(See maps & indexes p. 145, 148.)

COUNTRY SQUIRE MOTOR INN   (717)354-4166 **26**
◈ Motel. **Address:** 504 E Main St 17557

WHERE TO EAT

PALERMO PIZZA   717/354-2680 **21**
◈ Italian. Quick Serve. **Address:** 351 W Main St 17557

NEW HOPE (G-12) pop. 2,528, elev. 86'
• Part of Philadelphia area — see map p. 154

The picturesque town of New Hope, an artists' and writers' colony, is a favorite spot for antiques hunting. The village along the banks of the Delaware River across the river from the antique-rich Lambertville, N.J. features lovely guest homes and charming restaurants; make reservations early for these popular eateries.

Bucks County Playhouse stages its performances on the site of a former mill dating from the 1780s. Broadway productions are staged April through December; phone (215) 862-2121.

New Hope Visitors Center: 1 W. Mechanic St., New Hope, PA 18938. **Phone:** (215) 862-5030.

1870 WEDGWOOD INN OF NEW HOPE   215/862-2570
◈◈◈ Historic Bed & Breakfast. **Address:** 111 W Bridge St (SR 179) 18938

AARON BURR HOUSE INN   215/862-2343
◈◈◈ Historic Bed & Breakfast. **Address:** 80 W Bridge St (SR 179) 18938

FOX & HOUND BED & BREAKFAST OF NEW HOPE
                                  (215)862-5082
◈◈◈◈ Bed & Breakfast. **Address:** 246 W Bridge St 18938

THE INN AT BOWMAN'S HILL   215/862-8090
◈◈◈ ◈◈◈
Bed & Breakfast
Rates not provided
Address: 518 Lurgan Rd 18938 **Location:** 2.9 mi s on S Main St/River Rd, 0.5 mi w. **Facility:** This is an absolutely breathtaking B&B featuring precise attention to detail in its elegant room decor. The grounds include colorful landscaping, a gorgeous koi pond and a stunning outdoor pool. 8 units, some two bedrooms. 2 stories (no elevator), interior corridors. **Terms:** age restrictions may apply. **Amenities:** safes. **Pool:** heated outdoor. **Activities:** hot tub, bicycles, massage. **Featured Amenity:** full hot breakfast.

SAVE ┃↑┃ CALL 🛆 🌊 HS 📶

WHERE TO EAT

BOWMAN'S TAVERN   215/862-2972
◈◈ American. Casual Dining. **Address:** 1600 River Rd 18938

CENTRE BRIDGE INN   215/862-2048
◈◈◈ Continental. Fine Dining. **Address:** 2998 N River Rd 18938

HAVANA BAR   215/862-9897
◈◈ Cuban. Casual Dining. **Address:** 105 S Main St 18938

THE LANDING RESTAURANT   215/862-5711
◈◈ Regional American. Casual Dining. **Address:** 22 N Main St 18938

MARSHA BROWN CREOLE KITCHEN   215/862-7044
◈◈◈ Creole. Fine Dining. **Address:** 15 S Main St 18938

MARTINE'S RIVER HOUSE   215/862-2966
◈◈ Continental. Casual Dining. **Address:** 14 E Ferry St 18938

TRIUMPH BREWING COMPANY   215/862-8300
◈◈ American. Brewpub. **Address:** 400 Union Square Dr 18938

NEW KENSINGTON pop. 13,116
• Part of Pittsburgh area — see map p. 225

KING'S FAMILY RESTAURANT   724/339-2234
◈◈ American. Casual Dining. **Address:** 2400 Leechburg Rd, Suite 1000 15068

NEW MILFORD pop. 868

HOLIDAY INN EXPRESS GIBSON   (570)465-5544
◈◈◈ Hotel. **Address:** 1561 Oliver Rd 18834

WHERE TO EAT

ARMETTA'S PIZZERIA & PUB   570/465-5492
◈ Italian. Casual Dining. **Address:** 2092 SR 848 18834

NEW SMITHVILLE

DE MARCO'S ITALIAN RESTAURANT, PIZZERIA & BAR
                                  610/285-2278
◈◈ Italian. Casual Dining. **Address:** 10240 Old Rt 22 19530

NEW STANTON pop. 2,173

FAIRFIELD INN & SUITES BY MARRIOTT PITTSBURGH/NEW STANTON   (724)755-0800
◈◈◈ Hotel. **Address:** 107 Bair Blvd 15672
AAA Benefit: Members save 5% or more!

WHERE TO EAT

EAT'N PARK   724/925-1060
◈◈ American. Casual Dining. **Address:** 111 W Byers Ave 15672

LA TAVOLA RISTORANTE   724/925-9440
◈◈◈ Northern Italian. Casual Dining. **Address:** 400 S Center Ave 15672

NEWTOWN (BUCKS COUNTY)
• Part of Philadelphia area — see map p. 154

HOMEWOOD SUITES BY HILTON-NEWTOWN   (215)860-5080
◈◈◈ Extended Stay Hotel. **Address:** 110 Pheasant Run 18940
AAA Benefit: Members save up to 10%!

NORTH EAST (C-2) pop. 4,294, elev. 803'

North East and the vicinity grow an abundance of fruit and vegetables—especially grapes. With the help of Lake Erie's moderating effect on the climate and proper soil conditions, grape production is thriving. The first vines were planted in 1850 and today there are thousands of acres of vineyards, several wineries and a large Welch's processing plant. Locals take pride in their agricultural region: More than two dozen banners sporting an image of a large grape bunch are displayed around downtown and public school students are known as the Grapepickers. Local produce can be bought at markets, farms (including pick-your-own fruit and vegetable farms) and roadside stands. A farmers market is held Thursdays noon-7 from early June through mid-August in Gibson Park. Bicyclists and motorists on SR 5, which parallels Lake Erie and is part of the Great Lakes Seaway Trail (a national scenic byway), get great views of the sprawling vineyards and lake.

Recreational opportunities are certainly not lacking. Lake Erie offers boating, fishing and swimming. North East Marina, 11950 E. Lake Rd., provides various marine services, including fishing charters and free access to four boat ramps. The season runs mid-April to mid-October; phone (814) 725-8244. Freeport Beach is about 2 miles west of the marina at the end of SR 89. Lifeguards are on duty 10 a.m. until dusk early June through Labor Day. The adjacent Halli Reid Park, named for the first woman to swim across Lake Erie from Canada, has a playground, covered picnic areas and grills. There are several other small parks in the area, and North East has places to camp, golf, hike, hunt and cross-country ski as well. Tributary streams 16-Mile Creek and 20-Mile Creek can be used for steelhead trout fishing.

North East is home to a branch of Erie's Mercyhurst University. The 84-acre Catholic-affiliated Mercyhurst North East campus, which opened in 1991, was home to St. Mary's Seminary until the mid-1980s. Some of the historic buildings date between 1868 and 1920.

Lake Erie Speedway, 10700 Delmas Dr., hosts auto racing in six divisions Saturday evenings on its 3/8-mile asphalt track; the stands can seat up to 8,000. Pop into the post office lobby at 38 S. Lake St. to see a sculpture of a town crier, created during the Great Depression as part of President Roosevelt's WPA program; it resides above the drop-off area.

The extensive calendar of events in North East includes two festivals celebrating local agriculture. The North East Cherry Festival takes place in mid-July and the Wine Country Harvest Festival is held the last full weekend in September.

North East Area Chamber of Commerce: 44 W. Main St., North East, PA 16428. **Phone:** (814) 725-4262.

Self-guiding tours: Pick up a brochure, which includes a detailed map of the area, at the chamber of commerce and enjoy the exteriors of downtown's

many historic buildings, including the library, Masonic Temple and several churches and residences.

Shopping: In addition to all the edible goodies you can find in North East, there are boutiques and antique shops in some of the downtown historic buildings. More antiques can be found at Interstate Antique Mall, 5446 Station Rd. (SR 89), just off I-90.

HOLIDAY INN EXPRESS & SUITES - NORTH EAST (ERIE) (814)725-4400

Hotel
$100-$300

Address: 6310 Old Station Rd NE 16428 **Location:** I-90 exit 41, just n on SR 89. **Facility:** 123 units. 4 stories, interior corridors. **Amenities:** safes. **Pool:** heated indoor. **Activities:** sauna, hot tub, exercise room. **Guest Services:** valet and coin laundry. **Featured Amenity: full hot breakfast.**

NORTHERN CAMBRIA pop. 3,835

CITY HOTEL BAR & GRILL   814/951-0303
Hotel. **Address:** 1014 Maple Ave 15714

NORTH HUNTINGDON
• Part of Pittsburgh area — see map p. 225

HAMPTON INN & SUITES NORTH HUNTINGDON-IRWIN
724/863-9900
Hotel. **Address:** 8441 Country Club Dr 15642

AAA Benefit: Members save up to 10%!

HOLIDAY INN EXPRESS IRWIN   724/861-9000
Hotel. **Address:** 8400 US 30 15642

NORTHUMBERLAND pop. 3,804, elev. 452'

FRONT STREET STATION   570/473-3626
American. Casual Dining. **Address:** 2 Front St 17857

NORTH VERSAILLES pop. 10,229
• Part of Pittsburgh area — see map p. 225

KING'S FAMILY RESTAURANT   412/823-0324
American. Casual Dining. **Address:** 1820 Lincoln Hwy 15137

PRIMANTI BROS.   412/829-4700
American. Casual Dining. **Address:** 921 E Pittsburgh McKeesport Blvd 15137

NORTH WALES pop. 3,229
• Restaurants p. 140
• Part of Philadelphia area — see map p. 154

HAMPTON INN PHILADELPHIA MONTGOMERYVILLE
215/412-8255
Hotel. **Address:** 121 Garden Golf Blvd 19454

AAA Benefit: Members save up to 10%!

JOSEPH AMBLER INN   215/362-7500
Historic Boutique Bed & Breakfast. **Address:** 1005 Horsham Rd 19454

JOSEPH AMBLER INN   215/362-7500
 American. Casual Dining. **Address:** 1005 Horsham Rd 19454

NOTTINGHAM (I-10) elev. 551'
• Part of Philadelphia area — see map p. 154

Nottingham County Park *(see Recreation Areas Chart)* offers opportunities for bicycling, cross-country skiing, fishing, hiking and horseback riding, and it is also home to Nottingham Serpentine Barrens. The 630-acre site is rare because its desert-like landscape looks nothing like the typical surroundings of Southeastern Pennsylvania. The plants you'll find here have become highly adaptive to their environment because the soil is low in nutrients and high in metals; prairie grasses and pitch pines are common. The park, 150 Park Rd., is open daily 8 a.m.-dusk.

OAKDALE (G-1) pop. 1,459, elev. 899'
• Part of Pittsburgh area — see map p. 225

Oakdale is a southeastern suburb of Pittsburgh, and self identifies as "America's hometown." The rural borough still has a main street with a local hardware store, hanging flower baskets and American flags, and a gazebo in the center of town.

KING'S FAMILY RESTAURANT   724/695-3922
 American. Casual Dining. **Address:** 500 Marketplace Dr 15071

OAKMONT pop. 6,303
• Hotels & Restaurants map & index p. 246
• Part of Pittsburgh area — see map p. 225

DOONE'S INN AT OAKMONT   412/828-0410 **60**
 Bed & Breakfast. **Address:** 300 Rt 909 15147

CHELSEA GRILLE   412/828-0570 **62**
 American. Casual Dining. **Address:** 515 Allegheny Ave 15139

SOMMA PIZZA & SPORTS BAR   412/826-1500 **61**
 American. Sports Bar. **Address:** 380 Rt 909 15147

OAKS
• Part of Philadelphia area — see map p. 154

HAMPTON INN & SUITES-VALLEY FORGE/OAKS
                                    (610)676-0900

Hotel
$99-$139

  AAA Benefit: Members save up to 10%!

Address: 100 Cresson Blvd 19456 **Location:** US 422 exit Oaks. Located in a commercial area. **Facility:** 107 units, some efficiencies. 5 stories, interior corridors. **Terms:** 1-7 night minimum stay, cancellation fee imposed. **Pool:** outdoor. **Activities:** exercise room. **Guest Services:** valet and coin laundry. **Featured Amenity:** full hot breakfast.

HILTON GARDEN INN VALLEY FORGE/OAKS
                                    (610)650-0880

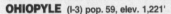
Hotel
$129-$199

  AAA Benefit: Members save up to 10%!

Address: 500 Cresson Blvd 19456 **Location:** US 422 exit Oaks. **Facility:** 135 units. 5 stories, interior corridors. **Terms:** 1-7 night minimum stay, cancellation fee imposed. **Pool:** heated indoor. **Activities:** hot tub, exercise room. **Guest Services:** valet and coin laundry, area transportation.

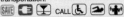

OHIOPYLE (I-3) pop. 59, elev. 1,221'

Ohiopyle is part of the Laurel Highlands *(see place listing p. 122)*. Once a hunting area of the Delaware, Shawnee and Iroquois, the area was named Ohiopehhle by the Native Americans for the white frothy water of the Youghiogheny River. Ohiopyle State Park *(see Recreation Areas Chart)* provides overlook platforms to the falls. It also is a trailhead for the Great Allegheny Passage and the Laurel Highlands Hiking Trail.

Ohiopyle is best known as a popular starting point for white-water rafting. Trips can be arranged through several outfitters in town.

Laurel Highlands Visitors Center: 124 Main St., Ohiopyle, PA 15470. **Phone:** (724) 238-5661 or (800) 333-5661.

The visitors center is in Ohiopyle State Park; it is not staffed during the off-season but brochures are available.

INSIDER INFO:
Great Allegheny Passage

The Great Allegheny Passage is one of the longest multipurpose recreational trails in the eastern United States, spanning 150 continuous miles between Pittsburgh and Cumberland, Md. Bicyclists, cross-country skiers, walkers and, in some places, equestrians travel through the Laurel Highlands along the scenic Youghiogheny and Casselman rivers. The 3,200-foot Big Savage Tunnel near the Mason-Dixon Line is usually closed Dec. 15-April 10; there is no alternate route.

The passage connects with the C&O Canal Towpath, providing a 334.5-mile motor-free route to Washington, D.C. Restrooms and facilities are available at several towns along the trail, which include (running west to east) the Pittsburgh riverfront; McKeesport; Boston; Cedar Creek Park; Whitsett; Connellsville; Ohiopyle; Confluence; Rockwood; Meyersdale; Frostburg, Md.; and Cumberland, Md. The trail passes through Ohiopyle State Park *(see Recreation Areas Chart)*, which offers white-water rafting and cottages for camping. Fallingwater, one of Frank Lloyd Wright's architectural landmarks, also is nearby.

For more information contact the Allegheny Trail Alliance at P.O. Box 228, Homestead, PA 15120.

OIL CITY (E-2) pop. 10,557, elev. 1,028'

The discovery of oil in 1860 precipitated the almost overnight settlement of Oil City. The narrow ravine of Oil Creek became the busiest valley on the continent and in a short time was covered with derricks from Oil City to Titusville. From 1860 to 1870, 17 million barrels of oil were shipped from this region to Pittsburgh. McClintock Well No. 1, drilled in 1861, is still producing.

The Oil Creek and Titusville Railroad offers 3-hour round-trips in restored 1930s passenger cars between Titusville and Rynd Farm in Oil City. Along the way there are stops at Drake Well Park and Petroleum Centre Station in Oil Creek State Park.

Hasson Park Arboretum on E. Bissell Avenue bursts into color in the spring when more than 500 rhododendron bloom. Summer and winter recreational activities are offered at Oil Creek State Park *(see Recreation Areas Chart)* off SR 8 between Oil City and Titusville; phone (814) 676-5915.

Oil Region Alliance of Business, Industry and Tourism: 217 Elm St., Oil City, PA 16301-1412. **Phone:** (814) 677-3152 or (800) 483-6264.

OLD FORGE pop. 8,313

ARCARO & GENELL   570/457-5555
♦♦ Italian. Casual Dining. **Address:** 443 S Main St 18518

ORRTANNA pop. 173, elev. 670'

HICKORY BRIDGE FARM BED & BREAKFAST   717/642-5261
♦♦♦ Historic Country Inn. **Address:** 96 Hickory Bridge Rd 17353

WHERE TO EAT

HICKORY BRIDGE FARM RESTAURANT   717/642-5261
♦♦ American. Casual Dining. **Address:** 96 Hickory Bridge Rd 17353

ORWIGSBURG pop. 3,099

OAK HILL INN   570/366-3881
♦♦♦ American. Casual Dining. **Address:** 655 Rt 61 S 17961

OSTERBURG

SLICK'S IVY STONE RESTAURANT   814/276-3131
♦♦ American. Casual Dining. **Address:** 8785 William Penn Rd 16667

PALMYRA (LEBANON COUNTY) (H-9)
pop. 7,320, elev. 450'

Founded by John Palm in the late 1700s, Palmyra bases its economy on food manufacturing and farming. Of interest 3 miles north of Main and Railroad streets is the 1803 Bindnagles Evangelical Lutheran Church, a two-story brick structure with round arch windows and doors. The grave of John Palm is in the churchyard.

AMERICAS BEST VALUE INN   (717)838-4761
♦♦ Motel. **Address:** 2951 Horseshoe Pike 17078

KNIGHTS INN   (717)838-1324
♦♦ Motel. **Address:** 1071 E Main St 17078

THE LONDONDERRY INN   717/838-7500
♦♦♦ Bed & Breakfast. **Address:** 2764 Horseshoe Pike 17078

WHERE TO EAT

HOMETOWN FAMILY RESTAURANT   717/838-0877
♦♦ American. Casual Dining. **Address:** 1 N Londonderry Square 17078

PAOLI (B-9) pop. 5,575, elev. 541'
• Part of Philadelphia area — see map p. 154

A short distance from Valley Forge National Historical Park near the junction of US 76 and 276 is the rustic Wharton Esherick Studio. Esherick, known as the "dean of American craftsmen" worked here until his death in 1970. Displayed are more than 200 of his pieces, including paintings, woodcuts, ceramics, sculpture, furniture and utensils. Guided studio tours are available. Reservations with 48-hour notice are required; phone (610) 644-5822 for more information.

Just west of Paoli in Malvern *(see page p. 127.)* at the junction of Monument and Wayne avenues is Paoli Battlefield Historic Site, the scene of the Battle of Paoli during the American Revolution. The grounds contain plaques describing the massacre. The oldest monument on the grounds dates to 1817. The site is open daily dawn to dusk; phone (484) 320-7173.

LE SAIGON   610/889-4870
♦♦ Vietnamese. Casual Dining. **Address:** 82 E Lancaster Ave 19301

SUSHI NAMI JAPANESE RESTAURANT   610/889-9800
♦♦ Japanese. Casual Dining. **Address:** 19 Lancaster Ave 19301

PARADISE (LANCASTER COUNTY)
pop. 1,129, elev. 457'
• Restaurants p. 142
• Hotels & Restaurants map & index p. 148

BEST WESTERN PLUS REVERE INN & SUITES
                                    (717)687-7683 [55]

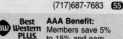

♦♦♦ Hotel $109-$199 | Best Western PLUS | **AAA Benefit:** Members save 5% to 15% and earn 10% bonus points!

Address: 3063 Lincoln Hwy E (Rt 30) 17562 **Location:** On US 30 (Lincoln Hwy), 0.3 mi w. Located in a commercial area. **Facility:** 95 units, some two bedrooms. 2-3 stories (no elevator), interior/exterior corridors. **Terms:** cancellation fee imposed. **Dining:** Revere Tavern, see separate listing. **Pool:** heated outdoor, heated indoor. **Activities:** hot tub, game room, exercise room. **Guest Services:** coin laundry. **Featured Amenity:** breakfast buffet.

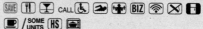

(See map & index p. 148.)

WHERE TO EAT

REVERE TAVERN   717/687-8601   ③⑦

◆◆

American Casual Dining
$7-$33

AAA Inspector Notes: *Historic.* This restaurant is found within a stone building built in 1740 as a stagecoach inn. Prior to his presidency, James Buchanan owned the building. His sister-in-law's brother, Stephen Foster, wrote some of his songs here. The menu features steaks, veal, pork, seafood and chicken. Try the veal Capri, tender medallions of veal, jumbo gulf shrimp and diced tomatoes sautéed in a tarragon cream sauce. **Features:** full bar. **Address:** 3063 Lincoln Hwy E (Rt 30) 17562 **Location:** On US 30 (Lincoln Hwy), 0.3 mi w; in Best Western Plus Revere Inn & Suites.

Ⓛ Ⓓ

TWO COUSINS PIZZA   717/687-8606   ㉘
🍝 Italian. Quick Serve. **Address:** 3099 Lincoln Hwy E 17562

PENNS CREEK (F-8) pop. 715, elev. 568'

Named for the stream that flows nearby, Penns Creek is surrounded by rich, rolling farmland. Just east at US 11 and US 15 is the site where the Penns Creek Massacre occurred Oct. 16, 1755, when Native Americans killed or captured 26 settlers.

PENNSYLVANIA DUTCH COUNTRY

The simple lifestyle of the Pennsylvania Dutch defines this bucolic area in southeastern Pennsylvania. Well-kept white farmhouses with expansive porches and black roofs dot the gently rolling hills. Tall silos stand like sentinels next to barns and neat vegetable gardens border houses, sharing space with clotheslines filled with dark trousers and prim dresses drying in the breeze.

Meandering two-lane roads wind past fields where bearded men in broad-brimmed hats guide plows pulled by teams of hard-working horses or mules. Horse-drawn carriages hospitably share roads with cars and trucks, the noisy clatter of the buggy's wheels against the pavement practically drowning out the rhythmic clip-clop of the horse's hooves.

The Amish settled this rich farmland in the early 18th century, coming here mainly from Germany in response to William Penn's promise of religious tolerance. Actually, the Amish were one of three similar spiritual groups who left Germany in search of freedom of worship in this new land. All three faiths-the Amish, the Mennonites and the Brethren-share the same beliefs concerning baptism, the importance of family and community, and the authority of the Bible.

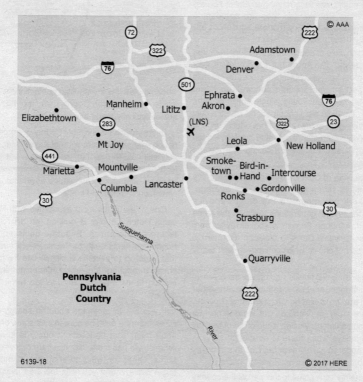

This map shows cities in the Pennsylvania Dutch Country where you will find attractions, hotels and restaurants. Cities are listed alphabetically in this book on the following pages.

Where the groups differ is in how much they allow the "outside world" to touch their everyday lives. The devout Amish are the most conservative of the groups. While most Mennonites and Brethren wear clothing much like their "English" (i.e., non-Amish) counterparts, Amish men are easily recognizable by their distinctive plain dark suits, solid-color shirts, suspenders and wide-brimmed hats. Amish women favor modest attire, generally consisting of long-sleeved dresses with full skirts (no prints), a cape and an apron, their hair hidden by demure prayer coverings.

Many Mennonites and Brethren allow contemporary conveniences such as electricity, phones and cars, but the Amish restrict such technology to reinforce their separation from the rest of the world. You won't see any power lines running to Amish homes, but the "Plain People" (as they are sometimes called) do manage to enjoy modern household appliances by using propane instead of electricity.

The Amish view of education also differs from that of the "English." The Amish build and operate their own one-room schools, which are placed every mile or two apart so that children can walk to them; teachers are generally young, single Amish women. Students (about 30 per school) attend classes only through the eighth grade; any further education, it is believed, would threaten their value system, loosen tight family ties and cause the children to become more secular.

And speaking of children, the Amish tend to have large families-seven or eight kids are average. Families are paramount to the group, and it's common for several generations to live in the same household. Although English is spoken away from home, Pennsylvania Dutch (a dialect of German) is the language of choice when conversing with family members.

Approximately 25 families comprise each Amish church district. Services, conducted every other Sunday, are held in church members' homes. Hymns are sung (in German), but there is no musical accompaniment. Visiting is the order of the day on the Sundays when there is no church service, and the children take advantage of this time by playing softball, volleyball or, in winter, hockey.

You certainly can't come to this part of the country without sampling the justly famous Pennsylvania Dutch cuisine. Numerous restaurants feature traditional Amish cooking served family style. Diners, seated at long tables, share heaping platters of all-you-can-eat down-home cooking, beginning with local delicacies such as chow chow, a mix of pickled vegetables, and homemade bread and apple butter. Dishes overflowing with fried chicken, sausages, mashed potatoes, bread stuffing, noodles with browned butter and fresh, seasonal veggies follow, not to mention shoofly pie for dessert. Other regional specialties to try include pretzels (the first pretzel bakery was established in Lititz in 1861),

whoopie pies (the cream-filled confections were first made in Lancaster County) and schnitz, dried apples typically made into pies.

Pennsylvania's Lancaster County is home to the nation's largest concentration of Amish. Many of the sect still hold to their farming heritage, but the majority now are spread out among the community and work in such diverse industries as manufacturing, construction, retail and crafts.

One of the crafts most associated with Pennsylvania Dutch Country is quilting, an art form perfected by the Amish. Beautiful quilts and other handmade items such as "quillows" (a small quilt that folds up to become a pillow) can be found in shops throughout the region. Other quality handcrafted items made locally include furniture and pottery.

If you like to rummage about in search of treasures from the past, be sure to visit some of the antique malls that Lancaster County is known for. Adamstown has more than its share of these emporiums. Other fun ways to shop are at the area's outlet malls and, if you're in the area in spring, at "mud sales." Named after the condition of the ground as it thaws out from the cold winter, these sales are typically held to benefit local volunteer fire departments. You'll find a mixture of Amish and English checking out everything from buggies to quilts to baked goods.

A ride through the rolling farmland of Pennsylvania Dutch Country, whether in a car or as part of a horse-drawn buggy tour, often reveals some of Lancaster County's hidden treasures-more than two dozen historic covered bridges. The Discover Lancaster Visitors Center has several self-guiding driving tours available.

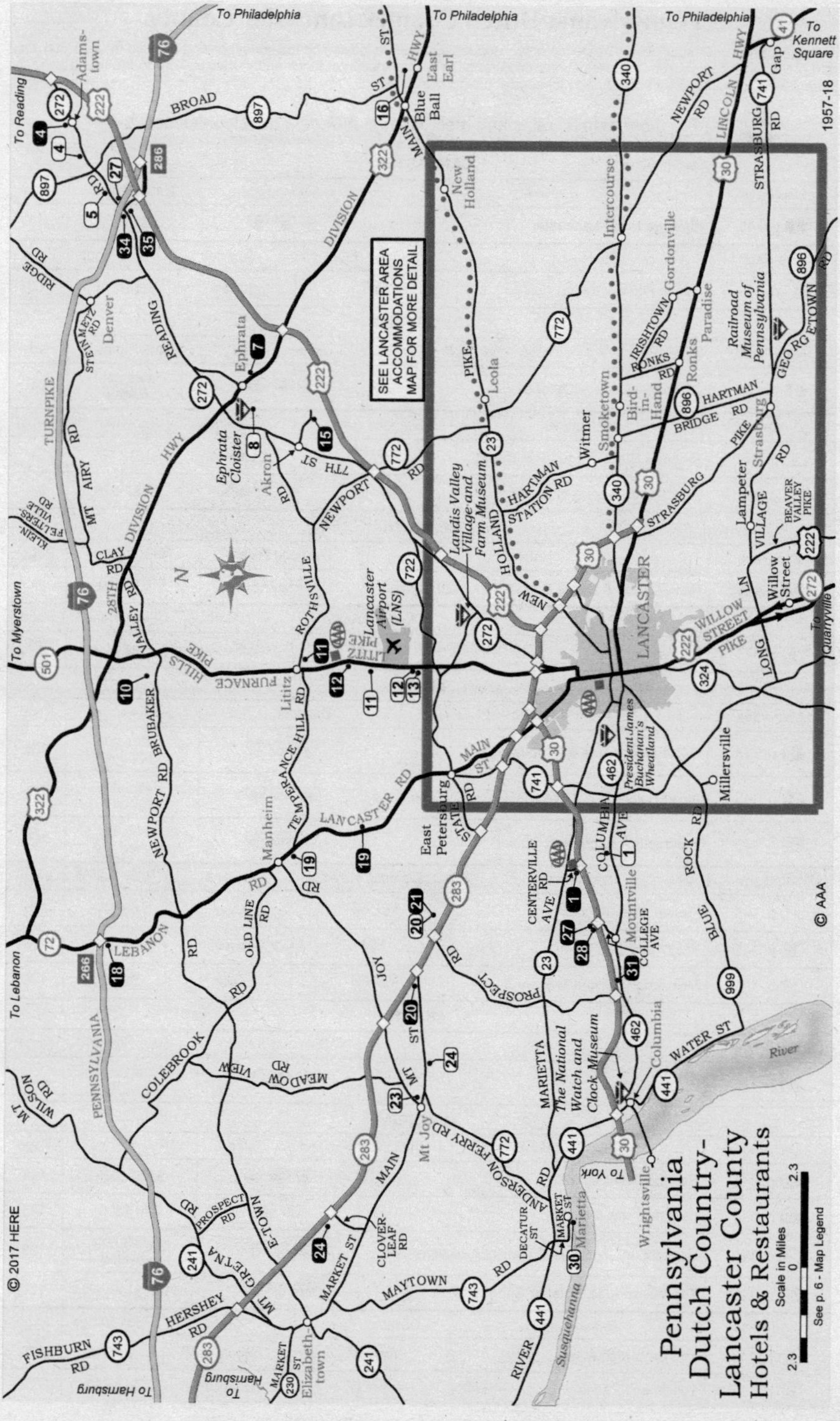

Pennsylvania Dutch Country-Lancaster County Hotels & Restaurants
SEE LANCASTER AREA ACCOMMODATIONS MAP FOR MORE DETAIL
Scale in Miles
2.3
0
2.3
See p. 6 - Map Legend
1957-18
© 2017 HERE
© AAA
To Philadelphia
To Reading
To Kennett Square
To Myerstown
To Lebanon
To Harrisburg
To York
To Quarryville
Adamstown
Denver
Ephrata
Ephrata Cloister
Akron
Blue Ball
East Earl
New Holland
Leola
Intercourse
Gordonville
Paradise
Ronks
Bird-in-Hand
Smoketown
Witmer
Gap
Railroad Museum of Pennsylvania
Strasburg
Lampeter
Willow Street
Lancaster
Lancaster Airport (LNS)
Landis Valley Village and Farm Museum
Lititz
Manheim
East Petersburg
Millersville
President James Buchanan's Wheatland
Mountville
Columbia
The National Watch and Clock Museum
Wrightsville
Marietta
Mt Joy
Elizabethtown
Susquehanna River
PENNSYLVANIA TURNPIKE
DIVISION HWY
LINCOLN HWY
NEWPORT RD
STRASBURG RD
HARTMAN BRIDGE RD
GEORGETOWN RD
LANCASTER RD
TEMPERANCE HILL RD
FURNACE HILLS PIKE
LITITZ PIKE
ROTHSVILLE RD
NEWPORT RD
BRUBAKER RD
VALLEY RD
28TH RD
CLAY RD
MT AIRY RD
STEINMETZ RD
RIDGE RD
BROAD ST
READING RD
7TH ST
NEW HOLLAND PIKE
HARTMAN STATION RD
MAIN ST
STATE RD
COLUMBIA AVE
CENTERVILLE RD
COLLEGE AVE
ROCK RD
BLUE RD
WATER ST
WILLOW STREET PIKE
LONG LN
VILLAGE RD
BEAVER VALLEY PIKE
IRISHTOWN RD
RONKS RD
OLD LINE RD
LEBANON RD
JOY RD
PROSPECT RD
MARIETTA AVE
ANDERSON FERRY RD
MAYTOWN RD
DECATUR ST
MARKET ST
RIVER RD
MT GRETNA RD
E-TOWN RD
PROSPECT RD
HERSHEY RD
FISHBURN RD
COLEBROOK RD
MEADOW VIEW RD
MT WILSON RD
CLOVERLEAF RD
MT JOY ST
KLEINFELTERSVILLE RD

Pennsylvania Dutch Country-Lancaster County

This index helps you "spot" where approved hotels and restaurants are located on the corresponding detailed maps. Hotel daily rate range is for comparison only. Restaurant price range is a combination of lunch and/or dinner. Turn to the listing page for more information and consult display ads for special promotions.

 For more details, rates and reservations: AAA.com/travelguides/hotels

LANCASTER

Map Page	Hotel	Diamond Rated	Rate Range	Page
1 p. 145	**Heritage Hotel Lancaster**	◈◈◈	$135-$165 [SAVE]	119

Map Page	Restaurant	Diamond Rated	Cuisine	Price Range	Page
1 p. 145	Venice Pizza & Pasta	◈	Italian	$6-$23	120

ADAMSTOWN

Map Page	Hotel	Diamond Rated	Rate Range	Page
4 p. 145	Adamstown Inns & Cottages	◈◈◈	Rates not provided	34

Map Page	Restaurants	Diamond Rated	Cuisine	Price Range	Page
4 p. 145	**Stoudt's Black Angus Restaurant**	◈◈	American	$12-$39	34
5 p. 145	Zia Maria's Italian Restaurant	◈◈	Italian	$7-$26	34

EPHRATA

Map Page	Hotel	Diamond Rated	Rate Range	Page
7 p. 145	Hampton Inn & Suites Ephrata-Mountain Springs	◈◈◈	$109-$189	71

Map Page	Restaurant	Diamond Rated	Cuisine	Price Range	Page
8 p. 145	Aromas del Sur	◈◈	Colombian	$9-$22	71

LITITZ

Map Page	Hotels	Diamond Rated	Rate Range	Page
10 p. 145	Swiss Woods Bed & Breakfast	◈◈◈	Rates not provided	126
11 p. 145	Alden House Bed & Breakfast	◈◈◈	Rates not provided	126
12 p. 145	**Holiday Inn Express & Suites**	◈◈◈	Rates not provided [SAVE]	126

Map Page	Restaurants	Diamond Rated	Cuisine	Price Range	Page
11 p. 145	Kanpai Asian Kitchen	◈◈	Asian	$5-$20	126
12 p. 145	Knight and Day Diner	◈	American	$4-$18	126
13 p. 145	Mojo Asian Cuisine & Sushi Bar	◈◈	Asian	$8-$20	126

AKRON

Map Page	Hotel	Diamond Rated	Rate Range	Page
15 p. 145	Boxwood Inn	◈◈◈	Rates not provided	34

MANHEIM

Map Page	Hotels	Diamond Rated	Rate Range	Page
18 p. 145	Hampton Inn-Manheim	◈◈◈	$129-$329	128
19 p. 145	Lancaster Inn & Suites	◈◈	$99-$209	128
20 p. 145	Hampton Inn & Suites Mount Joy/Lancaster West	◈◈◈	Rates not provided	128
21 p. 145	**The Warehouse Hotel at Spooky Nook**	◈◈◈	$109-$199 [SAVE]	128

Map Page	Restaurants	Diamond Rated	Cuisine	Price Range	Page
19 p. 145	The Cat's Meow	◈◈	American	$8-$24	128
20 p. 145	Forklift and Palate	◈◈	American	$10-$30	128

ELIZABETHTOWN

Map Page	Hotel	Diamond Rated	Rate Range	Page
24 p. 145	**SureStay Plus Hotel Elizabethtown-Hershey**	◇◇	Rates not provided [SAVE]	70

MOUNTVILLE

Map Page	Hotels	Diamond Rated	Rate Range	Page
27 p. 145	**Sleep Inn & Suites Lancaster County**	◇◇	$75-$190 [SAVE]	136
28 p. 145	**MainStay Suites**	◇◇	$69-$209 [SAVE]	136

COLUMBIA

Map Page	Hotel	Diamond Rated	Rate Range	Page
31 p. 145	Comfort Inn Lancaster County	◇◇	$90-$210	59

DENVER

Map Page	Hotels	Diamond Rated	Rate Range	Page
34 p. 145	Comfort Inn Lancaster County North	◇◇◇	$104-$185	65
35 p. 145	Red Roof Inn Denver	◇◇	$40-$160	65

Map Page	Restaurant	Diamond Rated	Cuisine	Price Range	Page
27 p. 145	The Black Horse Restaurant & Tavern	◇◇	American	$14-$34	65

EAST EARL

Map Page	Restaurant	Diamond Rated	Cuisine	Price Range	Page
16 p. 145	**Shady Maple Smorgasbord**	◇◇	American	$10-$24	67

MOUNT JOY

Map Page	Restaurants	Diamond Rated	Cuisine	Price Range	Page
23 p. 145	The Catacombs	◇◇	American	$22-$40	135
24 p. 145	Country Table Restaurant	◇◇	Regional American	$4-$13	135

MARIETTA

Map Page	Restaurant	Diamond Rated	Cuisine	Price Range	Page
30 p. 145	Railroad House Restaurant Bed & Breakfast	◇◇	American	$8-$25	129

Pennsylvania Dutch
Country - Lancaster Area
Hotels & Restaurants

See p. 6 - Map Legend

Scale in Miles

Pennsylvania Dutch Country-Lancaster Area

This index helps you "spot" where approved hotels and restaurants are located on the corresponding detailed maps. Hotel daily rate range is for comparison only. Restaurant price range is a combination of lunch and/or dinner. Turn to the listing page for more information and consult display ads for special promotions.

 For more details, rates and reservations: AAA.com/travelguides/hotels

LANCASTER

Map Page	Hotels	Diamond Rated	Rate Range	Page
1 p. 148	Homewood Suites by Hilton Lancaster	💎💎💎	$139-$309	119
2 p. 148	Fairfield Inn & Suites by Marriott Lancaster	💎💎💎	$100-$255	118
3 p. 148	Hilton Garden Inn Lancaster	💎💎💎	$149-$225	119
4 p. 148	Eden Resort & Suites, BW Premier Collection	💎💎💎	$109-$224	118
5 p. 148	Hampton Inn-Lancaster	💎💎💎	$159-$250	118
6 p. 148	**Courtyard by Marriott-Lancaster**	💎💎💎	$94-$287 [SAVE]	117
7 p. 148	Country Living Inn	💎💎	Rates not provided	117
8 p. 148	Cork Factory Hotel	💎💎💎	$129-$219	117
9 p. 148	**Lancaster Arts Hotel**	💎💎💎	$169-$369 [SAVE]	119
10 p. 148	The Lancaster Bed and Breakfast	💎💎💎	$145-$175	119
11 p. 148	King's Cottage Bed and Breakfast	💎💎💎	$175-$289	119
12 p. 148	**Hawthorn Suites by Wyndham**	💎💎	$90-$170 [SAVE]	118
13 p. 148	**Country Inn of Lancaster**	💎💎	Rates not provided [SAVE]	117
14 p. 148	**Wingate by Wyndham Lancaster**	💎💎💎	$109-$205 [SAVE]	119
15 p. 148	Comfort Suites Amish Country	💎💎💎	$104-$288	117
16 p. 148	**Continental Inn** *(See ad p. 118.)*	💎💎	$75-$145 [SAVE]	117
17 p. 148	**Country Inn & Suites By Carlson**	💎💎	$89-$299 [SAVE]	117
18 p. 148	Fairfield Inn & Suites by Marriott Lancaster East at The Outlets	💎💎💎	$85-$286	118
19 p. 148	Fulton Steamboat Inn	💎💎💎	Rates not provided	118
20 p. 148	Comfort Inn Lancaster - Rockvale Outlets	💎💎💎	$94-$234	117
21 p. 148	**Lancaster Marriott at Penn Square**	💎💎💎	$125-$303 [SAVE]	119
22 p. 148	Australian Walkabout Inn B&B	💎💎💎	$129-$229	117
23 p. 148	**DoubleTree Resort by Hilton Hotel Lancaster**	💎💎💎	$109-$180 [SAVE]	118

Map Page	Restaurants	Diamond Rated	Cuisine	Price Range	Page
1 p. 148	Arthur's Terrace Restaurant	💎💎	American	$10-$30	119
2 p. 148	Rice & Noodles	💎💎	Vietnamese	$5-$13	120
3 p. 148	DJ's Taste of the 50s	💎	American	$4-$8	119
4 p. 148	**Stockyard Inn**	💎💎💎	Steak Seafood	$8-$45	120
5 p. 148	Gibraltar	💎💎💎	Seafood	$15-$33	119
6 p. 148	Four54 Grill	💎	American	$6-$14	119
7 p. 148	Checkers Bistro	💎💎💎	French	$14-$35	119
8 p. 148	Lancaster Brewing Company	💎💎	Regional American	$9-$28	120
9 p. 148	Horse Inn Restaurant	💎💎	American	$18-$40	119
10 p. 148	The Belvedere Inn	💎💎💎	Continental	$7-$36	119

Map Page	Restaurants (cont'd)	Diamond Rated	Cuisine	Price Range	Page
⑪ p. 148	**The Brasserie Restaurant & Bar**	◆◆	American	$10-$29	119
⑫ p. 148	Lancaster Brewing Company Taproom & Grill	◆◆	American	$6-$24	120
⑬ p. 148	Manor Buffet	◆◆	Asian	$17	120
⑭ p. 148	**Tony Wang's Chinese Restaurant**	◆◆	Chinese	$6-$24	120
⑮ p. 148	Issei Noodle	◆◆	Asian Noodles	$6-$12	120
⑯ p. 148	The Pressroom	◆◆	American	$10-$34	120
⑰ p. 148	El Serrano Restaurante	◆◆	Mexican	$7-$20	119
⑱ p. 148	Tobias S Frogg	◆◆	American	$8-$25	120

NEW HOLLAND

Map Page	Hotels	Diamond Rated	Rate Range	Page
㉖ p. 148	Country Squire Motor Inn	◆	$63-$95	138
㉗ p. 148	Comfort Inn Amish Country	◆◆◆	$109-$213	137

Map Page	Restaurant	Diamond Rated	Cuisine	Price Range	Page
㉑ p. 148	Palermo Pizza	◆	Italian	$6-$18	138

LEOLA

Map Page	Hotel	Diamond Rated	Rate Range	Page
㉚ p. 148	**The Inn at Leola Village**	◆◆◆◆	$169-$369 [SAVE]	123

Map Page	Restaurants	Diamond Rated	Cuisine	Price Range	Page
㉔ p. 148	**TÈ**	◆◆◆◆◆	Italian	$129-$189	123
㉕ p. 148	Gracie's on West Main	◆◆	American	$7-$20	123

INTERCOURSE

Map Page	Hotels	Diamond Rated	Rate Range	Page
㉝ p. 148	Travelers Rest Motel	◆◆	$83-$149	110
㉞ p. 148	The Inn at Kitchen Kettle Village	◆◆◆	Rates not provided	110
㉟ p. 148	**Best Western Plus Intercourse Village Inn & Suites** (See ad p. 109.)	◆◆◆	$119-$299 [SAVE]	109
㊱ p. 148	The Inn & Spa at Intercourse Village	◆◆◆	Rates not provided	109

Map Page	Restaurant	Diamond Rated	Cuisine	Price Range	Page
㉘ p. 148	The Kling House Restaurant	◆◆	Regional American	$6-$13	110

BIRD-IN-HAND

Map Page	Hotels	Diamond Rated	Rate Range	Page
㊴ p. 148	Leaman's Lancaster Country Lodging	◆◆◆	$69-$89	48
㊵ p. 148	**Amish View Inn & Suites** (See ad p. 117.)	◆◆◆	$104-$214 [SAVE]	48
㊶ p. 148	Amish Country Motel	◆◆	$94-$129	48
㊷ p. 148	Bird-In-Hand Village Inn & Suites	◆◆◆	$99-$199	48
㊸ p. 148	Bird-In-Hand Family Inn	◆◆	$79-$199	48

Map Page	Restaurant	Diamond Rated	Cuisine	Price Range	Page
㉛ p. 148	**Smokehouse BBQ and Brews**	◆◆	Regional American	$7-$19	48

SMOKETOWN

Map Page	Hotels	Diamond Rated	Rate Range	Page
㊻ p. 148	**Smoketown Inn (of Lancaster County)**	◆◆	$82-$109 [SAVE]	279
㊼ p. 148	Mill Stream Country Inn	◆◆	Rates not provided	279

Map Page	Restaurant	Diamond Rated	Cuisine	Price Range	Page
㉞ p. 148	**Good 'N Plenty Restaurant**	♦♦	Regional American	$8-$21	279

GORDONVILLE

Map Page	Hotels	Diamond Rated	Rate Range	Page
㊿ p. 148	**Harvest Drive Family Inn**	♦♦	Rates not provided [SAVE]	89
(51) p. 148	Motel 6-Lancaster #4174	♦♦	Rates not provided	89
(52) p. 148	After Eight B&B	♦♦♦	$108-$260	89

PARADISE (LANCASTER COUNTY)

Map Page	Hotel	Diamond Rated	Rate Range	Page
�55 p. 148	**Best Western Plus Revere Inn & Suites**	♦♦♦	$109-$199 [SAVE]	141

Map Page	Restaurants	Diamond Rated	Cuisine	Price Range	Page
㊲ p. 148	**Revere Tavern**	♦♦	American	$7-$33	142
㊳ p. 148	Two Cousins Pizza	♦	Italian	$5-$12	142

STRASBURG

Map Page	Hotel	Diamond Rated	Rate Range	Page
㊽ p. 148	Holiday Inn Express & Suites Lancaster East Strasburg	♦♦♦	Rates not provided	286

Map Page	Restaurant	Diamond Rated	Cuisine	Price Range	Page
㊶ p. 148	Fireside Tavern	♦♦	American	$6-$25	286

RONKS

Map Page	Hotels	Diamond Rated	Rate Range	Page
㊱ p. 148	Quiet Haven Motel	♦	$58-$99	273
㊶ p. 148	**Days Inn Ronks Dutch Country**	♦♦	$59-$169 [SAVE]	273
㊳ p. 148	**La Quinta Inn & Suites**	♦♦♦	$75-$195 [SAVE]	273
㊴ p. 148	Eastbrook Inn	♦♦	Rates not provided	273
㊵ p. 148	**Hershey Farm Inn**	♦♦	$50-$180 [SAVE]	273

Map Page	Restaurants	Diamond Rated	Cuisine	Price Range	Page
㊹ p. 148	Route 30 Diner	♦♦	American	$6-$17	273
㊺ p. 148	**Miller's Smorgasbord & Bakery**	♦♦	Regional American	$8-$24	273
㊻ p. 148	Dienner's Country Restaurant	♦♦	American	$3-$12	273
㊼ p. 148	Katie's Kitchen	♦♦	American	$7-$13	273
㊽ p. 148	**Hershey Farm Restaurant**	♦♦	Regional American	$6-$26	273

Make the Conn🔗ction

Find this symbol for places to look, book and save on AAA.com.

PERKASIE (G-11) pop. 8,511, elev. 414'
• Part of Philadelphia area — see map p. 154

• Part of Philadelphia area — see map p. 154

SAVE THE PEARL S. BUCK HOUSE, 1 mi. s.w. of SR 313 at 520 Dublin Rd., was the home of author and humanitarian Pearl S. Buck. The 1825 stone farmhouse displays her Nobel and Pulitzer prizes and many personal mementos collected in China, including decorative screens, rare Asian artwork and porcelain. The desk and typewriter on which she wrote "The Good Earth" are displayed, and her personal collection of Pennsylvania country furniture also is featured. During the Festival of Trees display in November and December, the house is decorated for the holidays and includes more than a dozen trees. A welcome center features exhibits.

Hours: Guided tours are offered Mon.-Sat. at 11, 1 and 2, Sun. at 1 and 2. Hours may vary during special events; phone ahead. Closed major holidays. **Cost:** $15; $12 (ages 62+); $7 (students with ID). Fees may vary during special events. **Phone:** (215) 249-0100. GT

PERRYOPOLIS pop. 1,784

LENORA'S   724/736-2509
American. Fine Dining. **Address:** 301 Liberty St 15473

PETERSBURG (G-6) pop. 480, elev. 680'

SHAVER'S CREEK ENVIRONMENTAL CENTER is off SR 26, then 1.7 mi. w. on SR 1029 to Stone Valley Recreation Area east entrance. Walking trails wind through woodlands, hillsides and marshes. A raptor center houses injured birds of prey. Bird feeding stations, bat boxes and interactive exhibits are offered. Seasonal walks and events also are featured throughout the year. **Hours:** Daily 10-5, mid-Feb. to mid-Dec. Closed Thanksgiving. **Cost:** Free. **Phone:** (814) 863-2000 or (814) 667-3424.

Philadelphia

Then & Now

So, why is the Liberty Bell cracked?

There are many tales concerning the circumstances of the bell's first crack, but consensus has it that the fracture dangerously expanded and ultimately rendered the bell unusable after it rang in 1846 to commemorate George Washington's birthday. It was probably a fitting occasion for its final performance.

Philadelphia teems with icons like this hallowed bell that inspire an undeniable sense of history and awe. These vestiges of the past send shivers down the spines of visitors and residents alike as it hits home that this is indeed America's birthplace. Have lunch at City Tavern like Washington did, or tour Christ Church, where he was a parishioner, along with Benjamin Franklin and some members of Congress. Then wander inside the Betsy Ross House to learn about the woman who reputedly sewed the first stars and stripes on Old Glory.

To experience Philadelphia to the fullest, a good place to start is where it all began: Independence National Historical Park. You can easily spend the entire day here, exploring landmarks that represent the nation's founding. There's Congress Hall, the site that hosted the inauguration of John Adams and the second inauguration of Washington, and of course, that famous bell.

AAA.com/travelguides—
more ways to look, book and save

Outside of this historic square mile, there are other nooks and crannies of the Old City ripe for exploration. Stroll down narrow Elfreth's Alley, said to be America's oldest continuously inhabited residential street. Take the self-guiding tour at the U.S. Mint to see the birth of currency, or learn about Quaker life at the brick Historic Arch Street Meeting House, built as a gathering spot in 1804.

Now that you have a sense of the old, you can appreciate the new. Skyscrapers like Comcast Center, One Liberty Place (with its new 57-story-tall One Liberty Observation Deck) and Three Logan Square soar over Center City, and statues of historical figures meld with those of modern day heroes. You can get a closer look at the commanding statue of city founder William Penn presiding over his "City of Brotherly Love" from a perch atop City Hall's clock tower.

Penn's brotherly love and the strong sense of family and tradition instilled by the Quakers are still values held near and dear to Philadelphians. Philly's neighborhoods have histories of their

Liberty Bell

(Continued on p. 156.)

Destination Philadelphia

This map shows cities in the Philadelphia vicinity where you will find attractions, hotels and restaurants. Cities are listed alphabetically in this book on the following pages.

© AAA

Nearby New Jersey

6129-18

Fast Facts

ABOUT THE CITY

POP: 1,526,006 ▪ **ELEV:** 39 ft.

MONEY

SALES TAX: Pennsylvania's statewide sales tax is 6 percent. An additional 2 percent is collected by Philadelphia County, as is an 8.5 percent hotel tax.

WHOM TO CALL

EMERGENCY: 911

POLICE (non-emergency): 311

HOSPITALS: Aria Health (Torresdale Campus), (215) 612-4000 ▪ Hospital of the University of Pennsylvania, (215) 662-4000 ▪ Methodist Hospital, (215) 952-9000 ▪ Pennsylvania Hospital, (215) 829-3000 ▪ Roxborough Memorial Hospital, (215) 483-9900 ▪ Temple University Hospital, (215) 707-2000.

WHERE TO LOOK AND LISTEN

NEWSPAPERS: Philadelphia has two daily papers: the Philadelphia *Inquirer (online at www.philly.com)* and the *Daily News (online at www.philly.com/dailynews).*

RADIO: Philadelphia radio station KYW (1060 AM) is an all-news/weather station ▪ WHYY (90.9 FM) is a member of National Public Radio.

VISITOR INFORMATION

Independence Visitor Center: One N. Independence Mall W., Philadelphia, PA 19106. **Phone:** (800) 537-7676.

Tours of area attractions, including Independence National Historical Park, may be booked here. It's open daily 8:30-7, Memorial Day-Labor Day; 8:30-6, rest of year.

Visit Philadelphia also provides information at the center about the city's attractions, neighborhoods, hotels, restaurants and events and neighboring Bucks, Chester, Delaware and Montgomery Counties.

TRANSPORTATION

AIR TRAVEL: Philadelphia International Airport (PHL) is 6.5 miles south of the business district via I-76 (Schuylkill Expressway) and SR 291 (Penrose Avenue). SEPTA's airport rail line runs daily on the half-hour 5 a.m.-midnight between the airport and Center City. Advance fare $9; onboard fare $10. Discounted fares are available for children, senior citizens and disabled guests.

RENTAL CARS: Hertz, at the Philadelphia International Airport, (215) 492-7205 or (800) 654-3080, offers discounts to AAA members.

 Book and save at **AAA.com/hertz**

RAIL SERVICE: Amtrak trains pull into both the main 30th Street Station terminal at 30th and Market streets and the North Philadelphia Station at N. Broad Street and W. Glenwood Avenue. If your destination is mid-city, disembark at 30th Street Station. Phone (800) 872-7245, or TTY (800) 523-6590.

BUSES: The major bus terminal is Greyhound Lines Inc., (215) 931-4075, at 10th and Filbert streets. Peter Pan Bus Lines, (800) 343-9999, also serves the city. New Jersey Transit buses, (973) 275-5555, depart for southern New Jersey and shore points.

TAXIS: Yellow Cab Co., (215) 333-8294, charges a $2.70 base rate plus $2.30 per mile. A fuel surcharge also may be added. One-way fares between the airport and central Philadelphia locations are a flat $49 fee.

PUBLIC TRANSPORTATION: A system of buses, trolleys, subways and regional rails serves Philadelphia. Operated by the Southeastern Pennsylvania Transportation Authority (SEPTA), buses, trolleys and subways charge $2.50, plus $1 for a transfer; exact change is required. Senior citizens ride free. Regional rail fares vary by zone; phone (215) 580-7800 for fare information. RiverLink Ferry offers ferry service from Penn's Landing to the Adventure Aquarium in Camden, N.J. *See Public Transportation.*

(Continued from p. 153.)
own. To the south, there's Bella Vista, characterized by the colorful, aromatic Italian Market. In Chinatown, diners can indulge culinary cravings at all hours. Handsome 18th-century Colonials flanked by quaint courtyards grace the fashionably preserved Society Hill area, while Rittenhouse Square exudes luxury and wealth.

Although many head to Philadelphia to explore attractions focusing on history and patriotism, a healthy shopping, dining, cultural and sports scene also are part of the mix. The Philadelphia Museum

of Art houses great works of art, and immortalizes fictional boxer Rocky Balboa with his larger-than-life likeness at the base of its steps. The Philadelphia Orchestra offers a popular summer concert series, and the Pennsylvania Ballet's annual "Nutcracker" performances enchant holiday audiences. The Franklin Institute and Philadelphia Zoo stimulate the imaginations of all ages.

And Philadelphians turn out in droves to show their love for the Phillies (baseball), Eagles (football), Flyers (hockey), 76ers (basketball) and Union (soccer).

Must Do: AAA Editor's Picks

- Book your tickets in advance to see one of the world's most celebrated collections of post-impressionist and early modern art at ⏦ **The Barnes Foundation** (2025 Benjamin Franklin Pkwy.). You'll be mesmerized by a diverse ensemble of works that spans multiple cultures and time periods.

- Stroll down **South Street** between Front and 9th, the "hippest street in town." After checking out the funky boutiques and tattoo parlors, pull up a chair at one of the outdoor cafés or bars. In the City of Brotherly Love, this is where you go for people watching, and you'll see it all—preppies, punk rockers, old hippies, pierced skateboarders and lawyers in business suits.

- For romance, hail a **horse-drawn cab** at 5th and Chestnut streets. As the horse trots down Society Hill's 18th-century cobblestone streets, enjoy the sights: Colonial and Federal architecture, row houses and intimate courtyards. Other routes include a trip through Independence National Historical Park's tree-lined lanes and a peek at the bustling Old City area, featuring such sites as the **Betsy Ross House** (239 Arch St.) and **Elfreth's Alley** (off 2nd St. between Arch and Race sts.).

- Think about it—or go to the **Rodin Museum** (in Fairmount Park at Benjamin Franklin Pkwy. & 22nd St.) and leave the pondering to Auguste Rodin's best-known sculpture, "The Thinker." While you're here, tour the museum and discover other sculptures to consider, contemplate and regard.

- Cheer for one of Philly's **sports teams**. If there's a nip in the air, you can head to **Lincoln Financial Field** (1020 Pattison Ave.) and take your chances on tickets for an Eagles game. And if football's not your thing, applaud at **Wells Fargo Center** (3601 S. Broad St.) as a 76er dunks the ball or a Flyer hooks the puck. In spring and summer, go to a Phillies game at **Citizens Bank Park** (1 Citizens Bank Way) and catch a foul ball on the third base line. The latest addition for area sports fans is the region's first Major League Soccer club, the Philadelphia Union, that plays at **Talen Energy Stadium** (1 Stadium Dr.). Warning: Philadelphia sports fans are *very* loyal to their teams.

- Jog to the top of the steps at the ⏦ **Philadelphia Museum of Art** (2600 Benjamin Franklin Pkwy.) and—like Rocky Balboa in the movie—pump your arms in the air! Once you catch your breath, enter the museum to enjoy one of the world's premier art collections. With some 240,000 objects on-site, it's a challenge to see everything, so consider joining one of the daily tours.

- Enjoy music the old-fashioned way at Macy's twice daily **Wanamaker Organ** recitals Monday through Saturday. One of the largest musical instruments in the world, this grand organ fills the store atrium with classical and contemporary tunes from seven floors above the cosmetic counters, downtown at 13th and Market streets. During the holidays, there's a light show to go along with the musical numbers.

- There's no better way to experience the founding of our nation than to visit ⏦ **Independence National Historical Park** (145 S. 3rd St.). It's packed full of history, Colonial architecture and iconic sights like the Liberty Bell.

- Chow down on a **Philly cheesesteak**, the famous hoagie made with thinly sliced rib eye, melted cheese and grilled onions. Most South Philly sandwich shops are open 24-7-365 (and most claim *they* cooked up the original idea). Two of the best are **Pat's King of Steaks** (1237 E. Passyunk Ave.) and **Geno's Steaks** (1219 9th St.).

- Gawk at the strange, spine-tingling exhibits at the **Mütter Museum of The College of Physicians of Philadelphia** (19 S. 22nd St.). Exhibits at this College of Physicians of Philadelphia museum include the Soap Lady, celebrity body parts and casts of patients who suffered from gigantism, eye diseases and other deformities.

Philadelphia Museum of Art

Philadelphia 1-day Itinerary

AAA editors suggest these activities for a great short vacation experience. Those staying in the area for a longer visit can access a 3-day itinerary at AAA.com/TravelGuide.

Morning

- Begin your first day in the City of Brotherly Love at **Independence Visitor Center** in ▽ **Independence National Historical Park** located at the corner of 6th and Market streets in Center City. Arrive early to beat the crowds. Get free tickets and sign up for a National Park Service walking tour; for a historical overview, catch a film that runs throughout the day.

- Head to ▽ **Independence Hall** (Chestnut & 5th sts.). Many landmark events in American history occurred within these halls: On July 4, 1776, the Declaration of Independence was adopted in the Assembly Room of this Georgian structure; the Articles of Confederation and the U.S. Constitution sprang to life in the same room.

- Your next stop should be ▽ **Liberty Bell Center** (6th & Market sts.). In the late 1800s, the 2,000-pound bell made a pilgrimage from its perch in the Pennsylvania State House to various states in the union, holding court at events to heal the nation after the Civil War. In 1915, Philadelphia became the revered symbol of liberty's final resting place.

- Continue touring the historical park and see the following: ▽ **National Constitution Center** (525 Arch St.), where hands-on activities and a self-guiding audio tour provide a unique historical perspective; ▽ **Congress Hall** (6th & Chestnut sts.), where you can participate in a ranger-led program; and the ▽ **Second Bank of the United States Portrait Gallery** (420 Chestnut St.), featuring the "People of Independence" display, an assortment of paintings highlighting early leaders who influenced the nation.

Afternoon

- Walk north on 5th Street. Stop at Christ Church's modest burial ground, where Benjamin Franklin and other signers of the Declaration of Independence are interred.

- For lunch, head back to Market or Chestnut streets to dine in an Old City casual diner or sandwich joints. If you're in the mood for a Philly cheesesteak try **Sonny's Famous Steaks.** Try **Farmicia** for a more leisurely lunch of tasty American cuisine.

- After lunch, walk (or bus it) back to ▽ **Christ Church** (20 N. American St.). This time go inside to see where the American Episcopal Church got its start and where some of the Founding Fathers worshipped. Then tour the **Betsy Ross House** (239 Arch St.) to experience 18th-century life. Afterward, stroll down **Elfreth's Alley** (off 2nd St. between Arch and Race sts.), America's oldest continually inhabited street.

Independence Hall

- In the late afternoon, head southeast to Head House Square (Lombard and S. 3rd streets). Need to rest your feet? Take a romantic horse-drawn carriage ride from Independence Park on Market Street between 5th and 6th streets. You'll meander through Society Hill's 18th-century cobblestone streets; the architecture, row houses and intimate courtyards cast fabulous shadows as twilight beckons. For a modern vibe, grab a cab to Center City to ascend to the **One Liberty Observation Deck** (1650 Market St.) for a 360-degree view, 57 flights above the city.

Evening

- For dinner, try one of Old City's restaurants, which are all near Independence National Historical Park. If you're in the mood for some spicy Asian cuisine, try **Han Dynasty.** If you're looking for a more formal meal of modern American cuisine, then **Fork** is the answer. **Amada** is perfect for a lively meal of Spanish tapas and wine, or you can enjoy sushi and sake at **Morimoto.** After dinner, visit **Penn's Landing** on the waterfront, scene of Friday night concerts all summer and Thursday film screenings under the stars in July and August. In the winter, you can practice your turns on the outdoor ice-skating rink.

- An alternative is to head to Fishtown to enjoy a meal at **Kensington Quarters** or a sandwich and one of the small-batch beers at the casual **Kraftwork.** Those looking to keep the party going will want to head to Frankford and Girard avenues to grab a cocktail at some of the most popular bars in town.

Top Picks for Kids

Under 13

- Thrill wee ones with a trip to **Sesame Place** (100 Sesame Rd.) in nearby **Langhorne.** Rides and waterslides entertain tots, as do huggable Sesame Street friends like Big Bird, Elmo and Cookie Monster. For an educational experience that's also tons of fun, attend the Neighborhood Street Party parade.

- Ages 5-12 will have a blast at ⌁ **The Franklin Institute** (222 N. 20th St.). The Train Factory mesmerizes young conductors as they learn about operating a 350-ton locomotive, while aspiring astronauts can command a mission and examine space expedition equipment. Kids can also walk through a two-story-high giant heart with sound and lighting effects or peer through a telescope in the fourth-floor observatory.

- The **Please Touch Museum** (in Fairmount Park at 4231 Avenue of the Republic) amuses young children with interactive exhibits that stimulate learning through touching and playing. Explore a neighborhood in City Capers, experiment with movement at Space Station or wind through Wonderland's maze.

Teens

- Teens love intrigue, and they'll find it at **Ghost Tours of Philadelphia** (5th & Chestnut sts.). And what's more, they'll be exposed to a little history in addition to pondering such dilemmas as whether Edgar Allan Poe's spirit lingers in the Old City. Guides conduct a candlelit stroll past Philly's spooky nooks and crannies, telling tales of haunted houses and ghostly encounters. And,

of course, there's the requisite cemetery stop.

- Philadelphia is known for its iconic treats, and **Reading Terminal Market** (51 N. 12th St.) is the perfect venue in which to sample the city's delectable tidbits. In this enclosed historic farmers market built underneath the Reading Railroad's train shed, you'll find everything from cheesesteaks to soft pretzels to whoopie pies.

- Guided tours aboard the cruiser *Olympia* and the World War II submarine *Becuna* at the **Independence Seaport Museum** (211 S. Columbus Blvd.) spark the imaginations of students as they investigate these historic vessels. The "Ship Via Philadelphia" display features hands-on activities—including a miniature cargo crane—that illustrate the concepts of commerce and trade.

- For a buggy endeavor, head to the **Philadelphia Insectarium and Butterfly Pavilion** (8046 Frankford Ave.) a museum devoted entirely to creepy-crawlies and butterflies. You can handle some of the live creatures if you choose, but if you'd rather admire them from afar there are plenty of exhibits, including mounted specimens.

All Ages

- ⌁ **Independence National Historical Park** (145 S. 3rd St.) awes history buffs with the revered Liberty Bell and sites like ⌁ **Independence Hall** that played a pivotal role in the nation's development.

- The 42-foot-long T. rex welcoming visitors into **The Academy of Natural Sciences of Drexel University** (1900 Benjamin Franklin Pkwy.) certainly makes a lasting impression, as do the other residents in Dinosaur Hall. Or, maybe it's The Big Dig, an indoor fossil-finding activity for kid-sized anthropologists. An animal care center housing critters that have been injured or born in captivity provides an inside look into their care and feeding, and a tropical butterfly garden presents a palette of vibrant color.

- At the **Philadelphia Zoo** (3400 W. Girard Ave.), rides like the carousel, train and swan boats excite tots, while older kids are eager to saddle up on a pony or camel. Habitats are plentiful, and you'll even come face to face with the endangered inhabitants.

- Several Philly events bring joy to the entire crew. The **Mummers Parade** on New Year's Day is a merry extravaganza with colorful costumes, elaborate floats and entertainment. **Odunde**, held during the second Sunday in June, is one of the country's largest African-American festivals. **Wawa Welcome America** around July 4 has a number of fun activities leading up to its Independence Day festivities. For the culturally inclined, the Philadelphia Orchestra Family Concert Series on occasional Saturdays from October through April or May makes for a nice outing.

Philadelphia Zoo

Arriving
By Car

I-95 is the major route from the northeast and south, connecting the city with Philadelphia International Airport. From New Jersey on the east, I-676 joins US 30 and traverses the north side of downtown as the Vine Street Expressway (I-676). From the northwest, I-76 leaves the Pennsylvania Turnpike at Valley Forge and enters Philadelphia at the Schuylkill Expressway. Follow either I-95 or I-76 to I-676 to the city center; enter the business district at 15th Street.

US 1 (Roosevelt Boulevard) traverses northeast Philadelphia, but both the north and south entrances into town are heavily commercialized and rather slow. From the east both the New Jersey Turnpike and I-295, which run north-south in New Jersey, provide ready access to either US 30, which enters the city center via the Benjamin Franklin Bridge and I-676, or to New Jersey SR 42 (North-South Freeway or Atlantic City Expressway), which approaches the Walt Whitman Bridge and south Philadelphia. When crossing either bridge from New Jersey, there is a $5 toll for passenger vehicles.

Getting Around
Street System

It would be wise to leave your automobile behind when going downtown because the old streets, though arrow straight, are very narrow. Unless you *must* have your car, allow a bus or cab driver to negotiate the congested, often two-lane, streets.

Most north-south streets, beginning with Front Street west of the Delaware River, are numbered;

Benjamin Franklin Bridge

east-west streets are named. Broad Street, the major north-south artery, is the equivalent of 14th Street. All downtown north-south streets are alternate one-way with the exception of Broad, which has two lanes in each direction. Market Street is one-way eastbound between 20th and 15th streets. Westbound motorists should use JFK Boulevard at this point. Chestnut Street is closed to all traffic except buses between 8th and 18th streets from 6 a.m. to 7 p.m.

Since Market Street is the principal east-west artery, north and south numbering begins at this street. Westward numbering begins at Front Street.

Right turns on red are permitted after a full stop, unless otherwise posted. Rush hours in general are 7-9:30 a.m. and 4-6:30 p.m. The speed limit on most streets is 25 mph, or as posted.

Parking

Though chances of getting on-street parking on the clogged streets are virtually zero, some metered parking is permitted on side streets and less traveled avenues: Parking meter rates in Center City are $2.50 per hour. Rates in the numerous lots and garages range from about $4-$6 for 30 minutes; $9-$24 for 2 hours; $18-$26 for 12 hours and $22-$28 for 24 hours.

Public Transportation

A SEPTA Independence Pass provides unlimited rides on all SEPTA buses, trolleys and subways for one day; the pass is $13 for individuals and $30 for a family of five (one person, but no more than two people, must be age 18+). For information about schedules, routes and locations where day pass and tokens may be purchased, phone (215) 580-7800, or TTY (215) 580-7853.

The Speedline, operated by Port Authority Transit Corporation (PATCO), connects with SEPTA's subway with three stops on Locust St. between 9th and 16th sts. and one at 8th and Market sts. One-way fare between any Philadelphia station $1.40; free (ages 0-5). One-way fare from Philadelphia into New Jersey $2.25-$3. Phone (215) 922-4600 or (856) 772-6900.

PHLASH, the downtown visitor shuttle, services 22 key locations, including attractions, hotels, shopping, cultural sites and historic districts. Passengers may board at any stop. Buses run daily 10-6, May 1-early Sept. and late Nov.-Dec. 31; Fri.-Sun., 10-6, mid-Mar. through Apr. 30 and early Sept.-late Nov. Fare (single-trip) $2; free (ages 0-4 and 65+). All-day pass $5; phone (484) 881-3574 to confirm information.

RiverLink Ferry offers ferry service from Penn's Landing to the Adventure Aquarium in Camden, N.J. *(see attraction listing p. 217).* Weather permitting, the ferry departs Penn's Landing daily on the hour 10-6 (also Sat.-Sun. at 7) and departs Camden daily on the half-hour 9:30-5:30 (also Sat.-Sun. at 6:30), Memorial Day through Labor Day. Hours may vary during special events; phone ahead. The ferry also runs on weekends early May-day before Memorial

Day and day after Labor Day-late Sept. and during concerts and special events; phone for schedule. Tickets may be purchased at either terminal or at the Independence Visitor Center. Fare $9; $7 (ages 3-12 and 65+). Phone (215) 928-8804.

Shopping

Sure, big name department stores like Macy's and Nordstrom are available at the area malls. But those on the hunt for fabulous finds know that the heart and soul of Philly shopping lies in its unique neighborhoods and its nearby suburbs.

Oh, and did we mention that there's no sales tax on clothing or shoes in Pennsylvania?

Even if you're not in the market, Center City's quaint **Antique Row**, bordered by Locust and Lombard streets from 9th to Broad streets, delights with its engaging window displays. Here, anything goes, from kitschy bargains to refined elegance: You can pick up an unusual $4 china plate or a $40,000 Chippendale highboy, barter for a mustache cup or negotiate for a priceless silver service. Historic samplers and needlework are the specialty at **M. Finkel & Daughter** (936 Pine St.), while stained glass and porcelain entice at **Kohn & Kohn** (1112 Pine).

The section of **Chestnut Street** from 8th to 18th streets is a busy corridor where Philadelphians find a mixed bag of stores in a range of tastes.

Bargain shoppers and fashionistas rejoiced at the end of 2015 when the **Bloomingdale's Outlet** opened in Center City's **Shops at Liberty Place** (1625 Chestnut). With nearly 23,000 square feet of women's, men's, children's and home goods at discounts of 20 to 70 percent off to choose from, there's almost nothing you can't find. The urban mall with the typical retail potpourri is further enhanced by a stunning glass atrium.

Lapstone & Hammer (1106 Chestnut) is a fashionable man's paradise, with both high-end sneakers and Italian leather products, as well as men's grooming products. Athletes and sports fans sprint to **Mitchell & Ness** (1201 Chestnut) to ogle the amazing collection of reproduction pro jerseys and jackets. It makes sense to open a flagship store of **Five Below** (1529 Chestnut) just blocks from its headquarters on a grand scale—this one in a two-story 1915 theater is nearly twice as big as all the others, selling all of its goods for $5 or less. International clothier **Uniqlo** (1608 Chestnut) has three stories of functional, simple men's, women's and kids fashions to explore. If you'd like to create a tranquil, cool, space of your own at home, step into **The Shade Store** (1725 Chestnut), which expanded to Philadelphia from its New York space in 2015.

The **Market & Shops at Comcast Center,** farther north at John F. Kennedy Boulevard and N. 17 Street, has a handful of shops and eateries catering to downtown office workers.

Jewelers' Row, on Sansom between 7th and 8th streets (between Chestnut and Walnut streets), is Center City's diamond district, second in size only to New York's and reputedly the nation's oldest. You'll

Shops at Liberty Place

surely find a trinket that tickles your fancy in this treasure trove of shops, many operated by the same Philadelphia families for generations. Don't buy on first impulse—checking out the competition generally pays off, since many of the jewelers do offer discounts.

Those inclined toward high-end tidbits land in the **Rittenhouse Square** area, in a class all its own. As you browse along Walnut Street from Broad to 20th, you'll come across fashion-forward designs at **Diesel, Urban Outfitters** (originally launched in Pennsylvania) and a multitude of other chic retailers. For some great deals, peruse the sale racks in the lower level of **Anthropologie** (1801 Walnut), another sophisticated chain born in the Keystone State. Pricey designs with an edgy flair are all the rage at **Joan Shepp** (1811 Chestnut), while **Boyd's** (1818 Chestnut) is the arbiter of classic elegance amid upper crust digs complete with chandeliers. Savor some lunch or the luxury goods of **Tiffany & Co.** and other upscale merchants at **Shops at the Bellevue,** (Broad and Walnut streets). The **Apple Store** (16th and Walnut) draws the technically savvy masses into its packed quarters.

Even more style moved in in 2015; try **Shop Sixty Five** (128 S. 17th St.) for expertly curated womenswear, denim and accessories by stylist Linda La Rosa Bidlo; and the trendy **Skirt** boutique (212 S. 17th St.) where you can work with a stylist to create a perfect wardrobe.

Shoppers looking for something a little more worldly in their home goods, beauty products and stationery will be thrilled to hear that Japanese goods seller **Rikumo** has moved and expanded from its Spring Garden store to a shop in Center City (1216 Walnut).

Foodies must stop by the happily bustling [SAVE] **Reading Terminal Market** (12th and Arch streets), a cornucopia of palate-pleasing sensations. Indulge in a steaming cheese steak, freshly baked soft pretzels, succulent pastry and other culinary treats. (Hint: It's also an affordable breakfast stop.) The [SAVE] **Hard Rock Cafe Philadelphia,** is located nearby at 12th and Market streets.

For a slice of history with your purchases, duck into **Macy's Center City** in the Wanamaker Building (1300 Market St.), where you are serenaded by the music of the Wanamaker Grand Organ as you shop. Out-of-state visitors get extra discounts.

Young hipsters love to pop into the trendy emporiums clustered about **Old City** to search for modish clothes, new age home designs and vintage furniture. This neighborhood just north of Independence National Historical Park also is dotted with some of the most happening galleries in Philly's art scene. If you're around, you can sample wine and hors d'oeuvres during the "First Friday" evening of the month, when galleries host an open house that turns into a wandering street party. **The Bourse,** a renovated 1895 grain and stock exchange just across from the Liberty Bell at 21 S. 5th St., is a good place for tourists to pick up some souvenirs. Weary shoppers seek refuge in the food court, a comfortable oasis within a stylish multilevel atrium.

Those in the know who also want to feel good about themselves when they shop stop into **The Wardrobe Boutique** (1822 Spring Garden St.), near the Philadelphia Museum of Art. Proceeds from sales of the gently-used clothing and accessories goes to help local women - and these designer duds can perk up any closet.

South Street, just south of Society Hill, has an eclectic assortment of funky shops with unique baubles. If you're into vintage and have a hankering for the exotic, this is your turf—the scene heats up at night. You can't help but notice **Philadelphia's Magic Gardens,** a folk art gallery and sculpture garden housed within a whimsical building adorned with mosaics. Antique hounds should note that a few dealers branch off the main drag.

Head a little farther south and you'll come across the Bella Vista neighborhood, home of the **9th Street Italian Market.** Running along 9th from Wharton to Fitzwater streets, the market tantalizes your senses with the aromas of garlic and freshly baked bread along with the colorful displays of fresh vegetables, pastas, spices and cheeses. For culinary delights sure to tease your taste buds, stop by Di Bruno Bros., a foodie haven brimming with cheeses and other gourmet specialties. The market's a great lunch spot—roasted garlic pizza is a hit at Sarcone's, while locals swear by both Pat's King of Steaks and Geno's Steaks for mouthwatering cheese steaks, a short jaunt south down 9th Street. **Fabric Row,** at S. 4th Street and Fitzwater, is a hub of textile-related concerns featuring custom draperies, tailors, designer fabrics and sewing supplies. Also in South Philly is the new Miss Demeanor (1729 E. Passyunk), in the old Tom's Prime Meats building—though it's been transformed from a butcher shop to a place for fair-trade dresses and other made-in-America women's clothes.

In Philadelphia's Northern Liberties neighborhood, a few blocks north of the Old City, the **Piazza at Schmidt's Commons** (2nd Street and Germantown Avenue) is a landscaped open-air plaza surrounded by art studios and boutiques; it's also the site of concerts, festivals and other events. **Liberties Walk,** 1040 N. American St., is a pedestrian walkway that travels past boutiques and restaurants.

On the fringes of Philly, wander the charming cobblestone streets of pretty **Chestnut Hill** and relish the assortment of some 125 shops. An easy trip from downtown, this northwest enclave with a moneyed vibe attracts those on the prowl for art and antiques, suburbanites out for a spin, and those just happy to park in a quaint café and do a little people watching. Individually owned boutiques touting specialized merchandise co-exist with established chains. About 7 miles northwest of Center City, **Main Street Manayunk** offers an assortment of galleries and shops interspersed with restaurants. You can browse for home furnishings, jewelry, boutique-style fashions, and vintage and consignment finds.

If you only visit one suburban shopping mall, make it the **King of Prussia** (US 202 at Schuylkill Expressway), a monstrous labyrinth of stores that makes fighting traffic almost worthwhile. Reputedly the East Coast's largest, the megamall features

9th Street Italian Market

more than 350 shops and seven major anchors, including Bloomingdale's, Lord & Taylor and Neiman Marcus. You can replenish your energy in one of the numerous eateries, including upscale steakhouse Morton's of Chicago.

Nightlife

Philly is a drinking town, as evidenced by the number of handsome brewpubs and classy lounges. But the city which gave birth to television sensation "American Bandstand" also continues to party hearty with a decent selection of trendy dance clubs and good ol' rock 'n' roll.

Clubs providing entertainment may include cover charges, and usually require drink or food minimums. To avoid surprises, phone ahead and confirm prices, opening hours, scheduled acts and dress codes.

Nowadays, you never know where you'll find great late-night places to eat or drink as pop-up restaurants and food trucks and beer gardens have been sprouting up everywhere.

Case in point: **The Independence Beer Garden** (Independence Mall West/(215) 922-7100) offers 20,000 square feet of space to relax and unwind with 40 beers on tap. The new space also offers food and other cocktails for those who aren't into hops.

In fact, every neighborhood has its favorite brewpub, but there are definitely standouts. Homey touches like an antique wooden bar, brick accents and an inviting fireplace make young movers and shakers want to snuggle up with a cold one and some first-rate munchies at **The Black Sheep Pub & Restaurant** (Rittenhouse Square/(215) 545-9473). **Fergie's Pub** (Center City/(215) 928-8118), a rip-roaring Irish pub, throws quite a party on St. Pat's Day—the jovial spot attracts a multifarious gang, including those eager for some good music or fresh mussels along with their brew. Savor one of Philly's best burgers with your brew at **Good Dog Bar & Restaurant** (Center City/(215) 985-9600), where youngish patrons like to shoot pool and select tunes from an Internet jukebox amid canine-inspired decor. The packed taproom at **Monk's Cafe** (Center City/(215) 545-7005) specializes in beer from Belgium, with one of the ales actually custom brewed in that country—you might be able to escape the throngs of kids by nabbing a seat at the back bar. An edgy, 20-to-30 something set hangs out at **Standard Tap** (Northern Liberties/(215) 238-0630), home of well-crafted drafts and a cranking jukebox—the pub grub is heavenly, from the roast pork sandwich to the duck confit salad. **U-Bahn** (Center City/(215) 800-1079) offers local beer, local food and even local music; singer/songwriters perform several times a week.

If your idea of fun is a little more physical—more specifically, a sea of bodies gyrating to a thumping beat—then you'll find bliss partying in Philadelphia's dance clubs. Philly's most colorful DJs spin funk, punk, rock 'n' roll, trance, progressive and what not in this sleek, high-tech danceteria serving up potent

The Independence Beer Garden

drinks. The party begins behind the retro façade of **Silk City Diner, Bar & Lounge** (Northern Liberties/(215) 592-8838). Grab a nosh at the diner and then migrate to the club, where you can burn the calories on a dance floor accented by disco balls, neon lighting, DJs and live music performances. **District N9NE** (Callowhill/(215) 769-2780) features electronic dance music along with a great sound and lighting system to match.

Jazz aficionados head to **Chris' Jazz Café** (Center City/(215) 568-3131), a locally touted joint featuring top hometown acts and the occasional touring show in cozy digs. It's not the tasty soul food that has them singing the blues at **Warmdaddy's** (South Philly/(215) 462-2000)—it's the top-notch sound system. Jam sessions showcase local cool cats at this down-home find with a laid-back vibe during Friday and Saturday evenings and Sunday brunches. **The Raven Lounge** (Rittenhouse Square/(215) 840-3577), which draws a disparate bunch in search of tunes in an unpretentious atmosphere, has been known to put up a live jazz or blues ensemble on its music stage upstairs. You can take a trip through time and a far-away place to 1930s France by visiting the **Paris Bistro & Jazz Café**, offering music, French food and drinks every Thursday-Sunday (Chestnut Hill/(215) 242-6200). For cuisine of a more southern American flavor, have a serving of **Relish** (West Oak Lane/(215) 276-0170) and live jazz Thursday-Saturday. Slip into an intimate jazz parlor six nights at **South** (Spring Garden/(215) 600-0220) and move out to the bar or dining hall for some food from that region.

For those who like to sit and sip, Philly offers plenty of swank lounges and happening bars. In summer, the rooftop deck at **Continental Mid-town** (Center City/(215) 567-1800) is a major hangout—inside, a trendy crowd sips apple martinis and soaks up the ambiance of the chicly decorated space. Mellow-minded hipsters who would rather skip the scene, settle in a comfy chair and peruse a decent wine list choose **L'Etage** (South Street/(215) 592-0656) for a low-key evening with a French flair. For drinkable assets, brave the line at **The Franklin Bar** (Rittenhouse Square/(267) 467-3277), a snug and dimly lit subterranean speakeasy that captivates patrons with designer cocktails.

If you're not averse to spending some serious coin, you'll relish a costly libation amid Victorian décor reminiscent of the Prohibition era at **Vango Skybar & Lounge** (Rittenhouse Square/(215) 568-1020). Vango features an outdoor lounge on the top level, where you can sink into plush couches and appreciate a skyline panorama—get there early if you want to avoid the crowd and gaze at the twinkling lights of Center City in peace.

The Old World style wine bar at **Panorama** (Old City/(215) 922-7800) in the Penn's View Hotel impresses oenophiles with its state-of-the-art dispensing system—if you are new to the wine game, this is a great place to order a "flight," a sampling of five different vintages to taste. Eclectic touches like a wine bottle chandelier, stamped-tin ceiling and exposed brick walls entice connoisseurs at the **Vintage Wine Bar & Bistro** (Center City/(215) 922-3095), where Old City character melds with a new Philadelphia vibe. Reasonable prices along with open-air seating, yummy nibbles and a popular happy hour draw a youngish clientele to **Jet Wine**

PHS Philadelphia Flower Show

Bar (South Street/(215) 735-1116), a friendly and funky neighborhood nook just right for quiet conversation. **Tria Cafe Rittenhouse** (Center City/(215) 972-8742) delights foodies who like to select from the tempting assortment of cheeses and appetizers to pair with their wine (or beer).

You might not expect to find a country bar in Philly—but you'd be wrong; **Boot & Saddle** (Bella Vista/(267) 639-4528) is a restaurant and bar, and a venue for live music.

But it's rock 'n' roll that's still alive and kicking in the City of Brotherly Love. Twenty-something punkers and rockers infiltrate **Trocadero Theatre** (Chinatown/(215) 922-6888) in hopes of discovering hard-hitting, edgy talent—the roomy Chinatown club's ornate accents hint at its past stint as a burlesque house. Bigger names are now filling the likes of **The Fillmore Philly** (Northern Liberties/(215) 309-0150) that seats 2,500 or the only slightly larger **Electric Factory** (Franklin Square/(215) 627-1332).

The focus isn't on mainstream tunes at **World Cafe Live** (University City/(215) 222-1400), a modernistic live-music venue hosting a diverse global line-up, from indie bands to hip-hop to acoustical performances. Happy hours are a hot bargain. **Johnny Brenda's** (Northern Liberties/(215) 739-9684) is a gastro-pub that also happens to have a concert hall upstairs—the small Fishtown space has a welcoming, relaxed feel and showcases indie rock acts and the latest in Philly's rock scene at a value.

Philly's sports fans are fanatical, and there are lots of watering holes where they like to go get their game on. **XFINITY Live!** (South Philadelphia/(267) 443-6415), a dining and entertainment complex with a sports theme, presents a range of options for your viewing pleasure—wherever you land, you can rest assured you'll receive a healthy dose of team spirit. In the same part of town, hungry fans ease their jitters by cracking crabs at **Chickie's and Pete's Crab House & Sports Bar** (South Philadelphia/(215) 218-0500), probably the next best place to catch an Eagles game if home field tickets aren't available. Downtown at **Locust Rendezvous** (Center City/(215) 985-1163), revved-up spectators are lured by the dive-bar ambiance, ample big screens, cheap beverages and decent vittles. And **McGillin's Olde Ale House** (Center City/(215) 735-5562), a tried-and-true pick that's been serving drafts since the 1860s, always throws open a welcoming door for Philly's "phanatics."

For something completely different, **The Rotunda** (University City) offers world music, spoken word and theatrical performances and even art exhibits. Admission is free at most events at this alcohol-free venue.

Big Events

Philadelphia's calendar is packed throughout the year with events including the huge Mummers and Thanksgiving Day parades, flower and antiques shows, and folk festivals.

The brightly colored ⏞ **Mummers Parade** starts off the new year and attracts some 15,000 costumed Mummers String Bands, fancies and comics. The **Philadelphia International Auto Show** begins in late January at the **Pennsylvania Convention Center.** Philadelphia then settles down for the **Philadelphia Home Show** in mid-January.

February is **Black History Month,** observed in Philadelphia with exhibitions, lectures and music at **The African American Museum in Philadelphia.**

The **PHS Philadelphia Flower Show,** held in early March at the convention center, is one of the world's largest indoor flower exhibitions.

The wearing of the green is toasted during the **Philadelphia St. Patrick's Day Parade.** The **Easter Promenade** offers music, entertainment, pony rides and a petting zoo on **Head House Square** on Easter Sunday.

The **Penn Relays** at **Franklin Field** in late April is one of the world's oldest and largest track meets. In mid-April, vintage hounds come out in droves for the **Philadelphia Antiques Show** is conducted in a tented area of **The Navy Yard** at the **Marine Parade Grounds,** 4747 S. Broad St.

In May, the city's historic homes open their doors during the **Society Hill Open House and Garden Tour.**

The **Dad Vail Regatta,** held in mid-May, is one of the largest college regattas in the country. High school rowers get their turn in the spotlight shortly thereafter when the ⏞ **Stotesbury Cup Regatta** takes place on the **Schuylkill River** in mid-May. This event has been taking place annually since 1927.

Also in May, the **Rittenhouse Square Flower Market** is an open market featuring plants, food and entertainment in addition to a variety of blooms. Look for the tents at 18th and Walnut streets at **Rittenhouse Square.** The **Philadelphia International Children's Festival** at the **Annenberg Center,** 3680 Walnut St., features kids' activities and theater performances.

Summer kicks off in June with the **Rittenhouse Square Fine Arts Show** (also held in September) and **Elfreth's Alley Fête Days.** The latter celebrates patriotism and Colonial history; events include tours of private homes.

The **Odunde Festival,** held the second Sunday in June, is a 12-block African street festival filled with music, dance, food, crafts and culture. The day kicks off with a procession to celebrate the Yoruba New Year.

⏞ **Wawa Welcome America!** explodes the first week in July to celebrate the country's birth in its hometown. Parades, concerts and fireworks displays are among the more than 40 scheduled events. Mid-August brings the **Philadelphia Folk Festival,** which features folk music concerts and workshops at suburban **Old Poole Farm** in Upper Salford Township (near Schwenksville).

Philadelphia International Auto Show

The **Fringe Arts Festival** is in September. Philly festivities go on the move in late September through October, when the **Puerto Rican Day Parade,** the **Pulaski Day Parade,** the **Columbus Day Parade** and the **German-American Parade** all take place.

The Convention Center stages the **Philadelphia Museum of Art Crafts Show** in early November, a major exhibition of crafts by the nation's top artisans. Later in November the holidays begin in grand and traditional fashion with the ⏞ **Philadelphia Thanksgiving Day Parade,** complete with celebrities, enormous balloons and floats.

The Philadelphia holiday season begins at Thanksgiving and includes various events, including a tree lighting ceremony at **Macy's Center City** (also Macy's Christmas Light Show and the Dickens Village inside the store), seasonal pop-up and craft markets like the **Christmas Village** in LOVE Park. The **Franklin Square Holiday Festival and Electrical Spectacle Holiday Light Show** electrifies Franklin Square starting in mid-November through December, while skaters make new designs of their own on the ice in starting in late November at the **Blue Cross RiverRink Winterfest.**

The city is proud to be awarded title of host city of the ⏞ **Army-Navy Game** in which the military branches face off in a football game in early December at **Lincoln Financial Field.**

Sports & Rec

Philadelphia, with a representative in every major sports league—**baseball, football, hockey, basketball** and **soccer**—is a paradise for spirited spectator sports fans. The NFL Super Bowl LII champion **Eagles** play at Philadelphia's **Lincoln Financial**

Field at S. Broad and Pattison streets; and the **Phillies** of baseball's National League suit up at **Citizens Bank Park,** 10th Street and Pattison Avenue. The **Wells Fargo Center,** also at S. Broad and Pattison streets, plays host to the NHL's **Flyers** and the NBA's **76ers.** For ticket information, phone (215) 463-1000 for the Phillies; (267) 570-4150 for the Eagles; (215) 339-7676 for the 76ers; and (215) 218-7825 for the Flyers. Philly's newest team, the **Philadelphia Union,** plays soccer at **Talen Energy Stadium** in nearby Chester; (877) 218-6466.

Rowing is popular on the **Schuylkill River;** sculls are often seen skimming the water. Periodic races and spectacular annual rowing regattas can be seen from Fairmount Park.

Polo is played by the suburban **Brandywine Polo Club,** which has games on Sunday afternoons June through September; phone (610) 268-8692. **Cricket** matches are held in **Fairmount Park** on weekends in the summer.

Fairmount Park caters to nearly everyone's recreational appetite, with **archery, bicycling, canoeing, fishing, golf, hiking, horseback riding, lawn bowling** and **tennis.**

From the **Schuylkill River Trail** (a small portion of which runs through Philadelphia) to the **D&L Trail,** there are plenty of hiking, **jogging** and **biking** opportunities. Maps showing good routes for **running** and **walking** are available at downtown hotels. Runners enjoy the Philadelphia **Rock 'n' Roll Half-Marathon** in September and the full **Philadelphia Marathon** through the historic city each November. **Note:** The Bartram Trail section of the Schuylkill River Trail is near, or crosses, state game lands, so wearing blaze orange is recommended during hunting seasons; contact the Pennsylvania Game Commission, (717) 787-4250, for details.

You can rent a bike through Indego, the city's bike share program; phone (844) 446-3346.

If you want to play the ponies, **Parx Casino and Racing** in Bensalem offers **Thoroughbred racing** all year; phone (215) 639-9000. **Delaware Park,** near Wilmington, Del., offers Thoroughbred races summer through fall; phone (800) 417-5687.

Note: Policies concerning admittance of children to pari-mutuel betting facilities vary. Phone for information.

Performing Arts

The **Philadelphia Orchestra,** one of the country's finest symphonies, presents its main season (May-September) in **The Kimmel Center for the Performing Arts** (see attraction listing p. 178). The **Philly Pops Christmas Spectacular** is popular for families. The Kimmel Center also hosts Broadway musicals, speakers and special concerts; phone (215) 731-3333 for tickets. **Opera Philadelphia** and the **Pennsylvania Ballet** perform at the **Academy of Music,** one block north of Broad and Locust streets; phone (215) 893-1999 for orchestra, opera and ballet tickets.

In summer, the orchestra's rich tones ring through Fairmount Park's **Mann Center for the Performing Arts** (see attraction listing p. 171). Tickets are sold at the box office, 52nd street and Parkside Avenue; phone (215) 546-7900. Summer concerts are also held at **RiverStage at the Great Plaza** at Penn's Landing. Check at the visitor center for times.

Philadelphia theater is popular. The **Forrest Theatre** presents pre-Broadway and hit shows with name stars; national touring companies appear at the **Annenberg Center** and the **Merriam Theater.**

There also are numerous regional and community theater companies, including the **Arden Theatre Company,** the **Bristol Riverside Theatre,** the **Hedgerow Theatre,** the **New Freedom Theatre,** the **People's Light,** the **Philadelphia Theatre Company,** the **Prince Theater,** the **Walnut Street Theatre** and the **Wilma Theater.** College theater can be enjoyed at **Temple University** or **Villanova University.**

Painted Bride Art Center presents an array of performing arts and music performances as well as art exhibits.

The biggest concerts often come to the **Wells Fargo Center,** which also plays host to the city's sports teams. Call (800) 298-4200 for tickets.

INSIDER INFO:
CityPASS

Philadelphia CityPASS offers savings to those who plan to visit many Philadelphia attractions. Visitors may buy a three-, four- or five-attraction ticket and can select from the following: The Academy of Natural Sciences of Drexel University, Adventure Aquarium (in Camden, N.J.), The Barnes Foundation, Battleship New Jersey (in Camden, N.J.), The Big Bus Co. and Philadelphia Trolley Works, Eastern State Penitentiary, The Franklin Institute, Museum of the American Revolution, National Constitution Center, One Liberty Observation Deck, Philadelphia Zoo and Please Touch Museum.

The pass, valid for 9 consecutive days from first date of use, will save travelers 45 percent off the combined cost of purchasing individual tickets to all of the included attractions. Philadelphia CityPASS can only be purchased online.

ATTRACTIONS

For a complete list of attractions, visit AAA.com/travelguides/attractions

SAVE **THE ACADEMY OF NATURAL SCIENCES OF DREXEL UNIVERSITY** is at 19th St. and Benjamin Franklin Pkwy. Founded in 1812, it is said to be the oldest natural history museum in America. Outstanding among the natural science exhibits are the children's discovery center, Outside In; and Dinosaur Hall, where fossils of prehistoric giants are displayed. The Butterflies! exhibit is a walk-through tropical garden with live butterflies from around the world and a display of live pupae. Marveling at Mollusks features specimens of clams, scallops, chambered nautiluses and other mollusks. Changing exhibits, live animal shows, historical dioramas, films and special programs also are offered.

Time: Allow 1 hour, 30 minutes minimum. **Hours:** Mon.-Fri. 10-4:30, Sat.-Sun. and holidays 10-5. Closed Jan. 1, Thanksgiving and Christmas. **Cost:** Mon.-Fri. $17.95; $14.95 (ages 65+ and students and military with ID); $13.95 (ages 3-12). Sat.-Sun. $19.95; $16.95 (ages 65+ and students and military with ID); $15.95 (ages 3-12). Additional fees for some exhibits. **Phone:** (215) 299-1000.
[TI] [🎦] 19th, 69

AMERICAN PHILOSOPHICAL SOCIETY (APS) MUSEUM—see Independence National Historical Park p. 174.

AWBURY ARBORETUM, 1 Awbury Rd., is a 55-acre public garden with several trails among indigenous trees, flowers and plants. There also is a secret garden, bird sanctuary and ponds. The 19th-century Francis Cope House is on the grounds and visitors can get information about the Cope family as well as trail maps. Pets on leashes are permitted. **Time:** Allow 2 hours minimum. **Hours:** Grounds daily dawn-dusk. Cope house Tues.-Fri. 9-5 (also Mon. 9-5, Apr.-Nov.); closed major holidays. **Cost:** Free. **Phone:** (215) 849-2855.
[🐾] [🎦] [🎦] Washington Lane, 266

[SAVE] **EASTERN STATE PENITENTIARY,** 2027 Fairmount Ave., opened in 1829 with a revolutionary design in prison facilities: private cells with skylights, individual recreation areas and cellblocks radiating from a central rotunda. Also new was the reform concept that replaced brutality with isolation and productive work. Multimedia displays and art exhibitions portray life on the inside. Original cell blocks, center surveillance hub, a baseball diamond, Al Capone's cell and Death Row can be seen. An audio tour, a 1-hour guided tour and interactive exhibits are available.

Note: The building is unheated, and access to tour sites may change due to weather.

Time: Allow 1 hour, 30 minutes minimum. **Hours:** Daily 10-5. Guided tours depart daily at 2; phone ahead to confirm schedule. Last admission is 1 hour before closing. Closed Jan. 1, Thanksgiving, Christmas Eve and Christmas. **Cost:** (includes audio tour, guided tour and exhibits) $16; $14 (ages 62+); $12 (ages 7-12 and students with ID). Tour is not recommended for children ages 0-6. **Phone:** (215) 236-3300. [GT] [🎦] Fairmount, 121

[GEM] **FAIRMOUNT PARK** is reached by Benjamin Franklin Pkwy. This beautiful park system covers 9,200 acres throughout the city. It is threaded by miles of scenic drives, walks, a bicycle route and horse trails. Visitors can see sculls racing on the

Schuylkill, hear band concerts in Pastorious Park or symphony orchestras at Mann Center for the Performing Arts, or visit numerous museums and historic houses.

The park system, founded in 1876, was the site of the Centennial Exposition. Of almost 200 buildings erected for the fair, only Memorial Hall and the Ohio House remain. Glendenning Rock Garden and Horticultural Hall Gardens are noteworthy. Within the park boundaries are several Colonial estates (see *Fairmount Park Historic Houses*) and public squares, including Franklin Square, which features a carousel and playgrounds, and Logan Square, with the beautiful Swann Memorial Fountain that is lit at night.

Historic RittenhouseTown, on Wissahickon Avenue, was the site of America's first paper mill. Today seven buildings remain and can be viewed from the outside via a guided walking tour on summer weekends. The boat houses along the Schuylkill River are lit at night with strings of white lights that reflect in the water; they are best seen from the Schuylkill Expressway across the river. **Cost:** Fairmount Square, free. Rittenhouse Town tours $5; $2.50 (ages 0-11 and senior citizens). Cash only. **Phone:** (215) 438-5711 for Historic RittenhouseTown. [🚫] [🎦]

[GEM] **The Barnes Foundation,** 2025 Benjamin Franklin Pkwy. within Fairmount Park, displays an extensive collection of early Impressionist, Post-Impressionist and Early Modern paintings, that includes 181 works by Pierre Auguste Renoir, 69 by Paul Cézanne, 59 by Henri Matisse and 46 by Pablo Picasso. Other artists represented include Edgar Degas, Amedeo Modigliani, Claude Monet, Georges Seurat and Vincent Van Gogh. Native American pottery, Pennsylvania German decorative furniture, sculpture, ceramics and metalwork are displayed. Other noted collections include art from Africa, Central America, China, Greece and Rome.

What differentiates this art collection from most others is the way the pieces are displayed; each room displays American and European furniture and metalwork in ways that enhance and accentuate characteristics of the artworks. Therefore, don't be surprised to see painting masterpieces next to an antique tool or a chest from Pennsylvania Dutch country. The presentation is unconventional— exactly the way founder Dr. Albert C. Barnes wanted it to be.

Time: Allow 1 hour, 30 minutes minimum. **Hours:** Wed.-Mon. 11-5 (also 6-9 p.m. first Fri. of the month). Phone ahead to confirm schedule. **Cost:** $25; $23 (ages 65+); $5 (ages 13-18 and college students with ID); free (active military with ID and family, Memorial Day-Labor Day). Guided 1-hour tour $45; 90-minute tour $60. First Friday events $28; $10 (students with ID). Reservations are required for tours. Phone ahead to confirm rates. **Parking:** $12 for up to 4 hours. **Phone:** (215) 278-7000. [GT] [TI] [🎦] 19th, 69

Philadelphia SEPTA System Map

Legend

- Market-Frankford Line
- Broad Street Line & Broad-Ridge Spur
- Norristown High Speed Line
- Trolley Lines
- PATCO Line
- Regional Rail Lines

① Station   ① Transfer Station

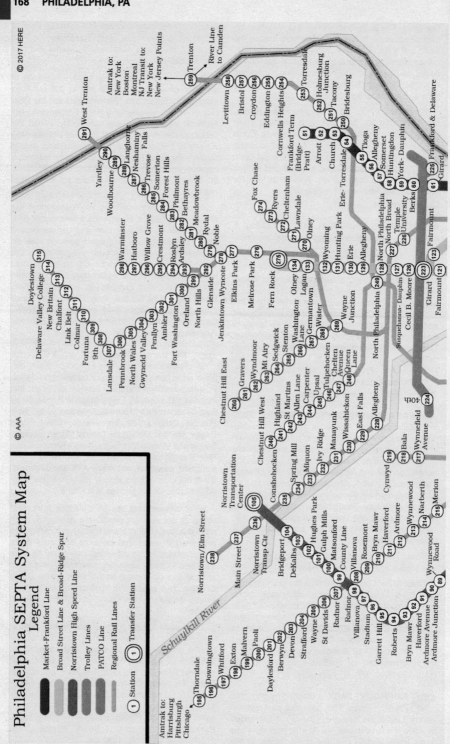

© 2017 HERE

© AAA

1320-18

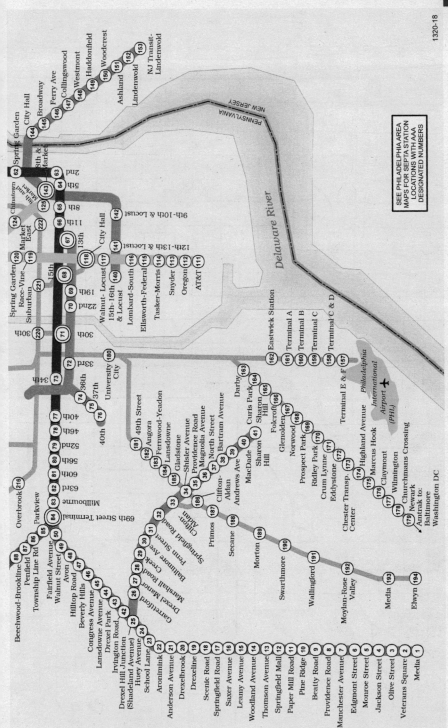

Delaware River

PENNSYLVANIA
NEW JERSEY

153 NJ Transit-Lindenwold
152 Lindenwold
151 Ashland
150 Woodcrest
149 Haddonfield
148 Westmont
147 Collingswood
146 Ferry Ave
145 Broadway
144 City Hall
Spring Garden

62 8th & Market
Spring Garden
63 2nd
64 5th
143
125
222 8th
124 Chinatown
Market East
120 Spring Garden
119 Race-Vine
15th
68
69 19th
70 22nd
71 30th
72 33rd
73 34th
74 36th
75 37th
76 40th

65 8th
66 11th
67 13th
142 9th-10th & Locust
118 City Hall
117 12th-13th & Locust
141
140 Walnut-Locust
116 15th-16th & Locust
115 Lombard-South
114 Ellsworth-Federal
113 Tasker-Morris
112 Snyder
111 Oregon
AT&T

180 University City
220 30th

162 Eastwick Station
161 Terminal A
160 Terminal B
159 Terminal C
158 Terminal C & D
157 Terminal E & F
Philadelphia International Airport (PHL)

77 40th
78 46th
79 52nd
80 56th
81 60th
82 63rd
83 Millbourne
84 69th Street Terminal
85 Parkview
216 Overbrook

163 Darby
164 Curtis Park
165 Sharon Hill
166 Folcroft
167 Glenolden
168 Norwood
169 Prospect Park
170 Ridley Park
171 Crum Lynne
172 Eddystone
173 Chester Transp. Center
174 Highland Avenue
175 Marcus Hook
176 Claymont
177 Wilmington
178 Churchmans Crossing
179 Newark
Amtrak to:
Baltimore
Washington DC

181 49th Street
182 Angora
183 Fernwood-Yeadon
184 Lansdowne
185 Gladstone
186 Clifton-Aldan
187 Primos
188 Secane
189 Morton
190 Swarthmore
191 Wallingford
192 Moylan-Rose Valley
193 Media
194 Elwyn

49 49th Street
41 Sharon Hill
40 MacDade
39 Andrews Ave
38 Bartram Avenue
37 North Street
36 Magnolia Avenue
35 Providence Road
34 Shisler Avenue
33
32 Springfield Road
31 Penn Street
30 Baltimore Ave
29 Creek Road
28 Marshall Road
27 Drexel Manor
26 Cartreford
25
24 School Lane
23 Huey Avenue

88 Beechwood-Brookline
87 Penfield
86 Township Line Rd
50 Fairfield Avenue
49 Walnut Street
48 Avon
47 Hilltop Road
46 Beverly Hills
45 Congress Avenue
44 Lansdowne Avenue
43 Irvington Road
42 Drexel Hill Junction (Shadeland Avenue)

22 Aronimink
21 Anderson Avenue
20 Drexelbrook
19 Drexeline
18 Scenic Road
17 Springfield Road
16 Saxer Avenue
15 Leamy Avenue
14 Woodland Avenue
13 Thomson Avenue
12 Springfield Mall
11 Paper Mill Road
10 Pine Ridge
9 Beatty Road
8 Providence Road
7 Manchester Avenue
6 Edgmont Street
5 Monroe Street
4 Jackson Street
3 Olive Street
2 Veterans Square
1 Media

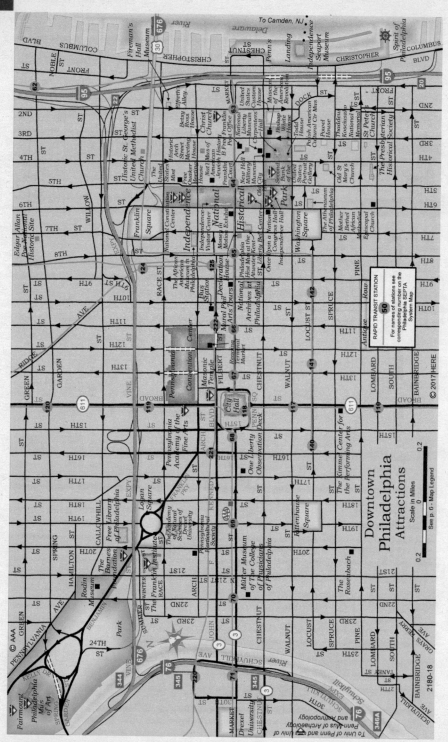

Downtown
Philadelphia
Attractions

Scale in Miles

See p. 6 - Map Legend

RAPID TRANSIT STATION

For names of stations see
corresponding number on the
Philadelphia SEPTA
System Map

© 2017 HERE

2180-18

© AAA

To Camden, NJ

Fairmount Water Works Interpretive Center is within Fairmount Park behind the Philadelphia Museum of Art at 640 Waterworks Dr. Serving as a model for more than 30 other American water delivery systems, the Fairmont Water Works was a 19th-century engineering wonder providing clean water to the growing Philadelphia vicinity.

Operating 1815-1909, it now houses historical and interactive environmental exhibits, galleries, a theater, a freshwater mussel hatchery and displays that invite visitors to discover the wonders of water. Guided tours are available upon request. **Time:** Allow 2 hours minimum. **Hours:** Tues.-Sat. 10-5, Sun. 1-5. Closed major holidays. **Cost:** Free. **Phone:** (215) 685-0723. GT ⊞ 30th, 220

Horticulture Center, 100 N. Horticultural Dr. at jct. Belmont Ave. and Montgomery Dr. within Fairmount Park, includes a landscaped arboretum with a large reflecting pool, seasonal greenhouse displays and outdoor gardens. **Time:** Allow 30 minutes minimum. **Hours:** Grounds daily 7-6, Mar.-Oct.; 7-5, rest of year. Display house daily 9-3. Closed major holidays. **Cost:** Donations. **Phone:** (215) 685-0096.

Laurel Hill Cemetery, 3822 Ridge Ave. within Fairmount Park, incorporates striking architecture and landscape design elements into its 78 acres. The cemetery represents one of the nation's earliest examples of landscape architecture. It is shaded by large trees and contains interesting statuary. Many notable historical figures are buried here, including 40 Civil War-era generals, Philadelphia industrialists and six passengers aboard the RMS *Titanic*.

A cemetery map is available at the office. An audio tour by cellphone also is available. **Hours:** Grounds Mon.-Fri. 8-4:30, Sat.-Sun. 9:30-4:30. Tours at 10 a.m., fourth Fri. and second Sat. of every month. Closed major holidays. Phone ahead to confirm schedule. **Cost:** Grounds free. Guided tour $12; $10 (ages 65+ and students). Phone ahead to confirm rates. **Phone:** (215) 228-8200. GT ⊞ East Falls, 229

Mann Center for the Performing Arts, 52nd St. and Parkside Ave. within Fairmount Park, is an outdoor cultural arts center that presents summer concerts and arts festivals. **Note:** Picnicking is permitted at specified orchestra concerts only. **Hours:** The season runs May-Oct.; phone for schedules. **Cost:** Ticket prices $12-$150. **Phone:** (215) 546-7900 for general information, or (800) 745-3000 for tickets. ⊼ ⊞ Wynnefield Ave, 217

GEM SAVE **Philadelphia Museum of Art,** end of Benjamin Franklin Pkwy. at 26th St., in Fairmount Park, ranks among the largest art museums in the United States. Founded in 1876, the museum's collections offer a full range of both fine and decorative arts from Asia, Europe and the United States. Spanning more than 2,000 years, the museum is home to more than 240,000 objects, including masterpieces of painting, sculpture, works on paper, arms and armor, costumes and textiles.

Included are works by Paul Cézanne, Claude Monet, Pierre Auguste Renoir, Pablo Picasso, Marcel Duchamp, Henri Matisse and Joan Miró as well as those by modern artists. The American collections survey three centuries of paintings, furniture and decorative arts with an emphasis on Philadelphia's traditions. Special exhibitions are offered. Special programs for children and families, lectures, concerts and films also are presented.

Note: Sign-language interpreted tours can be arranged with advanced notice. Audio tours by cellphone also are available. **Hours:** Tues.-Sun. and some Mon. holidays 10-5 (also Wed. and Fri. 5-8:45). Closed July 4, Thanksgiving and Christmas. **Cost:** (includes Rodin Museum, the Ruth and Raymond G. Perelman Building and Mount Pleasant and Cedar Grove historic houses), valid for 2 consecutive days, $20; $18 (ages 65+); $14 (ages 13-18 and students with ID); visitors pay what they wish (first Sun. of the month and Wed. after 5 p.m.). Additional fees may be charged for special exhibitions. Cash only. **Parking:** $12 for up to 4 hours. **Phone:** (215) 763-8100 or TTY (215) 763-7600. GT ⊤⊤ ⊞ 30th, 220

Philadelphia Zoo, 3400 Girard Ave. W. within Fairmount Park, first opened on July 1, 1874. Today the 42-acre Victorian garden is home to nearly 1,300, including many rare and endangered species. Zoo360 is an animal trail system that enables primates and big cats to roam above the zoo, creating interesting viewing opportunities for visitors. KeyBank Big Cat Falls offers guests an up close look at endangered cats from around the globe. PECO Primate Reserve offers an encounter with primates and the McNeil Avian Center provides lush walk-through habitats where visitors discover more than 100 birds, many of them rare and endangered. Visitors can feed exotic birds in Wings of Asia, and Outback Outpost houses animals native to Australia. KidZooU features hands-on experiences for children, wildlife displays and rare breeds.

Time: Allow 2 hours minimum. **Hours:** Daily 9:30-5, Mar.-Oct.; 9:30-4, rest of year. Phone for special activity schedules. Closed Jan. 1, Thanksgiving, Christmas Eve, Christmas and Dec. 31. **Cost:** Mar.-Oct. $23; $21 (active military with ID); $19 (ages 2-11). Rest of year $16; $14 (active military with ID); free (ages 0-1). **Parking:** $16. **Phone:** (215) 243-1100. *(See ad on inside front cover.)* ⊤⊤ ⊞ 40th, 224

SAVE **Please Touch Museum,** 4231 Avenue of the Republic (formerly N. Concourse Dr.) at Memorial Hall in Fairmount Park, occupies a building used as an art gallery during the 1876 Centennial Exhibition. Abundant hands-on educational activities encourage children under age 8 and their families to use their senses as they play. Children can run a supermarket, medical practice or construction site. Space Station focuses on movement, height and flight. Older children and adults will enjoy Centennial Exploration, which showcases the historical World's Fair building.

Events and daily theater performances also are offered. **Time:** Allow 3 hours minimum. **Hours:** Mon.-Sat. 9-5 (also first Wed. of the month 5-7), Sun. 11-5 (9-3, Christmas Eve and Dec. 31). Closed Thanksgiving and Christmas. **Cost:** $19; $2 (first Wed. of the month 4-7); free (under 1). Carousel $3 (per ride). Every five children must be accompanied by one adult. **Parking:** $12. **Phone:** (215) 581-3181. ⓣ

Rodin Museum, 2151 Benjamin Franklin Pkwy. at jct. 22nd St. in Fairmount Park, is a Beaux Arts-style building displaying a priceless collection of Auguste Rodin originals and casts, one of the largest collections outside Paris. Many sculptures are housed in the garden, including casts of "The Burghers of Calais" and "The Thinker."

Rodin worked on "The Gates of Hell," a pair of doors intended for a Paris museum, for 37 years, but it was only cast in bronze after his death. The piece measures nearly 21 feet tall and 13 feet wide and contains more than 200 sculptures of human figures. A tour introduces visitors to the history of the work that consumed so much of Rodin's career.

An audio tour by cellphone is available. Photography is permitted. **Time:** Allow 30 minutes minimum. **Hours:** Wed.-Mon. 10-5. The Rodin, the Sculptor and His Models tour departs at noon. Closed July 4, Thanksgiving and Christmas.

Cost: Museum and Gardens, donations. Combination ticket with the Philadelphia Museum of Art, the Ruth and Raymond G. Perelman Building and the Mount Pleasant and Cedar Grove historic houses, valid for 2 consecutive days, $20; $18 (ages 65+); $14 (ages 13-18 and students with ID); visitors pay what they wish (first Sun. of the month). **Parking:** $12 for up to 4 hours. **Phone:** (215) 763-8100 or TTY (215) 763-7600. ⒼⓉ 🚇 30th, 220

Ruth and Raymond G. Perelman Building is at 2525 Pennsylvania Ave. at jct. Fairmount Ave., across from the Philadelphia Museum of Art. This 1927 Art Deco building (formerly the Fidelity Mutual Life Insurance Co.) is an extension of the art museum and features frequently changed exhibitions of contemporary art, including costumes, textiles, photography and fine craft. An art library contains about 200,000 items, including books and periodicals dating as far back as the 16th century as well as a full range of electronic resources.

An audio tour by cellphone is available. **Time:** Allow 1 hour, 30 minutes minimum. **Hours:** Museum Tues.-Sun. 10-5; closed July 4, Thanksgiving and Christmas. Library Tues.-Fri. 10-4 (also Sat. 10-4, mid-Sept. to mid-May); closed Nov. 24-28, Christmas Eve, Christmas and day after Christmas.

Cost: $10; $8 (ages 65+); $6 (ages 13-18 and students with ID); visitors pay what they wish (first Sun. of the month). Combination ticket with the Philadelphia Museum of Art, Rodin Museum, Mount Pleasant and Cedar Grove historic houses valid for 2 consecutive days, $20; $18 (ages 65+); $14 (ages 13-18 and students with ID); visitors pay what they wish (first Sun. of the month). Additional fees may be charged for special exhibitions. Cash only. **Parking:** $12 for up to 4 hours. **Phone:** (215) 763-8100. ⒼⓉ ⓣ 🚇 30th, 220

Shofuso Japanese House and Garden is off Montgomery Dr. at Belmont Mansion Dr. next to the Horticulture Center within Fairmount Park. The house was built in Japan in 1953 in a style that would have been intended for an educated upper-class person living in the 16th- or 17th century; the house displays a combination of elements from both centuries. The America-Japan Society of Tokyo gave it to New York's Museum of Modern Art for an exhibition, and afterward it was moved to Philadelphia.

A tea house adjoins the main house. A pond and ornamental garden also are on the grounds. A tea ceremony is held on occasional Sunday afternoons by reservation. **Time:** Allow 1 hour minimum. **Hours:** Wed.-Fri. 10-4, Sat.-Sun. 11-5, in Apr. and Oct. Closed major holidays. Phone ahead to confirm schedule. **Cost:** $10; $5 (ages 3-17, ages 65+ and students with ID). An additional fee is charged for tea ceremony. **Phone:** (215) 878-5097. ⒼⓉ

FAIRMOUNT PARK HISTORIC HOUSES, along the banks of the Schuylkill River within Fairmount Park, are the former homes of wealthy 18th- and 19th-century Philadelphians. They include Cedar Grove, Laurel Hill, Lemon Hill, Mount Pleasant, Strawberry Mansion and Woodford Mansion. **Hours:** Hours vary per house. **Cost:** $5-$8 per house. **Phone:** (215) 684-7926, or (215) 685-0274 for Sweetbriar Mansion.

Cedar Grove, at 1 Cedar Grove Dr. within Fairmount Park, is an 18th-century summer home that served five generations of the same Quaker family. It features many original family furnishings, household articles and decorative arts. **Hours:** Tours Thurs.-Sun. at 11, 1 and 2:30, Apr.-Dec. (also 10-4, first Sun. of the month). Closed July 4, Thanksgiving and Christmas. **Cost:** $8; $5 (ages 13-18, ages 65+ and students with ID); visitors pay what they wish (first Sun. of the month). Combination ticket with Philadelphia Museum of Art, Rodin Museum, Ruth and Raymond G. Perelman building and Mount Pleasant historic house, valid for 2 consecutive days, $20; $18 (ages 65+); $14 (ages 13-18 and students with ID); visitors pay what they wish (first Sun. of the month). **Phone:** (215) 763-8100 or (215) 684-7926. ⒼⓉ

Laurel Hill, 7201 N. Randolph Dr. within Fairmount Park, offers views of the Schuylkill River and features paneling, an 1818 Broadwood fortepiano, a 1783 Philadelphia tall chest and an octagonal drawing room with Federal architectural details. Tours of the home are conducted by docents.

Hours: Thurs.-Sun. 10-4, early Apr.-late Dec. Closed federal holidays. **Cost:** $8; $5 (ages 13-17, ages 65+ and students with ID). **Phone:** (215) 235-1776. GT

Lemon Hill, jct. Kelly and Sedgley drs. within Fairmount Park, is a masterpiece of 19th-century architecture with three oval-shaped rooms crafted with curved fireplaces, windows and doors. Staffordshire dishware with scenes of old Philadelphia and a 200-piece set of Chinese dinnerware also are on display. Tours are offered by docents. **Hours:** Thurs.-Sun. 10-4, early Apr.-late Dec. Closed federal holidays. **Cost:** $8; $5 (ages 13-17, ages 65+ and students with ID). **Phone:** (215) 232-4337. GT 🚇 40th, 224

Mount Pleasant, off Kelly Dr. to 3800 Mt. Pleasant Dr. within Fairmount Park, was built 1762-65 by Scottish sea captain John Macpherson. The Middle Georgian mansion features classical architecture and craftsmanship of Colonial Philadelphia. **Note:** Mount Pleasant is closed for renovations but program programs are offered. **Hours:** Phone for program schedule. **Phone:** (215) 763-8100 or (215) 684-7926.

Strawberry Mansion, at 2450 Strawberry Mansion Dr. within Fairmount Park, is the largest of the Fairmount Park historic mansions and is furnished in Empire style. The house features period furnishings, a doll collection, antique toys and other early American artifacts. **Hours:** Guided tours Tues.-Sun. on the hour 10-4, mid-Apr. through Dec. 31; Tues.-Sat. on the hour 10-4, Sun. by appointment, rest of year. Last tour departs 1 hour before closing. Closed major holidays. **Cost:** $8; $5 (ages 13-17, ages 65+ and students with ID). **Phone:** (215) 228-8364. GT

Woodford Mansion, jct. 33rd St. and W. Dauphin Dr. within Fairmount Park, is a fine example of Colonial architecture and is decorated with a collection of 18th-century American crafted furniture, 17th- and 18th-century Delftware, and Colonial pewter and clocks. **Hours:** Wed.-Sun. 10-4. Closed major holidays. **Cost:** $8; $5 (ages 13-17, ages 65+ and students with ID). **Phone:** (215) 229-6115. GT

◤GEM **THE FRANKLIN INSTITUTE** is at N. 20th St. and Benjamin Franklin Pkwy. Three floors of interactive exhibits are offered. SportsZone offers a 40-foot long race challenge, a pitching cage and other interactive displays; Your Brain explores developments in neuroscience; The Train Factory features a 350-ton moving locomotive; The Franklin Air Show includes an aircraft hangar, a midway, and a pilot training area where visitors can try various maneuvers in a flight simulator; and SkyBike is a two-wheel bicycle that balances riders on a 28-foot-high cable. The Franklin 3D Theater, the Joel N. Bloom Observatory, Sir Isaac's Loft and a giant walk-through heart also are featured.

Other exhibits relate to astronomy, aviation, electricity, math and physics. The Benjamin Franklin National Memorial, in the museum's rotunda, features a 20-foot-tall statue of Franklin. Fels Planetarium and Tuttleman Dome IMAX Theater are other highlights. An escape room experience also is available.

Time: Allow 4 hours minimum. **Hours:** Museum daily 9:30-5. Planetarium and theater show times vary; phone ahead. Closed Jan. 1, Thanksgiving, Christmas Eve and Christmas. **Cost:** (includes Fels Planetarium) $20; $16 (ages 3-11). IMAX theater additional $6. Franklin 3D Theater additional $6. IMAX theater or Franklin 3D Theater only, $10; price varies for feature films. SkyBike additional $3 (riders must be at least 56 inches tall). Flight simulator additional $5. Phone for special exhibition pricing; advance ticket purchase is strongly recommended. **Phone:** (215) 448-1200. *(See ad on inside front cover.)* 🚇 19th, 69

Fels Planetarium, 222 N. 20th St. at The Franklin Institute, presents multimedia shows about astronomy and the night skies. The Space Command Exhibit simulates life on an Earth-orbiting research station. **Hours:** Show times vary; phone ahead. Closed Jan. 1, Thanksgiving, Christmas Eve and Christmas.

Cost: (includes The Franklin Institute) $20; $16 (ages 3-11). **Phone:** (215) 448-1200. 🚇 19th, 69

Tuttleman Dome IMAX Theater, 222 N. 20th St. at The Franklin Institute, projects films about science and adventure onto a four-story, 79-foot-wide dome screen with 56 audio speakers. Diverse topics include space exploration, nature and technology.

Hours: Show times vary; phone ahead. Closed Jan. 1, Thanksgiving, Christmas Eve and Christmas.

Lemon Hill at Fairmount Park

Cost: Theater only, $10; with museum admission $6. Price varies for feature-length major motion pictures. **Phone:** (215) 448-1200 for show information. 🖼 19th, 69

HISTORIC ST. GEORGE'S UNITED METHODIST CHURCH, 235 N. 4th St. at the Benjamin Franklin Bridge, was dedicated in 1769 and is said to be the oldest Methodist church used continuously for worship. The church museum contains historic artifacts, including a bible presented to the church by Francis Asbury, one of the first Methodist bishops in the United States. A historical library and archives are available.

For guide service ring the bell at the side entrance on New Street. **Time:** Allow 30 minutes minimum. **Hours:** Tues.-Fri. 10-4. Sun. services at 10. Last admission for archives research 1 hour before closing. Closed Jan. 1, Thanksgiving and Christmas. Phone ahead to confirm schedule. **Cost:** Donations. A fee is charged for research. **Phone:** (215) 925-7788. 🖼 5th, 64

◤GEM◢ **INDEPENDENCE NATIONAL HISTORICAL PARK,** with its main area extending from 2nd to 6th sts. between Walnut and Arch sts., includes some 20 buildings that are closely associated with the Colonial period, the founding of the nation and Philadelphia's early role as the U.S. capital. It features the nation's best-known symbol of freedom—the Liberty Bell—as well as Independence Hall, where the Declaration of Independence and the U.S. Constitution were created. Within the 54-acre park is a site where Benjamin Franklin's home once stood; exhibits here depict his life and teachings.

The centerpiece in Washington Square is the memorial to George Washington and the unknown soldiers of the American Revolution. Walkways under mature trees lead to the memorial, where a statue of Washington stands guard over the tomb of one unknown soldier.

Free, timed tickets are required for tours of Independence Hall from March through December. Tickets are available at the Independence Visitor Center *(see attraction listing)*, at 6th and Market streets, or may be ordered in advance for a small fee through the National Park Reservation Service. The visitor center, open daily, presents exhibits and continuous showings of a 30-minute John Huston film, "Independence." Inquire at the center for a walking tour map and the latest information about events, attractions and activities in the Philadelphia region.

Note: Access to Congress Hall, Independence Hall and the Liberty Bell Center requires visitors to pass through security screening. The security entrance for Independence Square is at 5th and Chestnut streets. For the Liberty Bell Center, the security entrance is at 6th and Market streets.

Time: Allow 5 hours minimum. **Hours:** Many buildings are open daily 9-5. Hours may be extended in summer and reduced other times of year. Closed Christmas. Phone ahead to confirm schedule. **Cost:** All attractions are free except the National Constitution Center and the Benjamin Franklin Museum in Franklin Court. **Phone:** (215) 965-2305, or (877) 444-6777 for National Park Reservation Service. 🖼 5th, 64

American Philosophical Society (APS) Museum is at 104 S. 5th St. at jct. Chestnut St., adjacent to Independence Hall; the museum falls within the boundaries of Independence National Historical Park but is not part of the park. This scholarly society, founded in 1743 by Benjamin Franklin, included John Adams, Thomas Jefferson and many other prominent early Americans. Rotating exhibits are created from the society's collection, which includes artworks, 300,000 books, important documents, 11 million manuscripts, maps, scientific specimens and instruments, and other items tracing American history from the Founding Fathers to the computer age. Exhibitions showcase the connections between history, science and art.

Time: Allow 1 hour minimum. **Hours:** Thurs.-Sun. 10-4, early Apr.-late Dec. (also 4-5, Memorial Day-Labor Day). Guided tours are available by 2-week advance reservation Mon.-Wed. 10-4 (requires a minimum of five participants). Closed holidays and when exhibitions are being changed. Phone ahead to confirm schedule. **Cost:** Donations. Guided tours $5; $2 (students with ID). **Phone:** (215) 440-3440. GT 🖼 5th, 64

B. Free Franklin Post Office, 316 Market St. within Independence National Historical Park, commemorates Franklin's 1775 appointment as first postmaster general. Said to be the only post office operated by the U.S. Postal Service that does not fly the American flag, it is named after Franklin's unique signature. It is assumed that his use of Free as part of his signature referred to America's struggle for freedom. Philatelists prize the hand-canceled letters from this post office.

Hours: Mon.-Sat. 9-5. Closed major holidays. Phone ahead to confirm schedule. **Cost:** Free. **Phone:** (215) 965-2305 for visitor information. 🖼 5th, 64

Bishop White House, 309 Walnut St. within Independence National Historical Park, was built by Pennsylvania's first Protestant Episcopal bishop in 1787; he was also the rector of Christ Church and St. Peter's Church. The restored house contains many original articles.

Time: Allow 1 hour minimum. **Hours:** Same-day reservations to see the house can be made at the Independence Visitor Center. Hours vary. Phone ahead to confirm schedule. **Cost:** Free. **Phone:** (215) 965-2305 for visitor information. 🖼 2nd, 63

Carpenters' Hall, 320 Chestnut St. within Independence National Historical Park, was lent by the Carpenters' Co. of Philadelphia for the First Continental Congress in 1774. A collection of early carpentry tools as well as chairs used by the Congress are inside. An 11-minute video presentation chronicles the history of the Carpenters' Co., which still owns and operates the hall.

Hours: Tues.-Sun. 10-4, Mar.-Dec.; Wed.-Sun. 10-4, rest of year. Closed Jan. 1, Easter, Thanksgiving, Christmas Eve and Christmas. **Cost:** Free. **Phone:** (215) 925-0167. 🚇 5th, 64

Christ Church (Episcopal), on 2nd St. between Market and Arch sts. within Independence National Historical Park, was the house of worship of 15 signers of the Declaration of Independence. Brass plaques mark the pews once occupied by Benjamin Franklin, Betsy Ross and George Washington. The 1727 structure typifies early Georgian architecture. It has one of the oldest Palladian windows in North America. It also contains the font from which William Penn was baptized in 1644 in London.

Christ Church Burial Ground, 5th and Arch streets, contains the graves of Benjamin Franklin and four other signers of the Declaration of Independence. Guided tours of the church and of the burial ground are offered.

Time: Allow 30 minutes minimum. **Hours:** Church Mon.-Sat. 9-5, Sun. 1-5, Mar.-Dec.; Wed.-Sat. 9-5, Sun. 1-5, rest of year. Services Sun. at 9 and 11 a.m., Wed. at noon. Burial ground (weather permitting) Mon.-Sat. 10-4, Sun. noon-4, Mar.-Nov. Burial ground guided tours depart Mon.-Sat. 11-3:30, Sun. noon-3:30, Mar.-Nov.; last tour begins at 3:30. Closed Jan. 1, Easter, Thanksgiving and Christmas. **Cost:** Church by donation. Burial ground admission $3; $1 (ages 5-12). Guided burial ground tour (includes admission) $8; $3 (ages 5-12). **Phone:** (215) 922-1695. GT 🚇 2nd, 63

Congress Hall, 6th and Chestnut sts. within Independence National Historical Park, was built 1787-89 as the Philadelphia County Court House but was occupied by the U.S. Congress 1790-1800 until Congress was moved to Washington, D.C. On the first floor is the chamber of the House of Representatives; the second floor contains the elaborate chamber of the Senate and various committee rooms. The hall was the setting for the inaugurations of George Washington (his second) and John Adams.

Note: Access requires visitors to pass through security screening. **Hours:** Daily 9-5. Guided tours depart every 20 to 30 minutes, Mar.-Dec.; self-guiding tours (rangers are available to answer questions) are available rest of year. Closed major holidays. Phone ahead to confirm schedule. **Cost:** Free. **Phone:** (215) 965-2305. GT 🚇 5th, 64

Declaration House, s.w. corner of 7th and Market sts. within Independence National Historical Park, is

Bishop White House

a partial reconstruction of the dwelling in which Thomas Jefferson drafted the Declaration of Independence in June 1776. **Hours:** Hours vary seasonally; phone ahead for schedule. **Cost:** Free. **Phone:** (215) 965-2305. 🚇 8th, 65

Franklin Court, between 3rd, 4th, Chestnut and Market sts. within Independence National Historical Park, was once owned by Benjamin Franklin. This was his home when he was part of the Continental Congress and Constitutional Convention until his death in 1790. The brick house was demolished in 1812 and there are no records describing the architectural appearance, but the foundation can be seen and a 54-foot-tall steel skeletal structure provides an outline to give visitors a feel for the space it once occupied.

The complex includes the Benjamin Franklin Museum as well as five Market Street houses, the exteriors of which have been restored to period. The buildings contain the refinished *Aurora* newspaper office historically operated by Franklin's grandson, a working reproduction of an 18th-century printing press and bindery operation and a post office.

Hours: Daily 9-5. Printing office daily 10-5 with last printing demonstration at 4:30; hours may vary in winter. Closed Jan. 1, Thanksgiving and Christmas. Phone ahead to confirm schedule. **Cost:** Franklin Court (including Market Street buildings) free. Benjamin Franklin Museum $5; $2 (ages 4-16). **Phone:** (215) 965-2305. 🚇 5th, 64

Free Quaker Meeting House is at 500 Arch St. at jct. 5th St. within Independence National Historical Park. Built in 1783, the building served as a meeting and worship house for the 30 to 50 men and women, including Betsy Ross, who had been disowned by the Quakers for going against their principle of pacifism and supporting the Colonial militia. Displays detail Quaker history, including their role in the American Revolution.

A guide dressed in 18th-century Quaker attire is available to answer questions and share information about Quaker religious beliefs and the revolution. **Hours:** Hours vary. Phone ahead to confirm schedule. **Cost:** Free. **Phone:** (215) 965-2305. [GT] [🚇] 5th, 64

Independence Archeology Lab, 313 Walnut St. within Independence National Historical Park, is a laboratory where you can watch archeologists at work and learn how the small artifacts they study help piece together what life was like in 18th- and 19th-century Philadelphia. The items being studied were excavated 2000-03 before and during the National Constitution Center construction. Visitors may see archeologists at work in the park (weather permitting).

Time: Allow 30 minutes minimum. **Hours:** Entrance is by appointment only. Tours are offered Mon.-Fri. on a space-available basis to visitors ages 16 and older in groups up to 4 persons; one-week advance reservation is required. **Cost:** Free. **Phone:** (215) 861-4956 for tour reservations. [GT] [🚇] 2nd, 63

Independence Hall is between 5th and 6th sts. on Chestnut St. on Independence Square within Independence National Historical Park. Within this graceful 1732 brick building, built as the Pennsylvania State House, the Second Continental Congress voted to break with England, the Declaration of Independence and Constitution were signed, and George Washington accepted the role of commander in chief of the Colonial armies. The Assembly Room has been restored to look as it did when used by the founding fathers 1775-87. It contains the original Rising Sun chair that Washington occupied during the drafting of the Constitution.

Across the hallway is the restored Pennsylvania Supreme Court Chamber. Upstairs, the Governor's Council Chamber, Long Room and Committee Room have been restored and furnished in period. The west wing's Great Essentials Exhibit features original rare, printed copies of the Declaration of Independence, the Articles of Confederation and the Constitution as well as the silver inkstand that is believed to have been used by the signers of the Declaration of Independence and the Constitution.

Note: Access requires visitors to pass through security screening. Admission is by guided tour only (except for the west wing). Tickets are issued for specific times and are available at the Independence Visitor Center at 6th and Market streets. For a small handling fee, the National Park Reservation Service will arrange advance tickets (tickets are not necessary Jan.-Feb.). **Hours:** Daily 9-5. Phone ahead to confirm extended hours in summer. Closed

Christmas. **Cost:** Free. **Phone:** (215) 965-2305, or (877) 444-6777 for National Park Reservation Service. [GT] [🚇] 5th, 64

Independence Visitor Center, jct. 6th and Market sts. at 1 N. Independence Mall W. within Independence National Historical Park, is a 50,000-square-foot facility that provides a range of tourism services for Independence National Historic Park and the Philadelphia region. These include orientation films, hotel and dining reservations, tour and attraction information and ticket sales. The visitor center is the only location to obtain free timed tickets for Independence Hall on the day of your visit.

Time: Allow 30 minutes minimum. **Hours:** Daily 8:30-7, Memorial Day-Labor Day; 8:30-6, rest of year. Closed Thanksgiving and Christmas. **Cost:** Free. **Phone:** (215) 965-2305 or (800) 537-7676. [🍴] [🚇] 5th, 64

[GEM] **Liberty Bell Center,** on 6th St. between Chestnut and Market sts. within Independence National Historical Park, houses the renowned bell that announced America's birth as a new nation in 1776 and was used as a symbol in the 19th-century abolition movement. Today the 2,080-pound bell is encased in a glass chamber, and admirers will see Independence Hall in the background. The bell's yoke, made of American elm, is believed to be the original.

The center includes exhibits about the bell's significance as a worldwide symbol of freedom. An 11-minute video presentation, available in a dozen languages, tells the story of its origins. **Note:** Access requires visitors to pass through security screening. **Time:** Allow 30 minutes minimum. **Hours:** Daily 9-5. Closed Christmas. **Cost:** Free. **Phone:** (215) 965-2305. [🚇] 5th, 64

[GEM] **National Constitution Center** occupies a city block between 5th and 6th sts. at 525 Arch St. within Independence National Historical Park. Devoted to preserving the legacy of the U.S. Constitution and inspiring active citizenship, this museum features hundreds of interactive exhibits, rare artifacts and films. Signers' Hall is sure to amaze with its 42 life-size bronze sculptures of the nation's founding fathers. Don't miss the 17-minute presentation of "Freedom Rising," a 360-degree theatrical production illustrating important milestones in American history.

Audio tours by cellphone are available. **Time:** Allow 2 hours, 30 minutes minimum. **Hours:** Mon.-Sat. 9:30-5, Sun. noon-5. Closed Jan. 1, Thanksgiving and Christmas. **Cost:** $14.50; $13 (ages 65+ and college students with ID); $11 (ages 6-18); free (active military with ID). **Parking:** $8-$18. **Phone:** (215) 409-6700 for ticket information. [🍴] [🏞] [🚇] 5th, 64

New Hall Military Museum, on Chestnut St. between 3rd and 4th sts. within Independence National Historical Park, is a reconstruction of a 1791

building. The museum commemorates the history of the U.S. Army, Navy and Marine Corps 1775-1805. **Hours:** Hours vary. Phone ahead to confirm schedule. **Cost:** Free. **Phone:** (215) 965-2305. 5th, 64

Old City Hall, s.w. corner of 5th and Chestnut sts. within Independence National Historical Park, was the home of the U.S. Supreme Court 1791-1800. The exterior and the room used by the Supreme Court have been restored. **Hours:** Daily 9-5, July-Aug.; hours vary rest of year. Closed major holidays. Phone ahead to confirm schedule. **Cost:** Free. **Phone:** (215) 965-2305. 5th, 64

President's House Site, 600 Market St. at jct. 6th St. within Independence National Historical Park, is the site of the former residence of Presidents George Washington and John Adams 1790-1800. Although the structure no longer exists, the exhibit "Freedom and Slavery in the Making of a New Nation," which features video installations, panels and illustrated glass, tells the story of their time here. Archeological fragments unearthed from the site in 2007 can be viewed in a glass enclosure.

The contradiction of Washington's belief in freedom with his use of slaves is pointed out, profiling nearly a dozen of the Africans who worked here. A memorial honors all the enslaved who lived on the grounds. A cellphone audio tour is available. Note: the attraction is outdoors and offers no shelter from inclement weather. **Time:** Allow 45 minutes minimum. **Hours:** Daily 24 hours. **Cost:** Free. **Phone:** (215) 965-2305. 5th, 64

Second Bank of the United States Portrait Gallery is at 420 Chestnut St. within Independence National Historical Park. The 1824 structure, modeled after the Parthenon, now houses the People of Independence 1750-1840 collection. Nearly 200 late 18th- and early 19th-century sculptures and portraits, many by Charles Willson Peale, illustrate Philadelphia's role as the capital city 1790-1800. Many of the works represent members of the military and signers of the Declaration of Independence and Constitution. Works by artists James Sharples and Thomas Sully also are included.

Hours: Schedule varies; phone ahead. **Cost:** Free. **Phone:** (215) 965-2305. 5th, 64

Todd House, 4th and Walnut sts. within Independence National Historical Park, was the home of Dolley Payne Todd before her marriage to James Madison, fourth president of the United States. The restored 1775 home reflects life in the 18th century. Admission is by tour only and includes the Bishop White House.

Time: Allow 1 hour minimum. **Hours:** Same-day reservations to see the house can be made at the Independence Visitor Center. Hours vary. Phone ahead to confirm schedule. **Cost:** Free. **Phone:** (215) 956-2305 for visitor information. 5th, 64

National Constitution Center

INDEPENDENCE SEAPORT MUSEUM, on Penn's Landing at 211 S. Columbus Blvd. at jct. Walnut St., depicts the maritime heritage of the Delaware River, Delaware Bay and its tributaries. Visitors can climb aboard the World War II submarine *Becuna*, a Guppy-1A type submarine that went on missions in the Pacific before being refitted for missions during the Korean and Vietnam Wars, and *Olympia*, Adm. George Dewey's flagship during the Spanish-American War. Guided behind-the-scenes tours are available. History, science and art exhibits examine the area's waterways. In the Workshop on the Water, boat builders can be seen practicing their craft; models, blueprints and replicas of a variety of small watercraft pay tribute to generations of boat builders and enthusiasts.

Time: Allow 1 hour minimum. **Hours:** Daily 10-5, Apr.-Dec.; Tues.-Sun. (also Jan. 1, Martin Luther King Jr. Day and Presidents Day) 10-5, rest of year. Extended hours to tour ships are offered in summer; phone ahead. Behind-the-scenes tour first Sat. of the month; reservations are required. Closed Thanksgiving and Christmas. **Cost:** $17; $12 (ages 3-12 and 65+, college students and military with ID). Phone for behind-the-scenes tour rates. **Phone:** (215) 413-8655. GT 2nd, 63

JOHNSON HOUSE HISTORIC SITE is at 6306 Germantown Ave. The house was built in 1768 by a Quaker family and was used in the 1850s by slaves escaping the South. The tour provides insights into the Johnson family, the Underground Railroad and the abolitionist movement. **Time:** Allow 1 hour, 30 minutes minimum. **Hours:** Guided tours are offered Thurs.-Fri. 10-4, Sat. 1-4, early Feb. to mid-June and Labor Day-late Nov.; Sat. 1-4, rest of year. Phone ahead to confirm schedule. **Cost:** $8; $6 (ages 55+); $4 (ages 0-12). Cash only. **Phone:** (215) 438-1768. GT ♿ Upsal, 245

THE KIMMEL CENTER FOR THE PERFORMING ARTS, on Avenue of the Arts between S. Broad and Spruce sts., includes The Kimmel Center, Academy of Music and Merriman Theater and is home to the Philadelphia Orchestra, the Pennsylvania Ballet, Opera Philadelphia and several resident music and theater companies. The center houses the 2,500-seat Verizon Hall, the 650-seat Perelman Theater and the SEI Innovation Studio and is enclosed within an arched-glass atrium.

The Building and Theater tour gives an overview of the history of the Kimmel Center campus, and once a month begins with a 15-minute demonstration of the Fred J. Cooper Memorial Organ. Access to performance halls varies with event scheduling. The Art and Architecture tour focuses on the art displayed within the Kimmel and aspects of the building itself. **Time:** Allow 1 hour minimum. **Hours:** Daily 10-6. Building & Theater Tour departs daily at 1. Art & Architecture Tour departs Sat. at 10:30. Organ demonstrations are given some Sat. Closed major holidays. Phone ahead to confirm schedule. **Cost:** Free. **Phone:** (215) 893-1999 for tickets, or (215) 790-5886 for tour information.
GT ♟ ♿ Lombard-South, 116

MASONIC TEMPLE, 1 N. Broad St., was built 1868-73 and is one of the city's striking architectural landmarks. Each of the temple's seven lodge halls exemplifies a different architectural style—Corinthian, Ionic, Italian Renaissance, Norman, Gothic, Oriental and Egyptian. The hallways and stairways are enhanced by chandeliers, paintings, statuary and artwork. A large stained-glass window overlooks the marble grand staircase.

Tours of the building include the Grand Lodge Museum, which is a Byzantine room housing Masonic treasures. Included in the collection are jewels, George Washington's Masonic apron, furniture, Liverpool and Lowestoft ware, cut glass and statues by William Rush. Visitors must be accompanied by guides. **Hours:** Tours are offered Tues.-Sat. at 10, 11, 1, 2 and 3. Closed major holidays and special events. Phone ahead to confirm schedule. **Cost:** $15; $10 (ages 65+ and students with ID); $5 (ages 5-12); free (active military with ID); $35 (family, up to six people). Museum and library only, $7. **Phone:** (215) 988-1917. GT ♿ 13th, 67

MONEY IN MOTION EXHIBIT is in the Federal Reserve Bank at jct. 6th and Arch sts. America's financial history is presented through interactive exhibits. Topics include the role of the Federal Reserve Bank and the history of America's currency. Exhibits about counterfeit detection, electronic banking and monetary policy represent the more recent changes in

the nation's financial situation. Various types of currency are displayed; a highlight is currency that was used in the original 13 colonies.

Time: Allow 1 hour minimum. **Hours:** Mon.-Fri. 9:30-4:30, Mar.-Dec. (also Sat. 9-4:30, June-Aug.); Mon.-Fri. 10-2, rest of year. Last admission 30 minutes before closing. Phone for holiday schedule. **Cost:** Free. **Phone:** (215) 574-6441 or (866) 574-3727. ♿ 5th, 64

MUSEUM OF THE AMERICAN REVOLUTION is at 101 S. 3rd St.; parking is not available at the museum, but there are nearby parking lots and garages. The museum covers all aspects of the American Revolution—the causes of Colonial rebellion; the Revolutionary War itself; and the war's aftermath, both the good (creation of the United States) and the bad (the hardships felt by war veterans as well as the women, Native Americans and African Americans who did not receive full independence as a result of the American victory). Thousands of historical objects, including artwork and documents, are displayed in addition to creative interactive exhibits. Temporary exhibits also are offered.

Hours: Daily 9:30-6, mid-June through Labor Day; 10-5, rest of year. Extended hours offered some holiday weekends; phone ahead. Guided Highlights Tour Sat.-Sun. at 10 and 3. Early Access Guided Tour Tues., Thurs. and Sat. at 9. Closed Jan. 1, Thanksgiving and Christmas. Closes Christmas Eve at 3.

Cost: (valid for 2 consecutive days) $19; $17 (ages 65+ and students, teachers and military with ID); $12 (ages 6-17). Highlights tour additional $12. Early access tour (includes admission) $50. Timed entry tickets are required; last ticket is sold 1 hour before closing. Reservations are recommended for guided tours. **Phone:** (215) 253-6731 or (877) 740-1776. GT ♟ ♿ 2nd, 63

MÜTTER MUSEUM OF THE COLLEGE OF PHYSICIANS OF PHILADELPHIA is just s. of Market St. at 19 S. 22nd St. Thomas Dent Mütter, a professor of surgery at Jefferson Medical College, donated his collection of unique medical materials to The College of Physicians of Philadelphia in 1858. The collection now has more than 20,000 items, including medical instruments as well as anatomical and pathological specimens and models. Displays about diseases, viruses and treatment throughout history also can be seen. The building, designed by Cope & Stewardson, dates to 1908.

Time: Allow 1 hour, 30 minutes minimum. **Hours:** Daily 10-5. Closed Jan. 1, Thanksgiving, Christmas Eve and Christmas. **Cost:** $18; $16 (ages 65+); $15 (military with ID); $13 (ages 6-17 and students with ID). Combination ticket with the Penn Museum $26; $22 (ages 65+); $16 (ages 6-17 and students with ID). **Phone:** (215) 560-8564. ♿ 22nd, 70

NATIONAL LIBERTY MUSEUM is downtown at 321 Chestnut St. between 2nd and 3rd sts. Glass art, exhibits, films and interactive centers portray American democracy throughout the nation's history. The museum explores such topics as the relationship between character, leadership and heroism, and the potential for people of all ages and backgrounds to be heroes. The Welcome to Liberty Gallery features an immersive theater. A collection of contemporary glass art is on display, including a 20-foot glass sculpture by artist Dale Chihuly. The Live Like a Hero and Heroes of 9/11 exhibits and an original collection of presidential White House china also are featured.

Time: Allow 2 hours minimum. **Hours:** Daily 10-5. Phone for holiday hours. **Cost:** $7; $6 (ages 56+); $5 (students with ID); $2 (ages 5-17 with adult); $15 (family, two adults and their children). **Phone:** (215) 925-2800. 🚇 5th, 64

NATIONAL MUSEUM OF AMERICAN JEWISH HISTORY, 101 S. Independence Mall E. at jct. 5th and Market sts., is a Smithsonian affiliate and the only major museum dedicated to chronicling the American Jewish experience. The museum's four floors contain documents, artifacts, photographs, films and interactive exhibits preserving the history of Jewish life from the arrival of the first Jewish community in New York in 1654 to the present. The first floor exhibits feature items from prominent Jewish icons, including a pipe that belonged to Einstein and a piano that belonged to American composer Irving Berlin. Some of the topics covered include early Jewish lifestyles, the evolution of religious practices, and immigration obstacles and discrimination.

Time: Allow 1 hour, 30 minutes minimum. **Hours:** Wed.-Fri. 10-5, Sat.-Sun. 10-5:30. Museum open select Tues. during special exhibitions; phone ahead. Highlight tours are given at 11:30 and 2:30, subject to availability. Phone ahead to confirm schedule and for holiday hours and closings. **Cost:** $15; $13 (ages 13-21, ages 65+ and students with ID); free (active military with ID). **Parking:** Validation provided for a discount at The Bourse garage at 400 Ranstead St. **Phone:** (215) 923-3811. GT 🚇 5th, 64

ONE LIBERTY OBSERVATION DECK is on the 57th floor at 1650 Market St. See panoramic views of Philadelphia from the One Liberty Place skyscraper in the heart of Center City. An elevator takes guests 883 feet into the air (it takes about 75 seconds) where you'll be able to enjoy a 360-degree view from an enclosed deck. Interactive touch screens from multiple angles provide viewers information about what they're seeing. **Hours:** Daily 10-9, Apr.-Sept.; 10-8, rest of year. Last admission 30 minutes before closing. Guided tours are given on the hour 11-1 and 3-5. **Cost:** $14.50; $9.50 (ages 3-11). "Sun & Stars" (two visits within 48 hours) $20; $14 (ages 3-11). Family Four Pack (one visit) $40 (family, two adults and two children ages 3-11). Advance purchase tickets are available. **Phone:** (215) 561-3325. *(See ad on inside front cover.)* GT 🚇 Suburban, 221

PENNSYLVANIA ACADEMY OF THE FINE ARTS, 118-128 N. Broad St., was founded in 1805 and is the nation's first museum and school of fine arts. The majority of major American artists has studied, taught or exhibited here. The building, a Victorian Gothic beauty with all its exterior embellishments, dates to 1876 and houses art from the 18th century to the present. Changing exhibits of multimedia works by students, faculty and alumni can be viewed at the Samuel M.V. Hamilton Building.

The collection showcases American art since the 1760s. Among the PAFA founders was painter/scientist Charles Willson Peale; his self-portrait, "The Artist in His Museum," portrays him lifting a curtain to reveal scientific specimens. Other artists represented throughout the collection include Mary Cassatt, Thomas Eakins, Childe Hassam, Robert Henri, Edward Hopper, Georgia O'Keefe, William Rush, Henry Ossawa Tanner, Benjamin West and Andrew Wyeth. **Time:** Allow 1 hour minimum. **Hours:** Tues.-Fri. 10-5, Sat.-Sun. 11-5. Guided tours are offered Thurs.-Sat. at 1 and 2. Phone ahead to confirm tour schedule. Closed federal holidays. **Cost:** $15; $12 (ages 60+ and students with ID); $8 (ages 13-18); free (military with ID). **Phone:** (215) 972-7600, or (215) 972-2069 for tour information. GT 🚇 Race-Vine, 119

Samuel M.V. Hamilton Building, 128 N. Broad St., is part of the Pennsylvania Academy of the Fine Arts and features two floors of galleries with changing

National Liberty Museum

exhibits of multimedia works by American artists, including students, faculty and alumni. The early 20th-century building is a former automobile showroom and storage facility.

Time: Allow 1 hour minimum. **Hours:** Tues.-Fri. 10-5, Sat.-Sun. 11-5. Guided tours are offered Thurs.-Sat. at 1 and 2 when special exhibitions are on display. Phone ahead to confirm tour schedule. Closed federal holidays. **Cost:** $15; $12 (ages 60+ and students with ID); $8 (ages 13-18); free (military with ID). **Phone:** (215) 972-7600.
GT TI 🏛 Race-Vine, 119

🅂🄰🅅🄴 **PHILADELPHIA HISTORY MUSEUM AT THE ATWATER KENT,** 15 S. 7th St., includes over 100,000 objects hundreds of items covering 330 years of Philadelphia history. Portraiture, sports and political memorabilia are on display. Objects from the city's founders and residents include President George Washington's writing desk from the 1790s and Joe Frazier's boxing gloves from the 1970s. Themed galleries fitted with interactive elements tell stories about such topics as culture and local manufacturing. **Hours:** Tues.-Sat. 10:30-4:30. **Cost:** $10; $8 (ages 65+); $6 (ages 13-18 and students with ID); $20 (family, two adults and two children); free (active military with ID). **Phone:** (215) 685-4830. 🏛 8th, 65

 PHILADELPHIA MUSEUM OF ART—see Fairmount Park p. 171.

PHILADELPHIA ZOO—see Fairmount Park p. 171.

RODIN MUSEUM—see Fairmount Park p. 172.

RYERSS MUSEUM AND LIBRARY is at 7370 Central Ave. in Burholme Park. This Victorian house is on a hilltop and was built by the Ryerss family in 1859 to be used as a summer home. Since they loved animals, much of the interior is adorned with pieces related to animals including numerous portraits, and there is a pet cemetery on the grounds. Furnishings include Colonial and Victorian antiques as well as art and artifacts from Asia, the Americas and Europe. The house also includes a lending library.

Time: Allow 2 hours minimum. **Hours:** Fri.-Sun. 10-4. Self-guiding tours 10-3:30. Guided tours depart at 11 and 2. Closed major holidays. **Cost:** Free. **Phone:** (215) 685-0599 or (215) 685-0544.
GT 🏓 🏛 🏛 Ryers, 273

THE SCHUYLKILL CENTER FOR ENVIRONMENTAL EDUCATION is off the Schuylkill Expwy. (I-76) exit 338, .9 mi. e. on Green Ln., 2.3 mi. n. on Ridge Ave., .2 mi. w. on Port Royal Ave., then just n. to 8480 Hagy's Mill Rd., following signs. Covering 340 acres of fields and forests, the site features 3.5 miles of hiking trails, ponds, streams, wetlands, outdoor art installations and a 4-acre organic garden. Hickory, buttonwood, tulip, poplar and sumac trees are abundant, as are mica schist and quartzite rocks.

Previously an agricultural area, the center now houses a children's discovery center, an environmental art gallery, interactive exhibits and meeting space. Pets are not permitted. **Time:** Allow 1 hour, 30 minutes minimum. **Hours:** Trails daily dawn to dusk. Center Mon.-Sat. 9-5. Trail maps are available outside main building. Closed major holidays. **Cost:** Free. **Phone:** (215) 482-7300. 🏛

SCIENCE HISTORY INSTITUTE, 315 Chestnut St. between 3rd and 4th sts. in the renovated 1865 First National Bank building, offers a collection of exhibits to highlight the important role chemistry, chemical engineering and other related sciences has played in advancing everyday life. Historical items in the collection include scientific instruments, rare books, the personal papers of scientists and artwork. Temporary exhibits are included. Guest speakers discuss various topics the first Friday evening of each month from March through December.

Time: Allow 45 minutes minimum. **Hours:** Tues.-Sat. 10-5. (also first Fri. of the month 5-8, Mar.-Dec.). Guided tours are offered the last Sat. of the month at 2. Phone for holiday closures. **Cost:** Free. **Phone:** (215) 925-2222. GT 🏛 2nd, 63

THE UNITED STATES MINT is at 151 N. Independence Mall East between Arch and Race sts.; the entrance is at the corner of Fifth and Arch sts. Utilizing video, audio, photographs, historic documents and samples of currency, a self-guiding tour of the U.S. Mint gives visitors a thorough description of American coin production from the late 1700s to today. Visitors can watch coining operations from a vantage point 40 feet above the factory floor.

Note: A government-issued photo ID is required for ages 18+. Visitors must pass through a metal detector and are subject to search. Photography, food, drinks and large packages are not permitted. **Time:** Allow 1 hour minimum. **Hours:** Mon.-Sat. 9-4:30, Memorial Day-Labor Day (also Sun. 9-4:30, Memorial Day weekend and Labor Day weekend); Mon.-Fri. 9-4:30, rest of year. Last tour admittance is at 4:15. Closed federal holidays, except Memorial Day, Labor Day and July 4. Phone ahead to confirm schedule. **Cost:** Free. **Phone:** (215) 408-0112. 🏛 5th, 64

UNIVERSITY OF PENNSYLVANIA, bounded by Chestnut, Pine, 32nd and 40th sts., was founded in 1740 and is considered to be one of the nation's leading educational centers. In 1765 the country's first medical school was established here. The 299-acre main campus in west Philadelphia is composed of 215 buildings and the University of Pennsylvania Hospital. Tours of the campus are available through the Office of Undergraduate Admissions at 1 College Hall. **Hours:** Phone ahead for tour schedule. **Cost:** Free. **Phone:** (215) 898-7507. 🏛 36th, 74

Institute of Contemporary Art, 36th and Sansom sts. at the University of Pennsylvania, presents changing exhibitions of contemporary art. **Time:**

Allow 1 hour minimum. **Hours:** Wed.-Sun. 11-6 (also Wed. 6-8 p.m.). Guided tours are available with 2-week advance reservation. Closed Jan. 1, Thanksgiving, Christmas and when exhibitions are being changed. Phone ahead to confirm schedule. **Cost:** Free. **Phone:** (215) 898-7108, or (215) 746-5073 for tour reservations. GT 🚻 36th, 74

Penn Museum, 3260 South St. on the University of Pennsylvania urban campus, displays outstanding archeological and anthropological collections from around the world. Exhibits include artifacts from ancient Egypt, Asia, Central America, North America, Mesopotamia and the Mediterranean. Visitors can see conservators at work on ancient artifacts in a lab. Special events are held throughout the year.

Time: Allow 1 hour minimum. **Hours:** Tues.-Sun. 10-5 (also first Wed. of the month 5-8). Closed major holidays. **Cost:** $15; $13 (ages 65+); $10 (ages 6-17 and students with ID); free (active military with ID). Combination ticket with Mütter Museum of the College of Physicians of Philadelphia (on-site purchase only) $26; $22 (ages 65+); $16 (ages 6-17 and students with ID). **Phone:** (215) 898-4000. 🍴 🚻 University City, 180

WAGNER FREE INSTITUTE OF SCIENCE is at 1700 W. Montgomery Ave. Incorporated in 1855, the institute contains more than 100,000 mineral, fossil and zoological specimens. Displayed in cherry wood cases built in the 1880s, the exhibits include mounted animal skeletons and shells from around the world. As a continuing resource for scholarly research, it houses the Library and Archives, which also showcases items highlighting the history of the institution.

Evening and weekend events are held throughout the year. **Time:** Allow 1 hour, 30 minutes minimum. **Hours:** Museum Tues.-Fri. 9-4. Guided tours and library use are available by appointment; library appointments should be made at least 1 week in advance. Closed major holidays. **Cost:** Free. **Phone:** (215) 763-6529.
GT 🚻 Cecil B. Moore, 126

WOODMERE ART MUSEUM, 4 mi. s. of Pennsylvania Tpke./I-276 exit 333 at 9201 Germantown Ave., has paintings and decorative art spanning the 18th- through 20th centuries. The Victorian home and art collection of Charles Knox Smith form the nucleus of the museum. Of particular interest is the collection of 19th-century American paintings, which includes works by Thomas Anshutz, Frederic Church, Jasper Cropsey, Edward Moran and Benjamin West.

Changing exhibits often focus on local artists. **Time:** Allow 30 minutes minimum. **Hours:** Tues.-Fri. 10-5 (also Fri. 5-8:45), Sat. 10-6, Sun. 10-5. Jazz concerts are held select Fri. at 6 p.m. Closed major holidays. **Cost:** $10; $7 (ages 55+); free (ages 0-12, students with ID and to all Sun.). A fee is charged for jazz concerts. **Phone:** (215) 247-0476.
🚻 Chestnut Hill East, 260

Penn Museum

WYCK HOUSE, GARDEN, AND FARM, 6026 Germantown Ave., is the 2.5-acre estate that served as the home to nine generations of a prominent Quaker family who lived here 1689-1973. Tour guides show visitors through the house, which is filled with mementos and furniture offering a glimpse into American history. The grounds include a well-groomed rose garden widely recognized as the oldest rose garden growing in its original plan; a sprawling farm and woodlot; and several outbuildings, including a coach house, icehouse and smokehouse.

Time: Allow 2 hours minimum. **Hours:** House and garden guided tours are offered Thurs.-Sat. noon-4 and by appointment, early Apr.-Sat. before Thanksgiving. Closed major holidays. **Cost:** Free. **Phone:** (215) 848-1690. GT 🅰 🚻 Germantown, 267

Sightseeing
Boat Tours
The *Spirit of Philadelphia* offers narrated 2-hour lunch and dinner sightseeing cruises on the Delaware River. Cruises depart from Columbus Boulevard and Lombard Circle at Penn's Landing; phone (866) 394-8439.

Bus and Trolley Tours

MURAL ARTS PHILADELPHIA TOURS depart from the Hamilton Building at the Pennsylvania Academy of the Fine Arts, 128 N. Broad Street in Center City. Guided trolley and walking tours highlight community history and the stories behind the creation of the murals. The neighborhoods and themes of the 2-hour trolley tours vary each week, but all tours showcase a variety of murals. The

Journey South, Masterpiece East & West and Re-imagined Landscape trolley tours showcase about 35 of the murals. Other tours include Center City Mural Mile walking tours highlighting over 40 iconic Center City murals, and the Love Letter Train Tour featuring about 50 rooftop murals in West Philadelphia. Interactive painting activities and a scavenger hunt also are available.

Hours: Trolley tours depart Sat. at 10 (also Fri., mid-June through Aug. 31), Apr.-Nov. Mural Mile Center City walking tours depart Sat. at 11, Sun. at 11 and 4 (also other weekdays, mid-June through Aug. 31), Apr.-Nov. Love Letter tours depart Sat. at 10:30, Sun. at 1, Labor Day-Memorial Day. Phone ahead to confirm schedule. **Cost:** $22-$32. Reservations are strongly recommended. **Phone:** (215) 925-3633. GT 🚇 Race-Vine, 119

PHILADELPHIA TROLLEY WORKS, THE BIG BUS CO. AND 76 CARRIAGE CO. tours depart from jct. 5th and Market sts. with 27 stops along the loop. The 90-minute tour aboard a double-decker bus or a Victorian-style trolley passes and stops at most of Philadelphia's major attractions, from Independence Visitor Center to Philadelphia Zoo, and includes the Please Touch Museum, Philadelphia Museum of Art, The Franklin Institute, and Penn's Landing. Horse-drawn carriage and walking tours also are available.

Tickets can be purchased at the Independence Visitor Center. Free unlimited, interchangeable reboarding is permitted on the bus or trolley for the timeframe specified on the ticket. **Hours:** Daily 9:30-5:30 (also Sat.-Sun. 5:30-6), Memorial Day-Labor Day. Hours vary frequently rest of year; phone ahead to confirm schedule. Closed Jan. 1 and Christmas. **Cost:** Fare, valid for 24 hours, $32; $29 (senior citizens); $10 (ages 4-12). Fare, valid for 48 hours, $38; $35 (senior citizens); $15 (ages 4-12). A 72-hour fare also is available. Phone ahead to confirm rates. **Phone:** (215) 389-8687 for trolley, big bus and motor coach reservations, or (215) 923-8516 for horse-drawn carriage reservations. *(See ad on inside front cover.)* GT 🚇 40th, 76

Food Tours

TASTE OF PHILLY FOOD TOUR departs from the Reading Terminal Market welcome desk at jct. 12th and Filbert sts. The 75-minute walking tour, which provides a historical overview of the market includes stops at several of the market's vendors, including longtime merchants. Participants receive several small food bites so they can experience some of Philly's iconic treats. **Hours:** Wed. and Sat. at 10; additional tours are offered in summer. Phone ahead to confirm schedule. **Cost:** $16.95; $9.95 (ages 7-11). Advance purchase is required. Reservations are required. **Phone:** (215) 545-8007, or (800) 838-3006 for tickets. GT 🚇 Jefferson, 222

Guided Walking Tours

THE CONSTITUTIONAL WALKING TOUR departs from the main entrance of the National Constitution Center (near the stone benches) at 525 Arch St., and includes 21 stops on a 1.25-mile route. Knowledgeable and friendly guides provide historical context for some of the city's most prominent sites, including the Betsy Ross House, Christ Church and its nearby burial ground, Congress Hall, Declaration House, Franklin Court, Independence Hall, Liberty Bell Center, National Constitution Center and Old City Hall.

The tour does not include the interiors of any of the buildings. **Time:** Allow 1 hour, 15 minutes minimum. **Hours:** Tours depart Mon.-Sat. at 10, noon and 2, Sun. at 11, 1 and 3, Apr.-Nov. **Cost:** $19; $12.50 (ages 3-12); $55 (family, two adults and two children ages 3-12). Reservations are required. **Phone:** (215) 525-1776. GT 🚇 5th, 64

FRANKLIN'S FOOTSTEPS WALKING TOUR departs from the Independence Visitor Center at jct. 6th and Market sts.; tickets can be purchased inside the visitor center. The route includes more than 30 sites and offers visitors a thorough history of Revolutionary Philadelphia from the perspective of Benjamin Franklin, whose many titles include diplomat, inventor and philosopher. Detailed insights into Independence National Historical Park are shared at such stops as Carpenters' Hall, Christ Church, Independence Hall and Liberty Bell Center.

The tour does not include the interiors of any of the buildings. **Time:** Allow 1 hour, 30 minutes minimum. **Hours:** Tours depart daily at 11, 1 and 3, May-Oct.; Sat.-Sun. at 11, 1 and 3 in Apr. and Nov. Phone ahead to confirm schedule. **Cost:** $19; $17 (senior citizens); $12 (ages 4-12). Combination ticket with The Big Bus Co. $44; $20 (ages 4-12). **Phone:** (215) 389-8687. GT 🚇 5th, 64

GHOST TOURS OF PHILADELPHIA departs from Signers Garden at jct. 5th and Chestnut sts. This 90-minute candlelight walking tour through Society Hill, Old City and Independence National Historical Park takes visitors past places that are said to be haunted and includes a number of ghost stories. Stops on the route include Independence Hall, Washington Square and the cemetery at St. Peter's Church. Along the way you'll hear about early American history, folklore, and maybe even about Edgar Allan Poe's time in Philadelphia. Other tours also are offered on a more limited basis; phone for details.

The tour does not include the interiors of any of the buildings. **Hours:** Tours depart daily at 7:30 (also Thurs.-Sat. at 9:30), July-Aug.; daily at 7:30 (also Fri.-Sat. at 9:30) in June and Oct.; daily at 7:30 (also Sat. at 9:30), in Sept.; daily at 7:30, Apr.-May; Fri.-Sat. at 7:30 in Mar. and Nov. Visitors should arrive 15 minutes prior to departure. **Cost:** $17; $10 (ages 4-12). With advance reservations $15; $10 (ages 4-12). Reservations are required. **Phone:**

(215) 413-1997 for information or to purchase tickets. [GT] [🚍] 5th, 64

SPIRITS OF '76 GHOST TOUR departs from the Cosi Restaurant at 325 Chestnut St. at jct. 4th St. Guides share haunted Philadelphia facts and folklore, including tales about Edgar Allan Poe and the only prisoner to escape the city's Eastern State Penitentiary without being captured, on this tour through Old City. The route features more than 20 sites, some of which are said to be haunted.

The tour does not include the interiors of any of the buildings. **Time:** Allow 1 hour, 15 minutes minimum. **Hours:** Tours depart Mon.-Wed. at 7:30, Thurs.-Fri. at 7:30 and 9:30, Sat. at 6, 7:30 and 9:30, Sun. at 6 and 7:30, in Oct.; daily at 7:30 (also Thurs.-Sat. at 9:30), July-Aug.; Wed.-Sun. at 7:30, in June and Sept.; Thurs.-Sat. at 7:30, in May; Fri.-Sat. at 7:30, in Apr. and Nov. Phone ahead to confirm schedule. **Cost:** $19; $12.50 (ages 3-12); $55 (family, two adults and two children ages 3-12). Reservations are required. **Phone:** (215) 525-1776. [GT] [🚍] 5th, 64

Self-guiding Tours

The heart of historic Philadelphia lends itself to a walking tour. A stroll through the narrow cobblestone streets among restored Georgian and Colonial buildings is the best way to discover the essence of the city and to assimilate its 18th-century atmosphere. A good way to see historic Philadelphia is to combine the walking tour with stops at the attractions along the way. The names of sites listed in detail in the Attractions section are printed in bold type. Even if you do not tour a listed site, reading the attraction listing when you reach that point will make the tour more interesting. This tour takes approximately 5 hours, which allows for a leisurely pace.

Start at City Hall at Centre Square. Walking east on Market Street, you pass Macy's department store on the right. If you're in this area on a weekday morning, stop in for the 45-minute 11 a.m. tour of the historic Wanamaker building ($12); phone (215) 241-9000, ext. 2408. Advance reservations are recommended.

Continue east on Market Street to 7th Street, where you will find the **Declaration House.**

Cross 7th Street to the **Philadelphia History Museum at the Atwater Kent.** Upon leaving the museum, take the walkway to the right to 6th Street for a stop at the **Liberty Bell Center,** which houses the famous symbol of American freedom. From there, walk across Chestnut Street to **Independence Hall.**

Within the next 3 blocks of Chestnut are numerous historical buildings that are part of the **Independence National Historical Park.** They include **Congress Hall** and **Old City Hall,** which flank Independence Hall; **Second Bank of the United States Portrait Gallery;** the **New Hall Military Museum; Carpenters' Hall; Todd House;** and the **Bishop White House.**

Facing Independence Hall is the renovated Philadelphia Bourse. The historic merchants' exchange now houses shops, restaurants and an information center on the first floor.

Just east on Chestnut Street is a path leading to **Franklin Court,** where a steel frame suggests the shape of Franklin's home, destroyed in 1812. Traces of the original foundation are visible.

From Franklin Court, exit onto Market Street and walk east to 2nd Street. Take 2nd Street north to **Christ Church,** on the left. Continue north 1.5 blocks, then stroll through Elfreth's Alley on the right. The 6-foot-wide alley is lined with a number of quaint, modest houses from the early 1700s. Farther north on 2nd Street is Fireman's Hall Museum, a museum depicting the history of fire fighting in America with memorabilia, graphics, films and antique equipment.

From this point turn around and return to Arch Street. Turn right on Arch Street and walk a half-block to the Betsy Ross House, on your right. After a visit, proceed west and cross 3rd Street toward the Historic Arch Street Meeting House, a Quaker gathering place since the early 1800s, which is on the left. The next block is occupied by **The United States Mint,** where pocket change and commemorative coins are made.

To end the tour, walk south to Market Street on 5th Street. You will pass the **Free Quaker Meeting House** on the right. Once on Market Street you can rest your feet, relax and refresh at one of the many restaurants in the area. At City Tavern, tucked away at 2nd and Walnut, diners experience a taste of the Colonial past. The 1792 building was once an unofficial meeting place for the First Continental Congress.

Another excellent area for the visitor on foot is Penn's Landing, which hosts concerts and events during summer. Catch a glimpse of Philadelphia's nautical past at the **Independence Seaport Museum,** home to the World War II submarine *Becuna.* The Philadelphia Vietnam Veterans Memorial and Spruce Street Harbor Park, Columbus Boulevard and Spruce Street, also are at Penn's Landing.

Pennsylvania Quest for Freedom: Philadelphia, features stops showcasing African-American history, including the Underground Railroad. Brochures can be picked up at the Independence Visitor Center and at many of the tour's sites.

The Historic Philadelphia Center offers brochures about the Once Upon A Nation storytelling program. Between Memorial Day and Labor Day, there are 10 benches scattered throughout historic Philadelphia where passersby can stop to listen to stories about historic sites and influential people from the past.

Philadelphia boasts nearly 4,000 murals, with some 1,800 on display, so check some out while you're in the city. Forty murals in Center City make up Mural Mile; a plaque at each stop describes the work.

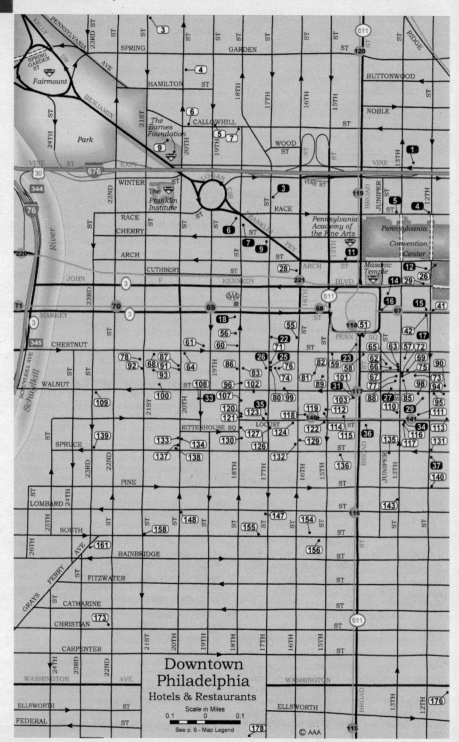

Downtown
Philadelphia
Hotels & Restaurants
Scale in Miles
0.1   0   0.1
See p. 6 - Map Legend
© AAA

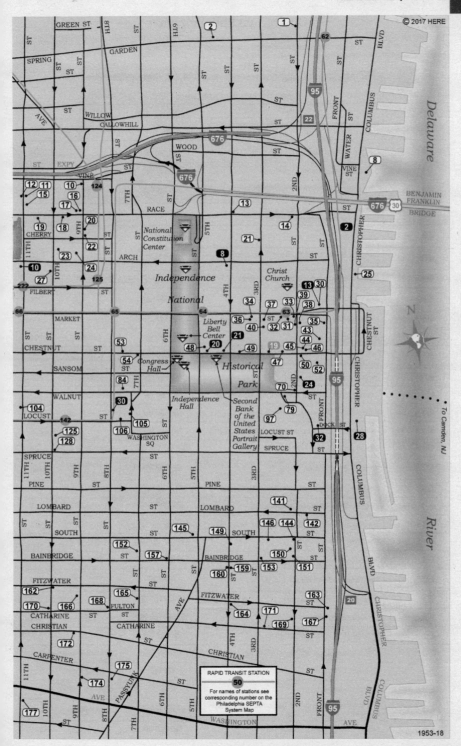

© 2017 HERE

1953-18

Downtown Philadelphia

This index helps you "spot" where approved hotels and restaurants are located on the corresponding detailed maps. Hotel daily rate range is for comparison only. Restaurant price range is a combination of lunch and/or dinner. Turn to the listing page for more information and consult display ads for special promotions.

 For more details, rates and reservations: AAA.com/travelguides/hotels

DOWNTOWN PHILADELPHIA

Map Page	Hotels	Diamond Rated	Rate Range	Page
1 p. 184	**Best Western Plus Philadelphia Convention Center Hotel**	◈◈◈	$119-$499 [SAVE]	202
2 p. 184	Holiday Inn Express Philadelphia - Penn's Landing	◈◈◈	Rates not provided	204
3 p. 184	**Sheraton Philadelphia Downtown**	◈◈◈	$109-$399 [SAVE]	205
4 p. 184	**Four Points by Sheraton-Philadelphia City Center**	◈◈◈	Rates not provided [SAVE]	203
5 p. 184	**Hampton Inn Philadelphia Center City/Convention Center** *(See ad p. 203.)*	◈◈◈	$139-$339 [SAVE]	203
6 p. 184	The Logan	◈◈◈◈	Rates not provided	204
7 p. 184	Embassy Suites Hotel by Hilton Philadelphia - Center City	◈◈◈	$169-$399	202
8 p. 184	**Wyndham Philadelphia Historic District**	◈◈◈	$129-$549 [SAVE]	206
9 p. 184	The Windsor Suites	◈◈◈	Rates not provided	206
10 p. 184	**Hilton Garden Inn Philadelphia Center City**	◈◈◈	$129-$299 [SAVE]	203
11 p. 184	Le Méridien Philadelphia	◈◈◈	$59-$699	204
12 p. 184	Home2 Suites by Hilton Philadelphia Convention Center	◈◈◈	$169-$499	204
13 p. 184	Penn's View Hotel	◈◈◈	$159-$399	205
14 p. 184	**Courtyard by Marriott Philadelphia Downtown**	◈◈◈	$96-$657 [SAVE]	202
15 p. 184	**Philadelphia Downtown Marriott Hotel**	◈◈◈	$79-$648 [SAVE]	205
16 p. 184	Residence Inn by Marriott Center City Philadelphia	◈◈◈	$92-$518	205
17 p. 184	**Loews Philadelphia Hotel**	◈◈◈◈	$149-$489 [SAVE]	204
18 p. 184	**Sonesta Philadelphia**	◈◈◈	Rates not provided [SAVE]	205
19 p. 184	**Best Western Plus Independence Park Hotel**	◈◈◈	$99-$499 [SAVE]	202
20 p. 184	**Kimpton Hotel Monaco Philadelphia**	◈◈◈◈	$179-$549 [SAVE]	204
21 p. 184	**The Franklin Hotel at Independence Park**	◈◈◈	$107-$719 [SAVE]	203
22 p. 184	**The Westin Philadelphia**	◈◈◈◈	$119-$999 [SAVE]	206
23 p. 184	The Ritz-Carlton Philadelphia	◈◈◈◈	$299-$609	205
24 p. 184	**The Thomas Bond House B & B**	◈◈	Rates not provided [SAVE]	205
25 p. 184	**Hotel Palomar-Philadelphia**	◈◈◈◈	$179-$549 [SAVE]	204
26 p. 184	**Sofitel Philadelphia**	◈◈◈◈	$159-$599 [SAVE]	204
27 p. 184	**Holiday Inn Express Midtown**	◈◈◈	$169-$399 [SAVE]	204
28 p. 184	**Hilton Philadelphia at Penn's Landing**	◈◈◈	$159-$599 [SAVE]	204
29 p. 184	Rodeway Inn	◈◈	$80-$1000	205
30 p. 184	**Morris House Hotel**	◈◈◈	$189-$429 [SAVE]	205
31 p. 184	**The Bellevue Hotel-in the Unbound Collection by Hyatt**	◈◈◈◈	$119-$449 [SAVE]	202
32 p. 184	Sheraton Philadelphia Society Hill	◈◈◈	$129-$229	205

DOWNTOWN PHILADELPHIA (cont'd)

Map Page	Hotels (cont'd)	Diamond Rated	Rate Range	Page
33 p. 184	The Rittenhouse	◆◆◆◆	$349-$3500	205
34 p. 184	**The Independent Hotel Philadelphia**	◆◆◆	Rates not provided SAVE	204
35 p. 184	**The Warwick Hotel Rittenhouse Square** *(See ad p. 206.)*	◆◆◆◆	Rates not provided SAVE	206
36 p. 184	**DoubleTree by Hilton Philadelphia Center City**	◆◆◆	$109-$399 SAVE	202
37 p. 184	**Alexander Inn**	◆◆◆	$139 SAVE	202

Map Page	Restaurants	Diamond Rated	Cuisine	Price Range	Page
1 p. 184	Seiko Japanese Restaurant	◆◆	Japanese	$7-$32	210
2 p. 184	Silk City Diner, Bar & Lounge	◆◆	American	$8-$18	210
3 p. 184	The Belgian Cafe	◆◆	Belgian	$9-$20	207
4 p. 184	McCrossen's Tavern	◆◆	American	$9-$19	209
5 p. 184	Rose Tattoo Cafe	◆◆	Continental	$11-$30	209
6 p. 184	Pizzeria Vetri	◆◆	Pizza	$8-$18	209
7 p. 184	Sabrina's Cafe & Spencer's Too	◆◆	American	$6-$18	210
8 p. 184	Morgan's Pier	◆◆	American	$9-$15	209
9 p. 184	The Garden Restaurant @ the Barnes Collection	◆◆◆	Mediterranean	$14-$19	208
10 p. 184	Sang Kee Peking Duck House	◆◆	Chinese	$7-$16	210
11 p. 184	Vietnam Restaurant	◆◆	Vietnamese	$8-$15	210
12 p. 184	Vietnam Palace Restaurant	◆◆	Vietnamese	$8-$16	210
13 p. 184	Kisso Sushi Bar	◆◆	Japanese	$7-$23	208
14 p. 184	Race Street Cafe	◆◆	American	$8-$19	209
15 p. 184	Yakitori Boy	◆◆	Japanese	$5-$18	210
16 p. 184	Terakawa Ramen	◆◆	Japanese	$8-$14	210
17 p. 184	Pho Xe Lua Viet Thai Restaurant	◆◆	Vietnamese	$5-$12	209
18 p. 184	Shiao Lan Kung	◆◆	Chinese	$8-$18	210
19 p. 184	Dim Sum Garden	◆◆	Chinese	$7-$11	208
20 p. 184	Ray's Cafe	◆◆	Regional Chinese	$8-$19	209
21 p. 184	La Locanda Del Ghiottone	◆◆	Italian	$16-$31	208
22 p. 184	New Harmony Vegetarian Restaurant	◆◆	Chinese Vegetarian	$6-$13	209
23 p. 184	Penang	◆◆	Asian	$6-$20	209
24 p. 184	Rangoon Burmese Restaurant	◆◆	Burmese	$7-$17	209
25 p. 184	La Veranda	◆◆◆	Italian	$10-$40	208
26 p. 184	Di Nic's Roast Beef & Pork	◆	Sandwiches	$5-$8	208
27 p. 184	QT Vietnamese Sandwich	◆	Vietnamese	$3-$8	209
28 p. 184	Tir na Nog, Bar & Grill	◆◆	Irish	$9-$27	210
29 p. 184	Maggiano's Little Italy	◆◆◆	Italian	$10-$47	208
30 p. 184	Panorama	◆◆◆	Regional Italian	$20-$30	209
31 p. 184	Campo's Deli	◆	Sandwiches	$7-$10	207
32 p. 184	Marmont Steakhouse & Bar	◆◆	American	$8-$45	209
33 p. 184	Revolution House	◆◆	American	$9-$22	209

Map Page	Restaurants (cont'd)	Diamond Rated	Cuisine	Price Range	Page
③④ p. 184	Fork	◆◆◆◆	New American	$16-$75	208
③⑤ p. 184	La Famiglia	◆◆◆	Italian	$7-$43	208
③⑥ p. 184	High Street on Market	◆◆◆	American	$6-$44	208
③⑦ p. 184	Karma Restaurant & Bar	◆◆	Indian	$11-$22	208
③⑧ p. 184	The Continental Restaurant & Martini Bar	◆◆◆	American	$9-$30	207
③⑨ p. 184	Cuba Libre Restaurant & Rum Bar	◆◆◆	Cuban	$8-$33	207
④⓪ p. 184	Farmicia	◆◆◆	Continental	$8-$25	208
④① p. 184	Hard Rock Cafe	◆◆	American	$15-$23 SAVE	208
④② p. 184	Bank and Bourbon	◆◆◆	American	$12-$34	207
④③ p. 184	Spasso Italian Grill	◆◆	Italian	$11-$29	210
④④ p. 184	Han Dynasty	◆◆◆	Szechuan	$12-$23	208
④⑤ p. 184	The Plough and The Stars Irish Restaurant & Bar	◆◆	Irish	$8-$24	209
④⑥ p. 184	2nd Story Brewing Company	◆◆	American	$10-$24	206
④⑦ p. 184	Amada	◆◆◆	Spanish Small Plates	$15-$45	206
④⑧ p. 184	Red Owl Tavern	◆◆	American	$14-$26	209
④⑨ p. 184	Buddakan	◆◆◆	Asian	$15-$48	207
⑤⓪ p. 184	Ariana Restaurant	◆◆	Afghan	$8-$16	207
⑤① p. 184	McCormick & Schmick's	◆◆◆	Seafood	$12-$46	209
⑤② p. 184	Kabul, Cuisine of Afghanistan	◆◆	Afghan	$15-$20	208
⑤③ p. 184	Morimoto	◆◆◆◆	Japanese	$26-$45	209
⑤④ p. 184	Jones	◆◆	American	$10-$26	208
⑤⑤ p. 184	R2L	◆◆◆	New American	$26-$42	209
⑤⑥ p. 184	Pastrami & Things	◆	Deli	$4-$10	209
⑤⑦ p. 184	Spice 28	◆◆	Asian Fusion	$8-$29	210
⑤⑧ p. 184	The Capital Grille	◆◆◆	Steak	$13-$60	207
⑤⑨ p. 184	Del Frisco's Double Eagle Steak House	◆◆◆	Steak	$14-$59	207
⑥⓪ p. 184	The Continental Midtown	◆◆	American	$9-$34	207
⑥① p. 184	Devil's Alley Bar and Grill	◆◆	American	$10-$19	207
⑥② p. 184	McGillin's Olde Ale House	◆◆	American	$6-$15	209
⑥③ p. 184	Lolita	◆◆◆	Mexican	$10-$24	208
⑥④ p. 184	Jane G's	◆◆	Chinese	$10-$29	208
⑥⑤ p. 184	Barbuzzo	◆◆◆	Mediterranean	$10-$22	207
⑥⑥ p. 184	Opa	◆◆◆	Greek Small Plates	$11-$35	209
⑥⑦ p. 184	Zavino	◆◆◆	Italian	$12-$18	210
⑥⑧ p. 184	Butcher Bar	◆◆	American	$12-$35	207
⑥⑨ p. 184	1225Raw Sushi & Sake Lounge	◆◆◆	Sushi	$10-$29	206
⑦⓪ p. 184	**City Tavern**	◆◆	American	$9-$27	207
⑦① p. 184	Davio's Northern Italian Steakhouse	◆◆◆	Northern Italian	$12-$55	207
⑦② p. 184	El Vez	◆◆◆	Mexican	$8-$28	208

Map Page	Restaurants (cont'd)	Diamond Rated	Cuisine	Price Range	Page
73 p. 184	Fergie's Pub	◆◆	Irish	$6-$14	208
74 p. 184	Dizengoff	◆	Middle Eastern	$10-$12	208
75 p. 184	Vintage Wine Bar & Bistro	◆◆	French	$11-$22	210
76 p. 184	Abe Fisher	◆◆◆	Jewish Small Plates	$14-$65	206
77 p. 184	Double Knot	◆◆	Asian	$7-$22	208
78 p. 184	Poi Dog Snack Shop	◆	Hawaiian	$14	209
79 p. 184	Positano Coast by Aldo Lamberti	◆◆◆	Southern Italian Small Plates	$7-$30	209
80 p. 184	Square 1682	◆◆	New American	$11-$32	210
81 p. 184	Mission Taqueria	◆◆	Mexican Small Plates	$6-$16	209
82 p. 184	Oyster House	◆◆	Seafood	$14-$28	209
83 p. 184	Tria Cafe Rittenhouse	◆◆◆	Continental	$6-$14	210
84 p. 184	El Fuego	◆	Mexican	$4-$10	208
85 p. 184	Charlie was a Sinner	◆◆	Vegan Small Plates	$7-$12	207
86 p. 184	The Dandelion	◆◆◆	American	$13-$28	207
87 p. 184	Tinto	◆◆◆	Spanish	$10-$55	210
88 p. 184	Sampan	◆◆◆	Asian	$10-$24	210
89 p. 184	Ocean Prime	◆◆◆	American	$27-$49	209
90 p. 184	Irish Pub	◆◆	Irish	$4-$9	208
91 p. 184	Village Whiskey	◆◆◆	American	$10-$26	210
92 p. 184	Day by Day	◆◆	American	$7-$15	207
93 p. 184	Porcini Restaurant	◆◆	Italian	$21-$26	209
94 p. 184	Moriarty's Restaurant & Irish Pub	◆◆	American	$8-$24	209
95 p. 184	Caribou Café	◆◆	French	$10-$27	207
96 p. 184	a.kitchen	◆◆◆	American	$15-$32	206
97 p. 184	Zahav	◆◆◆◆	Middle Eastern	$15-$45	210
98 p. 184	Aki Japanese Fusion Restaurant & Sake Bar	◆◆	Japanese	$9-$27	206
99 p. 184	Alma de Cuba	◆◆◆	Cuban	$23-$32	206
100 p. 184	Vernick Food & Drink	◆◆◆◆	New American	$28-$70	210
101 p. 184	**XIX (Nineteen) Restaurant**	◆◆◆	American	$14-$48	210
102 p. 184	Pietro's Coal Oven Pizzeria	◆◆	Italian	$9-$18	209
103 p. 184	The Palm Restaurant	◆◆◆	American	$31-$57	209
104 p. 184	Strangelove's	◆◆	American	$13-$19	210
105 p. 184	Talula's Garden	◆◆◆	American	$20-$50	210
106 p. 184	Ristorante La Buca	◆◆	Italian	$11-$38	209
107 p. 184	Rouge	◆◆◆	American	$12-$28	210
108 p. 184	Lacroix At The Rittenhouse	◆◆◆◆	Continental	$18-$105	208
109 p. 184	Res Ipsa	◆◆	Italian	$6-$50	209
110 p. 184	Green Eggs Cafe Midtown	◆◆	American	$10-$15	208
111 p. 184	Vedge	◆◆◆	Vegetarian Small Plates	$27-$45	210

Map Page	Restaurants (cont'd)	Diamond Rated	Cuisine	Price Range	Page
112 p. 184	Shiroi Hana Japanese Restaurant	◈◈	Japanese	$11-$35	210
113 p. 184	Garces Trading Company	◈◈	Continental	$8-$29	208
114 p. 184	Good Dog Bar & Restaurant	◈◈	American	$9-$21	208
115 p. 184	Estia	◈◈◈	Greek	$12-$45	208
116 p. 184	Bud & Marilyn's	◈◈◈	American	$16-$24	207
117 p. 184	Little Nonna's	◈◈◈	Italian	$11-$26	208
118 p. 184	Schlesinger's	◈◈	Deli	$7-$24	210
119 p. 184	Misconduct Tavern	◈◈	American	$8-$15	209
120 p. 184	Devon Seafood Grill	◈◈◈	Seafood	$13-$66	208
121 p. 184	Parc	◈◈◈	French	$11-$33	209
122 p. 184	Fado Irish Pub	◈◈	Irish	$10-$17	208
123 p. 184	The Prime Rib	◈◈◈	Steak	$20-$50	209
124 p. 184	Los Catrines Tequila's	◈◈◈	Mexican	$10-$28	208
125 p. 184	CHeU Noodle Bar	◈◈	Asian Fusion	$8-$16	207
126 p. 184	The Black Sheep Pub & Restaurant	◈◈	American	$8-$20	207
127 p. 184	Barclay Prime	◈◈◈◈	Steak	$32-$150	207
128 p. 184	Varga Bar	◈◈	American	$8-$21	210
129 p. 184	Bistro La Viola	◈◈	Italian	$14-$18	207
130 p. 184	Le Cheri	◈◈◈	French	$11-$38	208
131 p. 184	Tria	◈◈	Continental	$9-$11	210
132 p. 184	Monk's Cafe	◈◈	Belgian	$7-$24	209
133 p. 184	D'Angelo's Ristorante Italiano	◈◈	Italian	$10-$40	207
134 p. 184	Twenty Manning Grill	◈◈◈	American	$13-$27	210
135 p. 184	Vetri	◈◈◈◈◈	Italian	$155	210
136 p. 184	Volvér	◈◈◈	New International	$20-$125	210
137 p. 184	Seafood Unlimited	◈◈	Seafood	$11-$18	210
138 p. 184	Audrey Claire	◈◈◈	Mediterranean	$17-$26	207
139 p. 184	Mama Palma's	◈◈	Italian	$8-$25	208
140 p. 184	Mixto	◈◈	Latin American	$8-$24	209
141 p. 184	Pizzeria Stella	◈◈	Pizza	$9-$19	209
142 p. 184	**Bistro Romano**	◈◈◈	Regional Italian	$17-$29	207
143 p. 184	Amis	◈◈◈	Italian	$10-$26	207
144 p. 184	Bridget Foy's	fyi	American	$11-$22	207
145 p. 184	South Street Souvlaki	◈◈	Greek	$5-$25	210
146 p. 184	Lovash Indian Cuisine	◈◈	Northern Indian	$9-$25	208
147 p. 184	Bistro La Baia	◈◈	Italian	$11-$16	207
148 p. 184	Pub and Kitchen	◈◈◈	American	$9-$26	209
149 p. 184	Alyan's	◈	Middle Eastern	$5-$14	206
150 p. 184	Fez Moroccan Cuisine	◈◈	Moroccan	$13-$25	208
151 p. 184	Mustard Greens	◈◈	Chinese	$7-$24	209

Map Page	Restaurants (cont'd)	Diamond Rated	Cuisine	Price Range	Page
152 p. 184	The Good King Tavern	♦♦♦	French	$10-$24	208
153 p. 184	ELA	♦♦♦	American	$16-$26	208
154 p. 184	Jet Wine Bar	♦♦	Small Plates	$11-$18	208
155 p. 184	Pumpkin	♦♦	Mediterranean	$30-$50	209
156 p. 184	The Cambridge	♦♦	American	$13-$25	207
157 p. 184	Beau Monde	♦♦	Northern French	$10-$29	207
158 p. 184	Ten Stone	♦♦	American	$8-$12	210
159 p. 184	Southwark	♦♦♦	Continental	$12-$27	210
160 p. 184	Famous 4th Street Delicatessen	♦♦	Jewish Deli	$9-$27	208
161 p. 184	Grace Tavern	♦♦	American	$5-$14	208
162 p. 184	Sam's Morning Glory Diner	♦♦	American	$5-$15	210
163 p. 184	Kanella South	♦♦	Mediterranean	$9-$32	208
164 p. 184	Hungry Pigeon	♦♦	American	$8-$28	208
165 p. 184	Saloon	♦♦♦	Italian	$10-$45	210
166 p. 184	Ralph's Italian Restaurant	♦♦	Southern Italian	$9-$34	209
167 p. 184	Catahoula	♦♦	Creole	$10-$19	207
168 p. 184	Cucina Forte	♦♦	Italian	$13-$32	207
169 p. 184	Royal Sushi and Izakaya	♦♦	Japanese Small Plates	$10-$125	210
170 p. 184	Dante & Luigi's	♦♦	Italian	$7-$30	207
171 p. 184	Dmitri's	♦♦	Mediterranean	$8-$20	208
172 p. 184	Sabrina's Cafe	♦♦	American	$6-$13	210
173 p. 184	The Sidecar Bar and Grille	♦♦	American	$10-$18	210
174 p. 184	Paesano's	♦	Sandwiches	$7-$9	209
175 p. 184	Bibou	♦♦♦	French	$100	207
176 p. 184	Pho & Cafe Viet Huong	♦♦	Vietnamese	$4-$14	209
177 p. 184	Ratchada Thai & Laos Cuisine	♦♦	Asian	$9-$25	209
178 p. 184	American Sardine Bar	♦♦	American	$7-$15	207

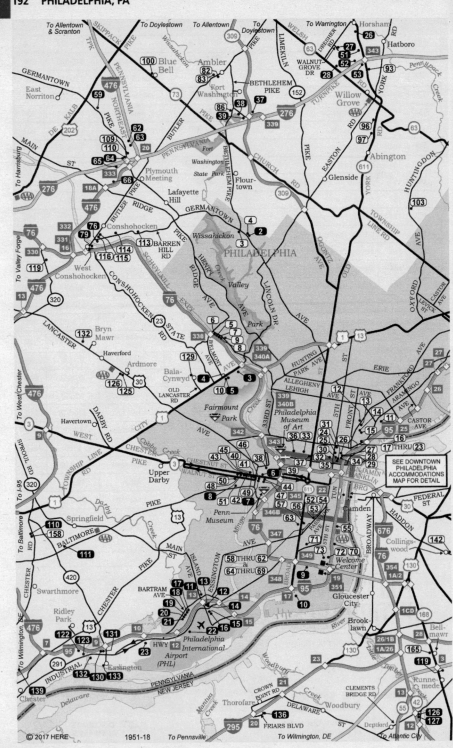

1951-18

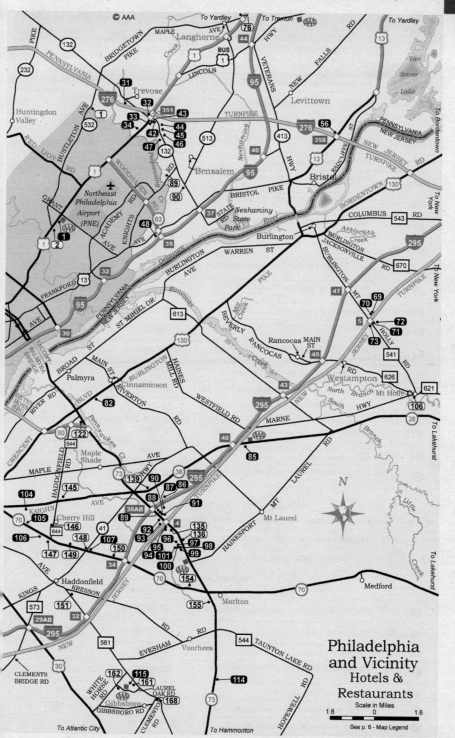

Philadelphia
and Vicinity
Hotels &
Restaurants

Scale in Miles

1.6   0   1.6

See p. 6 - Map Legend

✈ Airport Hotels

Map Page	PHILADELPHIA INTERNATIONAL (Maximum driving distance from airport: 5.9 mi)	Diamond Rated	Rate Range	Page
132 p. 192	**The Clarion Hotel Conference Center, 5.5 mi**	◈◈	$139-$549 SAVE	74
133 p. 192	Holiday Inn Express Philadelphia Airport, 5.0 mi	◈◈◈	Rates not provided	74
130 p. 192	**Red Roof PLUS+ Philadelphia Airport, 4.9 mi**	◈◈	$85-$109 SAVE	74
131 p. 192	Wyndham Garden Hotel Philadelphia Airport, 4.7 mi	◈◈◈	$89-$265	74
13 p. 192	**Aloft Philadelphia Airport, 2.2 mi**	◈◈◈	$139-$189 SAVE	211
20 p. 192	**Courtyard by Marriott Philadelphia Airport, 3.6 mi**	◈◈◈	$86-$475 SAVE	211
10 p. 192	Courtyard by Marriott Philadelphia South at the Navy Yard, 5.9 mi	◈◈◈	$99-$1309	211
15 p. 192	**DoubleTree by Hilton Philadelphia Airport, 2.0 mi**	◈◈◈	$99-$199 SAVE	211
21 p. 192	Embassy Suites by Hilton-Philadelphia Airport, 3.4 mi	◈◈◈	$149-$279	211
19 p. 192	Fairfield Inn by Marriott - Philadelphia Airport, 3.6 mi	◈◈◈	$83-$322	211
12 p. 192	**Four Points by Sheraton Philadelphia Airport, 2.1 mi**	◈◈◈	$129-$169 SAVE	211
18 p. 192	Hampton Inn-Philadelphia Airport, 2.9 mi	◈◈◈	$129-$229	211
16 p. 192	Hawthorn Suites by Wyndham Philadelphia Airport, 2.2 mi	◈◈	$129-$229	211
17 p. 192	Microtel Inn & Suites by Wyndham Philadelphia Airport, 3.0 mi	◈◈	$70-$125	212
22 p. 192	**Philadelphia Airport Marriott Hotel, 2.6 mi**	◈◈◈	$109-$429 SAVE	213
23 p. 192	**Renaissance Hotel Philadelphia Airport, 3.3 mi**	◈◈◈	$80-$344 SAVE	213
11 p. 192	Residence Inn by Marriott Philadelphia Airport, 2.3 mi	◈◈◈	$102-$334	213
14 p. 192	**Sheraton Suites Philadelphia Airport, 2.0 mi**	◈◈◈	Rates not provided SAVE	213
122 p. 192	Microtel Inn & Suites by Wyndham, Philadelphia Airport Ridley Park, 5.7 mi	◈◈	$150-$170	272
123 p. 192	SpringHill Suites by Marriott Philadelphia Airport/ Ridley Park, 5.5 mi	◈◈◈	$96-$309	272

Philadelphia and Vicinity

This index helps you "spot" where approved hotels and restaurants are located on the corresponding detailed maps. Hotel daily rate range is for comparison only. Restaurant price range is a combination of lunch and/or dinner. Turn to the listing page for more information and consult display ads for special promotions.

 For more details, rates and reservations: AAA.com/travelguides/hotels

PHILADELPHIA

Map Page	Hotels	Diamond Rated	Rate Range	Page
1 p. 192	Four Points by Sheraton Philadelphia Northeast	◈◈◈	Rates not provided	211
2 p. 192	Chestnut Hill Hotel	◈◈◈	Rates not provided	211
3 p. 192	Courtyard by Marriott Philadelphia City Ave	◈◈◈	$106-$330	211
4 p. 192	Homewood Suites by Hilton/Philadelphia City Avenue	◈◈◈	$139-$259	212
5 p. 192	Hilton Philadelphia City Avenue	◈◈◈	$149-$239	211
6 p. 192	**Sheraton Philadelphia University City Hotel**	◈◈◈	$79-$489 SAVE	213
7 p. 192	**The Inn at Penn, A Hilton Hotel** *(See ad p. 212.)*	◈◈◈◈	$179-$369 SAVE	212

PHILADELPHIA (cont'd)

Map Page	Hotels (cont'd)	Diamond Rated	Rate Range	Page
8 p. 192	**Homewood Suites by Hilton University City Philadelphia**	◈◈◈	$159-$344 [SAVE]	212
9 p. 192	Holiday Inn Philadelphia Stadium	◈◈◈	$129-$999	212
10 p. 192	Courtyard by Marriott Philadelphia South at the Navy Yard	◈◈◈	$99-$1309	211
11 p. 192	Residence Inn by Marriott Philadelphia Airport	◈◈◈	$102-$334	213
12 p. 192	**Four Points by Sheraton Philadelphia Airport**	◈◈◈	$129-$169 [SAVE]	211
13 p. 192	**Aloft Philadelphia Airport**	◈◈◈	$139-$189 [SAVE]	211
14 p. 192	**Sheraton Suites Philadelphia Airport** (See ad p. 213.)	◈◈◈	Rates not provided [SAVE]	213
15 p. 192	**DoubleTree by Hilton Philadelphia Airport**	◈◈◈	$99-$199 [SAVE]	211
16 p. 192	Hawthorn Suites by Wyndham Philadelphia Airport	◈◈	$129-$229	211
17 p. 192	Microtel Inn & Suites by Wyndham Philadelphia Airport	◈◈	$70-$125	212
18 p. 192	Hampton Inn-Philadelphia Airport	◈◈◈	$129-$229	211
19 p. 192	Fairfield Inn by Marriott - Philadelphia Airport	◈◈◈	$83-$322	211
20 p. 192	**Courtyard by Marriott Philadelphia Airport**	◈◈◈	$86-$475 [SAVE]	211
21 p. 192	Embassy Suites by Hilton-Philadelphia Airport	◈◈◈	$149-$279	211
22 p. 192	**Philadelphia Airport Marriott Hotel**	◈◈◈	$109-$429 [SAVE]	213
23 p. 192	**Renaissance Hotel Philadelphia Airport**	◈◈◈	$80-$344 [SAVE]	213

Map Page	Restaurants	Diamond Rated	Cuisine	Price Range	Page
1 p. 192	Pho Palace	◈◈	Vietnamese	$7-$20	215
2 p. 192	Las Margaritas	◈◈	Mexican	$5-$17	214
3 p. 192	McNally's Tavern	◈◈	Sandwiches	$4-$12	215
4 p. 192	Chestnut Grill and Sidewalk Cafe	◈◈	American	$8-$20	214
5 p. 192	Zesty's	◈◈◈	Mediterranean	$13-$32	215
6 p. 192	Taqueria Feliz	◈◈	Mexican	$6-$18	215
7 p. 192	Jake's & Cooper's Wine Bar	◈◈◈	American	$10-$34	214
8 p. 192	Winnie's Le Bus	◈◈	American	$10-$26	215
9 p. 192	The Goat's Beard	◈◈	American	$9-$25	214
10 p. 192	Delmonico's Steak House	◈◈◈	Steak	$15-$35	214
11 p. 192	Bait & Switch	◈◈	Seafood	$8-$20	214
12 p. 192	Martha	◈◈◈	American Small Plates	$10-$16	214
13 p. 192	Pizza Brain	◈	Pizza	$4-$24	215
14 p. 192	Andy's Chicken	◈	Korean	$7-$12	214
15 p. 192	Cedar Point Bar & Kitchen	◈◈	American	$7-$15	214
16 p. 192	Kraftwork	◈◈	American	$10-$22	214
17 p. 192	CHeU Fishtown	◈◈	Asian Fusion	$12-$26	214
18 p. 192	Wm. Mulherin's Sons	◈◈◈	Italian	$18-$45	215
19 p. 192	Kensington Quarters	◈◈◈	American	$12-$30	214
20 p. 192	Cake Life Bake Shop	◈	Breads/Pastries	$3-$8	214
21 p. 192	Girard	◈◈	American	$6-$13	214
22 p. 192	Root	◈◈◈	Continental	$14-$28	215

Map Page	Restaurants (cont'd)	Diamond Rated	Cuisine	Price Range	Page
㉓ p. 192	Sancho Pistola's	◆◆	Mexican	$8-$18	215
㉔ p. 192	Las Cazuelas Restaurant	◆◆	Mexican	$7-$19	214
㉕ p. 192	Bardot Cafe	◆◆	American	$10-$20	214
㉖ p. 192	Poke Bowl	◆	Hawaiian Specialty	$9-$12	215
㉗ p. 192	Cantina Dos Segundos	◆◆	Mexican	$12-$24	214
㉘ p. 192	Standard Tap	◆◆	American	$8-$26	215
㉙ p. 192	Circles Contemporary Asian	◆◆	Asian Fusion	$8-$19	214
㉚ p. 192	Honey's Sit 'n Eat	◆◆	Comfort Food	$6-$16	214
㉛ p. 192	North 3rd	◆◆	American	$10-$22	215
㉜ p. 192	Federal Donuts	◆	Comfort Food	$2-$10	214
㉝ p. 192	Bar Hygge	◆◆	American	$10-$24	214
㉞ p. 192	Green Eggs Cafe	◆◆	Breakfast	$9-$13	214
㉟ p. 192	The Abbaye	◆◆	American	$5-$20	214
㊱ p. 192	Jack's Firehouse Restaurant	◆◆◆	American	$8-$32	214
㊲ p. 192	Osteria	◆◆◆	Italian	$12-$30	215
㊳ p. 192	Sabrina's Cafe @ Powelton	◆◆	American	$7-$20	215
㊴ p. 192	JG Domestic	◆◆	American	$12-$22	214
㊵ p. 192	Distrito	◆◆◆	New Mexican	$8-$32	214
㊶ p. 192	Thai Singha House	◆◆	Thai	$4-$19	215
㊷ p. 192	New Delhi	◆	Indian	$10-$15	215
㊸ p. 192	Pattaya Thai Cuisine	◆◆	Thai	$8-$17	215
㊹ p. 192	New Deck Tavern	◆◆	American	$8-$17	215
㊺ p. 192	Tandoor India	◆◆	Indian	$9-$16	215
㊻ p. 192	Pod	◆◆◆	Japanese	$9-$30	215
㊼ p. 192	White Dog Cafe	◆◆	American	$12-$32	215
㊽ p. 192	The Restaurant School At Walnut Hill College	◆◆◆	Continental	$13-$21	215
㊾ p. 192	Bobby's Burger Palace	◆	Burgers	$6-$9	214
㊿ p. 192	Abyssinia Ethiopian Restaurant	◆◆	Ethiopian	$6-$15	214
51 p. 192	Marigold Kitchen	◆◆◆	American	$24-$45	214
52 p. 192	Bitar's	◆	Eastern Mediterranean	$4-$9	214
53 p. 192	Geno's Steaks	◆	Sandwiches	$10-$13	214
54 p. 192	Pat's King of Steaks	◆	Sandwiches	$10-$13	215
55 p. 192	Warmdaddy's	◆◆	Southern American	$8-$23	215
56 p. 192	The Victor Cafe	◆◆◆	Italian	$17-$36	215
57 p. 192	Green Eggs Cafe	◆◆	Breakfast	$9-$16	214
58 p. 192	Brigantessa	◆◆◆	Southern Italian	$12-$32	214
59 p. 192	Fond	◆◆◆	New American	$28-$32	214
60 p. 192	Noord eetcafe	◆◆	Scandinavian	$18-$30	215
61 p. 192	ITV (In the Valley)	◆◆◆	New Continental	$18-$25	214

Map Page	Restaurants (cont'd)	Diamond Rated	Cuisine	Price Range	Page
62 p. 192	Laurel	◈◈◈◈	New French	$96	214
63 p. 192	Circles	◈◈◈	Asian	$8-$19	214
64 p. 192	Capogiro	◈	Desserts	$5-$9	214
65 p. 192	Mr. Martino's Trattoria	◈◈	Italian	$11-$22	215
66 p. 192	Bing Bing Dim Sum	◈◈	Asian Small Plates	$9-$16	214
67 p. 192	Los Caballitos Cantina	◈◈	Mexican	$7-$23	214
68 p. 192	Marra's Cucina Italiana	◈◈	Italian	$8-$21	214
69 p. 192	Le Virtù	◈◈◈	New Italian	$18-$40	214
70 p. 192	John's Roast Pork	◈	Sandwiches	$5-$10	214
71 p. 192	Bomb Bomb Bar-b-que Grill	◈◈	Italian Barbecue	$8-$26	214
72 p. 192	Tony Luke's	◈	Sandwiches	$6-$10	215
73 p. 192	Oregon Diner	◈◈	American	$5-$18	215

HORSHAM

Map Page	Hotels	Diamond Rated	Rate Range	Page
26 p. 192	Days Inn-Horsham/Philadelphia	◈◈	$59-$99	107
27 p. 192	Residence Inn by Marriott-Willow Grove	◈◈◈	$59-$336	107
28 p. 192	Extended Stay America-Philadelphia/Horsham	◈◈	$70-$170	107

TREVOSE

Map Page	Hotels	Diamond Rated	Rate Range	Page
31 p. 192	**Wyndham Philadelphia-Bucks County, PA**	◈◈◈	$104-$149 (SAVE)	290
32 p. 192	**Red Roof Inn Philadelphia Trevose**	◈◈	$63-$99 (SAVE)	290
33 p. 192	Comfort Inn Trevose	◈◈◈	$80-$211	289
34 p. 192	Radisson Hotel Philadelphia Northeast	◈◈◈	Rates not provided	289

FORT WASHINGTON

Map Page	Hotels	Diamond Rated	Rate Range	Page
37 p. 192	**Best Western Fort Washington Inn**	◈◈◈	$89-$105 (SAVE)	76
38 p. 192	Holiday Inn Express & Suites Ft. Washington-Philadelphia	◈◈◈	$109-$189	76
39 p. 192	**Hilton Garden Inn Philadelphia/Fort Washington**	◈◈◈	$99-$259 (SAVE)	76

Map Page	Restaurant	Diamond Rated	Cuisine	Price Range	Page
86 p. 192	Cantina Feliz	◈◈◈	Mexican	$11-$24	76

BENSALEM

Map Page	Hotels	Diamond Rated	Rate Range	Page
42 p. 192	Hampton Inn & Suites Philadelphia/Bensalem	◈◈◈	Rates not provided	44
43 p. 192	Inn of the Dove	◈◈◈	Rates not provided	44
44 p. 192	**Best Western Plus Philadelphia Bensalem**	◈◈◈	$89-$199 (SAVE)	44
45 p. 192	Sleep Inn & Suites-Bensalem	◈◈	$80-$160	44
46 p. 192	Holiday Inn Bensalem-Philadelphia Area	◈◈◈	Rates not provided	44
47 p. 192	Extended Stay America-Philadelphia/Bensalem	◈◈	$60-$140	44
48 p. 192	Holiday Inn Express Philadelphia Northeast/ Bensalem	◈◈◈	$119-$179	44

Map Page	Restaurants	Diamond Rated	Cuisine	Price Range	Page
(89) p. 192	Spice Rack	♦♦	Indian	$7-$15	44
(90) p. 192	Fisher's Tudor House	♦♦	American	$10-$22	44

WILLOW GROVE

Map Page	Hotels	Diamond Rated	Rate Range	Page
(51) p. 192	Courtyard by Marriott Philadelphia Willow Grove	♦♦♦	$85-$282	303
(52) p. 192	SpringHill Suites by Marriott Philadelphia Willow Grove	♦♦♦	$76-$249	303
(53) p. 192	Hampton Inn-Willow Grove	♦♦♦	$84-$159	303

Map Page	Restaurant	Diamond Rated	Cuisine	Price Range	Page
(93) p. 192	Ooka Japanese Sushi & Hibachi Steak House	♦♦	Japanese	$13-$29	303

LEVITTOWN

Map Page	Hotel	Diamond Rated	Rate Range	Page
(56) p. 192	**Ramada Inn**	♦♦	$69-$119 (SAVE)	123

EAST NORRITON

Map Page	Hotel	Diamond Rated	Rate Range	Page
(59) p. 192	**Hyatt House Philadelphia/Plymouth Meeting**	♦♦♦	$94-$299 (SAVE)	67

PLYMOUTH MEETING

Map Page	Hotels	Diamond Rated	Rate Range	Page
(62) p. 192	Courtyard by Marriott-Philadelphia/Plymouth Meeting	♦♦♦	$79-$281	263
(63) p. 192	DoubleTree Suites by Hilton Philadelphia West	♦♦♦	$99-$179	263
(64) p. 192	SpringHill Suites by Marriott Philadelphia/Plymouth Meeting	♦♦♦	$77-$277	263
(65) p. 192	Homewood Suites by Hilton Philadelphia/Plymouth Meeting	♦♦♦	Rates not provided	263
(66) p. 192	Hampton Inn Plymouth Meeting	♦♦♦	$139-$209	263

Map Page	Restaurants	Diamond Rated	Cuisine	Price Range	Page
(109) p. 192	Redstone American Grill	♦♦	American	$13-$42	263
(110) p. 192	Fat Daddy's Deli	♦	Sandwiches	$5-$17	263

WESTAMPTON, NJ

Map Page	Hotels	Diamond Rated	Rate Range	Page
(69) p. 192	Courtyard by Marriott Burlington Mt. Holly/Westampton	♦♦♦	$73-$271	222
(70) p. 192	**Holiday Inn Express Hotel & Suites Burlington/ Mt. Holly**	♦♦♦	Rates not provided (SAVE)	222
(71) p. 192	**Best Western Burlington Inn**	♦♦	$89-$129 (SAVE)	222
(72) p. 192	Hilton Garden Inn Mt. Holly/Westampton	♦♦♦	$109-$259	222
(73) p. 192	Red Roof Inn & Suites Westhampton	♦♦	$90-$130	222

CONSHOHOCKEN

Map Page	Hotel	Diamond Rated	Rate Range	Page
(76) p. 192	**Residence Inn by Marriott Philadelphia/Conshohocken**	♦♦♦	$98-$276 (SAVE)	60

Map Page	Restaurants	Diamond Rated	Cuisine	Price Range	Page
(113) p. 192	Spring Mill Cafe	♦♦♦	French	$12-$37	60
(114) p. 192	Coyote Crossing	♦♦	Mexican	$8-$28	60
(115) p. 192	Blackfish	♦♦♦	Continental	$10-$32	60
(116) p. 192	El Limon	♦	Mexican	$8-$14	60

WEST CONSHOHOCKEN

Map Page	Hotel	Diamond Rated	Rate Range	Page
79 p. 192	**Philadelphia Marriott West**	◆◆◆	$59-$509 SAVE	298

Map Page	Restaurant	Diamond Rated	Cuisine	Price Range	Page
119 p. 192	Savona	◆◆◆	Northern Italian	$20-$55	299

CINNAMINSON, NJ

Map Page	Hotel	Diamond Rated	Rate Range	Page
82 p. 192	**Sleep Inn**	◆◆	$84-$175 SAVE	219

Map Page	Restaurant	Diamond Rated	Cuisine	Price Range	Page
122 p. 192	The Jug Handle Inn	◆◆	American	$7-$20	219

MOUNT LAUREL, NJ

Map Page	Hotels	Diamond Rated	Rate Range	Page
85 p. 192	Residence Inn by Marriott Mount Laurel at Bishop's Gate	◆◆◆	$91-$244	221
86 p. 192	Homewood Suites by Hilton Philadelphia/Mount Laurel	◆◆◆	$109-$299	220
87 p. 192	**DoubleTree Suites by Hilton Hotel Mt. Laurel**	◆◆◆	$109-$299 SAVE	220
88 p. 192	**Hotel ML**	◆◆◆	$64-$199 SAVE	220
89 p. 192	**The Westin Mount Laurel**	◆◆◆	$149-$189 SAVE	221
90 p. 192	Super 8	◆◆	$69-$109	221
91 p. 192	**Aloft Mount Laurel**	◆◆◆	Rates not provided SAVE	220
92 p. 192	Courtyard by Marriott Mt. Laurel	◆◆◆	$90-$378	220
93 p. 192	Fairfield Inn & Suites by Marriott Mt. Laurel	◆◆◆	$82-$239	220
94 p. 192	**La Quinta Inn & Suites Mt. Laurel-Philadelphia**	◆◆◆	$75-$159 SAVE	221
95 p. 192	**Staybridge Suites - Mt. Laurel**	◆◆◆	Rates not provided SAVE	221
96 p. 192	Hilton Garden Inn-Mt. Laurel	◆◆◆	$99-$179	220
97 p. 192	Extended Stay America Pacilli Place Philadelphia/Mt. Laurel	◆◆	$60-$100	220
98 p. 192	Hampton Inn by Hilton Philadelphia/Mt. Laurel	◆◆◆	$129-$159	220
99 p. 192	**Hyatt Place Mt. Laurel**	◆◆◆	$99-$199 SAVE	221
100 p. 192	**Hyatt House Mt. Laurel**	◆◆◆	$99-$299 SAVE	221
101 p. 192	Candlewood Suites Mt. Laurel	◆◆	Rates not provided	220

Map Page	Restaurants	Diamond Rated	Cuisine	Price Range	Page
135 p. 192	Sage Diner	◆◆	American	$6-$27	221
136 p. 192	Singapore Restaurant and Sushi Bar	◆◆◆	Japanese	$8-$24	221

CHERRY HILL, NJ

Map Page	Hotels	Diamond Rated	Rate Range	Page
104 p. 192	**Days Inn & Suites**	◆◆	$80-$105 SAVE	218
105 p. 192	Crowne Plaza Philadelphia/Cherry Hill	◆◆◆	Rates not provided	218
106 p. 192	Holiday Inn Philadelphia-Cherry Hill	◆◆◆	$99-$159	218
107 p. 192	Extended Stay America-Philadelphia/Cherry Hill	◆◆	$60-$125	218

Map Page	Restaurants	Diamond Rated	Cuisine	Price Range	Page
145 p. 192	Seasons 52 Fresh Grill	◆◆◆	New American	$10-$30	219
146 p. 192	Brio Tuscan Grille	◆◆◆	Italian	$10-$29	218

Map Page	Restaurants (cont'd)	Diamond Rated	Cuisine	Price Range	Page
(147) p. 192	Caffe Aldo Lamberti	◆◆◆	Italian	$10-$43	218
(148) p. 192	Norma's	◆◆	Eastern Mediterranean	$7-$24	218
(149) p. 192	Chick's Deli	◆	Deli	$5-$12	218
(150) p. 192	The Farm & Fisherman Tavern + Market	◆◆◆	American	$12-$28	218
(151) p. 192	Il Villaggio	◆◆◆	Italian	$12-$43	218

SPRINGFIELD (DELAWARE COUNTY)

Map Page	Hotels	Diamond Rated	Rate Range	Page
(110) p. 192	Courtyard by Marriott Philadelphia Springfield	◆◆◆	$111-$360	280
(111) p. 192	Days Inn Springfield/Philadelphia Int'l Airport	◆◆	$90-$179	280

Map Page	Restaurant	Diamond Rated	Cuisine	Price Range	Page
(158) p. 192	Tavola Restaurant and Bar	◆◆	American	$12-$37	280

VOORHEES, NJ

Map Page	Hotels	Diamond Rated	Rate Range	Page
(114) p. 192	Hampton Inn Philadelphia/Voorhees	◆◆◆	Rates not provided	222
(115) p. 192	Springhill Suites by Marriott Voorhees Mt. Laurel/Cherry Hill	◆◆◆	$62-$420	222

Map Page	Restaurants	Diamond Rated	Cuisine	Price Range	Page
(161) p. 192	Black Olive	◆◆	Greek	$8-$28	222
(162) p. 192	Passariello's Pizzeria & Italian Eatery	◆	Italian	$7-$16	222

RUNNEMEDE, NJ

Map Page	Hotel	Diamond Rated	Rate Range	Page
(119) p. 192	Comfort Inn & Suites	◆◆◆	$79-$169	221

RIDLEY PARK

Map Page	Hotels	Diamond Rated	Rate Range	Page
(122) p. 192	Microtel Inn & Suites by Wyndham, Philadelphia Airport Ridley Park	◆◆	$150-$170	272
(123) p. 192	SpringHill Suites by Marriott Philadelphia Airport/Ridley Park	◆◆◆	$96-$309	272

DEPTFORD, NJ

Map Page	Hotels	Diamond Rated	Rate Range	Page
(126) p. 192	Residence Inn by Marriott Deptford	◆◆◆	$95-$440	219
(127) p. 192	Fairfield Inn by Marriott Philadelphia/Deptford	◆◆	$81-$352	219

ESSINGTON

Map Page	Hotels	Diamond Rated	Rate Range	Page
(130) p. 192	**Red Roof PLUS+ Philadelphia Airport**	◆◆	$85-$109 [SAVE]	74
(131) p. 192	Wyndham Garden Hotel Philadelphia Airport	◆◆◆	$89-$265	74
(132) p. 192	**The Clarion Hotel Conference Center**	◆◆	$139-$549 [SAVE]	74
(133) p. 192	Holiday Inn Express Philadelphia Airport	◆◆◆	Rates not provided	74

THOROFARE, NJ

Map Page	Hotel	Diamond Rated	Rate Range	Page
(136) p. 192	**Best Western West Deptford Inn**	◆◆	$119-$150 [SAVE]	222

CHESTER

Map Page	Hotel	Diamond Rated	Rate Range	Page
(139) p. 192	**Best Western Plus Philadelphia Airport South at Widener University**	◆◆◆	$109-$139 [SAVE]	57

LANGHORNE

Map Page	Restaurant	Diamond Rated	Cuisine	Price Range	Page
⑦⑥ p. 192	J. B. Dawson's	◆◆	American	$9-$28	121

AMBLER

Map Page	Restaurants	Diamond Rated	Cuisine	Price Range	Page
⑧② p. 192	Bridget's Steakhouse	◆◆◆	Steak	$11-$39	41
⑧③ p. 192	Trax Restaurant and Cafe	◆◆◆	American	$23-$33	41

ABINGTON

Map Page	Restaurants	Diamond Rated	Cuisine	Price Range	Page
⑨⑥ p. 192	Lee's Hoagie House	◆	Sandwiches	$5-$17	34
⑨⑦ p. 192	Kitchen Bar	◆◆	American	$9-$20	34

BLUE BELL

Map Page	Restaurant	Diamond Rated	Cuisine	Price Range	Page
⑩⑩ p. 192	Blue Bell Inn	◆◆◆	Steak Seafood	$11-$40	49

HUNTINGDON VALLEY

Map Page	Restaurant	Diamond Rated	Cuisine	Price Range	Page
⑩③ p. 192	White Elephant Restaurant	◆◆	Thai	$9-$25	108

MOUNT HOLLY, NJ

Map Page	Restaurant	Diamond Rated	Cuisine	Price Range	Page
⑩⑥ p. 192	Robin's Nest	◆◆	American	$10-$33	220

ARDMORE

Map Page	Restaurants	Diamond Rated	Cuisine	Price Range	Page
①②⑤ p. 192	Mikado Thai Pepper	◆◆	Asian	$8-$20	41
①②⑥ p. 192	Tired Hands Fermentaria	◆◆	American	$6-$18	41

BALA-CYNWYD

Map Page	Restaurant	Diamond Rated	Cuisine	Price Range	Page
①②⑨ p. 192	Al Dar Bistro	◆◆	Mediterranean	$7-$24	41

BRYN MAWR

Map Page	Restaurant	Diamond Rated	Cuisine	Price Range	Page
①③② p. 192	Tango	◆◆◆	American	$7-$29	51

MAPLE SHADE, NJ

Map Page	Restaurant	Diamond Rated	Cuisine	Price Range	Page
①③⑨ p. 192	P.J. Whelihan's Pub & Restaurant	◆◆	American	$6-$19	219

COLLINGSWOOD, NJ

Map Page	Restaurant	Diamond Rated	Cuisine	Price Range	Page
①④② p. 192	The Pop Shop	◆◆	Comfort Food	$6-$18	219

MARLTON, NJ

Map Page	Restaurants	Diamond Rated	Cuisine	Price Range	Page
①⑤④ p. 192	Mexican Food Factory	◆◆	Mexican	$9-$25	219
①⑤⑤ p. 192	Joe's Peking Duck House	◆◆	Chinese	$9-$29	219

BELLMAWR, NJ

Map Page	Restaurant	Diamond Rated	Cuisine	Price Range	Page
①⑥⑤ p. 192	Club Diner	◆◆	American	$6-$13	216

GIBBSBORO, NJ

Map Page	Restaurant	Diamond Rated	Cuisine	Price Range	Page
①⑥⑧ p. 192	The ChopHouse	◆◆◆	Steak	$13-$50	219

DOWNTOWN PHILADELPHIA
- Restaurants p. 206
- Hotels & Restaurants map & index p. 184

ALEXANDER INN
(215)923-3535 **37**

Historic Boutique Hotel
$139

Address: 301 S 12th St 19107 **Location:** Jct Spruce and 12th sts. 12th-13th & Locust, 141. **Facility:** A fireplace is featured in the lobby of this seven-story brick building, which was constructed in 1900. Some rooms are compact. All feature comfortable beds and light wood furnishings. 48 units. 7 stories, interior corridors. **Parking:** no self-parking. **Terms:** cancellation fee imposed. **Amenities:** safes. **Activities:** exercise room. **Guest Services:** valet laundry. **Featured Amenity:** breakfast buffet.

Located in the heart of the City near the Historic District, theatres, restaurants and shopping.

THE BELLEVUE HOTEL-IN THE UNBOUND COLLECTION BY HYATT
(215)893-1234 **31**

Historic Hotel
$119-$449

AAA Benefit: Members save 10%!

Address: 200 S Broad St 19102 **Location:** Between Walnut and Locust sts. Walnut-Locust, 117. **Facility:** Built in 1906, this hotel began as the Bellevue Hotel. Keep your eyes open for original details and unique artwork. Rooms are modern with large flat-screen TVs and lots of outlets for your devices. 172 units. 6 stories, interior corridors. **Parking:** on-site (fee) and valet. **Terms:** cancellation fee imposed. **Amenities:** safes. **Dining:** XIX (Nineteen) Restaurant, see separate listing. **Pool:** heated indoor. **Activities:** health club, spa. **Guest Services:** valet laundry.

BEST WESTERN PLUS INDEPENDENCE PARK HOTEL
(215)922-4443 **19**

Historic Hotel
$99-$499

Best Western PLUS AAA Benefit: Members save 5% to 15% and earn 10% bonus points!

Address: 235 Chestnut St 19106 **Location:** Between 2nd and 3rd sts. Located in Old City Historic District. 2nd, 63. **Facility:** Built in 1856, this small property boasts a boutique-style appeal. Guest rooms vary in size, but all are designed in traditional American décor and feature beautiful high ceilings and windows. 36 units. 5 stories, interior corridors. **Parking:** street only. **Terms:** cancellation fee imposed. **Guest Services:** valet laundry.

BEST WESTERN PLUS PHILADELPHIA CONVENTION CENTER HOTEL
(215)398-3080 **1**

Hotel
$119-$499

Best Western PLUS. AAA Benefit: Members save 5% to 15% and earn 10% bonus points!

Address: 1225 Vine St 19107 **Location:** Just w of jct 12th St. Race-Vine, 119. **Facility:** 107 units. 7 stories, interior corridors. **Parking:** on-site (fee) and valet. **Terms:** 4 night minimum stay - seasonal, 3 day cancellation notice-fee imposed. **Amenities:** safes. **Activities:** exercise room. **Guest Services:** valet laundry. **Featured Amenity:** breakfast buffet.

COURTYARD BY MARRIOTT PHILADELPHIA DOWNTOWN
(215)496-3200 **14**

Hotel
$96-$657

COURTYARD Marriott AAA Benefit: Members save 5% or more!

Address: 21 N Juniper St 19107 **Location:** Just n of Market St. Adjacent to City Hall. 13th, 67. **Facility:** 499 units. 17 stories, interior corridors. **Parking:** valet only. **Terms:** check-in 4 pm, 3 day cancellation notice-fee imposed. **Amenities:** Some: safes. **Activities:** exercise room. **Guest Services:** valet and coin laundry.

DOUBLETREE BY HILTON PHILADELPHIA CENTER CITY
(215)893-1600 **36**

Hotel
$109-$399

DOUBLETREE BY HILTON AAA Benefit: Members save 5% or more!

Address: 237 S Broad St 19107 **Location:** Jct Broad and Locust sts. Located on Avenue of the Arts. Walnut-Locust, 117. **Facility:** 481 units. 26 stories, interior corridors. **Parking:** on-site (fee) and valet. **Terms:** check-in 4 pm, 1-7 night minimum stay, cancellation fee imposed. **Amenities:** safes. **Dining:** 2 restaurants. **Pool:** heated indoor. **Activities:** sauna, health club. **Guest Services:** valet laundry.

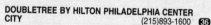

EMBASSY SUITES HOTEL BY HILTON PHILADELPHIA - CENTER CITY
(215)561-1776 **7**

Hotel. **Address:** 1776 Benjamin Franklin Pkwy 19103

AAA Benefit: Members save 5% or more!

(See map & index p. 184.)

FOUR POINTS BY SHERATON-PHILADELPHIA CITY CENTER
215/496-2700

Hotel
Rates not provided

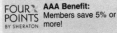

AAA Benefit: Members save 5% or more!

Address: 1201 Race St 19107 **Location:** Jct 12th St; just n to entrance. Race-Vine, 119. **Facility:** 92 units. 10 stories, interior corridors. **Parking:** street only. **Amenities:** safes. **Activities:** exercise room. **Guest Services:** valet laundry.

THE FRANKLIN HOTEL AT INDEPENDENCE PARK
(215)925-0000   **21**

Hotel
$107-$719

MARRIOTT

AAA Benefit: Members save 5% or more!

Address: 401 Chestnut St 19106 **Location:** Jct 4th St. 5th, 64. **Facility:** Located in Independence National Historical Park, near multiple historic attractions, this full-service hotel offers guest rooms with pillow-top mattresses; many have lovely views of the park. 152 units. 13 stories, interior corridors. **Parking:** valet only. **Terms:** cancellation fee imposed. **Amenities:** safes. **Pool:** heated indoor. **Activities:** sauna, hot tub, exercise room. **Guest Services:** valet laundry.

HAMPTON INN PHILADELPHIA CENTER CITY/ CONVENTION CENTER
(215)665-9100   **5**

Hotel
$139-$339

Hampton

AAA Benefit: Members save up to 10%!

Address: 1301 Race St 19107 **Location:** At 13th and Race sts. Race-Vine, 119. **Facility:** 250 units. 12 stories, interior corridors. **Parking:** on-site (fee) and valet. **Terms:** check-in 4 pm, 1-7 night minimum stay, cancellation fee imposed. **Amenities:** safes. **Pool:** heated indoor. **Activities:** hot tub, exercise room. **Guest Services:** valet and coin laundry. **Featured Amenity:** breakfast buffet. *(See ad this page.)*

HILTON GARDEN INN PHILADELPHIA CENTER CITY
(215)923-0100   **10**

Hotel
$129-$299

Hilton Garden Inn

AAA Benefit: Members save up to 10%!

Address: 1100 Arch St 19107 **Location:** At Arch and 11th sts. Adjacent to convention center. Jefferson, 222. **Facility:** 279 units. 7-10 stories, interior corridors. **Parking:** on-site (fee). **Terms:** check-in 4 pm, 1-7 night minimum stay, cancellation fee imposed. **Pool:** heated indoor. **Activities:** hot tub, exercise room. **Guest Services:** valet and coin laundry.

▼ See AAA listing this page ▼

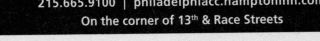
For complete hotel, dining and attraction listings: **AAA.com/travelguides**

(See map & index p. 184.)

HILTON PHILADELPHIA AT PENN'S LANDING
(215)521-6500 **28**

Hotel
$159-$599

AAA Benefit: Members save 5% or more!

Address: 201 S Columbus Blvd 19106 **Location:** Waterfront. Jct S Columbus Blvd and Dock St. Located at Penn's Landing-Delaware River. 2nd, 63. **Facility:** 350 units. 22 stories, interior corridors. **Parking:** on-site (fee) and valet. **Terms:** 1-7 night minimum stay, cancellation fee imposed. **Amenities:** safes. **Pool:** heated indoor. **Activities:** sauna, exercise room, massage. **Guest Services:** valet laundry, rental car service, area transportation.

HOLIDAY INN EXPRESS MIDTOWN
(215)735-9300 **27**

Hotel
$169-$399

Address: 1305 Walnut St 19107 **Location:** Just e of Broad St. Walnut-Locust, 117. **Facility:** 168 units. 20 stories, interior corridors. **Parking:** on-site (fee). **Terms:** cancellation fee imposed. **Amenities:** safes. **Pool:** outdoor. **Activities:** exercise room. **Guest Services:** valet laundry. **Featured Amenity:** breakfast buffet.

HOLIDAY INN EXPRESS PHILADELPHIA - PENN'S LANDING
215/627-7900 **2**

Hotel. **Address:** 100 N Columbus Blvd 19106

HOME2 SUITES BY HILTON PHILADELPHIA CONVENTION CENTER
(215)627-1850 **12**

Extended Stay Hotel. **Address:** 1200 Arch St 19107

AAA Benefit: Members save up to 10%!

HOTEL PALOMAR-PHILADELPHIA
(215)563-5006 **25**

Historic Boutique Hotel
$179-$549

Address: 117 S 17th St 19103 **Location:** Corner of 17th and Samson sts. 15th-16th & Locust, 140. **Facility:** Located in Center City, this lovely hotel is in the former Architects Building and successfully combines the property's historical Art Deco design with modern décor. 230 units. 25 stories, interior corridors. **Parking:** valet only. **Terms:** 3 day cancellation notice-fee imposed. **Amenities:** safes. **Dining:** Square 1682, see separate listing. **Activities:** exercise room. **Guest Services:** valet laundry.

THE INDEPENDENT HOTEL PHILADELPHIA
215/772-1440 **34**

Boutique Hotel
Rates not provided

Address: 1234 Locust St 19107 **Location:** Just e of jct 13th St. 12th-13th & Locust, 141. **Facility:** Hardwood floors, elegant décor and plush bedding add warmth to the guest rooms at this former printing press cum hotel in Center City. Breakfast can be delivered to your room during your stay. 24 units. 5 stories, interior corridors. *Bath:* shower only. **Parking:** street only. **Dining:** 2 restaurants, also, Bud & Marilyn's, Little Nonna's, see separate listings. **Guest Services:** valet laundry. **Featured Amenity:** continental breakfast.

KIMPTON HOTEL MONACO PHILADELPHIA
(215)925-2111 **20**

Historic Boutique Hotel
$179-$549

Address: 433 Chestnut St 19106 **Location:** Jct 5th and Chestnut sts. 5th, 64. **Facility:** This hotel is the perfect base for exploring neighboring Independence Hall and Old City attractions. Originally built in 1907, this hotel features plush fabrics, sleek designs and bold colors. 268 units. 9 stories, interior corridors. **Parking:** valet only. **Terms:** 3 day cancellation notice-fee imposed. **Amenities:** safes. **Dining:** Red Owl Tavern, see separate listing. **Activities:** bicycles, exercise room. **Guest Services:** valet laundry.

LE MÉRIDIEN PHILADELPHIA
(215)422-8200 **11**

Historic Boutique Hotel. **Address:** 1421 Arch St 19102

AAA Benefit: Members save 5% or more!

LOEWS PHILADELPHIA HOTEL
(215)627-1200 **17**

Historic Hotel
$149-$489

Address: 1200 Market St 19107 **Location:** Corner of 12th and Market sts. 13th, 67. **Facility:** One of America's first skyscrapers, this hotel features the original PSFS sign from 1932 on its roof. Rooms are decorated in bright white with locally themed art, many offering sweeping city views. 581 units, some two bedrooms. 33 stories, interior corridors. **Parking:** valet only. **Terms:** check-in 4 pm, cancellation fee imposed. **Amenities:** video games, safes. **Dining:** Bank and Bourbon, see separate listing. **Pool:** heated indoor. **Activities:** sauna, steamroom, exercise room, spa. **Guest Services:** valet laundry.

THE LOGAN
215/963-1500 **6**

Boutique Hotel. **Address:** 1 Logan Square 19103

AAA Benefit: Members save 5% or more!

Use the free online TripTik Travel Planner at AAA.com/maps

(See map & index p. 184.)

MORRIS HOUSE HOTEL

(215)922-2446 **30**

Historic Bed & Breakfast
$189-$429

Address: 225 S 8th St 19106 **Location:** Jct 8th and Locust sts; entrance on St. James Pl. ⊞ 9th-10th & Locust, 142. **Facility:** Built in 1787, this inn was home to the Morris family for more than 120 years. You'll find rooms with original details like wood moldings as well as modern, spacious suites in another building. 17 units, some efficiencies and kitchens. 3 stories (no elevator), interior corridors. **Parking:** street only. **Terms:** 7 day cancellation notice-fee imposed, resort fee. **Guest Services:** coin laundry. **Featured Amenity: continental breakfast.**

PENN'S VIEW HOTEL

(215)922-7600 **13**

Historic Hotel. **Address:** 14 N Front St 19106

PHILADELPHIA DOWNTOWN MARRIOTT HOTEL

(215)625-2900 **15**

Hotel
$79-$648

AAA Benefit: Members save 5% or more!

Address: 1201 Market St 19107 **Location:** Between 12th and 13th sts. Adjacent to convention center. ⊞ 13th, 67. **Facility:** 1408 units. 23 stories, interior corridors. **Parking:** valet only. **Terms:** check-in 4 pm, 3 day cancellation notice-fee imposed. **Amenities:** safes. **Pool:** heated indoor. **Activities:** exercise room. **Guest Services:** valet and coin laundry.

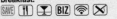

RESIDENCE INN BY MARRIOTT CENTER CITY PHILADELPHIA

(215)557-0005 **16**

Extended Stay Hotel. **Address:** 1 E Penn Square 19107

AAA Benefit: Members save 5% or more!

THE RITTENHOUSE

(215)546-9000 **33**

Historic Hotel. **Address:** 210 W Rittenhouse Square 19103

THE RITZ-CARLTON PHILADELPHIA

(215)523-8000 **23**

Classic Historic Hotel. **Address:** Ten Avenue of the Arts 19102

AAA Benefit: Unequaled service at special member savings!

RODEWAY INN

(215)546-7000 **29**

Hotel. **Address:** 1208 Walnut St 19107

🔗 **For complete hotel, dining and attraction listings:**

AAA.com/travelguides

SHERATON PHILADELPHIA DOWNTOWN

(215)448-2000 **3**

Hotel
$109-$399

Sheraton

AAA Benefit: Members save 5% or more!

Address: 201 N 17th St 19103 **Location:** Jct 17th and Race sts. ⊞ Race-Vine, 119. **Facility:** 757 units. 29 stories, interior corridors. **Parking:** on-site (fee) and valet. **Terms:** cancellation fee imposed. **Amenities:** *Some:* safes. **Dining:** 2 restaurants. **Pool:** indoor. **Activities:** health club. **Guest Services:** valet laundry.

SHERATON PHILADELPHIA SOCIETY HILL

(215)238-6000 **32**

Hotel. **Address:** One Dock St 19106

AAA Benefit: Members save 5% or more!

SOFITEL PHILADELPHIA

(215)569-8300 **26**

Contemporary Hotel
$159-$599

Address: 120 S 17th St 19103 **Location:** Jct Sansom and 17th sts. ⊞ 15th-16th & Locust, 140. **Facility:** This former home of the Philadelphia Stock Exchange now features elegantly appointed guest rooms with feather-top beds and upscale modern furnishings. 306 units. 13 stories, interior corridors. **Parking:** valet only. **Terms:** cancellation fee imposed. **Amenities:** safes. **Dining:** 2 restaurants. **Activities:** exercise room, massage. **Guest Services:** valet laundry.

SONESTA PHILADELPHIA

215/561-7500 **18**

Boutique Hotel
Rates not provided

Address: 1800 Market St 19103 **Location:** Between 18th and 19th sts. ⊞ 19th, 69. **Facility:** This downtown hotel features sleek, red-and-white décor with many artistic accents throughout. Guest rooms include locally themed artwork, modern furnishings and gorgeous Center City views. 439 units. 8-25 stories, interior corridors. **Parking:** valet only. **Terms:** check-in 4 pm. **Amenities:** safes. **Dining:** 2 restaurants. **Pool:** outdoor. **Activities:** exercise room. **Guest Services:** valet laundry.

THE THOMAS BOND HOUSE B & B

215/923-8523 **24**

Historic Bed & Breakfast
Rates not provided

Address: 129 S 2nd St 19106 **Location:** Between Walnut and Chestnut sts; in Old City Historic District. ⊞ 2nd, 63. **Facility:** This 1769 Georgian Revival home has rooms that range in size from petite to sizeable, and is convenient to many Olde City attractions. Rooms are attractively furnished with antiques and reproductions. 12 units. 4 stories (no elevator), interior corridors. **Parking:** on-site (fee). **Terms:** age restrictions may apply.

(See map & index p. 184.)

THE WARWICK HOTEL RITTENHOUSE SQUARE

215/735-6000 **35**

Historic Hotel
Rates not provided

Address: 220 S 17th St 19103 **Location:** Between Walnut and Locust sts; main entrance on 17th St. 15th-16th & Locust, 140. **Facility:** Steps from Rittenhouse Square, this hotel has a sleek lobby design with modern furnishings and blue lighting accents. Guest rooms are well appointed, but some are small. 301 units. 12 stories. Interior corridors. **Parking:** on-site (fee) and valet. **Amenities:** safes. **Dining:** 2 restaurants, also, The Prime Rib, see separate listing. **Activities:** health club, spa. **Guest Services:** valet and coin laundry. (See ad this page.)

SAVE ECO 🍴 ⬆️ 🍸 CALL ♿ 👪 BIZ 🛜 ✕
🛏️ ☕ / SOME UNITS 🐾 🖼️ 🚉

THE WESTIN PHILADELPHIA

(215)563-1600 **22**

Hotel
$119-$999

WESTIN
HOTELS & RESORTS

AAA Benefit:
Members save 5% or more!

Address: 99 S 17th St at Liberty Pl 19103 **Location:** Between Market and Chestnut sts. 15th, 68. **Facility:** A modern lounge with marble floors and elegant furnishings set the luxurious tone at this downtown hotel. Rooms maintain the same upscale appointments and feature their signature "Heavenly Bed". 294 units. 15 stories. Interior corridors. **Parking:** valet only. **Terms:** cancellation fee imposed. **Amenities:** safes. **Activities:** sauna, exercise room, massage. **Guest Services:** valet laundry.

SAVE 🍴 ⬆️ 🍸 CALL ♿ 👪 BIZ 🛜 ✕ 📹
☕ / SOME UNITS 🐾 🖼️ 🚉

THE WINDSOR SUITES

215/981-5678 **9**

Extended Stay Contemporary Hotel. **Address:** 1700 Benjamin Franklin Pkwy 19103

WYNDHAM PHILADELPHIA HISTORIC DISTRICT

(215)923-8660 **8**

Hotel
$129-$549

Address: 400 Arch St 19106 **Location:** Jct 4th and Arch sts. 5th, 64. **Facility:** 364 units. 8 stories, interior corridors. **Parking:** on-site (fee). **Terms:** check-in 4 pm, cancellation fee imposed. **Amenities:** safes. **Pool:** outdoor. **Activities:** exercise room. **Guest Services:** valet and coin laundry.

SAVE 🍴 ⬆️ 🍸 CALL ♿ 🏊
👪 BIZ 🛜 ✕ 📹 ☕
/ SOME UNITS HS 🖼️ 🚉

WHERE TO EAT

1225RAW SUSHI & SAKE LOUNGE   215/238-1903 **69**
Sushi. Casual Dining. **Address:** 1225 Sansom St 19107

2ND STORY BREWING COMPANY   267/314-5770 **46**
American. Gastropub. **Address:** 117 Chestnut St 19106

ABE FISHER   215/867-0088 **76**
Jewish Small Plates. Fine Dining. **Address:** 1623 Sansom St 19103

AKI JAPANESE FUSION RESTAURANT & SAKE BAR
215/985-1838 **98**
Japanese. Casual Dining. **Address:** 1210 Walnut St 19107

A.KITCHEN   215/825-7030 **96**
American. Casual Dining. **Address:** 135 S 18th St 19103

ALMA DE CUBA   215/988-1799 **99**
Cuban. Fine Dining. **Address:** 1623 Walnut St 19103

ALYAN'S   215/922-3553 **149**
Middle Eastern. Casual Dining. **Address:** 603 S 4th St 19147

AMADA   215/625-2450 **47**
Spanish Small Plates. Fine Dining. **Address:** 217 Chestnut St 19106

▼ See AAA listing this page ▼

(See map & index p. 184.)

AMERICAN SARDINE BAR   215/334-2337 178
♥♥♥ American. Gastropub. Address: 1800 Federal St 19146

AMIS   215/732-2647 143
♥♥♥ Italian. Casual Dining. Address: 412 S 13th St 19147

ARIANA RESTAURANT   215/922-1535 50
♥♥ Afghan. Casual Dining. Address: 134 Chestnut St 19106

AUDREY CLAIRE   215/731-1222 138
♥♥♥ Mediterranean. Casual Dining. Address: 276 S 20th St 19103

BANK AND BOURBON   215/231-7300 42
♥♥♥ American. Casual Dining. Address: 1200 Market St 19107

BARBUZZO   215/546-9300 65
♥♥♥ Mediterranean. Fine Dining. Address: 110 S 13th St 19107

BARCLAY PRIME   215/732-7560 127
♥♥♥♥ Steak. Fine Dining. Address: 237 S 18th St 19103

BEAU MONDE   215/592-0656 157
♥♥ Northern French. Casual Dining. Address: 624 S 6th St 19147

THE BELGIAN CAFE   215/235-3500 3
♥♥ Belgian. Casual Dining. Address: 601 N 21st St 19130

BIBOU   215/965-8290 175
♥♥♥ French. Fine Dining. Address: 1009 S 8th St 19147

BISTRO LA BAIA   215/546-0496 147
♥♥ Italian. Casual Dining. Address: 1700 Lombard St 19146

BISTRO LA VIOLA   215/735-8630 129
♥♥ Italian. Casual Dining. Address: 253 S 16th St 19102

BISTRO ROMANO   215/925-8880 142

♥♥♥
**Regional
Italian
Fine Dining
$17-$29**

AAA Inspector Notes: Located in an early 1700s granary appointed with lots of brick, stone, exposed wood ceiling beams and soft lighting, the below-ground dining room offers a warm, intimate setting. The upstairs lounge features a beautiful, intricately carved, painted oak bar from an early 20th-century Great Lakes steamship. The acclaimed Caesar salad is the most popular menu item and is prepared table-side. Call ahead for a variety of budget-conscious weekly specials, including Lobsterfest on Tuesday nights. **Features:** full bar, happy hour. **Reservations:** suggested, weekends. **Address:** 120 Lombard St 19147 **Location:** Between Front and 2nd sts. 🚇 2nd, 63. **Parking:** on-site (fee) and street.

D 🚌

**Regional Italian Cuisine
in Historic 1700's Granary**

THE BLACK SHEEP PUB & RESTAURANT
                                    215/545-9473 126
♥♥ American. Casual Dining. Address: 247 S 17th St 19103

BRIDGET FOY'S   215/922-1813 144
fyi American. Casual Dining. Under major renovation, scheduled to be completed June 2018. Last rated: ♥♥ Address: 200 South St 19147

BUD & MARILYN'S   215/546-2220 116
♥♥♥ American. Casual Dining. Address: 1234 Locust St 19107

BUDDAKAN   215/574-9440 49
♥♥♥ Asian. Fine Dining. Address: 325 Chestnut St 19106

BUTCHER BAR   215/563-6328 68
♥♥ American. Casual Dining. Address: 2034 Chestnut St 19103

THE CAMBRIDGE   267/455-0647 156
♥♥♥ American. Casual Dining. Address: 1508 South St 19146

CAMPO'S DELI   215/923-1000 31
♥ Sandwiches. Quick Serve. Address: 214 Market St 19106

THE CAPITAL GRILLE   215/545-9588 58
♥♥♥ Steak. Fine Dining. Address: 1338 Chestnut St 19107

CARIBOU CAFÉ   215/625-9535 95
♥♥ French. Casual Dining. Address: 1126 Walnut St 19107

CATAHOULA   215/271-9300 167
♥♥♥ Creole. Casual Dining. Address: 775 S Front St 19147

CHARLIE WAS A SINNER   267/758-5372 85
♥♥ Vegan Small Plates. Casual Dining. Address: 131 S 13th St 19147

CHEU NOODLE BAR   267/639-4136 125
♥ Asian Fusion. Gastropub. Address: 255 S 10th St 19107

CITY TAVERN   215/413-1443 70

♥♥
**American
Casual Dining
$9-$27**

AAA Inspector Notes: Many a founding father patronized the original City Tavern, which opened its doors on a prominent Independence Square spot in 1773. The tradition continues today in this re-creation, which aptly captures the Colonial spirit and style of its predecessor. Enjoy unique 18th century dishes such as lobster pie served in a pewter pot, roast lamb or venison, glazed duck, fried oysters or Sally Lunn bread. **Features:** full bar, patio dining. **Reservations:** suggested. **Address:** 138 S 2nd St 19106 **Location:** Corner of 2nd and Walnut sts. 🚇 2nd, 63. **Parking:** valet and street only. L D 🚌 🚌

THE CONTINENTAL MIDTOWN   215/567-1800 60
♥♥♥ American. Casual Dining. Address: 1801 Chestnut St 19102

THE CONTINENTAL RESTAURANT & MARTINI BAR
                                    215/923-6069 38
♥♥♥ American. Casual Dining. Address: 138 Market St 19106

CUBA LIBRE RESTAURANT & RUM BAR   215/627-0666 39
♥♥♥ Cuban. Casual Dining. Address: 10 S 2nd St 19106

CUCINA FORTE   215/238-0778 168
♥♥ Italian. Casual Dining. Address: 768 S 8th St 19147

THE DANDELION   215/558-2500 86
♥♥♥ American. Gastropub. Address: 124 S 18th St 19103

D'ANGELO'S RISTORANTE ITALIANO   215/546-3935 133
♥♥ Italian. Casual Dining. Address: 256 S 20th St 19103

DANTE & LUIGI'S   215/922-9501 170
♥♥ Italian. Casual Dining. Address: 762 S 10th St 19147

DAVIO'S NORTHERN ITALIAN STEAKHOUSE
                                    215/563-4810 71
♥♥♥ Northern Italian. Fine Dining. Address: 111 S 17th St 19103

DAY BY DAY   215/564-5540 92
♥♥ American. Casual Dining. Address: 2101 Sansom St 19103

DEL FRISCO'S DOUBLE EAGLE STEAK HOUSE
                                    215/246-0533 59
♥♥♥ Steak. Fine Dining. Address: 1426 Chestnut St 19102

DEVIL'S ALLEY BAR AND GRILL   215/751-0707 61
♥♥ American. Casual Dining. Address: 1907 Chestnut St 19103

(See map & index p. 184.)

DEVON SEAFOOD GRILL 215/546-5940 `120`
Seafood. Fine Dining. **Address:** 225 S 18th St 19103

DIM SUM GARDEN 215/873-0258 `19`
Chinese. Casual Dining. **Address:** 1020 Race St 19107

DI NIC'S ROAST BEEF & PORK 215/923-6175 `26`
Sandwiches. Quick Serve. **Address:** 51 N 12th St 19107

DIZENGOFF 215/867-8181 `74`
Middle Eastern. Quick Serve. **Address:** 1625 Sansom St 19103

DMITRI'S 215/625-0556 `171`
Mediterranean. Casual Dining. **Address:** 795 S 3rd St 19147

DOUBLE KNOT 215/631-3868 `77`
Asian. Quick Serve. **Address:** 120 S 13th St 19107

ELA 267/687-8512 `153`
American. Gastropub. **Address:** 627 S 3rd St 19147

EL FUEGO 215/592-1901 `84`
Mexican. Quick Serve. **Address:** 723 Walnut St 19106

EL VEZ 215/928-9800 `72`
Mexican. Casual Dining. **Address:** 121 S 13th St 19107

ESTIA 215/735-7700 `115`
Greek. Fine Dining. **Address:** 1405 Locust St 19102

FADO IRISH PUB 215/893-9700 `122`
Irish. Casual Dining. **Address:** 1500 Locust St 19103

FAMOUS 4TH STREET DELICATESSEN 215/922-3274 `160`
Jewish Deli. Casual Dining. **Address:** 700 S 4th St 19147

FARMICIA 215/627-6274 `40`
Continental. Casual Dining. **Address:** 15 S 3rd St 19106

FERGIE'S PUB 215/928-8118 `73`
Irish. Casual Dining. **Address:** 1214 Sansom St 19107

FEZ MOROCCAN CUISINE 215/925-5367 `150`
Moroccan. Casual Dining. **Address:** 620 S 2nd St 19147

FORK 215/625-9425 `34`
New American. Fine Dining. **Address:** 306 Market St 19106

GARCES TRADING COMPANY 215/574-1099 `113`
Continental. Casual Dining. **Address:** 1111 Locust St 19107

THE GARDEN RESTAURANT @ THE BARNES COLLECTION 215/278-7082 `9`
Mediterranean. Casual Dining. **Address:** 2025 Benjamin Franklin Pkwy 19130

GOOD DOG BAR & RESTAURANT 215/985-9600 `114`
American. Casual Dining. **Address:** 224 S 15th St 19102

THE GOOD KING TAVERN 215/625-3700 `152`
French. Gastropub. **Address:** 614 S 7th St 19147

GRACE TAVERN 215/893-9580 `161`
American. Gastropub. **Address:** 2229 Gray's Ferry Ave 19146

GREEN EGGS CAFE MIDTOWN 267/861-0314 `110`
American. Casual Dining. **Address:** 212 S 13th St 19107

HAN DYNASTY 215/922-1888 `44`
Szechuan. Casual Dining. **Address:** 123 Chestnut St 19106

HARD ROCK CAFE 215/238-1000 `41`
SAVE American. Casual Dining. **Address:** 1113-31 Market St 19107

HIGH STREET ON MARKET 215/625-0988 `36`
American. Fine Dining. **Address:** 308 Market St 19106

HUNGRY PIGEON 215/278-2736 `164`
American. Casual Dining. **Address:** 743 S 4th St 19147

IRISH PUB 215/925-3311 `90`
Irish. Casual Dining. **Address:** 1123 Walnut St 19107

JANE G'S 215/563-8800 `64`
Chinese. Casual Dining. **Address:** 1930 Chestnut St 19103

JET WINE BAR 215/735-1116 `154`
Small Plates. Casual Dining. **Address:** 1525 South St 19146

JONES 215/223-5663 `54`
American. Casual Dining. **Address:** 700 Chestnut St 19106

KABUL, CUISINE OF AFGHANISTAN 215/922-3676 `52`
Afghan. Casual Dining. **Address:** 106 Chestnut St 19106

KANELLA SOUTH 215/644-8949 `163`
Mediterranean. Casual Dining. **Address:** 757 S Front St 19147

KARMA RESTAURANT & BAR 215/925-1444 `37`
Indian. Casual Dining. **Address:** 246 Market St 19106

KISSO SUSHI BAR 215/922-1770 `13`
Japanese. Casual Dining. **Address:** 205 N 4th St 19106

LACROIX AT THE RITTENHOUSE 215/790-2533 `108`
Continental. Fine Dining. **Address:** 210 W Rittenhouse Square 19103

LA FAMIGLIA 215/922-2803 `35`
Italian. Fine Dining. **Address:** 8 S Front St 19106

LA LOCANDA DEL GHIOTTONE 215/829-1465 `21`
Italian. Casual Dining. **Address:** 130 N 3rd St 19106

LA VERANDA 215/351-1898 `25`
Italian. Fine Dining. **Address:** 5 N Columbus Blvd 19106

LE CHERI 215/546-7700 `130`
French. Fine Dining. **Address:** 251 S 18th St 19103

LITTLE NONNA'S 215/546-2100 `117`
Italian. Casual Dining. **Address:** 1234 Locust St 19107

LOLITA 215/546-7100 `63`
Mexican. Casual Dining. **Address:** 106 S 13th St 19107

LOS CATRINES TEQUILA'S 215/546-0181 `124`
Mexican. Fine Dining. **Address:** 1602 Locust St 19103

LOVASH INDIAN CUISINE 215/925-3881 `146`
Northern Indian. Casual Dining. **Address:** 236 South St 19147

MAGGIANO'S LITTLE ITALY 215/567-2020 `29`
Italian. Fine Dining. **Address:** 1201 Filbert St 19107

MAMA PALMA'S 215/735-7357 `139`
Italian. Casual Dining. **Address:** 2229 Spruce St 19103

MARATHON GRILL
American. Casual Dining.
LOCATIONS:
Address: 121 S 16th St 19102 **Phone:** 215/569-3278
Address: 1818 Market St 19103 **Phone:** 215/561-1818

(See map & index p. 184.)

MARMONT STEAKHOUSE & BAR 215/923-1100 [32]
♛♛ American. Casual Dining. **Address:** 222 Market St 19106

MCCORMICK & SCHMICK'S 215/568-6888 [51]
♛♛♛ Seafood. Fine Dining. **Address:** One S Broad St 19107

MCCROSSEN'S TAVERN 215/854-0923 [4]
♛♛ American. Gastropub. **Address:** 529 N 20th St 19130

MCGILLIN'S OLDE ALE HOUSE 215/735-5562 [62]
♛♛ American. Sports Bar. **Address:** 1310 Drury St 19107

MISCONDUCT TAVERN 215/732-5797 [119]
♛♛ American. Casual Dining. **Address:** 1511 Locust St 19102

MISSION TAQUERIA 215/383-1200 [81]
♛♛ Mexican Small Plates. Casual Dining. **Address:** 1516 Sansom St 19102

MIXTO 215/592-0363 [140]
♛♛ Latin American. Casual Dining. **Address:** 1141 Pine St 19107

MONK'S CAFE 215/545-7005 [132]
♛♛ Belgian. Gastropub. **Address:** 264 S 16th St 19102

MORGAN'S PIER 215/279-7134 [8]
♛♛ American. Casual Dining. **Address:** 221 N Columbus Blvd 19123

MORIARTY'S RESTAURANT & IRISH PUB 215/627-7676 [94]
♛♛ American. Casual Dining. **Address:** 1116 Walnut St 19107

MORIMOTO 215/413-9070 [53]
♛♛♛♛ Japanese. Fine Dining. **Address:** 723 Chestnut St 19106

MUSTARD GREENS 215/627-0833 [151]
♛♛ Chinese. Casual Dining. **Address:** 622 S 2nd St 19147

NEW HARMONY VEGETARIAN RESTAURANT 215/627-4520 [22]
♛♛ Chinese Vegetarian. Casual Dining. **Address:** 135 N 9th St 19107

OCEAN PRIME 215/563-0163 [89]
♛♛♛ American. Fine Dining. **Address:** 124 S 15th St 19102

OPA 215/545-0170 [66]
♛♛♛ Greek Small Plates. Casual Dining. **Address:** 1311 Sansom St 19107

OYSTER HOUSE 215/567-7683 [82]
♛♛ Seafood. Casual Dining. **Address:** 1516 Sansom St 19102

PAESANO'S 215/440-0371 [174]
♛ Sandwiches. Quick Serve. **Address:** 1017 S 9th St 19147

THE PALM RESTAURANT 215/546-7256 [103]
♛♛♛ American. Fine Dining. **Address:** 200 S Broad St 19102

PANORAMA 215/922-7800 [30]
♛♛♛ Regional Italian. Fine Dining. **Address:** 14 N Front St 19106

PARC 215/545-2262 [121]
♛♛♛ French. Casual Dining. **Address:** 227 S 18th St 19103

PASTRAMI & THINGS 215/405-0544 [56]
♛ Deli. Quick Serve. **Address:** 24 S 18th St 19103

PENANG 215/413-2531 [23]
♛♛ Asian. Casual Dining. **Address:** 117 N 10th St 19107

PHO & CAFE VIET HUONG 215/336-5030 [176]
♛♛ Vietnamese. Casual Dining. **Address:** 1110 Washington Ave 19147

PHO XE LUA VIET THAI RESTAURANT 215/627-8883 [17]
♛♛ Vietnamese. Casual Dining. **Address:** 907 Race St 19107

PIETRO'S COAL OVEN PIZZERIA 215/735-8090 [102]
♛♛ Italian. Casual Dining. **Address:** 1714 Walnut St 19103

PIZZERIA STELLA 215/320-8000 [141]
♛♛ Pizza. Casual Dining. **Address:** 420 S 2nd St 19106

PIZZERIA VETRI 215/600-2629 [6]
♛♛ Pizza. Casual Dining. **Address:** 1939 Callowhill St 19130

THE PLOUGH AND THE STARS IRISH RESTAURANT & BAR 215/733-0300 [45]
♛♛ Irish. Casual Dining. **Address:** 123 Chestnut St 19106

POI DOG SNACK SHOP 215/279-7015 [78]
♛ Hawaiian. Quick Serve. **Address:** 100 1/2 S 21st St 19103

PORCINI RESTAURANT 215/751-1175 [93]
♛♛ Italian. Casual Dining. **Address:** 2048 Sansom St 19103

POSITANO COAST BY ALDO LAMBERTI 215/238-0499 [79]
♛♛♛ Southern Italian Small Plates. Casual Dining. **Address:** 212 Walnut St 19106

THE PRIME RIB 215/772-1701 [123]
♛♛♛ Steak. Fine Dining. **Address:** 1701 Locust St 19103

PUB AND KITCHEN 215/545-0350 [148]
♛♛ American. Gastropub. **Address:** 1946 Lombard St 19146

PUMPKIN 215/545-4448 [155]
♛♛ Mediterranean. Casual Dining. **Address:** 1713 South St 19146

QT VIETNAMESE SANDWICH 267/639-4520 [27]
♛♛ Vietnamese. Quick Serve. **Address:** 48 N 10th St 19107

R2L 215/564-5337 [55]
♛♛♛ New American. Fine Dining. **Address:** 50 S 16th St 19102

RACE STREET CAFE 215/627-6181 [14]
♛♛ American. Gastropub. **Address:** 208 Race St 19106

RALPH'S ITALIAN RESTAURANT 215/627-6011 [166]
♛♛ Southern Italian. Casual Dining. **Address:** 760 S 9th St 19147

RANGOON BURMESE RESTAURANT 215/829-8939 [24]
♛♛ Burmese. Casual Dining. **Address:** 112 N 9th St 19107

RATCHADA THAI & LAOS CUISINE 215/467-1546 [177]
♛♛ Asian. Casual Dining. **Address:** 1117 S 11th St 19147

RAY'S CAFE 215/922-5122 [20]
♛♛ Regional Chinese. Casual Dining. **Address:** 141 N 9th St 19107

RED OWL TAVERN 215/923-2267 [48]
♛♛ American. Casual Dining. **Address:** 433 Chestnut St 19106

RES IPSA 267/519-0329 [109]
♛♛ Italian. Casual Dining. **Address:** 2218 Walnut St 19103

REVOLUTION HOUSE 215/625-4566 [33]
♛♛ American. Gastropub. **Address:** 200 Market St 19106

RISTORANTE LA BUCA 215/928-0556 [106]
♛♛ Italian. Fine Dining. **Address:** 711 Locust St 19106

ROSE TATTOO CAFE 215/569-8939 [5]
♛♛ Continental. Casual Dining. **Address:** 1847 Callowhill St 19130

(See map & index p. 184.)

ROUGE 215/732-6622 (107)
▼▼ American. Casual Dining. **Address:** 205 S 18th St 19103

ROYAL SUSHI AND IZAKAYA 267/909-9002 (169)
▼▼ Japanese Small Plates. Gastropub. **Address:** 780 S 2nd St 19147

SABRINA'S CAFE 215/574-1599 (172)
▼▼ American. Casual Dining. **Address:** 910 Christian St 19147

SABRINA'S CAFE & SPENCER'S TOO 215/636-9061 (7)
▼▼ American. Casual Dining. **Address:** 1804 Callowhill St 19130

SALOON 215/627-1811 (165)
▼▼▼ Italian. Fine Dining. **Address:** 750 S 7th St 19147

SAMPAN 215/732-3501 (88)
▼▼▼ Asian. Fine Dining. **Address:** 124 S 13th St 19107

SAM'S MORNING GLORY DINER 215/413-3999 (162)
▼▼ American. Casual Dining. **Address:** 735 S 10th St 19147

SANG KEE PEKING DUCK HOUSE 215/925-7532 (10)
▼▼ Chinese. Casual Dining. **Address:** 238 N 9th St 19107

SCHLESINGER'S 215/735-7305 (118)
▼▼ Deli. Casual Dining. **Address:** 1521 Locust St 19102

SEAFOOD UNLIMITED 215/732-3663 (137)
▼▼ Seafood. Casual Dining. **Address:** 270 S 20th St 19103

SEIKO JAPANESE RESTAURANT 215/413-1606 (1)
▼▼ Japanese. Casual Dining. **Address:** 604 N 2nd St 19123

SHIAO LAN KUNG 215/928-0282 (18)
▼▼ Chinese. Casual Dining. **Address:** 930 Race St 19107

SHIROI HANA JAPANESE RESTAURANT 215/735-4444 (112)
▼▼ Japanese. Casual Dining. **Address:** 222 S 15th St 19102

THE SIDECAR BAR AND GRILLE 215/732-3429 (173)
▼▼ American. Gastropub. **Address:** 2201 Christian St 19146

SILK CITY DINER, BAR & LOUNGE 215/592-8838 (2)
▼▼ American. Gastropub. **Address:** 435 Spring Garden St 19123

SOUTH STREET SOUVLAKI 215/925-3026 (145)
▼▼ Greek. Casual Dining. **Address:** 509 South St 19147

SOUTHWARK 267/930-8538 (159)
▼▼▼ Continental. Fine Dining. **Address:** 701 S 4th St 19147

SPASSO ITALIAN GRILL 215/592-7661 (43)
▼▼ Italian. Casual Dining. **Address:** 34 S Front St 19106

SPICE 28 215/928-8880 (57)
▼▼ Asian Fusion. Casual Dining. **Address:** 1228 Chestnut St 19107

SQUARE 1682 215/563-5008 (80)
▼▼ New American. Casual Dining. **Address:** 121 S 17th St 19103

STRANGELOVE'S 215/873-0404 (104)
▼▼ American. Gastropub. **Address:** 216 S 11th St 19107

TALULA'S GARDEN 215/592-7787 (105)
▼▼▼ American. Fine Dining. **Address:** 210 W Washington Square 19106

TEN STONE 215/735-9939 (158)
▼▼ American. Casual Dining. **Address:** 2063 South St 19146

TERAKAWA RAMEN 267/687-1355 (16)
▼▼ Japanese. Casual Dining. **Address:** 204 N 9th St 19107

TINTO 215/665-9150 (87)
▼▼▼ Spanish. Fine Dining. **Address:** 114 S 20th St 19103

TIR NA NOG, BAR & GRILL 267/514-1700 (28)
▼▼ Irish. Casual Dining. **Address:** 1600 Arch St 19103

TRIA 215/629-9200 (131)
▼▼ Continental. Casual Dining. **Address:** 1137 Spruce St 19107

TRIA CAFE RITTENHOUSE 215/972-8742 (83)
▼▼ Continental. Casual Dining. **Address:** 123 S 18th St 19103

TWENTY MANNING GRILL 215/731-0900 (134)
▼▼ American. Casual Dining. **Address:** 261 S 20th St 19103

VARGA BAR 215/627-5200 (128)
▼▼ American. Casual Dining. **Address:** 941 Spruce St 19107

VEDGE 215/320-7500 (111)
▼▼▼ Vegetarian Small Plates. Fine Dining. **Address:** 1221 Locust St 19107

VERNICK FOOD & DRINK 267/639-6644 (100)
▼▼▼▼ New American. Fine Dining. **Address:** 2031 Walnut St 19103

VETRI 215/732-3478 (135)
▼▼▼▼ Italian. Fine Dining. **Address:** 1312 Spruce St 19107

VIETNAM PALACE RESTAURANT 215/592-9596 (12)
▼▼ Vietnamese. Casual Dining. **Address:** 222 N 11th St 19107

VIETNAM RESTAURANT 215/592-1163 (11)
▼▼ Vietnamese. Casual Dining. **Address:** 221 N 11th St 19107

VILLAGE WHISKEY 215/665-1088 (91)
▼▼▼ American. Gastropub. **Address:** 118 S 20th St 19103

VINTAGE WINE BAR & BISTRO 215/922-3095 (75)
▼▼ French. Casual Dining. **Address:** 129 S 13th St 19107

VOLVÉR 215/670-2302 (136)
▼▼▼▼ New International. Fine Dining. **Address:** 300 S Broad St 19102

XIX (NINETEEN) RESTAURANT 215/790-1919 (101)

▼▼▼▼
**American
Fine Dining
$14-$48**

AAA Inspector Notes: Atop the historic Hyatt at the Bellevue hotel, this elegant restaurant boasts a domed ceiling and fabulous views of the city. The menu features typically prepared seafood and chops complemented nicely by an extensive wine list. The environment is lovely, but be prepared for some noise due to the acoustics of the aforementioned dining room dome. **Features:** full bar, Sunday brunch, happy hour. **Reservations:** suggested. **Address:** 200 S Broad St 19102 **Location:** Between Walnut and Locust sts; in The Bellevue Hotel-in the Unbound Collection by Hyatt. ⊞ Walnut-Locust, 117. **Parking:** on-site (fee) and valet.

B L D ⊞

YAKITORI BOY 215/923-8088 (15)
▼▼ Japanese. Casual Dining. **Address:** 211 N 11th St 19107

ZAHAV 215/625-8800 (97)
▼▼▼▼ Middle Eastern. Fine Dining. **Address:** 237 St. James Pl 19106

ZAVINO 215/732-2400 (67)
▼▼▼ Italian. Casual Dining. **Address:** 112 S 13th St 19107

PHILADELPHIA elev. 39'

- Restaurants p. 214
- Hotels & Restaurants map & index p. 192

ALOFT PHILADELPHIA AIRPORT (267)298-1700

Hotel
$139-$189

 **AAA Benefit:** Members save 5% or more!

Address: 4301 Island Ave 19153 **Location:** Jct I-95 and SR 291 exit 13 northbound; exit 15 southbound. Eastwick, 161. **Facility:** 136 units. 5 stories, interior corridors. **Parking:** on-site (fee). **Terms:** cancellation fee imposed. **Amenities:** safes. **Pool:** heated indoor. **Activities:** exercise room. **Guest Services:** valet and coin laundry.

CHESTNUT HILL HOTEL   215/242-5905 ②
Historic Hotel. **Address:** 8229 Germantown Ave 19118

COURTYARD BY MARRIOTT PHILADELPHIA AIRPORT (215)365-2200 ㉒

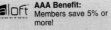
Hotel
$86-$475

COURTYARD Marriott **AAA Benefit:** Members save 5% or more!

Address: 8900 Bartram Ave 19153 **Location:** I-95 exit 12B (airport) southbound; exit 10 northbound, follow SR 291 E, then 1 mi n. Located in a commercial area. Eastwick, 161. **Facility:** 152 units. 4 stories, interior corridors. **Parking:** on-site (fee). **Terms:** 3 day cancellation notice-fee imposed. **Pool:** heated indoor. **Activities:** exercise room. **Guest Services:** valet and coin laundry, boarding pass kiosk, area transportation.

COURTYARD BY MARRIOTT PHILADELPHIA CITY AVE
(215)477-0200 ③
Hotel. **Address:** 4100 Presidential Blvd 19131
AAA Benefit: Members save 5% or more!

COURTYARD BY MARRIOTT PHILADELPHIA SOUTH AT THE NAVY YARD (215)644-9200 ⑩
Hotel. **Address:** 1001 Intrepid Ave 19112
AAA Benefit: Members save 5% or more!

AAA.com/ TourBook Comments
Let Your Voice Be Heard

If your visit to a TourBook-listed property doesn't meet your expectations, tell us about it.

AAA.com/TourBookComments

DOUBLETREE BY HILTON PHILADELPHIA AIRPORT (215)365-4150 ⑮

Hotel
$99-$199

 AAA Benefit: Members save 5% or more!

Address: 4509 Island Ave 19153 **Location:** I-95 exit 13 northbound; exit 15 southbound, 0.5 mi e; just e of SR 291. Eastwick, 161. **Facility:** 331 units. 9 stories, interior corridors. **Parking:** on-site (fee) and valet. **Terms:** 1-7 night minimum stay, cancellation fee imposed. **Amenities:** safes. **Dining:** 2 restaurants. **Pool:** heated indoor. **Activities:** exercise room. **Guest Services:** valet laundry.

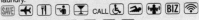

EMBASSY SUITES BY HILTON-PHILADELPHIA AIRPORT
(215)365-4500 ㉑
Hotel. **Address:** 9000 Bartram Ave 19153
AAA Benefit: Members save 5% or more!

FAIRFIELD INN BY MARRIOTT - PHILADELPHIA AIRPORT
(215)365-2254 ⑲
Hotel. **Address:** 8800 Bartram Ave 19153
AAA Benefit: Members save 5% or more!

FOUR POINTS BY SHERATON PHILADELPHIA AIRPORT (215)492-0400 ⑫

Hotel
$129-$169

FOUR POINTS BY SHERATON **AAA Benefit:** Members save 5% or more!

Address: 4105 Island Ave 19153 **Location:** Jct I-95 and SR 291 exit 13 northbound; exit 15 southbound. Located in a commercial area. Eastwick, 161. **Facility:** 177 units. 5 stories, interior corridors. **Parking:** on-site (fee). **Terms:** cancellation fee imposed. **Amenities:** safes. **Pool:** outdoor. **Activities:** exercise room. **Guest Services:** valet laundry, rental car service.

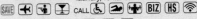

FOUR POINTS BY SHERATON PHILADELPHIA NORTHEAST
215/671-9600 ①
Hotel. **Address:** 9461 E Roosevelt Blvd 19114
AAA Benefit: Members save 5% or more!

HAMPTON INN-PHILADELPHIA AIRPORT (215)966-1300 ⑱
Hotel. **Address:** 8600 Bartram Ave 19153
AAA Benefit: Members save up to 10%!

HAWTHORN SUITES BY WYNDHAM PHILADELPHIA AIRPORT
(215)492-1611 ⑯
Extended Stay Hotel. **Address:** 4630 Island Ave 19153

HILTON PHILADELPHIA CITY AVENUE (215)879-4000 ⑤
Hotel. **Address:** 4200 City Ave 19131
AAA Benefit: Members save 5% or more!

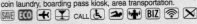

(See map & index p. 192.)

HOLIDAY INN PHILADELPHIA STADIUM (215)755-9500 **9**
▼▼▼ Hotel. **Address:** 900 Packer Ave 19148

HOMEWOOD SUITES BY HILTON/PHILADELPHIA CITY AVENUE (215)966-3000 **4**
▼▼ Extended Stay Hotel. **Address:** 4200 City Ave 19131

 AAA Benefit: Members save up to 10%!

HOMEWOOD SUITES BY HILTON UNIVERSITY CITY PHILADELPHIA (215)382-1111 **8**

▼▼▼
Extended Stay Hotel
$159-$344

 HOMEWOOD SUITES BY HILTON™ **AAA Benefit:** Members save up to 10%!

 Address: 4109 Walnut St 19104 **Location:** I-76 (Schuylkill Expwy) exit 345 eastbound; exit 346A (Sansom St) westbound; jct 41st St. ⬚ 40th, 77. **Facility:** 136 efficiencies. 11 stories, interior corridors. **Parking:** valet only. **Terms:** check-in 4 pm, 1-7 night minimum stay, cancellation fee imposed. **Pool:** heated indoor. **Activities:** hot tub, exercise room. **Guest Services:** valet and coin laundry, area transportation. **Featured Amenity:** breakfast buffet.

THE INN AT PENN, A HILTON HOTEL (215)222-0200 **7**

▼▼▼▼
Hotel
$179-$369

AAA Benefit: Members save 5% or more!

Address: 3600 Sansom St 19104 **Location:** I-76 (Schuylkill Expwy) exit 345 eastbound; exit 346A (Sansom St) westbound; between 36th and 37th sts. ⬚ 36th, 74. **Facility:** This elegant hotel has a spacious library area with seating, space to work and an honor bar. Guest rooms are stylish and include an iPad that can be used as an alarm, radio and to order room service. 245 units. 6 stories, interior corridors. **Parking:** valet only. **Terms:** check-in 4 pm, 1-7 night minimum stay, cancellation fee imposed. **Amenities:** safes. **Activities:** exercise room, massage. **Guest Services:** valet laundry. (See ad this page.)

SAVE ⬚ ⬚ CALL ⬚ ⬚ BIZ HS 🛜 ✕ ⬚ ⬚ ⬚/SOME UNITS ⬚ ⬚

THE INN AT PENN A Hilton Hotel **Located on U Penn's campus. Easy walk to center city, restaurants and nightlife.**

MICROTEL INN & SUITES BY WYNDHAM PHILADELPHIA AIRPORT (215)492-0700 **17**
▼▼ Hotel. **Address:** 8840 Tinicum Blvd 19153

(See map & index p. 192.)

PHILADELPHIA AIRPORT MARRIOTT HOTEL
(215)492-9000 **22**

Hotel
$109-$429

AAA Benefit: Members save 5% or more!

Address: 1 Arrivals Rd 19153 **Location:** I-95 exit 10 northbound; exit 12A southbound. Terminal B, 159. **Facility:** 419 units. 14 stories, interior corridors. **Parking:** on-site (fee). **Terms:** check-in 4 pm, 3 day cancellation notice-fee imposed. **Amenities:** safes. **Activities:** exercise room. **Guest Services:** complimentary and valet laundry, boarding pass kiosk.

RENAISSANCE HOTEL PHILADELPHIA AIRPORT
(610)521-5900 **23**

Hotel
$80-$344

RENAISSANCE HOTELS

AAA Benefit: Members save 5% or more!

Address: 500 Stevens Dr 19113 **Location:** I-95 exit 9A (Essington/SR 420), just e on Wanamaker Ave, then 1.4 mi n on Industrial Way. Located in a commercial area. **Facility:** 349 units. 12 stories, interior corridors. **Terms:** cancellation fee imposed. **Amenities:** Some: safes. **Dining:** 2 restaurants. **Pool:** heated indoor. **Activities:** exercise room. **Guest Services:** valet laundry.

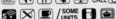 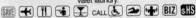

RESIDENCE INN BY MARRIOTT PHILADELPHIA AIRPORT
(215)921-8011 **11**

 Extended Stay Contemporary Hotel. **Address:** 3701 Island Ave 19153

AAA Benefit: Members save 5% or more!

SHERATON PHILADELPHIA UNIVERSITY CITY HOTEL
(215)387-8000 **6**

Hotel
$79-$489

Sheraton

AAA Benefit: Members save 5% or more!

Address: 3549 Chestnut St 19104 **Location:** I-76 (Schuylkill Expwy) exit 345, 0.5 mi w; jct 36th St; at University of Pennsylvania. 36th, 74. **Facility:** 332 units. 20 stories, interior corridors. **Parking:** on-site (fee). **Terms:** cancellation fee imposed. **Amenities:** safes. **Pool:** outdoor. **Activities:** exercise room. **Guest Services:** valet and coin laundry.

SHERATON SUITES PHILADELPHIA AIRPORT
215/365-6600 **14**

Hotel
Rates not provided

Sheraton

AAA Benefit: Members save 5% or more!

Address: 4101 Island Ave 19153 **Location:** Jct I-95 and SR 291 exit 13 northbound; exit 15 southbound. Located in a commercial area. Eastwick, 161. **Facility:** 250 units. 8 stories, interior corridors. **Parking:** on-site (fee). **Amenities:** safes. **Pool:** heated indoor. **Activities:** exercise room. **Guest Services:** valet laundry, area transportation. (See ad this page.)

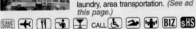

▼ See AAA listing p. 214 ▼

(See map & index p. 192.)

WHERE TO EAT

THE ABBAYE   215/627-6711 (35)
American. Casual Dining. **Address:** 637 N 3rd St 19123

ABYSSINIA ETHIOPIAN RESTAURANT   215/387-2424 (50)
Ethiopian. Casual Dining. **Address:** 229 S 45th St 19104

ANDY'S CHICKEN   215/291-0700 (14)
Korean. Quick Serve. **Address:** 2001 Memphis St 19125

BAIT & SWITCH   267/639-5041 (11)
Seafood. Casual Dining. **Address:** 2537 E Somerset St 19134

BARDOT CAFE   267/639-4772 (25)
American. Gastropub. **Address:** 447 Poplar St 19123

BAR HYGGE   215/765-2274 (33)
American. Gastropub. **Address:** 1720 Fairmount Ave 19130

BING BING DIM SUM   215/279-7702 (66)
Asian Small Plates. Casual Dining. **Address:** 1648 E Passyunk Ave 19148

BITAR'S   215/755-1121 (52)
Eastern Mediterranean. Quick Serve. **Address:** 947 Federal St 19147

BOBBY'S BURGER PALACE   215/387-0378 (49)
Burgers. Quick Serve. **Address:** 3925 Walnut St 19104

BOMB BOMB BAR-B-QUE GRILL   215/463-1311 (71)
Italian Barbecue. Casual Dining. **Address:** 1026 Wolf St 19148

BRIGANTESSA   267/318-7341 (58)
Southern Italian. Casual Dining. **Address:** 1520 E Passyunk Ave 19147

CAKE LIFE BAKE SHOP   215/278-2580 (20)
Breads/Pastries. Quick Serve. **Address:** 1306 Frankford Ave 19125

CANTINA DOS SEGUNDOS   215/629-0500 (27)
Mexican. Casual Dining. **Address:** 931 N 2nd St 19123

CAPOGIRO   215/462-3790 (64)
Desserts. Quick Serve. **Address:** 1625 E Passyunk Ave 19148

CEDAR POINT BAR & KITCHEN   215/423-5400 (15)
American. Gastropub. **Address:** 2370 E Norris St 19125

CHESTNUT GRILL AND SIDEWALK CAFE   215/247-7570 (4)
American. Casual Dining. **Address:** 8229 Germantown Ave 19118

CHEU FISHTOWN   267/758-2269 (17)
Asian Fusion. Gastropub. **Address:** 1416 Frankford Ave 19125

CHICKIE'S AND PETE'S CRAB HOUSE & SPORTS BAR
American. Casual Dining.
LOCATIONS:
Address: 11000 Roosevelt Blvd 19116 **Phone:** 215/856-9890
Address: 1526 Packer Ave 19145 **Phone:** 215/218-0500
Address: 4010 Robbins Ave 19135 **Phone:** 215/338-3060

CIRCLES   267/687-1778 (63)
Asian. Casual Dining. **Address:** 1514 Tasker St 19145

CIRCLES CONTEMPORARY ASIAN   267/687-1309 (29)
Asian Fusion. Casual Dining. **Address:** 812 N 2nd St 19123

DELMONICO'S STEAK HOUSE   215/879-4000 (10)
Steak. Fine Dining. **Address:** 4200 City Ave 19131

DISTRITO   215/222-1657 (40)
New Mexican. Casual Dining. **Address:** 3945 Chestnut St 19104

FEDERAL DONUTS   267/275-8489 (32)
Comfort Food. Quick Serve. **Address:** 701 N 7th St 19123

FOND   215/551-5000 (59)
New American. Fine Dining. **Address:** 1537 S 11th St 19147

GENO'S STEAKS   215/389-0659 (53)
Sandwiches. Quick Serve. **Address:** 1219 9th St 19147

GIRARD   267/457-2486 (21)
American. Casual Dining. **Address:** 300 E Girard Ave 19125

THE GOAT'S BEARD   267/323-2495 (9)
American. Casual Dining. **Address:** 4201 Main St 19127

GREEN EGGS CAFE   215/226-3447 (57)
Breakfast. Casual Dining. **Address:** 1306 Dickinson St 19147

GREEN EGGS CAFE   215/922-3447 (34)
Breakfast. Casual Dining. **Address:** 719 N 2nd St 19123

HONEY'S SIT 'N EAT   215/925-1150 (30)
Comfort Food. Casual Dining. **Address:** 800 N 4th St 19123

ITV (IN THE VALLEY)   267/858-0669 (61)
New Continental. Casual Dining. **Address:** 1615 E Passyunk Ave 19148

JACK'S FIREHOUSE RESTAURANT   215/232-9000 (36)
American. Fine Dining. **Address:** 2130 Fairmount Ave 19130

JAKE'S & COOPER'S WINE BAR   215/483-0444 (7)
American. Fine Dining. **Address:** 4365 Main St 19127

JG DOMESTIC   215/222-2363 (39)
American. Casual Dining. **Address:** 2929 Arch St 19104

JOHN'S ROAST PORK   215/463-1951 (70)
Sandwiches. Quick Serve. **Address:** 14 E Snyder Ave 19148

KENSINGTON QUARTERS   267/314-5086 (19)
American. Fine Dining. **Address:** 1310 Frankford Ave 19125

KRAFTWORK   215/739-1700 (16)
American. Gastropub. **Address:** 541 E Girard Ave 19125

LAS CAZUELAS RESTAURANT   215/351-9144 (24)
Mexican. Casual Dining. **Address:** 426 W Girard Ave 19123

LAS MARGARITAS   215/969-6600 (2)
Mexican. Casual Dining. **Address:** 2538 Welsh Rd, Suite 40 19152

LAUREL   215/271-8299 (62)
New French. Fine Dining. **Address:** 1617 E Passyunk Ave 19148

LE VIRTÙ   215/271-5626 (69)
New Italian. Fine Dining. **Address:** 1927 E Passyunk Ave 19148

LOS CABALLITOS CANTINA   215/755-3550 (67)
Mexican. Casual Dining. **Address:** 1651 E Passyunk Ave 19148

MARIGOLD KITCHEN   215/222-3699 (51)
American. Fine Dining. **Address:** 501 S 45th St 19104

MARRA'S CUCINA ITALIANA   215/463-9249 (68)
Italian. Casual Dining. **Address:** 1734 E Passyunk Ave 19148

MARTHA   215/867-8881 (12)
American Small Plates. Gastropub. **Address:** 2113 E York St 19125

(See map & index p. 192.)

MCNALLY'S TAVERN 215/247-9736 ③
◆◆ Sandwiches. Casual Dining. **Address:** 8634 Germantown Ave 19118

MR. MARTINO'S TRATTORIA 215/755-0663 (65)
◆◆ Italian. Casual Dining. **Address:** 1646 E Passyunk Ave 19148

NEW DECK TAVERN 215/386-4600 ㊹
◆◆ American. Casual Dining. **Address:** 3408 Sansom St 19104

NEW DELHI 215/386-1941 ㊷
◆ Indian. Casual Dining. **Address:** 4004 Chestnut St 19104

NIFTY FIFTY'S 215/676-1950
◆◆ American. Casual Dining. **Address:** 2491 Grant Ave 19114

NOORD EETCAFE 267/909-9704 (60)
◆◆ Scandinavian. Casual Dining. **Address:** 1046 Tasker St 19148

NORTH 3RD 215/413-3666 ㉛
◆◆ American. Gastropub. **Address:** 801 N 3rd St 19123

OREGON DINER 215/462-5566 (73)
◆◆ American. Casual Dining. **Address:** 302 W Oregon Ave 19148

OSTERIA 215/763-0920 ㊲
◆◆◆ Italian. Fine Dining. **Address:** 640 N Broad St 19130

PAT'S KING OF STEAKS 215/468-1546 (54)
◆ Sandwiches. Quick Serve. **Address:** 1237 E Passyunk Ave 19147

PATTAYA THAI CUISINE 215/387-8533 ㊸
◆◆ Thai. Casual Dining. **Address:** 4006 Chestnut St 19104

PHO PALACE 215/437-1898 ①
◆◆ Vietnamese. Casual Dining. **Address:** 15501 Bustleton Ave 19116

PIZZA BRAIN 215/291-2965 ⑬
◆ Pizza. Quick Serve. **Address:** 2313 Frankford Ave 19125

POD 215/387-1803 ㊻
◆◆◆ Japanese. Casual Dining. **Address:** 3636 Sansom St 19104

POKE BOWL 267/319-9943 ㉖
◆ Hawaiian Specialty. Quick Serve. **Address:** 958 N 2nd St 19123

THE RESTAURANT SCHOOL AT WALNUT HILL COLLEGE 215/222-4200 ㊽
◆◆◆ Continental. Fine Dining. **Address:** 4207 Walnut St 19104

ROOT 215/515-3452 ㉒
◆◆◆ Continental. Fine Dining. **Address:** 1206 Frankford Ave 19125

SABRINA'S CAFE @ POWELTON 215/222-1022 ㊳
◆◆ American. Casual Dining. **Address:** 227 N 34th St 19104

SANCHO PISTOLA'S 267/324-3530 ㉓
◆◆ Mexican. Gastropub. **Address:** 19 W Girard Ave 19125

STANDARD TAP 215/238-0630 ㉘
◆◆ American. Gastropub. **Address:** 901 N 2nd St 19123

TANDOOR INDIA 215/222-7122 ㊺
◆◆ Indian. Casual Dining. **Address:** 106 S 40th St 19104

TAQUERIA FELIZ 267/331-5874 ⑥
◆◆ Mexican. Casual Dining. **Address:** 4410 Main St 19127

THAI SINGHA HOUSE 215/382-8001 ㊶
◆◆ Thai. Casual Dining. **Address:** 3906B Chestnut St 19104

TONY LUKE'S 215/551-5725 (72)
◆ Sandwiches. Quick Serve. **Address:** 39 E Oregon Ave 19148

THE VICTOR CAFE 215/468-3040 (56)
◆◆◆ Italian. Casual Dining. **Address:** 1303 Dickinson St 19147

WARMDADDY'S 215/462-2000 (55)
◆◆ Southern American. Casual Dining. **Address:** 1400 S Columbus Blvd 19147

WHITE DOG CAFE 215/386-9224 ㊼
◆◆ American. Casual Dining. **Address:** 3420 Sansom St 19104

WINNIE'S LE BUS 215/487-2663 ⑧
◆◆ American. Casual Dining. **Address:** 4266 Main St 19127

WM. MULHERIN'S SONS 215/291-1355 ⑱
◆◆◆ Italian. Fine Dining. **Address:** 1355 N Front St 19122

ZESTY'S 215/483-6226 ⑤
◆◆◆ Mediterranean. Casual Dining. **Address:** 4382 Main St 19127

Nearby New Jersey

BATSTO elev. 13'

• Part of Philadelphia area — see map p. 154

Established in 1766, Batsto became a prominent iron foundry and was of great military importance to the Patriots' cause during the Revolution. The village's prosperity grew after the war, a time when ironworks, glassworks, a brickyard, a gristmill and a sawmill provided livelihoods for nearly 1,000 people.

Fortunes dwindled when competition from cheap Pennsylvania coal forced the town's more expensive charcoal-fired furnaces to close in 1855. An 1874 fire burned half of Batsto to the ground, but 2 years later wealthy Philadelphia financier Joseph Wharton purchased the town site and the surrounding 100,000 acres.

INSIDER INFO:
The Pine Barrens

If most people don't know about New Jersey's Pine Barrens, it could be because the 450,000 year-round residents of this national reserve that overlies more than a million acres of the state's bottom half, prefer to keep a good thing to themselves.

Wedged between the roar of traffic along the New Jersey Turnpike and the Garden State Parkway, this quiet wilderness shows little evidence of the human settlement and enterprise that have occurred. Yet the Pines are far from barren.

The area's heart is a tapestry of impenetrable scrub and pitch pine, rivers, swamps and bogs where rebelling Colonials mined iron to make cannonballs. Villages, foundries and glassworks churned out the region's products until the late 1800s, after which the forest resumed full reign.

Local residents, affectionately called the "Pineys," learned to "work the woods" by selling its seasonal gifts and tending its cranberry and blueberry crops. Cranberries have been commercially raised in the Pine Barrens since about 1835, while the first commercial blueberry planting was made in 1916. The Pine Barrens account for approximately 25 percent of the state's agricultural income.

Many recreational opportunities exist in the Pine Barrens. Boating, canoeing, swimming, fishing and hunting are popular activities. Hikers can enjoy the Batona Trail, a marked wilderness trail that traverses the Pine Barrens, or explore old abandoned towns and the restored Batsto Village. More than 1,000 known sites in the vicinity show that man lived in this area as early as 10,000 B.C.

Left undisturbed are the woodland's wonders: a confusing tangle of sand roads cut during Colonial times, 12,000 acres of stunted pygmy pines in an area called the Plains, insectivorous plants, exotic orchids, ventriloquist tree frogs found almost nowhere else and a legendary winged creature known as the "Jersey Devil."

The muck soil in the Pine Barrens produces monobactum, a microorganism expected to revolutionize the antibiotics industry. An aquifer inside the Pine's deep sand beds holds 17 trillion gallons of water with the purity of glacial ice. The water in this shallow aquifer usually is at or near the surface, producing bogs, marshes and swamps. A maze of serpentine streams fed by the aquifer, stained the color of tea by cedar sap, rises within the low dome of land on which the Pines exist.

With development encroaching on all sides, the Pines' uniqueness becomes more apparent each year—except to local residents, who have always known it.

BATSTO HISTORIC VILLAGE is off CR 542 on Batsto Rd. This restored 19th-century village within Wharton State Forest *(see Recreation Areas Chart)* grew up around the Batsto Iron Works. Buildings include an iron master's mansion, a sawmill, a church, a gristmill, a general store, an icehouse, a post office and workers' houses. The visitor center houses a museum with permanent and changing historical exhibits. Visitors can take a smartphone audio/video tour.

Time: Allow 2 hours minimum. **Hours:** Grounds daily dawn-dusk. Visitor center open daily 9-4. Mansion tours are given when staff is available. Closed Jan. 1, Thanksgiving, Christmas and state holidays. Phone ahead to confirm schedule. **Cost:** Grounds and visitor center free. Mansion tour $3; $1 (ages 6-11). **Parking:** Sat.-Sun. and holidays $5, Memorial Day-Labor Day. **Phone:** (609) 561-3262 or (609) 561-0024.

BELLMAWR pop. 11,583
• **Hotels & Restaurants map & index p. 192**
• **Part of Philadelphia area — see map p. 154**

CLUB DINER   856/931-2880   (165)
American. Casual Dining. **Address:** 20 N Black Horse Pike 08031

BLACKWOOD pop. 4,545
• **Part of Philadelphia area — see map p. 154**

HAMPTON INN BY HILTON-TURNERSVILLE   (856)228-4200
Hotel. **Address:** 5800 Black Horse Pike 08012

AAA Benefit:
Members save up to 10%!

BORDENTOWN pop. 3,924
• **Part of Philadelphia area — see map p. 154**

BEST WESTERN BORDENTOWN INN   (609)298-8000

Motel
$79-$150

Best Western. AAA Benefit: Members save 5% to 15% and earn 10% bonus points!

Address: 1068 US Hwy 206 S 08505 **Location:** New Jersey Tpke exit 7, 0.8 mi n. Next to a park. **Facility:** 100 units. 2 stories (no elevator), exterior corridors. **Terms:** cancellation fee imposed. **Pool:** heated indoor. **Activities:** sauna, hot tub, exercise room. **Guest Services:** valet and coin laundry.

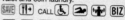

/ SOME UNITS

COMFORT INN   (609)298-9111
Hotel. **Address:** 1009 US 206 08505

HAMPTON INN BORDENTOWN   (609)298-4000
Hotel. **Address:** 2004 US Hwy 206 S 08505

AAA Benefit:
Members save up to 10%!

WHERE TO EAT

THE FARNSWORTH HOUSE RESTAURANT   609/291-9232
Italian. Casual Dining. **Address:** 135 Farnsworth Ave 08505

MASTORIS DINER RESTAURANT   609/298-4650
American. Casual Dining. **Address:** 144 Rt 130 08505

BRIDGEPORT
• **Part of Philadelphia area — see map p. 154**

HAMPTON INN-BRIDGEPORT   (856)467-6200
Hotel. **Address:** 2 Pureland Dr 08085

AAA Benefit:
Members save up to 10%!

BURLINGTON pop. 9,920, elev. 13'
• **Part of Philadelphia area — see map p. 154**

One of the first permanent settlements in the western part of the colony, Burlington was established by members of the Society of Friends in 1677. It became the capital of West Jersey and shared that status with Perth Amboy after East and West Jersey united. A strategic location on the Delaware River between Trenton and Camden made the flourishing port so prosperous that its citizens—primarily Quaker settlers and pacifists—were relatively uninvolved in the Revolution.

Venerable buildings that are open to the public by appointment include the 1703 Old St. Mary's Church, at Broad and Wood streets; the 1685 Revell House, in the 200 block of Wood Street; the 1785 Friends Meeting House, on High Street near Broad Street; the 1797 John Hoskins House, 202 High St.; the 1792 Friends School, at York and Penn streets; and the restored carriage house on Smith's Alley between High and Wood streets.

Burlington County Regional Chamber of Commerce: 520 Fellowship Rd., Suite E502, Mount Laurel, NJ 08054. **Phone:** (856) 439-2520.

BURLINGTON COUNTY HISTORICAL SOCIETY COMPLEX is 2 blks. n. of US 130 at 451-459 High St. The Corson Poley Center contains a library, museum, Children's History Center and three historic houses: the Bard-How House, the Capt. James Lawrence House and the James Fenimore Cooper House. The museum displays a locally made jinrikisha—an Asian hand-pulled carriage—as well as a collection of tall case clocks and quilts. Another exhibit, The American Revolution: A Global Conflict, explores early American history. The Children's History Center offers interactive experiences for children ages 2 and up.

The library's genealogical records are available for research. **Hours:** Guided museum and 40-minute house tours are offered Tues.-Sat. 10-5. Children's History Center open Tues.-Sat. 10-5. Library open Wed.-Thurs. 1-5. Closed major holidays. **Cost:** Fee for house tour, Children's History Center or library and gallery $5. House tour, library and gallery $5. **Phone:** (609) 386-4773.

Bard-How House, 453 High St. in the Burlington County Historical Society Complex, was built around 1743 for merchant Bennett Bard and his wife, Sarah Pattison Bard. It was purchased in 1756 by butcher and tavern owner Samuel How. Period furnishings and other accessories decorate the restored house, including a tall case clock that dates from 1740.

Hours: Guided house tours are offered Tues.-Sat. 10-5. Closed major holidays. **Cost:** (includes Capt. James Lawrence House, James Fenimore Cooper House, and Burlington County Historical Society Complex library and gallery) $5. Tour only (includes Capt. James Lawrence House and James Fenimore Cooper House) $5. **Phone:** (609) 386-4773.

Capt. James Lawrence House, 459 High St. in the Burlington County Historical Society Complex, is the birthplace of the American naval hero of the War of 1812. The commander of the USS *Chesapeake* engaged in battle against the HMS *Shannon,* and the mortally wounded Lawrence issued his famous last command, remembered as "Don't give up the ship." The house is furnished in period and also contains a toy collection.

Hours: Guided house tours are offered Tues.-Sat. 10-5. Closed major holidays. **Cost:** (includes Bard-How House, James Fenimore Cooper House, and Burlington County Historical Society Complex library and gallery) $5. Tour only (includes Bard-How House and James Fenimore Cooper House) $5. **Phone:** (609) 386-4773.

James Fenimore Cooper House, 457 High St. in the Burlington County Historical Society Complex, is the birthplace of the author of the "Leatherstocking Tales," novels depicting the era of American frontiersmen and Native Americans. "The Last of the Mohicans" and "The Deerslayer" are among the best known titles in the series, written 1826-41. The 1780 Cooper House has five museum rooms.

Hours: Guided house tours are offered Tues.-Sat. 10-5. Closed major holidays. **Cost:** (includes Bard-How House, Capt. James Lawrence House, and Burlington County Historical Society Complex library and gallery) $5. Tour only (includes Bard-How House and Capt. James Lawrence House) $5. **Phone:** (609) 386-4773.

CAMDEN pop. 77,344, elev. 25'
• Part of Philadelphia area — see map p. 154

The site of William Cooper's ferryboat operation on the Delaware River in the 1680s grew into a city well-established in industry and transportation, especially after becoming the terminus for the Camden & Amboy Railroad in 1834. Yet echoes of the city's shipbuilding past remain ever-present.

Port facilities along the deep, broad Delaware River led to a boom in shipbuilding during World Wars I and II. The first nuclear-powered merchant ship, the *Savannah,* was built in Camden. On the cultural side, poet Walt Whitman—whose unfettered, subjective style revolutionized poetic expression in the mid-19th century—lived his last years in Camden. The tomb of the good gray poet is in Harleigh Cemetery on Haddon Avenue.

ADVENTURE AQUARIUM is on the banks of the Delaware River at 1 Riverside Dr. Sea life and wildlife can be seen and touched in a variety of exhibits, including KidZone, an interactive exhibit designed specifically for kids. Shark Realm, a 40-foot walk-through tunnel, houses more than 20 sharks and 850 other marine animals. For an alternate view of the exhibit, guests can walk above it on the rope-suspension Shark Bridge. Hippo Haven houses hippopotamuses and porcupines. Little Blue Beach is home to tiny blue penguins. Films shown in a 4-D theater depict the wonders of underwater life. A Swim with the Sharks snorkeling program and special behind-the-scenes animal adventures also are offered.

Ferry/trolley service to the museum is available to and from the riverfront in Philadelphia Memorial Day through Labor Day. **Time:** Allow 2 hours minimum. **Hours:** Daily 10-5. **Cost:** $26.95; $19.95 (ages 2-12). Adventure Combo with 4-D theater ticket $29.45; $22.45 (ages 2-12). **Parking:** $10. **Phone:** (856) 365-3300 or (800) 616-5297. **(See ad on inside front cover.)** 🍴 🚇 City Hall, 144

BATTLESHIP *NEW JERSEY* is berthed at 62 Battleship Pl. on the Camden waterfront. This Iowa Class vessel, launched from the Philadelphia Navy Yard in 1942, is celebrated as the U.S. Navy's most decorated battleship. After serving in World War II, Korea, Vietnam and the Persian Gulf, the ship was decommissioned in 1990. Gun turrets, bridge communications, captain's and admiral's cabins, and enlisted men's bunks and mess area can be seen.

The 2-hour Fire Power Tour offers an in-depth look at the ship's weapons systems and the combat engagement center. The 90-minute Turret II Experience explores the battleship's legendary 16-inch gun turret.

Note: Video cameras, bags, backpacks and baby strollers are not permitted. Comfortable dress and shoes are recommended. A video version is available for those physically unable to take the tour. **Time:** Allow 2 hours minimum. **Hours:** Tours are offered every 15 minutes daily 9:30-5, May 1-Labor Day; daily 9:30-3, in Apr., day after Labor Day-Oct. 31 and Dec. 26-Dec. 31; Sat.-Sun. (also Presidents Day) 9:30-3, Nov. 1-Dec. 24 and early Feb.-Mar. 31. Turret II Experience tours are offered Sat.-Sun. and holidays at 11. Closed Jan. 1, Thanksgiving and Christmas. **Cost:** Fire Power Tour $21.95; $17 (ages 5-11 and 62+ and retired military with ID); free (ages 0-4 and active military with ID). Turret II Experience $29.95; $25.95 (ages 5-11 and 62+ and retired military with ID); free (ages 0-4 and active military with ID). **Parking:** Fees vary by garage. **Phone:** (856) 966-1652 or (866) 877-6262. GT 🚇 City Hall, 144

CAMDEN CHILDREN'S GARDEN is on the riverfront at 3 Riverside Dr., adjacent to Adventure Aquarium. It features a variety of themed gardens designed for children ages 12 and under, including a dinosaur garden, a fitness garden and a picnic garden. Storybook Gardens features the Giant's Garden, Three Little Pigs Garden and an English-style garden like the one depicted in the different versions of the movie "The Secret Garden." There also is a butterfly garden, a maze and a tree house. Indoor exhibits include the Philadelphia Eagles Butterfly House, Benjamin Franklin's Secret Workshop and the tropically landscaped Plaza de Aibonito.

Visitors also can ride the Garden Carousel, the Arrow River Train and the Spring Butterfly Ride, which raises riders 30 feet in the air to provide a butterfly's-eye view of the gardens. **Time:** Allow 2 hours minimum. **Hours:** Wed.-Sun. 10-5. Closed Thanksgiving and Christmas. Phone ahead to confirm schedule. **Cost:** $8; $6 (Camden residents with

ID); $4 (visitors with a paid admission to Adventure Aquarium arriving through the Garden Gate); free (ages 0-2). **Phone:** (856) 365-8733. 🌳 🚇 City Hall, 144

CARNEYS POINT pop. 7,382
• **Part of Philadelphia area — see map p. 154**

COMFORT INN & SUITES	(856)299-8282
🔻🔻🔻 Hotel. **Address:** 634 Sodders Rd 08069	
HOLIDAY INN EXPRESS HOTEL & SUITES	856/351-9222
🔻🔻🔻 Hotel. **Address:** 506 S Pennsville-Auburn Rd 08069	

WHERE TO EAT

LAPP'S OLYMPIA DAIRY MARKET	856/514-3448
🔻 Burgers. Quick Serve. **Address:** 1073 US 40 08069	

CHERRY HILL elev. 56'
• **Hotels & Restaurants map & index p. 192**
• **Part of Philadelphia area — see map p. 154**

CROWNE PLAZA PHILADELPHIA/CHERRY HILL	856/665-6666 **105**
🔻🔻🔻 Hotel. **Address:** 2349 W Marlton Pike (SR 70) 08002	
DAYS INN & SUITES	(856)663-0100 **104**

🔻 🔻
Motel
$80-$105

Address: 525 SR 38 E 08002 **Location:** I-295 exit 34B, 4 mi w on SR 70 to Cuthbert Blvd (SR 38 E), then just ne. **Facility:** 86 units, some two bedrooms. 2 stories (no elevator), exterior corridors. **Terms:** cancellation fee imposed. **Pool:** outdoor. **Activities:** exercise room. **Guest Services:** coin laundry. **Featured Amenity:** continental breakfast.

SAVE 🍴➕ 🛏 📶 BIZ HS 🛜
✉ 🔒 🖥 🖨

EXTENDED STAY AMERICA-PHILADELPHIA/CHERRY HILL	(856)616-1200 **107**
🔻🔻 Extended Stay Hotel. **Address:** 1653 E SR 70 (Marlton Pike) 08034	
HOLIDAY INN PHILADELPHIA-CHERRY HILL	(856)663-5300 **106**
🔻🔻🔻 Hotel. **Address:** 2175 W Marlton Pike 08002	

WHERE TO EAT

BRIO TUSCAN GRILLE	856/910-8166 **146**
🔻🔻🔻 Italian. Fine Dining. **Address:** 901 Haddonfield Rd 08002	
CAFFE ALDO LAMBERTI	856/663-1747 **147**
🔻🔻🔻 Italian. Fine Dining. **Address:** 2011 Rt 70 W 08002	
CHICK'S DELI	856/429-2022 **149**
🔻 Deli. Quick Serve. **Address:** 906 Township Ln 08002	
THE FARM & FISHERMAN TAVERN + MARKET	856/356-2282 **150**
🔻🔻🔻 American. Gastropub. **Address:** 1442 Marlton Pike E 08034	
IL VILLAGGIO	856/795-1778 **151**
🔻🔻 Italian. Fine Dining. **Address:** 211 Haddonfield-Berlin Rd 08034	
NORMA'S	856/795-1373 **148**
🔻🔻 Eastern Mediterranean. Casual Dining. **Address:** 145 Barclay Farms Shopping Center (SR 70) 08002	

(See map & index p. 192.)

SEASONS 52 FRESH GRILL   856/665-1052 (145)
♦♦♦♦ New American. Fine Dining. **Address:** 2000 Rt 38, Suite 1145 08002

SILVER DINER   856/910-1240
♦♦ American. Casual Dining. **Address:** 2131 SR 38 E 08002

CINNAMINSON
• Hotels & Restaurants map & index p. 192
• Part of Philadelphia area — see map p. 154

SLEEP INN   (856)829-0717 (82)

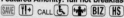

♦♦♦ Hotel $84-$175

Address: 208 Rt 130 N 08077 **Location:** 0.9 mi n of jct SR 73. **Facility:** 52 units. 2 stories, interior corridors. *Bath:* shower only. **Activities:** exercise room. **Featured Amenity:** full hot breakfast.

SAVE ▮ CALL ☾ ☖ BIZ HS
🛜 ▯ ▭ ▭

WHERE TO EAT

THE JUG HANDLE INN   856/665-8696 (122)
♦♦ American. Casual Dining. **Address:** 1018 S Fork Landing Rd 08077

COLLINGSWOOD   pop. 13,926
• Hotels & Restaurants map & index p. 192
• Part of Philadelphia area — see map p. 154

THE POP SHOP   856/869-0111 (142)
♦♦ Comfort Food. Casual Dining. **Address:** 729 Haddon Ave 08108

DEPTFORD
• Hotels & Restaurants map & index p. 192
• Part of Philadelphia area — see map p. 154

FAIRFIELD INN BY MARRIOTT PHILADELPHIA/DEPTFORD
(856)686-9050 (127)
♦♦ Hotel. **Address:** 1160 Hurffville Rd 08096

AAA Benefit: Members save 5% or more!

RESIDENCE INN BY MARRIOTT DEPTFORD
(856)686-9188 (126)
♦♦♦ Extended Stay Hotel. **Address:** 1154 Hurffville Rd 08096

AAA Benefit: Members save 5% or more!

GIBBSBORO   pop. 2,274
• Hotels & Restaurants map & index p. 192
• Part of Philadelphia area — see map p. 154

THE CHOPHOUSE   856/566-7300 (168)
♦♦♦ Steak. Fine Dining. **Address:** 4 Lakeview Dr S 08026

HADDONFIELD   pop. 11,593, elev. 74'
• Part of Philadelphia area — see map p. 154

In 1701, Elizabeth Haddon was sent from England by her father—who had no sons—to develop 550 acres southeast of Camden. In less than a year the industrious Quaker lass had built a house, begun the colony and proposed marriage to Quaker missionary John Estaugh (he accepted). Their romance is at the center of "The Theologian's Tale" in Henry Wadsworth Longfellow's "Tales of a Wayside Inn."

MAPLE SHADE
• Hotels & Restaurants map & index p. 192
• Part of Philadelphia area — see map p. 154

P.J. WHELIHAN'S PUB & RESTAURANT   856/234-2345 (139)
♦♦ American. Casual Dining. **Address:** 396 S Lenola Rd 08052

MARLTON   pop. 10,133
• Hotels & Restaurants map & index p. 192
• Part of Philadelphia area — see map p. 154

JOE'S PEKING DUCK HOUSE   856/985-1551 (155)
♦♦♦ Chinese. Casual Dining. **Address:** 145 Rt 73 S 08053

MEXICAN FOOD FACTORY   856/983-9222 (154)
♦♦ Mexican. Casual Dining. **Address:** 601 W SR 70 08053

MOUNT HOLLY   elev. 45'
• Restaurants p. 220
• Hotels & Restaurants map & index p. 192
• Part of Philadelphia area — see map p. 154

Sharing the name of a nearby hill, Mount Holly was first settled by Quakers in 1676 and served as the capital of the state for 2 months in 1779. John Woolman, a Quaker abolitionist known for his 1774 journal, taught at the Old School House at 35 Brainerd St. Other historic buildings include the 18th- and 19th-century county buildings on High Street between Garden and Union streets.

Smithville Mansion, 2 miles east at 803 Smithville Rd. in nearby Eastampton's Smithville County Park, was the Greek Revival home of Hezekiah B. Smith, former owner of a local foundry and operator of the factory that produced the first "American Star" bicycles; one example of which can be seen within the home. Guided tours are available May through October; phone (609) 261-3295. Also within the restored mansion are period furnishings, including President James K. Polk's bed, and an art gallery. Christmas and candlelight tours are offered in December.

HISTORIC BURLINGTON COUNTY PRISON MUSEUM is at 128 High St. The museum's interior still looks much the same as it did during its years as a prison. Exhibits includes a re-created warden's office and adjacent home, a maximum-security cell and a kitchen. One display details changes to American prison cells throughout history. Architect Robert Mills also designed several Washington, D.C.-area buildings as well as the Washington Monument.

Time: Allow 45 minutes minimum. **Hours:** Thurs.-Sat. 10-4, Sun. noon-4. Closed major holidays. **Cost:** $5; $3 (ages 65+ and military with ID); $2 (students with ID); free (ages 0-4). Audio tour additional $3. **Phone:** (609) 265-5476 or (609) 265-5858.

(See map & index p. 192.)

CHARLIE BROWN'S STEAKHOUSE   609/265-1100
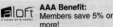 Steak. Casual Dining. **Address:** 949 Rt 541 08060

ROBIN'S NEST   609/261-6149   106
American. Casual Dining. **Address:** 2 Washington St 08060

MOUNT LAUREL elev. 82'
- Hotels & Restaurants map & index p. 192
- Part of Philadelphia area — see map p. 154

The Lenni-Lenape first called the Delaware Valley home until the 1700s when early European settlers, notably the Dutch, arrived fleeing religious persecution. Its proximity to Philadelphia helped increase the city's growth. The New Jersey Turnpike and I-295 both go through the community.

Laurel Acres Park, 1045 S. Church St., with its lake and grassy hill provide recreational opportunities such as fishing and, in winter, sledding. Concerts occur at the park, mainly in July and August. There's also a Veterans Memorial on-site. Phone (856) 234-0001, ext. 1220.

ALOFT MOUNT LAUREL   856/234-1880   91

Hotel
Rates not provided

 aloft **AAA Benefit:** Members save 5% or more!

Address: 558 Fellowship Rd 08054 **Location:** I-295 exit 36A, just se on SR 73 to Fellowship Rd, then just n. **Facility:** 154 units. 6 stories, interior corridors. **Bath:** shower only. **Amenities:** safes. **Pool:** heated indoor. **Activities:** exercise room. **Guest Services:** valet and coin laundry, area transportation.

CANDLEWOOD SUITES MT. LAUREL   856/642-7567   101
Extended Stay Hotel. **Address:** 4000 Crawford Pl 08054

COURTYARD BY MARRIOTT MT. LAUREL   (856)273-4400   92
Hotel. **Address:** 1000 Century Pkwy 08054

AAA Benefit: Members save 5% or more!

DOUBLETREE SUITES BY HILTON HOTEL MT. LAUREL   (856)778-8999   87

Hotel
$109-$299

DOUBLETREE BY HILTON

AAA Benefit: Members save 5% or more!

Address: 515 Fellowship Rd N 08054 **Location:** I-295 exit 36A, just se on SR 73 to Fellowship Rd, then just n. **Facility:** 204 units. 3 stories, interior corridors. **Terms:** 1-7 night minimum stay, cancellation fee imposed. **Amenities:** safes. **Pool:** heated indoor. **Activities:** hot tub, exercise room. **Guest Services:** valet and coin laundry.

EXTENDED STAY AMERICA PACILLI PLACE PHILADELPHIA/MT. LAUREL   (856)608-9820   97
Extended Stay Hotel. **Address:** 500 Diemer Dr 08054

FAIRFIELD INN & SUITES BY MARRIOTT MT. LAUREL   (856)642-0600   93
Hotel. **Address:** 350 Century Pkwy 08054

AAA Benefit: Members save 5% or more!

HAMPTON INN BY HILTON PHILADELPHIA/MT. LAUREL   (856)778-5535   98
Hotel. **Address:** 5000 Crawford Pl 08054

AAA Benefit: Members save up to 10%!

HILTON GARDEN INN-MT. LAUREL   (856)234-4788   96
Hotel. **Address:** 4000 Atrium Way 08054

AAA Benefit: Members save up to 10%!

HOMEWOOD SUITES BY HILTON PHILADELPHIA/MOUNT LAUREL   (856)222-9001   86
Extended Stay Hotel. **Address:** 1422 Nixon Dr 08054

AAA Benefit: Members save up to 10%!

HOTEL ML   (856)234-7300   88

Hotel
$64-$199

Address: 915 SR 73 N 08054 **Location:** New Jersey Tpke exit 4, northeast corner; I-295 exit 36A, just se. **Facility:** 280 units, some efficiencies. 10 stories, interior corridors. **Terms:** check-in 4 pm, cancellation fee imposed. **Amenities:** Some: safes. **Pool:** heated outdoor. **Activities:** exercise room. **Guest Services:** valet and coin laundry, area transportation.

(See map & index p. 192.)

HYATT HOUSE MT. LAUREL (856)222-1313 `100`

Extended Stay Hotel
$99-$299

HYATT house™
AAA Benefit: Members save 10%!

Address: 3000 Crawford Pl 08054 **Location:** I-295 exit 36A, 1.5 mi s on SR 73. **Facility:** 116 kitchen units, some two bedrooms. 3 stories (no elevator), exterior corridors. **Terms:** cancellation fee imposed. **Pool:** outdoor. **Activities:** picnic facilities, exercise room. **Guest Services:** valet and coin laundry. **Featured Amenity:** breakfast buffet.

HYATT PLACE MT. LAUREL (856)840-0770 `99`

Hotel
$99-$199

HYATT PLACE®
AAA Benefit: Members save 10%!

Address: 8000 Crawford Pl 08054 **Location:** I-295 exit 36A, 1.5 mi s on SR 73. **Facility:** 124 units. 6 stories, interior corridors. **Terms:** cancellation fee imposed. **Pool:** outdoor. **Activities:** exercise room. **Guest Services:** valet laundry. **Featured Amenity:** breakfast buffet.

/SOME UNITS

LA QUINTA INN & SUITES MT. LAUREL-PHILADELPHIA (856)235-7500 `94`

Hotel
$75-$159

Address: 5000 Clover Rd 08054 **Location:** New Jersey Tpke exit 4, just se; I-295 exit 36A, 0.8 mi se. **Facility:** 63 units, some two bedrooms. 3 stories, interior corridors. **Amenities:** safes. **Activities:** exercise room. **Guest Services:** valet and coin laundry. **Featured Amenity:** full hot breakfast.

/SOME UNITS

RESIDENCE INN BY MARRIOTT MOUNT LAUREL AT BISHOP'S GATE (856)234-1025 `85`

Extended Stay Hotel. **Address:** 1000 Bishops Gate Blvd 08054

AAA Benefit: Members save 5% or more!

STAYBRIDGE SUITES - MT. LAUREL 856)722-1900 `95`

Extended Stay Hotel
Rates not provided

Address: 4115 Church Rd 08054 **Location:** New Jersey Tpke exit 4, 0.5 mi s on SR 73, then 0.5 mi w. **Facility:** 99 efficiencies, some two bedrooms. 3 stories, interior corridors. **Terms:** check-in 4 pm. **Pool:** heated indoor. **Activities:** exercise room. **Guest Services:** complimentary and valet laundry. **Featured Amenity:** full hot breakfast.

/SOME UNITS

SUPER 8 (856)802-2800 `90`

Hotel. **Address:** 560 Fellowship Rd 08054

THE WESTIN MOUNT LAUREL (856)778-7300 `89`

Hotel
$149-$189

WESTIN HOTELS & RESORTS
AAA Benefit: Members save 5% or more!

Address: 555 Fellowship Rd 08054 **Location:** I-295 exit 36A, just se on SR 73 to Fellowship Rd, then just n. **Facility:** 173 units. 7 stories, interior corridors. **Parking:** on-site and valet. **Terms:** cancellation fee imposed. **Amenities:** safes. **Pool:** heated indoor. **Activities:** hot tub, exercise room. **Guest Services:** valet laundry.

/SOME UNITS

WHERE TO EAT

SAGE DINER 856/727-0770 `135`

American. Casual Dining. **Address:** 1170 Rt 73 & Church Rd 08054

SINGAPORE RESTAURANT AND SUSHI BAR 856/802-2888 `136`

Japanese. Casual Dining. **Address:** 1215 SR 73 08054

PENNSVILLE pop. 11,888, elev. 19'
• Part of Philadelphia area — see map p. 154

HAMPTON INN (856)351-1700

Hotel. **Address:** 429 N Broadway 08070

AAA Benefit: Members save up to 10%!

SUPER 8 PENNSVILLE/WILMINGTON (856)299-2992

Hotel. **Address:** 413 N Broadway 08070

RUNNEMEDE pop. 8,468
• Hotels & Restaurants map & index p. 192
• Part of Philadelphia area — see map p. 154

COMFORT INN & SUITES (856)312-8521 `119`

Hotel. **Address:** 109 E 9th Ave 08078

SALEM pop. 5,146, elev. 14'
• Part of Philadelphia area — see map p. 154

Settled in 1675 by Quakers, Salem is one of the oldest English settlements on the Delaware River. Its early importance as a port made it a prize during the Revolutionary War, when the city was occupied by the British. After the war Camden surpassed Salem as a shipping center, and attention turned to agriculture.

The restored 1721 Alexander Grant House, 4 miles south of town at 79-83 Market St., displays objects from the Colonial and Federal periods. Hancock House State Historic Site was the scene of a British-led massacre during the Revolutionary War. In retaliation against the Quaker community for supplying cattle to Gen. George Washington's starving troops at Valley Forge, 300 men under Maj. John Simcoe surprised and killed some 30 local militiamen asleep in the house;

among the dead was homeowner Judge William Hancock.

Built in 1734, the Hancock House is an excellent example of the English Quaker style of dwelling once prominent in the Lower Delaware Valley, which incorporated a distinctive feature of zigzagging lines of bricks at each end. The house is located at 3 Front St. in the nearby town of Hancocks Bridge, south of Salem via SR 49 to CR 658. It is open Wed.-Sun. 9-4; phone (856) 935-4373.

One survivor of this bygone era is an oak tree estimated to be more than 5 centuries old. It stands at the entrance to the Friends Burial Ground, 112 W. Broadway. Beneath its branches early settler John Fenwick bargained with the Lenni-Lenape people for the land on which Salem was established.

Salem County Chamber of Commerce: 174 E. Broadway, P.O. Box 71, Salem, NJ 08079. **Phone:** (856) 351-2245.

THOROFARE
• **Hotels & Restaurants map & index p. 192**
• **Part of Philadelphia area — see map p. 154**

BEST WESTERN WEST DEPTFORD INN
(856)848-4111 **136**

Hotel
$119-$150

 Best Western. AAA Benefit: Members save 5% to 15% and earn 10% bonus points!

Address: 98 Friars Blvd 08086 **Location:** I-295 exit 20, just e on Mid Atlantic Pkwy, then 0.4 mi n. **Facility:** 100 units. 2 stories, interior corridors. **Terms:** cancellation fee imposed. **Pool:** outdoor. **Activities:** limited exercise equipment. **Guest Services:** valet and coin laundry. **Featured Amenity:** breakfast buffet.

VOORHEES
• **Hotels & Restaurants map & index p. 192**
• **Part of Philadelphia area — see map p. 154**

HAMPTON INN PHILADELPHIA/VOORHEES
856/751-1212 **114**

Hotel. **Address:** 320 Rt 73 S 08043

AAA Benefit: Members save up to 10%!

SPRINGHILL SUITES BY MARRIOTT VOORHEES MT. LAUREL/CHERRY HILL
(856)782-2555 **115**

Hotel. **Address:** 1031 Voorhees Dr 08043

AAA Benefit: Members save 5% or more!

WHERE TO EAT

BLACK OLIVE   856/435-5500 **161**

Greek. Casual Dining. **Address:** 910 Haddonfield Berlin Rd 08043

PASSARIELLO'S PIZZERIA & ITALIAN EATERY
856/784-7272 **162**

Italian. Buffet Style. **Address:** 111 Laurel Oak Rd 08043

WESTAMPTON

• **Hotels & Restaurants map & index p. 192**
• **Part of Philadelphia area — see map p. 154**

BEST WESTERN BURLINGTON INN
(609)261-3800 **71**

Hotel
$89-$129

 Best Western. AAA Benefit: Members save 5% to 15% and earn 10% bonus points!

Address: 2020 Burlington Mt Holly Rd 08060 **Location:** New Jersey Tpke exit 5, just n. **Facility:** 87 units. 2 stories, interior corridors. **Terms:** cancellation fee imposed. **Pool:** heated indoor. **Activities:** exercise room. **Guest Services:** coin laundry.

COURTYARD BY MARRIOTT BURLINGTON MT. HOLLY/WESTAMPTON
(609)261-6161 **69**

Hotel. **Address:** 30 Western Dr 08060

AAA Benefit: Members save 5% or more!

HILTON GARDEN INN MT. HOLLY/WESTAMPTON
(609)702-1600 **72**

Hotel. **Address:** 111 Hancock Ln 08060

AAA Benefit: Members save up to 10%!

HOLIDAY INN EXPRESS HOTEL & SUITES BURLINGTON/MT. HOLLY
609/702-5800 **70**

Hotel
Rates not provided

Address: 18 Western Dr 08060 **Location:** New Jersey Tpke exit 5, 0.3 mi n. **Facility:** 76 units. 3 stories, interior corridors. **Amenities:** safes. **Pool:** heated indoor. **Activities:** exercise room. **Guest Services:** valet and coin laundry. **Featured Amenity:** breakfast buffet.

RED ROOF INN & SUITES WESTHAMPTON
(609)845-9400 **73**

Hotel. **Address:** 2015 Burlington Mt Holly Rd 08060

WILLIAMSTOWN pop. 15,567
• **Part of Philadelphia area — see map p. 154**

BEST WESTERN MONROE INN & SUITES
(856)340-7900

Hotel
$90-$260

 Best Western. AAA Benefit: Members save 5% to 15% and earn 10% bonus points!

Address: 1151 N Black Horse Pike 08094 **Location:** New Jersey Tpke exit 3, 3.2 mi s on SR 168, then 9 mi s on SR 42; 2 mi s of jct CR 689. **Facility:** 44 units. 2 stories, interior corridors. **Terms:** cancellation fee imposed. **Pool:** heated indoor. **Activities:** exercise room. **Guest Services:** coin laundry.

WOODBURY pop. 10,174, elev. 34'
• Part of Philadelphia area — see map p. 154

Woodbury was occupied by British troops in November 1777. Gen. Charles Cornwallis chose as his headquarters the home of John Cooper, a Continental Congress member denounced for his patriotism by his pacifist Quaker friends. A number of Revolutionary War-era buildings have been preserved.

"Light Horse" Harry Lee, father of Robert E. Lee, made Woodbury his headquarters during military campaigns in South Jersey in 1779. Other local notables include Commodore Stephen Decatur and Capt. James Lawrence, both of whom attended Woodbury Academy. The Hunter-Lawrence-Jessup House, 58 N. Broad St., was the boyhood home of Lawrence, known for his dying command "Don't give up the ship," uttered during the War of 1812. His former home now houses the Gloucester County Historical Society Museum. Exhibits include textiles, samplers, toys, dolls, military artifacts and a Colonial-era kitchen; phone (856) 848-8531.

Greater Woodbury Chamber of Commerce: P.O. Box 363, Woodbury, NJ 08096. **Phone:** (856) 845-4056.

CHARLIE BROWN'S STEAKHOUSE   856/853-8505
Steak. Casual Dining. **Address:** 111 N Broad St 08096

This ends the Philadelphia section and resumes the alphabetical city listings for Pennsylvania.

PINE FORGE

GRACIE'S 21ST CENTURY CAFE AND CATERING
610/323-4004
American. Fine Dining. **Address:** Manatawny Rd 19548

PINE GROVE pop. 2,186

COMFORT INN   (570)345-8031

Hotel
$80-$200

Address: 433 Suedberg Rd 17963 **Location:** I-81 exit 100, just e. **Facility:** 68 units. 3 stories, interior corridors. **Amenities:** safes. **Pool:** heated indoor. **Activities:** game room, exercise room. **Featured Amenity:** continental breakfast.

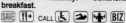

HAMPTON INN PINE GROVE   (570)345-4505
Hotel. **Address:** 481 Suedberg Rd 17963

AAA Benefit: Members save up to 10%!

Pittsburgh

Then & Now

The view of Pittsburgh's skyline is stunning as you emerge from the Fort Pitt Tunnel, where the Allegheny, Monongahela and Ohio rivers converge and modern monoliths soar majestically beyond. Shame on visitors expecting to see a gritty steel mill town engulfed in smoke for Pittsburgh doesn't deserve the bad rap of its past—the city has cleaned itself up and undergone a renaissance. Steel mills have been replaced by high-tech and healthcare concerns, and more than 30 institutions of higher learning now exist in "The College City."

Pittsburgh has received accolades for urban beauty, and a prime example is Point State Park, flanked by the three mighty rivers, a majestic fountain at one end and the skyscrapers of the downtown Golden Triangle at the other. The Three Rivers Heritage Trail guides hikers, joggers and cyclists along 24 miles of riverfront turf, while locals and tourists alike enjoy the equestrian paths and the occasional evening jazz concert at Riverview Park. An extensive trail system snakes through woodlands and steep valleys at Frick Park, while peaceful urban exploration via kayak or canoe is an option on the Allegheny River Trail.

AAA.com/travelguides—
more ways to look, book and save

Many names gracing buildings and other venues serve as reminders of the philanthropic families that figured prominently in the city's development. There's Heinz Hall, home of the Pittsburgh Symphony Orchestra; Senator John Heinz History Center; and football arena Heinz Field. Mellon Bank Center carves out a space in the skyline and Mellon Square is a modernist rooftop garden plaza. Carnegie Mellon University is one of the area's leading educational institutions, and the Carnegie Museums of Pittsburgh offer are a treasure to anyone captivated by art, science and natural history.

Point State Park fountain

What's nice about Pittsburgh is that it has big-city amenities, yet retains a small-town feel. The city's unique neighborhoods stand as proud symbols of ethnic diversity: Squirrel Hill, home of one of the region's largest Jewish populations; Bloomfield, known as "Little Italy"; the North Side, with traces of the old German community that immigrated in the early 19th century; and Polish Hill, where Polish immigrants settled in the late 1800s. In all, Pittsburgh has nearly 90 neighborhoods.

All Pittsburghers come together to demonstrate spirit for their beloved sports teams: the Steelers (football), Penguins (hockey) and Pirates (baseball). Home games are a sea of black

(Continued on p. 226.)

Destination Pittsburgh

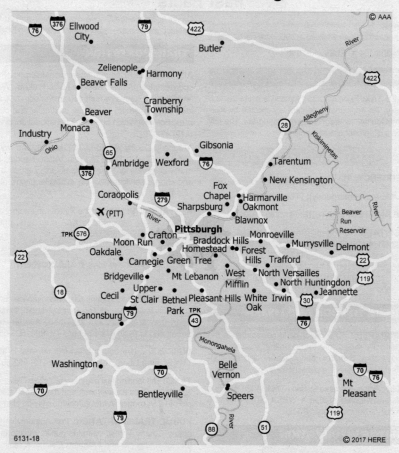

This map shows cities in the Pittsburgh vicinity where you will find attractions, hotels and restaurants. Cities are listed alphabetically in this book on the following pages.

Fast Facts

ABOUT THE CITY

POP: 305,704 ■ **ELEV:** 1,370 ft.

MONEY

SALES TAX: Pennsylvania's statewide sales tax is 6 percent. An additional 1 percent is collected by Allegheny County, as is a 7 percent lodging tax. The city levies a 5 percent amusements tax.

WHOM TO CALL

EMERGENCY: 911

POLICE (non-emergency): (412) 323-7800

TIME AND TEMPERATURE: (412) 391-9500

HOSPITALS: Allegheny General Hospital, (412) 359-3131 ■ UPMC Mercy, (412) 232-8111 ■ UPMC Passavant—McCandless, (412) 367-6700 ■ UPMC Presbyterian, (412) 647-2345 ■ UPMC St. Margaret, (412) 784-4000 ■ West Penn Hospital, (412) 578-5000.

WHERE TO LOOK AND LISTEN

NEWSPAPERS: The major daily newspaper is the morning *Post-Gazette,* found online at www.post-gazette.com. Smaller daily, weekly and special-interest papers also are published.

RADIO: Pittsburgh radio station KDKA (1020 AM) is a news/talk/weather station ■ WESA (90.5 FM) is a member of National Public Radio.

VISITOR INFORMATION

Welcome Pittsburgh Information Center and Gift Shop: 120 Fifth Ave., Pittsburgh, PA 15222. **Phone:** (412) 281-7711 or (800) 359-0758.

Three other visitor centers also provide maps, brochures, event schedules and sightseeing companies. They're at the Pittsburgh International Airport, at the David L. Lawrence Convention Center and at the Senator John Heinz History Center in the Strip District.

TRANSPORTATION

AIR TRAVEL: Pittsburgh International Airport (PIT), approximately 19 miles west via I-376 (Parkway West) and SR 60 is served by numerous major domestic and international carriers as well as commuter and cargo lines. For information on ground transportation, phone (412) 472-3525.

Allegheny County Airport (AGC), south of the city on Lebanon Church Road in West Mifflin, handles primarily corporate or private aircraft, although air taxis and charter services also are available; phone (412) 466-1275.

RENTAL CARS: Hertz, at the Pittsburgh International Airport, offers discounts to AAA members; phone (412) 472-5955 or (800) 654-3080.

 Book and save at AAA.com/hertz

RAIL SERVICE: An Amtrak passenger service station is on the lower level of The Pennsylvanian, formerly Penn Central Station, at 1100 Liberty Ave. at Grant Street; phone (800) 872-7245 or TTY (800) 523-6590.

BUSES: The Greyhound Lines Inc. terminal is at 55 11th St. near Liberty Avenue; phone (412) 392-6514.

TAXIS: The leading taxi company is Yellow Cab, (412) 321-8100. Cabs are metered, and the base rate is $4 plus $1.75 per mile. A fuel surcharge may be charged.

PUBLIC TRANSPORTATION: Port Authority of Allegheny County Transit operates public transportation throughout the city and Allegheny County. A section of downtown Pittsburgh is a fare free zone. Other areas have a base fare of $2.75; exact change is required. Discounted fares are available through the purchase of weekly or monthly passes, which can be purchased at the transit's downtown service center at 534 Smithfield St. For route information, phone (412) 442-2000.

(Continued from p. 224.)

and gold as devoted fans show off the colors adopted by all three teams—it's a brave soul who dons an opposing team's jersey.

Tradition also plays a part in the form of food icons and the friendly neighborhood grocer. Pittsburghers grew up with Isaly's Chipped Chopped Ham in the fridge, a household staple since the 1930s still satisfying cravings today. Many locals consider Sarris Candies to be one of the nation's best confectioners, and numerous pubs and restaurants continue to serve pierogis, those soul-satisfying dumplings filled with such ingredients as potatoes, cheese, bacon and sauerkraut. Generations of Pittsburghers have sampled the namesake beer of Iron City Brewing Co., a fixture since 1861 and once delivered to homes via horse-drawn carriage. In the Strip District, named for a narrow plot of land between the river and the hillside, you'll find mom and pop businesses devoted entirely to popcorn, cheese, freshly baked bread, biscotti, coffee and other culinary delights. Stores like Pennsylvania Macaroni Co., with its remarkable selection of pastas, olive oil and all things Italian, and Wholey's fish market, where patrons still line up and take a number on busy Saturdays to snare a fresh catch, are like family to Strip District shoppers.

Must Do: AAA Editor's Picks

- Introduce yourself to Pittsburgh by visiting 🐾 **Point State Park** (601 Commonwealth Pl.), an urban green space with a dramatic view—this is where the Monongahela, Allegheny and Ohio rivers converge. Visit the 🐾 **Fort Pitt Museum**, stroll along riverside walkways or take a seat by the fountain at the park's edge, where you'll spy such sites as PNC Park, Heinz Field and the 🐾 **Carnegie Science Center** across the water.

- Spend time in the **Strip District** (around 21st St. & Penn Ave.) and explore its delightful mom-and-pop groceries, bakeries and restaurants touting everything from homemade lasagna to first-rate espresso. Do as the locals do and grab a hearty breakfast at **Deluca's Diner** (2015 Penn Ave.), shop for culinary specialties at the Pennsylvania Macaroni Company (2010 Penn Ave.), and appreciate the circuslike atmosphere at **Wholey's** (1711 Penn Ave.), a fish market.

- **See a game.** Whether you prefer hockey (Penguins), football (Steelers) or baseball (Pirates), this town comes to a standstill when its beloved sports teams are playing. And Pittsburgh has definitely earned bragging rights: the Steelers won the Super Bowl in 2009, with the Penguins following suit by nabbing the Stanley Cup title in June 2009, 2016 and 2017.

- Explore Pittsburgh's **Golden Triangle** area in the heart of downtown. The cultural district presents an assortment of trendy restaurants and nightlife opportunities—the Benedum Center for the Performing Arts (237 7th St.) hosts ballet and Broadway performances, while the Cabaret at Theater Square (655 Penn Ave.) offers year-round musical productions.

- Ride the city's 2 remaining inclines—there were once 15 scaling the steep hills. The **Duquesne Incline** (1197 W. Carson St.), facing the Ohio River, offers dramatic views of the city. The city's other funicular, the **Monongahela Incline** (W. Carson & Smithfield sts.), is the steepest in the United States.

- Tour the 🐾 **Cathedral of Learning** (4200 5th Ave.) at the University of Pittsburgh. You can't miss the massive Gothic Revival structure—the 42-story behemoth is said to be the world's second tallest educational building. Inside, you can explore some 30 nationality classrooms and learn about the culture and heritage of Pittsburgh's ethnic communities.

- Immerse yourself on **Carson Street** in "the Burgh's" South Side. Lined with funky shops, nightspots and eateries, Carson has a bit of a bohemian flair. The main drag is sandwiched between two large shopping complexes, Station Square (near the Smithfield Street Bridge) and SouthSide Works at the east end.

- **Cruise Pittsburgh's three mighty rivers**—the Monongahela, Allegheny and Ohio. The riverboat captains of 🐾 **Gateway Clipper Fleet** (350 W. Station Square Dr.) provide historical anecdotes as well as information about various landmarks during your sightseeing trip. **Just Ducky Tours** (125 W. Station Square Dr.) supplies amphibious vehicles that can explore city streets as well as slide into the water.

- View thousands of stunning art and science objects at the 🐾 **Carnegie Museums of Pittsburgh** (4400 Forbes Ave.). Discover the world of pop art at **The Andy Warhol Museum**, experience American and European works at the **Carnegie Museum of Art**, gaze at dinosaur fossils at the 🐾 **Carnegie Museum of Natural History** and see a laser show, visit the planetarium or explore the **USS Requin** submarine at the 🐾 **Carnegie Science Center.**

- Celebrate the city's ethnic diversity by visiting some of its vibrant **neighborhoods.** Traces of Germany are reflected in the schnitzel, sausages and tasty brews of the North Side; Bloomfield's "Little Italy" houses an assortment of Italian groceries; and while Squirrel Hill is the epicenter of the city's Jewish population, you'll also find Chinese, Middle Eastern and Greek culinary offerings.

Fort Pitt Museum

Pittsburgh 1-day Itinerary

AAA editors suggest these activities for a great short vacation experience.

Morning

- Start your day by visiting ⟲ **Point State Park** (601 Commonwealth Pl.) to get your bearings while enjoying a scenic perspective of Pittsburgh's epicenter. The triangular-shaped park juts forth from downtown's edge, with a majestic fountain marking the point where the Allegheny, Monongahela and Ohio rivers meet. With a backdrop of soaring skyscrapers behind you, you'll have fun identifying landmarks across the water like Heinz Field and PNC Park on the North Shore. Visit the ⟲ **Fort Pitt Museum** to learn how the fort's strategic position played an integral role in our nation's history.

- It's a quick hop over the Fort Duquesne Bridge to investigate a few of the attractions you likely glimpsed from the park. On the North Shore, explore your choice of facilities affiliated with the ⟲ **Carnegie Museums of Pittsburgh** (4400 Forbes Ave.). The ⟲ **Carnegie Science Center** spans a variety of topics; whether you're intrigued by miniature railroads, sports challenges or aquarium life, you can tailor your experience to be as laid-back or interactive as you wish—and the matinee and night laser shows dazzle viewers. Navigate your way through the **USS Requin**, a Tench-class submarine launched in 1945 now docked adjacent to the museum. If pop art captures your attention, swing by **The Andy Warhol Museum**, a shrine to the artist's various pursuits, including sculpture, painting, photography, film and video.

- If you're in an outdoors frame of mind, another option is to take one of the sightseeing cruises offered by the ⟲ **Gateway Clipper Fleet** (350 W. Station Square Dr.), departing from the city's South Shore across the Fort Pitt Bridge. In addition to appreciating prime city views, you'll learn about local history and the three rivers the vessel sails upon.

Afternoon

- For a real slice of Pittsburgh life, head to the **Strip District,** a narrow, mile-long pocket just northeast of downtown wedged between 11th and 33rd Streets. Most of the action takes place on the main drags of Smallman Street and Penn Avenue.

- Since the Strip is all about food, it's a phenomenal lunch stop, with plenty of options on Penn Avenue. Seafood aficionados on the run should stop by **Wholey's** (1711 Penn Ave.), a market that also happens to serve up a mighty fine fish sandwich. If you're in the mood for a deli sandwich, burger or entrée salad, try **Deluca's Diner** (2015 Penn Ave.), a local favorite that's also a popular breakfast haunt. To sample innovative Caribbean fare in an eclectic setting, head to **Kaya Restaurant,** around the corner at 2000 Smallman St.

The Andy Warhol Museum

- After lunch, wander around the district and peruse the sidewalk vendors—a great place to grab that Steelers T-Shirt or whatever souvenir catches your eye. It's fun to browse the locally owned Italian groceries and sample such delectable goods as cheeses, olive oils, espresso, freshly baked breads, biscotti, chocolate and other confections. A sprinkling of unique shops offers fashion accessories and trinkets for the home and garden.

- You could also visit the University of Pittsburgh campus, about 3 miles east of downtown in the Oakland neighborhood. The must-see here is the ⟲ **Cathedral of Learning** (4200 5th Ave.), the campus' regal centerpiece and one of the world's tallest educational structures. A self-guiding tour will lead you through Nationality Rooms where you can learn about the cultures represented.

Evening

- The South Side is a prime evening destination. Eateries and clubs are scattered along the stretch of Carson Street between the Station Square and SouthSide Works shopping and entertainment complexes. The **Hard Rock Cafe** at Station Square offers crowds, lively music and typical American fare. For more of a funky neighborhood feel, check out **Primanti Bros.** (2 S. Market Sq.), known for sliding French fries into their sandwiches; it has been a hit with Pittsburghers since 1933. After dinner, join the pub crawl among the street's cornucopia of nightspots.

Arriving
By Car

The primary highway from the north or the south is I-79, which passes through the western edge of the metropolitan area. Intersecting with east-west routes I-76 (Pennsylvania Turnpike) on the north and with I-70 on the south, I-79 funnels traffic into Pittsburgh via controlled-access I-279 (Parkway West) and the Fort Pitt Tunnel from Carnegie.

A second approach is I-279 (Parkway North) from Cranberry, and from the south via Banksville Road and I-279. US 19 Truck Route, using East Street from the north and West Liberty Avenue from the south, carries heavy commercial and industrial traffic into the city.

I-76 carries the bulk of east-west traffic through the area, interchanging en route with all major arteries; I-376 through the eastern suburbs provides the principal link to the heart of the city, arriving downtown via Grant Street exit 1C. Two other important east-west highways are US 22 and US 30, which combine upon nearing the city, then join expressways I-376 before entering the downtown area.

SR 28, first as the Allegheny Valley Expressway, then as E. Ohio Street, follows the north bank of the Allegheny River into the city's North Side, providing a route from northeast suburbs. Similarly, SR 60 makes an easy connection from the northwestern suburbs along the south side of the Ohio River, picking up airport traffic before joining with US 22/30.

Getting Around
Street System

Pittsburgh's topography—a maze of hills and ravines sliced at an acute angle by two rivers converging to form a third—permits no consistent geometrical street layout. Instead, there is a patchwork of patterns dictated mainly by the lay of the land. A good street map is necessary for travel in this city.

From the Golden Triangle major thoroughfares fan out more or less parallel to the Allegheny and Monongahela rivers, with intervening streets perpendicular to the rivers near the Point but following the contours of the hills farther out. Fifth Avenue and Liberty Avenue are the primary arteries.

On the north side, at least the sections nearest the river, the picture is more regular, with avenues running parallel to the Allegheny River and streets perpendicular to it. All the major thoroughfares seem to converge on Allegheny Center, framed by N., E., S. and W. Commons. E. Ohio Street and Western Avenue feed in from the east and west, respectively; East Street, Federal Street, Brighton Avenue and Allegheny Avenue reach the center from the north.

The near edge of the hilly south side is the only part of the city that employs the designations East and West, using the Smithfield Street Bridge as the dividing line. Carson Street (SR 837), parallel to the river, is the main artery through this area.

Smithfield Street Bridge

Most of Pittsburgh's streets are named; there are relatively few areas of consecutively numbered thoroughfares. Two such locations are on the Point, where 1st through 7th avenues are numbered northward from the Monongahela River, and inland from the Allegheny River, where numbered streets increase as they proceed upstream.

A series of marked alternate routes known as the "Belt Routes" were developed to relieve congestion on the major highways and to aid travelers in and around the city. The five Belt Routes that loop Greater Pittsburgh and link various towns and highways are posted throughout the metropolitan area with color-coded signs (red, green, blue, yellow and orange). The purple belt circles the Golden Triangle.

The downtown speed limit, unless otherwise posted, is 25 mph, and on major thoroughfares, 35 mph. Unless a sign prohibits it, turning right at a red light after coming to a complete stop is legal. Similarly, so is turning left from one one-way street onto another. Pedestrians always have the right-of-way, particularly at marked crosswalks. Jaywalking, however, is illegal, and the law is strictly enforced. Driving during rush hours, about 6:30-9 a.m. and 4-6:30 p.m., should be avoided if possible.

Parking

As in any big city, parking downtown or near the major attractions is at a premium. On-street parking, when a space can be found, is governed by the meter system. However, commercial parking lots and garages are plentiful throughout. Rates cost about $5-$6 per hour to $25 per day.

Shopping

Pittsburgh's neighborhoods provide happy hunting grounds for those inclined to pop into trendy boutiques, bookstores and locally owned mom and pops offering unique home furnishings and all forms of bric-a-brac. You'll mostly find malls and their anchors in the suburbs, while themed complexes downtown and in its environs offer the shopper a little something extra—entertainment, cute bistros and other diversions amid popular chains and specialty retailers.

The downtown **Golden Triangle** is defined as the area roughly from Point State Park to Crosstown Boulevard, tucked between the Allegheny River on the north and the Monongahela River on the south. If you're in the market for some classy baubles, make a beeline to the **Clark Building** at Liberty Avenue and Seventh Street. Considered the city's "diamond district," the art deco structure contains retail, wholesale and estate jewelers.

Fifth Avenue Place reigns proudly at Fifth and Liberty, an impressive landmark crowned with a massive pyramid and steeple. It's a favorite haunt of downtown professionals who dash in during lunch to search for clothes and gifts.

Forbes Avenue, near Carnegie Mellon University in the **Oakland** neighborhood is south of Fifth Avenue, and features shopping and dining near the school and medical centers.

East of downtown, there are several neighborhoods chock full of shopping delights. Closest to the Golden Triangle is the thriving **Strip District** (named for a narrow, mile-long stretch), where you'll find a delectable selection of culinary items—locals come here for pastas, exotic coffees, luscious pastries, gourmet finds and ethnic specialties. The Strip is in full swing on Saturday mornings, a colorful array of street performers, food and knick-knack vendors, and farmers displaying fresh produce. The **16:62 Design Zone**, extending from the district's 16th Street Bridge to the 62nd Street Bridge in Lawrenceville, hosts a plethora of businesses focusing on furniture and home décor. One of the city's oldest neighborhoods, **Lawrenceville** also contributes to the retail scene by way of eclectic boutiques and art studios—you'll find them dotted along Butler Street, Penn Avenue and Hatfield Street.

The **Shadyside** neighborhood is about 15 minutes east of downtown. Popular chains and specialty stores are sprinkled throughout upscale **Walnut Street**, with trendy cafés in-between perfect for refueling. **Ellsworth Avenue** presents a more local spin, punctuated with home accessory shops, art galleries and the occasional coffee place. You'll also stumble across some unique finds on the area's side streets.

The **South Craig Street** business district is the commercial hub of **Oakland**, another East End neighborhood. Refurbished row houses contain funky little bistros frequented by University of Pittsburgh and Carnegie Mellon University students, while businesses tout books, gifts and other knick-knacks. The shops of **Squirrel Hill**, east of Oakland, are mainly situated on Murray and Forbes. Kosher groceries, ethnic eateries and locally owned businesses selling novelty items from a variety of cultures give the area a real international flair, and it's fun hunting for resale clothing and souvenirs while indulging your sweet tooth at a bakery or coffeehouse.

The area south of downtown across the Monongahela River also holds allure for shoppers. Conveniently, there's a subway ("T") stop at the [SAVE] **Shops at Station Square**, situated on Carson Street at the Smithfield Street Bridge. Savor the view of Pittsburgh's skyline from this refurbished 19th-century railroad station with some 20 retailers, including [SAVE] **Hard Rock Cafe**. Station Square is also a popular dining, entertainment and nightlife venue. **SouthSide Works**, East Carson and 27th streets, is an outdoor complex complete with town square. High-end boutiques of both national and local stature are the draw here, and you'll also have your pick of the best-loved chains. Those just along for the ride can enjoy a movie or a meal. (Incidentally, the stretch of **East Carson Street** linking Station Square with SouthSide Works is inhabited by jewelry, antique and novelty stores as well as plenty of cafes, bars and coffeehouses.) Farther southeast across the Homestead Grays Bridge (formerly the High-Level Bridge) and recognizable by its massive brick smokestacks, **The Waterfront** provides open-air shopping and entertainment bordering the Monongahela River on the site of a former steel mill; the 260-acre retail behemoth's temptations are enhanced by the sweeping river view.

The suburban mall is alive and kicking in Pittsburgh, and if you arrived via plane you probably had

Stop for coffee in the Strip District

your first taste of mall mania as you wandered past the vast assortment of shops and restaurants at **Fraport USA** (formerly the AIRMALL). Near the airport off SR 60, **Robinson Town Centre** and **The Mall at Robinson** serve the western suburbs. The southern suburbs tout the 130-store **South Hills Village,** off US 19 between Upper St. Clair and Bethel Park. In Bethel Park at the intersection of US 19 and Fort Couch Road, **Village Square** specializes in such discounters as Burlington and Kohl's. In the South Hills off US 19 is the **Galleria of Mt. Lebanon,** which features Ann Taylor, Williams-Sonoma and other chains.

Heading east on US 22 near the Pennsylvania Turnpike is **Monroeville Mall;** its 160 establishments are the commercial heart of this suburban region. Northeast of Pittsburgh off SR 28 exit 12A in Tarentum is **Galleria at Pittsburgh Mills,** with JC-Penney and Macy's. Farther out tucked into the North Hills are **McIntyre Square, North Hills Village, The Block Northway** and the upscale **Ross Park Mall**—all on McKnight Road. Branches of most large department stores can be found amid these four shopping complexes.

Nightlife

Pittsburghers like to mingle, and the city's thriving brew pubs and neighborhood bars provide the perfect setting for a game of pool, some friendly chat or nibbling on homemade pierogis and other flavorsome bites. Those musically inclined can opt for an evening at one of the live music venues or dance the night away to the pulsating beat of DJ-inspired tunes. Clubs providing entertainment may include cover charges and usually require drink minimums. To avoid surprises, phone ahead and confirm prices, opening hours, scheduled acts and dress codes.

If you appreciate well-crafted drafts, you've come to the right place. Ironically, copper tanks have replaced the altar at **Church Brew Works** (Lawrenceville/(412) 688-8200). Instead of sermons, this former cathedral now serves up piously named house brews and creative pub grub under its soaring ceilings—fans of dark lager should try the heavenly Pious Monk Dunkel. **Fat Head's Saloon** (South Side/(412) 431-7433) attracts all walks, from business types to partying sports fans. Knowledgeable bartenders in this bustling spot will provide tips on which of the tapped beers, bottles or artery-clogging headwiches (head-size sandwiches) are right for you.

German-style lagers are showcased at (North Side/(412) 237-9400), where live polka tunes and an outdoor biergarten add to the merriment in a family style atmosphere—try their top-notch Penn Pilsner along with some authentic German fare. No more authentic German experience will be found though, than at the **Hofbrauhaus Pittsburgh** (South Side/(412) 224-2328), modeled after the famous beerhall in Munich. **Piper's Pub** (South Side/(412) 381-3977), offering a solid selection of English draughts and bottles, entertains a jolly assortment of British expats who gather to watch soccer and feast

Shop at Village Square

on across-the-pond favorites like bangers and mash. Belgian beer fans can indulge themselves with hard-to-find concoctions at **Sharp Edge Beer Emporium** (Friendship/(412) 661-3537), but whatever your preference, it's hard to go away unhappy with a menu touting some 300 international choices. The budget-minded should hit the weekday happy hour (4:30-6:30) for half-off Belgian and craft drafts.

Pittsburgh's dance clubs appeal mostly to 20- and 30-somethings looking for a rousing party scene. If you want some fog with your colored lights, check out **Diesel Club Lounge** (South Side/(412) 651-4713), a big-city style multilevel club. Whether you're there for the stellar sound system, DJ-inspired gyrating or concerts appealing to varied age groups, you can check out the action from the catwalks looming above.

Pittsburgh offers a decent selection of live music venues showcasing diverse talent. Hipsters interested in listening to underground, alternative and indie bands frequent **Brillobox** (Lawrenceville/(412) 621-4900)—downstairs caters to diners, so venture upstairs to catch live acts. If you like the type of place where you're just a stone's throw away from the performers, **Club Café** (South Side/(412) 431-4950) hosts emerging and established artists presenting everything from jazz to blues to pop in a stylishly cozy spot catering to the sophisticated urbanite. **Moondog's** (Blawnox area/(412) 828-2040) is a little out of the way—you'll definitely need a set of wheels to get there—but the journey to this no-frills neighborhood pub is worth it for fans of quality rhythm and blues, country and rock.

The congregation at **Mr. Smalls** (Millvale/(412) 821-4447), in a former Catholic church, is now made up of reggae, punk, rock and hip-hop followers—the great acoustics also make this a popular concert stop for nationally known bands. The art deco inspired **Rex Theater** (South Side/(412) 381-6811), a Pittsburgh institution that has been around since the early 1900s, also delights with an array of local and national acts in a refurbished movie house.

If you're into sipping an inventive cocktail, chatting with friends or just plain people watching, Pittsburgh has a healthy sampling of lounges to choose from. Martinis of all colors mixed with 80s music are a stable at the **Lava Lounge** (South Side/(412) 431-5282). If you like to get in on the act with a little piano bar/karaoke fun, pop into **Howl at the Moon** (Downtown/(412) 586-5692) for your shot at local stardom for a night. Downtown professionals decompress at **Olive or Twist** (Downtown/(412) 255-0525), an upscale enclave known for its tantalizing menu of classic and contemporary martinis. Oenophiles usually land at the classy lounge at **Le Lyonnais** (Downtown/(412) 697-1336), boasting some 100 wines by the glass with a collection largely influenced by West Coast vintners. For a tropical twist, head to **Tiki Lounge** (South Side/(412) 381-8454), where the South Pacific ambience will ease you into an island state of mind. Cocktails with names like Coconut Kiss, Head Hunter and Blue Shark help you unwind, and you get to keep the kitschy yet fun drink container as a souvenir.

Big Events

The **David L. Lawrence Convention Center** hosts many public events throughout the year. In mid-January there is the **Pittsburgh RV Show,**

Enjoy a drink a Tiki Lounge

which features motor homes, travel trailers and fifth wheels as well as accessories. The **Pittsburgh International Auto Show,** held in early February, gives car enthusiasts the opportunity to view new car, truck and motorcycle models. In early March, the **Pittsburgh Home and Garden Show** fills the center.

Over ten days in early June Pittsburgh celebrates the ▽ **Three Rivers Arts Festival** at **Gateway Center** and **Point State Park** as well as throughout the **Cultural District:** There are programs and productions of just about everything cultural the city has to offer, including art, dance, music, theater and mime.

The ▽ **Pittsburgh Three Rivers Regatta** occurs over the first weekend in August at Point State Park. In addition to the regatta, dozens of other events are held as well.

In late August, sample Mediterranean cuisine at the **Taste of Greece Festival,** and experience **Shadyside Art Festival on Walnut Street,** which attracts artists, craftsmen, browsers and music aficionados. The **Pittsburgh Irish Festival** is held in early September at **The Riverplex at Sandcastle.** Mid-November begins the holiday season as downtown buildings show off their light displays at **Light Up Night.**

Sports & Rec

That Pittsburghers are avid sports lovers is well known from the citywide celebrations that followed all the Steelers' Super Bowl victories and the Penguins' Stanley Cup victories. However, the city offers abundant and convenient opportunities for recreational pursuits as well; nearly every imaginable sport or recreational pastime is available. **Boating** is very popular on Pittsburgh's three rivers.

The focus for much recreation is the city and county parks. **Frick, Highland** and **Schenley** parks offer ball fields, **tennis** courts, **golf** courses and trails for **bicycling** and **hiking.** In winter, golf courses and hilly areas are popular for **cross-country skiing.** Information about facilities and current activities in the city parks can be obtained from the City Parks and Recreation Department; phone (412) 255-2539.

Allegheny County's **North Park** and **South Park** have plenty of the above activities as well as **swimming** pools, nearby bicycle rentals, **ice-skating** in winter and game preserves. In addition, North Park's lake offers **fishing,** boating and boat rentals. For more information about county park programs and activities contact Allegheny County Parks; phone (412) 350-7275. **The Rink at PPG Place,** (412) 394-3641, and **Schenley Park Rink,** (412) 422-6523, also offer ice-skating late November through early March.

Bicycling devotees have the advantage of a city bicycle route that links Highland, **Mellon,** Frick and Schenley parks. Near Highland Park is the **Washington Boulevard Cycling Track,** a half-mile slightly banked oval. The City Parks and Recreation

Department can provide route information; phone (412) 255-2539. **Riverview Park** on the city's North Side features hiking trails and the Allegheny Observatory, an astronomy research center. Tours are offered April through October (by reservation only); phone (412) 321-2400.

Hiking is popular, as the number of hiking groups and programs attest. The Sierra Club and Venture Outdoors can furnish information about hiking, **canoeing** and **camping** in the area. In winter many of the city's hiking paths become **ski** trails. Besides the cross-country skiing provided by the city and county park areas, Allegheny County's **Boyce Park,** on Old Frankstown Road in nearby Plum, offers downhill skiing, cross-country skiing and **snow tubing.** Instruction and equipment rental are offered; phone (724) 327-0338 for general information or (724) 733-4665 for snow conditions. Equipment also can be rented at several ski shops, some of which also arrange ski trips and tours.

The **Three Rivers Heritage Trail** caters to bicyclists as well as walkers and joggers with its 24 miles of bicycle and pedestrian pathways; **in-line skating** is possible on some portions, too. The trail runs along the Allegheny, Monongahela and Ohio rivers. For route details and other information contact the Friends of the Riverfront Inc. at (412) 488-0212.

In addition to the courses in the parks, golf is available at a number of excellent public courses. Inquire at your hotel, for some might have a reciprocal golf club agreement for their guests with one of the local private or semiprivate courses.

Horseback riding is available at various stables and riding academies. Those who would rather watch equines than ride one can go to the **harness races** at **The Meadows Racetrack & Casino,** 25 miles south of Pittsburgh in Washington, where live harness racing is held year-round; for more information phone (724) 503-1200 or (877) 824-5050. There is **Thoroughbred racing** throughout the year at **Mountaineer Race Track and Gaming Resort** near Chester, W.Va., about an hour from Pittsburgh; phone (800) 804-0468.

Note: Policies concerning admittance of children to pari-mutuel betting facilities vary. Phone for information.

Among the swimming pools in Allegheny County, those in Boyce, **Settler's Cabin** and South Park provide waves for those who yearn for the surf. The fee for nonresidents is $8; $6 (ages 6–17); $4 (ages 60+); $1 (ages 0-5). Swimmers can choose a pool with or without waves.

Pittsburgh has 78 tennis courts in Schenley, Frick, Highland, **McKinley** and Mellon parks. Within Allegheny County you will find regional tennis courts at **West Park** and other public parks. Courts operate on a first-come, first-served basis. Because some require permits, it is a good idea to check with the city or county parks departments first; phone (412) 255-2539 or (412) 350-2455, respectively.

In-line skating at Three Rivers Heritage Trail

The National Football League's **Steelers** are popular among **football** fans; their home games are played at **Heinz Field.** Thanks to their sixth win in 2009, the Steelers have more Super Bowl victories than any other NFL franchise. Major League Baseball's **Pirates** are the stars during the **baseball** season; they play at **PNC Park.** The National Hockey League's **Penguins** play **hockey** at **PPG Paints Arena.** College sports also are big attractions, particularly the games played by the University of Pittsburgh's **Panthers.**

Performing Arts

The city's arts scene is growing, becoming more varied, more vital and more progressive. This is perhaps most apparent in Pittsburgh's theater offerings.

The **Pittsburgh Public Theatre** is a professional Equity company offering classical and modern dramas, including a new play each year. Its home is in the downtown **O'Reilly Theater,** designed by noted architect Michael Graves; phone (412) 316-1600 for ticket information. On the South Side, contemporary American plays are presented by the **City Theatre Company** during its late September to early June season; phone (412) 431-2489. The always-interesting **Quantum Theatre** moves from one unique venue to another; phone (412) 362-1713. **Carnegie Mellon University's** theater is as active and excellent as ever; phone (412) 268-2082. **Point Park University's Pittsburgh Playhouse** in Oakland is the site of a wide range of classical and contemporary productions; phone (412) 392-8000 for ticket information. **University of**

Pittsburgh Stages (formerly the University of Pittsburgh Repertory Theatre) performs at the **Stephen Foster Memorial**; phone (412) 624-7529.

Dance of many kinds, from folk to modern, also is available. As they have for more than 80 years, **The Tamburitzans** bring to vivid life the folk dances, songs and music of Old Eastern Europe at several venues, including Duquesne University; phone (412) 224-2071. The lavish **Benedum Center for the Performing Arts,** formerly the Stanley Theatre, is home to the acclaimed **Pittsburgh Ballet Theatre,** which performs October through April or early May; phone (412) 281-0360. The **Pittsburgh Dance Council** performs at the **Byham Theater;** phone (412) 456-6666 for the box office.

The **August Wilson Center for African American Culture,** (412) 258-2700, named for the Pittsburgh native and playwright, is housed in a contemporary facility downtown on Liberty Avenue. Its offerings include dance, music and theater performances.

For orchestral music at its best, the **Pittsburgh Symphony** has few rivals. This orchestra packs the opulent 1926 **Heinz Hall**, 600 Penn Ave., September through June for its regular program series as well as for its Pops, Schooltime Concerts and Tiny Tots' series. Its excellent acoustics, elegant decor and dramatic architecture now form the backdrop for much of Pittsburgh's cultural activity. A courtyard with wrought-iron benches and water sculptures have been added to the hall. Phone (412) 392-4900 for ticket information.

The **Pittsburgh Opera** performs also at the Benedum Center for the Performing Arts. The **Pittsburgh Civic Light Opera** (CLO) also performs at the Benedum as well as at the Byham Theater.

The **CLO Cabaret** always entertains at the intimate **Cabaret at Theater Square.**

Contemporary American music is the specialty of the **Pittsburgh New Music Ensemble,** which performs at the **City Theatre** in July; phone (888) 718-4253. Free chamber music concerts are held at The Frick Art Museum on Sundays, October through April. The Summer Concert in the Parks series provides a variety of free concerts, including bluegrass, folk and jazz in several of the city and county parks.

These are only a few of the possibilities; *Pittsburgh* magazine and the newspaper carry complete lists.

ATTRACTIONS

 For a complete list of attractions, visit AAA.com/travelguides/attractions

CARNEGIE MUSEUMS OF PITTSBURGH, 4400 Forbes Ave. in Oakland, is based in the heart of the university area and is composed of several cultural institutions. Adjoining contemporary and 19th-century buildings house Carnegie Museum of Art and Carnegie Museum of Natural History; the Andy Warhol Museum and Carnegie Science Center are located in the city's North Side district. Also included at 4400 Forbes Ave. are Carnegie Library and Carnegie Music Hall. **Hours:** Vary per museum. **Cost:** Varies per museum. **Phone:** (412) 622-3131.

The Andy Warhol Museum is at 117 Sandusky St. on the city's North Shore and is part of the Carnegie Museums of Pittsburgh. The facility is devoted to the life and work of one of the most influential artists of the second half of the 20th century. Installation art, extensive archival material and more than 500 canvases present the entire range of the Pittsburgh native's creative endeavors as a graphic artist, fine artist, filmmaker, music producer, stage designer, author and publisher.

Time: Allow 1 hour minimum. **Hours:** Tues.-Sun. 10-5 (also Fri. 5-10). Closed Jan. 1, Martin Luther King Jr. Day, Easter, Memorial Day, July 4, Labor Day, Thanksgiving and Christmas. Phone ahead to confirm schedule. **Cost:** $20; $10 (ages 3-18, ages 65+ and students with ID); half-price (Fri. 5-10). Phone ahead to confirm rates. **Phone:** (412) 237-8300. North Side, 2

Carnegie Library of Pittsburgh, 4400 Forbes Ave., was constructed in 1895 and is one of the nation's foremost public libraries. It contains nearly 5 million items, including archives, audio recordings, books, electronic resources, magazines, newspapers and photographs. Cultural, educational and recreational programs also are offered throughout the year.

Pittsburgh Symphony

Guided tours are available by appointment. **Time:** Allow 1 hour minimum. **Hours:** Mon.-Thurs. 10-8, Fri.-Sat. 10-5:30, Sun. noon-5. **Cost:** Free. **Phone:** (412) 622-3114. 🔲 GT

Carnegie Museum of Art, 4400 Forbes Ave., part of the Carnegie Museums of Pittsburgh, displays international paintings, sculpture and decorative arts from the 16th century to the present. The Hall of Architecture's collection of monumental architectural casts is said to be one of three such collections worldwide. Changing exhibitions are presented throughout the year.

The Heinz Architectural Center surveys past and current architectural expression through the exhibition of drawings, models, photographs and related materials. Free gallery tours are given regularly. **Time:** Allow 3 hours minimum. **Hours:** Daily 10-5 (also Thurs. 5-8), Memorial Day-Labor Day; Wed.-Mon. 10-5 (also Thurs. 5-8), rest of year. Closed Jan. 1, Easter, Thanksgiving and Christmas. **Cost:** (includes Carnegie Museum of Natural History) $19.95; $14.95 (ages 65+); $11.95 (ages 3-18 and students with ID). Mon.-Fri. after 3 p.m. half-price. **Phone:** (412) 622-3131. 🔲 GT 🍴

▼GEM **Carnegie Museum of Natural History,** 4400 Forbes Ave., part of the Carnegie Museums of Pittsburgh, is known for its exhibits about earth sciences, life sciences and anthropology. Masterpiece specimens sparkle in Hillman Hall of Minerals and Gems where visitors can explore crystallography and mineral formations.

The Halls of African and North American Wildlife show animals in dioramas depicting realistic habitats. Mummies and other treasures from ancient Egypt are displayed in the Walton Hall of Ancient Egypt. The Alcoa Foundation Hall of American Indians includes exhibits about four societies: Tlingit of the Northwest Coast, Hopi of the Southwest, Lakota of the Plains and Iroquois of the Northeast. Polar World: Wyckoff Hall of Arctic Life traces the cultural history of Inuit peoples and their adaptation to the Arctic. Dinosaurs in Their Time presents fossils in scientifically-accurate poses, the result of current evidence.

Time: Allow 3 hours minimum. **Hours:** Daily 10-5 (also Thurs. 5-8), Memorial Day-Labor Day; Wed.-Mon. 10-5 (also Thurs. 5-8), rest of year. Guided 1-hour gallery tours are given Sat. at noon and 2, Sun. at 2:30. Guided 30-minute gallery tours are given Sat. at 10:30, 11, 12:30 and 1, Sun. at 1 and 1:30. Closed Jan. 1, Easter, Thanksgiving and Christmas. **Cost:** (includes Carnegie Museum of Art) $19.95; $14.95 (ages 65+); $11.95 (ages 3-18 and students with ID). Mon.-Fri. after 3 p.m. half-price. **Phone:** (412) 622-3131. 🔲 GT

▼GEM **Carnegie Science Center** is at 1 Allegheny Ave. on the North Shore next to Heinz Field and is part of the Carnegie Museums of Pittsburgh. There are hundreds of hands-on exhibits covering the science of space flight, geology, physics, biology and energy; there are three live demonstration theaters, a laser

show display and an authentic Cold War-era submarine. Temporary exhibits also are presented. Documentaries, Hollywood blockbusters and live performances are shown in the four-story Rangos Giant Cinema theater.

The Buhl Planetarium offers high-definition, full-dome planetarium experiences. Model railroads and village scenes depicting turn-of-the-20th-century western Pennsylvania are displayed at the Miniature Railroad and Village.

SpacePlace includes a weightlessness simulation activity and walk-in replicas of two modules of the International Space Station. H2Oh! explores the science of water and how rivers create the habitats of the Pittsburgh region. BodyWorks describes the workings of the human body. SportsWorks offers more than 30 interactive sports challenges.

Hours: Science Center daily 10-5 (also Fri.-Sat. 5-7), Memorial Day-Labor Day; 10-5, rest of year. Phone for Giant Cinema daily performance schedule and laser matinee and evening show times. Closed Thanksgiving, Christmas and during Steelers home games with 1 and 4 p.m. kickoff times. **Cost:** (includes USS *Requin*) $19.95; $11.95 (ages 3-12). Discover More combination ticket with Science Center, USS *Requin* and one laser show $24.95; $16.95 (ages 3-12). Giant Cinema only $9.95-$13.95; $7.95-$11.95 (ages 3-12 and 65+). Educational movie only $9.95; $7.95 (ages 3-12 and 65+). Other combination tickets are available. **Parking:** $5. **Phone:** (412) 237-3400. 🔲 🍴 ♿ Allegheny, 1

USS *Requin* is part of the Carnegie Science Center at 1 Allegheny Ave.; the science center is one of four Carnegie Museums of Pittsburgh. The vessel features kiosks with touch screens offering visitors an opportunity to connect with submarine veterans and learn about the history of the *Requin* as well as submarines in general.

Note: Below-deck views of the submarine require full mobility. A video tour in the main building is offered for those unable to navigate the vessel. **Hours:** Daily 10-4:30 (weather and river conditions permitting). Closed Thanksgiving, Christmas and during Steelers home games with afternoon kickoff times. Phone ahead to confirm schedule. **Cost:** USS *Requin* only, $7. Combination ticket with Carnegie Science Center $19.95; $11.95 (ages 3-12). **Phone:** (412) 237-3400. ♿ Allegheny, 1

▼GEM **CATHEDRAL OF LEARNING** is on a 14-acre quadrangle at Bigelow Blvd., 5th Ave., Bellefield Ave. and Forbes Ave. The University of Pittsburgh's 42-story truncated Gothic stone tower was once known as the world's tallest schoolhouse.

Encircling the dramatic, Gothic-inspired Commons Room are 30 nationality classrooms, which reflect architectural and decorative styles ranging from classical, Byzantine and Romanesque to Renaissance, Tudor, Empire and folk. Based on cultural periods prior to 1787, each room was designed by artists and architects from nations that represent

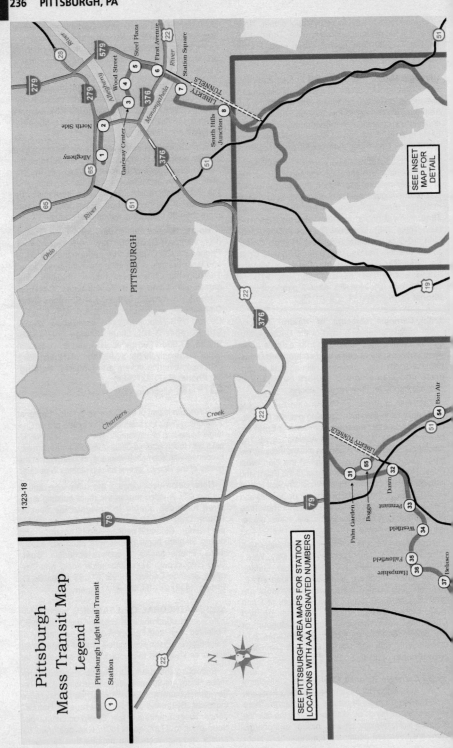

Pittsburgh
Mass Transit Map

Legend

▬▬ Pittsburgh Light Rail Transit

① Station

PITTSBURGH

1323-18

SEE PITTSBURGH AREA MAPS FOR STATION
LOCATIONS WITH AAA DESIGNATED NUMBERS

SEE INSET MAP FOR DETAIL

Stations:
① Allegheny
② North Side
③ Gateway Center
④ Wood Street
⑤ Steel Plaza
⑥ First Avenue
⑦ Station Square
⑧ South Hills Junction
579

LIBERTY TUNNELS

Allegheny River
Monongahela River
Ohio River
Chartiers Creek

㉛ Palm Garden
㉟ Boggs
㉜ Dawn
㉝ Pennant
㉞ Westfield
㉟ Fallowfield
㊱ Hampshire
㊲ Belasco
㊴ Bon Air

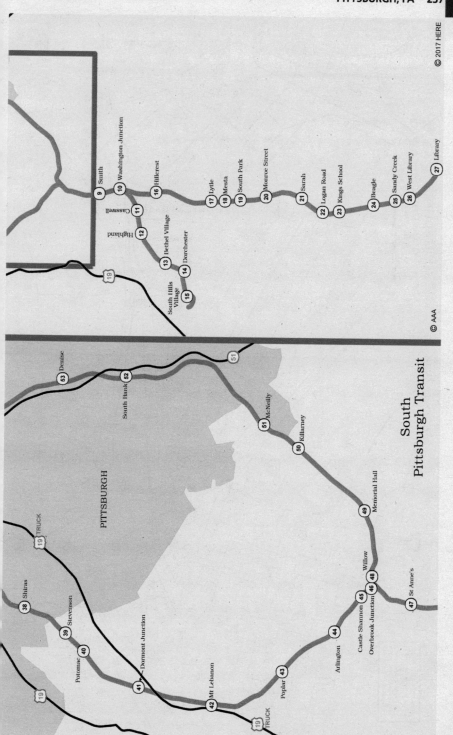

© 2017 HERE

© AAA

South
Pittsburgh Transit

PITTSBURGH

(9) Smith
(10) Washington Junction
(11) Casswell
(16) Hillcrest
(12) Highland
(13) Bethel Village
(14) Dorchester
(15) South Hills Village
(17) Lytle
(18) Mesta
(19) South Park
(20) Monroe Street
(21) Sarah
(22) Logan Road
(23) Kings School
(24) Beagle
(25) Sandy Creek
(26) West Library
(27) Library

(51)
(53) Denise
(52) South Bank
(51) McNeilly
(50) Killarney
(49) Memorial Hall
(48) St Anne's
(45) Castle Shannon
(46) Overbrook Junction
(47) St Anne's
(44) Arlington
(43) Poplar
(42) Mt Lebanon
(41) Dormont Junction
(40) Potomac
(39) Stevenson
(38) Shiras

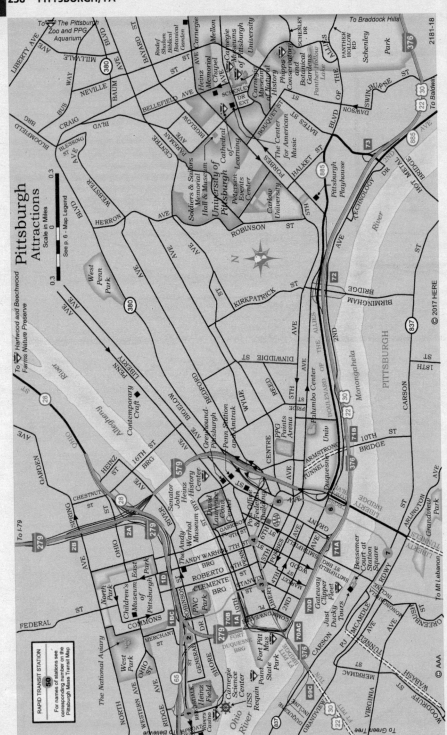

Pittsburgh's ethnic heritages and includes authentic period furnishings.

Visitors may lift the toggle switch as they enter each third floor room to activate a taped narration that describes the various room features. Third floor rooms explore such cultures as Austria, India, Africa, Israel and Japan. A sampling of heritages reflected in the first-floor classrooms, with audio descriptions and in-room written descriptions, includes Italy, Scotland, Greece, France, England and Germany. Between mid-November and mid-January, the rooms are decorated in the traditional holiday manner of each nation represented.

Time: Allow 1 hour, 30 minutes minimum. **Hours:** Narrated audio tours of Nationality Rooms Mon.-Sat. 9-2:30, Sun. and holidays 11-2:30, late Apr.-late Aug.; Sat. 9-2:30, Sun. and holidays 11-2:30, rest of year. Walk-in guided tours are offered 10:30-2:30 the day after Thanksgiving and Dec. 27-31. Closed Jan. 1, Thanksgiving, Christmas Eve, Christmas and day after Christmas. Phone ahead to confirm schedule. **Cost:** Free. Guided or audio tour $4; $2 (ages 6-18). **Phone:** (412) 624-6000. GT

THE FRICK PITTSBURGH, 7227 Reynolds St. in Point Breeze, is a 6-acre complex that includes Pittsburgh industrialist Henry Clay Frick's restored 19th-century home, Clayton; The Frick Art Museum; the reconstructed Alden and Harlow 1897 Greenhouse; and a welcome center. The Car and Carriage Museum features carriages and vintage automobiles. The Frick Art Museum contains Helen Clay Frick's art collection and hosts traveling exhibitions; docent-led tours of the permanent collection are available by appointment.

Hours: Tues.-Sun. 10-5 (also Fri. 5-9). Closed Jan. 1, Thanksgiving, Christmas Eve and Christmas. **Cost:** Clayton $15; $13 (senior citizens and students and active military with ID); $8 (ages 6-16). The Frick Art Museum and Car and Carriage Museum are free. A fee is charged for The Frick Art Museum guided tour. Reservations are strongly recommended for Clayton and are required for The Frick Art Museum guided tour. **Phone:** (412) 371-0600. GT ✕

Car and Carriage Museum, 7227 Reynolds St. at The Frick Pittsburgh, displays classic automobiles, including Henry Clay Frick's 1914 Rolls Royce Silver Ghost Touring Car. **Time:** Allow 1 hour minimum. **Hours:** Tues.-Sun. 10-5 (also Fri. 5-9). Closed Jan. 1, Thanksgiving, Christmas Eve and Christmas. **Cost:** Free. **Phone:** (412) 371-0600.

Clayton, 7227 Reynolds St. at The Frick Pittsburgh, is the former estate of industrialist Henry Clay Frick and his family, who lived here 1883-1905. Visitors are introduced to the restored Victorian home, the only surviving home along Pittsburgh's once famous Millionaire's Row, on 75-minute guided tours. When the family moved into the Italianate-style house, there were 11 rooms; in

1891, architect Frederick J. Osterling built an additional 12 rooms. Most of the artifacts, furnishings and personal mementos of the Frick family are original to the house.

Hours: Guided tours are offered Tues.-Sun. 10-5 (also Fri. 5-9). Closed Jan. 1, Thanksgiving, Christmas Eve and Christmas. **Cost:** $15; $13 (senior citizens and students and active military with ID); $8 (ages 6-16). Reservations are strongly recommended. **Phone:** (412) 371-0600. GT

The Frick Art Museum, 7227 Reynolds St. at The Frick Pittsburgh, presents Italian, Flemish and French paintings dating from the early Renaissance through the 18th century. Temporary exhibitions, concerts and lectures also are presented. Docent-led tours of the permanent collection are available by appointment. **Time:** Allow 1 hour minimum. **Hours:** Tues.-Sun. 10-5 (also Fri. 5-9). Temporary exhibition tours Wed. and Sat.-Sun. at 2 when temporary exhibitions are on display; phone ahead. Closed Jan. 1, Thanksgiving, Christmas Eve and Christmas. **Cost:** Permanent collection free. A fee is charged for temporary exhibitions and for permanent collection guided tours. Reservations are required for permanent collection guided tours. **Phone:** (412) 371-0600. GT

HARTWOOD, 200 Hartwood Acres, is a 629-acre estate designed in the style of a 16th-century English country manor. A 1-hour tour includes the Gothic Tudor mansion and its collection of antiques. Wooded trails are on the grounds. Concerts are given in summer.

Time: Allow 1 hour minimum. **Hours:** Park daily 8-dusk. Guided mansion tours are given Mon.-Sat. on the hour 10-3, Sun. noon-3. Candlelight tours are offered select evenings Nov.-Dec.; phone for schedule. Stable tours are offered on a limited basis; phone for schedule. Closed most federal holidays. The mansion may close for private events; phone ahead. **Cost:** $8; $5 (ages 13-17 and 60+); $3 (ages 6-12); $1 (ages 0-5). Candlelight tour $8. Reservations are required for tours. Cash only. **Phone:** (412) 767-9200. GT

THE NATIONAL AVIARY is at Allegheny Commons West at 700 Arch St. at jct. Ridge Ave. The bird zoo houses more than 500 birds from more than 150 species, many of them threatened or endangered. Visitors can participate in daily feedings, bird shows and interactive encounters. A bird flight simulator also is offered. **Time:** Allow 1 hour minimum. **Hours:** Daily 10-5 (10-3 on Dec. 31). Closed Thanksgiving, Christmas Eve and Christmas. **Cost:** Aviary $15; $14 (ages 2-12 and 60+). Aviary and bird show $20; $19 (ages 2-12 and 60+). Bird feeding additional $3-$5. Simulator additional $8. **Phone:** (412) 323-7235. ✕ 🚫 North Side, 2

PHIPPS CONSERVATORY AND BOTANICAL GARDENS—see Schenley Park p. 241.

The Pittsburgh Zoo & PPG Aquarium

THE PITTSBURGH ZOO & PPG AQUARIUM is off Butler St. w. of the Highland Park Bridge. The 77-acre site is home to 9,000 animals representing 900 species. Animals are featured in naturalistic exhibits such as a tropical forest, Asian forest and an African savanna. The Kids Kingdom offers sea lions and a petting zoo with deer and goats as well as a play area. The Islands exhibit features warty pigs, siamang gibbons and Philippine crocodiles. Capybaras, fossae, giant anteaters, a pygmy hippo and ocelots are found at Jungle Odyssey.

The PPG Aquarium features species from habitats such as the Amazon River, Antarctica, the tropics and Pennsylvania streams and rivers. The Water's Edge exhibit offers up-close views of polar bears, sea otters and a northern elephant seal; two underwater tunnels afford views of the bears and seal swimming overhead and around visitors.

A tram provides transportation within the park spring through fall. **Time:** Allow 2 hours minimum. **Hours:** Daily 9:30-6, Memorial Day weekend-Labor Day; 9-5, Apr. 1-Fri. before Memorial Day and day after Labor Day-Dec. 31; 9-4, rest of year. Gates close 1 hour, 30 minutes before closing time, Memorial Day weekend-Labor Day; gates close 1 hour before closing time, rest of year. Closed Jan. 1, Thanksgiving and Christmas. **Cost:** Apr.-Nov. $16; $15 (ages 60+); $14 (ages 2-13). Rest of year $13; $12 (ages 60+); $14 (ages 2-13). **Phone:** (412) 665-3640. [T]

POINT STATE PARK is at the confluence of the Allegheny, Monongahela and Ohio rivers. The 36-acre park occupies land that was extremely valuable in the mid-18th century. In 1754 the French seized the area from the British, beginning events that led to the French and Indian War. The British regained supremacy in 1758 and one year later erected a new fort, which they named Fort Pitt for William Pitt, prime minister of England and friend of the Colonies. The fort served the frontier for the next three decades in the following struggles: Dunmore's War, Pontiac's Uprising, the Revolutionary War and the Indian wars of the late 18th century.

Fort Pitt Block House and Fort Pitt Museum *(see attraction listings)* as well as plaques, markers and other features interpret the history and significance of the area. One of the nation's largest fountains serves as the park's focal point and symbolizes the city's revitalized Golden Triangle. Set at the confluence of the three rivers, the fountain propels plumes of water to heights of 120 feet and is illuminated at night with white lights. It operates daily mid-April through Veterans Day (weather permitting).

Benches around the lawn areas and stone bleachers overlooking the Allegheny River and the North Side provide seating for the park's many outdoor events. Bicycle and footpaths connect to other recreation trails that traverse the city. **Hours:** Park daily dawn-dusk. **Cost:** Free. **Phone:** (412) 565-2850. [🚇] Gateway Center, 3

Fort Pitt Block House, 601 Commonwealth Pl. in Point State Park, was built in 1764 and is all that remains of Fort Pitt, the last vestige of British rule in western Pennsylvania. A significant amount of original architecture remains, and visitors can view 18th-century construction techniques. Exhibits, period artifacts and digital presentations are included, and educators are on site to assist with interpretation.

The Fort Pitt Society of the Daughters of the American Revolution have owned and preserved the site since 1894. **Hours:** Wed.-Sat. 10:30-4:30, Apr.-Oct.; Fri.-Sat. 10:30-4:30, rest of year. Phone ahead to confirm schedule. **Cost:** Free. **Phone:** (412) 471-1764. [🚇] Gateway Center, 3

Fort Pitt Museum, 601 Commonwealth Pl. in Point State Park, focuses on the early history of western Pennsylvania from the mid-1700s to the early 1800s. Exhibits illustrate the initial struggle between three groups, the French, English and Native Americans, who fought to lay claim to the region. Artifacts, dioramas, audiovisual presentations and computer simulations depict such events as the French and Indian War, Pontiac's Rebellion, the Revolutionary War, the early Native American wars in Ohio and Pittsburgh's early development as the "Gateway to the West." The museum is in a reproduction of one of the original bastions.

Hours: Daily 10-5. Guided tours are offered Sat.-Sun., June-Aug.; phone for times. Closed Jan. 1, Easter, Thanksgiving and Christmas. **Cost:** $8; $7 (ages 62+); $6 (retired and active military); $4.50 (ages 6-17 and students with ID). **Phone:** (412) 281-9284. [GT] [🚇] Gateway Center, 3

SCHENLEY PARK, on Schenley Dr., is one of the city's most popular green spaces. Among its amenities are playgrounds, a swimming pool, 13 tennis courts, an all-weather track, bridle trails, a golf course and an 18-hole disc golf course. During the winter there are opportunities for ice-skating and cross-country skiing. **Hours:** Park daily dawn-dusk. Phone ahead to confirm schedule. **Phone:** (412) 682-7275 for park and event information, or (412) 255-2539 for Parks and Recreation Department. 🍴 ⊠ 🎣 🏛

Phipps Conservatory and Botanical Gardens, in Schenley Park at 1 Schenley Park, was donated to the city in 1893 by industrialist Henry Phipps. The grounds feature outdoor gardens and a 17-room Victorian glasshouse with exotic and native plants as well as several works of glass sculptures by artist Dale Chihuly, including a chandelier in the welcome center. Some of the conservatory's themed rooms are dedicated to ferns, orchids, palms and tropical forest plants. The Stove Room showcases plants found in the deep tropics, and it is transformed into a butterfly forest between spring and fall. A Japanese courtyard garden features bonsai. The Victoria Room recalls the Victorian era while the Broderie Room typifies gardens enjoyed by the French nobility during Louis XIV's reign.

Fountains, streams and waterfalls are incorporated throughout the themed areas, and many displays change seasonally. The Center for Sustainable Landscapes features an art gallery, and its surrounding grounds offer a lagoon and native plants. The Discovery Garden, geared toward children, has been designed with hands-on elements to allow youngsters to learn and play. In summer visitors get to enjoy the Aquatic Garden's water and floating plants in addition to the century-old statue of Neptune, the Roman sea god.

Guided tours are offered by appointment. **Time:** Allow 1 hour minimum. **Hours:** Grounds daily 9:30-5 (also Fri. 5-10). Extended evening hours during the winter flower show late Nov.-late Dec.; phone ahead. Butterfly exhibit open late Apr.-Labor Day. Phone ahead for tour times. Closed Thanksgiving and Christmas. **Cost:** $17.95; $16.95 (ages 62+ and students with ID); $11.95 (ages 2-18). An additional fee is charged for some guided tours. **Phone:** (412) 622-6914. GT 🍴 🏛

SENATOR JOHN HEINZ HISTORY CENTER, 1212 Smallman St., is an affiliate of the Smithsonian Institution and is the state's largest history museum. It features six floors of permanent and changing exhibits devoted to the history and heritage of western Pennsylvania; a library and archives; and the Western Pennsylvania Sports Museum, chronicling the region's professional and amateur sports figures.

The Pittsburgh: A Tradition of Innovation exhibition celebrates 250 years of Pittsburgh inventors and innovations that have changed the world, including the first liver transplant, the Polio vaccine, the nation's first radio station and the Ferris wheel. A large collection of glass along with interactive exhibits recall the days when Pittsburgh was known as America's Glass City. The Heinz exhibit chronicles the history of Pittsburgh's H. J. Heinz Co. Interactive exhibits and games in Discovery Place help children understand how people in different times lived, worked and played.

Hours: Daily 10-5. Library and archives Wed.-Sat. 10-5. Closed Jan. 1, Easter, Thanksgiving and Christmas. **Cost:** $16; $14 (ages 62+); $6.50 (ages 6-17 and students with ID). **Phone:** (412) 454-6000. 🍴 🚃 Steel Plaza, 5

Sightseeing

Visitors who prefer sightseeing on their own should stop at VisitPittsburgh's Welcome Pittsburgh Information Center and Gift Shop at 120 Fifth Ave. Other branches are at the Pittsburgh International Airport, at the David L. Lawrence Convention Center and in Senator John Heinz History Center; phone (412) 281-7711 or (800) 359-0758. All centers provide brochures and maps of the Golden Triangle, Strip District, Design Zone (the city's interior design district) and Mount Washington. The Pittsburgh History and Landmarks Foundation, in Station Square, offers self-guiding tours and customized bus and walking tours for sites in western Pennsylvania; phone (412) 471-5808.

Boat Tours

GATEWAY CLIPPER FLEET departs from 350 W. Station Square Dr. Narrated 1-hour sightseeing cruises on the city's three rivers are offered aboard a fleet of riverboats. Other cruises also are available, including kids' character cruises, specialty entertainment cruises, and lunch and dinner cruises.

Hours: Sightseeing cruise departs daily at 10:30, 11:45, 1, 2:15 and 3:30, Apr.-Oct. Evening sightseeing tours also are offered; phone for schedules. Passengers should arrive 30 minutes before departure to board. **Cost:** Sightseeing cruise $22; $12 (ages 3-12). **Phone:** (412) 355-7980. GT 🚃 Station Square, 7

JUST DUCKY TOURS departs from Station Square at 125 W. Station Square Dr. Fully narrated 1-hour city tours are offered aboard restored World War II amphibious vehicles, known as DUKWs (pronounced "ducks"), which traverse downtown streets then splash into the rivers. Landside highlights include PPG Tower, Grant Street and the theater district. After launching into one of three rivers near Heinz Field and PNC Park, the water cruise provides an offshore perspective of the Golden Triangle.

Time: Allow 1 hour minimum. **Hours:** Tours depart Mon.-Fri. at 10:30, noon, 1:30, 3, 4 and 6, Sat.-Sun. at 10:30, noon, 1:30, 3, 4:30 and 6, Apr.-Nov. Phone ahead to confirm schedule. **Cost:** $25; $15 (ages 3-12); $5 (ages 0-2). Reservations are recommended. **Phone:** (412) 402-3825. GT 🚃 Station Square, 7

Bus Tours

The Pittsburgh History and Landmarks Foundation, in Station Square, offers bus and walking tours for a range of historical sites in western Pennsylvania; phone (412) 471-5808.

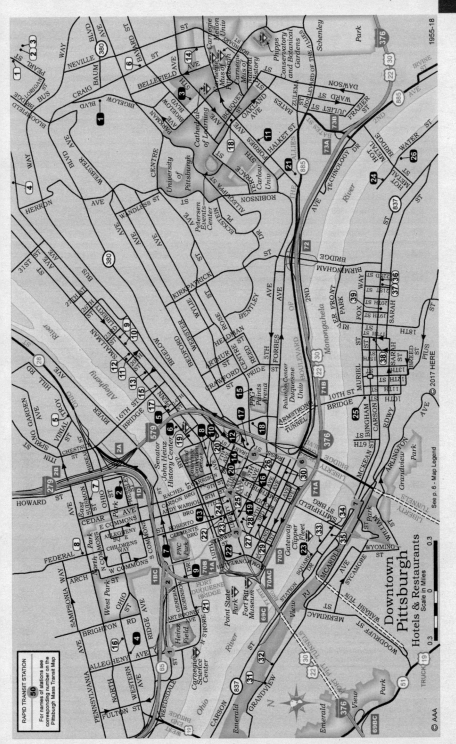

Downtown Pittsburgh

This index helps you "spot" where approved hotels and restaurants are located on the corresponding detailed maps. Hotel daily rate range is for comparison only. Restaurant price range is a combination of lunch and/or dinner. Turn to the listing page for more information and consult display ads for special promotions.

 For more details, rates and reservations: **AAA.com/travelguides/hotels**

DOWNTOWN PITTSBURGH

Map Page	Hotels	Diamond Rated	Rate Range	Page
1 p. 243	**Residence Inn by Marriott Pittsburgh University/Medical Center**	◈◈◈	$89-$386 SAVE	256
2 p. 243	**The Priory Hotel**	◈◈◈	$145-$210 SAVE	256
3 p. 243	Wyndham Pittsburgh University Center	◈◈◈	$99-$349	257
4 p. 243	The Parador Inn	◈◈◈	$160-$210	255
5 p. 243	Homewood Suites by Hilton Pittsburgh Downtown	◈◈◈	Rates not provided	254
6 p. 243	**Hampton Inn & Suites Pittsburgh-Downtown**	◈◈◈	$139-$259 SAVE	254
7 p. 243	**SpringHill Suites by Marriott Pittsburgh North Shore**	◈◈◈	$90-$525 SAVE	257
8 p. 243	**The Westin Convention Center Pittsburgh**	◈◈◈	Rates not provided SAVE	257
9 p. 243	**Hyatt Place Pittsburgh-North Shore**	◈◈◈	$84-$229 SAVE	255
10 p. 243	Courtyard by Marriott Pittsburgh Downtown	◈◈◈	$98-$437	254
11 p. 243	Hilton Garden Inn Pittsburgh University Place	◈◈◈	$109-$299	254
12 p. 243	**Drury Plaza Hotel Pittsburgh Downtown**	◈◈◈	$119-$259 SAVE	254
13 p. 243	**Renaissance Pittsburgh Hotel**	◈◈◈◈	$141-$602 SAVE	256
14 p. 243	**Kimpton Hotel Monaco Pittsburgh**	◈◈◈◈	$189-$399 SAVE	255
15 p. 243	Cambria Hotel & Suites Pittsburgh at PPG Paints Arena	◈◈◈	$159-$709	254
16 p. 243	Embassy Suites by Hilton Pittsburgh Downtown	◈◈◈	Rates not provided	254
17 p. 243	DoubleTree by Hilton Hotel & Suites Pittsburgh Downtown	◈◈◈	$159-$169	254
18 p. 243	**Pittsburgh Marriott City Center**	◈◈◈	$100-$449 SAVE	255
19 p. 243	**Fairmont Pittsburgh**	◈◈◈◈	$209-$599 SAVE	254
20 p. 243	Omni William Penn Hotel	◈◈◈◈	Rates not provided	255
21 p. 243	Hampton Inn Pittsburgh University/Medical Center	◈◈◈	$139-$199	254
22 p. 243	**Wyndham Grand Pittsburgh Downtown**	◈◈◈	$99-$459 SAVE	257
23 p. 243	**Sheraton Pittsburgh Hotel at Station Square**	◈◈◈	Rates not provided SAVE	256
24 p. 243	**Hyatt House Pittsburgh-South Side**	◈◈◈	$139-$399 SAVE	255
25 p. 243	Holiday Inn Express Hotel & Suites Pittsburgh/South Side *(See ad p. 255.)*	◈◈◈	$109-$199 SAVE	254
26 p. 243	**SpringHill Suites by Marriott - Pittsburgh Southside Works** *(See ad p. 257.)*	◈◈◈	$73-$329 SAVE	257

Map Page	Restaurants	Diamond Rated	Cuisine	Price Range	Page
① p. 243	Caliente Pizza & Draft House	◈◈	Pizza	$7-$18	258
② p. 243	Ginza	◈◈	Japanese	$8-$21	258
③ p. 243	Station	◈◈	New American	$10-$28	258

Map Page	Restaurants (cont'd)	Diamond Rated	Cuisine	Price Range	Page
④ p. 243	The Church Brew Works	♦♦♦	American	$9-$34	258
⑤ p. 243	Penn Brewery Restaurant	♦♦	German	$9-$19	258
⑥ p. 243	Legume	♦♦♦	New American	$14-$55	258
⑦ p. 243	Max's Allegheny Tavern	♦♦	German	$5-$18	258
⑧ p. 243	El Burro Comedor	♦	Mexican	$4-$10	258
⑨ p. 243	Penn Avenue Fish Company	♦	Seafood	$8-$16	258
⑩ p. 243	Luke Wholey's Wild Alaskan Grille	♦♦	Seafood	$9-$45	258
⑪ p. 243	Kaya Restaurant	♦♦	Caribbean	$10-$29	258
⑫ p. 243	Deluca's Diner	♦	American	$6-$12	258
⑬ p. 243	Wholey's	♦	Seafood	$6-$12	259
⑭ p. 243	Ali Baba Restaurant	♦♦	Middle Eastern Comfort Food	$5-$16	258
⑮ p. 243	Gaucho Parrilla Argentina	♦♦	Argentine	$8-$40	258
⑯ p. 243	Nicky's Thai Kitchen	♦♦	Thai	$5-$19	258
⑰ p. 243	Lidia's	♦♦♦	Northern Italian	$19-$45	258
⑱ p. 243	Oishii Bento	♦	Asian	$5-$14	258
⑲ p. 243	Eleven	♦♦♦♦	New American	$12-$45	258
⑳ p. 243	Sienna Mercato	♦♦	Italian	$7-$32	258
㉑ p. 243	Jerome Bettis' Grille 36	♦♦	American	$7-$25	258
㉒ p. 243	Olive or Twist	♦♦	American	$12-$28	258
㉓ p. 243	Six Penn Kitchen	♦♦♦	New American	$9-$30	258
㉔ p. 243	Morton's The Steakhouse	♦♦♦	Steak	$27-$48	258
㉕ p. 243	Täkō	♦♦	Mexican	$8-$18	259
㉖ p. 243	The Terrace Room	♦♦♦	Continental	$13-$34	259
㉗ p. 243	Sienna on the Square	♦♦♦	Italian	$10-$45	258
㉘ p. 243	NOLA On The Square	♦♦	New Creole	$9-$34	258
㉙ p. 243	Ruth's Chris Steak House	♦♦♦	Steak	$10-$60	258
㉚ p. 243	Chinatown Inn	♦♦	Chinese	$8-$20	258
㉛ p. 243	Monterey Bay Fish Grotto	♦♦♦	Seafood	$28-$50	258
㉜ p. 243	**Altius**	♦♦♦♦	American	$24-$44	258
㉝ p. 243	Hard Rock Cafe	♦♦	American	$13-$24 SAVE	258
㉞ p. 243	Grand Concourse Restaurant & Gandy Dancer Saloon	♦♦♦	American	$9-$42	258
㉟ p. 243	Kiku's of Japan	♦♦	Sushi	$14-$35	258
㊱ p. 243	Little Tokyo Bistro	♦♦	Sushi	$12-$35	258
㊲ p. 243	Stagioni	♦♦♦	Italian	$12-$32	258
㊳ p. 243	Nakama Japanese Steakhouse and Sushi Bar	♦♦	Japanese	$9-$46	258
㊴ p. 243	Carmella's Plates & Pints	♦♦♦	New American	$15-$25	258

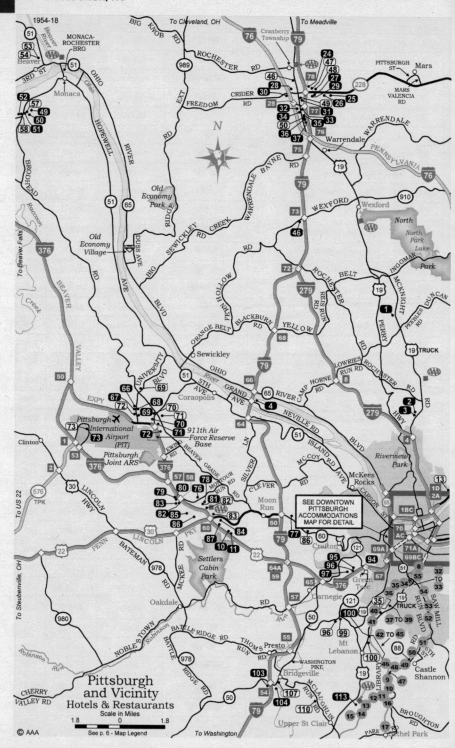

Pittsburgh
and Vicinity
Hotels & Restaurants
Scale in Miles
1.8   0   1.8
© AAA   See p. 6 - Map Legend

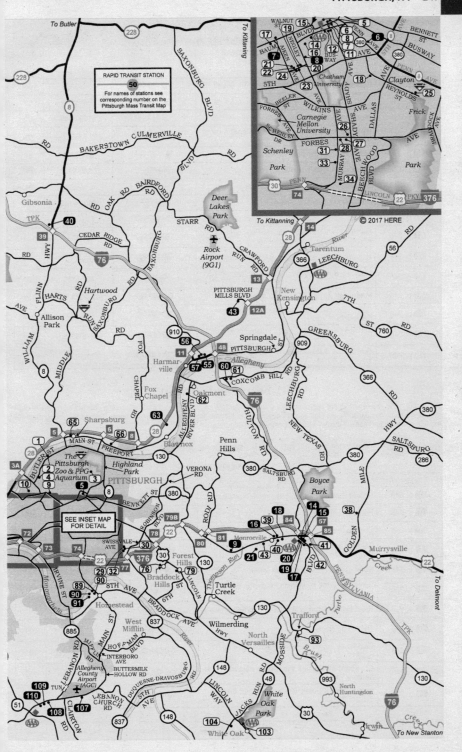

RAPID TRANSIT STATION

50

For names of stations see
corresponding number on the
Pittsburgh Mass Transit Map

© 2017 HERE

✈ Airport Hotels

Map Page	PITTSBURGH INTERNATIONAL (Maximum driving distance from airport: 8.9 mi)	Diamond Rated	Rate Range	Page
71 p. 246	Courtyard by Marriott Pittsburgh Airport, 8.8 mi	◈◈◈	$80-$303	60
66 p. 246	DoubleTree by Hilton Pittsburgh Airport, 7.4 mi	◈◈◈	$99-$299	60
67 p. 246	Hampton Inn Pittsburgh Airport, 7.4 mi	◈◈◈	$109-$149	60
73 p. 246	Hyatt Regency Pittsburgh International Airport, 0.7 mi	◈◈◈	$99-$359 [SAVE]	61
68 p. 246	La Quinta Inn Pittsburgh Airport, 7.4 mi	◈◈◈	$59-$129	61
69 p. 246	Pittsburgh Airport Super 8, 7.0 mi	◈◈	$60-$90	61
70 p. 246	Sheraton Pittsburgh Airport Hotel, 8.9 mi	◈◈◈	$79-$239	61
85 p. 246	Candlewood Suites, 8.6 mi	◈◈	$109-$159	134
80 p. 246	Comfort Suites, 7.3 mi	◈◈◈	$89-$189	134
81 p. 246	Fairfield Inn & Suites by Marriott Pittsburgh Airport/Robinson Township, 8.7 mi	◈◈◈	$68-$232	134
76 p. 246	Homewood Suites by Hilton, 8.8 mi	◈◈◈	Rates not provided	134
83 p. 246	MainStay Suites/Sleep Inn Pittsburgh Airport, 7.5 mi	◈◈	$59-$159	134
79 p. 246	**Pittsburgh Airport Marriott, 7.4 mi**	◈◈◈	$79-$314 [SAVE]	134
82 p. 246	Residence Inn by Marriott Pittsburgh Airport Coraopolis, 7.7 mi	◈◈◈	$78-$242	135
86 p. 246	SpringHill Suites by Marriott - Pittsburgh Airport, 8.5 mi	◈◈◈	$75-$306	135
78 p. 246	TownePlace Suites Pittsburgh Airport/Robinson Township, 8.7 mi	◈◈◈	$79-$204	135

Pittsburgh and Vicinity

This index helps you "spot" where approved hotels and restaurants are located on the corresponding detailed maps. Hotel daily rate range is for comparison only. Restaurant price range is a combination of lunch and/or dinner. Turn to the listing page for more information and consult display ads for special promotions.

 For more details, rates and reservations: AAA.com/travelguides/hotels

PITTSBURGH

Map Page	Hotels	Diamond Rated	Rate Range	Page
1 p. 246	Home2 Suites by Hilton Pittsburgh/McCandless	◈◈◈	$109-$139	261
2 p. 246	Hampton Inn	◈◈◈	$119-$193	259
3 p. 246	Comfort Inn	◈◈◈	$99-$159	259
4 p. 246	**Fairfield Inn & Suites by Marriott Pittsburgh Neville Island**	◈◈◈	$76-$254 [SAVE]	259
5 p. 246	**Hotel Indigo Pittsburgh East Liberty**	◈◈◈	$109-$289 [SAVE]	261
6 p. 246	SpringHill Suites by Marriott Pittsburgh Bakery Square	◈◈◈	$97-$311	261
7 p. 246	**Hyatt House Pittsburgh/Bloomfield/Shadyside**	◈◈◈	$139-$399 [SAVE]	261
8 p. 246	The Inn on Negley	◈◈◈◈	Rates not provided	261
9 p. 246	**Residence Inn by Marriott-Wilkins** *(See ad p. 259.)*	◈◈◈	$105-$316 [SAVE]	261
10 p. 246	**Courtyard by Marriott Pittsburgh Airport Settlers Ridge**	◈◈◈	$62-$292 [SAVE]	259
11 p. 246	Hampton Inn & Suites Pittsburgh Airport South/Settlers Ridge	◈◈◈	Rates not provided	259

Map Page	Restaurants	Diamond Rated	Cuisine	Price Range	Page
1 p. 246	Cure	◈◈◈	New American	$12-$38	262

Map Page	Restaurants (cont'd)	Diamond Rated	Cuisine	Price Range	Page
② p. 246	Pusadee's Garden	◈◈	Thai	$12-$24	262
③ p. 246	Joseph Tambellini Restaurant	◈◈◈	Italian	$24-$42	262
④ p. 246	Banh Mi & Ti	◈	Vietnamese Coffee/Tea	$6-$8	262
⑤ p. 246	Tana Ethiopian Cuisine	◈◈	Ethiopian	$12-$20	262
⑥ p. 246	Muddy Waters Oyster Bar	◈◈	Cajun	$11-$29	262
⑦ p. 246	Spoon	◈◈◈	New American	$15-$65	262
⑧ p. 246	Kelly's Bar & Lounge	◈◈	American	$6-$11	262
⑨ p. 246	Tessaro's	◈◈	American	$10-$26	262
⑩ p. 246	Morcilla	◈◈◈	Spanish Small Plates	$14-$28	262
⑪ p. 246	Casbah Mediterranean Kitchen & Wine Bar	◈◈◈	Mediterranean	$8-$30	262
⑫ p. 246	Buffalo Blues	◈◈	Wings	$7-$21	262
⑬ p. 246	Scratch Food & Beverage	◈◈	American	$8-$30	262
⑭ p. 246	Umi	◈◈	Japanese	$20-$40	262
⑮ p. 246	Soba	◈◈	New Asian	$13-$38	262
⑯ p. 246	Harris Grill	◈◈	American	$8-$22	262
⑰ p. 246	Cafe Sam	◈◈◈	International	$6-$25	262
⑱ p. 246	Point Brugge Cafe	◈◈	Belgian	$8-$32	262
⑲ p. 246	La Feria	◈◈	Peruvian	$10-$15	262
⑳ p. 246	Pamela's Diner	◈	American	$6-$10	262
㉑ p. 246	Girasole	◈◈	Northern Italian	$10-$22	262
㉒ p. 246	Cappy's Cafe	◈	American	$6-$9	262
㉓ p. 246	Shady Grove	◈◈	American	$10-$18	262
㉔ p. 246	Sushi Too	◈◈	Japanese	$7-$25	262
㉕ p. 246	The Cafe at The Frick Art & Historical Center	◈◈	New American	$11-$28	262
㉖ p. 246	Everyday Noodles	◈◈	Asian	$7-$12	262
㉗ p. 246	Ramen Bar	◈◈	Asian Soup	$5-$12	262
㉘ p. 246	Uncle Sam's Sandwich Bar	◈	Sandwiches	$6-$12	262
㉙ p. 246	El Burro Numero Dos	◈	Mexican	$4-$10	262
㉚ p. 246	Square Cafe	◈◈	Breakfast	$6-$14	262
㉛ p. 246	Sichuan Gourmet	◈◈	Szechuan	$6-$29	262
㉜ p. 246	D's Six Pax & Dogz	◈◈	American	$7-$20	262
㉝ p. 246	Tan Lac Vien Vietnamese Bistro	◈◈	Vietnamese	$10-$17	262
㉞ p. 246	Chengdu Gourmet	◈	Szechuan	$10-$22	262
㉟ p. 246	The Dor-Stop Restaurant	◈	Breakfast Sandwiches	$5-$14	262

MONROEVILLE

Map Page	Hotels	Diamond Rated	Rate Range	Page
⑭ p. 246	Hampton Inn Monroeville/Pittsburgh	◈◈◈	$119-$179	133
⑮ p. 246	Holiday Inn Pittsburgh-Monroeville	◈◈◈	Rates not provided	133
⑯ p. 246	Extended Stay America Pittsburgh-Monroeville	◈◈	$75-$115	133

MONROEVILLE (cont'd)

Map Page	Hotels (cont'd)	Diamond Rated	Rate Range	Page
17 p. 246	**SpringHill Suites by Marriott Pittsburgh Monroeville** *(See ad p. 259.)*	◈◈◈	$79-$245 [SAVE]	133
18 p. 246	**Courtyard by Marriott Pittsburgh Monroeville** *(See ad p. 259.)*	◈◈◈	$90-$340 [SAVE]	133
19 p. 246	Comfort Suites Monroeville	◈◈◈	$104-$179	133
20 p. 246	**Red Roof PLUS+ Pittsburgh East - Monroeville**	◈◈	$52-$157 [SAVE]	133
21 p. 246	**DoubleTree by Hilton Hotel Pittsburgh - Monroeville Convention Center**	◈◈◈	$109-$189 [SAVE]	133

Map Page	Restaurants	Diamond Rated	Cuisine	Price Range	Page
38 p. 246	Eighty Acres Kitchen & Bar	◈◈◈	New American	$8-$35	133
39 p. 246	Blaze Pizza	◈	Pizza	$8	133
40 p. 246	Rudy's Submarines	◈	Sandwiches	$4-$10	133
41 p. 246	Dad's Pub & Grub	◈◈	American	$8-$22	133
42 p. 246	Gateway Grill	◈◈	American	$7-$20	133
43 p. 246	Taipei -Tokyo	◈◈	Chinese	$5-$22	133

CRANBERRY TOWNSHIP

Map Page	Hotels	Diamond Rated	Rate Range	Page
24 p. 246	TownePlace Suites by Marriott Pittsburgh Cranberry Township	◈◈◈	$94-$165	63
25 p. 246	Hilton Garden Inn Pittsburgh/Cranberry	◈◈◈	$139	62
26 p. 246	Home2 Suites by Hilton Pittsburgh Cranberry, PA	◈◈◈	Rates not provided	62
27 p. 246	Pittsburgh Marriott North	◈◈◈	$89-$340	63
28 p. 246	Hampton Inn Cranberry	◈◈◈	$109-$149	62
29 p. 246	**Courtyard by Marriott Pittsburgh North/Cranberry Woods**	◈◈◈	$80-$323 [SAVE]	62
30 p. 246	Residence Inn by Marriott Pittsburgh Cranberry Township	◈◈◈	$87-$408	63
31 p. 246	Quality Inn	◈◈◈	$79-$119	63
32 p. 246	**Hyatt Place Pittsburgh/Cranberry**	◈◈◈	$129-$649 [SAVE]	63
33 p. 246	Candlewood Suites	◈◈◈	Rates not provided	62
34 p. 246	Clarion Inn	◈◈	$109-$129	62
35 p. 246	Super 8-Cranberry	◈◈	$90-$230	63
36 p. 246	Comfort Inn Cranberry Township	◈◈◈	$89-$134	62
37 p. 246	**DoubleTree Cranberry**	◈◈◈	$99-$179 [SAVE]	62

Map Page	Restaurants	Diamond Rated	Cuisine	Price Range	Page
46 p. 246	Monte Cello's Cranberry	◈◈	Italian	$5-$15	63
47 p. 246	Firebirds Wood Fired Grill	◈◈◈	Steak	$8-$30	63
48 p. 246	Juniper Grill	◈◈◈	American	$4-$22	63
49 p. 246	Tamarind	◈◈	Indian	$10-$15	63
50 p. 246	Pig Iron Public House	◈◈◈	American	$4-$18	63

GIBSONIA

Map Page	Hotel	Diamond Rated	Rate Range	Page
40 p. 246	Quality Inn & Suites Pittsburgh-Gibsonia	◈◈	$84-$180	88

TARENTUM

Map Page	Hotel	Diamond Rated	Rate Range	Page
43 p. 246	**SpringHill Suites by Marriott Pittsburgh Mills** (See ad p. 261.)	♦♦♦	$93-$458 SAVE	289

WEXFORD

Map Page	Hotel	Diamond Rated	Rate Range	Page
46 p. 246	Hampton Inn by Hilton Wexford	♦♦♦	Rates not provided	299

MONACA

Map Page	Hotels	Diamond Rated	Rate Range	Page
49 p. 246	Comfort Suites	♦♦♦	$79-$159	132
50 p. 246	Fairfield Inn & Suites by Marriott	♦♦♦	$76-$230	132
51 p. 246	**Holiday Inn Express Hotel & Suites-Center Township**	♦♦♦	$104-$139 SAVE	133
52 p. 246	Hampton Inn Beaver Valley/Pittsburgh	♦♦♦	$104-$164	132

Map Page	Restaurants	Diamond Rated	Cuisine	Price Range	Page
57 p. 246	Bowser's	♦	American	$7-$11	133
58 p. 246	Rainaldi's Restaurant	♦♦	Italian	$9-$25	133

HARMARVILLE

Map Page	Hotels	Diamond Rated	Rate Range	Page
55 p. 246	Holiday Inn Express	♦♦♦	Rates not provided	92
56 p. 246	Hampton Inn & Suites Pittsburgh/Harmarville	♦♦♦	Rates not provided	92
57 p. 246	TownePlace Suites by Marriott	♦♦♦	$93-$241	92

OAKMONT

Map Page	Hotel	Diamond Rated	Rate Range	Page
60 p. 246	Doone's Inn at Oakmont	♦♦♦	Rates not provided	140

Map Page	Restaurants	Diamond Rated	Cuisine	Price Range	Page
61 p. 246	Somma Pizza & Sports Bar	♦♦	American	$5-$18	140
62 p. 246	Chelsea Grille	♦♦	American	$7-$30	140

BLAWNOX

Map Page	Hotel	Diamond Rated	Rate Range	Page
63 p. 246	Comfort Inn & Suites	♦♦♦	$89-$179	48

CORAOPOLIS

Map Page	Hotels	Diamond Rated	Rate Range	Page
66 p. 246	DoubleTree by Hilton Pittsburgh Airport	♦♦♦	$99-$299	60
67 p. 246	Hampton Inn Pittsburgh Airport	♦♦♦	$109-$149	60
68 p. 246	La Quinta Inn Pittsburgh Airport	♦♦♦	$59-$129	61
69 p. 246	Pittsburgh Airport Super 8	♦♦	$60-$90	61
70 p. 246	Sheraton Pittsburgh Airport Hotel	♦♦♦	$79-$239	61
71 p. 246	Courtyard by Marriott Pittsburgh Airport	♦♦♦	$80-$303	60
72 p. 246	Embassy Suites by Hilton Pittsburgh International Airport	♦♦♦	$119-$199	60
73 p. 246	**Hyatt Regency Pittsburgh International Airport**	♦♦♦	$99-$359 SAVE	61

Map Page	Restaurants	Diamond Rated	Cuisine	Price Range	Page
69 p. 246	Kiyoshi	♦♦	Asian	$8-$19	61
70 p. 246	Armstrong's Restaurant	♦♦	American	$6-$20	61

Map Page	Restaurants (cont'd)	Diamond Rated	Cuisine	Price Range	Page
71 p. 246	Hyeholde Restaurant	◆◆◆	Continental	$25-$44	61
72 p. 246	Wings, Suds & Spuds	◆	American	$5-$12	61
73 p. 246	bellfarm Kitchen/Bar	◆◆◆	American	$8-$35	61

MOON RUN

Map Page	Hotels	Diamond Rated	Rate Range	Page
76 p. 246	Homewood Suites by Hilton	◆◆◆	Rates not provided	134
77 p. 246	Pittsburgh Comfort Inn	◆◆	$89-$199	134
78 p. 246	TownePlace Suites Pittsburgh Airport/Robinson Township	◆◆◆	$79-$204	135
79 p. 246	**Pittsburgh Airport Marriott**	◆◆◆	$79-$314 [SAVE]	134
80 p. 246	Comfort Suites	◆◆◆	$89-$189	134
81 p. 246	Fairfield Inn & Suites by Marriott Pittsburgh Airport/Robinson Township	◆◆◆	$68-$232	134
82 p. 246	Residence Inn by Marriott Pittsburgh Airport Coraopolis	◆◆◆	$78-$242	135
83 p. 246	MainStay Suites/Sleep Inn Pittsburgh Airport	◆◆	$59-$159	134
84 p. 246	**Hyatt Place Pittsburgh Airport**	◆◆◆	$79-$259 [SAVE]	134
85 p. 246	Candlewood Suites	◆◆	$109-$159	134
86 p. 246	SpringHill Suites by Marriott - Pittsburgh Airport	◆◆◆	$75-$306	135
87 p. 246	Holiday Inn Express & Suites - Pittsburgh Airport	◆◆◆	Rates not provided	134

Map Page	Restaurants	Diamond Rated	Cuisine	Price Range	Page
82 p. 246	Ya Fei	◆◆	Chinese	$7-$20	135
83 p. 246	Ditka's Restaurant	◆◆◆	Steak	$12-$60	135

HOMESTEAD

Map Page	Hotels	Diamond Rated	Rate Range	Page
90 p. 246	Hampton Inn & Suites Pittsburgh Waterfront	◆◆◆	$119-$209	106
91 p. 246	Courtyard by Marriott Pittsburgh-Waterfront	◆◆◆	$86-$311	106

Map Page	Restaurants	Diamond Rated	Cuisine	Price Range	Page
89 p. 246	Mitchell's Fish Market	◆◆◆	Seafood	$10-$35	106
90 p. 246	P.F. Chang's China Bistro	◆◆◆	Chinese	$10-$27	106

GREEN TREE

Map Page	Hotels	Diamond Rated	Rate Range	Page
94 p. 246	Holiday Inn Express Hotel & Suites Pittsburgh West-Greentree	◆◆◆	Rates not provided	90
95 p. 246	Crowne Plaza Pittsburgh West-Green Tree	◆◆◆	Rates not provided	90
96 p. 246	Hampton Inn Pittsburgh Green Tree	◆◆◆	$109-$159	90
97 p. 246	**DoubleTree by Hilton Pittsburgh-Green Tree**	◆◆◆	$99-$149 [SAVE]	90

Map Page	Restaurant	Diamond Rated	Cuisine	Price Range	Page
96 p. 246	Tamarind Savoring India	◆◆	Indian	$7-$15	90

MOUNT LEBANON

Map Page	Hotel	Diamond Rated	Rate Range	Page
100 p. 246	**SpringHill Suites by Marriott Pittsburgh Mt. Lebanon** (See ad p. 260.)	◆◆◆	$93-$273 [SAVE]	136

Map Page	Restaurants	Diamond Rated	Cuisine	Price Range	Page
99 p. 246	DeBlasio's	◆◆	Italian	$6-$30	136

Map Page	Restaurants (cont'd)	Diamond Rated	Cuisine	Price Range	Page
100 p. 246	Il Pizzaiolo	♦♦	Italian	$12-$24	136

BRIDGEVILLE

Map Page	Hotels	Diamond Rated	Rate Range	Page
103 p. 246	Hampton Inn	♦♦♦	Rates not provided	50
104 p. 246	Holiday Inn Express	♦♦♦	Rates not provided	50

Map Page	Restaurant	Diamond Rated	Cuisine	Price Range	Page
107 p. 246	LaBella Bean Coffee House & Eatery	♦	American	$3-$10	51

WEST MIFFLIN

Map Page	Hotels	Diamond Rated	Rate Range	Page
107 p. 246	Holiday Inn Express Hotel & Suites	♦♦♦	Rates not provided	299
108 p. 246	SpringHill Suites by Marriott-West Mifflin	♦♦♦	$80-$250	299
109 p. 246	Hampton Inn - West Mifflin	♦♦♦	$119-$159	299
110 p. 246	Comfort Inn-West Mifflin	♦♦	$94-$176	299

BETHEL PARK

Map Page	Hotel	Diamond Rated	Rate Range	Page
113 p. 246	**Crowne Plaza Hotel & Suites Pittsburgh South**	♦♦♦	$119-$179 SAVE	45

BEAVER

Map Page	Restaurants	Diamond Rated	Cuisine	Price Range	Page
53 p. 246	Bert's Wooden Indian	♦♦	American	$4-$15	42
54 p. 246	The Wooden Angel	♦♦	American	$12-$40	42

SHARPSBURG

Map Page	Restaurants	Diamond Rated	Cuisine	Price Range	Page
65 p. 246	Gran Canal Caffe	♦♦	Italian	$14-$25	277
66 p. 246	Cornerstone Restaurant & Bar	♦♦	American	$8-$30	277

BRADDOCK HILLS

Map Page	Restaurant	Diamond Rated	Cuisine	Price Range	Page
76 p. 246	Veltre's Pizza	♦	Pizza	$4-$16	49

FOREST HILLS

Map Page	Restaurant	Diamond Rated	Cuisine	Price Range	Page
79 p. 246	Drews Family Restaurant	♦♦	American	$4-$16	76

CRAFTON

Map Page	Restaurant	Diamond Rated	Cuisine	Price Range	Page
86 p. 246	Sapporo Japanese Steakhouse	♦♦	Japanese	$7-$38	61

TRAFFORD

Map Page	Restaurant	Diamond Rated	Cuisine	Price Range	Page
93 p. 246	Parente's Ristorante	♦♦	Italian	$7-$24	289

WHITE OAK

Map Page	Restaurants	Diamond Rated	Cuisine	Price Range	Page
103 p. 246	China House	♦♦	Chinese	$3-$15	300
104 p. 246	Luciano's Italian Brick Oven	♦♦	Italian	$5-$20	300

UPPER ST. CLAIR

Map Page	Restaurant	Diamond Rated	Cuisine	Price Range	Page
110 p. 246	Piccolina's	♦♦♦	Northern Italian	$10-$33	291

DOWNTOWN PITTSBURGH
- Restaurants p. 258
- Hotels & Restaurants map & index p. 243

CAMBRIA HOTEL & SUITES PITTSBURGH AT PPG PAINTS ARENA (412)381-6687 **15**

◆◆◆ Hotel. **Address:** 1320 Centre Ave 15219

COURTYARD BY MARRIOTT PITTSBURGH DOWNTOWN (412)434-5551 **10**

◆◆◆ Hotel. **Address:** 945 Penn Ave 15222

AAA Benefit: Members save 5% or more!

DOUBLETREE BY HILTON HOTEL & SUITES PITTSBURGH DOWNTOWN (412)281-5800 **17**

◆◆◆ Hotel. **Address:** One Bigelow Square 15219

AAA Benefit: Members save 5% or more!

DRURY PLAZA HOTEL PITTSBURGH DOWNTOWN (412)281-2900 **12**

◆◆◆
Hotel
$119-$259

Address: 745 Grant St 15219 **Location:** Across from Penn Station and County Courthouse. 🚇 Steel Plaza, 5. **Facility:** 207 units. 10 stories, interior corridors. **Parking:** valet only. **Terms:** cancellation fee imposed. **Pool:** indoor. **Activities:** hot tub, exercise room. **Guest Services:** valet and coin laundry.

SAVE 🍸 CALL 🛗 🏊 💪 BIZ
HS 📶 ✕ 🍴 🖥 📺
/ SOME UNITS 🐾 🚍

EMBASSY SUITES BY HILTON PITTSBURGH DOWNTOWN 412/338-2200 **16**

◆◆◆ Hotel. **Address:** 535 Smithfield St 15222

AAA Benefit: Members save 5% or more!

FAIRMONT PITTSBURGH (412)773-8800 **19**

◆◆◆◆
Contemporary
Hotel
$209-$599

Address: 510 Market St 15222 **Location:** Between Market St and 5th Ave; in cultural district. 🚇 Gateway Center, 3. **Facility:** While hip and modern in design, you'll find nods to the city's history with Andy Warhol prints and artifacts unearthed during the hotel's construction. Rooms offer lush bedding and big windows. 185 units. 14-23 stories, interior corridors. **Parking:** on-site (fee) and valet. **Terms:** cancellation fee imposed. **Amenities:** safes. **Activities:** sauna, steamroom, health club, spa. **Guest Services:** valet laundry.

SAVE ECO 🍴 💪 🍸 CALL 🛗
💪 BIZ HS 📶 ✕ 🎥 🖥
/ SOME UNITS 🐾 🍴 🖥 🚍

HAMPTON INN & SUITES PITTSBURGH-DOWNTOWN (412)288-4350 **6**

◆◆◆
Hotel
$139-$259

AAA Benefit: Members save up to 10%!

Address: 1247 Smallman St 15222 **Location:** Jct 11th and Smallman sts, just e. 🚇 Steel Plaza, 5. **Facility:** 143 units. 8 stories, interior corridors. **Terms:** check-in 4 pm, 1-7 night minimum stay, cancellation fee imposed. **Pool:** heated indoor. **Activities:** hot tub, exercise room. **Guest Services:** valet and coin laundry. **Featured Amenity:** breakfast buffet.

SAVE 🍴 CALL 🛗 🏊 💪 BIZ HS 📶 🎥 🖥
/ SOME UNITS 🍴 🖥 🚍

HAMPTON INN PITTSBURGH UNIVERSITY/MEDICAL CENTER (412)681-1000 **21**

◆◆◆ Hotel. **Address:** 3315 Hamlet St 15213

AAA Benefit: Members save up to 10%!

HILTON GARDEN INN PITTSBURGH UNIVERSITY PLACE (412)683-2040 **11**

◆◆◆ Hotel. **Address:** 3454 Forbes Ave 15213

AAA Benefit: Members save up to 10%!

HOLIDAY INN EXPRESS HOTEL & SUITES PITTSBURGH/SOUTH SIDE (412)488-1130 **25**

◆◆◆
Hotel
$109-$199

Address: 20 S 10th St 15203 **Location:** At 10th St Bridge; in South Side. 🚇 First Avenue, 6. **Facility:** 125 units. 6 stories, interior corridors. **Parking:** on-site (fee). **Terms:** check-in 4 pm. **Pool:** heated indoor. **Activities:** exercise room. **Guest Services:** valet and coin laundry, area transportation. *(See ad p. 255.)*

SAVE 🍴 CALL 🛗 🏊 💪
BIZ HS 📶 ✕ 🎥 🖥
🖥 📺 🚍

HOMEWOOD SUITES BY HILTON PITTSBURGH DOWNTOWN 412/232-0200 **5**

◆◆◆ Extended Stay Contemporary Hotel. **Address:** 1410 Smallman St 15222

AAA Benefit: Members save up to 10%!

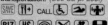

🔗 **For complete hotel, dining and attraction listings: AAA.com/travelguides**

(See map & index p. 243.)

HYATT HOUSE PITTSBURGH-SOUTH SIDE
(412)390-2477 **24**

Extended Stay Hotel
$139-$399

 **HYATT house™**

AAA Benefit: Members save 10%!

Address: 2795 S Water St 15203 **Location:** I-376 exit 72A, right on 2nd Ave, then just s. **Facility:** 136 efficiencies, some two bedrooms. 6 stories, interior corridors. **Parking:** valet only. **Terms:** cancellation fee imposed. **Pool:** heated indoor. **Activities:** exercise room. **Guest Services:** valet and coin laundry, area transportation. **Featured Amenity:** breakfast buffet.

[SAVE] [ICONS]

HYATT PLACE PITTSBURGH-NORTH SHORE
(412)321-3000 **9**

Hotel
$84-$229

HYATT PLACE®

AAA Benefit: Members save 10%!

Address: 260 N Shore Dr 15212 **Location:** I-279/376 exit 70B (Fort Duquesne Blvd), exit 6C, stay right, n on 6th St/Roberto Clemente Bridge (which becomes Federal St), w on W General Robinson St, s on Mazeroski Way, then just w. Across from PNC Park. North Side, 2. **Facility:** 178 units. 7 stories, interior corridors. **Parking:** on-site (fee). **Terms:** cancellation fee imposed. **Pool:** heated indoor. **Activities:** exercise room. **Guest Services:** valet laundry, area transportation. **Featured Amenity:** breakfast buffet.

[SAVE] [ICONS]

KIMPTON HOTEL MONACO PITTSBURGH
(412)471-1170 **14**

Boutique Contemporary Hotel
$189-$399

Address: 620 William Penn Pl 15219 **Location:** Jct Sixth Ave. Steel Plaza, 5. **Facility:** With a location perfect for business travelers or theatergoers, this hotel gives a nod to local culture. Its unique décor includes black and gold armoires in each room. 248 units. 9 stories, interior corridors. **Parking:** valet only. **Terms:** cancellation fee imposed. **Amenities:** safes. **Activities:** exercise room. **Guest Services:** valet laundry.

[SAVE] [ICONS]

OMNI WILLIAM PENN HOTEL
412/281-7100 **20**

Classic Historic Hotel. **Address:** 530 William Penn Pl 15219

THE PARADOR INN
(412)231-4800 **4**

Bed & Breakfast. **Address:** 939 Western Ave 15233

PITTSBURGH MARRIOTT CITY CENTER
(412)471-4000 **18**

Hotel
$100-$449

 MARRIOTT

AAA Benefit: Members save 5% or more!

Address: 112 Washington Pl 15219 **Location:** Center Ave; just e of Crosstown Blvd. Steel Plaza, 5. **Facility:** 402 units. 10-21 stories, interior corridors. **Parking:** on-site (fee) and valet. **Terms:** check-in 4 pm, cancellation fee imposed. **Dining:** 2 restaurants. **Pool:** heated indoor. **Activities:** sauna, exercise room. **Guest Services:** valet and coin laundry, area transportation.

[SAVE] [ICONS]

▼ See AAA listing p. 254 ▼

(See map & index p. 243.)

THE PRIORY HOTEL
(412)231-3338 **2**

Historic Country Inn
$145-$210

Address: 614 Pressley St 15212 **Location:** I-376 exit 70B, 3 blks w on E Ohio St to Cedar Ave, then 3 blks s. North Side, 2. **Facility:** Built in 1888 to house Benedictine priests, the inn has been restored and the beautifully decorated rooms include modern touches like luxurious bedding, free Wi-Fi and flat panel TVs. 42 units, some kitchens. 4 stories, interior corridors. **Terms:** cancellation fee imposed. **Amenities:** safes. **Activities:** exercise room. **Guest Services:** valet laundry, area transportation. **Featured Amenity: continental breakfast.**

RENAISSANCE PITTSBURGH HOTEL
(412)562-1200 **13**

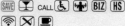

Historic Hotel
$141-$602

RENAISSANCE® HOTELS

AAA Benefit: Members save 5% or more!

Address: 107 Sixth St 15222 **Location:** I-376 E exit 70B (Liberty Ave), just e, then just n. Gateway Center, 3. **Facility:** This historic hotel's lobby offers a gorgeous 1906 rotunda, white marble walls and a mosaic ceiling. Rooms have incredibly soft triple-sheeted bedding, and some have views of PNC Park or the river. 300 units. 14 stories, interior corridors. **Parking:** valet only. **Terms:** check-in 4 pm, cancellation fee imposed. **Amenities:** safes. **Activities:** exercise room. **Guest Services:** valet laundry.

RESIDENCE INN BY MARRIOTT PITTSBURGH UNIVERSITY/MEDICAL CENTER
(412)621-2200 **1**

Extended Stay Hotel
$89-$386

Residence Inn® Marriott

AAA Benefit: Members save 5% or more!

Address: 3896 Bigelow Blvd 15213 **Location:** On SR 380. **Facility:** 171 kitchen units, some two bedrooms. 9 stories, interior corridors. **Parking:** onsite (fee). **Terms:** cancellation fee imposed. **Amenities:** safes. **Pool:** heated indoor. **Activities:** hot tub, exercise room. **Guest Services:** valet and coin laundry, area transportation. **Featured Amenity: full hot breakfast.**

SHERATON PITTSBURGH HOTEL AT STATION SQUARE
412/261-2000 **23**

Hotel
Rates not provided

Sheraton®

AAA Benefit: Members save 5% or more!

Address: 300 W Station Square Dr 15219 **Location:** I-376 exit Grant St, south end of Smithfield Street Bridge. Located on Monongahela River. Station Square, 7. **Facility:** 399 units. 9-15 stories, interior corridors. **Parking:** onsite (fee). **Amenities:** safes. **Pool:** heated indoor. **Activities:** hot tub, exercise room. **Guest Services:** valet laundry, area transportation.

(See map & index p. 243.)

SPRINGHILL SUITES BY MARRIOTT PITTSBURGH NORTH SHORE
(412)323-9005 **7**

Hotel
$90-$525

 AAA Benefit: Members save 5% or more!

Address: 223 Federal St 15212 **Location:** Corner of Federal and General Robinson sts. Across from PNC Park. North Side, 2. **Facility:** 198 units. 10 stories, interior corridors. **Parking:** on-site (fee). **Terms:** cancellation fee imposed. **Pool:** heated indoor. **Activities:** exercise room. **Guest Services:** valet and coin laundry, area transportation. **Featured Amenity:** breakfast buffet.

SPRINGHILL SUITES BY MARRIOTT - PITTSBURGH SOUTHSIDE WORKS
(412)488-8003 **26**

Hotel
$73-$329

SPRINGHILL SUITES MARRIOTT AAA Benefit: Members save 5% or more!

Address: 2950 S Water St 15203 **Location:** US 22/30 exit 2A (Forbes Ave), right to McDevitt Pl, left to CR 885, right to Hot Metal St, then left. **Facility:** 115 units. 6 stories, interior corridors. **Parking:** on-site (fee). **Terms:** cancellation fee imposed. **Pool:** heated indoor. **Activities:** exercise room. **Guest Services:** valet and coin laundry, area transportation.

(See ad this page.)

THE WESTIN CONVENTION CENTER PITTSBURGH
412/281-3700 **8**

Hotel
Rates not provided

 WESTIN HOTELS & RESORTS **AAA Benefit:** Members save 5% or more!

Address: 1000 Penn Ave 15222 **Location:** Jct 10th St; at Liberty Center. Adjacent to convention center. Wood Street, 4. **Facility:** 616 units. 26 stories, interior corridors. **Parking:** on-site (fee) and valet. **Amenities:** safes. **Pool:** heated indoor. **Activities:** sauna, steamroom, health club, massage. **Guest Services:** valet laundry, area transportation.

WYNDHAM GRAND PITTSBURGH DOWNTOWN
(412)391-4600 **22**

Hotel
$99-$459

Address: 600 Commonwealth Pl 15222 **Location:** Jct I-279/376/SR 885; in Gateway Center. Opposite Point State Park. Gateway Center, 3. **Facility:** 712 units, some two bedrooms and kitchens. 24 stories, interior corridors. **Parking:** valet only. **Terms:** check-in 4 pm, cancellation fee imposed. **Pool:** heated indoor. **Activities:** hot tub, exercise room. **Guest Services:** valet laundry, area transportation.

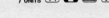

WYNDHAM PITTSBURGH UNIVERSITY CENTER
(412)682-6200 **3**

Hotel. **Address:** 100 Lytton Ave 15213

(See map & index p. 243.)

WHERE TO EAT

ALI BABA RESTAURANT   412/682-2829   (14)
Middle Eastern Comfort Food. Casual Dining. **Address:** 404 S Craig St 15213

ALTIUS   412/904-4442   (32)

American Fine Dining $24-$44

AAA Inspector Notes: Want to impress your date? This is the place to be. You'll immediately be wowed by the floor-to-ceiling windows that offer a breathtaking view of the city skyline and the Three Rivers area, and the kitchen will continue to impress you throughout your visit. The menu offerings are straightforward enough with chops, pasta dishes and seafood, as the chef focuses on using the freshest ingredients of the season to ensure that the flavors in every single dish are at their peak. **Features:** full bar. **Reservations:** suggested. **Address:** 1230 Grandview Ave 15211 **Location:** Atop Mt. Washington; adjacent to Duquesne Incline. Allegheny, 1. **Parking:** valet and street only. D

Elevated cuisine, spectacular views of Pittsburgh

CALIENTE PIZZA & DRAFT HOUSE   412/682-1414   (1)
Pizza. Casual Dining. **Address:** 4624 Liberty Ave 15224

CARMELLA'S PLATES & PINTS   412/918-1215   (39)
New American. Casual Dining. **Address:** 1908 E Carson St 15203

CHINATOWN INN   412/261-1292   (30)
Chinese. Casual Dining. **Address:** 522 3rd Ave 15219

THE CHURCH BREW WORKS   412/688-8200   (4)
American. Gastropub. **Address:** 3525 Liberty Ave 15201

DELUCA'S DINER   412/566-2195   (12)
American. Casual Dining. **Address:** 2015 Penn Ave 15222

EL BURRO COMEDOR   412/904-3451   (8)
Mexican. Quick Serve. **Address:** 1108 Federal St 15212

ELEVEN   412/201-5656   (19)
New American. Fine Dining. **Address:** 1150 Smallman St 15222

GAUCHO PARRILLA ARGENTINA   412/709-6622   (15)
Argentine. Casual Dining. **Address:** 1601 Penn Ave 15222

GINZA   412/688-7272   (2)
Japanese. Casual Dining. **Address:** 4734 Liberty Ave 15224

GRAND CONCOURSE RESTAURANT & GANDY DANCER SALOON   412/261-1717   (34)
American. Casual Dining. **Address:** 100 W Station Square Dr 15219

HARD ROCK CAFE   412/481-7625   (33)
[SAVE] American. Casual Dining. **Address:** 230 W Station Square Dr 15219

JEROME BETTIS' GRILLE 36   412/224-6287   (21)
American. Sports Bar. **Address:** 393 N Shore Dr 15212

KAYA RESTAURANT   412/261-6565   (11)
Caribbean. Casual Dining. **Address:** 2000 Smallman St 15222

KIKU'S OF JAPAN   412/765-3200   (35)
Sushi. Casual Dining. **Address:** 225 W Station Square Dr 15219

LEGUME   412/621-2700   (6)
New American. Fine Dining. **Address:** 214 N Craig St 15213

LIDIA'S   412/552-0150   (17)
Northern Italian. Fine Dining. **Address:** 1400 Smallman St 15222

LITTLE TOKYO BISTRO   412/488-9986   (36)
Sushi. Casual Dining. **Address:** 2122 E Carson St 15203

LUKE WHOLEY'S WILD ALASKAN GRILLE   412/904-4509   (10)
Seafood. Casual Dining. **Address:** 2106 Penn Ave 15222

MAX'S ALLEGHENY TAVERN   412/231-1899   (7)
German. Casual Dining. **Address:** 537 Suismon St 15212

MONTEREY BAY FISH GROTTO   412/481-4414   (31)
Seafood. Fine Dining. **Address:** 1411 Grandview Ave 15211

MORTON'S THE STEAKHOUSE   412/261-7141   (24)
Steak. Fine Dining. **Address:** 625 Liberty Ave 15222

NAKAMA JAPANESE STEAKHOUSE AND SUSHI BAR   412/381-6000   (38)
Japanese. Casual Dining. **Address:** 1611 E Carson St 15203

NICKY'S THAI KITCHEN   412/321-8424   (16)
Thai. Casual Dining. **Address:** 856 Western Ave 15233

NOLA ON THE SQUARE   412/471-9100   (28)
New Creole. Casual Dining. **Address:** 24 Market Square 15222

OISHII BENTO   412/687-3335   (18)
Asian. Quick Serve. **Address:** 119 Oakland Ave 15213

OLIVE OR TWIST   412/255-0525   (22)
American. Casual Dining. **Address:** 140 6th St 15222

PENN AVENUE FISH COMPANY   412/434-7200   (9)
Seafood. Quick Serve. **Address:** 2208 Penn Ave 15222

PENN BREWERY RESTAURANT   412/237-9400   (5)
German. Brewpub. **Address:** 800 Vinial St 15212

PRIMANTI BROS.
American. Casual Dining.
LOCATIONS:
Address: 3803 Forbes Ave 15213 **Phone:** 412/621-4444
Address: 2 S Market Square 15222 **Phone:** 412/261-1599
Address: 1832 E Carson St 15203 **Phone:** 412/381-2583
Address: 46 18th St 15230 **Phone:** 412/263-2142

RUTH'S CHRIS STEAK HOUSE   412/391-4800   (29)
Steak. Fine Dining. **Address:** 6 PPG Pl 15222

SIENNA MERCATO   412/281-2810   (20)
Italian. Casual Dining. **Address:** 942 Penn Ave 15222

SIENNA ON THE SQUARE   412/281-6363   (27)
Italian. Casual Dining. **Address:** 22 Market Square 15222

SIX PENN KITCHEN   412/566-7366   (23)
New American. Casual Dining. **Address:** 146 6th St 15222

STAGIONI   412/586-4738   (37)
Italian. Fine Dining. **Address:** 2104 E Carson St 15203

STATION   412/251-0540   (3)
New American. Casual Dining. **Address:** 4744 Liberty Ave 15224

(See map & index p. 243.)

THE TERRACE ROOM   412/553-5235 26
◇◇◇ Continental. Fine Dining. **Address:** 530 William Penn Pl 15219

TÄKÓ   412/471-8256 25
◇◇ Mexican. Casual Dining. **Address:** 214 Sixth St 15222

WHOLEY'S   412/391-3737 13
◇ Seafood. Quick Serve. **Address:** 1711 Penn Ave 15222

PITTSBURGH elev. 764'
- **Restaurants p. 262**
- **Hotels & Restaurants map & index p. 246**

COMFORT INN   (412)415-3867 3
◇◇◇ Hotel. **Address:** 4607 McKnight Rd 15237

COURTYARD BY MARRIOTT PITTSBURGH AIRPORT SETTLERS RIDGE   (412)788-4404 10

◇◇◇
Hotel
$62-$292

 COURTYARD Marriott **AAA Benefit:** Members save 5% or more!

Address: 5100 Campbells Run Rd 15205 **Location:** I-376 exit 60B (Crafton/SR 60 S), just n. **Facility:** 124 units. 5 stories, interior corridors. **Terms:** cancellation fee imposed. **Pool:** heated indoor. **Activities:** exercise room. **Guest Services:** valet and coin laundry, boarding pass kiosk, area transportation.

SAVE 🚫 ⦿ 🍴 🍸 CALL 👤 🏊
👥 BIZ HS 📶 ✕ 🖥 💻 /SOME UNITS 📷

FAIRFIELD INN & SUITES BY MARRIOTT PITTSBURGH NEVILLE ISLAND   (412)264-4722 4

◇◇◇
Hotel
$76-$254

 FAIRFIELD INN & SUITES Marriott **AAA Benefit:** Members save 5% or more!

Address: 5850 Grand Ave 15225 **Location:** Waterfront. I-79 exit 65, 0.5 mi ne towards Neville Island. **Facility:** 110 units. 4 stories, interior corridors. **Terms:** cancellation fee imposed. **Pool:** heated indoor. **Activities:** hot tub, exercise room. **Guest Services:** valet and coin laundry, area transportation.

SAVE ⦿ CALL 👤 🏊 👥 BIZ
HS 📶 ✕ 🖥 💻 📷

HAMPTON INN   (412)939-3200 2
◇◇◇ Hotel. **Address:** 4575 McKnight Rd 15237

AAA Benefit: Members save up to 10%!

HAMPTON INN & SUITES PITTSBURGH AIRPORT SOUTH/ SETTLERS RIDGE   412/788-4440 11
◇◇◇ Hotel. **Address:** 5000 Campbells Run Rd 15205

AAA Benefit: Members save up to 10%!

🔗 **AAA.com/maps—Dream, plan, go with TripTik Travel Planner**

▼ See AAA listing p. 289 ▼

(See map & index p. 246.)

HOME2 SUITES BY HILTON PITTSBURGH/MCCANDLESS
(412)630-8400 **1**

 Extended Stay Hotel. **Address:** 8630 Duncan Ave 15237

AAA Benefit: Members save up to 10%!

HOTEL INDIGO PITTSBURGH EAST LIBERTY
(412)665-0555 **5**

Contemporary Hotel
$109-$289

Address: 123 N Highland Ave 15206 **Location:** Jct Penn Ave, just n. **Facility:** 135 units. 6 stories, interior corridors. **Parking:** valet and street only. **Terms:** cancellation fee imposed. **Amenities:** safes. **Activities:** exercise room. **Guest Services:** valet and coin laundry, boarding pass kiosk, area transportation.

HYATT HOUSE PITTSBURGH/BLOOMFIELD/SHADYSIDE
(412)621-9900 **7**

Extended Stay Hotel
$139-$399

HYATT house
AAA Benefit: Members save 10%!

Address: 5335 Baum Blvd 15224 **Location:** Jct Liberty Ave. **Facility:** 128 units, some efficiencies. 5 stories, interior corridors. **Parking:** on-site (fee). **Terms:** cancellation fee imposed. **Pool:** heated indoor. **Activities:** exercise room. **Guest Services:** valet and coin laundry, area transportation. **Featured Amenity:** breakfast buffet.

THE INN ON NEGLEY
412/661-0631 **8**

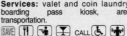 Bed & Breakfast. **Address:** 703 S Negley Ave 15232

RESIDENCE INN BY MARRIOTT-WILKINS
(412)816-1300 **9**

Extended Stay Hotel
$105-$316

Residence Inn Marriott **AAA Benefit:** Members save 5% or more!

Address: 3455 William Penn Hwy 15235 **Location:** I-76 (Pennsylvania Tpke) exit 57, 3.5 mi n. **Facility:** 124 units, some two bedrooms, efficiencies and kitchens. 4 stories, interior corridors. **Terms:** check-in 4 pm, cancellation fee imposed. **Amenities:** safes. **Pool:** heated indoor. **Activities:** exercise room. **Guest Services:** valet and coin laundry. *(See ad p. 259.)*

SPRINGHILL SUITES BY MARRIOTT PITTSBURGH BAKERY SQUARE
(412)362-8600 **6**

 Hotel. **Address:** 134 Bakery Square Blvd 15206

AAA Benefit: Members save 5% or more!

(See map & index p. 246.)

WHERE TO EAT

ALADDIN'S EATERY   412/421-5100
♦♦ Lebanese. Casual Dining. **Address:** 5878 Forbes Ave 15217

BANH MI & TI   412/251-5030   (4)
♦ Vietnamese Coffee/Tea. Quick Serve. **Address:** 4502 Butler St 15201

BUFFALO BLUES   412/362-5837   (12)
♦♦ Wings. Casual Dining. **Address:** 216 S Highland Ave 15206

THE CAFE AT THE FRICK ART & HISTORICAL CENTER
    412/371-0600   (25)
♦♦ New American. Casual Dining. **Address:** 7227 Reynolds St 15208

CAFE SAM   412/621-2000   (17)
♦♦♦ International. Casual Dining. **Address:** 5242 Baum Blvd 15224

CAPPY'S CAFE   412/621-1188   (22)
♦ American. Casual Dining. **Address:** 5431 Walnut St 15232

CASBAH MEDITERRANEAN KITCHEN & WINE BAR
    412/661-5656   (11)
♦♦♦ Mediterranean. Fine Dining. **Address:** 229 S Highland Ave 15206

CHENGDU GOURMET   412/521-2088   (34)
♦ Szechuan. Casual Dining. **Address:** 5840 Forward Ave 15217

CURE   412/252-2595   (1)
♦♦♦ New American. Casual Dining. **Address:** 5336 Butler St 15201

THE DOR-STOP RESTAURANT   412/561-9320   (35)
♦ Breakfast Sandwiches. Casual Dining. **Address:** 1430 Potomac Ave 15216

D'S SIX PAX & DOGZ   412/241-4666   (32)
♦♦ American. Casual Dining. **Address:** 1118 S Braddock Ave 15218

EL BURRO NUMERO DOS   412/243-4348   (29)
♦ Mexican. Casual Dining. **Address:** 1113 S Braddock Ave 15218

EVERYDAY NOODLES   412/421-6668   (26)
♦♦ Asian. Casual Dining. **Address:** 5875 Forbes Ave 15217

GIRASOLE   412/682-2130   (21)
♦♦ Northern Italian. Casual Dining. **Address:** 733 Copeland St 15232

HARRIS GRILL   412/362-5273   (16)
♦♦ American. Gastropub. **Address:** 5747 Ellsworth Ave 15232

JOSEPH TAMBELLINI RESTAURANT   412/665-9000   (3)
♦♦♦ Italian. Fine Dining. **Address:** 5701 Bryant St 15206

KELLY'S BAR & LOUNGE   412/363-6012   (8)
♦ American. Casual Dining. **Address:** 6012 Penn Cir S 15206

LA FERIA   412/682-4501   (19)
♦♦ Peruvian. Casual Dining. **Address:** 5527 Walnut St 15232

MAD MEX   412/366-5656
♦♦ Mexican. Casual Dining. **Address:** 7905 McKnight Rd 15237

MORCILLA   412/652-9924   (10)
♦♦♦ Spanish Small Plates. Casual Dining. **Address:** 3519 Butler St 15201

MUDDY WATERS OYSTER BAR   412/361-0555   (6)
♦♦ Cajun. Casual Dining. **Address:** 130 S Highland Ave 15206

PAMELA'S DINER   412/683-1003   (20)
♦ American. Casual Dining. **Address:** 5527 Walnut St 15232

POINT BRUGGE CAFE   412/441-3334   (18)
♦♦ Belgian. Gastropub. **Address:** 401 Hastings St 15206

PUSADEE'S GARDEN   412/781-8724   (2)
♦♦ Thai. Casual Dining. **Address:** 5321 Butler St 15201

RAMEN BAR   412/521-5138   (27)
♦♦ Asian Soup. Casual Dining. **Address:** 5860 Forbes Ave 15217

SCRATCH FOOD & BEVERAGE   412/251-0822   (13)
♦♦ American. Casual Dining. **Address:** 1720 Lowrie St 15212

SHADY GROVE   412/697-0909   (23)
♦♦ American. Casual Dining. **Address:** 5500 Walnut St 15232

SICHUAN GOURMET   412/521-1313   (31)
♦♦ Szechuan. Casual Dining. **Address:** 1900 Murray Ave 15217

SOBA   412/362-5656   (15)
♦♦♦ New Asian. Fine Dining. **Address:** 5847 Ellsworth Ave 15232

SPOON   412/362-6001   (7)
♦♦♦ New American. Fine Dining. **Address:** 134 S Highland Ave 15206

SQUARE CAFE   412/244-8002   (30)
♦♦ Breakfast. Casual Dining. **Address:** 1137 S Braddock Ave 15218

SUSHI TOO   412/687-8744   (24)
♦♦ Japanese. Casual Dining. **Address:** 5432 Walnut St 15232

TANA ETHIOPIAN CUISINE   412/665-2770   (5)
♦♦ Ethiopian. Casual Dining. **Address:** 5929 Baum Blvd 15206

TAN LAC VIEN VIETNAMESE BISTRO   412/521-8888   (33)
♦♦ Vietnamese. Casual Dining. **Address:** 2114 Murray Ave 15217

TESSARO'S   412/682-6809   (9)
♦♦ American. Casual Dining. **Address:** 4601 Liberty Ave 15224

UMI   412/362-6198   (14)
♦♦ Japanese. Fine Dining. **Address:** 5849 Ellsworth Ave 15232

UNCLE SAM'S SANDWICH BAR   412/521-7827   (28)
♦ Sandwiches. Quick Serve. **Address:** 5808 Forbes Ave 15217

PITTSTON pop. 7,739

COMFORT INN PITTSTON   (570)655-1234
♦♦ Hotel. **Address:** 400 Hwy 315 18640

PLEASANT HILLS pop. 8,268
• Part of Pittsburgh area — see map p. 225

PRIMANTI BROS.   412/653-6779
♦ American. Casual Dining. **Address:** 830 Clairton Blvd (Rt 51) 15236

PLYMOUTH MEETING pop. 6,177
- Hotels & Restaurants map & index p. 192
- Part of Philadelphia area — see map p. 154

COURTYARD BY MARRIOTT-PHILADELPHIA/PLYMOUTH MEETING   (610)238-0695   **62**
◆◆◆ Hotel. **Address:** 651 Fountain Rd 19462

AAA Benefit: Members save 5% or more!

DOUBLETREE SUITES BY HILTON PHILADELPHIA WEST   (610)834-8300   **63**
◆◆◆ Hotel. **Address:** 640 Fountain Rd 19462

AAA Benefit: Members save 5% or more!

HAMPTON INN PLYMOUTH MEETING   (610)567-0900   **66**
◆◆◆◆ Hotel. **Address:** 2055 Chemical Rd 19462

AAA Benefit: Members save up to 10%!

HOMEWOOD SUITES BY HILTON PHILADELPHIA/PLYMOUTH MEETING   610-828-9600   **65**
◆◆◆ Extended Stay Hotel. **Address:** 200 Lee Dr 19462

AAA Benefit: Members save up to 10%!

SPRINGHILL SUITES BY MARRIOTT PHILADELPHIA/PLYMOUTH MEETING   (610)940-0400   **64**
◆◆◆ Hotel. **Address:** 430 Plymouth Rd 19462

AAA Benefit: Members save 5% or more!

WHERE TO EAT

FAT DADDY'S DELI   610/941-3278   **110**
◆ Sandwiches. Quick Serve. **Address:** 405 W Germantown Pike 19462

REDSTONE AMERICAN GRILL   610/941-4400   **109**
◆◆ American. Casual Dining. **Address:** 512 W Germantown Pike 19462

POCONO MOUNTAINS AREA

The name Poconos comes from a Native American word meaning "a stream runs between two mountains." In this case the stream is the Delaware River, which separates Pennsylvania from New Jersey, cutting through a ridge of the Appalachian Mountains and, in the process, forming Mount Minsi in Pennsylvania and Mount Tammany in New Jersey.

The area's 2,400 square miles, spread out among northeast Pennsylvania's Carbon, Monroe, Pike and Wayne counties, encompass rolling hills and some of the loveliest waterfalls in the East.

Folks have been coming to these mountains for rest and recreation since the mid-19th-century. Just 2 hours from both New York City and Philadelphia, the area was (and is today) a ready-made respite for big-city residents eager for a nearby escape.

Summer resorts and boardinghouses near the Delaware River opened to handle the vacationers who came by railroad to relax in the fresh, crisp mountain air and enjoy Mother Nature's bounties. Travelers still come to savor the great outdoors, but they now come year-round and more than likely arrive by car-all the better to explore this vacationland's vast mix of activities.

This map shows cities in the Pocono Mountains Area where you will find attractions, hotels and restaurants. Cities are listed alphabetically in this book on the following pages.

And the choice of accommodations has expanded as well. Today's visitors can select from plush lodges (many with their own golf courses and spas), historic country inns, quaint bed and breakfasts, simple mom and pop motels, an assortment of chain hotels-and, of course, the romantic couples-only resorts with their heart-shaped tubs and 7-foot-tall champagne glass whirlpool towers that have lured honeymooners to the area since the early 1960s.

You won't find any large cities here (all the better for relaxation). Stroudsburg and East Stroudsburg are about as big as it gets, but there are plenty of small, friendly towns to explore, brimming with Victorian architecture, galleries, historic homes, museums and shops.

If it's recreation you're seeking, though, a good place to begin is at the eastern edge of the area at Delaware Water Gap National Recreation Area, which Pennsylvania shares with New Jersey. The Delaware River and US 209 bisect this 40-mile-long parcel which includes a 27-mile portion of the Appalachian Trail.

And it's just a short drive (or hike) off US 209 to some of the area's most beautiful waterfalls. Bushkill, Raymondskill and Dingmans falls can all be admired from numerous vantage points. Trails and boardwalks suitable for all skill levels lead to scenic overlooks.

If water sports are on your agenda, the place to go is Lake Wallenpaupack, near Hawley in the northern part of the Poconos. One of the state's largest man-made lakes, it was created in 1926 to provide hydroelectric power. With 52 miles of shoreline and a maximum depth of 60 feet, it's a huge watery playground.

Winter brings skiing to the Pocono Mountains. While the Pennsylvania slopes will never rival those in the Rockies (the tallest mountains here are just over 2,000 feet and artificial snow is often used), Pocono ski resorts are known for their family-friendly atmosphere. An assortment of state parks, state forests, rivers, streams, and lakes provide a rich backdrop for white-water rafting, canoeing, horseback riding, hiking, golfing and biking.

Or, if you prefer spectator sports and you're a NASCAR fan, Pocono Raceway (known as the "Tricky Triangle") near Long Pond is the site of two Monster Energy NASCAR Cup Series races, the Pocono 400 held in June and the Overton's 400 in July.

Shopping and being pampered in a spa are also high on many vacationers' lists. Outlets, malls and specialty shops cater to all tastes and budgets, and a popular pastime is combing the boutiques and the antiques and arts and crafts stores along the area's historic main streets. And spending an afternoon in a luxurious spa is a relaxing way to rejuvenate after taking in all the activities the Poconos have to offer.

Though beautiful all year, the Poconos are particularly scenic in the fall when the leaves change to blazing crimson, gold and orange.

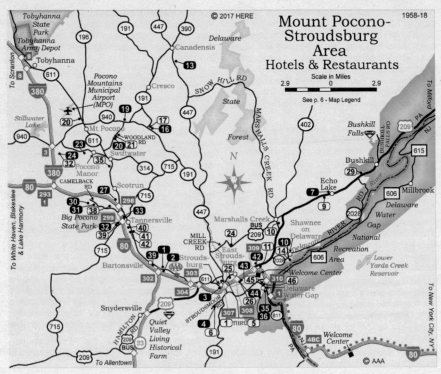

© 2017 HERE

Mount Pocono-Stroudsburg Area
Hotels & Restaurants

1958-18

Scale in Miles
2.9   0   2.9

See p. 6 - Map Legend

© AAA

Mount Pocono-Stroudsburg Area

This index helps you "spot" where approved hotels and restaurants are located on the corresponding detailed maps. Hotel daily rate range is for comparison only. Restaurant price range is a combination of lunch and/or dinner. Turn to the listing page for more information and consult display ads for special promotions.

 For more details, rates and reservations: AAA.com/travelguides/hotels

STROUDSBURG

Map Page	Hotels	Diamond Rated	Rate Range	Page
1 this page	Fairfield Inn & Suites by Marriott - Stroudsburg Bartonsville Poconos	◈◈◈	$99-$348	287
2 this page	Hampton Inn & Suites Stroudsburg/Bartonsville	◈◈◈	Rates not provided	287
3 this page	Hampton Inn - Stroudsburg/Poconos	◈◈◈	$119-$199	287
4 this page	Stroudsmoor Country Inn	◈◈◈	$90-$330	287

Map Page	Restaurants	Diamond Rated	Cuisine	Price Range	Page
① this page	Sarah Street Grill	◈◈	American	$9-$26	287
② this page	Café Duet	◈	Coffee/Tea Sandwiches	$5-$10	287
③ this page	Marco Antonio's	◈◈	Spanish	$15-$44	287
④ this page	Newberry's Yard of Ale	◈◈	American	$10-$25	287
⑤ this page	Siamsa Irish Pub	◈◈	Irish Fish & Chips Steak	$9-$29	287
⑥ this page	Stroudsmoor Country Inn	◈◈◈	Traditional American	$11-$44	287

MARSHALLS CREEK

Map Page	Hotel	Diamond Rated	Rate Range	Page
7 this page	**Pocono Palace Resort**	◈◈	Rates not provided SAVE	129

Map Page	Restaurants	Diamond Rated	Cuisine	Price Range	Page
⑨ p. 266	Big "A" Grillehouse	◈	Italian Steak Seafood	$8-$43	129
⑩ p. 266	Alaska Pete's	◈◈◈	Seafood Steak	$12-$35	129
⑪ p. 266	Landmark Restaurant	◈	New Breakfast Comfort Food	$5-$12	129

SHAWNEE ON DELAWARE

Map Page	Hotel		Diamond Rated	Rate Range	Page
⑩ p. 266	The Shawnee Inn and Golf Resort		◈◈◈	Rates not provided	277

Map Page	Restaurant	Diamond Rated	Cuisine	Price Range	Page
⑭ p. 266	The Gem & Keystone Brewpub	◈◈	American	$8-$26	277

CANADENSIS

Map Page	Hotel		Diamond Rated	Rate Range	Page
⑬ p. 266	Brookview Manor Inn		◈◈◈	$165-$289	53

CRESCO

Map Page	Hotel		Diamond Rated	Rate Range	Page
⑯ p. 266	Crescent Lodge		◈◈◈	Rates not provided	63

Map Page	Restaurant	Diamond Rated	Cuisine	Price Range	Page
⑰ p. 266	Crescent Lodge	◈◈◈	Continental	$16-$29	63

MOUNT POCONO

Map Page	Hotels		Diamond Rated	Rate Range	Page
⑲ p. 266	**Paradise Stream Resort**		◈◈	Rates not provided [SAVE]	136
⑳ p. 266	**Mount Airy Casino Resort**		◈◈◈◈	$99-$699 [SAVE]	136

Map Page	Restaurants	Diamond Rated	Cuisine	Price Range	Page
⑳ p. 266	Baileys Rib & Steakhouse	◈◈	Steak	$16-$36	136
㉑ p. 266	Guy Fieri's Mt. Pocono Kitchen	◈◈	New Comfort Food	$13-$28	136

POCONO MANOR

Map Page	Hotels		Diamond Rated	Rate Range	Page
㉓ p. 266	**Pocono Manor Resort & Spa**		◈◈◈	Rates not provided [SAVE]	269
㉔ p. 266	Kalahari Resort		◈◈◈	Rates not provided	269

Map Page	Restaurant	Diamond Rated	Cuisine	Price Range	Page
㉜ p. 266	Sortino's Italian Kitchen	◈◈	Italian Comfort Food	$15-$29	269

SCOTRUN

Map Page	Hotel		Diamond Rated	Rate Range	Page
㉗ p. 266	Great Wolf Lodge		◈◈◈	Rates not provided	274

TANNERSVILLE

Map Page	Hotels		Diamond Rated	Rate Range	Page
㉚ p. 266	The Chateau Resort & Conference Center		◈◈	Rates not provided	288
㉛ p. 266	Camelback Resort		◈◈◈	Rates not provided	288
㉜ p. 266	**Days Inn-Tannersville**		◈◈	$66-$150 [SAVE]	288
㉝ p. 266	**Best Western Plus Poconos Hotel**		◈◈	$90-$250 [SAVE]	288

Map Page	Restaurants	Diamond Rated	Cuisine	Price Range	Page
㊳ p. 266	**Barley Creek Brewing Company**	◈◈	American	$11-$24	288

Map Page	Restaurants (cont'd)	Diamond Rated	Cuisine	Price Range	Page
㉟ p. 266	**Tandoor Palace Restaurant & Bar**	◈	Indian	$12-$21	289
㊵ p. 266	Gabel's Ice Cream & Fast Food	◈	American	$3-$8	288
㊶ p. 266	Legendary Tannersville Inn	◈◈	American	$9-$33	288
㊷ p. 266	**Smuggler's Cove**	◈◈	Seafood	$7-$45	288

DELAWARE WATER GAP

Map Page	Hotels	Diamond Rated	Rate Range	Page
㉟ p. 266	Deer Head Inn	◈◈	Rates not provided	64
㊱ p. 266	Water Gap Country Club	◈◈	$69-$195	64

Map Page	Restaurants	Diamond Rated	Cuisine	Price Range	Page
㊺ p. 266	Apple Pie Cafe	◈	Breakfast Sandwiches	$5-$10	64
㊻ p. 266	Sycamore Grille	◈◈◈	American	$8-$30	64

BARTONSVILLE

Map Page	Hotel	Diamond Rated	Rate Range	Page
㊴ p. 266	**Baymont Inn & Suites**	◈◈	$90-$299 [SAVE]	42

EAST STROUDSBURG

Map Page	Hotels	Diamond Rated	Rate Range	Page
㊷ p. 266	**Days Inn East Stroudsburg**	◈◈	$60-$150 [SAVE]	69
㊸ p. 266	Super 8 East Stroudsburg	◈◈	$55-$145	69
㊹ p. 266	**Quality Inn Near Pocono Mountains**	◈◈◈	$70-$139 [SAVE]	69

Map Page	Restaurants	Diamond Rated	Cuisine	Price Range	Page
㉔ p. 266	**Peppe's Bistro**	◈◈◈	Northern Italian	$9-$33	69
㉕ p. 266	Holy Guacamole	◈	Mexican	$3-$7	69
㉖ p. 266	**The Roasted Tomato**	◈◈	American	$9-$22	69
㉙ p. 266	Petrizzo's Restaurant	◈◈	Italian Pizza	$10-$22	69

SWIFTWATER

Map Page	Restaurant	Diamond Rated	Cuisine	Price Range	Page
㉟ p. 266	Desaki	◈◈◈	Japanese Steak Sushi	$15-$50	288

POCONO MANOR

- Hotels & Restaurants map & index p. 266
- Part of Pocono Mountains Area — see map p. 264

KALAHARI RESORT   570/580-6000 **24**
▼▼▼▼ Resort Hotel. **Address:** 250 Kalahari Blvd 18349

POCONO MANOR RESORT & SPA   570/839-7111 **23**

▼▼▼
Historic Resort Hotel
Rates not provided

Address: 1 Manor Dr 18349 **Location:** I-380 exit 3, just e on SR 314, follow signs for 1.3 mi. **Facility:** Built in 1902, this resort offers a relaxed charm and sweeping views of the region. Extensive recreational facilities will keep the whole family occupied. Rooms have nice traditional appeal. 240 units, some two bedrooms and efficiencies. 7 stories, interior corridors. **Terms:** check-in 4 pm. **Dining:** 3 restaurants. **Pool:** outdoor, heated indoor. **Activities:** fishing, regulation golf, cross country skiing, ice skating, recreation programs in summer, bicycles, playground, game room, trails, exercise room, spa. **Guest Services:** coin laundry, area transportation.

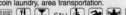

WHERE TO EAT

SORTINO'S ITALIAN KITCHEN   570/580-6085 **32**
▼▼ Italian Comfort Food. Casual Dining. **Address:** 250 Kalahari Blvd 18349

POCONO PINES pop. 1,409

- Part of Pocono Mountains Area — see map p. 264

VAN GILDER'S JUBILEE RESTAURANT & PUB   570/646-2377
▼▼ Comfort Food. Casual Dining. **Address:** 2067 Rt 940 18350

POINT MARION (I-2) pop. 1,159, elev. 817'

Point Marion is part of the Laurel Highlands *(see place listing p. 122).*

POINT PLEASANT (G-12) elev. 92'

- Part of Philadelphia area — see map p. 154

Before its settlement in the mid-1700s Point Pleasant was the site of Native American quarries for argillite, which was used in making arrowheads and knife blades. The Delaware River, another natural resource, provides many recreational opportunities for area visitors and residents.

POTTSTOWN (A-8) pop. 22,377, elev. 144'

- Part of Philadelphia area — see map p. 154

As early as 1714 an iron forge was established north of the present site of Pottstown, and iron making quickly became the area's principal industry. When Colonial ironmaster John Potts founded the city in 1752, he named it Pottsgrove. In 1815 it was incorporated as Pottstown. The city remains a busy industrial and trade center.

TriCounty Area Chamber of Commerce: 152 E. High St., Suite 360, Pottstown, PA 19464. **Phone:** (610) 326-2900.

Shopping: Coventry Mall, SR 100 and SR 724, is the major shopping center. It includes Boscov's and Kohl's.

COMFORT INN & SUITES   (610)326-5000
▼▼▼ Hotel. **Address:** 99 Robinson St 19464

WHERE TO EAT

COVENTRY PUB   610/323-5790
▼▼ American. Casual Dining. **Address:** 1440 S Hanover St 19465

SLY FOX BREWERY & TASTIN' ROOM   484/300-4644
▼ American. Brewpub. **Address:** 331 Circle of Progress Dr 19464

POTTSVILLE (G-9) pop. 14,324, elev. 636'

Pottsville was named for John Pott, a pioneer ironworker who built a small iron furnace in 1806. The founding of the city coincided with the beginning of the vital iron and steel industry, which prospered for more than a century.

Pottsville also was part of northeastern Pennsylvania's anthracite coal mining region. Pottsville sports the 90-foot-high Henry Clay Monument, a memorial to the presidential candidate who supported legislation favorable to the area's coal industry. The monument, built in 1855, is said to be the nation's oldest cast-iron statue.

Schuylkill County Visitors Bureau: Union Station Bldg., One Progress Cir., Suite 100, Pottsville, PA 17901. **Phone:** (570) 622-7700 or (800) 765-7282.

JERRY'S CLASSIC CARS AND COLLECTIBLES MUSEUM, downtown at 394 S. Centre St. (US 209), houses an impressive collection of more than 20,000 antiques and memorabilia on two floors. The majority of items relate to 1950s and '60s pop culture. The museum features hand-painted murals and themed sections, including a bandstand, kitchen and soda fountain. There are usually about 15 classic cars on display; the models chosen from the collection are changed regularly.

Time: Allow 1 hour minimum. **Hours:** Fri.-Sun. noon-5, May-Oct. **Cost:** $10; $8 (ages 6-12 and senior citizens); free (ages 0-5). **Phone:** (570) 628-2266. **GT**

PUNXSUTAWNEY (F-4) pop. 5,962, elev. 1,236'

Each Feb. 2, the nation awaits the prognostication of one of the town's most respected citizens: Punxsutawney Phil—the official groundhog of ▼ Groundhog Day. As they have each year since 1887, believers trek at dawn to Gobbler's Knob and rout the rodent from his den to determine whether there will be an early spring or 6 more weeks of winter, a legend based on the European tradition of Candlemas Day (Feb. 2), where a burrowing animal is used to predict the length of winter.

This annual occurrence was immortalized in the 1993 movie "Groundhog Day," in which a television weatherman (played by comedian Bill Murray) reluctantly comes to Punxsutawney to cover the event, only to awake the next morning and find himself reliving every facet of the preceding day over, again and again.

On the other 364 days of the year, Phil and his family reside at the "groundhog zoo" at the Punxsutawney Memorial Library, just off the town's historic Barclay Square at 301 E. Mahoning St. A glass window lets visitors see the animals and their habitat from either inside or outside the building.

A series of 32 colorful, larger-than-life fiberglass statues honoring Punxsutawney's most famous resident can be seen in public spaces around town. The chamber of commerce has maps that show the placement of each of the Phils, as they are called.

Area residents enjoy the outdoors year-round on the Mahoning Shadow Trail, a 15-mile rails-to-trails conversion that runs between Punxsutawney and Fordham, beckoning walkers, runners, bicyclists and cross-country skiers. The trail, which mostly follows Mahoning Creek, crosses a railroad bridge and passes coke ovens and a waterfall. Trail maps are available at the chamber of commerce office.

Punxsutawney Area Chamber of Commerce: 102 W. Mahoning St., Punxsutawney, PA 15767. **Phone:** (814) 938-7700.

PUNXSUTAWNEY WEATHER DISCOVERY CENTER, 201 N. Findley St., features interactive exhibits relating to weather forecasting—both the scientific kind and folklore (where Punxsutawney Phil comes in). Visitors can watch weather videos in the theater, experience the power of a tornado, create a thunderstorm and try their hand at giving a TV weather forecast. **Time:** Allow 1 hour minimum. **Hours:** Mon.-Sat. 10-4, June-Aug.; Mon.-Tues. and Thurs.-Sat. 10-4, Apr.-May and Sept.-Dec.; Mon. and Thurs.-Sat. 10-4, rest of year. Closed major holidays; phone ahead to confirm holiday schedule. **Cost:** $6; free (ages 0-1). **Phone:** (814) 938-1000.

QUAKERTOWN pop. 8,979
• Part of Philadelphia area — see map p. 154

ECONO LODGE	215/536-2500

▼▼ Hotel. **Address:** 1446 W Broad St 18951

HAMPTON INN-QUAKERTOWN	(215)536-7779

▼▼▼ Hotel. **Address:** 1915 John Fries Hwy (SR 663) 18951

> **AAA Benefit:** Members save up to 10%!

HOLIDAY INN EXPRESS HOTEL & SUITES QUAKERTOWN	215/529-7979

▼▼▼ Hotel. **Address:** 1918 John Fries Hwy (SR 663) 18951

QUALITY INN & SUITES	(215)538-3000

▼▼▼ Hotel. **Address:** 1905 John Fries Hwy (SR 663) 18951

SPRINGHILL SUITES BY MARRIOTT	(215)529-6800

▼▼▼ Hotel. **Address:** 1930 John Fries Hwy (SR 663) 18951

> **AAA Benefit:** Members save 5% or more!

WHERE TO EAT

THE SPINNERSTOWN HOTEL RESTAURANT & TAP ROOM	215/536-7242

▼▼ American. Casual Dining. **Address:** 2195 Spinnerstown Rd 18951

THE WEST END	267/347-4003

▼▼ American. Sports Bar. **Address:** 750 N West End Blvd 18951

QUARRYVILLE (I-10) pop. 2,576, elev. 488'
• Part of Pennsylvania Dutch Country area — see map p. 143

About 7 miles south on US 222 is the Robert Fulton Birthplace, the restored stone house where the artist, inventor and engineer was born in 1765. His drawings, miniature portraits and invention models, including the steamship *Clermont,* are exhibited on weekends during the summer; phone (717) 548-2679.

RADNOR
• Part of Philadelphia area — see map p. 154

RADNOR HOTEL   (610)688-5800
♦♦♦ Hotel. **Address:** 591 E Lancaster Ave 19087

WHERE TO EAT

GLENMORGAN BAR & GRILL   610/341-3188
♦♦ American. Casual Dining. **Address:** 593 E Lancaster Ave 19087

READING (H-10) pop. 88,082, elev. 237'

Thomas and Richard Penn, sons of William Penn, founded Reading in 1748 and named it for their ancestral home in England. The settlement was a supply base for forts along the Blue Mountains during the French and Indian War. In Reading originated the first Civil War regiment, volunteer band, flag and women's aid society. Modern Reading has become a major industrial center, with many clothing manufacturers maintaining retail outlet stores.

Reading contains a wealth of 18th- and 19th-century buildings, many noted for their elaborate use of decorative glass and wrought iron, in its five historic districts: Callowhill, which centers on the city's commercial area; Prince, which contains preserved 19th-century workers' homes, factories and commercial structures; Centre Park, which displays some of the city's finest Victorian structures; Penn's Common; and Queen Anne.

On the east side of Reading on the summit of Mount Penn is the Pagoda, a seven-story 1908 Japanese building that affords panoramas of the city and the Schuylkill Valley. Some 8 miles northwest via SR 183 is the Blue Marsh Lake Recreation Area *(see Recreation Areas Chart).*

The GoggleWorks Center for the Arts, (610) 374-4600, is an art gallery where you can watch artists at work; there also is a theater that shows foreign and independent films. The site comprises several buildings at the intersection of Washington and 2nd streets and includes the former Thomas A. Wilson & Co. factory, a company that produced optical glass in the late 19th century. The company quickly expanded its horizons to become an innovator in occupational safety products, the first of which was a protective lens that offered the vision of those working in metal processing. The front desk offers maps of the galleries. Guided tours are offered; phone for schedule.

Pennsylvania's Americana Region Visitor Center: 201 Washington St., Reading, PA 19601. The visitor center inside the GoggleWorks Center for the Arts is staffed on weekends; brochures available daily. **Phone:** (610) 375-4085 or (800) 443-6610.

Shopping: Carter's and Lee and Wrangler are among the stores that fill the more than 450,000 square feet of retail space at **VF Outlet Center**, 801 Hill Ave. Boscov's and Burlington Coat Factory anchor **Fairgrounds Square Mall**, 3050 N. Fifth Street Hwy.

SAVE **MID-ATLANTIC AIR MUSEUM,** SR 183 to the Reading Regional Airport at 11 Museum Dr., following signs, displays both military and civilian aircraft dating from 1917 to 2006. Among the more than 65 airplanes displayed are two classic commercial airliners, a 1952 Martin 4-0-4 and a Vickers Viscount; a 1944 Douglas DC-3; a 1943 North American B-25 Mitchell; and a 1944 P-61 Black Widow, the first "night fighter" ever built.

Note: When using GPS for directions, use 1054 Arnold Road, Reading PA, 19605. **Time:** Allow 1 hour minimum. **Hours:** Daily 9:30-4. Last tour begins 1 hour before closing. Closed major holidays. **Cost:** $10; $8 (ages 65+); $3 (ages 6-12). **Phone:** (610) 372-7333. GT

COMFORT INN   (610)371-0500

♦♦
Hotel
$105-$185

Address: 2200 Stacey Dr (5th Street Hwy) 19605 **Location:** US 222 business route, just s of Warren St Bypass (SR 12 E). Located in a commercial area. **Facility:** 60 units. 2 stories, interior corridors. **Amenities:** safes. **Activities:** exercise room. **Guest Services:** valet laundry. **Featured Amenity:** full hot breakfast.

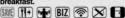

DOUBLETREE BY HILTON READING   610/375-8000
♦♦♦ Hotel. **Address:** 701 Penn St 19601

> **AAA Benefit:** Members save 5% or more!

FAIRFIELD INN & SUITES BY MARRIOTT READING/WYOMISSING   (610)376-4400
♦♦♦ Hotel. **Address:** 21 Meridian Blvd 19610

> **AAA Benefit:** Members save 5% or more!

HOLIDAY INN EXPRESS HOTEL & SUITES   (610)372-0700
♦♦♦ Hotel. **Address:** 2389 Bernville Rd (Rt 183) 19605

WHERE TO EAT

THE ABE SALOON AND VICTORIAN LOUNGE   610/372-7777
♦♦ American. Casual Dining. **Address:** 100 N 5th St 19601

ALEBRIJE MEXICAN RESTAURANT
♦♦ Mexican. Casual Dining.
LOCATIONS:
Address: 3805 Perkiomen Ave 19606 **Phone:** 610/370-0900
Address: 3225 N 5th Street Highway 19605
Phone: 610/939-9288

JUDY'S ON CHERRY   610/374-8511
♦♦ Mediterranean Small Plates. Fine Dining. **Address:** 332 Cherry St 19602

STOKESAY CASTLE LORD'S DINING ROOM
610/375-6100

♦♦♦ American Fine Dining $30-$48 | **AAA Inspector Notes:** As guests walk into the elegant dining room, they will be captivated by the wood-beam cathedral ceiling, upscale furnishings, beautiful stone fireplace and wrought iron chandeliers. The contemporary American-focused menu provides an abundance

of flavorful dishes including coffee-dusted sea scallops and roasted rack of wild boar. Those looking for a more casual dining experience may be interested in the Knight's Pub, located right next door. **Features:** full bar. **Reservations:** suggested. **Address:** 141 Stokesay Castle Ln 19606 **Location:** US 422 business route, 3.4 mi w of jct US 422. D CALL ♿

THAI CUISINE RESTAURANT   610/929-6993
♦♦ Thai. Casual Dining. **Address:** 502 Eisenbrown St 19605

TROOPER THORN'S   610/685-4944
♦♦ Irish. Casual Dining. **Address:** 451 Morgantown Rd 19611

UGLY OYSTER DRAFTHAUS   610/373-6791
♦♦ American. Gastropub. **Address:** 21 S 5th St 19602

RIDLEY PARK pop. 7,002
• Hotels & Restaurants map & index p. 192
• Part of Philadelphia area — see map p. 154

MICROTEL INN & SUITES BY WYNDHAM, PHILADELPHIA AIRPORT RIDLEY PARK   (610)595-0300 **122**
♦♦ Hotel. **Address:** 155 S Stewart Ave 19078

SPRINGHILL SUITES BY MARRIOTT PHILADELPHIA AIRPORT/ RIDLEY PARK   (610)915-6600 **123**
♦♦♦ Hotel. **Address:** 201 Industrial Hwy 19078

AAA Benefit: Members save 5% or more!

ROBESONIA pop. 2,061

OZGOOD'S NEIGHBORHOOD GRILL & BAR   610/693-6685
♦♦ American. Casual Dining. **Address:** 319 E Penn Ave 19551

RONKS (H-10) pop. 362, elev. 380'
• Hotels & Restaurants map & index p. 148
• Part of Pennsylvania Dutch Country area — see map p. 143

A restored 1738 water-driven gristmill and the largest covered bridge in Lancaster County is located .25 mi. s. of US 30 at jct. S. Ronks and S. Soudersburg rds. Buggy rides, tractor pulls and hayrides are available seasonally at Mill Bridge Camp Resort. Phone ahead to verify schedule; (717) 687-8181 or 800-645-2744.

THE AMISH VILLAGE, 199 Hartman Bridge Rd., offers 25-minute tours of an 1840 farmhouse furnished in the Old Order Amish style. The tour includes the great room (used for community meetings), kitchen, bedrooms and basement, and the guide offers insight into Amish history, clothing, furniture and their way of life. Other buildings include a barn, schoolhouse, blacksmith shop, store and springhouse. Visitors are permitted to feed the farm animals.

The 90-minute Backroads Bus Tour is a narrated tour in a 14-passenger bus along country roads where buggies and farmers are often seen. The tour includes at least one stop; options include a quilt shop, a pretzel bakery or a bake shop. Picnicking is permitted after tours. **Time:** Allow 1 hour, 30 minutes minimum. **Hours:** Village Mon.-Sat. 9-5, Sun. 10-5, Mar.-June and Sept.-Oct. (also 9-5, weekday holidays); Mon.-Sat. 9-6, Sun. 10-6, July-Aug. (also 9-6 on July 4); daily 9-4, in Nov.; daily 10-4, in Dec.; Sat.-Sun. 10-4, rest of year. Closed Jan. 1, Thanksgiving, Christmas Eve and Christmas. **Cost:** Amish Village tour $9.75; $6.25 (ages 5-12). Backroads Bus Tour $22; $15 (ages 0-12). Combination Amish Village and Backroads Bus Tour $28; $18 (ages 5-12); $15 (ages 0-4). Reservations are recommended for combination tours. **Phone:** (717) 687-8511. GT 🍴

(See map & index p. 148.)

DAYS INN RONKS DUTCH COUNTRY
(717)390-1800 62

Hotel
$59-$169

Address: 34 Eastbrook Rd 17572 Location: Jct US 30 (Lincoln Hwy), just n on SR 896. Located in a commercial tourist area. Facility: 52 units, some efficiencies. 2 stories (no elevator), interior corridors. Amenities: safes. Activities: exercise room. Guest Services: coin laundry.

EASTBROOK INN
717/393-2550 64

Motel. Address: 21 Eastbrook Rd 17572

HERSHEY FARM INN
(717)687-8635 65

Hotel
$50-$180

Address: 240 Hartman Bridge Rd 17572 Location: Jct US 30 (Lincoln Hwy), 1.5 mi s on SR 896. Facility: 60 units, some two bedrooms. 1-2 stories (no elevator), interior/exterior corridors. Terms: cancellation fee imposed. Dining: Hershey Farm Restaurant, see separate listing. Pool: outdoor. Activities: fishing, playground, trails. Guest Services: coin laundry. Featured Amenity: breakfast buffet.

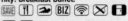

LA QUINTA INN & SUITES
(717)392-8100 63

Hotel
$75-$195

Address: 25 Eastbrook Rd 17572 Location: Jct US 30 (Lincoln Hwy), just n on SR 896. Facility: 77 units. 3 stories, interior corridors. Pool: heated indoor. Activities: hot tub, exercise room. Guest Services: coin laundry. Featured Amenity: continental breakfast.

QUIET HAVEN MOTEL
717/397-6231 61

Motel. Address: 2556 Siegrist Rd 17572

 WHERE TO EAT

DIENNER'S COUNTRY RESTAURANT
717/687-9571 46

American. Casual Dining. Address: 2855 Lincoln Hwy E 17572

HERSHEY FARM RESTAURANT
717/687-8635 48

Regional
American
Casual Dining
$6-$26

AAA Inspector Notes: This restaurant in the heart of Pennsylvania Dutch Country lays out a smorgasbord of home-cooked fare, including soups, salad and such hot dishes as sliced roast beef, fried chicken and pot pie. A country theme is prevalent in the warm, cozy dining room. Scenic trails with vegetable and flower gardens and a rustic waterfall wind out back. Reservations: suggested, weekends. Address: 240 Hartman Bridge Rd 17572 Location: Jct US 30 (Lincoln Hwy), 1.5 mi s on SR 896; in Hershey Farm Inn. B L D

KATIE'S KITCHEN
717/687-5333 47

American. Casual Dining. Address: 200 Hartman Bridge Rd 17572

MILLER'S SMORGASBORD & BAKERY
717/687-6621 45

Regional
American
Casual Dining
$8-$24

AAA Inspector Notes: The focus of the menu at this eatery is traditional Lancaster County favorites such as carved beef, turkey, ham, fried chicken, creamy cheesecake and gourmet apple pie. While the buffet is the most popular option, a la carte items also are available. The inviting building features traditional turn-of-the-20th-century architecture. Address: 2811 Lincoln Hwy E 17572 Location: US 30 (Lincoln Hwy), 1.8 mi e of jct SR 896. B L D

ROUTE 30 DINER
717/397-2507 44

American. Casual Dining. Address: 2575 Lincoln Hwy E 17572

ROYERSFORD pop. 4,752
• Part of Philadelphia area — see map p. 154

STAYBRIDGE SUITES ROYERSFORD/VALLEY FORGE
610/792-9300

Extended Stay Hotel. Address: 88 Anchor Pkwy 19468

ST. MARYS (E-5) pop. 13,070, elev. 1,702'

St. Marys was founded on December 8, 1842, by German immigrants escaping religious persecution; it was named in honor of the Blessed Virgin Mary. Today it is the industrial and retail hub of Elk County and in close proximity to the largest free-roaming elk herd east of the Mississippi.

St. Marys Area Chamber of Commerce: 53 S. St. Marys St., St. Marys, PA 15857. **Phone:** (814) 781-3804.

BEST WESTERN PLUS EXECUTIVE INN
(814)834-0000

Hotel
$110-$160

 Best Western PLUS.

AAA Benefit: Members save 5% to 15% and earn 10% bonus points!

Address: 1002 Earth Rd 15857 Location: SR 255, south end of town. Located in a commercial area. Facility: 57 units. 3 stories, interior corridors. Terms: cancellation fee imposed. Pool: heated outdoor. Activities: exercise room. Guest Services: valet laundry.

SARVER

KING'S FAMILY RESTAURANT
724/295-2220

American. Casual Dining. Address: 400 Buffalo Plaza 16055

🔗 **Save on travel, shopping, dining and more: AAA.com/discounts**

SAYRE   pop. 5,587

BEST WESTERN GRAND VICTORIAN INN
(570)888-7711

Hotel
$99-$109

Best Western. AAA Benefit: Members save 5% to 15% and earn 10% bonus points!

Address: 255 Spring St 18840 **Location:** SR 17 exit 61, just s. **Facility:** 100 units. 4 stories, interior corridors. **Terms:** cancellation fee imposed. **Pool:** heated indoor. **Activities:** sauna, hot tub, health club. **Guest Services:** valet laundry.

COMFORT INN & SUITES
(570)888-1100

Hotel
$89-$199

Address: 2160 Elmira St 18840 **Location:** I-86 exit 60, 0.4 mi s on US 220, just e, then 0.7 mi s. **Facility:** 85 units, some efficiencies. 3 stories, interior corridors. **Amenities:** safes. **Pool:** heated indoor. **Activities:** exercise room. **Guest Services:** coin laundry. **Featured Amenity: full hot breakfast.**

HAMPTON INN SAYRE
(570)882-1166

Hotel
$109-$169

Hampton AAA Benefit: Members save up to 10%!

Address: 3080 N Elmira St 18840 **Location:** US 220 exit Sayre/S Waverly, just n. **Facility:** 70 units. 4 stories, interior corridors. **Terms:** 1-7 night minimum stay, cancellation fee imposed. **Pool:** heated indoor. **Activities:** exercise room. **Guest Services:** valet and coin laundry. **Featured Amenity: breakfast buffet.**

MICROTEL INN & SUITES BY WYNDHAM
(570)888-0001
Hotel. **Address:** 1775 Elmira St 18840

WHERE TO EAT

THE BRI MARIE INN AND RESTAURANT   570/888-8800
New American. Fine Dining. **Address:** 119 S Elmer Ave 18840

THE GRILLE AT THE TRAIN STATION   570/888-3100
American. Casual Dining. **Address:** 718 N Lehigh Ave 18840

SCENERY HILL

CENTURY INN DINING ROOM   724/945-6600
American. Casual Dining. **Address:** 2175 E National Pike (US 40) 15360

SCHWENKSVILLE (A-9) pop. 1,385, elev. 148'
• **Part of Philadelphia area — see map p. 154**
PENNYPACKER MILLS, 5 Haldeman Rd., is the former home of Samuel W. Pennypacker, Pennsylvania's 25th governor. The house was built in the early 18th century and after Pennypacker bought the house in 1900 he had an architect transform it into a Georgian-style Colonial Revival mansion. Historical documents and original family furnishings and artifacts can be seen. Special events, educational activities and changing exhibits are offered throughout the year. **Time:** Allow 30 minutes minimum. **Hours:** Tues.-Sat. 10-4, Sun. 1-4. Closed major holidays. **Cost:** Donations. **Phone:** (610) 287-9349.

SCOTRUN
• **Hotels & Restaurants map & index p. 266**
• **Part of Pocono Mountains Area — see map p. 264**

GREAT WOLF LODGE   570/688-9899 **27**
Hotel. **Address:** 1 Great Wolf Dr 18355

SCOTTDALE (H-2) pop. 4,384, elev. 1,050'

Scottdale is part of the Laurel Highlands *(see place listing p. 122).*

SCRANTON (E-10) pop. 76,089, elev. 753'
• **Restaurants p. 276**

Scranton and Lackawanna County played an important part in the Industrial Revolution—four anthracite blast furnaces built in the 1840s and 1850s by the Scranton brothers helped supply more than 80 percent of the anthracite coal that fueled the growth of American industry. Miles of track, industrial sites and mine tunnels remain.

At 700 Lackawanna Ave. (I-81 exit 185) is the 1908 Lackawanna Station, a former railroad depot that has been restored and converted into the Radisson Lackawanna Station Hotel Scranton. The lobby of the neo-Classical structure displays a mosaic floor, a barrel-vaulted Tiffany stained-glass ceiling and Siena marble and faience tile murals; phone (570) 342-8300.

The Suraci Gallery, Mahady Gallery and The Maslow Study Gallery for Contemporary Art at Marywood University, the Linder Gallery at Keystone College and The Hope Horn Gallery at the University of Scranton feature paintings, sculpture, prints and photographs. Theater, concert and musical presentations are offered at the schools throughout the year. Phone (570) 348-6278 for Marywood University; (570) 945-8000 for Keystone College and (570) 941-7400 for Scranton University information.

Outdoor concerts are presented May through September at The Pavilion at Montage Mountain, (570) 961-9000. Additional theater, concert and musical presentations are offered at Peoples Security Bank Theater at Lackawanna College, (570) 955-1455; and Scranton Cultural Center, (570) 346-7369.

Pop culture has brought Scranton, which served as the fictional setting of the NBC comedy "The Office," a lot of attention in recent years. Though not filmed here, the show's characters often discussed local restaurants, attractions and the mining history. The sitcom's opening credits showed some of the city's landmarks.

Lots of recreational opportunities can be found at Lackawanna State Park *(see Recreation Areas Chart)*, McDade Park and Merli-Sarnoski Park. The PNC Field, off I-81 exit 182 at the base of Montage Mountain, plays host to the New York Yankees' class AAA-affiliate, the Scranton/Wilkes-Barre Rail-Riders, in spring and summer; phone (570) 969-2255.

Shopping: Viewmont Mall, on US 6 Bus. Rte. off I-81 exit 191A, features JCPenney and Macy's.

ANTHRACITE HERITAGE MUSEUM is at 22 Bald Mountain Rd. in McDade Park. The museum is dedicated to collecting, interpreting and preserving the history and culture of Pennsylvania's hard-coal region. Exhibits also highlight various immigrant groups who settled in the region and depict their influence on local history and industry. A brief film showcasing the industry's history also can be seen.

Guided tours are available by appointment. **Time:** Allow 1 hour minimum. **Hours:** Mon.-Sat. 9-5, Sun. noon-5, May-Sept.; Wed.-Sat. 9-5, Sun. noon-5, rest of year. Closed major holidays; phone ahead. **Cost:** $7; $6 (ages 65+); $5 (ages 3-11); free (active military with ID). Phone for guided tour rates. **Phone:** (570) 963-4804. ⒼⓉ

HOUDINI TOUR & MAGIC SHOW, off I-81 exit 190, then w. 2 mi. to 1433 N. Main Ave., is dedicated to the memory of famed escape artist and magician Harry Houdini. Guided tours showcase Houdini memorabilia, including photographs, props and posters. Rare Houdini films and a live magic show also are included. A 4-hour séance show also is offered Sat. by reservation only.

Hours: Daily 1-4, July 1-Labor Day weekend; Sat.-Sun. and holiday weekends 1-4, rest of year. Phone ahead to confirm schedule. **Cost:** $20; $14.95 (ages 0-11). **Phone:** (570) 342-5555, or (570) 383-1821 for show reservations.

STEAMTOWN NATIONAL HISTORIC SITE is off I-81 exit 185 at jct. Cliff and Lackawanna aves. The National Historic Site is on the railroad yard of the Delaware, Lackawanna and Western Railroad and covers more than 40 acres. It features one of the country's largest collections of period locomotives, freight and passenger cars and railway maintenance vehicles. A visitor center, turntable and roundhouse also can be seen.

History and technology museums detail many aspects of railroading, including advances in railroad development and the types of jobs that the industry required. "Steel and Steam," an 18-minute film chronicling the evolution of railroads in the early 1900s, is regularly shown in a 250-seat theater. Half-hour steam and diesel train excursions offer views of the grounds and traverse a portion of the former main line. Park rangers and volunteers lead several themed walking tours as well.

Ages 15 and under must be accompanied by an adult. **Time:** Allow 2 hours, 30 minutes minimum. **Hours:** Daily 9-5, Apr.-Dec.; 10-4, rest of year (weather permitting). Ticket office closes 1 hour before park closing. "Steel and Steam" is presented every 30 minutes 9:30-1 hour before closing. Train excursions are offered mid-Apr. to late Oct.; phone ahead for departure times. Walking tour schedules vary; phone ahead. Closed Jan. 1, Thanksgiving and Christmas.

Cost: Site free. Train excursion fare $5; free (ages 0-5). Additional fees for some excursions. **Phone:** (570) 340-5200, or (570) 340-5204 for train reservations. ⒼⓉ 🛤

Electric City Trolley Station and Museum is off I-81 exit 185 to Lackawanna Ave., following signs to 300 Cliff St., on the grounds of Steamtown National Historic Site. The facility displays trolleys, photographs and a model trolley that children can control. A 10-minute film details the history of trolleys. Approximately 10-mile 1-hour trolley excursion rides also are offered.

Although the museum is on the grounds of a national park, the site is operated by Lackawanna County; therefore, National Parks passes are not valid. **Time:** Allow 30 minutes minimum. **Hours:** Museum daily 9-4. Trolley rides depart Thurs.-Sun. at 10:30, noon, 1:30 and 3, late-Apr.-Oct 31. Tickets must be purchased 15 minutes before scheduled departures. Closed Jan. 1, Thanksgiving and Christmas. Phone ahead to confirm schedule. **Cost:** Museum $6; $5 (ages 62+); $4 (ages 4-17). Trolley ride $8; $7 (ages 62+); $6 (ages 4-17). Combination ticket $10; $9 (ages 62+); $8 (ages 4-17). **Phone:** (570) 963-6590.

 Get member rates and reservations

at AAA.com/hertz

COMFORT SUITES   (570)347-1551

♦♦♦♦
Hotel
$84-$269

Address: 44 Montage Mountain Rd 18507 **Location:** I-81 exit 182 northbound; exit 182A southbound. **Facility:** 100 units, some two bedrooms and efficiencies. 4 stories, interior corridors. **Pool:** heated indoor. **Activities:** hot tub, game room, exercise room. **Guest Services:** valet and coin laundry, area transportation. **Featured Amenity:** breakfast buffet.

[SAVE] [⟵] [↑↓] CALL [♿] [☄] [⊯]
[BIZ] [⊚] [✕] [🔌] [🛏] [💻]

COURTYARD BY MARRIOTT SCRANTON WILKES-BARRE
(570)969-2100

♦♦♦ Hotel. **Address:** 16 Glenmaura National Blvd 18507

AAA Benefit: Members save 5% or more!

HAMPTON INN-SCRANTON AT MONTAGE MOUNTAIN
(570)342-7002

♦♦♦ Hotel. **Address:** 22 Montage Mountain Rd 18507

AAA Benefit: Members save up to 10%!

HILTON SCRANTON & CONFERENCE CENTER
(570)343-3000

♦♦♦♦ Hotel. **Address:** 100 Adams Ave 18503

AAA Benefit: Members save 5% or more!

RADISSON LACKAWANNA STATION HOTEL SCRANTON
(570)342-8300

♦♦♦ Classic Historic Hotel. **Address:** 700 Lackawanna Ave 18503

SPRINGHILL SUITES BY MARRIOTT SCRANTON WILKES-BARRE
(570)207-1212

♦♦♦ Hotel. **Address:** 19 Radcliffe Dr 18507

AAA Benefit: Members save 5% or more!

TOWNEPLACE SUITES BY MARRIOTT SCRANTON WILKES-BARRE
(570)207-8500

♦♦♦ Extended Stay Hotel. **Address:** 26 Radcliffe Dr 18507

AAA Benefit: Members save 5% or more!

WHERE TO EAT

BLU WASABI   570/307-3282

♦♦ Japanese. Casual Dining. **Address:** 1008 Scranton Carbondale Hwy 18508

CARMEN'S 2.0 RESTAURANT   570/558-3929

♦♦ New Italian. Fine Dining. **Address:** 700 Lackawanna Ave 18503

CASA BELLA RISTORANTE   570/969-9006

♦♦ Italian. Casual Dining. **Address:** 330 W Market St N 18508

COOPER'S SEAFOOD HOUSE & SHIP'S PUB
570/346-6883

♦♦
Seafood
Casual Dining
$8-$34

AAA Inspector Notes: It's hard to imagine that any more mid-20th century kitsch could be stuffed into this fun, casual restaurant and tavern. The menu offers a fairly good selection of seafood dishes, both broiled and fried, and the selection of IPA beers is excellent. The walls are packed with a truly unique mix of nautical and pirate artifacts, old photos of Scranton, movie-star memorabilia and even some dioramas of popular TV shows. The men's room is a shrine to the Beatles; for the ladies' room it's Elvis. **Features:** full bar. **Address:** 701 N Washington Ave 18509 **Location:** At Washington Ave and Pine St; center. [L] [D] [LATE]

KILDARE'S IRISH PUB   570/344-4030

♦♦ Irish Comfort Food. Casual Dining. **Address:** 199 Jefferson Ave 18503

LA TOLTECA   570/969-0966

♦♦ Mexican. Casual Dining. **Address:** 46 Viewmont Dr 18508

NEW AMBER INDIAN RESTAURANT   570/344-7100

♦♦ Indian. Casual Dining. **Address:** 3505 Birney Ave 18507

SELINSGROVE pop. 5,654

COMFORT INN   (570)374-8880

♦♦ Hotel. **Address:** 613 N Susquehanna Tr 17870

HOLIDAY INN EXPRESS & SUITES SELINSGROVE
570/743-9275

♦♦♦ Hotel. **Address:** 651 N Susquehanna Tr 17870

WHERE TO EAT

BJ'S   570/374-9841

♦♦♦ Barbecue Seafood. Casual Dining. **Address:** 17 N Market St 17870

SELLERSVILLE pop. 4,249
• **Part of Philadelphia area — see map p. 154**

THE WASHINGTON HOUSE   215/257-3000

♦♦♦
American
Casual Dining
$7-$28

AAA Inspector Notes: Originally a farmhouse in the 1700s, this converted restaurant provides an intimate and homey atmosphere. Inside guests will find beautiful wood moldings, a decorative glass wine cellar and elaborate art pieces. The menu provides a variety of American cuisine with some European influences including Wiener schnitzel and Prussian peasant pork and noodles. **Features:** full bar, patio dining, Sunday brunch, happy hour. **Reservations:** suggested. **Address:** 136 N Main St 18960 **Location:** Just off SR 309 on Bethlehem Pike; midway between Quakertown and Montgomeryville. **Parking:** on-site and street.
[L] [D]

SEVEN SPRINGS (H-3) pop. 26, elev. 2,520'

Seven Springs is part of the Laurel Highlands (see place listing p. 122).

SHAMOKIN DAM pop. 1,686

ECONO LODGE INN & SUITES   (570)743-1111

♦♦ Hotel. **Address:** 3249 N Susquehanna Tr 17876

HAMPTON INN SELINSGROVE/SHAMOKIN DAM
(570)743-2223

Hotel
$109-$239

AAA Benefit:
Members save up to
10%!

Address: 3 Stettler Ave 17876 **Location:** US 11 and 15, 1 mi s of jct SR 61. Located in a commercial area. **Facility:** 75 units. 3 stories, interior corridors. **Terms:** 1-7 night minimum stay, cancellation fee imposed. **Pool:** heated indoor. **Activities:** hot tub, exercise room. **Guest Services:** valet and coin laundry. **Featured Amenity: full hot breakfast.**

WHERE TO EAT

SKEETER'S PIT BBQ   570/743-2727
Barbecue. Quick Serve. **Address:** 106 Victor Ln 17876

SHANKSVILLE (H-4) pop. 237, elev. 2,230'

Shanksville is part of the Laurel Highlands *(see place listing p. 122)*.

On Sept. 11, 2001, United Airlines Flight 93 crashed in a field in this rural farming and mining community. One of four commercial airliners hijacked that morning, Flight 93 was the only one that did not crash into a prominent American building. The plane left from Newark, N.J., bound for San Francisco, Calif., but its course was changed to Washington, D.C. by four terrorists. Passengers and crew members learned of the day's earlier attacks on the twin towers of the World Trade Center and the Pentagon when they telephoned authorities and family members. With extreme courage, they fought the four hijackers, thwarting their plan to fly the plane into a Washington, D.C. landmark. The crash site is now home to a temporary memorial to these 33 passengers and seven crew members. The first phase of a National Park Service permanent memorial was dedicated Sept. 10, 2011.

SHARON (E-1) pop. 14,038, elev. 854'

Evolving from a mill built on the Shenango River in 1802, Sharon is an industrial city that was founded on steel products. Frank H. Buhl, known as the father of industrial Shenango Valley, built a Romanesque castle in 1890 as a wedding present to his wife. One hundred years later the home was purchased and restored by Jim and Donna Winner. Buhl Mansion now operates as a luxury bed and breakfast and spa. Tours of the mansion, which showcases quality reproductions of works by some of the art world's greats, are available by appointment; phone (724) 346-3046.

VisitMercerCountyPA: 50 N. Water Ave., Sharon, PA 16146. **Phone:** (724) 346-3771.

Shopping: Reyers, in Sharon City Center at 40 S. Water Ave., stocks more than 100,000 pairs of shoes and carries hundreds of name brands. The Winner Outlet, in a four-story building at 32 W. State St., sells discount bridal, sport and cruise wear along with collectibles and giftware.

SHARPSBURG pop. 3,446
- **Hotels & Restaurants map & index p. 246**
- **Part of Pittsburgh area — see map p. 225**

CORNERSTONE RESTAURANT & BAR   412/408-3420 (66)
American. Casual Dining. **Address:** 301 Freeport Rd 15215

GRAN CANAL CAFFE   412/781-2546 (65)
Italian. Casual Dining. **Address:** 1021 N Canal St 15215

SHARTLESVILLE (G-10) pop. 455, elev. 568'

ROADSIDE AMERICA, off I-78/US 22 exit 23 at 109 Roadside Dr., is an extensive exhibit of miniature villages and towns depicting the growth and development of rural America. The 8,000-square-foot exhibit includes model trains that represent more than a half-century's work on the part of the builder. **Time:** Allow 1 hour minimum. **Hours:** Thurs.-Mon. 10-5 (also Sat.-Sun. 5-6). Hours may be extended in summer; phone ahead. Closed Jan. 1, Easter, Thanksgiving, Christmas Eve and Christmas. **Cost:** $8; $7 (senior citizens and military); $5 (ages 6-11). **Phone:** (610) 488-6241.

SHAWNEE ON DELAWARE (F-12) elev. 338'
- **Hotels & Restaurants map & index p. 266**
- **Part of Pocono Mountains Area — see map p. 264**

In this quaint town nestled in the foothills of the Poconos, visitors can secure outfitters for trips on the Delaware River as well as rent canoes, kayaks and other gear. River Road, which travels through Shawnee on Delaware, is a good route for navigating the adjacent Delaware Water Gap National Recreation Area.

The Shawnee Playhouse presents live theater performances, ballet, children's shows and other entertainment in a charming structure dating from 1904; for information phone (570) 421-5093.

THE SHAWNEE INN AND GOLF RESORT   570/424-4000 (10)
Historic Resort Hotel. **Address:** 100 Shawnee Inn Dr 18356

WHERE TO EAT

THE GEM & KEYSTONE BREWPUB   570/424-0990 (14)
American. Casual Dining. **Address:** 1 River Rd 18356

SHILLINGTON pop. 5,273
• Hotels p. 278 • Restaurants p. 278

BEST WESTERN PLUS READING INN & SUITES
(610)777-7888

Hotel
$95-$189

AAA Benefit: Members save 5% to 15% and earn 10% bonus points!

Address: 2299 Lancaster Pike 19607 **Location:** I-76 (Pennsylvania Tpke) exit 286, 9 mi n on US 222. Located in a commercial area. **Facility:** 142 units. 4 stories, interior corridors. **Terms:** cancellation fee imposed. **Amenities:** safes. **Pool:** outdoor. **Activities:** exercise room. **Guest Services:** valet and coin laundry.

 WHERE TO EAT

FLANAGAN'S PUB   610/777-6401
American. Sports Bar. **Address:** 41 W Lancaster Ave 19607

GIRALDI'S   610/816-5313
Italian. Quick Serve. **Address:** 2342 Lancaster Pike 19607

SHIPPENSBURG pop. 5,492

BEST WESTERN SHIPPENSBURG HOTEL
(717)532-5200

Hotel
$79-$159

Best Western. AAA Benefit: Members save 5% to 15% and earn 10% bonus points!

Address: 125 Walnut Bottom Rd 17257 **Location:** I-81 exit 29, 0.5 mi w on SR 174. **Facility:** 59 units. 2 stories (no elevator), interior corridors. **Terms:** 3 day cancellation notice-fee imposed. **Amenities:** safes. **Pool:** heated indoor. **Activities:** sauna, hot tub, exercise room. **Guest Services:** coin laundry.

COURTYARD BY MARRIOTT SHIPPENSBURG
(717)477-0680

Hotel
$62-$260

COURTYARD Marriott. AAA Benefit: Members save 5% or more!

Address: 503 Newburg Rd 17257 **Location:** 1.2 mi n on SR 696 from jct US 11 and SR 533 (King St). Next to the Conference Center at Shippensburg University. **Facility:** 110 units. 4 stories, interior corridors. **Terms:** cancellation fee imposed. **Pool:** heated indoor. **Activities:** hot tub, exercise room. **Guest Services:** coin laundry, boarding pass kiosk.

DYKEMAN HOUSE BED & BREAKFAST   717/530-1919
Historic Bed & Breakfast. **Address:** 6 W Dykeman Rd 17257

HOLIDAY INN EXPRESS & SUITES SHIPPENSBURG
717/532-1100

Hotel
Rates not provided

Address: 120 Walnut Bottom Rd 17257 **Location:** I-81 exit 29, 0.6 mi w on SR 174. **Facility:** 72 units, some two bedrooms. 3 stories, interior corridors. **Pool:** heated indoor. **Activities:** hot tub, exercise room. **Guest Services:** coin laundry. **Featured Amenity:** breakfast buffet.

MCLEAN HOUSE   (717)530-1390
Historic Bed & Breakfast. **Address:** 80 W King St 17257

QUALITY INN & SUITES SHIPPEN PLACE HOTEL
717/532-4141
Hotel. **Address:** 32 E King St 17257

WHERE TO EAT

CJ'S AMERICAN PUB & GRILL   717/532-5612
American. Casual Dining. **Address:** 487 E King St 17257

UNIVERSITY GRILLE   717/530-1148
American. Casual Dining. **Address:** 32 E King St 17257

SHIPPENVILLE pop. 480

SWEET BASIL FAMILY DINING AND JACK'S SALOTTO
814/226-7013
Italian. Casual Dining. **Address:** 21108 Paint Blvd (SR 66) 16254

SHREWSBURY pop. 3,823

HAMPTON INN BY HILTON   (717)235-9898
Hotel. **Address:** 1000 Far Hills Dr 17349

AAA Benefit: Members save up to 10%!

SIGEL

FARMER'S INN   814/752-2942
American. Casual Dining. **Address:** 759 Schaffer Rd 15860

SKYTOP
• Part of Pocono Mountains Area — see map p. 264

SKYTOP LODGE
(570)595-7401

Historic Resort Hotel
$189-$445

Address: One Skytop 18357 **Location:** On SR 390. **Facility:** Situated on a private mountaintop, this regal, stone-faced resort stands like a fortress overlooking the beautiful surrounding acreage. The restored grand hotel features contemporary rooms. 193 units. 1-4 stories, interior corridors. **Parking:** on-site and valet. **Terms:** check-in 4 pm, 2 night minimum stay - seasonal and/or weekends, cancellation fee imposed, resort fee. **Amenities:** safes. **Dining:** 4 restaurants, entertainment. **Pool:** heated outdoor, heated indoor. **Activities:** hot tub, regulation golf, miniature golf, tennis, downhill & cross country skiing, sledding, ice skating, recreation programs, bicycles, playground, game room, exercise room, spa. **Guest Services:** valet laundry.

SLIPPERY ROCK (F-2) pop. 3,625, elev. 1,299'

Four miles south of Slippery Rock near the junction of SRs 173 and 528, visitors will find the Old Stone House, built in 1822 by John K. Brown as a stagecoach stop on the Pittsburgh-Franklin Pike. The restored tavern and stagecoach stop is furnished in period. The Slippery Rock University History Department offers tours of the house during special events; phone (724) 738-4964.

APPLEBUTTER INN   724/794-1844
◆◆ Classic Country Inn. **Address:** 666 Centreville Pike 16057

FAIRFIELD INN & SUITES BY MARRIOTT SLIPPERY ROCK
(724)406-0535

◆◆◆ Hotel. **Address:** 1000 University Pkwy 16057

AAA Benefit:
Members save 5% or more!

WHERE TO EAT

NORTH COUNTRY BREWING COMPANY   724/794-2337
◆◆ American. Brewpub. **Address:** 141 S Main St 16057

SMETHPORT (D-5) pop. 1,655, elev. 1,560'

Smethport, first settled in 1811, quickly grew and became a thriving borough in 1853. Main Street is the Mansion District and is lined with Victorian mansions of former local barons. Hamlin Lake Park offers boating, fishing, in-line skating, swimming and tennis.

Just southwest of Smethport in Mount Jewett is Kinzua Bridge State Park, which covers 329 acres. Within the park is a visitor center as well as the Kinzua Sky Walk, a pedestrian walkway with railroad tracks built on the towers of the old Kinzua Viaduct, which upon completion in 1882 received worldwide acclaim for being the world's highest and longest railroad bridge. The Kinzua Sky Walk extends 624 feet and features an octagon-shaped overlook at the end. A section of the overlook's floor is made of glass so visitors can look down into the Kinzua Gorge. For more information phone (814) 778-5467.

Smethport Visitor Center: 119 W. Main St., Smethport, PA 16749. **Phone:** (814) 887-5630.

Self-guiding tours: Maps detailing a walking tour of the Mansion District are available at the Hamlin Memorial Library, McKean County Courthouse and Smethport Visitor Center.

SMOKETOWN pop. 357
• Hotels & Restaurants map & index p. 148
• Part of Pennsylvania Dutch Country area — see map p. 143

MILL STREAM COUNTRY INN   717/299-0931   **47**
◆◆ Hotel. **Address:** 170 Eastbrook Rd 17576

SMOKETOWN INN (OF LANCASTER COUNTY)
717/397-6944   **46**

◆◆ Hotel
$82-$109

Address: 190 Eastbrook Rd 17576 **Location:** Jct SR 340, just s on SR 896. **Facility:** 22 units, some two bedrooms, efficiencies and kitchens. 2 stories (no elevator), interior corridors. **Terms:** 2 night minimum stay - seasonal and/or weekends, 3 day cancellation notice. **Featured Amenity:** continental breakfast.

WHERE TO EAT

GOOD 'N PLENTY RESTAURANT   717/394-7111   **34**

◆◆
Regional American Casual Dining
$8-$21

AAA Inspector Notes: Crafts and quilts are on display in the country-cozy dining room where you'll sit for family-style meals presented on large platters. Those who would rather order from an individual menu can eat in the smaller dining room that offers the same country flair. Meat, relishes, homemade bread and starches are wholesome and filling, while the desserts are varied and tempting. **Address:** 150 Eastbrook Rd 17576 **Location:** US 30 (Lincoln Hwy), 1 mi n on SR 896; 0.5 mi s of SR 340. L D CALL

SOMERSET (H-4) pop. 6,277, elev. 2,250'
• Restaurants p. 280

Somerset is part of the Laurel Highlands *(see place listing p. 122).*

A-1 ECONOMY INN   814/445-4144

◆◆
Motel
Rates not provided

Address: 1138 N Center Ave 15501 **Location:** Just e via Water Works Rd, just n on SR 601. **Facility:** 19 units. 1 story, interior corridors. **Guest Services:** coin laundry. **Featured Amenity:** continental breakfast.

BUDGET HOST INN   (814)445-7988

 Motel. **Address:** 799 N Center Ave 15501

COMFORT INN   (814)445-9611

Hotel
$98-$180

Address: 202 Harmon St 15501 **Location:** I-70/76 (Pennsylvania Tpke) exit 110, just s. **Facility:** 102 units. 2-3 stories, interior corridors. **Pool:** outdoor. **Activities:** exercise room. **Guest Services:** valet laundry. **Featured Amenity:** continental breakfast.

[SAVE] [icons...] [BIZ] [HS] [icon]
[icons...] / SOME UNITS [icon]

GLADES PIKE INN   814/443-4978

 Historic Bed & Breakfast. **Address:** 2684 Glades Pike Rd 15501

HAMPTON INN   (814)445-9161

 Hotel. **Address:** 324 Laurel Crest Rd 15501

AAA Benefit:
Members save up to 10%!

QUILL HAVEN COUNTRY INN   (814)443-4514

 Historic Bed & Breakfast. **Address:** 1519 N Center Ave 15501

 WHERE TO EAT

HOSS'S FAMILY STEAK & SEA   814/445-3788

 Steak. Casual Dining. **Address:** 1222 N Center Ave 15501

KING'S FAMILY RESTAURANT   814/445-5311

 American. Casual Dining. **Address:** 1180 N Center Ave 15501

PINE GRILL RESTAURANT   814/445-2102

 American. Casual Dining. **Address:** 800 N Center Ave 15501

REY AZTECA   814/443-2329

 Mexican. Casual Dining. **Address:** 780 N Center Ave 15501

SOUTH STERLING
• Part of Pocono Mountains Area — see map p. 264

THE FRENCH MANOR INN AND SPA   (570)676-3244

Country Inn
$199-$410

Address: 50 Huntingdon Dr 18445 **Location:** SR 191, 0.4 mi w. **Facility:** This beautiful inn is fashioned after a stone château on the south of France. Rooms in the main house have a quaint and distinct charm. Out buildings have more space and balconies with stunning views. 19 units. 2 stories (no elevator), interior/exterior corridors. **Terms:** 2 night minimum stay - weekends, 14 day cancellation notice-fee imposed, resort fee. **Dining:** The French Manor Restaurant, see separate listing. **Pool:** heated indoor. **Activities:** hot tub, sledding, recreation programs in season, trails, spa. **Guest Services:** valet laundry, area transportation. **Featured Amenity:** full hot breakfast.

[SAVE] [icons...] CALL [icons...] [X]
/ SOME UNITS [HS] [icons...]

 WHERE TO EAT

THE FRENCH MANOR RESTAURANT   570/676-3244

French
Fine Dining
$35-$55

AAA Inspector Notes: *Historic.* This oasis of true refinement is set in a beautiful manor modeled after a château in the south of France. The dining room provides a stately atmosphere for elegant dining. The 30-foot vaulted ceiling, the dual fireplaces and the Pecky cypress wall paneling are impressive. The menu centers on gourmet cuisine and features such specialty items as filet mignon a la homard, seared sea bass, foaming escargot in pastry and prime beef. The service is skilled and diligent. **Features:** full bar, patio dining. **Reservations:** suggested. Semiformal attire. **Address:** 50 Huntingdon Dr 18445 **Location:** SR 191, 0.4 mi w; in The French Manor Inn and Spa. [icons...] [B] [D] CALL [icon]

SOUTH WILLIAMSPORT (E-8) pop. 6,379, elev. 522'

The city hosts the Little League World Series each summer.

[SAVE] **WORLD OF LITTLE LEAGUE MUSEUM** is at 525 US 15, next to the Little League World Series stadium. Displays and videos interpret the history and growth of Little League Baseball and Softball since the organization was founded in 1939. The museum includes uniforms, Major League Baseball players' Little League items, a 1934 Babe Ruth uniform and high-tech interactive experiences.

Time: Allow 1 hour minimum. **Hours:** Daily 9-5. Closed Jan. 1, Easter, Thanksgiving, Christmas Eve, Christmas and Dec. 31. Phone ahead to confirm schedule. **Cost:** $5; $3 (ages 62+); $2 (ages 5-12). Audio guide rental $3; free (AAA members). **Phone:** (570) 326-3607.

SPEERS pop. 1,154
• Part of Pittsburgh area — see map p. 225

THE BACK PORCH RESTAURANT   724/483-4500

 American. Casual Dining. **Address:** 114 Speers St 15012

SPRINGFIELD (DELAWARE COUNTY)
• Hotels & Restaurants map & index p. 192
• Part of Philadelphia area — see map p. 154

COURTYARD BY MARRIOTT PHILADELPHIA SPRINGFIELD
                                      (610)543-1080 [110]

 Hotel. **Address:** 400 W Sproul Rd 19064

AAA Benefit:
Members save 5% or more!

DAYS INN SPRINGFIELD/PHILADELPHIA INT'L AIRPORT
                                      (610)544-4700 [111]

 Hotel. **Address:** 650 Baltimore Pike 19064

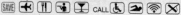 **WHERE TO EAT**

TAVOLA RESTAURANT AND BAR   610/543-1200 [158]

 American. Casual Dining. **Address:** 400 W Sproul Rd 19064

SPRINGS (I-3) elev. 2,474'

Springs is part of the Laurel Highlands *(see place listing p. 122).*

STARLIGHT
- Part of Pocono Mountains Area — see map p. 264

THE INN AT STARLIGHT LAKE   570/798-2519

♥♥ Historic Country Inn. **Address:** 289 Starlight Lake Rd 18461

STATE COLLEGE (F-6) pop. 42,034, elev. 1,174'
- Hotels p. 282 • Restaurants p. 285

The Pennsylvania State University *(see attraction listing)*, founded as an agricultural college in 1855, is located in the fertile Nittany Valley of central Pennsylvania. The school, established to teach methods of soil conservation, became Pennsylvania State College in 1874. A community slowly grew up around the school, and it was incorporated as the Borough of State College in 1896. Today Penn State University offers undergraduate degrees in more than 160 programs and some 160 graduate degree programs. The commonwealth's largest university, Penn State has more than 99,000 students at 27 locations statewide, including more than 46,600 at the University Park campus in State College.

State College features mountain bike trails and opportunities for fly-fishing.

Central Pennsylvania Convention & Visitors Bureau: 800 E. Park Ave., State College, PA 16803. **Phone:** (814) 231-1400 or (800) 358-5466.

THE PENNSYLVANIA STATE UNIVERSITY, at University Park, is the commonwealth's largest university and is noted for its beautiful campus. Campus parking is provided for a fee daily until 9 p.m. (central campus) and until 5 p.m. (other areas). **Phone:** (814) 865-4700.

The Arboretum at Penn State lies on the n.w. section of campus between Shortlidge and Bigler rds. Due to the great size of the project, portions of the 370-acre site are opening in phases. The 35-acre H.O. Smith Botanic Gardens is open, and it features more than 700 species and 17,000 plants, an overlook pavilion, fountain, boardwalk, rose and fragrance garden, lotus pond, esplanade, sub-tropical-themed terrace and pollinators' gardens. The Childhood's Gate Children's Garden is designed for visitors from ages 3 to 12, and includes information about the region's biodiversity. The main biking and hiking trail is the Bellefonte Central Rail Trail, a 1.3-mile crushed-limestone path following the old railroad bed.

Future additions will include additional themed gardens, an education center and a conservatory. **Time:** Allow 1 hour minimum. **Hours:** Daily dawn-dusk (weather permitting). **Cost:** Free. A free parking pass (available at the arboretum office at the Overlook Pavilion) is required Mon.-Fri. 8-5. **Phone:** (814) 865-9118.

The Berkey Creamery, Department of Food Science, College of Agricultural Sciences is at jct. Bigler and Curtin rds. on Penn State's University Park campus. Visitors can view the processing procedures at the creamery from the observation room. The creamery produces cheese, ice cream, milk, yogurt and other products. **Hours:** Observation room open Mon.-Fri. 8-5; phone ahead for extended hours and to see when ice cream production will be in progress. Closed major holidays and university breaks. **Cost:** Free. **Phone:** (814) 865-7535.

Earth and Mineral Sciences Museum and Art Gallery, on the ground floor of the Deike Building (Rooms 006 and 018) on Burrowes Rd. on Penn State's University Park campus, contains gemstones, minerals and fossils representing more than 20,000 specimens. Also on display are mineral industries-related art and mining and scientific equipment. Interactive earthquake, tornado and augmented reality sandbox exhibits are offered.

Time: Allow 30 minutes minimum. **Hours:** Mon.-Fri. 9:30-5. Closed major holidays and during university breaks. Phone ahead to confirm schedule. **Cost:** Free. **Phone:** (814) 865-6336.

Frost Entomological Museum, on Curtin Rd. on Penn State's University Park campus, houses more than 2 million insects in its collection, including mounted, live, land and aquatic specimens. There are numerous exhibits, photographs and models. **Note:** The museum is closed indefinitely for renovations; phone ahead for updates. **Time:** Allow 30 minutes minimum. **Hours:** Mon.-Fri. 9:30-4:30. Closed major holidays and university breaks. **Cost:** Free. **Phone:** (814) 865-1895.

Old Main is on Pollock Rd. on Penn State's University Park campus. It is the Central Administration building and was built 1856-63; it was rebuilt 1929-30. It contains the Land Grant Frescoes by American muralist Henry Varnum Poor. **Hours:** Mon.-Fri. 8-5. Closed major holidays. **Cost:** Free. **Phone:** (814) 865-7517.

Palmer Museum of Art, Penn State, on Curtin Rd. at Penn State's University Park campus, offers American and international exhibitions of paintings, sculpture, prints, drawings, photographs and ceramics. Special exhibitions feature works of art from other museums and public and private collections. Educational programs, films and musical performances also are presented. Guided tours are available with 2-week advance reservation (requires a minimum of 10 participants). **Time:** Allow 30 minutes minimum. **Hours:** Tues.-Sat. 10-4:30, Sun. noon-4. Closed some holidays. Phone ahead to confirm schedule Nov.-Jan. **Cost:** Free. **Phone:** (814) 865-7672. GT

Penn State All-Sports Museum, in Beaver Stadium on the University Park campus, contains memorabilia of the Penn State Nittany Lions sports teams, the Heisman trophy, photographs of former players and displays of more than 30 current and former varsity sports.

Time: Allow 30 minutes minimum. **Hours:** Tues.-Sat. 10-4, Sun. noon-4, mid-Mar. to mid-Jan.; Fri.-Sat. 10-4, Sun. noon-4, rest of year. Home football game weekend schedule varies; phone ahead. Closed university breaks and major holidays except July 4. **Cost:** $5; $3 (children, senior citizens and students with ID). **Phone:** (814) 865-0044.

Penn State University Special Collections Library is in the Paterno Library at jct. Curtin and Allen rds. on the University Park campus; parking is available at the Nittany Lion Inn parking deck. The library offers more than 200,000 printed volumes and millions of records, photographs and other items. The archives include collections documenting the history of Penn State, the State College area and national labor union history. **Time:** Allow 30 minutes minimum. **Hours:** Mon.-Fri. 9-5. Hours vary by semester; phone ahead for extended hours and to confirm schedule. Closed major holidays. **Cost:** Free. **Phone:** (814) 865-1793.

THE ATHERTON HOTEL   (814)231-2100

Hotel
$99-$179

Address: 125 S Atherton St 16801 **Location:** On US 322 business route, just w of jct SR 26; downtown. **Facility:** 149 units. 7 stories, interior corridors. **Parking:** on-site (fee). **Terms:** cancellation fee imposed. **Amenities:** video games. **Activities:** exercise room. **Guest Services:** valet laundry, area transportation.

BEST WESTERN PLUS UNIVERSITY PARK INN & SUITES   (814)234-8393

Hotel
$75-$350

AAA Benefit: Members save 5% to 15% and earn 10% bonus points!

Address: 115 Premiere Dr 16801 **Location:** I-99 exit 76 (Shiloh Rd), 0.6 mi e, then just n. **Facility:** 79 units. 4 stories, interior corridors. **Terms:** cancellation fee imposed. **Pool:** heated indoor. **Activities:** hot tub, exercise room. **Guest Services:** valet and coin laundry. *(See ad this page.)*

CARNEGIE INN & SPA, AN ASCEND HOTEL COLLECTION MEMBER   (814)234-2424

Contemporary
Country Inn
$119-$499

Address: 100 Cricklewood Dr 16803 **Location:** I-99/US 322 exit 71 (Toftrees/Woodycrest). **Facility:** Located next to a golf course, the contemporary property has the ambience of a Scottish country house. Offered is individually decorated, traditional-style guest rooms and a new full-service spa. 20 units. 3 stories, interior corridors. **Parking:** on-site and valet. **Terms:** 3 day cancellation notice. **Activities:** exercise room, spa. **Guest Services:** valet laundry, area transportation. **Featured Amenity:** full hot breakfast.

COMFORT SUITES   (814)235-1900
Hotel. **Address:** 132 Village Dr 16803

COUNTRY INN & SUITES BY CARLSON   814/234-6000
Hotel. **Address:** 1357 E College Ave 16801

▼ *See AAA listing this page* ▼

COURTYARD BY MARRIOTT (814)238-1881
 Hotel. **Address:** 1730 University Dr 16801

AAA Benefit: Members save 5% or more!

DAYS INN PENN STATE (814)238-8454
 Hotel. **Address:** 240 S Pugh St 16801

FAIRFIELD INN & SUITES BY MARRIOTT STATE COLLEGE (814)238-3871

Hotel
$80-$454

AAA Benefit: Members save 5% or more!

Address: 2215 N Atherton St 16803 **Location:** US 322 exit N Atherton St, 0.8 mi e. **Facility:** 83 units. 3 stories, interior corridors. **Terms:** cancellation fee imposed. **Pool:** heated indoor. **Activities:** hot tub, exercise room. **Guest Services:** valet and coin laundry. **Featured Amenity:** breakfast buffet.

HAMPTON INN & SUITES AT WILLIAMSBURG SQUARE (814)231-1899

Hotel
$99-$999

AAA Benefit: Members save up to 10%!

Address: 1955 Waddle Rd 16803 **Location:** US 322 Bypass exit Toftrees/Woodycrest, just s. **Facility:** 71 units. 4 stories, interior corridors. **Terms:** 1-7 night minimum stay, cancellation fee imposed. **Pool:** heated outdoor. **Activities:** exercise room. **Guest Services:** valet and coin laundry. **Featured Amenity:** breakfast buffet.

HAMPTON INN STATE COLLEGE (814)231-1590
 Hotel. **Address:** 1101 E College Ave 16801

AAA Benefit: Members save up to 10%!

HILTON GARDEN INN (814)272-1221

Hotel
$109-$499

AAA Benefit: Members save up to 10%!

Address: 1221 E College Ave 16801 **Location:** 0.5 mi off US 322 Bypass on SR 26 S. **Facility:** 103 units. 4 stories, interior corridors. **Terms:** 1-7 night minimum stay, cancellation fee imposed. **Pool:** heated indoor. **Activities:** hot tub, exercise room. **Guest Services:** valet and coin laundry.

HOLIDAY INN EXPRESS AT WILLIAMSBURG SQUARE (814)867-1800

Hotel
$89-$999

Address: 1925 Waddle Rd 16803 **Location:** US 322 Bypass exit Toftrees/Woodycrest, just s. **Facility:** 106 units. 4 stories, interior corridors. **Terms:** 30 day cancellation notice-fee imposed. **Activities:** exercise room. **Guest Services:** valet and coin laundry. **Featured Amenity:** breakfast buffet.

HYATT PLACE STATE COLLEGE 814/862-9808

Hotel
Rates not provided

AAA Benefit: Members save 10%!

Address: 219 W Beaver Ave 16801 **Location:** Just w of jct SR 26 and business route 322; downtown. **Facility:** 165 units. 8 stories, interior corridors. **Parking:** on-site (fee). **Activities:** exercise room. **Guest Services:** valet laundry. **Featured Amenity:** breakfast buffet.

NITTANY BUDGET MOTEL (814)238-0015

Motel
$49-$275

Address: 2070 Cato Ave 16801 **Location:** SR 26, 2.6 mi s of jct US 322 business route. **Facility:** 23 units. 1 story, exterior corridors. **Featured Amenity:** continental breakfast.

THE NITTANY LION INN OF THE PENNSYLVANIA STATE UNIVERSITY (814)865-8500

Historic Hotel
$129-$449

Address: 200 W Park Ave 16803 **Location:** US 322, 0.5 mi w of jct SR 26. **Facility:** Located on the campus of Penn State University, this 1931 Colonial-style inn offers traditional-style rooms decorated in PSU colors. Luxury bedding and upscale appointments in all rooms. 223 units. 3 stories, interior corridors. **Parking:** on-site and valet. **Terms:** check-in 4 pm, cancellation fee imposed. **Amenities:** video games. **Activities:** hot tub, regulation golf, exercise room. **Guest Services:** valet laundry, area transportation. *(See ad p. 284.)*

(See ad p. 284.)

🔗 **What's for dinner?** AAA.com/travelguides/restaurants

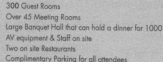

THE PENNSYLVANIA STATE UNIVERSITY-THE PENN STATER CONFERENCE CENTER HOTEL   (814)863-5000

Hotel
$119-$399

Address: 215 Innovation Blvd 16803 **Location:** US 322 E/220 N exit Penn State University/Innovation Park exit "A", 0.5 mi e. **Facility:** 300 units. 5 stories, interior corridors. **Parking:** on-site and valet. **Terms:** closed 12/24-1/2, cancellation fee imposed. **Dining:** 2 restaurants. **Pool:** heated indoor. **Activities:** hot tub, exercise room. **Guest Services:** valet laundry, area transportation. *(See ad p. 284.)*

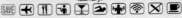

QUALITY INN PENN STATE   (814)234-1600

◆◆ Motel. **Address:** 1274 N Atherton St 16803

RAMADA CONFERENCE CENTER & GOLF HOTEL
(814)238-3001

◆◆◆ Hotel. **Address:** 1450 S Atherton St 16801

RESIDENCE INN BY MARRIOTT STATE COLLEGE
(814)235-6960

◆◆◆ Extended Stay Hotel. **Address:** 1555 University Dr 16801

AAA Benefit: Members save 5% or more!

SLEEP INN   (814)235-1020

◆◆◆ Hotel. **Address:** 111 Village Dr 16803

SPRINGHILL SUITES BY MARRIOTT STATE COLLEGE
(814)867-1807

SPRINGHILL SUITES
MARRIOTT

AAA Benefit: Members save 5% or more!

Hotel
$76-$284

Address: 1935 Waddle Rd 16803 **Location:** US 322 Bypass exit Toftrees/Woodycrest, just s; in Williamsburg Square. **Facility:** 72 efficiencies. 4 stories, interior corridors. **Terms:** cancellation fee imposed. **Pool:** heated indoor. **Activities:** exercise room. **Guest Services:** valet and coin laundry. **Featured Amenity:** breakfast buffet.

TOFTREES GOLF RESORT   (814)234-8000

◆◆◆
Resort Hotel
$79-$499

Address: 1 Country Club Ln 16803 **Location:** I-99/US 322 exit 71 (Toftrees/Woodycrest). **Facility:** This golf resort offers sprawling grounds, golf vista views and beautiful views of the Pennsylvania countryside. Rooms may be cozy, but come complete with plush bedding and either kings or doubles. 102 units. 2-3 stories (no elevator), interior corridors. **Terms:** check-in 4 pm. **Dining:** The Field Burger & Tap, see separate listing. **Pool:** heated outdoor. **Activities:** regulation golf, exercise room. **Guest Services:** valet and coin laundry.

WHERE TO EAT

THE ALLEN STREET GRILL   814/231-4745

◆◆ American. Casual Dining. **Address:** 100 W College Ave 16801

AMERICAN ALE HOUSE & GRILL   814/237-9701

◆◆◆
American Casual Dining
$9-$35

AAA Inspector Notes: The restaurant serves creative cuisine in a casual, bustling environment. Entrées include daily prime rib, scallops, octopus, pasta dishes, sandwiches and salads. Dining on the seasonal patio is a pleasant diversion. Entertainment provided many evenings. **Features:** full bar, happy hour. **Reservations:** suggested. **Address:** 821 Cricklewood 16803 **Location:** US 322 business route exit Toftrees/Woodycrest, just n to Toftrees, e to Cricklewood Dr, 0.5 mi n, then e. ⃞L ⃞D

THE DINER   814/238-5590

◆ Comfort Food. Buffet Style. **Address:** 126 W College Ave 16801

FACCIA LUNA PIZZERIA   814/234-9000

◆◆ Italian. Casual Dining. **Address:** 1229 S Atherton St 16801

THE FIELD BURGER & TAP   814/234-8000

◆◆
American Casual Dining
$9-$32

AAA Inspector Notes: The casual restaurant, overlooking the golf course, specializes in many types of burgers and fries as well as dirty milk shakes. Surroundings reflect deep color schemes like a steak house and your entrée arrives in a long slate plate board. **Features:** full bar. **Address:** 1 Country Club Ln 16803 **Location:** I-99/US 322 exit 71 (Toftrees/Woodycrest); in Toftrees Golf Resort.

⃞B ⃞L ⃞D CALL ♿

Burgers, Fries & Shakes made w/Fresh Local Ingredients

HERWIGS AUSTRIAN BISTRO   814/272-0738

◆◆ Austrian. Casual Dining. **Address:** 132 W College Ave 16801

MAD MEX   814/272-5656

◆◆ Mexican. Casual Dining. **Address:** 240 S Pugh St 16801

OLDE NEW YORK   814/237-1582

◆◆ International. Casual Dining. **Address:** 2298 E College Ave 16801

OTTO'S PUB AND BREWERY   814/867-6886

◆◆ American. Gastropub. **Address:** 2235 N Atherton St 16803

PENANG   814/861-6088

◆◆ Asian. Casual Dining. **Address:** 1221 N Atherton St 16803

THE TAVERN RESTAURANT   814/238-6116

◆◆ Traditional American. Casual Dining. **Address:** 220 E College Ave 16801

THE WAFFLE SHOP-NORTH   814/238-7460

◆◆ American. Casual Dining. **Address:** 1229 N Atherton St 16803

THE WAFFLE SHOP-WEST   814/235-1816

◆◆ American. Casual Dining. **Address:** 1610 W College Ave 16801

ZOLA KITCHEN & WINE BAR   814/237-8474

◆◆◆ New Mediterranean. Casual Dining. **Address:** 324 W College Ave 16801

STRASBURG (I-10) pop. 2,809, elev. 469'
- Hotels p. 286 • Restaurants p. 286
- Hotels & Restaurants map & index p. 148
- Part of Pennsylvania Dutch Country area — see map p. 143

Though first settled by French Huguenots, Strasburg evolved into a community of German immigrants in the Pennsylvania Dutch Country. The town

(See map & index p. 148.)

is noted for its quaint atmosphere; the availability of Amish food and arts and crafts; and its many railroad exhibits, both model and real. The Lancaster County Art Association, 149 Precision Ave. next to Strasburg Public Library, presents rotating exhibits of local artists' works. Classes, events and workshops are presented throughout the year. The gallery is open Thurs.-Sat. 11-4 and Sun. 1-4 except for major holidays and between Christmas and New Year's Day; phone (717) 687-7061.

[SAVE] **THE NATIONAL TOY TRAIN MUSEUM,** 1.5 mi. e. on SR 741 and .2 mi. n. on Paradise Ln., displays antique and contemporary toy trains. Six operating layouts can be viewed. A video about toy trains also is presented. **Time:** Allow 1 hour minimum. **Hours:** Daily 10-5, Memorial Day-Labor Day; Sat.-Sun. 10-5, Apr.-May and Sept.-Dec. (also day after Christmas-Dec. 31). Phone ahead for extended hours. Last admission 30 minutes before closing. Closed Christmas. **Cost:** $7; $6 (ages 65+); $4 (ages 6-12); $22 (family, two adults and three children). **Phone:** (717) 687-8976.

[GEM] [SAVE] **RAILROAD MUSEUM OF PENNSYLVANIA,** 1 mi. e. on SR 741E at 300 Gap Rd., traces the history of railroads in Pennsylvania through restored locomotives, railcars and artifacts. The museum takes visitors from the colorful era of 19th-century wood-burning engines to modern streamliners. An orientation video played in an early 20th-century passenger depot sets the tone.

The museum's collection of more than 100 vintage locomotives and railcars, which includes steam, diesel and electric locomotives, and passenger and freight cars, were all either made or operated in Pennsylvania. The beautifully restored rolling stock is displayed on five tracks inside the massive main hall. Additional pieces can be seen in the outdoor train yard with a working 1928 turntable.

Some of the cars are open for inspection—including the cab of a steam locomotive, a caboose and a passenger car—and can be walked through. Others can be seen up-close courtesy of stairways and platforms that allow for viewing the inside of the equipment. An observation bridge provides excellent views of the rolling stock from above.

Visitors can pretend to be an engineer and operate a train, including the throttle, brakes and horn, in the museum's cab simulator built from a Norfolk Southern diesel locomotive. In addition, the museum's education center in a late Victorian-era freight station has hands-on activities and an extensive model train layout. Railroad memorabilia such as lanterns, tools, china and clocks also can be seen. Special events are held throughout the year.

Note: The outdoor train yard is not always accessible due to weather or safety reasons. **Time:** Allow 1 hour, 30 minutes minimum. **Hours:** Mon.-Sat. 9-5, Sun. noon-5, Apr.-Oct.; Tues.-Sat. 9-5, Sun. noon-5, rest of year. Closed Jan. 1, Thanksgiving and Christmas. **Cost:** $10; $9 (ages 65+); $8 (ages 3-11). **Phone:** (717) 687-8628.

SIGHT & SOUND THEATRES, LANCASTER COUNTY, 300 Hartman Bridge Rd., presents live theatrical performances based on Bible stories in a 2,000-seat theater featuring a 300-foot wraparound stage and special effects. Live animals are part of the cast.

Hours: "Jesus" show Mar. 10, 2018-Jan. 5, 2019. Performances Tues.-Sat.; phone for curtain times. **Cost:** $59-$79; $26-$36 (ages 3-12). Reservations are recommended. **Phone:** (800) 377-1277.

HOLIDAY INN EXPRESS & SUITES LANCASTER EAST STRASBURG   717/455-4700 [58]
▼▼▼ Hotel. **Address:** 1900 Historic Dr 17579

WHERE TO EAT

FIRESIDE TAVERN   717/687-7979 [41]
▼▼ American. Gastropub. **Address:** 1500 Historic Dr 17579

ISAAC'S FAMOUS GRILLED SANDWICHES   717/687-7699
▼ Deli Sandwiches. Quick Serve. **Address:** Rt 741 E (226 Gap Rd) 17579

STROUDSBURG (F-11) pop. 5,567, elev. 420'
- Hotels & Restaurants map & index p. 266
- Part of Pocono Mountains Area — see map
p. 264

Col. Jacob Stroud, who served in the French and Indian War, settled in what is now Stroudsburg in 1769. Because of the strategic location 3 miles west of the Delaware Water Gap, Fort Penn was built around his home in 1776. Two years later the post sheltered refugees from the Wyoming Massacre (see Wyoming p. 303). The town was formally established in 1799 when Stroud and his son sold lots in their spaciously platted site.

The 1795 Stroud Mansion, built by the colonel for his son, still stands at 900 Main Street; it serves as headquarters for the Monroe County Historical Association. Artifacts are on display and a research library is on site. A 1-hour guided tour is offered Tuesday-Friday (also first and third Saturdays of the month) at 11 and 2. Phone (570) 421-7703.

The Sherman Theater, 524 Main St., opened in 1929. Among the evening's entertainment was a performance by comedians Stan Laurel and Oliver Hardy. Vaudeville shows were given in the theater's early days and then in later years the building became a movie house. These days live entertainment has returned, and performances are offered throughout the year. Phone (570) 420-2808.

Pocono Mountains Visitors Bureau: 1004 W. Main St., Stroudsburg, PA 18360. **Phone:** (570) 421-5791 or (800) 762-6667.

Self-guiding tours: Brochures about the area, including the historic downtown and hiking and biking in northeast Pennsylvania, are available at the visitors bureau.

Shopping: Downtown Stroudsburg's restored historic buildings are home to an array of antique, arts and crafts, apparel and specialty stores.

QUIET VALLEY LIVING HISTORICAL FARM is 3.5 mi. s.w. on US 209 Bus. Rte., then 1.5 mi. s.e. to 347 Quiet Valley Rd. This 115-acre living-history museum is a restored late 18th-through 19th-century Pennsylvania German farm. Guides in period clothing conduct tours of historic buildings, which include a house, barn, cabin, smoke house, springhouse, icehouse, dry house, maple sugar house and tool sheds. A bake oven can be seen, and crafts are demonstrated daily. Corn, flax, potatoes, rye and wheat are grown, and farm animals include chickens, goats, horses, pigs, rabbits, sheep, turkeys, a cow and a mule.

Special themed events are held select weekends throughout the year. During Farm Animal Frolic in May visitors can pet baby farm animals, enjoy pony or wagon rides, and watch sheep shearing. In October, Harvest Festival features folk entertainment, children's activities, and traditional craft demonstrations such as spinning, weaving and basket making. The Old Time Christmas celebration includes a living nativity scene and a visit from Pennsylvania German folk figure Belschnikel.

Pets and smoking are not permitted. **Time:** Allow 2 hours, 30 minutes minimum. **Hours:** Tours of historic farm museum Tues.-Sat. (also Labor Day) 10-5, Sun. noon-5, third Sat. in June-Labor Day. Farm Animal Frolic Sat. 10-4, Sun. noon-4, Memorial Day weekend and the previous weekend. Harvest Festival Sat.-Sun. 10-5, Columbus Day weekend. Old Time Christmas tours are offered every 15 minutes Sat.-Sun. 3-7, the first and second full weekends in Dec. **Cost:** $10; $5 (ages 3-12). Phone ahead to verify special event admission. **Phone:** (570) 992-6161. GT ⚓

FAIRFIELD INN & SUITES BY MARRIOTT - STROUDSBURG BARTONSVILLE POCONOS   (570)421-0100 **1**
◆◆◆ Hotel. **Address:** 294 Frantz Rd 18360

AAA Benefit: Members save 5% or more!

HAMPTON INN & SUITES STROUDSBURG/BARTONSVILLE   570/369-1400 **2**
◆◆◆ Hotel. **Address:** 700 Commerce Blvd 18360

AAA Benefit: Members save up to 10%!

HAMPTON INN - STROUDSBURG/POCONOS   (570)424-0400 **3**
◆◆◆ Hotel. **Address:** 114 S 8th St 18360

AAA Benefit: Members save up to 10%!

STROUDSMOOR COUNTRY INN   (570)421-6431 **4**
◆◆◆ Country Inn. **Address:** 231 Stroudsmoor Rd 18360

WHERE TO EAT

CAFÉ DUET   570/431-3442 **2**
◆ Coffee/Tea Sandwiches. Quick Serve. **Address:** 35 N 7th St 18360

MARCO ANTONIO'S   570/424-2415 **3**
◆◆ Spanish. Casual Dining. **Address:** 620 Main St 18360

NEWBERRY'S YARD OF ALE   570/517-0130 **4**
◆◆ American. Casual Dining. **Address:** 622 Main St 18360

SARAH STREET GRILL   570/424-9120 **1**
◆◆ American. Casual Dining. **Address:** 550 Quaker Alley 18360

SIAMSA IRISH PUB   570/421-8434 **5**
◆◆ Irish Fish & Chips Steak. Casual Dining. **Address:** 636 Main St 18360

STROUDSMOOR COUNTRY INN   570/421-6431 **6**
◆◆◆ Traditional American. Casual Dining. **Address:** 231 Stroudsmoor Rd 18360

SUGARLOAF

TOM'S KITCHEN FAMILY RESTAURANT   570/788-3808
◆◆ American. Casual Dining. **Address:** 656 State Rt 93 18249

SUNBURY (F-8) pop. 9,905, elev. 446'

Sunbury, on Shamokin Creek and the Susquehanna River, was the site of Pennsylvania's largest frontier fort, Fort Augusta. The powder magazine from the 1756 fort still stands. The Hunter House, 1150 N. Front St., contains a research library and a permanent exhibit of artifacts recovered from archaeological digs made on the site of the fort; phone (570) 286-4083.

Sunbury had one of the world's first central station incandescent electric lighting plants. It was built by Thomas Edison in 1883. The plant was treated with much suspicion by the townspeople, most of whom were afraid to cross the threshold to look inside.

At S. Second Street are the Keithan Bluebird Gardens, featuring a variety of trees, azaleas and rhododendrons. The gardens reach peak bloom March through May. On SR 147 is the Shikellamy Marina & Fabridam, where a 3,000-acre lake is formed by what is said to be the world's largest inflatable dam.

Shopping: Susquehanna Valley Mall, on US 11/15, is the town's main shopping center. Its major stores are The Bon-Ton and Boscov's.

SWARTHMORE pop. 6,194
- Hotels p. 288
- Part of Philadelphia area — see map p. 154

THE INN AT SWARTHMORE (610)543-7500
♦♦♦ Hotel. **Address:** 10 S Chester Rd 19081

SWIFTWATER
- Hotels & Restaurants map & index p. 266
- Part of Pocono Mountains Area — see map p. 264

DESAKI 570/839-2500 ③⑤
♦♦♦ Japanese Steak Sushi. Casual Dining. **Address:** 2054 Rt 611 18370

TAFTON (E-11) elev. 1,532'
- Part of Pocono Mountains Area — see map p. 264

Tafton is near Lake Wallenpaupack *(see Hawley p. 100 and Recreation Areas Chart)*, the state's third largest man-made lake. Preseason stocking makes this a good location for fishing.

TANNERSVILLE (F-11) elev. 1,276'
- Hotels & Restaurants map & index p. 266
- Part of Pocono Mountains Area — see map p. 264

Shopping: The Crossings Premium Outlets, I-80 exit 299, following signs, is a rambling, two-story shopping experience featuring approximately 100 high-end outlet stores. Shopping choices offering selections from head to toe include Ann Taylor, Brooks Brothers, Guess, Michael Kors, Polo Ralph Lauren and Tommy Hilfiger. Young fashionistas can shop at Carter's, Gymboree and OshKosh B'gosh,

while those in search of accessory, housewares and gift bargains can peruse the shelves at Coach, Corningware Corelle & More and Yankee Candle.

BEST WESTERN PLUS POCONOS HOTEL
(570)629-4100 ③③

Hotel
$90-$250

Best Western PLUS. **AAA Benefit:** Members save 5% to 15% and earn 10% bonus points!

Address: 2647 Rt 715 18372 **Location:** I-80 exit 299, just n. **Facility:** 90 units. 3 stories (no elevator), interior corridors. **Terms:** check-in 4 pm. **Amenities:** safes. **Pool:** heated indoor. **Activities:** exercise room. **Featured Amenity:** breakfast buffet.

CAMELBACK RESORT 570/517-1665 ③①
♦♦♦ Resort Hotel. **Address:** 193 Resort Dr 18372

THE CHATEAU RESORT & CONFERENCE CENTER
570/629-5900 ③⓪
♦♦ Resort Hotel. **Address:** 475 Camelback Rd 18372

DAYS INN-TANNERSVILLE (570)629-1667 ③②

♦♦ Hotel $66-$150

Address: 126 Hill Motor Lodge Rd 18372 **Location:** I-80 exit 299, just s on SR 715. **Facility:** 72 units. 1-2 stories (no elevator), exterior corridors. **Terms:** cancellation fee imposed. **Amenities:** safes. **Dining:** Tandoor Palace Restaurant & Bar, see separate listing. **Pool:** outdoor. **Guest Services:** coin laundry. **Featured Amenity:** continental breakfast.

WHERE TO EAT
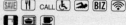

BARLEY CREEK BREWING COMPANY
570/629-9399 ③⑧

♦♦ American Gastropub $11-$24

AAA Inspector Notes: Popular with local families and the many tourists who flood the area, this bustling public house and eatery is near Camelback Mountain. With a fine selection of house-crafted brews, a broad pub menu is served in a high-ceilinged timber-frame building or, in the warmer months, in an outdoor garden with games for the kids and a covered deck to beat the heat. **Features:** full bar, happy hour. **Address:** 1774 Sullivan Tr 18372 **Location:** I-80 exit 299, just n on SR 715, then 1.1 mi w on Sullivan Tr to jct Camelback Rd. L D CALL&

GABEL'S ICE CREAM & FAST FOOD 570/629-0370 ④⓪
♦ American. Quick Serve. **Address:** SR 611 & Alger Ave 18372

LEGENDARY TANNERSVILLE INN 570/629-3131 ④①
♦♦ American. Casual Dining. **Address:** 2977 Rt 611 18372

SMUGGLER'S COVE 570/629-2277 ④②

♦♦ Seafood Casual Dining $7-$45

AAA Inspector Notes: Colorful posters, lobster tanks and nautical bric-a-brac dot the relaxed dining room here, and service is friendly and attentive. The menu features a very good choice of seafood, shellfish, salads, steaks and a variety of items for picky children. Specialties and daily selections include mahi-mahi, tuna, grilled salmon, escargots in their shell, lobster, prime rib, a fresh salad bar and crab cakes. Highly recommended if you enjoy seafood and are in the Poconos. **Features:** full bar, early bird specials. **Reservations:** suggested. **Address:** 2972 Rt 611 18372 **Location:** I-80 exit 299, just n on SR 715, then 1 mi s. L D CALL&

(See map & index p. 266.)

TANDOOR PALACE RESTAURANT & BAR

570/619-0068

Indian
Casual Dining
$12-$21

AAA Inspector Notes: Serving traditional Indian cuisine, the restaurant has two dining rooms: one in a 170-year-old railroad dining car and another decorated with Indian paintings. The menu lists tandoor preparations in addition to other chicken, lamb, goat, seafood and many vegetarian dishes. Good choices are tandoori chicken (chicken marinated overnight in yogurt and spices and roasted in a clay oven) and methi malai mutter (a rare blend of creamed, chopped fenugreek leaves, spinach and green peas). **Features:** full bar. **Address:** 126 Motor Hill Lodge Rd 18372 **Location:** I-80 exit 299, just s on SR 715; in Days Inn-Tannersville.

L   D

TARENTUM pop. 4,530, elev. 777'

- **Hotels & Restaurants map & index p. 246**
- **Part of Pittsburgh area — see map p. 225**

SPRINGHILL SUITES BY MARRIOTT PITTSBURGH MILLS

(724)274-1064 **43**

Hotel
$93-$458

SPRINGHILL SUITES
MARRIOTT

AAA Benefit: Members save 5% or more!

Address: 3015 Pittsburgh Mills Blvd 15084 **Location:** SR 28 exit Pittsburgh Mills Blvd. Located in Pittsburgh Mills shopping area. **Facility:** 115 units. 5 stories, interior corridors. **Terms:** cancellation fee imposed. **Pool:** heated indoor. **Activities:** exercise room. **Guest Services:** valet and coin laundry. *(See ad p. 261.)*

SAVE CALL

BIZ HS

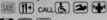

EAT'N PARK   724/275-1014
American. Casual Dining. **Address:** 3005 Pittsburgh Mills Blvd 15084

TITUSVILLE (D-2) pop. 5,601, elev. 1,174'

Native Americans used the slick film on Oil Creek to mix their war paints, and enterprising settlers bottled and sold it as a medicinal concoction called Seneca Oil. Not until 1859 when Col. Edwin Drake drilled a well, did oil begin to revolutionize industry and spur progress around the world. Titusville's status as birthplace of the oil industry earned Oil Creek Valley its title of "the valley that changed the world," and the city became a wealthy boom town. Pennsylvania was the nation's number one oil producer until 1901, when production peaked and the oil industry began striking richer fields in the West.

Today evidence of the town's wealth can be found downtown on Main and Perry streets, which are lined with mansions showcasing varying architectural designs, including Queen Anne and Victorian.

Titusville Area Chamber of Commerce: 202 W. Central Ave., Titusville, PA 16354. **Phone:** (814) 827-2941.

Self-guiding tours: Visitors can stroll past fine examples of architecture while touring the tree-lined streets of Titusville. A brochure is available at the chamber of commerce.

DRAKE WELL MUSEUM is at 202 Museum Ln. The museum marks the spot where Edwin Drake drilled the world's first commercially successful oil well in 1859. Photographs and outdoor working oil field equipment trace the evolution of the modern petroleum industry. The exhibit "There's a Drop of Oil and Gas in Your Life Every Day" features a multisensory orientation theater. A replica of Drake's well, an operating oil lease with pump jacks and a steel drilling rig and pumping jacks are also on display.

A 10-mile paved bicycle trail and 52 miles of hiking trails connect Drake Well and Oil Creek State Park *(see Recreation Areas Chart)*. **Hours:** Tues.-Sat. 9-5, Sun. noon-5, Mar.-Dec.; Sat. 9-5, Sun. noon-5, rest of year. Closed Jan. 1, Easter, Thanksgiving, day after Thanksgiving and Christmas. Phone ahead to confirm schedule. **Cost:** $10; $8 (ages 65+); $5 (ages 3-11); free (active military and their family with ID). **Phone:** (814) 827-2797.

TOWANDA (D-9) pop. 2,919, elev. 771'

Towanda was the boyhood home of composer Stephen Collins Foster and the home of staunch Abraham Lincoln supporter David Wilmot, who founded the Republican Party.

PARADISE INN & SUITES   570/268-7000
Hotel. **Address:** 44 Peace Ln 18848

WHERE TO EAT

RED ROSE DINER   570/265-7203
American. Casual Dining. **Address:** 526 Main St 18848

VILLA SENA   570/265-9986
Italian. Casual Dining. **Address:** 143 Villa Sena Blvd 18848

TRAFFORD pop. 3,174

- **Hotels & Restaurants map & index p. 246**
- **Part of Pittsburgh area — see map p. 225**

PARENTE'S RISTORANTE   412/373-0566 **93**
Italian. Casual Dining. **Address:** 427 Cavitt Ave 15085

TREVOSE pop. 3,550

- **Hotels & Restaurants map & index p. 192**
- **Part of Philadelphia area — see map p. 154**

COMFORT INN TREVOSE   (215)638-4554 **33**
Hotel. **Address:** 2779 Lincoln Hwy N 19053

RADISSON HOTEL PHILADELPHIA NORTHEAST
215/638-8300 **34**
Hotel. **Address:** 2400 Old Lincoln Hwy 19053

Get an expert view from AAA inspectors:
AAA.com/travelguides/hotels

(See map & index p. 192.)

RED ROOF INN PHILADELPHIA TREVOSE
(215)244-9422 **32**

Motel
$63-$99

Address: 3100 Lincoln Hwy 19053 **Location:** I-276 (Pennsylvania Tpke) exit 351, 0.5 mi s on US 1 at US 132. Located in a commercial area. Trevose, 286. **Facility:** 162 units. 2 stories (no elevator), exterior corridors. **Amenities:** video games, safes. **Guest Services:** coin laundry.

WYNDHAM PHILADELPHIA-BUCKS COUNTY, PA
(215)364-2000 **31**

Hotel
$104-$149

Address: 4700 Street Rd 19053 **Location:** I-276 (Pennsylvania Tpke) exit 351, just s on US 1, then 0.3 mi w on SR 132. Located in a commercial area. Trevose, 286. **Facility:** 214 units. 6 stories, interior corridors. **Terms:** check-in 4 pm. **Dining:** 2 restaurants. **Pool:** heated indoor. **Activities:** sauna, hot tub, game room, exercise room. **Guest Services:** valet and coin laundry, rental car service, area transportation. **Featured Amenity:** full hot breakfast.

TROUT RUN

FRY BROTHERS TURKEY RANCH
570/998-9400
American. Casual Dining. **Address:** 27 SR 184 17771

TUNKHANNOCK (WYOMING COUNTY)

COMFORT INN & SUITES TUNKHANNOCK
(570)836-4100
Hotel. **Address:** 5 N Eaton Rd 18657

HAMPTON INN TUNKHANNOCK
(570)996-5866
Hotel. **Address:** 209 E Tioga St 18657

AAA Benefit:
Members save up to 10%!

WHERE TO EAT

TWIGS RESTAURANT & CAFE
570/836-0433
American. Casual Dining. **Address:** 1 E Tioga St 18657

UNIONTOWN (I-2) pop. 10,372, elev. 1,022'

Uniontown is in the Laurel Highlands *(see place listing p. 122)* of southwestern Pennsylvania, an area filled with historic sites and outdoor recreation outlets. Spelunking, bicycling and white-water rafting are popular.

Founded in 1776, the town is on Route 40, the historic National Road, which was built 1811-18. It is the birthplace of Gen. George C. Marshall, who laid out the plan in which America would provide economic aid to Europe after World War II—the Marshall Plan. Southeast of town is the grave of Gen. Edward Braddock *(see Fort Necessity National Battlefield p. 76).* About 5 miles west on the National

Road/US 40 is Searights Toll House, one of two remaining such structures; there were originally six in the state.

Fayette Chamber of Commerce: 65 W. Main St., Uniontown, PA 15401. **Phone:** (724) 437-4571.

FAIRFIELD INN BY MARRIOTT UNIONTOWN
(724)434-1800
Hotel. **Address:** 283 McClellandtown Rd 15401

AAA Benefit:
Members save 5% or more!

HAMPTON INN
(724)430-1000
Hotel. **Address:** 698 W Main St (US 40) 15401

AAA Benefit:
Members save up to 10%!

INNE AT WATSON'S CHOICE AND HARVEST HOUSE BED & BREAKFAST
724/437-4999
Historic Bed & Breakfast. **Address:** 234 Balsinger Rd 15401

MG MOTEL
724/437-0506
Motel. **Address:** 7909 National Pike (US 40) 15401

SUPER 8
(724)425-0261
Hotel. **Address:** 701 W Main St 15401

WHERE TO EAT

ALL STAR ASIAN BUFFET
724/430-8185
Asian. Casual Dining. **Address:** 203 Walmart Dr 15401

ANGELINA'S PICCOLO
724/437-2782
Italian. Casual Dining. **Address:** 104 Oliver Plaza 15401

DI MARCO'S BISTRO & CANTINA
724/438-1611
American. Casual Dining. **Address:** 26 Morgantown St 15401

EAT'N PARK
724/439-0440
American. Casual Dining. **Address:** 519 W Main St 15401

GENERATIONS, A RESTAURANT
724/437-3204
Italian. Casual Dining. **Address:** 181 W Main St 15401

MELONI'S
724/437-2061

Italian
Casual Dining
$7-$20

AAA Inspector Notes: This restaurant is located in an old-fashioned neighborhood, where the service and atmosphere are casual and the food is tasty and filling. Lasagna, spaghetti and Italian sausage sandwiches are specialties. The menu also lists a handful of American choices. There is a good selection of beer and wines to choose from at the bar. **Features:** full bar. **Address:** 105 W Main St 15401 **Location:** Center. L D

MING HING CHINESE RESTAURANT
724/438-8883
Chinese. Casual Dining. **Address:** 629 Pittsburgh Rd 15401

TITLOW TAVERN & GRILLE
724/437-6749
American. Casual Dining. **Address:** 92 W Main St 15401

UPPER BLACK EDDY
• Part of Philadelphia area — see map p. 154

THE BRIDGETON HOUSE ON THE DELAWARE
610/982-5856
Bed & Breakfast. **Address:** 1525 River Rd 18972

UPPER DELAWARE SCENIC AND RECREATIONAL RIVER (D-11)

The Upper Delaware Scenic and Recreational River comprises 73 miles of the Upper Delaware River from just north of Port Jervis, N.Y., to Hancock, N.Y. Along this stretch the river changes from long, placid eddies to swift water and challenging rapids. It is paralleled on the New York side by SR 97 (Upper Delaware Scenic Byway), which has several scenic overlooks. The best road from which to see the river on the Pennsylvania side is the northern section of SR 191, which at times is only a few feet above the water.

Almost all land along the river is privately owned; public river access areas are located on both the Pennsylvania and New York shores. Private campgrounds and canoe liveries are available near the river.

The Upper Delaware was an important transportation route for Native Americans and early settlers. In 1828 the Delaware and Hudson Canal opened, bringing coal-laden boats from the Pennsylvania interior to the port of New York. However, problems soon developed at the point where the canal crossed the river: Slow-moving boats being towed across the river were constantly colliding with the huge log and timber rafts that were coursing down the river to sawmills and shipyards in Trenton, N.J., and Philadelphia, Pa.

To solve the problem and improve the canal's efficiency, the company approved a plan to build the canal above the water. John Roebling, who later designed the Brooklyn Bridge, built the Delaware Aqueduct, known today as Roebling Bridge, to cross the river and carry canal traffic from Lackawaxen, Pa., to Minisink Ford, N.Y. The aqueduct is considered to be the oldest wire suspension bridge in America. The adjacent tollhouse contains exhibits interpreting the history of the Delaware and Hudson Canal, John Roebling and the Delaware Aqueduct.

Beavers, foxes, white-tailed deer, minks, muskrats, otters, rabbits and squirrels populate the area. Birds include bald eagles, great blue herons, Canada geese and several varieties of hawks and ducks.

On the banks of the Upper Delaware Scenic and Recreational River lies the Zane Grey Museum, in Lackawaxen, Pa. The renowned Western author began his writing career and lived at the site with his wife, Dolly, 1905-18.

Recreational opportunities include boating, canoeing, fishing and rafting. In summer the National Park Service offers a variety of programs and recreational activities, including cultural and natural history walks and guided hikes.

Information stations are located at some public boating access sites in Narrowsburg, N.Y. and Lackawaxen, Pa., and at the Zane Grey Museum on Scenic Dr. in Lackawaxen, Pa. Phone (570) 684-4871 for the museum or (845) 252-7100 for river conditions. The museum is open Wed.-Sun.

10-5, Memorial Day-Sept. 30; Sat.-Sun. 10-5, first three weekends in Oct.

UPPER ST. CLAIR pop. 19,229
- **Hotels & Restaurants map & index p. 246**
- **Part of Pittsburgh area — see map p. 225**

KING'S FAMILY RESTAURANT   412/833-9095
▼▼ American. Casual Dining. **Address:** 155 McMurray Rd 15241

PICCOLINA'S   412/257-1880   110
▼▼▼ Northern Italian. Fine Dining. **Address:** 1580 McLaughlin Run Rd 15241

VALLEY FORGE (A-9) elev. 98'
- **Part of Philadelphia area — see map p. 154**

Valley Forge began as an iron forge on Valley Creek in the 1740s. A sawmill and gristmill were added by the time of the Revolutionary War, making Valley Forge an important supply center for the Colonists. However, it did not escape the attention of the British, who destroyed the forge and mills in 1777. Only ruins marked the site when George Washington chose Valley Forge for his winter of 1777-78 encampment *(see Valley Forge National Historical Park this page)*. The Valley Forge Tourism & Convention Board is in King of Prussia *(place listing p. 112)*.

VALLEY FORGE NATIONAL HISTORICAL PARK (A-8) elev. 154'
- **Part of Philadelphia area — see map p. 154**

Extending east from the village of Valley Forge along SR 23, the 3,500-acre Valley Forge National Historical Park was the site of the 6-month winter/spring encampment by the Continental Army. From Dec. 19, 1777, to June 19, 1778, Gen. George Washington and 12,000 soldiers survived against terrible odds and kept the British Army contained in Philadelphia.

During that harsh winter some 2,000 troops died from disease brought on by supply shortages, exposure and poor sanitation. Still, during those 6 months the army was reorganized, Baron von Steuben developed a uniform system of drill and the Continental Army left Valley Forge better trained and more efficient.

The visitor center, at the junction of SR 23 and N. Gulph Road, has exhibits and presents a short film. Maps outlining a self-guiding driving tour, which includes the National Memorial Arch, Washington's Headquarters, Washington Memorial Chapel *(see attraction listings)*, the reconstructed huts of Muhlenberg's Brigade and the original entrenchment lines and fortifications are available here. One-hour audio driving tours on CD can also be purchased. Seasonal trolley tours begin from this location.

A stop at any of the Storytelling Benches located throughout the park will offer insight into the Valley Forge army encampment and its impact on the Revolutionary War. The Once Upon A Nation benches are staffed seasonally. Ranger-led tours begin at the Park Theater next to the visitor center and finish with a look at the Muhlenberg Brigade replica log huts.

Allow 2 hours minimum. Park open daily 7 a.m.-dusk. Visitor center open daily 9-6, in summer (based on staff availability); 9-5, rest of year. Washington's Headquarters open daily 9-5, early Mar.-Dec. 31 (also 5-6, in summer, based on staff availability). All buildings are closed Jan. 1, Thanksgiving and Christmas. Varnum's Quarters Sat.-Sun. noon-4, seasonally. Varnum's picnic area daily 7 a.m.-dusk, Apr.-Oct.; Sat.-Sun., 7-dusk, in Nov. March to Valley Forge .25-mile ranger-led tours depart daily at 10:50 and 2:50, mid-June through Labor Day; Sat.-Sun. at 10:50 and 2:50, late Mar.-early June. Narrated 90-minute trolley tours depart daily, early June-Labor Day; Sat.-Sun., late Mar.-early June and early Sept.-late Nov. (weather permitting). Phone for departure times. Holiday tours offered in late Nov. and late Dec. Phone for schedule of other tours.

Park free. Trolley tour $17.50; $14.50 (ages 62+, students and active military with ID); $9 (ages 0-11). Audio CD $14.95 (available at the Encampment Store). Phone (610) 783-1000 for the visitor center to confirm staff availability, or (610) 783-1074 for trolley tours.

NATIONAL MEMORIAL ARCH, off SR 23 in Valley Forge National Historical Park, commemorates the patriotism and suffering of George Washington and the men who were under his command; it was dedicated in 1917. The final design was inspired by the Arch of Titus in Rome. The inner walls of this 60-foot high granite memorial contain bronze plaques listing the names of the general officers at Valley Forge. **Hours:** Daily 7 a.m.-dusk. Park visitor center daily 9-6, in summer (based on staff availability); 9-5, rest of year. **Cost:** Free. **Phone:** (610) 783-1000 for the park visitor center.

WASHINGTON MEMORIAL CHAPEL is at 1600 Valley Forge Park Rd. (SR 23) within Valley Forge National Historical Park. The Episcopal chapel was built in 1903 as a memorial to Gen. George Washington and contains artifacts, relics, woodcarvings and windows depicting national history. The National Patriot's Bell Tower houses 58 bells and the Veteran's Wall of Honor. Guided tours are available by appointment. **Time:** Allow 30 minutes minimum. **Hours:** Daily 10-5. **Cost:** Donations. **Phone:** (610) 783-0120. GT

WASHINGTON'S HEADQUARTERS is 3 mi. w. of the visitor center on SR 23W in Valley Forge National Historical Park. The house, which contains Revolutionary War-era furnishings, was rented by Gen. George Washington during the Continental Army's encampment Dec. 19, 1777, to June 19, 1778, and served as his command post for coordinating the daily operations of the entire army.

The structure is also known as the Potts House. Park rangers are available to answer questions. Displays that chronicle Washington as a leader can be seen in the 1917 Valley Forge Train Station building next door. **Time:** Allow 30 minutes minimum. **Hours:** Daily 9-5, early Mar.-Dec. 31 (also 5-6, in summer, based on staff availability). Park visitor center daily 9-6, in summer (based on staff availability); 9-5, rest of year. Closed Jan. 1, Thanksgiving and Christmas. **Cost:** Free. **Phone:** (610) 783-1000 for the park visitor center.

VOLANT (F-1) pop. 168, elev. 1,033'

If you're traveling along I-79 or I-80 and have an itch to go shopping for something special that can't be found in every mall or chain store, take the nearest Volant exit to visit this quaint town with nearly two dozen specialty shops lining Main Street (SR 208). The focal point of the old-fashioned small town is Volant Mill, which dates back to 1812. Volant had a flourishing business district in the late 19th- and early 20th centuries thanks to the mill and the railroad, but with the Great Depression came less growth; the mill eventually closed in the 1960s, the trains ceased in the mid-1970s and Volant settled into its new role as a typical small rural town. However, in 1984 an antique and country gift store opened up in the Volant Mill building. More shops gradually opened along Main Street, creating a specialty shopping district which is a popular destination still.

Amish families reside on nearby farms, so horses and buggies are common sights in the area. Neshannock Creek, excellent for trout fishing, runs through Volant and fly fishing is quite popular. Also popular is the annual trout stocking day in March, which is just one of many planned festivities in a busy calendar of events schedule where almost every month offers at least one way to celebrate a holiday or the arrival of a new season.

Shopping: The Volant Village Shops include nearly two dozen specialty shops along Main Street (SR 208) with a wide assortment of merchandise, including furniture, leather goods, rugs, kitchen supplies, soaps and lotions, garden flags, scrapbook materials, collectibles, home furnishings, jewelry, handmade Amish goods and artwork by regional artists. There also are coffees, teas, spices, jams, relishes and nostalgic candies. During autumn, which is a particularly lovely time to visit the area, many of the shops' inventories are enhanced with Halloween, Thanksgiving and Christmas decorations.

WARMINSTER
• Part of Philadelphia area — see map p. 154

HOLIDAY INN EXPRESS & SUITES WARMINSTER-HORSHAM
215/443-4300
♦♦♦ Hotel. **Address:** 240 Veterans Way 18974

WARREN (D-3) pop. 9,710, elev. 1,174'

Kinzua Dam, 6 miles east on SR 59, offers scenic views of the dam and Allegheny Reservoir, and a wide variety of summer and winter recreational activities are available. A visitor center in the Big Bend Access Area is open based on the availability of volunteers; phone (814) 726-0678, or (814) 726-0164 for lake conditions. *See Allegheny National Forest p. 34 and Recreation Areas Chart.*

Warren County Visitors Bureau: 22045 US 6, Warren, PA 16365. **Phone:** (814) 726-1222 or (800) 624-7802.

DAYS INN WARREN   (814)726-3000
♦♦♦ Hotel. **Address:** 210 Ludlow St 16365

HAMPTON INN & SUITES OF WARREN   (814)723-2722
♦♦♦ Hotel. **Address:** 3291 Market
St 16365

| AAA Benefit: |
| Members save up to 10%! |

QUALITY INN & SUITES   (814)723-8881
♦♦ Motel. **Address:** 204 Struthers St 16365

CHIODO'S FERRO CUCINA   814/723-5773
♦♦ Italian. Casual Dining. **Address:** 1413 Pennsylvania Ave 16365

WARRINGTON
• Part of Philadelphia area — see map p. 154

HAMPTON INN - WARRINGTON/DOYLESTOWN
(215)343-8400
♦♦♦ Hotel. **Address:** 1570 Easton
Rd 18976

| AAA Benefit: |
| Members save up to 10%! |

HOMEWOOD SUITES WARRINGTON   (215)343-1300

♦♦♦
Extended Stay Hotel
$149-$219

HOMEWOOD SUITES BY HILTON
AAA Benefit: Members save up to 10%!

Address: 2650 Kelly Rd 18976 **Location:** 2.4 mi s of jct US 202 and SR 611. **Facility:** 96 efficiencies, some two bedrooms. 5 stories, interior corridors. **Terms:** 1-7 night minimum stay, cancellation fee imposed. **Pool:** heated indoor. **Activities:** game room, exercise room. **Guest Services:** valet and coin laundry. **Featured Amenity: continental breakfast.**

WASHINGTON (H-1) pop. 13,663, elev. 1,039'
• Restaurants p. 294
• Part of Pittsburgh area — see map p. 225

The Washington & Jefferson College U. Grant Miller Library was founded by a gift from Benjamin Franklin; phone (724) 223–6070. The school, which started in 1781, is said to be the oldest college west of the Allegheny Mountains.

The Duncan Miller Glass Museum, 525 Jefferson Ave., exhibits fine pressed and hand-blown glass made 1893-1955. It is open for guided tours Thurs.-Sun. 11-4 (except holidays), early Apr.-Dec. 31 and by appointment year-round. Phone (724) 225-9950. There is also an annual glass show and sale held at the nearby Washington County Fairgrounds in late July.

Self-guiding tours: Washington County is home to 23 of the state's nearly 200 covered bridges. A brochure highlighting their history is available at various information stands in the area, including Courthouse Square.

Shopping: [SAVE] Tanger Outlet Center, .5 mi. e. off I-79 exit 41 (Racetrack Rd.) at 2200 Tanger Blvd., features more than 75 stores, including Ann Taylor Factory Store, Coach, Gymboree Outlet, Michael Kors, Nine West Outlet, Old Navy and Nike Factory Store.

CAMBRIA HOTEL & SUITES WASHINGTON   (724)223-5555
♦♦♦ Hotel. **Address:** 451 Racetrack Rd 15301

CANDLEWOOD SUITES WASHINGTON NORTH 724/873-7300
♦♦♦ Extended Stay Hotel. **Address:** 255 Meadowland Blvd 15301

COMFORT INN & SUITES WASHINGTON   (724)884-0299
♦♦♦ Hotel. **Address:** 2110 N Franklin Dr 15301

COMFORT INN MEADOWLANDS   (724)746-9700
♦♦ Hotel. **Address:** 237 Meadowlands Blvd 15301

COUNTRY INN & SUITES BY CARLSON   724/884-1450
♦♦♦ Hotel. **Address:** 245 Meadowlands Blvd 15301

COURTYARD BY MARRIOTT PITTSBURGH/WASHINGTON
MEADOW LANDS   (724)222-5620
♦♦♦ Hotel. **Address:** 1800 Tanger
Blvd 15301

| AAA Benefit: |
| Members save 5% or more! |

DOUBLETREE BY HILTON HOTEL PITTSBURGH-MEADOW
LANDS   (724)222-6200
♦♦♦ Hotel. **Address:** 340 Race-
track Rd 15301

| AAA Benefit: |
| Members save 5% or more! |

HAMPTON INN & SUITES   (724)222-4014
♦♦♦ Hotel. **Address:** 475 Johnson
Rd 15301

| AAA Benefit: |
| Members save up to 10%! |

HYATT PLACE PITTSBURGH SOUTH/MEADOWS RACETRACK & CASINO
(724)222-7777

Hotel
$99-$329

Address: 212 Racetrack Rd 15301 **Location:** I-79 exit 41, just e. **Facility:** 155 units. 4 stories, interior corridors. **Terms:** cancellation fee imposed. **Amenities:** safes. **Pool:** heated indoor. **Activities:** exercise room. **Guest Services:** valet laundry, area transportation. **Featured Amenity:** breakfast buffet.

RAMADA
(724)225-9750

Hotel
$82-$89

Address: 1170 W Chestnut St 15301 **Location:** I-70 exit 15, 0.5 mi e. on US 40. **Facility:** 92 units. 2 stories (no elevator), interior/exterior corridors. **Pool:** outdoor. **Guest Services:** valet laundry. **Featured Amenity:** continental breakfast.

RED ROOF INN WASHINGTON, PA
(724)228-5750

Motel
$50-$105

Address: 1399 W Chestnut St 15301 **Location:** I-70 exit 15, just e on US 40. **Facility:** 110 units. 2 stories, interior/exterior corridors. **Amenities:** safes.

SPRINGHILL SUITES BY MARRIOTT
(724)223-7800
Hotel. **Address:** 16 Trinity Point Dr 15301

WHERE TO EAT

HOG FATHER'S OLD FASHIONED BBQ   724/229-1227
Barbecue. Casual Dining. **Address:** 1301 Jefferson Ave 15301

PALAZZO 1837 RISTORANTE   724/223-1837
Italian. Casual Dining. **Address:** 1445 Washington Rd 15301

UNION GRILL   724/222-2860
American. Casual Dining. **Address:** 13 1/2 E Wheeling St 15301

WASHINGTON CROSSING HISTORIC PARK (H-12) elev. 52'
• Part of Philadelphia area — see map p. 154

Washington Crossing Historic Park is divided into two areas: the Upper Park (Thompson's Mill Section) is 1.5 miles southeast of New Hope via SR 32, and the Lower Park (McConkey's Ferry Section) is 5 miles farther south on SR 32. A bridge crosses the Delaware River and allows visitors to enter New Jersey's Washington Crossing State Park. The 500-acre park is dedicated to the memory of George Washington and the 2,400 soldiers who crossed the Delaware on Christmas night in 1776 to attack and capture Trenton, N.J., then garrisoned by Hessian soldiers. A re-enactment of the crossing of the Delaware is held at 1 p.m. on Christmas. Other events are presented throughout the year. Picnicking is permitted.

The park and recreation areas are open daily dawn-dusk (weather permitting). The visitor center is open daily 10-5 (weather permitting); closed some holidays. Historic building schedules vary. Phone ahead to confirm schedules.

Grounds free. Historic building admission (which includes Bowman's Hill Tower, Durham Boat House, McConkey's Ferry Inn, Thompson-Neely Farmstead and Visitor Center) $11; $6 (ages 4-11); free (active military with ID). Bowman's Hill Tower, Durham Boat House, McConkey's Ferry Inn or Thompson-Neely Farmstead only, $6 each site. Visitor center only, free. Additional fees may be charged for special events. Phone (215) 493-4076.

MCCONKEY'S FERRY SECTION, 7 mi. s. of New Hope on SR 32 at 1112 River Rd. within Washington Crossing Historic Park, focuses on the site where Gen. George Washington and his troops embarked on their historic crossing. The Mahlon K. Taylor House, the restored 1817 home of an influential businessman of the period, can be viewed from the outside (it is only open to large tour groups). Also depicted is the 19th-century village of Taylorsville, which grew as the Delaware Canal prospered.

Hours: Tours daily 10:30-3:30, mid-Mar. through Dec. 31; Sat.-Sun. 10:30-3:30, rest of year. Last tour begins at closing. Closed some holidays. Phone ahead to confirm schedule. **Cost:** (includes all McConkey's Ferry section sites as well as Bowman's Hill Tower and Thompson-Neely Farmstead in the Thompson's Mill Section) $11; $6 (ages 4-11); free (active military with ID). McConkey's Ferry Section only, $6 each site. Additional fees may be charged for special events. **Phone:** (215) 493-4076.

Durham Boat House, within McConkey's Ferry Section of Washington Crossing Historic Park at 1104 Embarcation Rd., stores replicas of boats used to transport iron ore and other heavy cargo, such as those used by Washington during the Christmas crossing of the Delaware River.

Hours: Daily 10:30-3:30, mid-Mar. through Dec. 31; Sat.-Sun. 10:30-3:30, rest of year. Last tour begins at closing. Closed some holidays. Phone ahead to confirm schedule. **Cost:** (includes Bowman's Hill Tower, McConkey's Ferry Inn, Thompson-Neely Farmstead and Visitor Center) $11; $6 (ages 4-11); free (active military with ID). Durham Boat House or McConkey's Ferry Inn only, $6 each site. Visitor Center only free. Additional fees may be charged for special events. **Phone:** (215) 493-4076. GT

Hibbs House, within McConkey's Ferry Section of Washington Crossing Historic Park at 1108 Embarcation Rd., is a restored tenant house built in the late 1830s. **Note:** The Hibbs House is open for special events only. **Phone:** (215) 493-4076.

McConkey's Ferry Inn, within McConkey's Ferry Section of Washington Crossing Historic Park at 1325 SR 532, is a restored stone building, the earliest parts of which date from the 1750s. George Washington is believed to have dined at the inn before crossing the Delaware.

Hours: Daily 10:30-3:30, mid-Mar. through Dec. 31; Sat.-Sun. 10:30-3:30, rest of year. Last tour begins at closing. Closed some holidays. Phone ahead to confirm schedule. **Cost:** (includes Bowman's Hill Tower, Durham Boat House, Thompson-Neely Farmstead and Visitor Center) $11; $6 (ages 4-11); free (active military with ID). Durham Boat House or McConkey's Ferry Inn only, $6 each site. Visitor Center only, free. Additional fees may be charged for special events. **Phone:** (215) 493-4076. GT

Visitor Center, within McConkey's Ferry Section of Washington Crossing Historic Park at 1112 River Rd., features visitor facilities, an exhibits gallery and a film that depicts the sites' significance. **Hours:** Daily 10-5 (weather permitting). Closed some holidays. Phone ahead to confirm schedule. **Cost:** Bowman's Hill Tower, Durham Boat House, McConkey's Ferry Inn, Thompson-Neely Farmstead and Visitor Center (includes orientation film) $11; $6 (ages 4-11); free (active military with ID). Durham Boat House or McConkey's Ferry Inn only, $6 each site. Visitor center only, free. **Phone:** (215) 493-4076.

THOMPSON'S MILL SECTION, 1.5 mi. s.e. of New Hope on SR 32 within Washington Crossing Historic Park, preserves 18th-century buildings, Bowman's Hill Tower and Revolutionary soldiers' grave sites. Bowman's Hill Tower and Thompson Neely House are open to the public. Other locations are available for exterior grounds observation only. **Hours:** Schedule varies per site. Closed some holidays. Phone ahead to confirm schedule. **Cost:** (includes Bowman's Hill Tower and Thompson-Neely Farmstead in the Thompson's Mill Section as well as all McConkey's Ferry section sites) $11; $6 (ages 4-11); free (active military with ID). Additional fees may be charged for some activities. **Phone:** (215) 493-4076.

Bowman's Hill Tower, within Thompson's Mill Section of Washington Crossing Historic Park at River Rd. & Lurgan Rd., was completed in 1931 and presents a commanding 14-mile view of the Delaware

River Valley. Washington Crossing can be seen to the south. **Note:** Visitors must climb stairs to an observation point within the 125-foot tower; the top is then reached by 23 stone stairs At press time, the elevator to the tower's observation point was closed for repairs.

Hours: Daily 10-4, Apr.-Dec. (weather permitting). Last admission is 15 minutes before closing. Closed some holidays. Phone ahead to confirm schedule. **Cost:** (includes Durham Boat House, McConkey's Ferry Inn, Thompson-Neely Farmstead and Visitor Center) $11; $6 (ages 4-11); free (active military with ID). Tower only, $6. Additional fees may be charged for special events. **Phone:** (215) 862-3166.

Bowman's Hill Wildflower Preserve is within Thompson's Mill Section of Washington Crossing Historic Park at 1635 River Rd., across from Thompson-Neely Farmstead. It includes a 134-acre wildflower area with a visitor center, native plant nursery, about a dozen hiking trails, indoor exhibits and a bird observation window. Educational programs and special events are offered throughout the year. Picnicking is permitted in the front at the Captain James Moore Pavilion.

Hours: Preserve Tues.-Sun. 8:30-dusk. Visitor center Tues.-Sun. 9-5. Guided tours depart Tues.-Sun. at 2, Apr.-Oct. Closed Thanksgiving and Christmas Eve-New Year's Day. **Cost:** (includes guided tour) $6; $4 (ages 65+ and students with ID); $3 (ages 3-14). **Phone:** (215) 862-2924. GT 🏕

Soldiers' Graves, within Thompson's Mill Section of Washington Crossing Historic Park, mark the burial place of Continental soldiers who died during the encampment. **Hours:** Daily dawn-dusk. **Cost:** Free. **Phone:** (215) 493-4076.

Thompson-Neely Farmstead, within Thompson's Mill Section of Washington Crossing Historic Park at 1638 River Rd., built in the 1700s, was the scene of a military hospital during the Bucks County encampment. A barn, a reconstructed 19th-century gristmill and other restored farm outbuildings are nearby.

Hours: Daily 10-4, Apr.-Dec. Closed some holidays. Phone ahead to confirm schedule. **Cost:** (includes Bowman's Hill Tower, Durham Boat House, McConkey's Ferry Inn and Visitor Center) $11; $6 (ages 4-11); free (active military with ID). Farmstead only, $6. Additional fees may be charged for special events. **Phone:** (215) 493-4076. GT

WATERFORD (C-2) pop. 1,517, elev. 1,192'

In 1753 the French built Fort LeBoeuf, which eventually fell to the British. A 21-year-old George Washington, then a major in the British Virginia Militia, delivered a message from Gov. Robert Dinwiddie asking the French to withdraw from the area. The French refused, and eventually tensions erupted into the French and Indian War. A statue of Washington stands near the site.

Also of interest on S. High Street is the Amos Judson House, a restored two-story Federal Greek Revival home built in 1820. The museum contains circa 1840 furnishings and a model of the fort as well as a library with genealogical information. Next door is the Fort LeBoeuf Museum at 123 S. High St.; it sits on the original site of the French fort. Inside are exhibits related to Native Americans who lived in the area as well as the French and British fur trade. Across the street is the restored 1826 Eagle Hotel, a stone structure built in the Federal and Georgian styles. This once was an important stagecoach stop and now houses a restaurant.

Brotherton's Bridge, on Niemeyer Road, is a covered bridge over LeBoeuf Creek. **Note:** At press time, work was scheduled to begin in 2018 to make structural repairs. Swimming, boating, fishing and camping are available at nearby Lake LeBoeuf *(see Recreation Areas Chart).*

WAYNE (B-9) elev. 400'
• Part of Philadelphia area — see map p. 154

In the mid-1800s banker J. Henry Askin developed a community he named Louella, in honor of his two daughters, Louisa and Ella. With railroad connections to Philadelphia, the rural Victorian village was populated by the families of commuting businessmen. Askin's financial difficulties forced him to sell the property, but Louella continued to grow and attract urbanites. The town was later renamed for Revolutionary War general Anthony Wayne.

Wayne is home to Valley Forge Military Academy and College, site of a monument commemorating the World War II Battle of the Bulge. The Radnor Historical Society, 113 W. Beech Tree Ln., is housed in a 1789 farmhouse and provides information about area history Tuesday and Saturday; phone (610) 688–2668.

CHANTICLEER GARDEN, 786 Church Rd., is a 35-acre garden situated on the former estate of pharmaceutical magnate Adolph Rosengarten Sr. Included throughout the various gardens are landscaped courtyards; flowering trees and shrubs; vegetable and herb gardens; tropical plants; perennials and annuals; and woodlands and ponds. Minder

Ruin Garden displays plantings among the foundation of a razed stone house. The Rosengarten house contains family furniture, decorative arts and fresh flower arrangements from the garden; participants may tour the garden on their own following the house tour.

Time: Allow 1 hour minimum. **Hours:** Garden open Wed.-Sun. 10-5, late Mar.-late Oct. (also Fri. 5-8, early May-Labor Day). Tours Fri.-Sat. at 11. **Cost:** Garden $10 (ages 13+). House tour (includes general admission) $15. Reservations are recommended for house tours. **Phone:** (610) 687-4163.

WAYNESBORO (I-7) pop. 10,568, elev. 713'

Tucked into rolling hills and surrounded by peach and apple orchards, Waynesboro dates back to 1749. Like many other towns in the vicinity, it lays claim to a historical footnote; abolitionist John Brown taught Sunday school nearby while preparing for his ill-fated Harper's Ferry, W.Va., raid. Later, Waynesboro became an early 20th-century retreat for Washington, D.C., residents seeking escape from summer heat and humidity.

Greater Waynesboro Chamber of Commerce: 118 Walnut St., Waynesboro, PA 17268. **Phone:** (717) 762-7123.

WAYNESBURG (I-1) pop. 4,176, elev. 938'

Waynesburg was named for Revolutionary War hero Gen. "Mad" Anthony Wayne. The town is the seat of Greene County, named for another Revolutionary War hero, Gen. Nathanael Greene. A statue of Greene is atop the 1850 county courthouse, a fine example of Greek Revival architecture. The old log courthouse, 144 E. Greene Street, now houses the Cornerstone Genealogical Society; phone (724) 627-5653. Also in town is Waynesburg University, one of the first colleges in the United States to grant degrees to women.

Greene County Tourist Promotion Agency: 19 S. Washington St., Waynesburg, PA 15370. **Phone:** (724) 627-8687.

HAMPTON INN   (724)802-1010
ⱱ̃ⱱ̃ⱱ̃ Hotel. **Address:** 227 Greene Plaza 15370

AAA Benefit: Members save up to 10%!

MICROTEL INN & SUITES BY WYNDHAM WAYNESBURG
(724)627-0310
ⱱ̃ⱱ̃ Hotel. **Address:** 300 Comfort Ln 15370

QUALITY INN   (724)627-3700
ⱱ̃ⱱ̃ Hotel. **Address:** 100 Comfort Ln 15370

WHERE TO EAT

HOT ROD'S HOUSE OF BAR-B-QUE   724/852-2681
ⱱ̃ⱱ̃ Barbecue. Casual Dining. **Address:** 46 S Morris St 15370

WEATHERLY (F-10) pop. 2,525, elev. 1,086'
• Part of Pocono Mountains Area — see map p. 264

RECREATIONAL ACTIVITIES
White-water Rafting
• ⟨SAVE⟩ **Whitewater Challengers Raft Tours** is at 288 N. Stagecoach Rd.; visitors are then bused to the rafting location. Other activities also are available. **Hours:** Daily, Apr.-Oct.; phone for departure times. **Phone:** (570) 443-9532 or (800) 443-8554. ⟨GT⟩

WELLSBORO (D-7) pop. 3,263, elev. 1,315'

If Wellsboro's lantern-lit streets, town green and Victorian mansions seem vaguely reminiscent of Massachusetts or Vermont, it is because the town was founded by New England colonists in 1806. In the mountainous region of north-central Pennsylvania, Wellsboro is an all-year recreation center.

Visit Potter-Tioga: 2053 SR 660, Wellsboro, PA 16901. **Phone:** (570) 724-0635 or (888) 846-4228.

Self-guiding tours: Walking and driving tour information is available from the tourism office.

SHERWOOD MOTEL   (570)724-3424

Motel
$92-$120

Address: 2 Main St 16901 **Location:** Just n on US 6 and SR 287; downtown. **Facility:** 42 units, some two bedrooms. 2 stories (no elevator), interior/exterior corridors. **Terms:** cancellation fee imposed. **Pool:** heated outdoor. **Activities:** playground.

WHERE TO EAT

PENN WELLS DINING ROOM   570/724-2111
ⱱ̃ⱱ̃ American. Casual Dining. **Address:** 62 Main St 16901

THE STEAK HOUSE   570/724-9092
ⱱ̃ⱱ̃ Steak. Casual Dining. **Address:** 29 Main St 16901

TIMELESS DESTINATION   570/724-8499
ⱱ̃ⱱ̃ Italian. Casual Dining. **Address:** 77 Main St 16901

WEST CHESTER (B-8) pop. 18,461, elev. 424'
• Restaurants p. 298
• Part of Philadelphia area — see map p. 154

Graced by many handsome Greek Revival and Victorian houses, West Chester is surrounded by the rich farmland of Chester County. During the Revolutionary War several major skirmishes occurred nearby, including the battles of Brandywine and Paoli. In 1842 West Chester became the home of the *Jeffersonian*, one of the few newspapers in the North to support the South. A rioting mob soon wrecked the paper's offices, and eventually the postmaster general prohibited its distribution by mail.

A building of note is the Chester County Courthouse, built in 1724.

AMERICAN HELICOPTER MUSEUM & EDUCATION CENTER, 1220 American Blvd., demonstrates the past and future of rotor-wing aircraft. More than 35 civilian and military aircraft are displayed, including a rare V-22 Osprey with tilted rotors. Hands-on programs demonstrate helicopter design and operation. A theater and interactive exhibits are other highlights. Docents are available to answer questions. **Time:** Allow 1 hour minimum. **Hours:** Wed.-Sat. 10-5, Sun. noon-5. Last admission 1 hour before closing. **Closed** major holidays; phone for holiday schedule. **Cost:** $10; $8 (ages 2-11, senior citizens and students with ID). **Phone:** (610) 436-9600.

QVC STUDIO TOUR, 1200 Wilson Dr., provides a behind-the-scenes look inside the cable shopping channel's works. **Time:** Allow 1 hour minimum. **Hours:** Tours depart Mon.-Sat. at 10:30, noon and 2:30. Closed Jan. 1, Easter, Memorial Day, July 4, Labor Day, Thanksgiving and Christmas. **Cost:** $10; $8 (ages 7-12). Ages 17 and under must be accompanied by an adult. Advance purchase is recommended. **Phone:** (800) 600-9900. GT

BRINTON HOTEL & SUITES
484/301-9232

Extended Stay Hotel
Rates not provided

Address: 1516 Wilmington Pike 19382 **Location:** 0.9 mi n of jct US 1 and 202. **Facility:** 25 efficiencies. 2 stories (no elevator), interior corridors. **Guest Services:** coin laundry.

HOLIDAY INN EXPRESS & SUITES WEST CHESTER
(610)399-4600

Hotel
$139-$159

Address: 1310 Wilmington Pike 19382 **Location:** 3 mi s on US 202 and 322. Located in a commercial area. **Facility:** 75 units. 3 stories, interior corridors. **Terms:** cancellation fee imposed. **Amenities:** safes. **Pool:** heated indoor. **Activities:** exercise room. **Guest Services:** valet and coin laundry. **Featured Amenity:** full hot breakfast.

HOTEL WARNER
(610)692-6920

Historic Hotel
$119-$299

Address: 120 N High St 19382 **Location:** Between Chestnut St and Prescott Alley; downtown. Located within walking distance to restaurants, shops and art galleries. **Facility:** In the heart of downtown, this former movie theater now provides spacious and modern guest rooms with flat-panel televisions, oversize desks and large, comfortable beds. 80 units. 5 stories, interior corridors. **Parking:** on-site (fee). **Terms:** cancellation fee imposed, resort fee. **Amenities:** safes. **Pool:** heated indoor. **Activities:** limited exercise equipment. **Guest Services:** valet and coin laundry. **Featured Amenity:** breakfast buffet.

MICROTEL INN & SUITES BY WYNDHAM WEST CHESTER
(610)738-9111

Hotel
$79-$125

Address: 500 Willowbrook Ln 19382 **Location:** US 202 exit Matlack St, just se. Located in Willowbrook Industrial Park. **Facility:** 100 units. 3 stories, interior corridors. **Activities:** exercise room. **Guest Services:** coin laundry. **Featured Amenity:** continental breakfast.

QUALITY INN & CONFERENCE CENTER
610/692-1900

Hotel. **Address:** 943 S High St 19382

WHERE TO EAT

AVALON 610/436-4100
Italian. Fine Dining. **Address:** 116 E Gay St 19382

CARMINE'S PIZZA AND EATERY 610/436-6009
Italian. Casual Dining. **Address:** 947 Paoili Pike 19380

DILWORTHTOWN INN 610/399-1390
American. Fine Dining. **Address:** 1390 Old Wilmington Pike 19382

HIGH STREET CAFFE 610/696-7435
Cajun. Casual Dining. **Address:** 322 S High St 19382

IRON HILL BREWERY 610/738-9600
American. Casual Dining. **Address:** 3 W Gay St 19380

LANDMARK AMERICANA 610/701-9900
American. Sports Bar. **Address:** 158 W Gay St 19380

LIMONCELLO 610/436-6230
Italian. Fine Dining. **Address:** 9 N Walnut St 19380

PIETRO'S PRIME 484/760-6100
Steak Seafood. Fine Dining. **Address:** 125 W Market St 19382

TECA 610/738-8244
Italian. Casual Dining. **Address:** 38 E Gay St 19380

WEST CONSHOHOCKEN pop. 1,320
• **Hotels & Restaurants map & index p. 192**
• **Part of Philadelphia area — see map p. 154**

PHILADELPHIA MARRIOTT WEST
(610)941-5600 79

Hotel
$59-$509

MARRIOTT

AAA Benefit: Members save 5% or more!

Address: 111 Crawford Ave 19428 **Location:** I-76 (Schuylkill Expwy) exit 331B eastbound; exit 332 westbound, 0.5 mi e on SR 23. Located in a commercial area. Conshohocken, 235. **Facility:** 289 units. 17 stories, interior corridors. **Parking:** on-site (fee). **Terms:** 3 day cancellation notice-fee imposed. **Pool:** heated indoor. **Activities:** hot tub, exercise room. **Guest Services:** valet laundry.

(See map & index p. 192.)

SAVONA 610/520-1200 ⑲

◈◈◈
Northern Italian Fine Dining
$20-$55

AAA Inspector Notes: Inspired by the French and Italian Riviera, the menu ranges from sandwiches and salads to heftier fare like pizza, pasta and grilled meats. The filet mignon with caramelized onion tart and roasted baby lamb rack are tasty favorites. The extensive wine-by-the-bottle list features more than 1,000 international and domestic varieties. The atmosphere is sleek and modern. **Features:** full bar. **Reservations:** suggested. **Address:** 100 Old Gulph Rd 19428 **Location:** I-76 (Schuylkill Expwy) exit 330, 0.3 mi s on SR 320 to jct Old Gulph Rd; in Village of Gulph Mills. Matsonford, 100. **Parking:** valet only. Ⓛ Ⓓ 🚗

WEST HAZLETON pop. 4,594

CANDLEWOOD SUITES (570)459-1600
◈◈◈ Extended Stay Hotel. **Address:** 9 Bowman's Mill Rd 18202

FAIRFIELD INN & SUITES BY MARRIOTT - HAZLETON
(570)453-0300
◈◈◈ Hotel. **Address:** 1 Woodbine St 18202

AAA Benefit: Members save 5% or more!

HAMPTON INN HAZLETON (570)454-3449
◈◈◈ Hotel. **Address:** 1 Top of the 80s Rd 18202

AAA Benefit: Members save up to 10%!

WHERE TO EAT

TOP OF THE 80'S RESTAURANT 570/454-8795
◈◈ American. Casual Dining. **Address:** 3 Top of the 80s Rd 18202

WEST LAWN pop. 1,715

AUSTIN'S RESTAURANT & BAR 610/678-5500
◈◈ American. Casual Dining. **Address:** 1101 Snyder Rd 19609

WEST MIDDLESEX pop. 863

HOLIDAY INN EXPRESS HOTEL & SUITES (724)982-4600
◈◈◈ Hotel. **Address:** 3060 Spangler Rd 16159

PARK INN BY RADISSON SHARON (724)528-2501
◈◈◈ Hotel. **Address:** 3377 New Castle Rd 16159

SUPER 8-WEST MIDDLESEX (724)528-3888
◈◈ Hotel. **Address:** 3369 New Castle Rd 16159

WEST MIFFLIN pop. 20,313
• **Hotels & Restaurants map & index p. 246**
• **Part of Pittsburgh area — see map p. 225**

COMFORT INN-WEST MIFFLIN (412)653-6600 ⑩
◈◈ Hotel. **Address:** 1340 Lebanon Church Rd 15236

HAMPTON INN - WEST MIFFLIN (412)650-1000 ⑩⑨
◈◈◈ Hotel. **Address:** 1550 Lebanon Church Rd 15122

AAA Benefit: Members save up to 10%!

HOLIDAY INN EXPRESS HOTEL & SUITES
412/469-1900 ⑩⑦
◈◈ Hotel. **Address:** 3122 Lebanon Church Rd 15122

SPRINGHILL SUITES BY MARRIOTT-WEST MIFFLIN
(412)653-9800 ⑩⑧
◈◈ Hotel. **Address:** 1000 Regis Ave 15236

AAA Benefit: Members save 5% or more!

WEST READING pop. 4,212

CANDLEWOOD SUITES 610/898-1910
◈◈ Extended Stay Hotel. **Address:** 55 S 3rd Ave 19611

WHERE TO EAT

CHEF ALANS AMERICAN BISTRO 610/375-4012
◈◈ American. Casual Dining. **Address:** 525 Penn Ave 19611

GNA RISTORANTE & PIZZERIA 610/376-1155
◈◈ Italian. Casual Dining. **Address:** 421 Penn Ave 19611

GO FISH SUSHI BAR AND SEAFOOD MARKET 610/376-6446
◈◈ Seafood. Casual Dining. **Address:** 619 Penn Ave 19611

THIRD & SPRUCE CAFE 610/376-5254
◈◈ American. Casual Dining. **Address:** 238 S 3rd Ave 19611

VAN'S CAFE 610/741-6466
◈ Vietnamese. Quick Serve. **Address:** 506 Penn Ave 19611

WEST READING TAVERN 610/376-9232
◈◈ American. Casual Dining. **Address:** 606 Penn Ave 19611

WEXFORD
• **Hotels & Restaurants map & index p. 246**
• **Part of Pittsburgh area — see map p. 225**

HAMPTON INN BY HILTON WEXFORD 412/528-1901 ㊻
◈◈◈ Hotel. **Address:** 2622 Wexford Bayne Rd 15143

AAA Benefit: Members save up to 10%!

WHERE TO EAT

KING'S FAMILY RESTAURANT 724/935-0320
◈◈ American. Casual Dining. **Address:** 105 VIP Dr, Rt 910 15090

WHITE HAVEN (F-10) pop. 1,097, elev. 1,120'

White Haven is a year-round outdoor recreation destination. White-water rafting is popular on the Lehigh River spring through fall, and nearby Hickory Run State Park *(see Recreation Areas Chart)* offers ice fishing, snowmobiling and cross-country skiing in winter.

COMFORT INN-POCONO MOUNTAIN (570)443-8461
◈◈ Hotel. **Address:** Rt 940 at I-80 & 476 18661

HOLIDAY INN EXPRESS & SUITES-WHITE HAVEN/LAKE HARMONY 570/443-2100
◈◈◈ Hotel. **Address:** Rt 940 at I-80 & 476 18661

WHERE TO EAT

POWERHOUSE EATERY 570/443-4480
◈◈ American. Casual Dining. **Address:** 60 Powerhouse Rd 18661

WHITE OAK pop. 7,862

- Hotels & Restaurants map & index p. 246
- Part of Pittsburgh area — see map p. 225

CHINA HOUSE	412/678-8800	(103)

♦♦ Chinese. Casual Dining. **Address:** 2001 Lincoln Way 15131

LUCIANO'S ITALIAN BRICK OVEN	412/672-7428	(104)

♦♦ Italian. Casual Dining. **Address:** 1212 Long Run Rd 15131

WILKES-BARRE (E-10) pop. 41,498, elev. 593'

In the Wyoming Valley on the Susquehanna River, Wilkes-Barre was named for John Wilkes and Isaac Barre, members of the British Parliament and Colonial sympathizers. They also are honored by a monument in Public Square.

The Wyoming Valley was the scene of the Yankee-Pennamite Wars, a land struggle between Pennsylvania and Connecticut from 1769-85. Many skirmishes were fought on Wilkes-Barre's River Common, a 35-acre park on River Street between North and South streets. Within the park, which dates from 1770, are the Luzerne County Court House and numerous historic markers. Eventually Congress ruled in favor of Pennsylvania, though Connecticut did not relinquish its claims to the disputed area until 1800.

The F.M. Kirby Center for the Performing Arts is housed in a restored 1930s Art Deco movie palace. The center is one of the preferred venues for the Northeastern Pennsylvania Philharmonic Orchestra. It offers a full program of drama, comedy, opera and musicals by resident and touring companies; phone (570) 826-1100 for the box office.

The Luzerne County Historical Society operates a museum at 69 S. Franklin St. (rear) with changing exhibits as well as Native American artifacts, rocks, minerals and fossils of local origin; phone (570) 822-1727.

Frances Slocum State Park offers a variety of recreational facilities. *See Recreation Areas Chart.*

Visit Luzerne County: 56 Public Sq., Wilkes-Barre, PA 18701. **Phone:** (888) 905-2872.

Make the Conn⚭ction

Find this symbol for places to look, book and save on AAA.com.

Shopping: The Wyoming Valley Mall on SR 309 Bus. Rte. offers more than 70 stores, including The Bon-Ton, JCPenney, Macy's and Sears.

BEST WESTERN PLUS GENETTI HOTEL & CONFERENCE CENTER   (570)823-6152

♦♦♦ Hotel $95-$199

 AAA Benefit: Members save 5% to 15% and earn 10% bonus points!

Address: 77 E Market St 18701 **Location:** Jct Washington St; downtown. **Facility:** 72 units. 5 stories, interior corridors. **Terms:** cancellation fee imposed. **Pool:** heated outdoor. **Activities:** bicycles, exercise room. **Guest Services:** valet and coin laundry.

SAVE ⊁ ¶¶ ⌂ CALL ⟲ ⇔
⚑ BIZ 🛜 ✕ 🔒 📶 🖵
/SOME UNITS 🐾 HS

COMFORT INN & SUITES   (570)823-0500

♦♦ Hotel $84-$244

Address: 1067 Wilkes-Barre Township Blvd (Rt 309) 18702 **Location:** I-81 exit 165 southbound; exit 165B northbound on SR 309 business route. **Facility:** 65 units. 4 stories, interior corridors. **Pool:** heated indoor. **Activities:** exercise room. **Guest Services:** valet and coin laundry. **Featured Amenity:** breakfast buffet.

SAVE ¶¶ ⌂ CALL ⟲ ⇔ ⚑
BIZ 🛜 ✕ 🔒 📶 🖵

COURTYARD BY MARRIOTT WILKES-BARRE SCRANTON/ARENA   (570)235-6700

♦♦♦ Hotel. **Address:** 879 Schechter Dr 18702

AAA Benefit: Members save 5% or more!

DAYS INN   (570)826-0111

♦♦ Hotel $65-$111

Address: 760 Kidder St 18702 **Location:** I-81 exit 170B to exit 1 (SR 309 S business route), just w; I-76 (Pennsylvania Tpke) exit 105 to exit 1 (SR 115 N). Across from Wyoming Valley Mall. **Facility:** 75 units. 4 stories, interior corridors. **Amenities:** safes. **Guest Services:** coin laundry. **Featured Amenity:** continental breakfast.

SAVE ¶¶ CALL ⟲ 🛜 🔒 🖵
/SOME UNITS 🐾 📶

ECONO LODGE ARENA   (570)823-0600

♦♦ Hotel $62-$109

Address: 1075 Wilkes-Barre Township Blvd 18702 **Location:** I-81 exit 165 southbound; exit 165B northbound, on SR 309 business route. **Facility:** 102 units. 3 stories, interior corridors. **Guest Services:** valet and coin laundry. **Featured Amenity:** continental breakfast.

SAVE ¶¶ CALL ⟲ BIZ 🛜 🔒
📶 🖵 /SOME UNITS 🐾

EXTENDED STAY AMERICA WILKES-BARRE HWY 315
(570)970-2500

 Extended Stay Hotel. **Address:** 1067 Hwy 315 18702

FAIRFIELD INN & SUITES BY MARRIOTT WILKES-BARRE SCRANTON   (570)208-4455

Hotel
$72-$208

AAA Benefit:
Members save 5%
or more!

Address: 884 Kidder St 18702 **Location:** I-81 exit 170B to exit 1 (SR 309 S business route), then 0.5 mi w. **Facility:** 110 units. 4 stories, interior corridors. **Terms:** cancellation fee imposed. **Pool:** heated indoor. **Activities:** hot tub, exercise room. **Guest Services:** valet and coin laundry, area transportation. **Featured Amenity: full hot breakfast.**

HAMPTON INN & SUITES-WILKES-BARRE
(570)824-1005

Hotel
$99-$299

AAA Benefit:
Members save up to
10%!

Address: 876 Schechter Dr 18702 **Location:** I-81 exit 168 (Highland Park Blvd), just w. Across from Wyoming County Mall. **Facility:** 113 units. 5 stories, interior corridors. **Terms:** 1-7 night minimum stay, cancellation fee imposed. **Pool:** heated indoor. **Activities:** hot tub, exercise room. **Guest Services:** valet and coin laundry, area transportation. **Featured Amenity: breakfast buffet.**

HILTON GARDEN INN-WILKES-BARRE   (570)820-8595
Hotel. **Address:** 242 Highland Park Blvd 18702

AAA Benefit:
Members save up to
10%!

HOLIDAY INN EXPRESS EAST   (570)825-3838
Hotel. **Address:** 1063 Hwy 315 18702

HOLIDAY INN WILKES BARRE - EAST MOUNTAIN
(570)822-1011
Hotel. **Address:** 600 Wildflower Dr 18702

HOST INN ALL SUITES   (570)270-4678

Extended Stay
Hotel
$99-$149

Address: 860 Kidder St 18702 **Location:** I-81 exit 170B to exit 1 (SR 309 S business route), 0.5 mi w. **Facility:** 66 kitchen units. 3 stories, interior corridors. **Amenities:** safes. **Pool:** heated indoor. **Activities:** hot tub, exercise room. **Guest Services:** valet and coin laundry, area transportation. **Featured Amenity: continental breakfast.**

MICROTEL INN & SUITES BY WYNDHAM WILKES-BARRE
(570)970-3760
Hotel. **Address:** 1185 Rt 315 18702

MOHEGAN SUN POCONO   570/831-2100
Contemporary Hotel. **Address:** 1280 Hwy 315 18702

QUALITY INN & SUITES CONFERENCE CENTER
(570)824-8901

Hotel
$57-$101

Address: 880 Kidder St 18702 **Location:** I-81 exit 170B to exit 1 (SR 309 S business route) off expressway, 0.5 mi w. **Facility:** 118 units. 2 stories (no elevator), exterior corridors. **Amenities:** Some: safes. **Guest Services:** valet and coin laundry, area transportation. **Featured Amenity: continental breakfast.**

RED ROOF INN WILKES-BARRE ARENA   (570)829-6422

Motel
$49-$120

Address: 1035 Hwy 315 18702 **Location:** I-81 exit 170B to exit 1 (SR 309 S business route) to SR 315, just n. **Facility:** 115 units. 3 stories, exterior corridors. **Amenities:** safes.

THE WOODLANDS INN, AN ASCEND HOTEL COLLECTION MEMBER   (570)824-9831
Hotel. **Address:** 1073 Hwy 315 18702

WHERE TO EAT

CAFE TOSCANA   570/208-1252
Italian. Casual Dining. **Address:** 1 Public Square 18701

HAYSTACKS   570/822-4474
American. Buffet Style. **Address:** 116 Wilkes-Barre Township Blvd 18706

KATANA   570/825-9080
Japanese. Casual Dining. **Address:** 41 S Main St 18701

LE MANHATTAN BISTRO   570/706-9588
French. Casual Dining. **Address:** 268 S Main St 18701

MIRAKUYA JAPANESE RESTAURANT   570/820-0901
Japanese. Casual Dining. **Address:** 695 Kidder St 18702

MIZU SUSHI HIBACHI   570/822-3866
Japanese Sushi Steak. Casual Dining. **Address:** 244 Highland Park Blvd 18702

RUTH'S CHRIS STEAK HOUSE   570/208-2266
Steak. Fine Dining. **Address:** 1280 Hwy 315 18702

THAI THAI   570/824-9599
Thai. Casual Dining. **Address:** 41 S Main St 18701

WILLIAMSPORT (E-8) pop. 29,381, elev. 528'
• Hotels p. 302 • Restaurants p. 302

Once known as the lumber capital of the world, modern Williamsport's strong manufacturing base complements its rich history. Among its highlights is Millionaires' Row, a street lined with Victorian-era mansions built by lumber barons. The city also is the birthplace of Little League Baseball. On West Fourth Street south of Max M. Brown Memorial Park is Carl E. Stotz Field, the original Little League field named after the league's founder.

Lycoming County Visitors Information Center: 102 W. Fourth St., Williamsport, PA 17701. **Phone:** (570) 327-7700 or (800) 358-9900.

Shopping: A shopping area along W. Fourth Street features stores and boutiques within a historic district.

SAVE **THOMAS T. TABER MUSEUM OF THE LYCOMING COUNTY HISTORICAL SOCIETY,** SR 180 Maynard St. exit to 858 W. Fourth St., exhibits artifacts from 10,000 B.C. to the present. Exhibits include an art gallery, blacksmith shop, woodworking shop, Victorian parlor and gristmill. Displays about the lumber industry, Native Americans and The Shempp Toy Train Collection also are featured.

Time: Allow 1 hour minimum. **Hours:** Tues.-Fri. 9:30-4, Sat. 11-4 (also Sun. 1-4, May-Oct.). Closed major holidays. **Cost:** $7.50; $6 (ages 65+); $5 (ages 3-12); $20 (family, two adults and children ages 3-12). **Phone:** (570) 326-3326.

WORLD OF LITTLE LEAGUE MUSEUM—see South Williamsport p. 280.

BEST WESTERN WILLIAMSPORT INN   (570)326-1981

◇◇◇ **Hotel** **$79-$300**

BW **Best Western.** **AAA Benefit:** Members save 5% to 15% and earn 10% bonus points!

Address: 1840 E 3rd St 17701 **Location:** I-180 exit 25 (Faxon St), 0.5 mi e. **Facility:** 132 units. 2 stories (no elevator), exterior corridors. **Terms:** cancellation fee imposed. **Pool:** outdoor. **Activities:** exercise room. **Guest Services:** valet and coin laundry, area transportation.

SAVE ⊞ ❙❙ ⊤ CALL ⅙ ➤ ⊞ BIZ ⊚ ✕ ❚ ⊟ ▯

/ SOME UNITS ⊞

CANDLEWOOD SUITES WILLIAMSPORT   570/601-9100
◇◇ Extended Stay Hotel. **Address:** 1836 E 3rd St 17701

COMFORT INN   (570)601-9300
◇◇◇ Hotel. **Address:** 1959 E 3rd St 17701

FAIRFIELD INN & SUITES BY MARRIOTT WILLIAMSPORT   (570)601-9200
◇◇◇ Hotel. **Address:** 104 Maynard St 17701

AAA Benefit: Members save 5% or more!

GENETTI HOTEL & SUITES   570/326-6600
◇◇ Historic Hotel. **Address:** 200 W 4th St 17701

🔗 **Rest assured:**

AAA.com/travelguides/hotels

HAMPTON INN & SUITES WILLIAMSPORT - FAXON EXIT   570/601-5800
◇◇◇◇ Hotel. **Address:** 66 Liberty Ln 17701

AAA Benefit: Members save up to 10%!

HAMPTON INN WILLIAMSPORT DOWNTOWN   (570)323-6190
◇◇◇ Hotel. **Address:** 140 Via Bella 17701

AAA Benefit: Members save up to 10%!

HOLIDAY INN DOWNTOWN WILLIAMSPORT   570/327-8231
◇◇◇ Hotel. **Address:** 100 Pine St 17701

HOLIDAY INN EXPRESS & SUITES DOWNTOWN WILLIAMSPORT   (570)327-5292
◇◇◇ Hotel. **Address:** 90 Pine St 17701

MOTEL 6 MONTOURSVILLE   570/368-8111
◇◇ Hotel. **Address:** 2815 Old Montoursville Rd 17701

RESIDENCE INN BY MARRIOTT WILLIAMSPORT   (570)505-3140
◇◇◇ Extended Stay Hotel. **Address:** 150 W Church St 17701

AAA Benefit: Members save 5% or more!

TOWNEPLACE SUITES BY MARRIOTT WILLIAMSPORT   (570)567-7467
◇◇◇ Extended Stay Hotel. **Address:** 10 W Church St 17701

AAA Benefit: Members save 5% or more!

WHERE TO EAT

33 EAST   570/322-1900
◇◇◇ American. Fine Dining. **Address:** 33 E 3rd St 17701

BARREL 135   570/322-7131
◇◇ New American. Casual Dining. **Address:** 135 W 3rd St 17701

BULLFROG BREWERY & RESTAURANT   570/326-4700
◇◇ American. Casual Dining. **Address:** 229 W 4th St 17701

DI SALVO'S   570/327-1200

◇◇◇ **Italian Casual Dining** **$10-$40**

AAA Inspector Notes: On the edge of downtown, this large restaurant got its roots as a homemade pasta shop. It has evolved into a family passion for food prepared using family recipes with an imaginative flair. They make most of their pasta in house. The seafood is the freshest available in the area. A substantial wine list offers the best wines of Italy for pairing. The main dining room is staider while the downstairs bar room dining and seasonal outdoor patio have flair. **Features:** full bar, patio dining. **Reservations:** suggested. **Address:** 341 E 4th St 17701 **Location:** Between Penn and Basin sts; downtown. L D

LE JEUNE CHEF   570/320-2433

◇◇◇ **Continental Fine Dining** **$6-$30**

AAA Inspector Notes: This restaurant is a training facility on the campus of the Pennsylvania College of Technology, which allows student chefs to hone their skills. Nicely prepared and artistically presented classical cuisine is fittingly complemented by an extensive selection of wines. The menu also offers popular favorites like burgers, chicken paillard and grilled salmon. Desserts are proficiently made in-house. **Features:** full bar. **Reservations:** suggested. **Address:** One College Ave 17701 **Location:** Jct I-180, US 220 and 15 exit Maynard St, n to college entrance, follow signs; on Pennsylvania College of Technology campus. L D CALL ⅙

THE PETER HERDIC HOUSE   570/322-0165
▼▼▼ Continental. Fine Dining. **Address:** 407 W 4th St 17701

VINCENZO'S ITALIAN CUISINE   570/327-1551
▼▼ Italian. Casual Dining. **Address:** 99 Maynard St 17701

WILLOW GROVE pop. 15,726
• Hotels & Restaurants map & index p. 192
• Part of Philadelphia area — see map p. 154

COURTYARD BY MARRIOTT PHILADELPHIA WILLOW GROVE
                                           (215)830-0550 **51**
▼▼▼ Hotel. **Address:** 2350 Easton
Rd (Rt 611) 19090

> **AAA Benefit:**
> Members save 5%
> or more!

HAMPTON INN-WILLOW GROVE   (215)659-3535 **53**
▼▼▼ Hotel. **Address:** 1500 Easton
Rd 19090

> **AAA Benefit:**
> Members save up to
> 10%!

SPRINGHILL SUITES BY MARRIOTT PHILADELPHIA WILLOW
GROVE   (215)657-7800 **52**
▼▼▼ Hotel. **Address:** 2480 Mary-
land Rd 19090

> **AAA Benefit:**
> Members save 5%
> or more!

WHERE TO EAT

OOKA JAPANESE SUSHI & HIBACHI STEAK HOUSE
                                           215/659-7688 **93**
▼▼ Japanese. Casual Dining. **Address:** 1109 Easton Rd 19090

WINDBER pop. 4,138

RIZZO'S RESTAURANT   814/467-7908
▼▼ Italian. Casual Dining. **Address:** 2200 Graham Ave 15963

WIND GAP (F-11) pop. 2,720, elev. 745'
The 1,168-acre Jacobsburg Environmental Education Center, 835 Jacobsburg Rd., encompasses the remains of the 18th-century village of Jacobsburg and the site of the second Henry Gun Factory; phone (610) 746-2801.

RED CARPET INN   (610)863-7782
▼▼ Motel. **Address:** 1395 Jacobsburg Rd 18091

WOMELSDORF pop. 2,810, elev. 434'

THE STOUCH TAVERN 1785   610/589-4577
▼▼▼ American. Fine Dining. **Address:** 138 W High St 19567

WRIGHTSVILLE pop. 2,310

ACCOMAC INN   717/252-1521
▼▼▼ Continental. Casual Dining. **Address:** 6330 S River Dr 17368

WYOMING (E-10) pop. 3,073, elev. 557'
With the outbreak of the Revolution, the Wyoming Valley's importance as a granary led to a number of attacks by Tory and Native American forces. On July 3, 1778, 1,200 Native Americans and renegade whites defeated 300 frontiersmen 4 miles north of Kingston near Forty Fort, leaving the settlements of the Wyoming Valley unprotected. The next day the Native Americans passed up and down the valley in a series of raids that became known as the Wyoming Massacre. In reprisal, Gen. John Sullivan led an expedition up the Susquehanna River, devastating the area and breaking the Native Americans' grip on the region.

A monument at Fourth Street and Wyoming Avenue marks the site of a grave for victims of the Wyoming Massacre.

The Swetland Homestead at 885 Wyoming Ave. is the 1803 Swetland family home; additions were made as the family acquired additional members and wealth. The period rooms span 70 years and can be toured by appointment; phone (570) 823-6244, ext. 3.

WYOMISSING (H-10) pop. 10,461, elev. 299'
• Restaurants p. 304

The borough of Wyomissing, Penn., is a suburb of Reading. The headquarters of department store Boscov's and the hometown of songstress Taylor Swift, Wyomissing retains its small-town charm, but has access to shopping at the modern Berkshire Mall. The Tree City, U.S.A. community holds summer concerts in the park and puts on a July 4th parade with contests for best wagons, costumed pets, decorated cars and baby carriages.

COURTYARD BY MARRIOTT READING WYOMISSING
                                           (610)378-1137
▼▼▼ Hotel. **Address:** 150 N Park
Rd 19610

> **AAA Benefit:**
> Members save 5%
> or more!

CROWNE PLAZA READING HOTEL   (610)376-3811
◆◆◆ Hotel. **Address:** 1741 Papermill Rd 19610

DAYS INN READING/WYOMISSING   (610)374-1500
▼▼ Hotel. **Address:** 910 Woodland Rd 19610

HAMPTON INN BY HILTON   (610)374-8100
▼▼▼ Hotel. **Address:** 1800 Paper-
mill Rd 19610

> **AAA Benefit:**
> Members save up to
> 10%!

HOLIDAY INN EXPRESS & SUITES WYOMISSING
                                           (610)373-4444
▼▼▼ Hotel. **Address:** 405 N Park Rd 19610

HOMEWOOD SUITES-READING/WYOMISSING (610)736-3100
▼▼▼ Extended Stay Hotel. **Ad-
dress:** 2801 Papermill Rd 19610

> **AAA Benefit:**
> Members save up to
> 10%!

THE INN AT READING HOTEL & CONFERENCE CENTER
                                           (610)372-7811
▼▼ Hotel. **Address:** 1040 N Park Rd 19610

THE WORKS
610/375-2700

**American
Casual Dining
$9-$20**

AAA Inspector Notes: In a renovated historic factory building, this restaurant is a fun, friendly place to bring the family. The kitchen prepares a nice selection of sandwiches, pizza, entrées and children's meals, with most items made from scratch. The back section of the building houses more than 150 entertaining arcade games. **Features:** full bar. **Address:** 1109 Bern Rd 19610 **Location:** Off Penn Ave (SR 423 business route); just e of jct State Hill Rd.

WYSOX

COMFORT INN (570)265-5691

 Hotel. **Address:** 898 Golden Mile Rd 18854

FAIRFIELD INN & SUITES BY MARRIOTT TOWANDA WYSOX
(570)265-5553

**Hotel
$49-$165**

FAIRFIELD
INN & SUITES
Marriott

AAA Benefit: Members save 5% or more!

Address: 1248 Golden Mile Rd 18848 **Location:** On US 6 E. **Facility:** 88 units. 3 stories, interior corridors. **Terms:** cancellation fee imposed. **Pool:** heated indoor. **Activities:** exercise room. **Guest Services:** valet and coin laundry. **Featured Amenity:** breakfast buffet.

[SAVE] [¶↑] CALL [&] [🚗] [📶] [BIZ]
[📶] [✕] [📱] [📷] [💻]
/ SOME UNITS [HS]

STONE MOUNTAIN INN ON KEENE SUMMIT B&B
570/265-8846

 Classic Historic Bed & Breakfast. **Address:** 1995 Keene Summit Rd 18854

THE RIVER STONE INN 570/265-8882

 American. Casual Dining. **Address:** 47 Leisure Dr 18848

YARDLEY pop. 2,434
• Part of Philadelphia area — see map p. 154

HAMPTON INN & SUITES NEWTOWN (215)860-1700

**Hotel
$99-$219**

Hampton
by HILTON

AAA Benefit: Members save up to 10%!

Address: 1000 Stony Hill Rd 19067 **Location:** I-95 exit 49, just sw. Located in a commercial area. **Facility:** 137 units, some efficiencies. 3 stories, interior corridors. **Terms:** 1-7 night minimum stay, cancellation fee imposed. **Pool:** outdoor. **Activities:** exercise room. **Guest Services:** valet and coin laundry. **Featured Amenity:** breakfast buffet.

[SAVE] [¶↑] CALL [&] [🚗] [📶] [BIZ]
[📶] [✕] [📱] [📷] [💻]

CARLUCCI'S GRILL 215/321-9010

 Italian. Casual Dining. **Address:** 1633 Big Oak Rd 19067

YORK (I-8) pop. 43,718, elev. 375'
• Restaurants p. 306

York served as the national capital Sept. 30, 1777, to June 27, 1778, while the British occupied Philadelphia. It was in York that Congress received the news of Gen. John Burgoyne's surrender, adopted the Articles of Confederation, issued the first National Thanksgiving Proclamation and learned that France was to send aid to the Colonies.

Capitalizing on the region's legacy as an industrial and manufacturing center, today's York County bills itself as the Factory Tour Capital of the World. More than a dozen factories, producing everything from pretzels to motorcycles, welcome visitors. A booklet detailing all of the city's tours is available at the visitor information centers.

Strand-Capitol Performing Arts Center, jct. George and Philadelphia streets, features the historic 1906 Capitol Theatre and the 1925 Strand Theatre. Performances run throughout the year; phone (717) 846-1111.

Heritage Rail Trail County Park is a 21-mile biking, hiking and horseback riding trail that runs from the Colonial Courthouse to the Mason Dixon Line, where it connects to Maryland's 20-mile Northern Central Railroad Trail. In winter, cross-country skiing and snowshoeing are permitted. The trail runs along an operational railroad line, so never get too close to the tracks. The park is open daily 8 a.m.-dusk; phone (717) 840-7440.

York County Convention and Visitors Bureau: York County Visitor Information Center at Harley-Davidson, 1425 Eden Rd., York, PA 17402. Or visit the Downtown York Visitor Information Center at Central Market, 34 W. Philadelphia St.; phone (717) 852-9675 or (888) 858-9675. **Phone:** (717) 852-6006 or (888) 858-9675.

Self-guiding tours: Literature about self-guiding walking tours is available from the York County History Center, (717) 848-1587, at 250 E. Market St. The York County Convention and Visitors Bureau also usually stocks them at their two locations.

Shopping: The York Galleria, 2 miles east of I-83 on US 30, is the area's largest mall; anchor stores are The Bon-Ton, Boscov's and Sears. West Manchester Mall, 1 mile west of I-83 on US 30, features Kohl's.

Two miles east of I-83 on US 30 across from York Galleria, Christmas Tree Hill offers holiday-themed gifts and home decor in a post-Revolutionary War mansion.

Many farmers markets specialize in Pennsylvania Dutch and German cuisine and include Central Market House, 34 W. Philadelphia St., held Tues., Thurs. and Sat. 6-2; Market & Penn Farmers Market, 380 W. Market St., held Tues. and Fri.-Sat. 6-3; and New Eastern Market, 201 Memory Ln., held Fri. 7-6.

RICHARD M. NIXON ENVIRONMENTAL EDUCATION CENTER, on Nixon Dr. in Richard M. Nixon County Park, has 187 acres of undisturbed environment. Its goal is to conserve and preserve the area's flora and fauna and teach about the importance of our environment. A natural history museum features dioramas, interactive displays, geological specimens from the area and more than 180 mounted specimens representing 15 countries. A large collection of York County taxidermy mounts also are on display.

Dioramas represent views of the African savannah, Arctic Circle and Northern Rocky Mountains. A bird observation window, a working indoor honeybee hive, live snakes and a touch room are included. More than 6 miles of hiking trails also are on-site. **Time:** Allow 1 hour minimum. **Hours:** Park grounds 8-dusk. Center Tues.-Sat. 8:30-4:30, Sun. noon-4:30. Closed major holidays. **Cost:** Free. **Phone:** (717) 428-1961.

 YORK COUNTY HISTORY CENTER includes several properties on E. Market, W. Market and W. Princess sts. Exhibits at the Historical Society Museum depict life in York County up to the 20th century. A reproduction of the original York village square with a one-room cabin, print shop, apothecary and toy store can be viewed. Decorative arts, folk art and exhibits about York's role in the Revolutionary and Civil wars are displayed. The Library & Archives houses an extensive collection on a variety of topics, including genealogy, local history and military history.

The Agricultural & Industrial Museum highlights the Golden Age of industrial development from south central Pennsylvania's early years to the present. Exhibits showcase industrial equipment and the history of transportation and include a working three-story gristmill and a 72-ton giant A-frame ammonia compressor.

The Fire Museum in the 1903 station showcases more than 200 years of local firefighting with photographs, uniforms, vintage vehicles and the original fire-horse stalls. The Colonial Complex *(see attraction listing)* focuses on the Revolutionary period.

Tickets may be purchased at any of the sites. **Hours:** All museums except Fire Museum open early Tues.-Sat.; times vary by museum. Agricultural & Industrial Museum 10-4. Historical Society Museum and Library & Archives 9-5. Fire Museum open Sat. 10-4, Apr.-Nov. Closed major holidays.

Cost: One-day ticket (includes Colonial Complex and all open sites and museums) $15; $13 (senior citizens and college students, veterans and active military with ID); $7 (students ages 6-18). Library and archives $8. **Phone:** (717) 848-1587.

 Colonial Complex, 157 W. Market St., is part of York County History Center and consists of restored 18th- and 19th-century buildings and a replica of York's colonial courthouse that are seen by a guided tour. The 1741 half-timbered Golden Plough Tavern housed travelers passing through rural Pennsylvania. The stone circa 1751 General Horatio Gates House is the supposed site where the Marquis de Lafayette gave a toast, which prevented the overthrow of Gen. George Washington as head of the Continental Army. Gen. Gates was the hero of the Battle of Saratoga.

The Colonial Court House is a reproduction of the one in which the Second Continental Congress voted to adopt the Articles of Confederation in 1777 during the Congress' 9-month term in York.

Hours: Tours offered Tues.-Sat., Apr.-Nov. Phone ahead to confirm tour schedule. Closed major holidays. **Cost:** One-day ticket (includes all open York County History Center sites and museums) $15; $13 (senior citizens and college students, veterans and active military with ID); $7 (students ages 6-18). **Phone:** (717) 848-1587. (GT)

BEST WESTERN WESTGATE INN (717)767-6931

Hotel
$79-$149

 Best Western

AAA Benefit: Members save 5% to 15% and earn 10% bonus points!

Address: 1415 Kenneth Rd 17408 **Location:** I-83 exit 21B northbound, 2 mi w on US 30, then just n; exit 22 southbound, 0.5 mi s on SR 181, 1.7 mi w on US 30, then just n. Located in a commercial area. **Facility:** 104 units. 3 stories, interior corridors. **Terms:** cancellation fee imposed. **Activities:** exercise room. **Guest Services:** coin laundry.

COMFORT INN & SUITES (717)699-1919

Hotel. **Address:** 2250 N George St 17402

COUNTRY INN & SUITES BY CARLSON YORK 717/747-5833

Hotel. **Address:** 245 St. Charles Way 17402

COURTYARD BY MARRIOTT YORK (717)840-7840

Hotel. **Address:** 2799 Concord Rd 17402

AAA Benefit: Members save 5% or more!

FOUR POINTS BY SHERATON YORK 717/846-4940

Hotel
Rates not provided

FOUR POINTS BY SHERATON

AAA Benefit: Members save 5% or more!

Address: 1650 Toronita St 17402 **Location:** I-83 exit 21A northbound; exit 21 southbound, just ne. Located in a commercial area. **Facility:** 146 units. 5 stories, interior corridors. **Pool:** heated indoor. **Activities:** hot tub, exercise room. **Guest Services:** valet and coin laundry. **Featured Amenity:** full hot breakfast.

HAMPTON INN & SUITES YORK SOUTH   717/741-0900
▼◆▼▼ Hotel. **Address:** 2159 S Queen St 17403

AAA Benefit: Members save up to 10%!

HAMPTON INN YORK   (717)840-1500
▼▼▼ Hotel. **Address:** 1550 Mt. Zion Rd 17402

AAA Benefit: Members save up to 10%!

HERITAGE HILLS GOLF RESORT AND CONFERENCE CENTER   (717)755-0123

Resort Hotel
$210-$260

Address: 2700 Mount Rose Ave 17402 **Location:** I-83 exit 18, 1 mi e on SR 124. Located in a quiet area. **Facility:** Guest rooms are elegantly decorated with granite-top custom furniture and mounted flat-screen TVs. While there is no swimming pool, guests have complimentary access to the pools at nearby Wisehaven. 104 units, some efficiencies. 5 stories, interior corridors. **Terms:** check-in 4 pm, 3 day cancellation notice-fee imposed. **Dining:** 2 restaurants, also, oak., see separate listing. **Activities:** regulation golf, miniature golf, exercise room, spa. **Guest Services:** valet laundry.

[SAVE] [⑪] [📷] [Y] CALL [⑤] [📶] [BIZ] [HS] [📶] [✕]
[☐] [🖥] [📋] / SOME UNITS [🐕]

HOLIDAY INN EXPRESS & SUITES   717/741-1000
▼▼▼ Hotel. **Address:** 140 Leader Heights Rd 17403

HOME2 SUITES BY HILTON YORK   717/747-0360
▼▼▼ Extended Stay Hotel. **Address:** 212 Pauline Dr 17402

AAA Benefit: Members save up to 10%!

HOMEWOOD SUITES BY HILTON   (717)434-1800
▼▼▼ Extended Stay Hotel. **Address:** 200 Masonic Dr 17406

AAA Benefit: Members save up to 10%!

TOWNEPLACE SUITES BY MARRIOTT YORK   (717)840-1180
▼▼▼ Extended Stay Hotel. **Address:** 2789 Concord Rd 17402

AAA Benefit: Members save 5% or more!

WINGATE BY WYNDHAM YORK   (717)848-2100
▼◆▼▼ Hotel. **Address:** 105 State St 17404

WYNDHAM GARDEN YORK   (717)846-9500
▼▼▼ Hotel. **Address:** 2000 Loucks Rd 17408

WHERE TO EAT

CRIMSON AMERICAN GRILL   717/793-3605
▼▼▼ American. Casual Dining. **Address:** 1839 S Queen St 17403

EL SERRANO   717/757-4963
▼▼ Mexican Small Plates. Casual Dining. **Address:** 3410 E Market St 17402

THE FIRST POST   717/430-8115
▼▼ American. Gastropub. **Address:** 3691 E Market St 17402

FUJIHANA JAPANESE STEAKHOUSE AND SUSHI   717/845-8988
▼▼ Japanese. Casual Dining. **Address:** 935 Loucks Rd 17404

ISAAC'S FAMOUS GRILLED SANDWICHES   717/751-0515
▼ Deli Sandwiches. Quick Serve. **Address:** 2960 Whiteford Rd 17402

JR'S FRESH CUT FRENCH FRIES   717/741-2379
▼ American. Casual Dining. **Address:** 34 W Philadelphia St 17402

KELLY'S INN   717/755-3896
▼▼ American. Casual Dining. **Address:** 1906 N Sherman St 17406

THE LEFT BANK RESTAURANT & BAR   717/843-8010
▼▼▼ New American. Casual Dining. **Address:** 120 N George St 17401

MAPLE DONUTS   717/757-7826
▼ Breads/Pastries. Quick Serve. **Address:** 3455 E Market St 17402

OAK.   717/755-0123
▼▼▼ American. Casual Dining. **Address:** 2700 Mount Rose Ave 17402

ROUND THE CLOCK DINER & COFFEE SHOP   717/848-5344
▼ American. Casual Dining. **Address:** 222 Arsenal Rd (US 30) 17402

VIET THAI MARKET STREET   717/846-9302
▼▼ Thai. Casual Dining. **Address:** 2535 E Market St 17402

WHITE ROSE BAR AND GRILL   717/848-5369
▼▼ American. Casual Dining. **Address:** 48 N Beaver St 17401

ZELIENOPLE (F-1) pop. 3,812, elev. 911'
• Part of Pittsburgh area — see map p. 225

Zelienople was founded in 1802 by Baron Dettmar Basse and named for his daughter Zélie. The 10-room Federal period Passavant House was Basse's gift to Zélie in 1808. The 1805 three-story Buhl House was built by another founding father, Christian Buhl. Both are open for guided tours Mon.-Fri.; phone (724) 452-9457 for tour information.

🔗 **Save on travel, shopping and more:**

AAA.com/discounts

⟳ Offices

Main office listings are shown in **BOLD TYPE** and toll-free member service numbers appear in *ITALIC TYPE*.
All are closed Saturdays, Sundays and holidays unless otherwise indicated.
The addresses, phone numbers and hours for any AAA/CAA office are subject to change.
The type of service provided is designated below the name of the city where the office is located:

✚ Auto travel services, including books and maps, and on-demand TripTik® routings.
● Auto travel services, including selected books and maps, and on-demand TripTik® routings.
■ Books/maps only, no marked maps or on-demand TripTik® routings.
▲ Travel Agency Services, cruise, tour, air, car and rail reservations; domestic and international hotel reservations; passport photo services; international and domestic travel guides and maps; travel money products; and International Driving Permits. In addition, assistance with travel related insurance products including trip cancellation, travel accident, lost luggage, trip delay and assistance products.
✪ Insurance services provided. If only this icon appears, only insurance services are provided at that office.
⟨ Car Care Plus Facility provides car care services.
⊡ Electric vehicle charging station on premises.

AAA NATIONAL OFFICE: 1000 AAA DRIVE, HEATHROW, FLORIDA 32746-5063, (407) 444-7000

PENNSYLVANIA

ALLENTOWN—AAA EAST CENTRAL, 2072 DOWNYFLAKE LN, 18103. WEEKDAYS (M-F) 9:00-5:00, THU 9:00-8:00, SAT 10:00-2:00. (610) 434-5141 ✚ ▲ ✪

ALTOONA—AAA EAST CENTRAL, 1634 VALLEY VIEW BLVD, 16602. WEEKDAYS (M-F) 9:00-5:00, SAT 9:00-12:00. (814) 946-1277 ✚ ▲

ARDMORE—AAA CLUB ALLIANCE INC, 30 GREENFIELD AVE, 19003. WEEKDAYS (M-F) 8:30-5:00, THU 8:30-6:30, SAT 8:30-4:30. (610) 649-9000 ✚ ▲ ✪

BEDFORD—AAA SOUTHERN PENNSYLVANIA, 9613 LINCOLN HWY STE 103, 15522. WEEKDAYS (M-F) 9:00-5:00, WED 9:00-7:00, SAT 9:00-12:00. (814) 623-5196, *(800) 222-1469*. ✚ ▲ ✪

BETHLEHEM—AAA EAST CENTRAL, 1520 STEFKO BLVD, 18017. WEEKDAYS (M-F) 9:00-5:00, THU 9:00-8:00, SAT 10:00-2:00. (610) 867-7502 ✚ ▲ ✪

BLOOMSBURG—AAA CLUB ALLIANCE INC, 1040 SCOTT TOWN CENTER, 17815. WEEKDAYS (M-F) 9:00-5:30, SAT 9:00-3:00. (570) 784-3380 ✚ ▲ ✪

BRADFORD—AAA EAST CENTRAL, 587 SOUTH AVE, 16701. WEEKDAYS (M-F) 9:00-5:00. (814) 368-3113 ✚

BUTLER—AAA EAST CENTRAL, 138 CLEARVIEW CIR, 16001. WEEKDAYS (M-F) 9:00-5:30, SAT 9:00-12:30. (724) 287-2713 ✚ ▲ ✪

CAMP HILL—AAA CENTRAL PENN, 4680 E TRINDLE RD, 17011. WEEKDAYS (M-F) 9:00-5:00, WED 9:00-6:00, SAT 9:00-12:00. (717) 761-6811 ✚ ▲ ✪

CARBONDALE—AAA NORTH PENN, 18 S MAIN ST, 18407. WEEKDAYS (M-F) 9:00-5:00, SAT 9:00-12:00. (570) 282-1390 ✚ ▲ ✪

CARLISLE—AAA CENTRAL PENN, 1911 W TRINDLE RD, 17013. WEEKDAYS (M-F) 9:00-5:00, WED 9:00-6:00, SAT 9:00-12:00. (717) 243-1844 ✚ ▲ ✪

CHAMBERSBURG—AAA SOUTHERN PENNSYLVANIA, 1666 LINCOLN WAY E, 17202. WEEKDAYS (M-F) 9:00-6:00, WED 9:00-8:00, SAT 9:00-2:00. (717) 264-4191, *(800) 222-1469*. ✚ ▲ ✪

CLIFTON HEIGHTS—AAA CLUB ALLIANCE INC, 5233 W BALTIMORE AVE, 19018. WEEKDAYS (M-F) 7:00-7:00, SAT 8:00-5:00, SUN 10:00-4:00. (610) 605-2114 ✚ ▲ ✪ ⟨ ⊡

CRANBERRY TOWNSHIP—AAA EAST CENTRAL, 20510 RT 19 #103-104, 16066. WEEKDAYS (M-F) 9:00-7:00, SAT 9:00-3:00. (724) 772-1122 ✚ ▲ ✪

DOWNINGTOWN—AAA CLUB ALLIANCE INC, 105 QUARRY RD, 19335. WEEKDAYS (M-F) 7:00-7:00, SAT 8:00-5:00. (484) 237-2230 ✚ ▲ ✪ ⟨

EASTON—AAA NORTHAMPTON COUNTY, 3914 HECKTOWN RD, 18045. MON/WED/FRI 9:00-5:00, TUE/THU 9:00-7:30, SAT 9:00-1:00. (610) 258-2371 ✚ ▲ ✪

ERIE—AAA EAST CENTRAL, 4430 BUFFALO RD, 16510. WEEKDAYS (M-F) 9:00-5:00. (814) 897-9508 ✚ ▲

ERIE—AAA EAST CENTRAL, 6660 PEACH ST UNIT #2, 16509. WEEKDAYS (M-F) 9:00-5:00, SAT 9:00-1:00. (814) 866-0246 ✚ ▲ ✪

FAIRLESS HILLS—AAA CLUB ALLIANCE INC, 110 LINCOLN HWY, 19030. WEEKDAYS (M-F) 8:30-5:00, THU 8:30-6:30, SAT 8:30-4:30. (215) 269-2034 ✚ ▲ ✪

FRANKLIN—AAA EAST CENTRAL, 491 ALLEGHENY BLVD #200, 16323. WEEKDAYS (M-F) 8:30-5:00. (814) 432-3960 ✚

GETTYSBURG—AAA CENTRAL PENN, 1275 YORK RD #10, 17325. WEEKDAYS (M-F) 9:00-5:00, WED 9:00-6:00, SAT 9:00-12:00. (717) 334-1155 ✚ ▲ ✪

GLEN MILLS—AAA CLUB ALLIANCE INC, 1810 WILMINGTON PIKE, 19342. WEEKDAYS (M-F) 9:00-5:30, SAT 9:00-3:00. (610) 808-9000 ✚ ▲ ✪

GREENSBURG—AAA EAST CENTRAL, 5142 RT 30 #135, 15601. WEEKDAYS (M-F) 9:00-5:00, SAT 10:00-2:00. (724) 834-8300 ✚ ▲ ✪

GROVE CITY—AAA EAST CENTRAL, 24 PINE GROVE VILLAGE DR, 16127. WEEKDAYS (M-F) 8:30-5:00. (724) 458-8930 ✚

HANOVER—AAA SOUTHERN PENNSYLVANIA, 1000 CARLISLE ST, 17331. WEEKDAYS (M-F) 9:00-6:00, WED 9:00-8:00, SAT 9:00-2:00. (717) 637-2400, *(800) 222-1469*. ✚ ▲ ✪

HARRISBURG—**AAA CENTRAL PENN**, 2301 PAXTON CHURCH RD, 17110. WEEKDAYS (M-F) 9:00-5:00, WED 9:00-6:00, SAT 9:00-12:00. (717) 657-2244 ✚ ▲ ✪

HERMITAGE—AAA EAST CENTRAL, 1749 E STATE ST, 16148. WEEKDAYS (M-F) 8:30-5:00, SAT 8:30-12:00. (724) 981-9141 ✚ ✪

HONESDALE—AAA NORTH PENN, 1126 MAIN ST, 18431. WEEKDAYS (M-F) 9:00-5:00, SAT 9:00-12:00. (570) 253-0160 ✚ ▲ ✪

HUMMELSTOWN—AAA CENTRAL PENN, 1142 MAE ST, 17036. WEEKDAYS (M-F) 9:00-5:00, WED 9:00-6:00, SAT 9:00-12:00. (717) 533-3381 ✚ ▲ ✪

HUNTINGDON—AAA CENTRAL PENN, 608 WASHINGTON ST, 16652. WEEKDAYS (M-F) 9:00-5:00, WED 9:00-6:00, SAT 9:00-12:00. (814) 643-1030 ✚ ▲ ✪

INDIANA—AAA EAST CENTRAL, 1169 WAYNE AVE, 15701. WEEKDAYS (M-F) 8:30-5:00, THU 8:30-7:00, SAT 9:30-1:30. (724) 349-4193 ✚ ▲

JOHNSTOWN—AAA SOUTHERN PENNSYLVANIA, 500 GALLERIA DR #112, 15904. WEEKDAYS (M-F) 10:00-6:00, WED 10:00-8:00, SAT 10:00-2:00. (814) 269-3641, *(800) 222-1469.* ✚▲○

KING OF PRUSSIA—AAA CLUB ALLIANCE INC, 139 E DEKALB PIKE, 19406. WEEKDAYS (M-F) 9:00-5:30, SAT 9:00-3:00. (610) 337-6800 ✚○

KITTANNING—AAA EAST CENTRAL, 11 FRANKLIN VILLAGE MALL, 16201. WEEKDAYS (M-F) 8:30-5:00, SAT 8:30-12:00. (724) 543-1924 ✚▲

LANCASTER—AAA CENTRAL PENN, 101 W JAMES ST, 17603. WEEKDAYS (M-F) 9:00-5:00, WED 9:00-6:00, SAT 9:00-12:00. (717) 397-4444 ✚○

LANCASTER—AAA CENTRAL PENN, 804 ESTELLE DR, 17601. WEEKDAYS (M-F) 9:00-5:00, WED 9:00-6:00, SAT 9:00-12:00. (717) 898-6900 ✚▲○

LANSDALE—AAA EAST CENTRAL, 1250 N BROAD ST, 19446. WEEKDAYS (M-F) 9:00-5:00, THU 9:00-8:00, SAT 10:00-2:00. (215) 855-8600 ✚▲○

LEBANON—AAA CENTRAL PENN, 984 ISABEL DR, 17042. WEEKDAYS (M-F) 9:00-5:00, WED 9:00-6:00, SAT 9:00-12:00. (717) 273-8533 ✚▲○

LEWISBURG—AAA EAST CENTRAL, 530 1/2 N DERR DR, 17837. WEEKDAYS (M-F) 8:30-5:00. (570) 524-7455 ●

LEWISTOWN—AAA CENTRAL PENN, 33 N BROWN ST, 17044. WEEKDAYS (M-F) 9:00-5:00, WED 9:00-6:00, SAT 9:00-12:00. (717) 242-2221 ✚○

LITITZ—AAA CENTRAL PENN, 727 S BROAD ST, 17543. WEEKDAYS (M-F) 9:00-5:00, WED 9:00-6:00, SAT 9:00-12:00. (717) 626-3040 ✚▲○

LOCK HAVEN—AAA SOUTHERN PENNSYLVANIA, 12 ORIOLE RD, 17745. WEEKDAYS (M-F) 9:00-5:00. (570) 748-2405, *(800) 222-1469.* ✚▲○

LOWER BURRELL—AAA EAST CENTRAL, 2501 LEECHBURG RD STE E, 15068. WEEKDAYS (M-F) 9:00-5:00, SAT 9:00-2:00. (724) 339-4440 ✚▲

MEADVILLE—AAA EAST CENTRAL, 18939 PARK AVE PLZ #7, 16335. WEEKDAYS (M-F) 8:30-5:00, SAT 8:30-12:00. (814) 724-2247 ✚▲

MONROEVILLE—AAA EAST CENTRAL, 2725 MOSSIDE BLVD, 15146. WEEKDAYS (M-F) 9:00-7:00 (PLEASE CALL FOR DRIVER'S LIC PHOTO HOURS), SAT 9:00-3:00. (412) 858-4640 ✚▲○

NEW CASTLE—AAA EAST CENTRAL, 40 EAST ST, 16101. WEEKDAYS (M-F) 9:00-5:00, SAT 10:00-2:00. (724) 658-8551 ✚▲○

PHILADELPHIA—AAA CLUB ALLIANCE INC, 1601 S COLUMBUS BLVD, 19148. WEEKDAYS (M-F) 7:00-7:00, SAT 8:00-5:00, SUN 10:00-4:00. (215) 399-1000 ✚▲○€

PHILADELPHIA—AAA CLUB ALLIANCE INC, 1801 MARKET ST, 19103. WEEKDAYS (M-F) 9:00-5:00. (215) 399-1180 ✚▲○

PHILADELPHIA—AAA CLUB ALLIANCE INC, 9475 ROOSEVELT BLVD, 19114. WEEKDAYS (M-F) 8:30-5:00, THU 8:30-6:30, SAT 8:30-4:30. (215) 671-1700 ✚▲○

PITTSBURGH—AAA EAST CENTRAL, 160 FT COUCH RD, 15241. WEEKDAYS (M-F) 9:00-7:00, SAT 9:00-3:00. (412) 833-5203 ✚▲○

PITTSBURGH—AAA EAST CENTRAL, 1760 PARK MANOR BLVD, 15205. WEEKDAYS (M-F) 9:00-7:00, SAT 9:00-3:00. (412) 809-2800 ✚▲○

PITTSBURGH—AAA EAST CENTRAL, 4790 MCKNIGHT RD, 15237. WEEKDAYS (M-F) 9:00-7:00, SAT 9:00-3:00. (412) 367-7600 ✚▲○

PITTSBURGH—AAA EAST CENTRAL, 538 SMITHFIELD ST, 15222. WEEKDAYS (M-F) 8:30-5:00. (412) 338-4300 ✚▲○

PITTSBURGH—AAA EAST CENTRAL, 5900 BAUM BLVD, 15206. WEEKDAYS (M-F) 8:30-5:00 (PLEASE CALL FOR DRIVER'S LIC PHOTO HOURS), SAT 10:00-3:00. (412) 365-7196 ✚▲○

PITTSBURGH—AAA EAST CENTRAL, 9 CLAIRTON BLVD, 15236. WEEKDAYS (M-F) 9:00-7:00 (PLEASE CALL FOR DRIVER'S LIC PHOTO HOURS.), SAT 9:00-3:00. (412) 655-6100 ✚▲○

POTTSVILLE—AAA SCHUYLKILL COUNTY, 340 S CENTRE ST, 17901. WEEKDAYS (M-F) 8:30-5:00, SAT 9:00-12:00. (570) 622-4991 ✚▲○

QUAKERTOWN—AAA EAST CENTRAL, 632 NORTH WEST END BLVD, 18951. WEEKDAYS (M-F) 10:00-6:00, THU 10:00-8:00, SAT 10:00-2:00. (215) 538-5150 ✚▲○

READING—AAA READING-BERKS, 920 VAN REED RD, 19610. WEEKDAYS (M-F) 9:00-5:00, WED 9:00-7:00, SAT 9:00-12:00. (610) 374-4531 ✚▲○

ROCHESTER—AAA EAST CENTRAL, 300 ADAMS ST, 15074. WEEKDAYS (M-F) 9:00-5:00, SAT 10:00-2:00. (724) 775-8000 ✚▲○

ROYERSFORD—AAA EAST CENTRAL, 70 BUCKWALTER RD, 19468. WEEKDAYS (M-F) 10:00-6:00, THU 10:00-8:00, SAT 10:00-2:00. (610) 323-6300 ✚▲○

SCRANTON—AAA NORTH PENN, 1035 N WASHINGTON AVE, 18509. WEEKDAYS (M-F) 9:00-5:00, THU 9:00-7:00, SAT 9:00-1:00. (570) 348-2511 ✚▲○

SHREWSBURY—AAA SOUTHERN PENNSYLVANIA, 14625 MT AIRY RD STE #104, 17361. WEEKDAYS (M-F) 9:00-6:00, WED 9:00-8:00, SAT 9:00-2:00. (717) 235-7883, *(800) 222-1469.* ✚▲○

SOMERSET—AAA EAST CENTRAL, 110 N CENTER AVE, 15501. WEEKDAYS (M-F) 8:30-5:00, FRI 8:30-7:00. (814) 443-6526 ✚

SOUTH WILLIAMSPORT—AAA NORTH PENN, 1 E 6TH AVE, 17702. WEEKDAYS (M-F) 8:30-5:00, MON 8:30-8:00. (570) 323-8431 ✚▲○

ST. MARYS—AAA EAST CENTRAL, 1375 BUCKTAIL RD, 15857. WEEKDAYS (M-F) 8:30-5:00. (814) 834-7838 ✚▲

STATE COLLEGE—AAA SOUTHERN PENNSYLVANIA, 200 SHILOH RD, 16801. WEEKDAYS (M-F) 9:00-6:00, WED 9:00-8:00, SAT 9:00-2:00. (814) 237-0305, *(800) 222-1469.* ✚▲○

STROUDSBURG—AAA NORTH PENN, 1527 N 9TH ST, 18360. WEEKDAYS (M-F) 9:00-5:00, SAT 9:00-12:00. (570) 421-2500 ✚▲○

SUNBURY—AAA EAST CENTRAL, 1001 MARKET ST, 17801. WEEKDAYS (M-F) 8:00-5:00. (570) 286-4507 ✚▲

TOWANDA—AAA NORTH PENN, 306 ENNIS LN, 18848. WEEKDAYS (M-F) 9:00-5:00, SAT 9:00-12:00. (570) 265-6122 ✚▲○

TUNKHANNOCK—AAA NORTH PENN, 208 W TIOGA ST, 18657. WEEKDAYS (M-F) 9:00-5:00. (570) 836-5104 ✚▲○

UNIONTOWN—AAA EAST CENTRAL, 209 WAL-MART DR # C-10, 15401. WEEKDAYS (M-F) 10:00-6:00, SAT 10:00-2:00. (724) 438-8575 ✚▲

WARMINSTER—AAA CLUB ALLIANCE INC, 602 YORK RD, 18974. WEEKDAYS (M-F) 7:00-7:00, SAT 8:00-5:00. (215) 315-4060 ✚▲○€

WARREN—AAA EAST CENTRAL, 2285 MARKET ST, 16365. WEEKDAYS (M-F) 9:00-5:00. (814) 723-6660 ✚▲

WARRINGTON—AAA CLUB ALLIANCE INC, 865 EASTON RD STE 100, 18976. WEEKDAYS (M-F) 9:00-5:30, SAT 9:00-3:00. (215) 343-2660 ✚▲○

WASHINGTON—AAA EAST CENTRAL, 196 MURTLAND AVE, 15301. WEEKDAYS (M-F) 8:30-5:00, SAT 8:30-12:00. (724) 222-3800 ✚▲○

WAYNE—AAA CLUB ALLIANCE INC, 849 W LANCASTER AVE, 19087. WEEKDAYS (M-F) 7:00-7:00, SAT 8:00-5:00, SUN 10:00-4:00. (610) 263-8150 ✚▲○€ ▭

WELLSBORO—AAA NORTH PENN, 9 CHARLESTON ST, 16901. WEEKDAYS (M-F) 8:30-5:00. (570) 724-4134 ✛ ▲ ✿

WEST CHESTER—AAA CLUB ALLIANCE INC, 707 E GAY ST, 19380. WEEKDAYS (M-F) 7:00-7:00, SAT 8:00-5:00, SUN 10:00-4:00. (610) 696-8100 ✛ ▲ ✿ ✔

WEXFORD—AAA EAST CENTRAL, 10548 PERRY HWY, 15090. WEEKDAYS (M-F) 9:00-7:00, SAT 9:00-3:00. (724) 933-3000 ✛ ▲ ✿

WHITE OAK—AAA EAST CENTRAL, 2001 LINCOLN WAY #8, 15131. WEEKDAYS (M-F) 10:00-6:00, SAT 10:00-2:00. (412) 675-3400 ✛ ▲

WILKES-BARRE—AAA CLUB ALLIANCE INC, 679-E KIDDER ST, 18702. WEEKDAYS (M-F) 9:00-5:30, SAT 9:00-3:00. (570) 819-1920 ✛ ▲ ✿

WILLOW GROVE—AAA CLUB ALLIANCE INC, 2506 W MORELAND RD, 19090. WEEKDAYS (M-F) 7:00-7:00, SAT 8:00-5:00, SUN 10:00-4:00. (215) 392-9620 ✛ ▲ ✿ ✔

YORK—AAA SOUTHERN PENNSYLVANIA, 2840 EASTERN BLVD, 17402. WEEKDAYS (M-F) 9:00-6:00, WED 9:00-8:00, SAT 9:00-2:00. (717) 600-8700, *(800) 222-1469*. ✛ ▲ ✿

Photo Credits

Page numbers are in bold type. Picture credit abbreviations are as follows:
- (i) numeric sequence from top to bottom, left to right ■ (AAA) AAA Travel library.

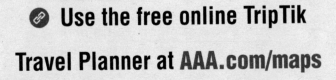

Use the free online TripTik

Travel Planner at AAA.com/maps

Be Vacation Ready
Know Before You Go

Before setting out on your trip, have your car checked out by a dependable **AAA/CAA Approved Auto Repair** facility.

AAA.com/autorepair

AAA Mobile
CAA Mobile

Let Your Voice Be Heard

We Want To Hear From You

- If a AAA listed establishment doesn't meet your expectations, send us the details so we can look into it.
- Or, if you've got a favorite hotel, restaurant or attraction you'd like us to consider for AAA inspection, send us your recommendation.

Visit us at **AAA.com/TourBookComments**

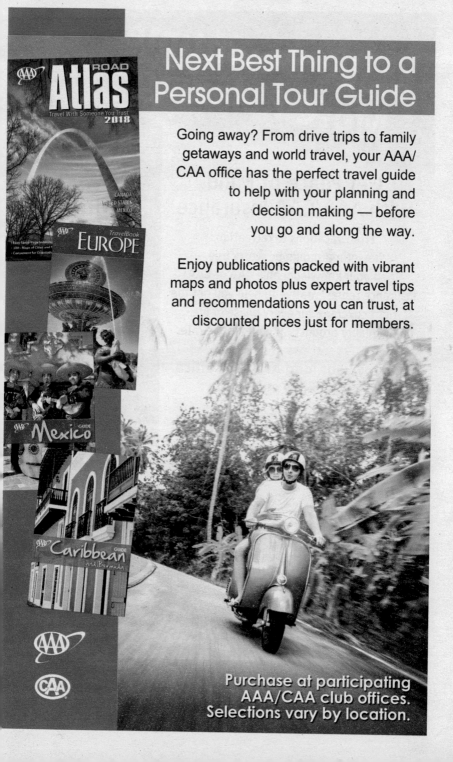

Love the Great Outdoors?

iStockphoto.com_pixelfit

When getting away means getting off the beaten path, visit **AAA.com/campgrounds** or **AAA.com/maps** for:

△ More than 20,000 places to camp across the U.S. and Canada

△ Complete mapping and travel information to plan your adventure

iStockphoto.com_welcomia

Look for locations with the trusted mark of approval.

Inspected & Approved

**Plan it, book it and save at
AAA.com/travel or CAA.ca/travel**

Circle the globe! Enjoy up to 25% savings with our exclusive offers on hotels, up to 20% on car rentals, and out-of-this-world deals on complete vacation packages. With a website that's easy to navigate and customer support you can trust, expect something more when you travel with AAA and CAA.

Hands-Free IS NOT Risk-Free

Not all voice-activated technologies are equal … complicated interactions can take your attention away from the road.

Use hands-free systems cautiously and keep your focus on the road when driving.

Learn more at
AAA.com/distraction

A REWARDING PARTNERSHIP.

DRIVING EXCLUSIVE SAVINGS AND BENEFITS FOR AAA MEMBERS.

- Save up to 20%* on base rate for car rentals
- Earn Hertz Gold Plus Rewards® points
- No charge for additional driver if AAA member
- Free use of one child seat
- Special daily rate of $6.99/ for NeverLost® navigation system

For discounts and reservations, visit AAA.com/hertz.